CONFLICTS OF INTEREST

CONFLICTS OF INTEREST

Fourth Edition

by

Charles Hollander Q.C.
M.A. Cantab.
Brick Court Chambers

&

Simon Salzedo, Q.C. FCA
B.A. Oxon, ACA, Dip. Law
Brick Court Chambers

LONDON
SWEET & MAXWELL
2011

First Edition 2000
Second Edition 2004
Third Edition 2008

Published in 2011 by
Sweet & Maxwell Limited of 100 Avenue Road, London NW3 3PF part of
Thomson Reuters (Professional) UK Limited
Registered in England & Wales, Company No 1679046.
Registered Office and address for service: Aldgate House, 33 Aldgate High Street,
London EC3N 1DL)

For further information on our products and services, visit
www.sweetandmaxwell.co.uk
Typeset by Servis Filmsetting Ltd, Stockport, Cheshire
Printed and bound in Great Britain by
CPI Group (UK) Ltd, Croydon, CR0 4YY.

No natural forests were destroyed to make this product;
only farmed timber was used and re-planted.

A CIP catalogue record of this book is available from the British Library

ISBN 978-0-414-023390

Thomson Reuters and the Thomson Reuters logo are trademarks of Thomson
Reuters.

Sweet & Maxwell ® is a registered trademark of Thomson Reuters (Professional)
UK Limited.

Crown copyright material is reproduced with the permission of the Controller of
HMSO and the Queen's Printer for Scotland.

All rights reserved. No part of this publication may be reproduced or transmitted,
in any form or by any means, or stored in any retrieval system of any nature,
without prior written permission, except for permitted fair dealing under the
Copyright, Designs and Patents Act 1988, or in accordance with the terms of a
license issued by the Copyright Licensing Agency in respect of photocopying and/or
reprographic reproduction. Application for permission for other use of copyright
material including permission to reproduce extracts in other published works shall
be made to the publishers. Full acknowledgment of author, publisher and source
must be given.

© 2011 Thomson Reuters (Professional) UK Limited

Preface to the Fourth Edition

Four editions in eleven years reflects the dynamism of this new area of law. This work as been judicially described by the Court of Appeal as "the leading book on the subject" which is of course flattering, but as far as we know it remains the only book on the subject.

In this new edition, the section of the work relating to judicial conflicts has been significantly expanded. Amongst the important new decisions are *BAA v Competition Commission, Helow v Secretary of State for the Home Department* and the criminal cases *Khan v R.* and *KC v R.* The single chapter in previous editions on judicial conflicts has now become three and a half chapters in response to the variety and frequency of modern day judicial challenges. The application of *Porter v Magill* to ever new situations seems to create far more legal difficulties than one might expect. Did jury members not send prosecuting counsel champagne and invitations to dinner after a trial in former times?

Another new development is a separate chapter on arbitration conflicts. This has become a hot topic in this jurisdiction. One of the reasons for this is the system whereby arbitrators and barristers may practice from the same chambers and increasingly appear as judge and advocate in the same case. Whilst permitted under English rules, it does not always sit comfortably with the expectations of foreign litigants and has given rise to problems. So the new arbitration conflicts chapter deals both with problems involving counsel and problems involving arbitrators. The chapters on fiduciary duties applied to conflicts of interest have also been significantly rewritten, as has the chapter on litigating conflicts.

There is another new code of conduct from the Solicitors' Regulation Authority. No sooner had the profession become comfortable with the previous rules, it now has to adjust to "outcomes focused regulation".

Important new authorities include *Virgin Media Communications v BSkyB,* where the Court of Appeal had frustratingly announced their decision but not their reasons at the time the last edition went to press (and the reasons turned out a little different from what had been anticipated), *Bloomsbury v Holyoake* (insolvency practitioners conflicted as a result of their firm's retainer to a person the administrators sued), *Meat Corp of Namibia v Dawn Meats* (expert witness conflict), *A v B* (arbitrator conflict) and from abroad *PCCW HK Telephone v Aitken* (Hong Kong CFA, applicability of *Bolkiah* test in other spheres) and *Radisich v Templeton* (duty to the other side in New Zealand).

Charles Hollander
Simon Salzedo
Brick Court Chambers
London

Foreword to the First Edition

by the Hon. Mr Justice Aikens

"*No man can serve two masters: for either he will hate the one and love the other; or else he will hold to the one, and despise the other*": St Matthew 6.24. So, as the authors remind us, proscriptions against serving two masters are hardly new or just rules of English law. But demands that the proscription be observed have become increasingly frequent and insistent in modern society. And nowadays if a modern "master" believes that his "servant" might be serving another and so causing loss to himself, the "master" will unhesitatingly resort to law, as the recent spate of highly publicised cases amply demonstrates. The claimant will allege that this duplicitous service has created a "conflict of interest" and he will seek redress. As the authors show conclusively, in today's commercial world no one who offers his services to another is immune from the issue of possible conflicts of interest.

This book is a trail-blazer. It is the first in which any concerted attempt has been made to explore the extent of the rules against "conflict of interest" in modern English law. It is the first to attempt a systematic analysis of why and how a person can be prevented from serving two masters. The authors are not afraid to suggest that the traditional legal analysis, which is based on the old equitable doctrine of the fiduciary's duties, has led, by a logical process of syllogisms, to legal rules that are both too severe and unjustifiable as a matter of common sense. So, they suggest, the current rules are in many cases inapt to deal with situations that arise in a modern sophisticated commercial society.

Charles Hollander Q.C. has wide experience in many areas of commercial law. Simon Salzedo practiced as an accountant before going to the Bar. So between them they are able to offer practical guidance on how the problems of conflicts of interest might be avoided or attenuated. They consider and, if necessary, criticise trenchantly professional and other regulations that deal with the problem of conflicts of interest. They also deal with the topical and important subject of "judicial" conflict of interest. I have no doubt that there will be further developments in the law on that topic.

As commercial competition becomes ever more keen in the new century, company directors, all types of advisors, judges and politicians will be forced to be even more scrupulous to avoid possible conflicts of interest. This new book is therefore very timely. I am sure that it will greatly assist

FOREWORD TO THE FIRST EDITION

all of us who need to know the rights and duties of service, whatever form it might take. I therefore welcome it warmly.

Richard Aikens
January 2000

Contents

Preface to the Fourth Edition	v
Foreword to the First Edition	vii
Table of Cases	xiii
Table of Statutes	xliii
Table of Statutory Instruments	xlv
Table of European Legislation	xlvii

Chapter 1: Conflicts of Interest: the Principles
1. Introduction to the law of conflicts of interest — 1–001
2. Conflicts rules in other jurisdictions — 1–009

Chapter 2: Existing Client Conflicts: the fiduciary obligation
1. The fiduciary relationship — 2–002
2. Existence of a fiduciary relationship: problem areas — 2–013
3. Fiduciary problems before, after and during the retainer — 2–018

Chapter 3: The Double Employment rule
1. Breach of the double employment rule — 3–002
2. What sort of conflict engages the double employment rule? — 3–011
3. Non-waivable conflicts and professional embarrassment — 3–017
4. Personal conflicts and the professional — 3–022

Chapter 4: Managing Conflicts by Contract
1. The retainer — 4–002
2. Consent as a defence to conflict — 4–008
3. Informed consent — 4–013
4. Undue influence as a restriction on consent — 4–015
5. Deemed consent — 4–016
6. Varying the terms by trade custom — 4–022
7. Exclusion and restriction of duties by contract — 4–023

Chapter 5: Perception of impropriety as a test for conflicts
1. The supervisory jurisdiction over solicitors — 5–001
2. Cases where the English court has adopted an appearance of impropriety — 5–008

3. Does the court in this jurisdiction retain an inherent jurisdiction to prevent solicitors from acting? 5–018

Chapter 6: The Obligation to Disclose Information
1. The obligation to transmit information learned from one client to another 6–001
2. The mortgage lending cases 6–004
3. *Barker Booth & Eastwood* 6–010
4. Disclosure of information problems after *Barker Booth & Eastwood* 6–015
5. Attribution of knowledge 6–022

Chapter 7: Information barriers
1. When information barriers become relevant 7–001
2. Confidential information 7–008
3. Features of an information barrier 7–014

Chapter 8: Litigating conflicts
1. Injunction 8–002
2. Remedies other than injunction 8–007
3. Litigation issues 8–014

Chapter 9: The Duty to the Other Side
1. A professional's duty to the other side? 9–001
2. Solicitors for liquidators 9–009

Chapter 10: Blowing the whistle on the client 10–001

Chapter 11: Judicial Conflicts: Bias and apparent bias
1. Bias, apparent bias and the impartial tribunal 11–002
2. Article 6 requirements 11–005
3. Apparent bias 11–010
4. Features of the *Magill* test 11–012

Chapter 12: Juries, tribunals and other decision-makers
1. Juries 12–001
2. Disciplinary tribunals 12–007
3. Councils and councillors 12–011
4. Coroners 12–012
5. Others involved in the administration of justice 12–013

Chapter 13: Judicial Conflicts: Applying the Principles
1. Applying the principles 13–001
2. Objections based on expressing prior views: keeping an open mind 13–006

3. Objections based on relationships and affiliations — 13–019

Chapter 14: Arbitrations
1. The impartial arbitrator — 14–002
2. Power of arbitrators to disqualify lawyers — 14–005
3. Conflicts through connections between arbitrators and counsel — 14–010

Chapter 15: Solicitors
1. The Code of Conduct — 15–002
2. SRA Code of Conduct Chapter 3: Conflicts of interest — 15–004
3. SRA Code of Conduct Chapter 4: The Confidentiality and Disclosure Rule — 15–009
4. The new rules—discussion — 15–012
5. EU and Cross-border practice — 15–013
6. Particular conflicts problems affecting solicitors outside the Code — 15–014

Chapter 16: Barristers — 16–001

Chapter 17: Accountants
1. The business of accountants — 17–001
2. Professional standards — 17–003
3. Investment advice and personal conflicts — 17–005
4. Existing client conflicts — 17–006
5. Does an auditor owe fiduciary duties? — 17–008
6. Former client conflicts — 17–011
7. Accountants as insolvency practitioners — 17–013

Chapter 18: Directors — 18–001

Chapter 19: Conflicts in the City
1. The regime under the Financial Services and Markets Act 2000 — 19–001
2. Takeovers — 19–009

Chapter 20: Estate Agents and Insurance Brokers
1. Estate Agents — 20–001
2. Insurance Brokers — 20–003

Index — 369

Table of Cases

A v B [2011] EWHC 2345 (Comm) 14–013
A-B v British Coal Corp [2006] EWCA Civ 172 CA (Civ Div) 13–010
Aberdeen Railway v Blaikie [1854] 1 Macq 461 .... 3–006, 3–007
Adam 12 Holdings Pty Ltd v Eat and Drink Pty Ltd [2006] V.S.C. 152 5–006
Adex International (Ireland) Ltd v IBM United Kingdom Ltd, unreported,
  November 17, 2000 CC 9–005
Admiral Management Services Ltd v Para Protect Europe Ltd [2002] EWHC
  233 (Ch); [2002] 1 W.L.R. 2722; [2003] 2 All E.R. 1017; [2002] C.P. Rep.
  37; [2003] 1 Costs L.R. 1; [2002] F.S.R. 59; (2002) 99(16) L.S.G. 37;
  (2002) 152 N.L.J. 518; (2002) 146 S.J.L.B. 93 Ch D 5–013
Advanced Housing Pty Ltd (in liquidation) v Newcastle Classic Developments
  Pty Ltd (1994) 14 A.C.S.R. 230 17–013
Advanced Housing Pty Ltd v Newcastle Classic Devts Pty [1994] 14 A.C.S.R.
  230 .... 5–016, 17–021
Akai Holdings Ltd v RSM Robson Rhodes LLP [2007] EWHC 1641 (Ch) Ch
  D 17–012
Albert v Belgium (A/58) (1983) 5 E.H.R.R. 533 ECHR 11–009
Alberta Ltd v Producers Pipelines Inc (1991) 80 D.L.R. (4th) 359 CA
  (Saskatchewan) 19–015
Ali Shipping Corp v Shipyard Trogir [1999] 1 W.L.R. 314; [1998] 2 All E.R.
  136; [1998] 1 Lloyd's Rep. 643; [1998] C.L.C. 566 CA (Civ Div) 9–008
Al-Kandari v JR Brown & Co [1988] Q.B. 665; [1988] 2 W.L.R. 671; [1988]
  1 All E.R. 833; [1988] Fam. Law 382; (1988) 85(14) L.S.G. 50; (1988) 138
  N.L.J. Rep. 62; (1988) 132 S.J. 462 CA (Civ Div) 9–001, 9–002
Allied Finance v Haddow [1983] N.Z.L.R. 22 9–002
Allied Maples Group Ltd v Simmons & Simmons [1995] 1 W.L.R. 1602;
  [1995] 4 All E.R. 907; [1996] C.L.C. 153; 46 Con. L.R. 134; [1955–95]
  P.N.L.R. 701; (1995) 145 N.L.J. 1646; [1995] N.P.C. 83; (1995) 70 P. &
  C.R. D14 CA (Civ Div) 8–009
Almeida v Opportunity Equity Partners Ltd [2006] UKPC 44 PC
  (Cayman) 13–015
AMEC Capital Projects Ltd v Whitefriars City Estates Ltd [2004] EWHC 393
  (TCC); (2004) 20 Const. L.J. 338 QBD 13–011
American Cyanamid Co v Ethicon Ltd (No.1) [1975] A.C. 396; [1975] 2
  W.L.R. 316; [1975] 1 All E.R. 504; [1975] F.S.R. 101; [1975] R.P.C. 513;
  (1975) 119 S.J. 136 HL 8–002
AMP Enterprises Ltd v Hoffman [2002] EWHC 1899 (Ch); [2002] B.C.C.
  996; [2003] 1 B.C.L.C. 319; [2003] B.P.I.R. 11; (2002) 99(36) L.S.G. 38;
  (2002) 146 S.J.L.B. 199 Ch D 5–016

Andrews v Ramsay [1903] 2 K.B. 635 8–013
Angelia, The. *See* Trade and Transport Inc v Iino Kaiun Kaisha Ltd
Anglo African Merchants Ltd v Bayley [1970] 1 Q.B. 311; [1969] 2 W.L.R. 686; [1969] 2 All E.R. 421; [1969] 1 Lloyd's Rep. 268; (1969) 113 S.J. 281 QBD 4–022, 20–004
Anglo Group Plc v Winther Browne & Co Ltd 72 Con. L.R. 118; [1999–2000] Info. T.L.R. 61; [2000] I.T.C.L.R. 559; [2000] Masons C.L.R. 13; (2000) 144 S.J.L.B. 197 QBD 5–013
Apple Corps Ltd v Apple Computer Inc (Use of Documents in EC Commission Proceedings) [1992] 1 C.M.L.R. 969; [1992] F.S.R. 389 Ch D.................. 9–004
Appleby v Cowley, The Times, April 14, 1982 Ch D 16–003
Aquachem Ltd v Delphis Bank Ltd (In Receivership) [2008] UKPC 7; [2008] B.C.C. 648 PC (Mauritius) 17–008
Arab Bank Plc v Zurich Insurance Co [1999] 1 Lloyd's Rep. 262; [1998] C.L.C. 1351 QBD 6–026
Architects of Wine Ltd v Barclays Bank Plc [2007] EWCA Civ 239; [2007] 2 All E.R. (Comm) 285; [2007] 2 Lloyd's Rep. 471; (2007) 151 S.J.L.B. 431; [2007] Bus. L.R. D37 CA (Civ Div)... 6–026
Arklow Investments Ltd v Maclean [2000] 1 W.L.R. 594; (2000) 144 S.J.L.B. 81 PC (NZ) 2–002, 2–003, 2–012, 2–013, 2–032, 9–004
Arkwright v Newbold (1881) L.R. 17 Ch. D. 301 CA 4–013
Armstrong v Strain [1952] 1 K.B. 232; [1952] 1 All E.R. 139; [1952] 1 T.L.R. 82 CA 6–026
Arrows Ltd, Re [1992] B.C.C. 121 Ch D 17–017, 17–018, 17–019
Asia Pacific Telcom v Optus Network [2005] N.S.W.S.C. 550....................... 5–006
ASM Shipping Ltd of India v TTMI Ltd of England [2005] EWHC 2238 (Comm); [2006] 2 All E.R. (Comm) 122; [2006] 1 Lloyd's Rep. 375; [2006] 1 C.L.C. 656 QBD... 14–002
ASM Shipping Ltd v Harris [2007] EWHC 1513 (Comm); [2008] 1 Lloyd's Rep. 61; [2007] 1 C.L.C. 1017; (2007) 23 Const. L.J. 533; [2007] Bus. L.R. D105 QBD 11–017, 14–003
AT&T Corp v Saudi Cable Co [2000] 1 All E.R. (Comm) 201; [2000] 1 Lloyd's Rep. 22; [2000] C.L.C. 220 QBD 14–002
Attorney General of Canada v The Information Commissioner of Canada [2002] F.C.T. 128... 9–004
Attorney General v Blake [1998] Ch. 439; [1998] 2 W.L.R. 805; [1998] 1 All E.R. 833; [1998] E.M.L.R. 309; (1998) 95(4) L.S.G. 33; (1998) 148 N.L.J. 15; (1998) 142 S.J.L.B. 35 CA (Civ Div) 2–010, 2–012, 2–020,
6–003, 8–011
Attorney General v Guardian. *See* Attorney General v Observer Ltd
Attorney General v Observer Ltd [1990] 1 A.C. 109; [1988] 3 W.L.R. 776; [1988] 3 All E.R. 545; [1989] 2 F.S.R. 181; (1988) 85(42) L.S.G. 45; (1988) 138 N.L.J. Rep. 296; (1988) 132 S.J. 1496 HL 2–030, 7–007
Auckland Casino v Casino Control Authority [1995] 1 N.Z.L.R. 142........ 11–003,
11–018
Australia & New Zealand Banking Group Ltd v P De Burgh Day, unreported, May 6, 1994, SC (Vict).. 17–015
Australian Breeders Co-operative Society v Jones (1997) 150 A.L.R. 488 4–002,
7–006

Australian Liquor Marketers Pty Ld v Tasman Liquor Traders Pty Ltd [2002]
  V.S.C. 324 3–013
Australian Securities and Investments Commission v Citigroup Global
  Markets Australia Pty Ltd (No.4) 2007 F.C.A. 963 .... 2–019, 4–024, 4–025
AWG Group Ltd (formerly Anglian Water Plc) v Morrison [2006] EWCA Civ
  6; [2006] 1 W.L.R. 1163; [2006] 1 All E.R. 967 CA (Civ Div) 11–016,
                                                                             13–015, 13–021
BAA Ltd v Competition Commission [2010] EWCA Civ 1097; [2011]
  U.K.C.L.R. 1 CA (Civ Div) 11–017, 11–018, 11–019, 14–003
Bagnall v Carlton (1877) L.R. 6 Ch. D. 371 CA 4–013
Bahain v Rashidian [1985] 1 W.L.R. 1337 .... 13–010, 13–013
Baker v Quantum Clothing Group Ltd [2009] EWCA Civ 499; [2009] P.I.Q.R.
  P19; (2009) 153(21) S.J.L.B. 29 CA (Civ Div) 11–019
Ball v Druces & Attlee (A Firm) (No.1) [2002] P.N.L.R. 23 QBD 7–010
Balogh v St Albans Crown Court [1975] Q.B. 73; [1974] 3 W.L.R. 314;
  [1974] 3 All E.R. 283; (1974) 118 S.J. 582 CA (Civ Div) 13–014
Bank of Credit and Commerce International SA (In Liquidation) v Ali (No.8)
  (2001) 151 N.L.J. 1852 Ch D 13–028
Bank of Montreal v Stuart [1911] A.C. 120 PC (Can) 4–015
Barclays Bank Plc v Eustice [1995] 1 W.L.R. 1238; [1995] 4 All E.R. 511;
  [1995] B.C.C. 978; [1995] 2 B.C.L.C. 630; (1995) 145 N.L.J. 1503; (1995)
  70 P. & C.R. D29 CA (Civ Div) 4–026
Baring v Stanton (1876) L.R. 3 Ch. D. 502 CA 4–013
Barings Plc (In Liquidation) v Coopers & Lybrand (No.1) [2000] 1 W.L.R.
  2353; [2000] 3 All E.R. 910; [2000] Lloyd's Rep. Bank. 225; (2000) 150
  N.L.J. 681 CA (Civ Div) 9–004
Barings Plc, Re [2001] 2 B.C.L.C. 159; [2002] B.P.I.R. 85 17–013
Baron Investments (Holdings) Ltd, Re [2000] 1 B.C.L.C. 272 Ch D 3–009,
                                                                                   9–007, 9–009
Bartram and Sons v Lloyd [1904] 90 T.L.R. 357 4–013
Batten v Wedgwood Coal & Iron Co (No.2) (1886) L.R. 31 Ch. D. 346
  Ch D 9–002
Bawden v London, Edinburgh and Glasgow Assurance Co [1892] 2 Q.B. 534
  CA 20–005
Beach Petroleum v Abbott Tout Russel Kennedy [1999] N.S.W.C.A. 408 2–004,
                                                                                    3–023, 4–002
Bebonis v Angelos [2003] N.S.W.C.A. 13 9–002
Beer v Ward 37 E.R. 779; (1821) Jac. 77 5–004
Begin v MCinnis, unreported, March 11, 1991 17–002
Belan v Casey [2002] N.S.W.S.C. 58 .... 5–006, 7–011
Belilos v Switzerland (A/132) (1988) 10 E.H.R.R. 466 ECHR 13–021
Bell v Lever Brothers Ltd [1932] A.C. 161 HL 18–003
Berg v IML London Ltd [2002] 1 W.L.R. 3271; [2002] 4 All E.R. 87
  QBD 13–012
Berry Taylor (A Firm) v Coleman [1997] P.N.L.R. 1 CA (Civ Div) 17–006
Bhullar v Bhullar [2003] EWCA Civ 424; [2003] B.C.C. 711; [2003] 2
  B.C.L.C. 241; [2003] W.T.L.R. 1397; (2003) 147 S.J.L.B. 421; [2003]
  N.P.C. 45 CA (Civ Div) 18–005
Bidermann Industries Licensing Inc v Amvar NV 173 A.D. 2d 401 14–008

TABLE OF CASES

Birmingham Midshires Mortgage Services Ltd v David Parry & Co [1998] P.N.L.R. 249; [1997] E.G. 150 (C.S.); [1997] N.P.C. 153 CA (Civ Div) 6–005
Birtchnell v The Equity Trustees Executors and Agency Co Ltd (1929) 42 C.L.R. 437 4–002
Black v Taylor [1993] 3 N.Z.L.R. 403 .... 1–012, 5–003, 5–006
Bloomsbury International Ltd, Re [2010] EWHC 1150 (Ch) Ch D 2–022, 5–016, 17–023
Boardman v Phipps [1967] 2 A.C. 46; [1966] 3 W.L.R. 1009; [1966] 3 All E.R. 721; (1966) 110 S.J. 853 HL 3–026, 4–011, 4–013, 17–003
Body v Bellbourne Group Ltd, unreported, July 28, 1998 17–002
Bogle v Coutts [2003] EWHC 1865 8–014
Boles and British Land Co's Contract, Re [1902] 1 Ch. 244 Ch D 2–021, 2–022
Bolkiah v KPMG [1999] 2 A.C. 222; [1999] 2 W.L.R. 215; [1999] 1 All E.R. 517; [1999] 1 B.C.L.C. 1; [1999] C.L.C. 175; [1999] P.N.L.R. 220; (1999) 149 N.L.J. 16; (1999) 143 S.J.L.B. 35 HL 1–001, 1–006, 1–008, 1–010, 1–011, 1–012, 2–005, 2–007, 2–018, 2–020, 2–022, 3–002, 3–009, 3–011, 3–012, 3–013, 3–023, 4–006, 4–007, 4–008, 4–010, 4–012, 4–017, 4–018, 4–020, 5–001, 5–002, 5–003, 5–004, 5–006, 5–007, 5–008, 5–011, 5–015, 5–018, 5–019, 5–020, 5–021, 6–002, 6–023, 6–024, 7–002, 7–003, 7–005, 7–007, 7–010, 7–015, 7–016, 7–017, 7–020, 8–002, 8–002, 8–003, 8–004, 8–005, 8–019, 9–006, 9–007, 9–009, 15–004, 15–010, 15–012, 15–014, 15–015, 16–004, 16–008, 17–003, 17–008, 17–023, 19–004, 19–007
Boulting v Association of Cinematograph Television and Allied Technicians [1963] 2 Q.B. 606; [1963] 2 W.L.R. 529; [1963] 1 All E.R. 716; (1963) 107 S.J. 133 CA 2–007, 3–008, 4–013, 18–007
Bovis Homes Ltd v New Forest DC [2002] EWHC 483 (Admin) QBD 12–011
Bowman v Fels [2005] EWCA Civ 226; [2005] 1 W.L.R. 3083; [2005] 4 All E.R. 609; [2005] 2 Cr. App. R. 19; [2005] 2 C.M.L.R. 23; [2005] 2 F.L.R. 247; [2005] W.T.L.R. 481; [2005] Fam. Law 546; (2005) 102(18) L.S.G. 24; (2005) 155 N.L.J. 413; (2005) 149 S.J.L.B. 357; [2005] N.P.C. 36 CA (Civ Div) 10–001, 10–005, 10–006
Boyce v Rendells (1983) 268 E.G. 268 6–002
Bradford v McLeod 1986 S.L.T. 244; 1985 S.C.C.R. 379; [1986] Crim. L.R. 690 HCJ 11–011
Breda v Breda (1997) 29 O.T.C. 223 .... 17–002, 17–011
Breen v Williams [1996] 186 C.L.R. 71 .... 2–010, 2–011, 3–023, 6–003
Breeze v Ahmad [2005] EWCA Civ 223; [2005] C.P. Rep. 29 CA (Civ Div) .. 5–013
Bricheno v Thorp 37 E.R. 864; (1821) Jac. 300 5–004
Brickenden v London Loan and Savings Co [1934] 3 D.L.R. 465 PC 3–023, 4–011, 4–013
Bristol & West Building Society v Mothew (t/a Stapley & Co) [1998] Ch. 1; [1997] 2 W.L.R. 436; [1996] 4 All E.R. 698; [1997] P.N.L.R. 11; (1998) 75 P. & C.R. 241; [1996] E.G. 136 (C.S.); (1996) 146 N.L.J. 1273; (1996) 140 S.J.L.B. 206; [1996] N.P.C. 126 CA (Civ Div) 1–001, 2–002, 2–005, 2–006, 2–007, 2–008, 2–009, 2–010, 3–001, 3–002, 3–005, 3–006, 3–019, 3–021, 4–010, 4–011, 4–013, 4–017, 6–003, 15–015, 15–018, 17–008, 17–009, 18–009

TABLE OF CASES

Bristol and West Building Society v Baden Barnes Groves & Co [2000] Lloyd's Rep. P.N. 788 Ch D 6–007, 6–009, 6–017
Bristol and West Building Society v Daniels & Co [1997] P.N.L.R. 323 Ch D 8–008
Bristol and West Building Society v Fancy & Jackson [1997] 4 All E.R. 582; [1997] N.P.C. 109 Ch D 8–008
Bristol and West Building Society v May May & Merrimans (No.1) [1996] 2 All E.R. 801; [1996] P.N.L.R. 138; [1996] E.G. 69 (C.S.); (1996) 93(19) L.S.G. 30; (1996) 146 N.L.J. 625; (1996) 140 S.J.L.B. 110 Ch D... 6–004, 6–007
British and American Tobacco Australia Services Ltd v Blanch [2004] N.S.W.S.C. 7 .... 5–006, 6–020, 7–012
British Midland Tool Ltd v Midland International Tooling Ltd [2003] EWHC 466 (Ch); [2003] 2 B.C.L.C. 523 Ch D 2–011, 18–003
British Sky Broadcasting Plc v Virgin Media Communications Ltd (formerly NTL Communications Ltd) [2008] EWCA Civ 612; [2008] 1 W.L.R. 2854; [2008] Bus. L.R. 1543; [2008] 4 All E.R. 1026; [2008] C.P. Rep. 34; (2008) 105(29) L.S.G. 33 CA (Civ Div) 3–015, 7–021, 8–003, 8–005, 9–004, 9–007
Broadcasting Station 2 GB Pty, Re (1964–65) N.S.W.R. 1648 18–007
Brown v Bennett The Times, November 2, Ch D 5–013
Brownie Mills v Shrimpton 1999 P.N.L.R. (NZCA) 9–002
Bruton Pty Ltd, Re (1990) 2 A.C.S.R. 277 17–018
Bryan v United Kingdom (A/335-A) (1996) 21 E.H.R.R. 342; [1996] 1 P.L.R. 47; [1996] 2 E.G.L.R. 123; [1996] 28 E.G. 137 ECHR 11–006, 11–009
BSB Holdings Ltd, Re [1996] 1 B.C.L.C. 155 Ch D 18–003, 19–010
BTR Industries South Africa (Pty) Ltd v Metal and Allied Workers' Union (1992) (3) S.A. 673 .... 11–003, 11–011
Buckle v Knoop (1866–67) L.R. 2 Ex. 125 4–022
Bulut v Austria (17358/90) (1997) 24 E.H.R.R. 84 ECHR 16–009
Bureau Interprofessionel des Vins de Bourgogne v Red Earth Nominees Pty Ltd (t/a Taltarni Vineyards) [2002] F.C.A. 588 .... 6–023, 7–007, 7–017
Burton v Chemical Vessel Services [1984] C.L.Y. 1525 5–013
Business Computers International Ltd v Registrar of Companies [1988] 1 Ch. 229 9–001
Button v Phelps [2006] EWHC 53 (Ch) Ch D 2–013
CA (Civ Div) 9–001
Caffrey v Darby 31 E.R. 1159; (1801) 6 Ves. Jr. 488 8–010
Calcraft v Guest [1898] 1 Q.B. 759 CA 15–018
Campbell v McCreath 1975 S.C. 81; 1975 S.L.T. (Notes) 5 6–025
Campbell v United Kingdom (A/80) (1985) 7 E.H.R.R. 165 ECHR 11–010
Canada Carlingwood Motors v Nissan Canada (2001) 52 O.R. (3d) 242 2–019
Canada Post Corp (2000) 89 L.A.C. (4th) 124 17–010
Canada Steamship Lines Ltd v King, The [1952] A.C. 192; [1952] 1 All E.R. 305; [1952] 1 Lloyd's Rep. 1; [1952] 1 T.L.R. 261; (1952) 96 S.J. 72 PC (Can) 4–026
Canadian Co-operative Leasing Services v Price Waterhouse (1992) 128 N.B.R. (2nd) 1 17–022
Canson Enterprises v Broughton & Co (1991) 85 D.L.R. (4th) 129 .... 8–010, 8–012
Caparo Industries Plc v Dickman [1990] 2 A.C. 605; [1990] 2 W.L.R. 358; [1990] 1 All E.R. 568; [1990] B.C.C. 164; [1990] B.C.L.C. 273; [1990]

xvii

TABLE OF CASES

E.C.C. 313; [1955–95] P.N.L.R. 523; (1990) 87(12) L.S.G. 42; (1990) 140 N.L.J. 248; (1990) 134 S.J. 494 HL 17–008
Carindale Country Club Estate Pty Ltd v Astill (1993) 115 A.L.R. 112 .... 5–004, 5–018, 7–003, 7–011
Carradine Properties Ltd v DJ Freeman & Co [1999] Lloyd's Rep. P.N. 483; [1955–95] P.N.L.R. 219; (1989) 5 Const. L.J. 267 CA (Civ Div) 4–002, 4–003, 4–027
Carter Holt Harvey Forests Ltd v Sunnex Logging Ltd [2001] 3 N.Z.L.R. 343 .... 1–012, 9–005, 9–006, 9–008
Carter v Palmer (1839) 1 Dr. & Wal. 722; (1841) 8 Cl. & Fin. 657 HL 16–003
Caruso v Tartaglia [2002] V.S.C. 91 5–003
Cayne v Global Natural Resources Plc [1984] 1 All E.R. 225 CA ... 8–002, 19–015
Chapman v United Kingdom (27238/95) (2001) 33 E.H.R.R. 18; 10 B.H.R.C. 48 ECHR 11–009
Charmae Investments Pty Ltd, unreported, November 12, 1990 17–015
Charterhouse Corporation v Lloyds Bank [1969] 2 All E.R. 1185 18–008
Christopher & Co v Essig [1948] W.N. 461; (1948) 92 S.J. 675 20–001
City Equitable Fire Insurance Co Ltd, Re [1925] Ch. 407; [1924] All E.R. Rep. 485 CA 4–025
Clarion Ltd v National Provident Institution [2000] 1 W.L.R. 1888; [2000] 2 All E.R. 265 Ch D 19–004
Clark Boyce v Mouat [1994] 1 A.C. 428; [1993] 3 W.L.R. 1021; [1993] 4 All E.R. 268; (1993) 143 N.L.J. 1440; (1993) 137 S.J.L.B. 231; [1993] N.P.C. 128 PC (NZ) 1–001, 2–007, 3–002, 3–013, 3–017, 3–018, 3–020, 3–023, 3–024, 3–026, 4–002, 4–008, 4–010, 4–010, 4–011, 4–012, 4–012, 4–014, 4–017, 4–019, 4–020, 4–027, 6–015
Clark v Smallfield [1861] 4 L.T. 405 4–022
Clenae Pty Ltd v Australia and New Zealand Banking Group (199) V.S.C.A. 35 SC (Vict) 11–003
Clenae Pty v Australia and New Zealand Banking Group (1999) V.S.C.A. 35 SC (Vict) 13–001
Cleveland Investments Global v Evans [2010] N.S.W.S.C. 567 5–006
Clough v Bond 40 E.R. 1016; (1838) 3 My. & C. 490 8–010
Club Superstores Australia Pty Ltd [1993] A.C.S.R. 930 .... 5–016, 17–021
Cobbetts LLP v Hodge [2009] EWHC 786 (Ch); [2010] 1 B.C.L.C. 30; (2009) 153(17) S.J.L.B. 29 Ch D 2–014
Coco v AN Clark (Engineers) Ltd [1968] F.S.R. 415; [1969] R.P.C. 41 Ch D 7–007
Collinson v Lister 44 E.R. 247; (1855) 7 De G.M. & G. 634 6–025
Colman v General Medical Council [2010] EWHC 1608 (QB); [2011] A.C.D. 38 QBD 12–009
Colman v Mills [1897] 1 Q.B. 396 19–004
Colonial Portfolio v Nissen [2000] N.S.W.S.C. 1047 8–017
Commission for the New Towns v Cooper (Great Britain) Ltd [1995] Ch. 259; [1995] 2 W.L.R. 677; [1995] 2 All E.R. 929; (1996) 72 P. & C.R. 270; [1995] 2 E.G.L.R. 113; [1995] E.G. 30 (C.S.); (1995) 139 S.J.L.B. 87; [1995] N.P.C. 34; (1995) 69 P. & C.R. D40 CA (Civ Div) 4–021
Commonwealth Bank of Australia v Smith (1991) 102 A.L.R. 453 Federal Court (Australia) 3–019

Connell v Odlum [1993] N.Z.L.R. 257 9–002
Connolly-Martin v Davis [1999] Lloyd's Rep. P.N. 790; [1999] P.N.L.R. 826;
  (1999) 96(23) L.S.G. 35 CA (Civ Div) 9–001
Cooke v Head (No.2) [1974] 1 W.L.R. 972; [1974] 2 All E.R. 1124; (1974)
  118 S.J. 366 CA (Civ Div) 5–003
Cote v Revenue Board, unreported, February 8, 199 17–002
County Personnel (Employment Agency) Ltd v Alan R Pulver & Co [1987] 1
  W.L.R. 916; [1987] 1 All E.R. 289; [1986] 2 E.G.L.R. 246; (1987) 84
  L.S.G. 1409; (1986) 136 N.L.J. 1138; (1987) 131 S.J. 474 CA (Civ Div) ... 4–002
Criterion Properties Plc v Stratford UK Properties LLC [2004] UKHL 28;
  [2004] 1 W.L.R. 1846; [2004] B.C.C. 570; [2006] 1 B.C.L.C. 729; (2004)
  101(26) L.S.G. 27; (2004) 148 S.J.L.B. 760; [2004] N.P.C. 96 HL 19–015
Cunliffe-Owen v Teather & Greenwood [1967] 1 W.L.R. 1421; [1967] 3 All
  E.R. 561; (1967) 111 S.J. 866 Ch D 4–020
Customs and Excise Commissioners v Barclays Bank Plc [2006] UKHL 28;
  [2007] 1 A.C. 181; [2006] 3 W.L.R. 1; [2006] 4 All E.R. 256; [2006] 2 All
  E.R. (Comm) 831; [2006] 2 Lloyd's Rep. 327; [2006] 1 C.L.C. 1096; (2006)
  103(27) L.S.G. 33; (2006) 156 N.L.J. 1060; (2006) 150 S.J.L.B. 859
  HL 9–003
D Ross v MicroFocus Ltd, unreported, November 18, 2009 13–015
D&J Construction Pty Ltd v Head (1987) 9 N.S.W.L.R. 118 .... 6–023, 8–004
D&J Constructions Pty Ltd v Clayton Utz (1987) 9 N.S.W.L.R. 118 5–003,
  5–004, 5–018
Dahl (t/a Dahl & Co) v Nelson, Donkin & Co (1879) L.R. 12 Ch. D. 568
  CA 4–022
Dairy Containers v NZI Bank [1995] 2 N.Z.L.R. 8 18–007
Dale v Inland Revenue Commissioners [1954] A.C. 11; [1953] 3 W.L.R. 448;
  [1953] 2 All E.R. 671; 46 R. & I.T. 513; 34 T.C. 468; (1953) 32 A.T.C.
  294; [1953] T.R. 269; (1953) 97 S.J. 538 HL 4–027
Darlington Building Society v O'Rourke James Scourfield & McCarthy [1999]
  Lloyd's Rep. P.N. 33; [1999] P.N.L.R. 365 CA (Civ Div) 6–008, 6–021
Davey v Woolley Harvey Dale & Dingwall (1982) 33 D.L.R. (3rd) 647 3–002,
  6–023, 6–025
David Lee & Co (Lincoln) Ltd v Coward Chance (A Firm) [1991] Ch. 259;
  [1990] 3 W.L.R. 1278; [1991] 1 All E.R. 668; [1990] B.C.L.C. 519; (1990)
  134 S.J. 1403 Ch D 4–008
Davidson v Scottish Ministers (No.2) [2004] UKHL 34; 2005 1 S.C. (H.L.) 7;
  2004 S.L.T. 895; 2004 S.C.L.R. 991; [2004] H.R.L.R. 34; [2004]
  U.K.H.R.R. 1079; [2005] A.C.D. 19; 2004 G.W.D. 27-572 HL 13–011
Davies v Clough 59 E.R. 105; (1837) 8 Sim. 262 .... 5–004, 6–023
Davies v Davies [2000] 1 F.L.R. 39; [1999] 3 F.C.R. 745; [2000] Fam. Law 23
  CA (Civ Div) 2–032
Dawson International v Coats Patons [1989] B.C.L.C. 233 19–011
Day v Mead [1987] 2 N.Z.L.R. 443 .... 3–002, 8–012
De Cubber v Belgium (A/86) (1985) 7 E.H.R.R. 236 ECHR 11–010
De Haes v Belgium (19983/92) (1998) 25 E.H.R.R. 1 ECHR 16–009
Dean v Allin & Watts [2001] EWCA Civ 758; [2001] 2 Lloyd's Rep. 249;
  [2001] Lloyd's Rep. P.N. 605; [2001] P.N.L.R. 39; (2001) 98(31) L.S.G.
  36; (2001) 145 S.J.L.B. 157 CA (Civ Div) 9–002

TABLE OF CASES

Deangrove Pty Ltd (Receivers and Managers Appointed) v Commonwealth Bank of Australia (2001) 108 F.C.R. 77 17–015
Deloitte & Touche AG v Johnson [1999] 1 W.L.R. 1605; [1999] B.C.C. 992; [2000] 1 B.C.L.C. 485; (1998–99) 1 I.T.E.L.R. 771 PC (Cayman) 5–016, 17–021
Demerara Bauxite Co Ltd v Hubbard [1923] A.C. 673 PC (West Indies) 2–027, 3–025, 4–013, 4–015
Dennard v PricewaterhouseCoopers LLP [2010] EWHC 812 (Ch) Ch D 3–022, 17–001, 17–007
Derby & Co Ltd v Weldon (No.2), unreported, October 19, 1988 Ch D 9–004
Diamantides v JP Morgan Chase Bank [2005] EWCA Civ 1612 CA (Civ Div) 2–023
Dimes v Grand Junction Canal Proprietors 10 E.R. 301; (1852) 3 H.L. Cas. 759 HL 11–002, 11–003, 11–004, 11–011
Director General of Fair Trading v Proprietary Association of Great Britain [2001] 1 W.L.R. 700; [2001] U.K.C.L.R. 550; [2001] I.C.R. 564; [2001] H.R.L.R. 17; [2001] U.K.H.R.R. 429; (2001) 3 L.G.L.R. 32; (2001) 98(7) L.S.G. 40; (2001) 151 N.L.J. 17; (2001) 145 S.J.L.B. 29 CA (Civ Div).... 11–011, 11–016, 11–017, 11–018, 12–003, 13–002
Discain Project Services Ltd v Opecprime Development Ltd (Application for Summary Judgment) [2000] B.L.R. 402; (2001) 3 T.C.L.R. 16 QBD 14–002
Dobbs v Triodos Bank [2005] EWCA 548 13–001
Doherty v McGlennan 1997 S.L.T. 444; 1996 S.C.C.R. 591 11–011
Domino Hire Pty Ltd v Pioneer Park Pty Ltd (in liquidation), unreported, December 15, 1999 17–022
Don King Productions Inc v Warren (No.1) [2000] Ch. 291; [1999] 3 W.L.R. 276; [1999] 2 All E.R. 218; [1999] 1 Lloyd's Rep. 588; [2000] 1 B.C.L.C. 607; [1999] E.M.L.R. 402 CA (Civ Div) 2–027, 3–025
Donnelly v Weybridge Construction Ltd (No.2) [2006] EWHC 2678 (TCC); 111 Con. L.R. 112; [2006] 46 E.G. 208 (C.S.) QBD 2–013
Downsview Nominees Ltd v First City Corp Ltd [1993] A.C. 295; [1993] 2 W.L.R. 86; [1993] 3 All E.R. 626; [1993] B.C.C. 46; [1994] 2 B.C.L.C. 49; (1992) 89(45) L.S.G. 26; (1992) 136 S.J.L.B. 324 PC (NZ) 17–015
Drabinsky v KPMG (1999) 56 C.L.A.S. 382; 87 A.C.W.S. 3d 1233 17–010
Dreiberg v Bettles and Carter (2007) N.S.W.S.C. 1204 17–018
Driscoll v Bromley (1837) 1 Jur. 238 4–013
Duncan v Hill (1872–73) L.R. 8 Ex. 242 4–020
Dunne v English (1874) L.R. 18 Eq. 524.. 4–013
Dunton Properties v Coles Knapp & Kennedy (1959) 174 E.G. 723 CA 20–001
Dwr Cymru Cyfyngedig v Albion Water [2008] EWCA Civ 97 CA (Civ Div) 13–009
Earl Cholmondeley v Lord Clinton 34 E.R. 515; (1815) 19 Ves. Jr. 261 .... 3–013, 5–004, 5–018, 6–023
Ebner, Re (1999) F.C.A. 110.. 13–001
El-Ajou v Dollar Land Holdings Plc (No.1) [1994] 2 All E.R. 685; [1994] B.C.C. 143; [1994] 1 B.C.L.C. 464; [1993] N.P.C. 165 CA 6–026
El-Farargy v El-Farargy [2007] EWCA Civ 1149; [2007] 3 F.C.R. 711; (2007) 104(46) L.S.G. 26; (2007) 151 S.J.L.B. 1500 CA...................................... 13–015

TABLE OF CASES

Elguzouli-Daf v Commissioner of Police of the Metropolis [1995] Q.B. 335; [1995] 2 W.L.R. 173; [1995] 1 All E.R. 833; (1995) 7 Admin. L.R. 421; (1995) 145 N.L.J. 151 CA (Civ Div) 9–001, 9–002
Emma Silver Mining Co v Grant (1879) L.R. 11 Ch. D. 918; (1879) 40 L.T. 804 Ch D 4–013
English & American Insurance Co Ltd v Herbert Smith & Co [1988] F.S.R. 232; (1987) 137 N.L.J. 148 Ch D 9–004
Eric Stansfield v South East Nursing Home Services Ltd [1986] 1 E.G.L.R. 29 8–013
Eric v Stansfield (A Firm) v South East Nursing Home Services [1986] 1 E.G.L.R. 29; (1985) 277 E.G. 311 20–001
Ernst & Young Inc v Royal Trust Corp of Canada (1997) 71 A.C.W.S. 3d 1079 17–012
Estate Realties v Wignall [1991] 3 N.Z.L.R. 482 .... 4–011, 4–013
EuroAfrica Shipping Lines Co Ltd v Zegluga Polska SA [2004] EWHC 385 (Comm); [2004] 2 B.C.L.C. 97 QBD 5–015
Everinghma v Ontario (1992) 88 D.L.R. (4th) 755 5–003
Ezsias v North Glamorgan NHS Trust [2007] EWCA Civ 330; [2007] 4 All E.R. 940; [2007] I.C.R. 1126; [2007] I.R.L.R. 603; (2007) 104(12) L.S.G. 34 CA (Civ Div) 13–008
Faccenda Chicken Ltd v Fowler [1987] Ch. 117; [1986] 3 W.L.R. 288; [1986] 1 All E.R. 617; [1986] I.C.R. 297; [1986] I.R.L.R. 69; [1986] F.S.R. 291; (1986) 83 L.S.G. 288; (1986) 136 N.L.J. 71; (1986) 130 S.J. 573 CA (Civ Div) 7–007
Factortame Ltd v Secretary of State for the Environment, Transport and the Regions (Costs) (No.2) [2002] EWCA Civ 932; [2003] Q.B. 381; [2002] 3 W.L.R. 1104; [2002] 4 All E.R. 97; [2003] B.L.R. 1; [2002] 3 Costs L.R. 467; (2002) 99(35) L.S.G. 34; (2002) 152 N.L.J. 1313; (2002) 146 S.J.L.B. 178 CA (Civ Div) 5–014
Farrer v Copley Singletons [1998] P.N.L.R. 22; (1998) 76 P. & C.R. 169; [1997] N.P.C. 113 CA (Civ Div) 4–006
Farrington v Row McBride [1985] 1 N.Z.L.R. 83 .... 3–002, 3–013, 3–023, 4–008, 4–011, 4–013
Ferguson v Paterson [1900] A.C. 271; (1900) 2 F. (H.L.) 37; (1900) 7 S.L.T. 472 HL 4–025
Fey v Austria (A/255–A) (1993) 16 E.H.R.R. 387 ECHR 11–010
Fields v Leeds CC, Independent, November 16, 1999 CA 5–013
Findlay v United Kingdom (22107/93) (1997) 24 E.H.R.R. 221 ECHR 11–005
Flaherty v National Greyhound Racing Club Ltd [2005] EWCA Civ 1117; (2005) 102(37) L.S.G. 31 CA (Civ Div) 12–007, 13–021, 14–003
Flame Bar-B-Q v Hoar's Estate (1978) 22 N.B.R. (2d) 595, 39 A.P.R. 595 17–002
Flanagan v Pioneer Building Society Ltd [2002] Q.S.C. 346 5–005
Foster Bryant Surveying Ltd v Bryant [2007] EWCA Civ 200; [2007] Bus. L.R. 1565; [2007] B.C.C. 804; [2007] 2 B.C.L.C. 239; [2007] I.R.L.R. 425; [2007] 12 E.G. 154 (C.S.); (2007) 104(13) L.S.G. 24 CA (Civ Div) 2–022, 18–001
Freudiana Holdings Ltd, Re [1994] N.P.C. 89 Ch D 13–013
Freuhauf Finance Corp Ltd v Feez Ruthning [1991] 1 Qd. 558 5–003

Fulham Football Club Ltd v Cabra Estates Plc [1992] B.C.C. 863; [1994] 1 B.C.L.C. 363; (1993) 65 P. & C.R. 284; [1993] 1 P.L.R. 29; (1992) 136 S.J.L.B. 267 CA 19–010
Fullwood v Hurley [1928] 1 K.B. 498 CA 3–013, 3–023, 4–011
Galloway v Barnet Enfield and Haringey Mental Health NHS Trust [2010] EWCA Civ 1368 CA (Civ Div) 12–010
Garbutt v Edwards [2005] EWCA Civ 1206; [2006] 1 W.L.R. 2907; [2006] 1 All E.R. 553; [2006] C.P. Rep. 8; [2006] 1 Costs L.R. 143; (2005) 102(43) L.S.G. 30; [2005] N.P.C. 122 CA 15–003
Garratt v Saxby [2004] EWCA Civ 341; [2004] 1 W.L.R. 2152; [2004] C.P. Rep. 32; (2004) 101(11) L.S.G. 35; (2004) 148 S.J.L.B. 237 CA (Civ Div) 13–012
Gartner v Ernst & Young [2003] F.C.A. 152 17–015
GBR Investment Ltd v Keung HC Christchurch Civ [2010] N.Z.H.C. 411 ... 1–012, 7–011
GE Capital Commercial Finance Ltd v Sutton [2004] EWCA Civ 315; [2004] 2 B.C.L.C. 662; (2004) 101(14) L.S.G. 25 CA (Civ Div) 17–015
Geelong School Supplies Pty v Dean [2006] F.C.A. 1404 5–006
General Reinsurance Corp v Forsakringsaktiebolaget Fennia Patria [1983] Q.B. 856; [1983] 3 W.L.R. 318; [1983] 2 Lloyd's Rep. 287; (1983) 127 S.J. 389 CA (Civ Div) 4–022
Geneva Finance Ltd, Re (1992) 7 A.C.S.R. 415 17–015
Georgiou v Enfield LBC [2004] EWHC 779 (Admin); [2004] B.L.G.R. 497; [2004] 2 P. & C.R. 21; [2005] J.P.L. 62; (2004) 101(17) L.S.G. 33 QBD 12–011
GH Renton & Co Ltd v Palmyra Trading Corp of Panama (The Caspiana) [1957] A.C. 149; [1957] 2 W.L.R. 45; [1956] 3 All E.R. 957; [1956] 2 Lloyd's Rep. 379 HL 4–027
Gibson v Robert Small and Others 10 E.R. 499; (1853) 4 H.L. Cas. 353 HL 4–022
Gill v Humanware Europe Ltd (Costs) [2010] EWCA Civ 799; [2010] I.C.R. 1343; [2010] I.R.L.R. 877 13–017
Gillies v Secretary of State for Work and Pensions [2006] UKHL 2; [2006] 1 W.L.R. 781; [2006] 1 All E.R. 731; 2006 S.C. (H.L.) 71; 2006 S.L.T. 77; 2006 S.C.L.R. 276; [2006] I.C.R. 267; (2006) 9 C.C.L. Rep. 404; (2006) 103(9) L.S.G. 33; (2006) 150 S.J.L.B. 127; 2006 G.W.D. 3–66 HL 11–014
Glennie v McDougall & Cowan Holdings Ltd [1935] 2 D.L.R. 561 .. 4–011, 4–013
Glentree Estates v Gee [1981] E.G.L.R. 28 20–001
Gluckstein v Barnes [1900] A.C. 240 HL 4–013
Goddard v Nationwide Building Society [1987] Q.B. 670; [1986] 3 W.L.R. 734; [1986] 3 All E.R. 264; (1986) 83 L.S.G. 3592; (1986) 137 N.L.J. 775; (1986) 130 S.J. 803 CA (Civ Div) 9–004
Goldcorp Exchange Ltd (In Receivership), Re [1995] 1 A.C. 74; [1994] 3 W.L.R. 199; [1994] 2 All E.R. 806; [1994] 2 B.C.L.C. 578; [1994] C.L.C. 591; (1994) 13 Tr. L.R. 434; (1994) 91(24) L.S.G. 46; (1994) 144 N.L.J. 792; (1994) 138 S.J.L.B. 127 PC (NZ) 2–016
Gordon & Breach Science Publishers Ltd, Re [1995] B.C.C. 261; [1995] 2 B.C.L.C. 189 Ch D 5–016

Gorham v British Telecommunications Plc [2000] 1 W.L.R. 2129; [2000] 4
All E.R. 867; [2001] Lloyd's Rep. I.R. 531; [2000] Lloyd's Rep. P.N. 897;
[2001] P.N.L.R. 2; [2000] Pens. L.R. 293; (2000) 97(38) L.S.G. 44; (2000)
144 S.J.L.B. 251 CA 19–004
Gould v O'Carroll [1964] N.S.W.R. 803 2–022
Gran Gelato Ltd v Richcliff (Group) Ltd [1992] Ch. 560; [1992] 2 W.L.R.
867; [1992] 1 All E.R. 865; [1992] 1 E.G.L.R. 297; [1991] E.G. 136 (C.S.);
(1992) 142 N.L.J. 51 Ch D 9–001, 9–002
Grant v Teacher's Appeals Tribunal [2006] UKPC 59 PC (Jamaica) 13–022
Gregory v United Kingdom (22299/93) (1998) 25 E.H.R.R. 577 ECHR 11–010,
12–002
Grey v Alexander [2000] Australian and New Zealand Conveyancing Reports
386 5–003
Griffiths v Griffiths 67 E.R. 242; (1843) 2 Hare 587 5–004
Grimwade v Meagher [1995] 1 V.R. 446 .... 5–003, 5–012
Grissell v Bristowe (1867–68) L.R. 3 C.P. 112 4–022
Groom v Crocker [1939] 1 K.B. 194; (1938) 60 Ll. L. Rep. 393 CA 15–018
Group Josi Re Co SA v Walbrook Insurance Co Ltd [1996] 1 W.L.R. 1152;
[1996] 1 All E.R. 791; [1996] 1 Lloyd's Rep. 345; [1995] C.L.C. 1532;
[1996] 5 Re. L.R. 91 CA (Civ Div) 6–026
Guerin v R. (1984) 13 D.L.R. (4th) 321 SC (Can) 8–010
Gus Consulting GmbH v Leboeuf Lamb Greene & Macrae [2006] EWCA Civ
683; [2006] C.P. Rep. 40; [2006] 2 C.L.C. 88; [2006] P.N.L.R. 32; [2006]
C.I.L.L. 2371; (2006) 103(25) L.S.G. 31 CA (Civ Div) 7–017
Haira v Burbey [1995] 3 N.Z.L.R. 396 3–002
Hakansson v Sweden (A/171) (1991) 13 E.H.R.R. 1 ECHR 11–018
Halewood International Ltd v Addleshaw Booth & Co (A Firm) [2000]
Lloyd's Rep. P.N. 298; [2000] P.N.L.R. 788 Ch D 7–007, 7–016,
7–017, 8–018
Hall & Barker, Re (1878) L.R. 9 Ch. D. 538 Ch D 15–017
Halstuk v Venvil. *See* Baron Investments (Holdings) Ltd, Re
Hamilton v GMB (Northern Region) [2007] I.R.L.R. 391 EAT 13–024
Hamilton v GRB [2007] I.R.L.R. 391 EAT 13–001
Hampshire CC v Gillingham, unreported, April 5, 2000 CA 13–003
Hampshire Land Co (No.2), Re [1896] 2 Ch. 743 Ch D 6–026
Hanson v Lorenz and Jones [1987] 1 F.T.L.R. 23; (1986) 136 N.L.J. 1088 CA
(Civ Div) 2–013
Harker v Edwards (1888) 57 L.J.Q.B. 147 4–020
Harmony Shipping Co SA v Davis [1979] 1 W.L.R. 1380; [1979] 3 All E.R.
177; [1980] 1 Lloyd's Rep. 44 CA (Civ Div) 5–013, 5–015
Harris v Harris [1931] P. 10 4–006
Harrods Ltd v Lemon [1931] 2 K.B. 157; 80 A.L.R. 1067 CA 3–013, 6–026
Hart v Relentless Records Ltd [2002] EWHC 1984 (Ch); [2003] F.S.R. 36;
(2002) 152 N.L.J. 1562 Ch D 11–014, 13–007, 13–008
Haslam & Hier-Evans, Re [1902] 1 Ch. 765 CA 2–007
Hauschildt v Denmark (A/154) (1990) 12 E.H.R.R. 266 ECHR 11–10
Haywood v Toadnight [1927] V.L.R. 512 3–023
Heath v Parkinson [1926] T.L.R. 693 20–001
Helow v Advocate General for Scotland [2008] UKHL 62; [2008] 1 W.L.R.

2416; [2009] 2 All E.R. 1031; 2009 S.C. (H.L.) 1; 2008 S.L.T. 967; 2008
S.C.L.R. 830; (2008) 152(41) S.J.L.B. 29; 2008 G.W.D. 35–520 HL 11–014,
11–015, 13–004, 13–005, 13–026
Hemsworth's Application for Judicial Review, Re [2009] NIQB 33; [2010]
Inquest L.R. 1 QBD.. 12–012
Henderson v Merrett Syndicates Ltd (No.1) [1995] 2 A.C. 145; [1994] 3
W.L.R. 761; [1994] 3 All E.R. 506; [1994] 2 Lloyd's Rep. 468; [1994]
C.L.C. 918; (1994) 144 N.L.J. 1204 HL 2–019, 9–002
Henry Smith & Son v Muskett [1981] E.G.L.R. 23.. 20–001
Heron International Ltd v Lord Grade [1983] B.C.L.C. 244; [1982] Com.
L.R. 108 CA 19–011
Heywood v Wellers [1976] Q.B. 446 8–013
HIH Casualty & General Insurance Ltd v JLT Risk Solutions Ltd (formerly
Lloyd Thompson Ltd) [2007] EWCA Civ 710; [2008] Bus. L.R. 180; [2007]
2 All E.R. (Comm) 1106; [2007] 2 Lloyd's Rep. 278; [2007] 2 C.L.C.
62; [2007] Lloyd's Rep. I.R. 717; [2008] P.N.L.R. 3; (2007) 104(30) L.S.G.
35 20–005
Hilton v Barker Booth & Eastwood [2005] UKHL 8; [2005] 1 W.L.R. 567;
[2005] 1 All E.R. 651; [2005] P.N.L.R. 23; [2006] Pens. L.R. 1; [2005] 6
E.G. 141 (C.S.); (2005) 102(14) L.S.G. 27; (2005) 155 N.L.J. 219; (2005)
149 S.J.L.B. 179; [2005] N.P.C. 14 HL 2–028, 6–009, 6–010, 6–014,
6–018, 8–009, 15–005, 15–009
Hippisley v Knee Bros [1905] 1 K.B. 1 8–013
Hitachi Ltd SMS v Schloemann Siemag Aktiengesellschaft, unreported, June
30, 1994 14–014
Hodgkinson v Simms (1994) 97 B.C.L.R. 1 17–005
Hogg v Cramphorn [1967] Ch. 254; [1966] 3 W.L.R. 995; [1966] 3 All E.R.
420; (1966) 110 S.J. 887 Ch D 19–015
Holder v Holder [1968] Ch. 353; [1968] 2 W.L.R. 237; [1968] 1 All E.R. 665;
(1968) 112 S.J. 17 CA (Civ Div) 2–022
Holdsworth v MR Anderson & Associates Pty Ltd 5–005
Hong Kong Re Luen Cheong Tai Construction Co Ltd [2002] 1354
H.K.C.U.1 17–019
Hood Sailmakers Ltd v Berthom Boat Co Ltd, *Independent*, May 10, 1999 .. 8–015
Horcal Ltd v Gatland (1984) 1 B.C.C. 99089; [1984] I.R.L.R. 288 CA (Civ
Div) 18–003
Hornan v Latif Group SL [2003] EWHC 536 (Ch); [2003] B.C.C. 976; [2003]
2 B.C.L.C. 186 Ch D 9–009
Hospital Products Ltd v United States Surgical Corp (1984) 156 C.L.R. 41
HCA... 2–004, 2–013, 2–015, 2–019, 5–015
Howard Smith Ltd v Ampol Petroleum Ltd [1974] A.C. 821; [1974] 2
W.L.R. 689; [1974] 1 All E.R. 1126; 118 S.J.L.B. 330; (1974) 118 S.J. 330
PC (Aus) 18–009, 19–015
Howell v Lees Millais [2007] EWCA Civ 720; (2007) 104(29) L.S.G. 24;
(2007) 151 S.J.L.B. 922; [2007] N.P.C. 88 CA (Civ Div) 13–015
Hrvatska Elektroprivreda dd v Republic of Slovenia, unreported, May 6,
2008 .... 14–012, 14–013, 14–014
Hurt, Re (1988) 80 A.L.R. 236 .... 17–002, 17–020
Hussain v Cuddy Woods & Cochrane [2001] Lloyd's Rep. P.N. 134 CA 16–005

IGI Insurance Ltd v Kirkland Timms Ltd, unreported, December 5, 1995 20–005
Ikarian Reefer. *See* National Justice Compania Naviera SA v Prudential Assurance Co Ltd
Imperial Mercantile Credit Association (In Liquidation) v Coleman (1873) L.R. 6 H.L. 189 HL 4–013
In Plus Group Ltd v Pyke [2002] EWCA Civ 370; [2003] B.C.C. 332; [2002] 2 B.C.L.C. 201 CA (Civ Div) 18–005
In the Marriage of A and B (1990) 13 Fam.L.R. 798 6–023
In the Marriage of Magro (1989) 93 F.L.R. 365 6–023
In the Marriage of Thevenaz [1986] F.L.C. 91–748 5–011
Indata Equipment Supplies Ltd (t/a Autofleet) v ACL Ltd [1998] 1 B.C.L.C. 412; [1998] F.S.R. 248; (1997) 141 S.J.L.B. 216 CA (Civ Div) 2–012, 2–013
Independent Management Resources Pty Ltd v Brown [1987] V.R. 605 7–011
Independent Pension Trustee Ltd v LAW Construction Co Ltd 1997 S.L.T. 1105 CS 17–015
Industrial Development Consultants Ltd v Cooley [1972] 1 W.L.R. 443; [1972] 2 All E.R. 162; (1972) 116 S.J. 255 Assizes (Birmingham) 2–014, 2–021, 2–022, 18–005
Island Export Finance v Umunna [1986] B.C.L.C. 460 18–005
Island Records Ltd v Tring International plc [1996] 1 W.L.R. 1256 8–011
Ismail Zai v State of Western Australia [2007] W.A.S.C.A. 150 .... 5–012, 7–013
Item Software (UK) Ltd v Fassihi [2004] EWCA Civ 1244; [2004] B.C.C. 994; [2005] 2 B.C.L.C. 91; [2005] I.C.R. 450; [2004] I.R.L.R. 928; (2004) 101(39) L.S.G. 34; (2004) 148 S.J.L.B. 1153 CA (Civ Div) 2–011, 6–003, 18–003, 18–005
J&P Avax SA v Societe Tecnimont SPA, unreported, February 12, 2009 CA (Paris) 14–002
Jaison Property Development Co Ltd v Swinhoe [2010] EWHC 2467 (QB) QBD 9–002
JD Wetherspoon Plc v Van de Berg & Co Ltd [2009] EWHC 639 (Ch); [2009] 16 E.G. 138 (C.S.) Ch D 2–023
Jewo Ferrous BV v Lewis Moore (A Firm) [2001] Lloyd's Rep. P.N. 6; [2001] P.N.L.R. 12 CA (Civ Div) 4–002
Jirna v Mister Donut of Canada (1971) 22 D.L.R. (3d) 639 CA (Ontario) 4–027
John Crowther Group v Carpets International [1990] B.C.L.C. 460 19–011
Johnson v Bingley [1997] P.N.L.R. 392; [1995] N.P.C. 27 QBD 15–003
Johnson v EBS Pensioner Trustees Ltd [2002] EWCA Civ 164; [2002] Lloyd's Rep. P.N. 309 CA (Civ Div) 3–023, 8–007
Johnson v Johnson [2000] 5 L.R.C. 223 11–014
Johnson, Assignees of Cochrane, a Bankrupt v Marriott 149 E.R. 725; (1833) 2 Cr. & M. 183 5–004
Jones v Canavan [1972] 2 N.S.W.L.R. 236 4–022
Jones v DAS Legal Expenses Insurance Co Ltd [2003] EWCA Civ 1071; [2004] I.R.L.R. 218; (2003) 147 S.J.L.B. 932 CA (Civ Div) 11–004, 11–012, 11–019, 11–020, 13–001
JRL Ex p. CJL, Re (1986) 161 C.L.R. 342 13–001
Kallinicos v Hunt [2005] N.S.W.S.C. 1181 5–006
Katz v McNally [1997] 2 B.C.L.C. 579 17–018

TABLE OF CASES

Kearney (Arthur) v HM Advocate [2006] UKPC D 1; 2006 S.C. (P.C.) 1; 2006 S.L.T. 499; 2006 S.C.C.R. 130; [2006] H.R.L.R. 15; 20 B.H.R.C. 157; 2006 G.W.D. 15–284 PC (Scotland) 11–008
Kelly v Cooper [1993] A.C. 205; [1992] 3 W.L.R. 936; [1994] 1 B.C.L.C. 395; [1992] E.G. 119 (C.S.); (1992) 136 S.J.L.B. 303; [1992] N.P.C. 134 PC (Bermuda) 1–001, 2–019, 3–011, 4–016, 4–017, 4–018, 4–019, 4–020, 6–002, 6–006, 6–015, 6–016, 6–019, 8–009, 8–013, 15–015, 17–008, 20–001
Kempe v Bailey [2003] 174 F.L.R. 460 11–019
Kenyon-Brown v Desmond Banks & Co (Undue Influence) (No.1) [2000] Lloyd's Rep. Bank. 80; [2000] Lloyd's Rep. P.N. 338; [2000] P.N.L.R. 266; (1999) 149 N.L.J. 1832; [1999] N.P.C. 140 CA (Civ Div) 4–011, 4–015
Keppel v Wheeler [1927] 1 K.B. 577 .... 8–013, 20–001
Kesselhaut v United States 555 F.2d 791 (Ct. Cl. 1977) 1–013
KFTCIC v Icori Estero SpA, unreported, June 28, 1991 13–002
Kingston Cotton Mill Co (No.2), Re [1896] 2 Ch. 279 CA 17–001
Koch Shipping Inc v Richards Butler [2002] EWCA Civ 1280; [2002] 2 All E.R. (Comm) 957; [2003] C.P. Rep. 10; [2002] Lloyd's Rep. P.N. 604; [2003] P.N.L.R. 11; (2002) 99(37) L.S.G. 39; (2002) 146 S.J.L.B. 197 CA (Civ Div) 7–007, 7–016, 7–017, 7–020
Konigsberg (A Bankrupt), Re [1989] 1 W.L.R. 1257; [1989] 3 All E.R. 289; [1990] Fam. Law 94; (1989) 86(40) L.S.G. 44; (1989) 139 N.L.J. 1302; (1989) 133 S.J. 1337 Ch D 4–006
Kooky Garments Ltd v Charlton [1994] N.Z.L.R. 587 5–003
KPMG v White, unreported, November 18, 1996 7–009
Kuwait Asia Bank EC v National Mutual Life Nominees Ltd [1991] 1 A.C. 187; [1990] 3 W.L.R. 297; [1990] 3 All E.R. 404; [1990] 2 Lloyd's Rep. 95; [1990] B.C.C. 567; [1990] B.C.L.C. 868 PC (NZ) 18–007
L (Children) (Care Proceedings: Cohabiting Solicitors), Re [2001] 1 W.L.R. 100; [2000] 2 F.L.R. 887; [2000] 3 F.C.R. 71; [2000] Fam. Law 810; (2000) 97(40) L.S.G. 42; (2000) 144 S.J.L.B. 238 Fam Div 5–009, 5–011, 16–009
Lac Minerals Ltd v International Corona Resources Ltd [1990] F.S.R. 441 SC (Can) 2–004, 2–012, 2–013
Laker Airways Inc v FLS Aerospace Ltd [2000] 1 W.L.R. 113; [1999] 2 Lloyd's Rep. 45; [1999] C.L.C. 1124 QBD 14–002, 14–010, 16–008
Lambert v Thurston 90 E.R. 667; (1690) Carth. 108 4–013
Lands Allotment Co, Re [1894] 1 Ch. 616 CA 18–001
Langborger v Sweden (A/155) (1990) 12 E.H.R.R. 416 ECHR 11–010
Lansing Linde Ltd v Kerr [1991] 1 W.L.R. 251; [1991] 1 All E.R. 418; [1991] I.C.R. 428; [1991] I.R.L.R. 80; (1990) 140 N.L.J. 1458 CA (Civ Div) 8–002
LaSalle National Bank v County of Lake 703 F.2d 252 (7th Cir. 1983) 1–013
Lascomme Ltd v United Dominions Trust (Ireland) Ltd [1993] 3 I.R. 412; [1994] 1 I.R.L.M. 227 17–015
Law Society of New South Wales v Harvey [1976] 2 N.S.W.L.R. 154 6–020
Law v Chartered Institute of Patent Agents [1919] 2 Ch. 276 Ch D 11–011
Lawal v Northern Spirit Ltd [2003] UKHL 35; [2004] 1 All E.R. 187; [2003] I.C.R. 856; [2003] I.R.L.R. 538; [2003] H.R.L.R. 29; [2003] U.K.H.R.R. 1024; (2003) 100(28) L.S.G. 30; (2003) 153 N.L.J. 1005; (2003) 147 S.J.L.B. 783 HL 13–020

Lawrence David Ltd v Ashton [1991] 1 All E.R. 385; [1989] I.C.R. 123; [1989] I.R.L.R. 22; [1989] 1 F.S.R. 87; (1988) 85(42) L.S.G. 48 CA (Civ Div) 8–002
L-B (Children) (Care Proceedings: Recusal), Re [2010] EWCA Civ 1118; [2011] 1 F.L.R. 889; [2011] Fam. Law 132; (2010) 154(37) S.J.L.B. 30 CA (Civ Div) 11–013
Lee Panavision Ltd v Lee Lighting Ltd [1991] B.C.C. 620; [1992] B.C.L.C. 22 CA (Civ Div) 18–009
Levy-Russell Ltd v Tecmotiv Inc (1994) 54 C.P.R. 3d 161 17–015
Lilly ICOS Ltd v Pfizer Ltd (No.1) [2001] F.S.R. 16; (2001) 59 B.M.L.R. 123; (2001) 24(1) I.P.D. 23006 Ch D 5–015
Lincoln v Holmesglen Institute of TAFE [1999] F.C.A. 601 5–003
Lively, ltd v City of Munich [1976] 1 W.L.R. 1004; [1976] 3 All E.R. 851; (1976) 120 S.J. 719 QBD 5–013
Liverpool Roman Catholic Archdiocesan Trustees Inc v Goldberg (No.3) [2001] 1 W.L.R. 2337; [2001] 4 All E.R. 950; [2001] B.L.R. 479; [2002] T.C.L.R. 4; (2001) 98(32) L.S.G. 37; (2001) 151 N.L.J. 1093 Ch D 5–013
Lloyds Bank Ltd v EB Savory & Co [1933] A.C. 201; (1932) 44 Ll. L. Rep. 231 HL 6–026
Locabail (UK) Ltd v Bayfield Properties Ltd (Leave to Appeal) [2000] Q.B. 451; [2000] 2 W.L.R. 870; [2000] 1 All E.R. 65; [2000] I.R.L.R. 96; [2000] H.R.L.R. 290; [2000] U.K.H.R.R. 300; 7 B.H.R.C. 583; (1999) 149 N.L.J. 1793; [1999] N.P.C. 143 CA (Civ Div) 7–020, 11–003, 11–004, 11–018, 13–001, 13–010, 13–018, 13–019, 13–027, 14–002
Lodwick v Southwark LBC [2004] EWCA Civ 306; [2004] I.C.R. 884; [2004] I.R.L.R. 554; (2004) 148 S.J.L.B. 385 CA (Civ Div) 13–003, 13–010
London & Mashonaland Exploration Co Ltd v Mashonaland Exploration Co Ltd [1891] W.N. 165 18–005
Longstaff v Birtles [2001] EWCA Civ 1219; [2002] 1 W.L.R. 470; [2001] 34 E.G. 98 (C.S.); (2001) 98(34) L.S.G. 43; (2001) 145 S.J.L.B. 210; [2001] N.P.C. 128 CA (Civ Div) 2–027
Lonrho Ltd v Shell Petroleum Co Ltd (No.1) [1980] 1 W.L.R. 627; (1980) 124 S.J. 412 HL 6–026
Loosemore v Financial Concepts [2001] Lloyd's Rep. P.N. 235 QBD 19–004
Lord Norreys v Hodgson [1897] 13 T.L.R. 421 4–013
Lowerstoft, Re 1986 B.C.L.C. 81 5–016
Lumley v Gye 118 E.R. 749; (1853) 2 El. & Bl. 216 2–025
Lumley v Wagner 42 E.R. 687; (1852) 1 De G.M. & G. 604 2–025
Luxor (Eastbourne) Ltd v Cooper [1941] A.C. 108 HL 17–008, 20–001
M(K) v M(H) (1992) 96 D.L.R. (4th) 289 2–004
Macmillan v Macmillan [2000] F.L.C. 93–048 5–011
Macquarie Bank Ltd v Myer [1994] 1 V.R. 350 5–005
Macro v Thompson (No.3) [1997] 2 B.C.L.C. 36 Ch D 13–023
Madhani v Pirani, unreported, October 16, 1997 17–005
Maes Finance Ltd v Sharp & Partners 69 Con. L.R. 46 QBD 6–005
Maguire v Makaronis [1955–95] P.N.L.R. 933 HC (Aus) 3–023
Mahli v Abbey Life Assurance Co Ltd [1996] L.R.L.R. 237; [1994] C.L.C. 615; [1995] 4 Re. L.R. 305 CA (Civ Div) 6–026
Mahomed v Morris (No.1) (2000) 97(7) L.S.G. 41 CA (Civ Div) 13–009

xxvii

Mallesons Stephen Jacques v KPMG Peat Marwick [1990] 4 W.A.R. 357.... 5–018, 6–023
Man O'War Station Ltd v Auckland City Council (No.1) [2002] UKPC 28 PC (NZ) 11–013, 13–002, 13–021
Mannesmann AG v Goldman Sachs International, unreported, November 18, 1999 .... 7–010, 8–018, 19–016
Marks & Spencer Plc v Freshfields Bruckhaus Deringer [2004] EWCA Civ 741; [2005] P.N.L.R. 4; (2004) 148 S.J.L.B. 788 CA (Civ Div) 3–010, 3–012, 4–010, 15–004, 19–017
Marwick Mitchell & Co v Superior Court 200 Cal.App.272, 293–4 (1988) 7–001
Maxwell Communications Corp Plc (No.1), Re [1992] B.C.C. 372; [1992] B.C.L.C. 465 Ch D 5–016, 9–009, 17–021, 17–023
McCullagh v Lane Fox (1995) 49 Con,L.R. 124 [1996] 1 E.G.L.R. 35 9–002
McDonald Estates v Martin [1990] 77 D.L.R. (4th) 249 .... 1–011, 5–003, 6–023, 6–025, 7–003, 7–014, 8–003, 17–012
McGrath v Shah (1989) 57 P. & C.R. 452 Ch D 4–027
McInerney v MacDonald (1992) 93 D.L.R. (4th) 415 .... 2–004, 2–010
McInerny v McDonald [1992] 2 S.C.R. 138 6–003
McMaster v Byrne [1952] 1 All E.R. 1362; [1952] W.N. 239; (1952) 96 S.J. 325 PC (Can).. 2–027, 3–025, 4–013, 4–015
McVeigh v Linen House Pty Ltd [1999] 3 V.R. 394....................................... 5–005
Meat Corp of Namibia Ltd v Dawn Meats (UK) Ltd [2011] EWHC 474 (Ch) Ch D 5–015, 8–005
Medicaments and Related Classes of Goods (No.2), Re. *See* Director General of Fair Trading v Proprietary Association of Great Britain
Meerabux v Attorney General of Belize [2005] UKPC 12; [2005] 2 A.C. 513; [2005] 2 W.L.R. 1307 PC (Belize) 11–004, 11–021
Mendoza & Co v Bell 159 E.G. 372; [1952] C.P.L. 334 20–001
Merck v Interpharm (1992) 44 C.P.R. (3d) 440; (1993) 46 C.P.R. (3d)513 ... 9–004
Meridian Global Funds Management Asia Ltd v Securities Commission [1995] 2 A.C. 500; [1995] 3 W.L.R. 413; [1995] 3 All E.R. 918; [1995] B.C.C. 942; [1995] 2 B.C.L.C. 116; (1995) 92(28) L.S.G. 39; (1995) 139 S.J.L.B. 152 PC (NZ) 6–026
Metropolitan Properties Co (FGC) Ltd v Lannon [1969] 1 Q.B. 577; [1968] 3 W.L.R. 694; [1968] 3 All E.R. 304; (1968) 19 P. & C.R. 856; [1968] R.V.R. 490; (1968) 112 S.J. 585 CA (Civ Div).. 11–011
Meyer v Scottish Cooperative Wholesale Society Ltd [1959] A.C. 324; [1958] 3 W.L.R. 404; [1958] 3 All E.R. 66; 1958 S.C. (H.L.) 40; 1958 S.L.T. 241; (1958) 102 S.J. 617 HL 18–009
MG v The Queen N.S.W.C.C.A 57 5–012
Michel v Lafrentz (1997) 199 A.R. 81 17–011
Micklefield v SAC Technology Ltd [1990] 1 W.L.R. 1002; [1991] 1 All E.R. 275; [1990] I.R.L.R. 218 Ch D.. 4–026
Midland Bank Trust Co Ltd v Hett Stubbs & Kemp [1979] Ch. 384; [1978] 3 W.L.R. 167; [1978] 3 All E.R. 571; [1955–95] P.N.L.R. 95; (1977) 121 S.J. 830 Ch D 4–027, 15–017, 15–018
Millar (David Cameron) v Dickson [2001] UKPC D 4; [2002] 1 W.L.R. 1615; [2002] 3 All E.R. 1041; 2002 S.C. (P.C.) 30; 2001 S.L.T. 988; 2001 S.C.C.R.

TABLE OF CASES

741; [2001] H.R.L.R. 59; [2001] U.K.H.R.R. 999; 2001 G.W.D. 26–1015 PC (Scotland).. 11–005, 11–018
Milner (JH) & Son v Bilton (Percy) Ltd [1966] 1 W.L.R. 1582; [1966] 2 All E.R. 894; (1966) 110 S.J. 635 QBD 15–017
Mintel International Group Ltd v Minter (Australia) Pty Ltd [2000] F.C.A 1410 7–013
Minter v Priest [1930] A.C. 558 HL 7–007
Mireskandari v Law Society [2009] EWCA Civ 864 CA (Civ Div)............. 11–012, 13–019
Mitchell v Pringle and Watt, unreported, May 3, 1991 17–007
Mixnam's Properties Ltd v Chertsey Urban DC [1965] A.C. 735; [1964] 2 W.L.R. 1210; [1964] 2 All E.R. 627; (1964) 128 J.P. 405; 62 L.G.R. 528; (1964) 15 P. & C.R. 331; [1964] R.V.R. 632; (1964) 108 S.J. 402 HL 19–004
Moch v Nedtravel (Pty) Ltd (1996) (3) S.A. 1 1–011
Molchan v Omega Oil and Gas [1988] 1 S.C.R. 348 4–027
Moody v Cox [1917] 2 Ch. 71 CA 3–013, 3–019, 3–022, 3–023, 4–013, 6–001, 6–007, 6–010, 6–014, 6–022
Moorgate Tobacco Co Ltd v Philip Morris Ltd (1984) 156 C.L.R. 414 2–013
Mortgage Express Ltd v Bowerman & Partners [1996] 2 All E.R. 836; [1996] E.C.C. 228; [1996] P.N.L.R. 62; [1996] 1 E.G.L.R. 126; [1996] 04 E.G. 126; [1995] E.G. 129 (C.S.); [1995] N.P.C. 129 CA (Civ Div) 6–004, 6–005, 6–006, 6–007, 6–009, 6–020
Moult v Halliday [1898] 1 Q.B. 125 QBD 4–022
Movitex v Bulfield (1986) 2 B.C.C. 99403; [1988] B.C.L.C. 104 Ch D 4–027
Moy v Pettman Smith (A Firm) [2002] EWCA Civ 875; [2002] C.P.L.R. 619; [2002] Lloyd's Rep. P.N. 513; [2002] P.N.L.R. 44 16–005
Mullins v Rothschild [2001] T.A.S.S.C. 76 .... 5–011, 5–012
Murad v Al-Saraj [2004] EWHC 1235 (Ch) Ch D 2–013
Murray v Macquarie Bank (1991) 33 F.C.R. 46 5–003
Mutual Life Insurance v Rank Organisation [1985] B.C.L.C. 11 19–010
Mutual Reinsurance Co Ltd v Peat Marwick Mitchell & Co [1997] 1 Lloyd's Rep. 253; [1996] B.C.C. 1010; [1997] 1 B.C.L.C. 1; [1997] P.N.L.R. 75 CA (Civ Div).. 17–008
National Home Loans Corp Plc v Giffen Couch & Archer [1998] 1 W.L.R. 207; [1997] 3 All E.R. 808; [1998] P.N.L.R. 111; [1997] N.P.C. 100 Court CA (Civ Div) 4–002, 4–003, 6–005, 6–009, 6–015
National Justice Compania Naviera SA v Prudential Assurance Co Ltd (The Ikarian Reefer) (No.1) [1993] 2 Lloyd's Rep. 68; [1993] F.S.R. 563; [1993] 37 E.G. 158 QBD 5–013
National Mutual Holdings Pty Ltd v Sentry Corp [1989] 22 F.C.R. 209 7–003
Nationwide Building Society v Balmer Radmore. See Nationwide Building Society v Various Solicitors (No.3)
Nationwide Building Society v Various Solicitors (No.3) [1999] Lloyd's Rep. P.N. 241; [1999] P.N.L.R. 606; [1999] E.G. 15 (C.S.); (1999) 96(9) L.S.G. 31; (1999) 143 S.J.L.B. 58; [1999] N.P.C. 15 Ch D............3–024, 6–007, 6–008, 6–021, 8–010, 8–012
Nema, The. See Pioneer Shipping Ltd v BTP Tioxide Ltd
New China Hong Kong Group v Ernst & Young [2003] H.K.C.U. 457 17–008

TABLE OF CASES

New Zealand Netherlands Society "Oranje" v Kuys [1973] 1 W.L.R. 1126; [1973] 2 All E.R. 1222; [1974] R.P.C. 272; (1973) 117 S.J. 565 PC (NZ)....4–013

Newhart Developments Ltd v Cooperative Commercial Bank Ltd [1978] Q.B. 814; [1978] 2 W.L.R. 636; [1978] 2 All E.R. 896; (1977) 121 S.J. 847 CA (Civ Div).. 17–014, 17–015

Newman v Phillips Fox (1999) 21 W.A.R. 309 .... 7–014, 7–018

Newsholme Bros v Road Transport & General Insurance Co Ltd [1929] 2 K.B. 356; (1929) 34 Ll. L. Rep. 247 CA 20–005

Nickel Mines Ltd, Re (1978) 3 A.C.L.R. 686 .... 17–018, 17–019

Nickleseekers Ltd v Vance 1985 1 QdR 272 11–019

Nida Pty Ltd, Re (1993) 10 A.C.S.R. 195 17–018

Nikolay v Peters [2010] S.G.H.C. 290 .... 3–013, 15–004

Noranda Australia Ltd v Lachlan Resources (1988) 13 N.S.W.L.R. 1............ 2–013

Norberg v Wynrib [1992] 2 S.C.R. 226 .... 2–013, 2–015

Norbrook Laboratories Ltd v Tank [2006] EWHC 1055 (Comm); [2006] 2 Lloyd's Rep. 485; [2006] B.L.R. 412 QBD 14–002

North & South Trust Co v Berkeley [1971] 1 W.L.R. 470; [1971] 1 All E.R. 980; [1970] 2 Lloyd's Rep. 467; (1970) 115 S.J. 244 QBD (CC)............... 3–013, 4–022, 6–002, 6–006, 20–004, 20–005

Northumberland Insurance v Alexander [1984] 8 A.C.L.R. 882..................... 6–025

NWL Ltd v Woods (The Nawala) (No.2) [1979] 1 W.L.R. 1294; [1979] 3 All E.R. 614; [1980] 1 Lloyd's Rep. 1; [1979] I.C.R. 867; [1979] I.R.L.R. 478; (1979) 123 S.J. 751 HL 8–002

O'Reilly v Law Society (1988) 24 N.S.W.L.R. 204 6–020

Oceanic v HIH [1999] N.S.W.S.C. 292....................5–003, 7–011, 15–018

Omega Trust Co Ltd v Wright Son & Pepper (No.2) [1998] P.N.L.R. 337 QBD 6–017, 6–018, 6–019, 15–003

Oppenheimer v Frazer & Wyatt [1907] 2 K.B. 50 CA 6–025

Orchard v South Eastern Electricity Board [1987] Q.B. 565; [1987] 2 W.L.R. 102; [1987] 1 All E.R. 95; (1986) 130 S.J. 956

Orient Power Holdings, Re [2008] H.K.C.U. 200 17–023

Orr v Ford (1989) 167 C.L.R. 340... 8–017

P v General Council of the Bar [2005] 1 W.L.R. 3019 12–008

P v P (Ancillary Relief: Proceeds of Crime) [2003] EWHC 2260 (Fam); [2004] Fam. 1; [2003] 3 W.L.R. 1350; [2003] 4 All E.R. 843; [2004] 1 F.L.R. 193; [2003] 3 F.C.R. 459; [2003] W.T.L.R. 1449; [2004] Fam. Law 9; (2003) 100(41) L.S.G. 33; (2003) 153 N.L.J. 1550; (2003) 147 S.J.L.B. 1206 Fam Div 10–001, 10–006, 10–007

P&V Industries Pty Ltd v Porto [2006] 14 V.R. 1 2–011

Pacific China Holdings Ltd v Grand Pacific Holdings Ltd HCCT 5/2007 SC (HK).. 14–002

Palmer Marine Surveys Ltd, Re [1986] 1 W.L.R. 573; (1985) 1 B.C.C. 99557; [1986] P.C.C. 317; (1986) 83 L.S.G. 1895; (1986) 130 S.J. 372 Ch D 5–016

Panton v Minister of Finance [2001] UKPC 33 PC (Jamaica)...................... 11–007

Paramount Acceptance Co Ltd v Souster [1981] 2 N.Z.L.R. 38................... 17–015

Parker v McKenna (1874–75) L.R. 10 Ch. App. 96 3–006

Parmalat Capital Finance Ltd v Food Holdings Ltd (In Liquidation) [2008] UKPC 23; [2008] B.C.C. 371; [2009] 1 B.C.L.C. 274; [2008] B.P.I.R. 641 PC (Cayman) 17–019

Pass v Dundas (1880) 43 L.T. 665 4–025
Pavel v Sony Corp (No.2) [1995] R.P.C. 500 CA 16–008
PCCW HKT Telephone Ltd v Aitken [2009] H.K.C.U. 198............... 8–005, 9–007
PCW Syndicates v PCW Reinsurers [1996] 1 W.L.R. 1136; [1996] 1 All E.R. 774; [1996] 1 Lloyd's Rep. 241; [1995] C.L.C. 1517; [1995] 4 Re. L.R. 373 CA (Civ Div) 6–026
Peek v Gurney (1873) L.R. 6 H.L. 377; [1861–1873] All E.R. Rep. 116 HL.. 4–013
Peet v Mid Kent Area Healthcare NHS Trust [2001] EWCA Civ 1703; [2002] 1 W.L.R. 210; [2002] 3 All E.R. 688; [2002] C.P.L.R. 27; [2002] Lloyd's Rep. Med. 33; (2002) 65 B.M.L.R. 43; (2001) 98(48) L.S.G. 29; (2001) 145 S.J.L.B. 261 CA (Civ Div).. 5–014
Peninsula Business Services v English [2008] EWHC 1824......................... 13–024
Perak Pioneer Ltd, Re (No.2) [1985] H.K.C. 430.. 17–019
Perot Systems Europe v Johnson, unreported, May 5, 2003 13–003
Perotti v Collyer-Bristow (A Firm) (Liability: Negligence) [2003] EWHC 25 (Ch); [2003] W.T.L.R. 1473 Ch D 2–025, 15–017
Perry v Barnett (1884–85) L.R. 15 Q.B.D. 388 CA 4–020
Perry v Edwin Coe Independent, April 1, 1994 Ch D................................ 4–006
Petroleum Wholesale Inc v Marshall 751 S.W. 2d 295, Texas Ct App (1988)... 7–019
Pfeifer & Plankl v Austria (1991) 19 E.H.R.R. 389 ECHR...................... 11–018
PG Prebble & Co (A Firm) v West 211 E.G. 831; (1969) 113 S.J. 657 CA (Civ Div) 20–001
Phillips Products v Hyland [1987] 1 W.L.R. 659; [1987] 2 All E.R. 620; (1988) 4 Const. L.J. 53; (1985) 82 L.S.G. 681; (1985) 129 S.J. 47; (1985) 4 Tr. L. 98 CA (Civ Div) 4–027
PhotoCure v Queen's University at Kingston [2002] I.P.R. 56 7–012
Piersack v Belgium (A/53) (1983) 5 E.H.R.R. 169 ECHR 11–010
Pilmer v Duke Group Ltd (in liquidation) [2001] 2 B.C.L.C. 73 17–009
Pilmer v Duke Group Ltd [2001] 207 C.L.R. 165 .... 2–010, 6–003
Pioneer Shipping Ltd v BTP Tioxide Ltd (The Nema) (No.2) [1982] A.C. 724; [1981] 3 W.L.R. 292; [1981] 2 All E.R. 1030; [1981] 2 Lloyd's Rep. 239; [1981] Com. L.R. 197; (1981) 125 S.J. 542 HL 4–027
Poche, Re [1984] 6 D.L.R. (4d) 40.. 4–025
Poland v Julien Praet et Cie SA [1961] 1 Lloyd's Rep. 187 CA 20–005
Polly Peck International Plc (In Administration) (No.1), Re [1991] B.C.C. 503 Ch D.. 9–009, 17–021
Porter v Magill [2001] UKHL 67; [2002] 2 A.C. 357; [2002] 2 W.L.R. 37; [2002] 1 All E.R. 465; [2002] H.R.L.R. 16; [2002] H.L.R. 16; [2002] B.L.G.R. 51; (2001) 151 N.L.J. 1886; [2001] N.P.C. 184 HL..................... 1–001, 5–014, 11–001, 11–005, 11–011, 11–013, 12–010, 13–002, 14–002, 14–004, 14–015, 17–009, 17–010, 17–011
Powell v May [1946] K.B. 330 KBD 19–004
Pradhan v Eastside Day Surgery Pty [1999] S.A.S.C. 256.................. 5–016, 7–014, 7–017, 17–011, 17–023
Prentice v Payne (2004) 120 L.Q.R. 198... 18–005
President of The Republic of South Africa v South African Rugby Football Union (1999) (7) B.C.L.R. (CC) 725 13–001

Price v Metropolitan House Investment and Agency Co (1907) 23 T.L.R. 630 20–001
Primrose Holdings v Ampers [2004] 3 N.Z.L.R. 521 9–002
Project v Hutt (2006) 150 S.J.L.B. 702 EAT 13–008
Pullar v United Kingdom (22399/93) 1996 S.C.C.R. 755; (1996) 22 E.H.R.R. 391 ECHR.. 12–003
R (on the application of Pounder) v Coroner for North and South Districts of Durham and Darlington [2010] EWHC 2419 12–012
R. (on the application of Brooke) v Parole Board [2007] EWHC 2036 (Admin); [2007] H.R.L.R. 46; [2008] Prison L.R. 76; [2007] A.C.D. 99; (2007) 157 N.L.J. 1463; (2007) 151 S.J.L.B. 1167; Times, October 18, 2007 DC.. 11–009
R. (on the application of Compton) v Wiltshire Primary Care Trust [2009] EWHC 1824 (Admin); [2010] P.T.S.R. (C.S.) 5 QBD 13–025
R. (on the application of Condron) v National Assembly for Wales [2006] EWCA Civ 1573; [2007] B.L.G.R. 87; [2007] 2 P. & C.R. 4; [2007] J.P.L. 938; [2006] 49 E.G. 94 (C.S.); [2006] N.P.C. 127; [2007] Env. L.R. D7 CA (Civ Div)..11–014, 12–010, 13–016
R. (on the application of Darsho Kaur) v Institute of Legal Executives [2011] EWCA Civ 116 .... 11–004, 12–004
R. (on the application of Holding & Barnes Plc) v Secretary of State for the Environment, Transport and the Regions [2001] UKHL 23; [2003] 2 A.C. 295; [2001] 2 W.L.R. 1389; [2001] 2 All E.R. 929; [2002] Env. L.R. 12; [2001] H.R.L.R. 45; [2001] U.K.H.R.R. 728; (2001) 3 L.G.L.R. 38; (2001) 82 P. & C.R. 40; [2001] 2 P.L.R. 76; [2001] J.P.L. 920; [2001] 20 E.G. 228 (C.S.); (2001) 98(24) L.S.G. 45; (2001) 151 N.L.J. 727; (2001) 145 S.J.L.B. 140; [2001] N.P.C. 90 HL 11–009
R. (on the application of Island Farm Development Ltd) v Bridgend CBC [2006] EWHC 2189 (Admin); [2007] B.L.G.R. 60; (2006) 103(36) L.S.G. 36; (2006) 150 S.J.L.B. 1153; [2006] N.P.C. 100 QBD 12–011
R. (on the application of Lewis) v Redcar and Cleveland BC [2007] EWHC 3166 (Admin); [2008] J.P.L. 1156; [2008] A.C.D. 38 QBD 12–011
R. (on the application of Paul) v Deputy Coroner of the Queen's Household [2007] EWHC 408 (Admin); [2008] Q.B. 172; [2007] 3 W.L.R. 503; [2007] 2 All E.R. 509; (2007) 95 B.M.L.R. 137; [2007] Inquest L.R. 17; (2007) 157 N.L.J. 366 DC 11–015
R. (on the application of PD) v West Midlands and North West Mental Health Review Tribunal [2004] EWCA Civ 311; [2004] M.H.L.R. 174; (2004) 148 S.J.L.B. 384 CA (Civ Div)... 12–010
R. v Abdroikov (Nurlon) [2007] UKHL 37; [2007] 1 W.L.R. 2679; [2008] 1 All E.R. 315; [2008] 1 Cr. App. R. 21; [2008] Inquest L.R. 1; [2008] Crim. L.R. 134; (2007) 151 S.J.L.B. 1365 ....12–003, 12–004, 12–008
R. v Alexander, unreported, July 28, 2004 CA.. 12–006
R. v Ali (Syed Shadat) [2009] EWCA Crim 1763; [2009] Inquest L.R. 228 CA (Civ Div) 12–004
R. v Amber Valley DC Ex p. Jackson [1985] 1 W.L.R. 298; [1984] 3 All E.R. 501; (1985) 50 P. & C.R. 136 QBD 12–010
R. v Bajwa (Narideep) [2007] EWCA Crim 1618 CA (Civ Div).................... 12–002
R. v Barnsley Licensing Justices Ex p. Barnsley and District Licensed Victuallers

Association [1960] 2 Q.B. 167; [1960] 3 W.L.R. 305; [1960] 2 All E.R. 703; (1960) 124 J.P. 359; 58 L.G.R. 285; (1960) 104 S.J. 583 CA 11–011
R. v Batt (Peter James) [1996] Crim. L.R. 910 CA 5–009, 5–012, 16–009
R. v Bow Street Metropolitan Stipendiary Magistrate Ex p. Pinochet Ugarte (No.2) [2000] 1 A.C. 119; [1999] 2 W.L.R. 272; [1999] 1 All E.R. 577; 6 B.H.R.C. 1; (1999) 11 Admin. L.R. 57; (1999) 96(6) L.S.G. 33; (1999) 149 N.L.J. 88 HL 1–001, 1–005, 11–001, 11–003, 11–004, 11–018
R. v Broadhead (Wayne) [2006] EWCA Crim 3062 CA 13–008
R. v Burcombe (Christopher John) [2010] EWCA Crim 2818 CA 11–015
R. v Byles (1911–1913) All E.R. Rep 430 11–019
R. v C [2009] EWCA Crim 2458; [2010] Crim. L.R. 504; (2009) 153(46) S.J.L.B. 32 CA 12–005
R. v Camborne Justices Ex p. Pearce [1955] 1 Q.B. 41; [1954] 3 W.L.R. 415; [1954] 2 All E.R. 850; (1954) 118 J.P. 488; (1954) 98 S.J. 577 QBD 11–003, 11–011
R. v Causey [1991] 1 W.L.R. 1551 10–005
R. v **Connor.** *See* R. v Mirza
R. v Dunstable Magistrates Court Ex p. Cox (1986) N.L.J. 310 8–015
R. v Essex Justices Ex p. Perkins [1927] 2 K.B. 475; (1927) 96 L.J. K.B. 530 KBD 11–018
R. v Gough (Robert) [1993] A.C. 646; [1993] 2 W.L.R. 883; [1993] 2 All E.R. 724; (1993) 97 Cr. App. R. 188; (1993) 157 J.P. 612; [1993] Crim. L.R. 886; (1993) 157 J.P.N. 394; (1993) 143 N.L.J. 775; (1993) 137 S.J.L.B. 168 HL............................. 11–004, 11–011, 12–001, 13–002, 14–002
R. v HM Coroner for Inner London West District Ex p. Dallaglio [1994] 4 All E.R. 139; (1995) 159 J.P. 133; (1995) 7 Admin. L.R. 256; [1995] C.O.D. 20 CA (Civ Div) 11–002, 11–003, 11–005, 12–015
R. v J [2009] EWCA Crim 1638 CA 12–004
R. v Kent Justices (1880) 44 J.P. 298 11–019
R. v Khan (Bakish Alla) [2008] EWCA Crim 531; [2008] 3 All E.R. 502; [2008] 2 Cr. App. R. 13; [2008] Inquest L.R. 25; [2008] Crim. L.R. 641; (2008) 152(12) S.J.L.B. 28 CA (Crim Div) 12–003, 12–004
R. v Khyam [2008] EWCA Crim 612 13–017
R. v King (David Andrew) [1983] 1 W.L.R. 411; [1983] 1 All E.R. 929; (1983) 77 Cr. App. R. 1; (1983) 147 J.P. 65; [1983] Crim. L.R. 326 CA (Civ Div) 5–013
R. v Lippe [1991] 2 S.C.R. 114 11–014
R. v Liverpool City Justices Ex p. Topping [1983] 1 W.L.R. 119; [1983] 1 All E.R. 490; (1983) 76 Cr. App. R. 170; (1983) 147 J.P. 154; [1983] Crim. L.R. 181; (1983) 127 S.J. 51 DC 11–011
R. v LL [2011] EWCA Crim 65 .... 11–009, 12–004
R. v Magistrates Court at Lilydale Ex p. Ciccone 1973 V.R. 122 11–019
R. v Mid Glamorgan Family Health Services Ex p. Martin [1993] P.I.Q.R. P426; [1994] C.O.D. 42; (1993) 90(27) L.S.G. 35; (1993) 137 S.J.L.B. 153 QBD 2–010, 6–003
R. v Mirza (Shabbir Ali) [2004] UKHL 2; [2004] 1 A.C. 1118; [2004] 2 W.L.R. 201; [2004] 1 All E.R. 925; [2004] 2 Cr. App. R. 8; [2004] H.R.L.R. 11; 16 B.H.R.C. 279; (2004) 101(7) L.S.G. 34; (2004) 154 N.L.J. 145; (2004) 148 S.J.L.B. 117 HL 12–001, 12–002

R. v Mulvihill (Thomas John) [1990] 1 W.L.R. 438; [1990] 1 All E.R. 436; (1990) 90 Cr. App. R. 372; (1989) 1 Admin. L.R. 33; [1989] Crim. L.R. 908; (1990) 134 S.J. 578 CA 11–011
R. v Neil [2002] 3 S.C.R. 631 ....3–014, 3–015, 4–005
R. v Neil [2002] S.C.C. 70 .... 2–004, 15–004
R. v Neil [2003] 218 D.L.R. (4th) 67.....................................1–011, 4–005, 5–007
R. v Price (Simon) [2009] EWCA Crim 2918; [2010] 2 Cr. App. R. (S.) 44; [2010] Crim. L.R. 522 CA (Civ Div) 12–006
R. v Rand (1865–66) L.R. 1 Q.B. 230 .... 11–003, 11–011
R. v Robinson, unreported, May 15,1995... 5–012
R. v Rodney (Roger) [1997] P.N.L.R. 489 CA 16–008
R. v S [2009] EWCA Crim 2377; [2010] 1 W.L.R. 2511; [2010] 1 All E.R. 1084; [2010] 1 Cr. App. R. 20; [2010] Crim. L.R. 643 CA 12–006
R. v S (RD) [1997] 3 S.C.T. 44 [116]-[119] 13–004
R. v Smith (Winston) (1975) 61 Cr. App. R. 128; [1975] Crim. L.R. 472; (1975) 119 S.J. 369 CA (Civ Div)... 5–009, 5–012
R. v Spear (John) [2002] UKHL 31; [2003] 1 A.C. 734; [2002] 3 W.L.R. 437; [2002] 3 All E.R. 1074; [2003] 1 Cr. App. R. 1; [2002] H.R.L.R. 40; [2002] H.R.L.R. 43; [2002] A.C.D. 97; (2002) 99(36) L.S.G. 38; (2002) 146 S.J.L.B. 193 HL 13–020
R. v Spencer (Alan Widdison) [1987] A.C. 128; [1986] 3 W.L.R. 348; [1986] 2 All E.R. 928; (1986) 83 Cr. App. R. 277; (1986) 130 S.J. 572 HL 11–011
R. v Sunderland Justices [1901] 2 K.B. 357 CA 11–011
R. v Sussex Justices Ex p. McCarthy [1924] 1 K.B. 256 KBD 11–011
R. v Waltham Forest LBC Ex p. Baxter [1988] Q.B. 419; [1988] 2 W.L.R. 257; [1987] 3 All E.R. 671; 86 L.G.R. 254; [1988] R.V.R. 6; (1987) 137 N.L.J. 947; (1988) 132 S.J. 227 CA (Civ Div) 12–010
R. v Watson Ex p. Armstrong (1976) 136 C.L.R. 248 11–011
R. v Williams Ex p. Phillips [1914] 1 K.B. 608 KBD 11–019
R. v Yemoh (Kurtis) [2009] EWCA Crim 930; [2009] Crim. L.R. 888 CA (Civ Div) 12–004
Raats v Gascoigne Wicks [2006] N.Z.H.C. 598............................... 4–007, 5–006
Rackham v Peek Foods [1990] B.C.L.C. 895 19–011
Radisich v Templeton [2009] N.Z.H.C. 654... 9–002
Rakusen v Ellis Munday & Clarke [1912] 1 Ch. 831 CA 5–004, 5–018, 7–002, 7–003, 7–016, 8–005
Ramsbottom's Application for Judicial Review, Re [2009] NIQB 55; [2010] Inquest L.R. 9 QBD 12–012
Ratiu v Conway [2005] EWCA Civ 1302; [2006] 1 All E.R. 571; [2006] 1 E.G.L.R. 125; [2006] W.T.L.R. 101; [2005] 46 E.G. 177 (C.S.) CA (Civ Div) 2–023, 2–024, 2–027, 2–030
Refugee Tribunal Ex p. H, Re [2000] A.L.R. 425 12–007
Regal (Hastings) Ltd v Gulliver [1967] 2 A.C. 134; [1942] 1 All E.R. 378 HL 4–011, 4–013
Regent Leisuretime Ltd v NatWest Finance Ltd (formerly County NatWest Ltd) [2003] EWCA Civ 391; [2003] B.C.C. 587; (2003) 147 S.J.L.B. 386 CA (Civ Div) 17–014
Regent Leisuretime Ltd v Skerrett [2006] EWCA Civ 1184; [2007] P.N.L.R. 9 CA 15–017

Regier v Campbell Stuart [1939] Ch. 766 Ch D 4–013
Regina and Speid, Re (1983) 43 O.R. (2d) 596 2–022
Remli v France (1996) 22 E.H.R.R. 253 ECHR 12–002
Rexstraw v Johnson [2003] N.S.W.C.A. 87 6–020
Richards v Law Society [2009] EWHC 2087 (Admin) DC 2–027
Roberts v Plaisted [1989] 2 Lloyd's Rep. 341 CA 20–005
Robertson v Hendrie EAT Scotland, unreported, February 7, 2007 13–015
Robins v Goldingham (1871–72) L.R. 13 Eq. 440 15–017
Robinson Scammell & Co v Ansell [1985] 2 E.G.L.R. 41; (1985) 275 E.G.
   369; (1985) 135 N.L.J. 752 CA (Civ Div) 8–013, 20–001
Robinson v Mollett (1874–75) L.R. 7 H.L. 802 HL 4–022, 4–025
Rochefoucauld v Boustead [1897] 1 Ch. 196 CA 4–006
Rompetrol Group NV v Romania, unreported, January 14, 2010 14–008
Rothschild v Brookman 6 E.R. 699; (1831) 2 Dow. & Cl. 188 HL 4–013
Royal Bank of Scotland Plc v Etridge (No.2) [2001] UKHL 44; [2002] 2 A.C.
   773; [2001] 3 W.L.R. 1021; [2001] 4 All E.R. 449; [2001] 2 All E.R.
   (Comm) 1061; [2002] 1 Lloyd's Rep. 343; [2001] 2 F.L.R. 1364; [2001] 3
   F.C.R. 481; [2002] H.L.R. 4; [2001] Fam. Law 880; [2001] 43 E.G. 184
   (C.S.); (2001) 151 N.L.J. 1538; [2001] N.P.C. 147; [2002] 1 P. & C.R.
   DG14 4–015
Russell McVeagh McKenzie Bartleet & Co v Tower Corporation [1998] 3
   N.Z.L.R. 641 .... 1–006, 1–007, 1–008, 1–011, 1–012, 5–018, 9–006
Rustal Trading Ltd v Gill & Duffus SA [2000] 1 Lloyd's Rep. 14; [2000]
   C.L.C. 231 QBD 14–002, 14–003
S Pearson & Son Ltd v Dublin Corp [1907] A.C. 351 HL 4–026
Sachs v Spielman [1889] 5 T.L.R. 487 4–013
Saffron Walden Second Benefit Building Society v Rayner (1880) L.R. 14 Ch.
   D. 406 CA 15–017
Sander v United Kingdom (34129/96) (2001) 31 E.H.R.R. 44; 8 B.H.R.C.
   279; [2000] Crim. L.R. 767 ECHR 12–002
Sasea Finance Ltd (In Liquidation) v KPMG (formerly KPMG Peat Marwick
   McLintock) (No.1) [1998] B.C.C. 216 Ch D 17–008
Save and Prosper Pensions Ltd v Homebase Ltd [2001] L. & T.R. 11
   Ch D 14–002
Save Guana Cay Reef Association v Queen, The [2009] UKPC 44 PC
   (Bahamas) 11–008
Savory Corporation v Development Underwriting Ltd [1963] N.S.W.R.
   138 19–015
Saxmere Company Ltd v Wool Board Disestablishment Co Ltd [2009]
   N.Z.L.R. 72 13–019
Scarth v Northland Bank, unreported, December 6, 1996 17–023
Schering Chemicals Ltd v Falkman Ltd [1982] Q.B. 1; [1981] 2 W.L.R. 848;
   [1981] 2 All E.R. 321; (1981) 125 S.J. 342 CA (Civ Div) 2–029
Scholes v Brook (1891) 63 L.T. 837 6–006
Schuppan (A Bankrupt) (No.1), Re [1996] 2 All E.R. 664; [1997] 1 B.C.L.C.
   211; [1996] B.P.I.R. 486 Ch D 9–004, 9–009
Secretary of State for Trade and Industry v Great Western Assurance Co SA
   [1997] 2 B.C.L.C. 685; [1999] Lloyd's Rep. I.R. 377; [1997] 6 Re. L.R. 197
   CA 20–004, 20–005

TABLE OF CASES

Seer Technologies Inc v Abbas (Leave to Appeal) [2001] C.P. Rep. 51 CA (Civ Div) 13–028
Sengupta v Holmes [2002] EWCA Civ 1104; (2002) 99(39) L.S.G. 39 CA (Civ Div) 11–014, 13–009, 13–010
Sent v John Fairfax Publications Pty Ltd [2002] V.S.C. 429....5–003, 5–006, 7–012
Seyfang v GD Searle & Co [1973] Q.B. 148; [1973] 2 W.L.R. 17; [1973] 1 All E.R. 290 QBD 5–013
Shanks v Central Regional Council [1987] S.L.T. 410 17–015
Shepherds Investments Ltd v Walters [2006] EWHC 836 (Ch); [2007] 2 B.C.L.C. 202; [2007] I.R.L.R. 110; [2007] F.S.R. 15; (2006) 150 S.J.L.B. 536 Ch D.. 2–011
Sheppard & Cooper Ltd v TSB Bank Plc [1996] B.C.C. 653; [1997] 2 B.C.L.C. 222; (1996) 93(12) L.S.G. 30 CA (Civ Div).. 17–020
Shrager v Basil Dighton Ltd [1924] 1 K.B. 274 CA 11–018
Sidaway v Board of Governors of the Bethlem Royal Hospital [1984] Q.B. 493; [1984] 2 W.L.R. 778; [1984] 1 All E.R. 1018; (1984) 81 L.S.G. 899; (1984) 128 S.J. 301 CA (Civ Div)... 2–004
Simner v New India Assurance Co Ltd [1995] L.R.L.R. 240 QBD 20–005
Sinclair Investment Holdings SA v Versailles Trade Finance Ltd (In Administrative Receivership) [2007] EWHC 915 (Ch); [2007] 2 All E.R. (Comm) 993; (2007–08) 10 I.T.E.L.R. 58 Ch D.. 2–013
Sintra Homes Ltd v Beard [2007] EWHC 3071 (Ch) Ch D 2–013
Sir John Moore Gold Mining, Re (1879) L.R. 12 Ch. D. 325 CA 17–013
Sisu Capital Fund v Tucker [2006] B.P.I.R. 154................. 17–013, 17–019, 17–020
Skjevesland v Geveran Trading Co Ltd (No.2) [2002] EWCA Civ 1567; [2003] 1 W.L.R. 912; [2003] 1 All E.R. 1; [2003] B.P.I.R. 238; (2002) 152 N.L.J. 1686; (2002) 146 S.J.L.B. 248 CA (Civ Div)............5–009, 5–011, 5–012, 5–017, 5–018, 16–009
Smith & Fawcett, Re [1942] Ch. 304 CA 19–015
Smith v Eric S Bush (A Firm) [1990] 1 A.C. 831; [1989] 2 W.L.R. 790; [1989] 2 All E.R. 514; (1989) 21 H.L.R. 424; 87 L.G.R. 685; [1955–95] P.N.L.R. 467; [1989] 18 E.G. 99; [1989] 17 E.G. 68; (1990) 9 Tr. L.R. 1; (1989) 153 L.G. Rev. 984; (1989) 139 N.L.J. 576; (1989) 133 S.J. 597 HL 4–026, 4–027
Smith v Kvaerner Cementation Foundations Ltd [2006] EWCA Civ 242; [2007] 1 W.L.R. 370; [2006] 3 All E.R. 593; [2006] C.P. Rep. 36; [2006] B.L.R. 244; [2006] A.C.D. 51; (2006) 103(14) L.S.G. 33; (2006) 156 N.L.J. 721; [2006] N.P.C. 35 CA (Civ Div) 11–013, 11–019, 11–020, 13–019, 14–011
Smith v Reynolds (1892) 66 L.T. 808 4–020
Smith v South Wales Switchgear Co Ltd. *See* Smith v UMB Chrysler (Scotland) Ltd
Smith v Stevens, unreported, May 15, 2001 5–014
Smith v UMB Chrysler (Scotland) Ltd [1978] 1 W.L.R. 165; [1978] 1 All E.R. 18; 1978 S.C. (H.L.) 1; 1978 S.L.T. 21; 8 B.L.R. 1; (1978) 122 S.J. 61 HL... 4–026
Smith v Wilson 110 E.R. 266; (1832) 3 B. & Ad. 728 4–022
Society of Lloyd's v Clementson (No.2) [1996] C.L.C. 1205 CA (Civ Div).... 5–013
Solicitor, Re, March 31, 1987 15–017

Solicitors (A Firm), Re [1992] Q.B. 959; [1992] 2 W.L.R. 809; [1992] 1 All E.R. 353; (1991) 141 N.L.J. 746; (1991) 135 S.J.L.B. 125 CA (Civ Div) .. 1–006, 6–023, 7–004, 15–014
Solicitors (A Firm), Re [2000] 1 Lloyd's Rep. 31 QBD 7–010, 7–017, 8–019
Solicitors, Re [1997] Ch. 1; [1996] 3 W.L.R. 16; [1995] 3 All E.R. 482; [1995] F.S.R. 783 Ch D 1–006, 3–023, 6–023, 7–003, 7–003, 7–004, 7–007, 7–009, 9–004
Solow v WR Grace & Co (1993) 597 N.Y.S.2d 361 5–018
South Blackwater Coal Limited v McCullough Robertson, unreported, May 8, 1997 8–017
South Island Commercial (2004) Ltd v Kiwi Green Island Club Ltd [2008] N.Z.S.C. 2032 9–005
Southwark LBC v Jiminez, unreported, April 8, 2003 CA 11–014, 13–007
Space Investments Ltd v Canadian Imperial Bank of Commerce Trust Co (Bahamas) Ltd [1986] 1 W.L.R. 1072; [1986] 3 All E.R. 75; (1986) 2 B.C.C. 99302; (1986) 83 L.S.G. 2567; (1986) 130 S.J. 612 PC (Bahamas) 4–027
Sparkes v Enterprise Newfoundland, unreported, June 16, 1994 17–002
SPE International Ltd v Professional Preparation Contractors (UK) Ltd [2002] EWHC 881 (Ch) Ch D 5–013
Spector v Ageda [1973] Ch. 30; [1971] 3 W.L.R. 498; [1971] 3 All E.R. 417; (1971) 22 P. & C.R. 1002; (1971) 115 S.J. 426 Ch D 3–022, 6–001, 6–002, 6–020, 6–022, 6–023
Spiliada Maritime Corp v Cansulex Ltd (The Spiliada) [1987] A.C. 460; [1986] 3 W.L.R. 972; [1986] 3 All E.R. 843; [1987] 1 Lloyd's Rep. 1; [1987] E.C.C. 168; [1987] 1 F.T.L.R. 103; (1987) 84 L.S.G. 113; (1986) 136 N.L.J. 1137; (1986) 130 S.J. 925 HL....................................... 3–009, 9–007
Spincode Pty Ltd v Look Software Ltd [2001] V.S.C.A. 248 .... 1–010, 2–022, 5–003, 5–004, 5–006, 5–006
Spring v Pride 46 E.R. 971; (1864) 4 De G.J. & S. 395 Court of Chancery.... 2–021
Sramek v Austria (A/84) (1985) 7 E.H.R.R. 351 ECHR 11–010, 13–021
St Margaret's Trust Ltd v Navigators and General Insurance Co Ltd (1948–49) 82 Ll. L. Rep. 752 KBD.. 20–005
Standard Investments v Canadian Imperial Bank of Commerce (1986) 22 D.L.R. (4d) 410 6–026
Starrs and Chalmers v Procurator Fiscal, unreported, November 16, 1999 .. 11–008
State of South Australia v Peat Marwick Mitchell & Co (1997) 24 A.C.S.R. 231 17–009
Steadman-Byrne v Amjad [2007] EWCA Civ 1148 .... 13–007, 13–008
Stena Finance BV v Sea Containers Ltd (1989) 39 W.I.R. 83 SC (Bermuda)... 19–015
Stevens v Gullis [2000] 1 All E.R. 527; [2001] C.P. Rep. 3; [1999] B.L.R. 394; (2000) 2 T.C.L.R. 385; 73 Con. L.R. 42; [2000] P.N.L.R. 229; [1999] 3 E.G.L.R. 71; [1999] 44 E.G. 143; (2000) 16 Const. L.J. 68 CA (Civ Div) 5–013
Stevens v Premium Real Estate Ltd [2009] N.Z.S.C. 15 4–019
Stewart v Canadian Broadcasting Commission [1997] 150 D.L.R. (4d) 24 ... 2–028, 6–011
Stiedl v Enyo Law LLP [2011] EWHC 2649 (Comm) 9–007
Stockton v Mason [1978] 2 Lloyd's Rep. 430; [1979] R.T.R. 130 CA 20–005

TABLE OF CASES

Stone v Reliance Mutual Insurance Society [1972] 1 Lloyd's Rep. 469 CA 20–005
Storey v Dorset Community NHS Trust [2000] C.L.Y. 304 CC (Plymouth) .. 5–013
Strother v 3464920 Canada Inc [2007] S.C.C. 24 4–004
Stubbs v Slater [1910] 1 Ch. 632 CA 4–013
Styles v O'Brien [2007] Tas.S.C. 67 5–006
Suisse Atlantique Societe d'Armement SA v NV Rotterdamsche Kolen Centrale [1967] 1 A.C. 361; [1966] 2 W.L.R. 944; [1966] 2 All E.R. 61; [1966] 1 Lloyd's Rep. 529; (1966) 110 S.J. 367 HL 4–026
Sumukan Ltd v Commonwealth Secretariat [2007] EWCA Civ 1148; [2008] Bus. L.R. 858; [2008] 2 All E.R. (Comm) 175; [2008] 1 Lloyd's Rep. 40; [2007] 2 C.L.C. 821; 116 Con. L.R. 17; (2007) 104(46) L.S.G. 26 CA (Civ Div) 11–018
Supasave Retail v Coward Chance (A Firm). *See* David Lee & Co (Lincoln) Ltd v Coward Chance (A Firm)
Surfing Hardware International Holdings v William McCausland (No 3) 5–006
Swain v Law Society [1983] 1 A.C. 598; [1982] 3 W.L.R. 261; [1982] 2 All E.R. 827; (1982) 79 L.S.G. 887; (1982) 126 S.J. 464 HL 15–003
Swain v West (Butchers) [1936] 3 All E.R. 261 CA 18–003
Swansea Council v Honey, unreported, November 7, 2008 EAT 13–024
Swindle v Harrison [1997] 4 All E.R. 705; [1997] P.N.L.R. 641; [1997] N.P.C. 50 CA (Civ Div) 8–010
Sybron Corp v Rochem Ltd [1984] Ch. 112; [1983] 3 W.L.R. 713; [1983] 2 All E.R. 707; [1983] I.C.R. 801; [1983] I.R.L.R. 253; (1983) 127 S.J. 391 CA (Civ Div) 18–003
Symphony Group Plc v Hodgson [1994] Q.B. 179; [1993] 3 W.L.R. 830; [1993] 4 All E.R. 143; [1997] Costs L.R. (Core Vol.) 319; (1993) 143 N.L.J. 725; (1993) 137 S.J.L.B. 134 CA (Civ Div) 13–013
Szarfer v Chodos (1986) 54 O.R. (2d) 663 16–003
T and A (Children) (Risk of Disclosure), Re [2000] 1 F.L.R. 859; [2000] 1 F.C.R. 659; [2000] Lloyd's Rep. P.N. 452; [2000] Fam. Law 398; (2000) 164 J.P.N. 426; (2000) 97(3) L.S.G. 37; (2000) 144 S.J.L.B. 49 CA (Civ Div) 5–011
Target Holdings Ltd v Redferns [1996] A.C. 421; [1995] 3 W.L.R. 352; [1995] 3 All E.R. 785; [1995] C.L.C. 1052; (1995) 139 S.J.L.B. 195; [1995] N.P.C. 136 HL 4–011, 4–013, 8–010
Tate v Williamson (1865–66) L.R. 1 Eq. 528 4–013
Taylor v Lawrence (Appeal: Jurisdiction to Reopen) [2002] EWCA Civ 90; [2003] Q.B. 528; [2002] 3 W.L.R. 640; [2002] 2 All E.R. 353; [2002] C.P. Rep. 29; (2002) 99(12) L.S.G. 35; (2002) 152 N.L.J. 221; (2002) 146 S.J.L.B. 50 CA (Civ Div) 13–001, 13–017, 13–019
Taylor v Williamsons (A Firm) [2002] EWCA Civ 1380; [2003] C.P. Rep. 20; (2002) 99(36) L.S.G. 39 CA (Civ Div) 11–014, 13–007
Teacher v Calder [1899] A.C. 451 8–011
Teck Corporation v Millar (1972) 33 D.L.R. (3d) 288 19–015
Tekni-Plex Inc v Meyer and Landis (1995) 632 N.Y.S.2d 565 5–018
Thames Trains Ltd v Adams [2006] EWHC 3291 (QB) QBD 9–001
Thompson v Collins [2009] EWCA Civ 525 CA 13–017
Thompson v Mikkelsen, unreported, October 3, 1974 7–014

Thompson v T Lohan (Plant Hire) Ltd [1987] 1 W.L.R. 649; [1987] 2 All E.R. 631; [1987] I.R.L.R. 148; (1987) 84 L.S.G. 979; (1987) 131 S.J. 358 CA (Civ Div) 4–027
Thomson v Berkhamsted Collegiate School [2009] EWHC 2374 (QB); [2010] C.P. Rep. 5; [2009] 6 Costs L.R. 859; (2009) 159 N.L.J. 1440 QBD 13–013
Thorby v Goldberg 112 C.L.R. 597 19–010
Times Newspapers Ltd v Singh & Choudry, unreported, December 17, 1999 CA 13–010
Toddglen Construction Ltd v Concord Adex Developments Corp [2003] Can.L.II 9525 .... 2–022, 5–007, 9–007
Torquay Local Board v Bridle (1882) 47 J.P. 183 19–004
Trade and Transport Inc v Iino Kaiun Kaisha Ltd (The Angelia) [1973] 1 W.L.R. 210; [1973] 2 All E.R. 144; [1972] 2 Lloyd's Rep. 154; (1972) 117 S.J. 123 QBD 4–027
Tricontinental Corporation Ltd v Holding Redlich, unreported, December 22, 1994 9–006
Trustor AB v Smallbone (No.4) [2001] 1 W.L.R. 1177; [2001] 3 All E.R. 987; [2002] B.C.C. 795; [2001] 2 B.C.L.C. 436; (2001) 98(20) L.S.G. 40; (2001) 151 N.L.J. 457; (2001) 145 S.J.L.B. 99 Ch D 2–024
TSB Bank Plc v Robert Irving & Burns [2000] 2 All E.R. 826; [1999] Lloyd's Rep. P.N. 956; [2000] P.N.L.R. 384 CA 4–006, 15–018, 20–004
Tudor Grange Holdings Ltd v Citibank NA [1992] Ch. 53; [1991] 3 W.L.R. 750; [1991] 4 All E.R. 1; [1991] B.C.L.C. 1009; (1991) 135 S.J.L.B. 3 Ch D 17–014, 17–015
Tufton v Sperni [1952] 2 T.L.R. 516; [1952] W.N. 439 CA 4–013
Tyrrell v Bank of London 11 E.R. 934; (1862) 10 H.L. Cas. 26 HL 6–020
Ultraframe (UK) Ltd v Fielding (Costs) [2006] EWCA Civ 1660; [2007] 2 All E.R. 983; [2007] C.P. Rep. 12; [2007] 2 Costs L.R. 264 CA (Civ Div) 2–015, 2–022
Uncle Toby's Co Pty Ltd v Trevor Jones Steel Fabrications Pty Ltd, unreported, October 12, 1995 5–003
Underwood Son & Piper v Lewis [1894] 2 Q.B. 306 CA 2–025, 15–017
Unioil v Deloitte Touche Tohmatsu (1997) 17 W.A.R. 98 .... 6–023, 6–025
United Australia v Barclays Bank [1941] A.C. 1 8–011
United Dominions Corporation v Brian Pty (1985) 157 C.L.R. 1 2–013
United Pan Europe Communications NV v Deutsche Bank AG [2000] 2 B.C.L.C. 461 CA (Civ Div) 8–006
United States Ex rel Cherry Hill Convalescent Center Inc v Healthcare Rehab System Inc (1997) 994 F.Supp.244 5–018
University of Nottingham v Fishel [2000] I.C.R. 1462; [2000] I.R.L.R. 471; [2001] R.P.C. 22; [2000] Ed. C.R. 505; [2000] E.L.R. 385; (2001) 24(2) I.P.D. 24009 QBD 2–014, 6–003, 8–008
Urbaser SA v Argentina ICSID, unreported 13–018
Vakauta v Kelly (1989) 167 C.L.R. 568 .... 13–003, 13–010, 13–018
Venables v News Group Newspapers Ltd [2001] Fam. 430; [2001] 2 W.L.R. 1038; [2001] 1 All E.R. 908; [2001] E.M.L.R. 10; [2001] 1 F.L.R. 791; [2002] 1 F.C.R. 333; [2001] H.R.L.R. 19; [2001] U.K.H.R.R. 628; 9 B.H.R.C. 587; [2001] Fam. Law 258; (2001) 98(12) L.S.G. 41; (2001) 151 N.L.J. 57; (2001) 145 S.J.L.B. 43 Fam Div 6–013

Vickery, Re [1931] 1 Ch. 572; [1931] All E.R. Rep. 562 Ch D 4–025
Virdi v Law Society [2010] EWCA Civ 100; [2010] 1 W.L.R. 2840; [2010] 3
 All E.R. 653; [2010] A.C.D. 38; (2010) 107(9) L.S.G. 14 CA (Civ Div) .. 11–015,
 12–009
Virgin Management Ltd v De Morgan Group Plc [1996] E.G. 16 (C.S.); [1996]
 N.P.C. 8 CA (Civ Div).. 4–002
Votraint v Commonwealth [2005] N.S.W.C.A. 249... 9–002
Wade v Poppleton & Appleby [2003] EWHC 3159 (Ch); [2004] 1 B.C.L.C.
 674; [2004] B.P.I.R. 642 Ch D 17–020, 17–022
Wallace Smith & Co, Re [1992] B.C.L.C. 970 .... 17–017, 17–018, 17–019
Wan v McDonald (1991) 33 F.C.R. 491 .... 5–003, 5–004
Warmington v McMurray [1963] 2 All E.R. 745 15–017
Warren v Mendy [1989] 1 W.L.R. 853; [1989] 3 All E.R. 103; [1989] I.C.R.
 525; [1989] I.R.L.R. 210; (1989) 133 S.J. 1261 CA (Civ Div) 2–025
Weatherill v Lloyds TSB Bank Plc [2000] C.P.L.R. 584 CA (Civ Div).......... 11–003
Webb v R. (1994) 181 C.L.R. 41 .... 11–004, 11–011
Weglarz v Bruck (1984) 470 N.E.2d 21 5–018
Weissfisch v Julius [2006] EWCA Civ 218; [2006] 2 All E.R. (Comm) 504;
 [2006] 1 Lloyd's Rep. 716; [2006] 1 C.L.C. 424 CA 14–002
Welsh v Chief Constable of Merseyside [1993] 1 All E.R. 692 QBD 9–002
Westend Entertainment Centre Pty Ltd v Equity Trustee Ltd [1999] V.S.C.
 514 3–013
Western Home Counties Developments Ltd v Stone Toms & Partners,
 unreported, March 19, 1984 2–017
White v Jones [1995] 2 A.C. 207; [1995] 2 W.L.R. 187; [1995] 1 All E.R. 691;
 [1995] 3 F.C.R. 51; (1995) 145 N.L.J. 251; (1995) 139 S.J.L.B. 83; [1995]
 N.P.C. 31 HL 9–001, 9–002
White v Morley [1899] 2 Q.B. 34 QBD 19–004
Wienerworld v Vision Video, unreported, July 24, 1997................................ 8–011
Wild v Simpson [1919] 2 K.B. 544 CA 15–017
Wilkie v Scottish Aviation Ltd 1956 S.C. 198; 1956 S.L.T. (Notes) 25 4–020
Wilkins v Wood [1848] 17 L.J.Q.B. 319 4–022
Williams v Hogg (1861) 5 L.T. 467 4–025
Williams v Scott [1900] A.C. 499 PC (Aus).. 4–013
Williamson v Official Solicitor, unreported, February 4, 2007 13–014
Wimmera Industrial Minerals Pty Ltd v Iluka Midwest [2002] F.C.A. 653,
 Fed Ct of Australia 2–013, 2–019, 5–015
Winters v Mishcon de Reya [2008] EWHC 2419 (Ch); (2008) 158 N.L.J.
 1494 Ch D 5–020
Wong Kok Chin v Singapore Society of Accountants [1990] 1 M.L.J. 456 ... 17–001
Wright v Morgan [1926] A.C. 788 PC (NZ) 2–022
Wyman v Paterson. *See* Ferguson v Paterson
X (formerly known as Mary Bell) v SO [2003] EWHC 1101 (QB); [2003]
 E.M.L.R. 37; [2003] 2 F.C.R. 686; [2003] A.C.D. 61 QBD 6–013
YBM Magnex International Inc, Re (2000) 275 A.R. 352............. 17–010, 17–022
Youell v Bland Welch & Co Ltd (No.2) [1990] 2 Lloyd's Rep. 431 QBD ... 20–005
Young v Robson Rhodes (A Firm) [1999] 3 All E.R. 524; [1999] Lloyd's Rep.
 P.N. 641 Ch D 2–022, 2–025, 7–006, 7–016, 8–006,
 8–009, 15–017, 17–011

Yukong Line Ltd of Korea v Rendsburg Investments Corp of Liberia (The Rialto) (Injunctive Relief) [2001] 2 Lloyd's Rep. 113 CA (Civ Div) 2–015
Yunghanns v Elfic Pty Ltd, unreported, 1998 .... 1–010, 7–001, 7–012
Z, Re [2009] EWHC 3621 (Fam); [2010] 2 F.L.R. 132; [2010] Fam. Law 458 Fam Div 7–017
Zeus Tradition Marine Ltd v Bell (The Zeus V) [1999] 1 Lloyd's Rep. 703; [1999] C.L.C. 391 QBD 20–005
Zivadinovich v Mehta (1997) 25 O.T.C. 198, (1999) 117 O. A.C. 328 17–005
Zurich GSG Ltd v Gray & Kellas (A Firm) [2007] CSOH 91; 2007 S.L.T. 917; [2008] P.N.L.R. 1; 2007 G.W.D. 26–460 6–025

Table of Statutes

1890	Partnership Act (c.39) 2–031		s.33 .... 14–005, 14–006, 14–007, 14–009
	s.16 6–025		(1)(b) 14–006
1925	Trustee Act (c.19)		s.34 14–006
	s.30(1) 4–025		s.68 14–009
	s.40 4–025		(2)(c) 14–009
1945	Law Reform (Contributory Negligence) Act (c.28) 8–012		s.73 .... 14–002, 14–003
			(1) 14–002
1972	European Communities Act (c.68) 10–001		s.103(2)(e) 14–009
			s.104 14–009
1974	Solicitors Act (c.47)		(3) 14–009
	Pt II 15–003	1998	Human Rights Act
	s.31 15–003		(c.42) 11–001, 11–005
	(2) 15–003	2000	Financial Services and Markets Act (c.8) ... 19–001
	s.65(2) 15–017		
1977	Unfair Contract Terms Act (c.50) 4–026, 4–027		s.118 19–004
			s.147 .... 19–001, 19–003, 19–004
	s.1(4) 4–026		
	s.2(2) 4–026		s.150 19–004
	s.3 4–026		s.397 19–004
	s.12 4–026	2002	Proceeds of Crime Act (c.29)
	Sch.1 para.1(a) 4–026		Pt 7 .... 10–001, 10–002, 10–006
	(e) 4–026		
1980	Insolvency Act (c.45) 17–014		s.327 .... 10–002, 10–003
	s.32(1) 17–014		ss.327–329 .. 10–002, 10–004
1981	Contempt of Court Act (c.49)		s.328 .... 10–002, 10–003, **10–004**, 10–006
	s.8(1) 12–001		s.329 10–003
1985	Administration of Justice Act (c.61)		s.330 .... **10–002**, 10–003
			(3) 10–006
	s.9 15–003		(5)(a) 10–006
	s.9A 15–003		(b) 10–006
1986	Financial Services Act (c.60) 19–001		(6) 10–006, 10–007
			s.333 10–007
	s.48(2)(h) 19–001, 19–003		s.333A 10–007
1996	Arbitration Act (c.23) ... 14–002, 14–008		s.333D(2) 10–007
			s.340 .... 10–003, 10–005
	s.24 14–001		(3) 10–002
	(1) 14–001, 14–002		s.342 10–007

xliii

	(3)(c) 10–007		(1) 18–005
	(4) 10–007		(5)–(6) 18–004
	Sch.9 10–002		(7) 18–005
	para.1(1) 10–003		s.176 .... 18–001, 18–005
2005	Serious Organised		s.177 .... 18–001, 18–006,
	Crime and Police Act		19–012
	(c.15) 10–001		s.178 18–006
2006	Companies Act (c.46) ... 18–001,		(1) 18–006
	19–009		(2) 18–006
	Pt 10 Ch.2 18–001		s.180 18–006
	s.170 18–001		s.182 .... 18–001, 18–006
	(2) 18–001, 18–005		s.183 18–001
	s.171–177 .... 18–001, 18–006		s.188 18–001
	s.172 .... 18–001, 18–002,		s.190 .... 18–001, 19–012
	18–003		ss.197–214 18–001
	(1) 19–010		s.228 18–001
	s.173 .... 18–001, 18–007,		s.237 18–001
	18–008, 18–009		Pt 28 19–009
	(2) 18–006		s.942 19–009
	s.174 18–001	2007	Legal Services Act
	s.175 .... 18–001, 18–004,		(c.29) 15–003, 16–001
	18–005		Sch.4 para.19 15–003

Table of Statutory Instruments

1990 Insurance Companies (Legal Expenses Insurance) Regulations (SI 1990/1159) 15–019
1994 Unfair Terms in Consumer Contracts Regulations (SI 1994/3159) 4–026
1998 Civil Procedure Rules (SI 1998/3132) 13–010
    r.31.22 9–004
    r.35.7 8–015
    Pt 36 13–012
1999 Unfair Terms in Consumer Contracts Regulations (SI 1999/2083) 4–026
2003 Money Laundering Regulations (SI 2003/3075) 10–001, 10–002
    reg.3 10–002
    (1)(c) 10–003
    (d) 10–003
    (9) 10–003
2006 Takeovers Directive (Interim Implementation) Regulations (SI 2006/1183) 19–009
2007 Money Laundering Regulations (SI 2007/2157) 10–001

Table of European Legislation

Treaties and Conventions

1950 European Convention on
Human Rights
art.6............ 11–005, 11–009,
12–013, 13–020,
16–009
(1)........................ 11–005

Directives

1987 Dir. 87/344 on the
coordination of
laws, regulations
and administrative
provisions relating
to legal expenses
insurance [1987] OJ
L185/77 15–019

1993 Dir. 93/13 on unfair terms
in consumer contracts
[1993] OJ L95/29 4–026
2001 Directive 2001/97 on
prevention of the
use of the financial
system for the
purpose of money
laundering [2001] OJ
L344/76 ... 10–001, 10–004
Recital 16 10–004
Recital 17 10–004
art.28........................ 10–007

xlvii

CHAPTER 1

Conflicts of Interest: the Principles

1. Introduction to the law of conflicts of interest

A. The modern law of conflicts

The law of conflicts of interest was little developed in English law until relatively recently. Until 1998, the leading case was a difficult to follow 1912 Court of Appeal decision, and challenges on grounds of conflict of interest were still relatively rare. Most of the authorities dealt with cases where the personal interest of the professional conflicted with the interest of the client. The increased sophistication and globalisation of modern commerce has given rise both to problems and solutions rarely necessary in the past. Challenges on grounds of conflict of interest nowadays are common, some genuine and some tactical.

1–001

Information barriers have rarely been greeted enthusiastically by the courts. But their use in the City, and their recognition under financial services legislation, has gradually involved their recognition and acceptance by the courts. Today large firms of professionals regularly and systematically deploy information barriers to the extent that fears expressed by the courts as to their efficacy seem outmoded.

The grandfather of the modern law of conflicts may be said to be Professor Paul Finn, an Australian academic and now judge, in his 1977 work *Fiduciary Obligations*. There are two Privy Council decisions in the early 1990s *Kelly v Cooper* and *Clark Boyce v Mouat*, but although both remain important decisions, their reasoning betrays the formative state of English conflict law at the time and is in many ways difficult to square with subsequent decisions. In the late 1990s there were two crucial decisions: *Bristol & West Building Society v Mothew* and *Prince Jefri Bolkiah v KPMG*. It is not a coincidence that the leading judgments in each of those decisions were given by Lord Millett. If one regards Professor Finn as the grandfather of the modern law, Lord Millett has a right to be treated as the father. Shortly after *Bolkiah,* which was the first case to set out clear conflicts principle both for existing and former client conflicts, two House of Lords decisions set the parameters for a different sort of conflict, the judicial conflict: *R. v Bow Street Metropolitan Magistrate Ex p. Pinochet Ugarte* and *Porter v Magill.*

This book was first published in 2000, in the wake of the *Bolkiah* and *Pinochet* decisions. Eleven years on, it is in its fourth edition. Conflicts committees and information barriers populate large firms in a way that was unnecessary in the past. It is increasingly important to understand how the law of conflicts of interest works.

This introductory chapter starts by considering the meaning of a number of the terms commonly used in connection with conflicts of interest. It then discusses the decision which is the foundation of the modern law of conflicts of interest, *Prince Jefri Bolkiah v KPMG.* Finally, it provides a brief overview of the rules on conflicts of interest in other important or analogous jurisdictions.

B. What is a conflict: definition of terms

1–002   The term "conflict of interest" is used in a number of wholly different contexts and to mean a number of different things. It is necessary, therefore to be precise and to define the terms which will be used throughout this book. It would be more appropriate to use the expression "conflict of duty" rather than "conflict of interest." However, because the term is used to include circumstances of conflict between the professional's duty to one client and his personal interest, "conflict of interest" is generally preferred.

The first type of conflict is an *existing client* conflict. The professional who acts for two clients at the same time will normally owe fiduciary duties to both. The precise scope and extent of the fiduciary duty may depend upon the terms of the retainer, but the most notable feature of the fiduciary duty is an obligation of loyalty. Where the professional is asked to act for two clients with conflicting interests at the same time, the fiduciary obligations of loyalty owed to each will clash, and there is an existing client conflict. If he accepts instructions for both, he will then be in breach of fiduciary duty to one or both clients and unable to carry out his obligations to both. The conflict is a conflict of the firm, partnership or company and not merely of the individual partner. For this reason, the conflict extends beyond the individuals within the firm who act for the client to the firm itself. It follows that to accept instructions for a second client where there is a conflict of interest gives rise to an automatic breach of fiduciary duty unless both clients have consented. Even when both clients have consented, there will be circumstances in which the professional cannot act, or continue to act, because he would be professionally embarrassed in doing so. These principles are nothing to do with whether the professional has obtained relevant confidential information. They are based on the fiduciary obligation of loyalty.

1–003 Where one client is a former client, so that there is no continuing relevant retainer, the position is different, and because in normal circumstances the fiduciary obligation no longer applies once the retainer ends, the problems are different. This is a *former client conflict*. The existing client conflict is to be contrasted with the former client conflict. Where the conflict is between the obligations owed to an existing client and the obligations owed to a former client, there are no competing fiduciary duties because there is generally no fiduciary obligation of loyalty to a former client, although there is an obligation to protect confidentiality, breach of this obligation being classified as a breach of fiduciary duty.

Here therefore the issue is quite different: does the professional have relevant confidential information obtained from the first retainer? If so, he cannot act for another client on a retainer where the confidential information is material unless he can show there is no real risk of disclosure. The risk must be a real one, not one that is merely fanciful or theoretical. The professional may be able to discharge this high burden by showing that effective internal measures are in place which will prevent disclosure, namely an *information barrier*.[1] The effect of such arrangements will be to create a firm within a firm.

As a matter of practicality, the courts have drawn a distinction between "structural" and "ad hoc" information barriers. The former are barriers which are regarded as part of the established structure of the firm (one partner in the Land's End office, the other in John O'Groats), the latter created for the very purpose of providing the particular information barrier required. In practice, the distinction is rarely black and white. But these measures will rarely be effective if organised solely on an ad hoc basis, as opposed to being part of the organisational structure of the firm.

1–004 Existing client and former client conflicts are concerned with the problems of two clients with different interests. A different problem is the conflict between the professional's own personal interest and that of his client. This can be referred to as a *personal conflict*. At one level, this sort of conflict is a facet of the professional's obligation as a fiduciary; he must not let his personal interest conflict with that of his client, and insofar as it does he must prefer the interest of the client. There are many personal conflicts which are unavoidable as part of everyday life. Any adviser who is paid by a success or percentage of deal fee[2] has a personal financial interest in the deal going ahead and to that extent a conflict of interest with that of the client. A large piece of litigation will attract substantial fees for the lawyers and

---

[1] The term "Chinese Wall" has recently fallen from favour. References are now made to "information barriers".
[2] This will not only cover investment bankers; it covers estate agents, for example, and a variety of other professionals.

expert witnesses and in giving advice they have a personal conflict in their interest in the litigation fighting rather than an early settlement. But there is no sensible means of eradicating these conflicts. Sometimes the perceived concerns as to impartiality require special measures to protect clients from these conflicts. Thus the concerns arising from lawyers accepting contingency fees in the United States have led to this sort of fee being outlawed by legislation. Here there is both conflict between the lawyer's personal interest and his duty to his client, and conflict between the lawyer's personal interest and his duty to the court. However, the legislature has recognised that there are practical advantages in lawyers' remuneration at times being dependent on success[3] and has thus permitted the more moderate conditional fees, whereby the lawyer may, in return for not receiving payment if the case is lost, agree to receive an enhanced fee of up to double his normal fee if successful.

The cases do not draw a clear distinction between the case where the conflict is that of the professional's client and that where the conflict is that of the professional himself; there is a personal conflict when the professional seeks to buy the client's property himself. Both are regarded as forms of existing client conflict. Personal conflicts are often faced by directors of companies.

Another animal may be described as the *commercial conflict*. The advertising executive knows that if he acts for Sainsburys he may not act for Tesco. He probably has never analysed precisely why not.[4] At one level, the problem is a commercial conflict simply because, whatever the legal analysis, Sainsburys would terminate his retainer if he did so. But the problem blends rapidly into the existing client conflict considered above, and the reason that neither the executive nor Sainsburys will permit the second retainer is often a recognition that it is not in practice possible for the professional loyally to pursue the advertising interests of both at the same time.

1–005   The expression is sometimes used *same matter conflict*. This raises the question whether a lawyer who has acted on one side of a matter can act on the other side in the same or a related matter. A same matter conflict involving two existing clients is an existing client conflict[5] and the rules are the same. A same matter conflict involving an existing and a former client is a confidential information issue. There are no special rules for same matter

---

[3] Namely, that in consequence lawyers will be willing to accept cases where legal aid is not available without cost to the litigant other than out of the proceeds of success.
[4] "It's not difficult to work out what a conflict is. You put yourself in the client's shoes, and ask yourself 'would he like you doing what the other client has asked you to do?' If the answer is 'no', you've probably got a conflict." (*Commercial Lawyer*, June 1999, quoting Alan Peck, a partner of city firm of solicitors Freshfields.)
[5] The Australian academic writer and more recently judge, Paul Finn, whose work is often referred to in connection with conflicts of interest, and is referred to on numerous occasions in this book, uses "same matter conflict" to mean an existing client conflict where the professional acts for two different interests in the same matter.

conflicts. So the expression can be confusing, and is not used in this book. However, the question whether the two matters are the same or related is evidentially significant and may be important in other jurisdictions.

The *non-waivable conflict* denotes a case where client consent is insufficient to enable a professional to act. Where the professional is unable to fulfil his obligations to both clients, their consent will not enable him to act. The related term *professional embarrassment* arises where the professional is personally inhibited from fulfilling his obligation to a client by reason either of his obligations to another client, or an obligation of confidence.

Completely different from any of these is the *judicial conflict*. This is the sort of conflict considered in the *Pinochet* case.[6] The principles are not limited to judges: they apply to any decision-making tribunal, and thus will include arbitrators as well as juries. Properly analysed, this is an issue of apparent bias rather than conflict of interest, and the principles are different.

C. The Bolkiah case

The *Bolkiah*[7] case is the foundation of the modern law of conflicts in this jurisdiction and is looked at on many occasions in this book. So it is convenient to explain the decision at the outset. Prince Jefri Bolkiah was the youngest brother of the Sultan of Brunei and was formerly chairman of the Brunei Investment Agency ("BIA"). The auditors of BIA were KPMG, one of the five largest firms of accountants in the world. KPMG had in the past as auditors for BIA accepted representations from Prince Jefri that certain substantial special transfers of funds from BIA had been made on behalf of the Brunei government. One of Prince Jefri's own companies had instructed KPMG in connection with major litigation between 1996 and 1998. This investigation, codenamed "Project Lucy", was conducted by KPMG's forensic accounting department. It involved 168 staff including 12 partners and £4.6m fees. The litigation settled in March 1998. Prince Jefri was subsequently removed from his post as chairman of BIA and partners of Arthur Andersen took control of his companies. In June 1998 the government of Brunei appointed a task force to investigate the activities of the BIA. KPMG performed certain further work described as "a natural extension of their audit function". KPMG were then asked to assist the task force in carrying out further investigations into the destination and present location of the money the subject of the special transfers. They accepted these instructions (this project was codenamed "Project Gemma") without contacting Prince Jefri. They established an information barrier within the firm to

1–006

---

[6] *R. v Bow Street Metropolitan Stipendiary Magistrate Ex p. Pinochet Ugarte* [2000] 1 A.C. 119, HL.
[7] *Prince Jefri Bolkiah v KPMG* [1999] 2 A.C. 222, HL.

protect Prince Jefri's confidentiality. It was apparent that the investigation might well lead to civil or criminal proceedings against Prince Jefri. KPMG employed 50 people on Project Gemma. Prince Jefri sought an injunction restraining KPMG from continuing with work on Project Gemma.

Pumfrey J. granted an injunction, holding that an accountant providing forensic services was in much the same position as a solicitor, and stating that once the court was satisfied, as was the case here, that KPMG were in possession of confidential information from Prince Jefri, there was a high burden on KPMG to satisfy the court that there was not a real risk of its disclosure, inadvertent or otherwise, and held that he was not so satisfied on the facts.[8]

This was reversed by a majority of the Court of Appeal.[9] Lord Woolf M.R. said there were three questions to be asked: (1) is there confidential information which if disclosed is likely to affect the former clients' interests adversely and (2) is there a real or appreciable risk that the confidential information will be disclosed; (3) does the nature and importance of the former fiduciary relationship mean that the confidential information should be protected by the court exercising its discretion and intervening? This was the analysis of the New Zealand Court of Appeal in *Russell McVeagh Bartleet & Co v Tower Corporation*,[10] which indicated that the three factors would overlap and led to a balancing exercise as to whether relief should be granted in the particular case. He held there was no real risk of disclosure on the facts. In respect of the balancing exercise, Lord Woolf M.R. said that this case was different from many others because KPMG did not go from working for one client to working for a competitor; they were working for BIA throughout, to the knowledge of Prince Jefri and he should have anticipated that if a conflict arose the BIA would wish to retain KPMG. Thus KPMG's duty should be limited to making reasonable efforts to protecting the confidential information and Prince Jefri would not be entitled to an injunction unless he really would suffer serious damage otherwise. On the facts the plaintiff would not suffer such prejudice. Otton L.J., adopting the *Russell McVeagh* test, agreed there was not a real or appreciable risk of disclosure. Waller L.J. dissented, holding that there was a real risk of disclosure, pointing out that the closeness of time between termination of Prince Jefri's retainer and the commencement of the BIA investigation almost made this a conflict between existing clients. He did not accept the argument that Prince Jefri should have anticipated the possibility of future conflict when he instructed KPMG.

1–007 The House of Lords unanimously restored the injunction prohibiting

---

[8] He followed *Re Solicitors (A Firm)* [1997] Ch. 1, Lightman J., especially at 9-10, and also *Re Solicitors (A Firm)* [1992] Q.B. 959, CA.
[9] The judgments of Pumfrey J. and the Court of Appeal (Lord Woolf M.R. and Otton L.J., Waller L.J. dissenting) can be found at [1999] B.C.L.C. 1.
[10] [1998] 3 N.Z.L.R. 641.

KPMG from continuing to act.[11] The leading speech was given by Lord Millett. The case was a former client conflict, because KPMG no longer acted for Prince Jefri. As the obligation of loyalty owed by a fiduciary came to an end on termination of the retainer, KPMG had no obligations to Prince Jefri as fiduciaries. The issue was thus one of confidential information. Although the position of a solicitor was regarded as not necessarily the same as that of an accountant, because the information relating to the solicitor's client's affairs will be privileged as well as confidential, some of the information obtained by KPMG from Prince Jefri was likely to have attracted litigation privilege and thus it was accepted that an accountant providing litigation support services was to be treated in the same way as a solicitor.[12]

Once it was established that the solicitors were in possession of relevant confidential information, and because the duty to preserve confidential information was unqualified, it was insufficient to show that reasonable steps had been taken to protect it. Lord Millett said that the court should intervene unless it is satisfied that there is no risk of disclosure. The risk must be a real one and not merely fanciful or theoretical. But it need not be substantial. No solicitor should, without the consent of his former client, accept instructions unless, viewed objectively, his doing so will not increase the risk that information which is confidential to the former client may come into the possession of a party with an adverse interest. On the facts, the House of Lords were not satisfied that the measures proposed and the undertakings offered by KPMG to protect confidentiality were adequate and granted the injunction.

Lord Millett regarded the exercise which had been carried out by the majority of the Court of Appeal as a "balancing" exercise. He said that there was no room for such an exercise. The fact that KPMG had acted for BIA throughout, to the knowledge of Prince Jefri, could only be relevant to the question whether Prince Jefri was to be taken to consent to KPMG acting in such circumstances (which on the facts he did not do); it was not relevant to the grant of injunctive relief. Thus he disagreed with the analysis of the New Zealand Court of Appeal in *Russell McVeagh*.

The factual issue which divided the courts which heard *Bolkiah* was the extent to which it was relevant that Prince Jefri had himself instructed the accountants knowing full well that they were longstanding auditors for the BIA, and thus likely to be the first port of call to be instructed by BIA in the event of any falling out between himself and the BIA. It was principally for that reason that the majority of the Court of Appeal were prepared to permit the accountants to continue acting. Although Lord Millett thought that the Court of Appeal had adopted the wrong test, in what he

1–008

---

[11] [1999] 2 A.C. 222.
[12] All the judges in the various courts said they accepted this although KPMG argued the contrary before Pumfrey J. and the Court of Appeal.

characterised as a "balancing exercise" in reliance on the New Zealand case *Russell McVeagh*,[13] what seems to have led to the divergence of view between the courts was what amounted to an implied consent issue: as Lord Millett put it, did Prince Jefri give inferred consent to KPMG acting for BIA in the circumstances which arose by instructing them himself in the full knowledge of their pre-existing relationship with BIA?

The sheer size of the operation made it very difficult for KPMG to justify an information barrier. The two projects involved 168 and 50 personnel respectively. The subject-matter of Project Gemma involved in part an asset-tracing operation. Preservation of confidentiality where the number of people in the office with relevant confidential information was so large and the number of people involved in the new project was also so large was always likely to be a Herculanean task.

The case is directly concerned with the rules as to former client conflicts. However, Lord Millett took the opportunity to set out the principles applicable to existing client conflicts too. It will be necessary to return to *Bolkiah* on a number of occasions. In summary, the principles established, which will be considered in detail in the course of this work, are as follows:

(a) Where the professional is asked to act for two clients with conflicting interests at the same time, the fiduciary obligations of loyalty owed to each will clash, and there is an existing client conflict. If he accepts instructions for both, he will then be in breach of fiduciary duty to one or both clients and unable to carry out his obligations to both. The problem is one of conflict, not merely confidential information. The conflict is a conflict of the firm, partnership or company and not merely of the individual partner. For this reason, the conflict extends beyond the individuals within the firm who act for the client to the firm itself.

(b) The professional who has an existing client conflict may not act without the informed consent of both clients. There are numerous ways of obtaining that consent expressly or by implication. If he has consent, in principle, he may act. But there will be circumstances where the conflict is such that he cannot act even with consent.

(c) The fiduciary obligation will come to an end upon the termination of the retainer, so thereafter there will be no basis for objection on that ground. If there is no relevant fiduciary obligation, the only basis for objection is risk of disclosure of confidential information.

(d) Where the conflict is between an existing client and a former client, there are no competing fiduciary duties because there is no fiduciary obligation of loyalty to a former client, although there is

---

[13] [1998] 3 N.Z.L.R. 641.

an obligation to protect confidentiality, breach of this obligation being classified as a breach of fiduciary duty.
(e) The professional who receives relevant confidential information from a former client may not act for a client whose interest conflicts with the former client unless the firm can show that there is no real risk of disclosure. The risk must be a real one, not one that is merely fanciful or theoretical. If the conflict is a former client conflict, it does not matter whether the second retainer relates to the same or a related matter—the issue is confidential information.
(f) The professional may be able to discharge this high burden by showing that effective internal measures are in place which will prevent disclosure, namely an information barrier. The effect of such arrangements will be to provide a firm within a firm. But these measures will rarely be effective if organised on an ad hoc basis, as opposed to being part of the organisational structure of the firm.
(g) There is no difference in the normal case between the rules which apply to lawyers and those which apply to other professionals.

2. Conflicts rules in other jurisdictions

It is not the intention of this book to provide an encyclopaedia of conflict rules in different jurisdictions. However, there are copious references in the course of the book to conflicts rules in other jurisdictions. It is therefore convenient to summarise briefly the conflict rules in the principal jurisdictions referred to in this work, so that references to authority from those jurisdictions within the book may be more readily understood. 1–009

A. Australia

There are far more decisions in Australia than in this jurisdiction, many of them judgments of high quality, and this book has increasingly used Australian authority as a valuable resource. Australian has a dual federal and state system, and the courts have always had a particular interest in the law of fiduciaries. Australia has largely followed the *Bolkiah* analysis. However in *Spincode Pty Ltd v Look Software Ltd*[14] in the Victoria Court of Appeal Brooking J.A. provided obiter a lengthy and well-reasoned critique of *Bolkiah,* pointing out that Lord Millett's analysis fails to deal with the court's longstanding supervisory jurisdiction over solicitors. After a shaky start, Australia has largely accepted this additional jurisdiction as a means of dealing with cases where there is an appearance of impropriety in 1–010

---

[14] [2001] V.S.C.A. 248.

counsel representing a client but no breach of the existing or former client principles enunciated in *Bolkiah*. Examples might be where the lawyer was likely to become a witness in the case or where he previously acted for two joint clients and seeks to act against one of those joint clients on a matter pertinent to the retainer even where there no confidential information. The test borrows from that applied in judicial conflicts:

> "whether a fair-minded reasonably well-informed member of the public would conclude that the proper administration of justice requires that a legal practitioner should be prevented from acting, in the interests of the protection of the integrity of the judicial process and the due administration of justice including the appearance of justice".[15]

There is also a suggestion in *Spincode* that the fiduciary obligation does not for all purposes come to an end upon the termination of the retainer, but not all subsequent Australian authority accepts this.

On occasion the Australian courts have adopted a more generous definition of confidential information than the English courts. In *Yunghanns v Elfic Pty Ltd*[16] Gillard J. said:

> "The degree of particularity of the confidential information must depend on all the circumstances. Often, it cannot be identified for fear of disclosure. In considering this factor it must be borne in mind that a solicitor makes notes, forms views and opinions of clients and observes things that the client may have forgotten or overlooked. In some cases, the circumstances of the retainer and the nature of the legal work will be sufficient to establish the nature of the confidential information. In this regard, the relationship between solicitor and client may be such that the solicitor learns a great deal about his client, his strengths, his weaknesses, his honesty or lack thereof, his reaction to crisis, pressures or tension, his attitude to litigation and settling cases and his tactics. These are factors which I would call the 'getting to know you' factors. The overall opinion formed by a solicitor of his client as a result of his contact may in the circumstances amount to confidential information that should not be disclosed or used against the client".

What is memorably described as "the getting to know you factors" would not be regarded in England as constituting confidential information. However, the view that Australia views the definition of confidential information more widely than this jurisdiction for purposes of conflicts of interest has not been universally accepted.[17]

---

[15] *Kallinicos v Hunt* [2005] N.S.W.S.C. 1181 at para. 76.
[16] 1998 Butterworths Cases 9803497.
[17] See 7–012.

B. Canada

In *Bolkiah* Lord Millett referred to the decision of the Supreme Court of Canada in *Macdonald Estates v Martin*.[18] For the majority, Sopinka J. said there were two rebuttable presumptions. First, that confidential information will have been communicated by the former client in the course of the retainer and second, that lawyers who work together share confidences. The burden is on the lawyer to rebut these presumptions. Sopinka J. said the court should restrain the firm from acting for the second client "unless satisfied on the basis of clear and convincing evidence that all reasonable measures have been taken to ensure that no disclosure will occur".

1–011

In *R. v Neil*[19] the Supreme Court of Canada considered whether the law firm could act in opposite sides on unrelated matters. Binnie J. went out of his way (the statement of principle was obiter) to identify a much more wide-ranging prohibition:

"... it is the firm not just the individual lawyer, that owes a fiduciary duty to its clients, and a bright line is required. The bright line is provided by the general rule that a lawyer may not represent one client whose interests are directly adverse to the immediate interests of another current client—*even if the two mandates are unrelated*—unless both clients consent after receiving full disclosure (and preferably independent legal advice) and the lawyer reasonably believes that he or she is able to represent each client without adversely affecting the other".[20]

Canada thus differs from this jurisdiction not merely in the test which applies for former client conflicts but in its "bright line" rule preventing a professional from acting for and against the same client at the same time on unrelated matters.[21]

C. New Zealand

In New Zealand the decision of the New Zealand Court of Appeal in *Russell McVeagh McKenzie Bartleet & Co v Tower Corp*[22] was adopted by the majority of the Court of Appeal in *Bolkiah* but rejected by the House of Lords. The stages were said to be, first, whether there was confidential

1–012

---

[18] [1990] 77 D.L.R. (4th) 249.
[19] [2003] 218 D.L.R. (4th) 67.
[20] At para. 29.
[21] Discussed at 3–014.
[22] [1998] 3 N.Z.L.R. 641.

information which, if disclosed, was likely to affect the interests of the former client adversely; secondly, whether there was a real or appreciable risk that the confidential information would be disclosed; and thirdly, whether the nature and importance of the former fiduciary relationship meant that the confidential information should be protected by an order of the kind sought. That was described as a "balancing test" by Lord Millett and not followed. The conflict between this approach and that taken by the House of Lords in *Bolkiah* does not yet seem to have been addressed.[23] In *Carter Holt Harvey Forests Ltd v Sunnex Logging Ltd*[24] the New Zealand Court of Appeal recognised the difference of approach but did not find it necessary to decide which to follow.

New Zealand has, until recently, used the Privy Council as a final court of appeal. So one might expect its approach to be similar to *Bolkiah*. However, although the position is less clear cut than in Australia, it has recognised a jurisdiction to intervene in the case of appearance of impropriety. Prior to *Bolkiah*, in *Black v Taylor*[25] the New Zealand Court of Appeal refused to permit a solicitor who had for decades acted as solicitor or counsel to family members from acting for the other side, founding itself on the inherent jurisdiction of the court to control its own processes and so prevent a practitioner from acting in a way which would cause reasonable members of the community to lose confidence in the judicial system. The case has been followed at first instance in New Zealand since *Bolkiah*.

D. United States

1–013   In the United States rules differ from state to state. The American Bar Association adopted Model Rules of Professional Conduct in 1983. A majority of states have adopted rules based on the Model Rules. Difficulties arise as a result of different rules from state to state. Federal rules are not necessarily the same as state rules. In general, the duty of loyalty survives termination of the attorney-client relationship and precludes a lawyer acting adversely to a former client in matters substantially related to the former representation. Model Rule[26] 1.6 precludes a lawyer from revealing information relating to the representation of a client unless the client gives informed consent. Rule 1.7 provides that a lawyer shall not represent a client if the representation involves a concurrent conflict of interest; a concurrent interest exists if the representation of one client will be directly

---

[23] In *GBR Investment Ltd v Keung* HC Christchurch CIV [2010] N.Z.H.C. 411 Associate Judge Bell recognised that he was bound by *Russell McVeagh* but sought to deal with the case in a manner also consistent with *Bolkiah*.
[24] [2001] 3 N.Z.L.R. 343.
[25] [1993] 3 N.Z.L.R. 403.
[26] *ABA Model Rules*, 2007 edition with 2009 revisions.

adverse to another client or there is a significant risk that the representation of one client will be materially limited by the lawyer's responsibilities to another client, a former client or a third person or by a personal interest of the lawyer. Notwithstanding this, a lawyer may represent a client if the lawyer believes that he will be able to provide competent and diligent representation to each affected client and each affected client gives informed consent confirmed in writing. Rule 1.9 provides that a lawyer who has formerly represented a client shall not represent another person in the same or a substantially related matter if that person's interests are materially adverse to the interests of the former client unless the former client gives informed consent confirmed in writing. Rule 1.10 provides that while lawyers are associated in a firm, none of them shall knowingly represent a client when any one of them practising alone would be prohibited from doing so by Rules 1.7 or 1.9[27] unless the disqualification is waived in the same way as in 1.7 and 1.10.

The US position is in general stricter than elsewhere. There is no formal recognition of information barriers,[28] and recognition by some US courts of the propriety of information barriers under strictly defined controls has come only recently.[29] Many courts remain wary of the efficacy of information barriers.[30] Most professional litigants seeking approval of information barriers continue to fail.[31] Under US practice, the availability of an information barrier as a means to avoid disqualification of a firm is never certain, and in certain jurisdictions is never available even under the most benign circumstances.

The US attitude to litigation has an effect with regard to conflicts which goes beyond construction of the rules. The threat of malpractice suits means that clients and former clients can recover substantial damages in claims from juries against law firms.[32] It is said that conflicts of interest have great "jury appeal" and that juries naturally identify with plaintiffs claiming that law firms' explanations or defensive engagement letters are insufficient

---

[27] Subject to limited exceptions where the prohibition is based on the personal interest of the disqualified lawyer or his association with a prior firm.
[28] Save in the context of protecting former government employees and their law firm employees from disqualification because of potential conflicts: see Model Rule 1.11.
[29] The first case was *Kesselhaut v United States* 555 F.2d 791 (Ct. Cl. 1977).
[30] See, e.g. *LaSalle National Bank v County of Lake* 703 F.2d 252 (7th Cir. 1983).
[31] J.R. Parker, "Private Sector Chinese Walls: Their efficacy as a method of avoiding imputed disqualification" 19 J. Legal Prof. 345, 349 (1995).
[32] See for example the 1998 Texas jury which awarded $59.5m against a Texas firm for an undisclosed conflict of interest. The verdict arose out of a common issue: does the firm represent the entity, the individual investors or both. Representatives of the defendant firm stated that the engagement letter covering the matter stated clearly that the entity was the client. The individual plaintiff claimed he never received the engagement letter notwithstanding evidence from the law firm that it had been sent and he claimed that the firm never told him that they did not represent him individually: see "Irate Jury Slams Gardere: Firm Hit with $59.5 million Malpractice Verdict in Conflict of Interest Case," Texas Lawyer, November 9, 1998.

adequately to warn plaintiffs, and especially individuals, of the nature of the legal representation and the possible need to obtain separate counsel. Experts regard such claims as among the most difficult to defend and some of the most expensive to resolve.[33]

---

[33] See A.E. Davis, "Personal, Business or Financial Conflicts of Interest", New York Law Journal, May 3, 1999.

CHAPTER 2

Existing Client Conflicts: the fiduciary obligation

The professional will owe two sets of duties to the client. One set is based in contract, and is derived from the express and implied terms of the retainer. These contractual duties may themselves give rise to obligations in tort as well. The other set is the fiduciary obligation. An appreciation of the inter-relationship between these sets of duties is crucial in an understanding of the law on conflicts of interest.

2–001

This chapter considers what is meant by a fiduciary relationship, who owes a fiduciary obligation in what circumstances, its effect and the obligations which attach to a fiduciary relationship. As it is crucial for the purpose of conflicts of interest for a professional to know whether he owes a fiduciary obligation at any particular time, the chapter goes on to consider problems in determining when fiduciary obligations commence, and to which legal entity they are owed. It then goes on to consider problem issues in termination of fiduciary obligations, and the rare circumstances when a fiduciary obligation may exist after the termination of a retainer.

1. The fiduciary relationship

A. What is a fiduciary?

A person who acts for another is to be regarded as a fiduciary. The Australian academic Professor Paul Finn[1], now Mr Justice Finn, who has contributed so much to the law on conflicts of interest, stated that a

2–002

---

[1] *Fiduciary Obligations* (1977).

fiduciary is, "someone who undertakes to act for or on behalf of another in some particular matter or matters".

This definition was widely followed, although Professor Finn himself points out[2] that a difficulty is that this definition suggests fiduciary responsibility may be voluntarily undertaken, whereas the nature of fiduciary regulation is that obligations are imposed on an individual in equity in given circumstances. Professor Finn provided the following revised definition:

"A person will be a fiduciary in his relationship with another when and in so far as that other is entitled to expect that he will act in that other's interests or (as in a partnership) in their joint interests, to the exclusion of his own several interest".[3]

In *Arklow v Maclean*[4] the Privy Council said that the fiduciary concept:

"encaptures a situation where one person is in a relationship with another which gives rise to a legitimate expectation, which equity will recognise, that the fiduciary will not utilise his or her position in such a way which is adverse to the interests of the principal".

Almost all of the relationships canvassed in this book will involve fiduciary relationships, so for purposes of conflicts of interest the position will usually be a relatively straightforward one. This is because a fiduciary relationship will arise where one party *acts for* another in a particular respect. In *Bristol and West Building Society v Mothew*[5] Millett L.J. said:

"A fiduciary is someone who has undertaken to act for or on behalf of another in a particular matter in circumstances which give rise to a relationship of trust and confidence. The distinguishing obligation of a fiduciary is the obligation of loyalty".

B. What gives rise to a fiduciary relationship?

2–003   The first, and most important, circumstance in which a fiduciary relationship arises is the relationship of trust and confidence. Such a relationship arises when one party undertakes to act in the interests of another, or where he places himself in a position where he is obliged to act in the interests of another, and the core obligation is the obligation of loyalty. Thus the

---

[2] "The Fiduciary Principle" in Youdan T.G. ed, *Equity, Fiduciaries and Trusts* (1989).
[3] "Fiduciary Law and the Modern Commercial World" in *Commercial Aspects of Trusts and Fiduciary Obligations* (McKendrick edn., 1992).
[4] [2000] 1 W.L.R. 594.
[5] [1998] Ch. 1, 18

professional, whether solicitor, barrister or advising accountant[6] will owe a fiduciary duty to his client. Where one party instructs another to act for him, and thus gives to the agent or professional man some form of power or delegated authority, or merely gives him a job to do on his behalf (such as the negotiation of a contract) a fiduciary relationship will be created. So too when the client gives to the professional property and relies on the professional to deal with the property for the benefit of the client. The relationship of fiduciary is present both where the professional acts for the client in the performance of a task which involves a measure of delegation to the professional, and also where the professional is instructed merely to advise the client as to a proposed course of action. Here the relationship of confidence and the dependence upon information and advice gives rise to the same type of obligation.

In a well-known 1998 article in the Law Quarterly Review, Lord Millett[7] identified two further categories of fiduciary relationship: *influence* and *confidentiality*.

A relationship of influence has as its defining characteristic vulnerability. Equity is jealous to prevent the exploitation of the vulnerable. It is unconscionable for a party to exploit the influence which he may have over another for the benefit of himself and not that other. The relationship does not depend on any undertaking by one party to act in the interests of another; it is rather a relationship of ascendancy and dependency. Thus cases involving family members, husband and wife, and elderly or vulnerable people, may be fiduciary relationship based on influence. There are cases where a client has entered into a transaction with a solicitor even when there is no continuing retainer which may be treated as within this principle.

The final category referred to by Lord Millett was the relationship of confidentiality whenever information is imparted by one person to another in confidence. The obligation to respect confidentiality has several juridical bases. It may be contractual or equitable. It may arise from the circumstances in which the information was imparted, or from the obviously confidential nature of the information. Lord Millett's inclusion of this third category must now be read subject to the views of the Privy Council in *Arklow Investments Ltd v Maclean*[8] where the relationship between confidentiality and fiduciary duties was considered.[9]

A distinction is sometimes drawn between fiduciary relationships based on the *status* of the parties, namely circumstances in which one party acting in a particular capacity to the other brings with it the obligations of fiduciary, such as trustee and beneficiary, solicitor and client, agent and principal,

2–004

---

[6] An auditor's position is different because of his statutory obligations: see 17–008.
[7] "Equity's Place in the Law of Commerce" (1998) L.Q.R. 214.
[8] [2000] 1 W.L.R. 594.
[9] Discussed at 2–012 below.

director and company, partner and partner, employee and employer, from those circumstances in which the special facts give rise to a fiduciary relationship, namely because the factual situation of the particular relationship is such that the law will require the imposition of a fiduciary relationship. Thus it was recognised in both *Lac Minerals Ltd v International Corona Resources Ltd*[10] and *Hospital Products Ltd v United States Surgical Corp*[11] that even if the relationship between the parties did not of itself fall within any of the classes which gave rise to fiduciary relationships, the presence of certain factors in what would otherwise be a non-fiduciary relationship would give rise to fiduciary obligations, such as an undertaking by the fiduciary to act on behalf of or for the benefit of another person, a discretion or power which affected the interests of that person, and the peculiar vulnerability of that other person to the fiduciary, such as in undue influence cases. In other areas of the law, the distinction between "status" based fiduciaries and "fact" based fiduciaries is of significance, but cases involving professional and client will normally fall within the former category,[12] and thus the distinction will not generally be material.[13]

It has been said that the English courts have not generally imposed fiduciary obligations of undivided loyalty outside cases where, at least when the fiduciary relationship is first applied, the beneficiary entrusted the fiduciary with control and management of property or money[14] and it has been suggested that this is the reason why the English courts have not imposed fiduciary obligations of loyalty on doctors.[15] Whilst this analysis may well be historically correct, practical application of such a test today is dangerous: solicitors and barristers who are involved in criminal cases do not have control or management of property or money, but it has not been suggested that their fiduciary obligations are different from those involved in commercial litigation.[16]

---

[10] [1990] F.S.R. 441; [1989] 2 S.C.R. 574.
[11] (1984) 156 C.L.R. 41, HCA.
[12] See *Beach Petroleum v Abbott Tout Russel Kennedy* [1999] N.S.W.C.A. 408.
[13] But see 4–024 where the distinction was crucial in determining whether an investment bank owed a fiduciary duty to a client in making full disclosure in relation to exclusions of liability in the engagement letter.
[14] Pattenden, *The Law of Professional Client Confidentiality* (2003) para.5.80. The Canadian courts have taken a different view recognising fiduciary relationships in a variety of circumstances not involving property or money: eg *M(K) v M(H)* (1992) 96 D.L.R. (4th) 289; *McInerney v MacDonald* (1992) 93 D.L.R. (4th) 415.
[15] *Sidaway v Bethlem Royal Hospital Governors* [1984] 1 All E.R. 1018 at 1032. There might however be circumstances in which there was a fiduciary obligation between doctor and patient based on vulnerability, so as to apply where the patient sought to leave money to the doctor in a will.
[16] Pattenden, *The Law of Professional Client Confidentiality*, at para.5.80 fn.316 accepts that solicitors owe fiduciary duties where they represent clients in criminal matters: see for example the decision of the Canadian Supreme Court in *R. v Neil*, [2002] S.C.C. 70, para.12. She suggests that the solicitor-client relationship may originally have gained this characterisation because solicitors have responsibility for the economic well-being of their clients.

C. What does a fiduciary duty mean?

Sir Anthony Mason, former Chief Justice of Australia, pithily commented that "the fiduciary relationship is a concept in search of a principle".[17] The purpose and effect of fiduciary obligations has sometimes been misunderstood. The seminal modern analysis of fiduciary obligations is to be found in the judgment of Millett L.J. in *Bristol & West Building Society v Mothew*.[18] The judgment of Millett L.J. in *Mothew* was approved by the House of Lords (Lord Millett giving the leading speech) in *Bolkiah*. Building on the *Mothew* analysis, it has been said that it is wrong in principle to treat fiduciary duties as simply the duties owed by persons in trustee-like positions:

2–005

> "The distinctive remedial regime applicable to breach of a fiduciary's duty is more readily explained if fiduciary doctrine's remedies are available from breaches of duties that apply only to fiduciaries . . . restricting the language of fiduciary duties to those duties that are applied consistently across the spectrum of fiduciary relationships allows both an explanation of the standards that apply differently to different fiduciary relationships".[19]

Fiduciary obligations, therefore, can be seen as the obligations peculiar to those who are in fiduciary positions. As Millett L.J. put it in *Mothew:*

> "The expression "fiduciary duty" is properly confined to those duties which are peculiar to fiduciaries and the breach of which attracts legal consequences differing from those consequent upon the breach of other duties. Unless the expression is so limited it is lacking in practical utility. In this sense it is obvious that not every breach of duty by a fiduciary is a breach of fiduciary duty".

The duty which is particular to a fiduciary is the duty of loyalty. Millett L.J. continued:

> "The distinguishing obligation of a fiduciary is the obligation of loyalty. This core liability has several facets. A fiduciary must act in good faith; he must not make a profit out of his trust; he must not place himself in a position where his duty and his interest may conflict; he may not act for his own benefit or the benefit of a third person without the informed consent of his principal".

---

[17] Mason, "Themes and Prospects" in Essays in Equity (Finn ed., 1985).
[18] [1998] Ch 1.
[19] Conaglen, *Fiduciary Loyalty* (2010) pp. 27–28. Matthew Conaglen's new book on fiduciary loyalty is an outstanding and valuable analysis of fiduciary obligations and is relied on heavily in this book.

2–006   Thus the professional will normally owe both fiduciary and non-fiduciary duties. The remedies available are different in each case. It is apparent from the analysis in *Mothew* that it is necessary to understand the distinction in order to resolve the trickier problems of analysis in conflicts of interest. The duty to exercise reasonable skill and care is not a fiduciary obligation, so breach of that obligation does not give rise to a breach of fiduciary duty. The duty on the professional to perform the task undertaken under the retainer is not a fiduciary duty. The duty of good faith is a little trickier: it is often said that a fiduciary owes a duty of good faith to his principal, but duties of good faith are not peculiar to fiduciaries. Many non-fiduciaries owe duties of good faith to their principals. Someone who owes duties akin to a trustee will owe obligations to act in good faith; it is inconceivable that such a person will be permitted to act in bad faith when performing those duties. But it has been said that there is nothing peculiar to a trustee in such a duty and thus such duties do not require detailed consideration in the context of an analysis of peculiarly fiduciary duties.[20]

The duty which is peculiar to a fiduciary is the duty of loyalty: a fiduciary is not permitted to make any unauthorised profit from his position and is not allowed to put himself in a position where his interest and duty conflict.

D. Bristol & West Building Society v Mothew

2–007   Apart perhaps from *Bolkiah*, the most important case in English law on conflicts of interest is *Bristol & West Building Society v Mothew*.[21] *Mothew* was decided shortly before *Bolkiah* and focuses on the effect of a fiduciary obligation on conflicts of interest. The leading speech in *Bolkiah* was given by Lord Millett, in *Mothew* by Millett L.J.

The solicitor defendant acted for both lender and borrower on the purchase of a property to the knowledge of each. The lender's instructions required the balance of the purchase money to be paid by the borrower without resort to further borrowing. It followed that the solicitor was bound to disclose any further borrowing by the borrower to the lender. The solicitor became aware that the borrower was obtaining a portion of the purchase money from another source but failed to disclose this to the lender. The borrower later defaulted and the lender sued the solicitor both at common law and in equity. The judge at first instance had held that the solicitor was in breach of fiduciary duty in failing to disclose information to the lender as to the second loan. In the Court of Appeal, Millett L.J. made clear that breach of fiduciary duty was only properly referable to breach of the duty which is particular to a fiduciary, the duty of loyalty:

---

[20] See Conaglen, *Fiduciary Loyalty* p.44.
[21] [1998] Ch. 1.

"The nature of the fiduciary obligation determines the nature of the breach. The various obligations of a fiduciary merely reflect different aspects of his core duties of loyalty and fidelity. Breach of fiduciary obligation, therefore, connotes disloyalty or infidelity. Mere incompetence is not enough. A servant who loyally does his incompetent best for his master is not unfaithful and is not guilty of a breach of fiduciary duty".

Breach of fiduciary duty, therefore, is not about incompetent fiduciaries; the incompetent fiduciary will be liable for breach of duty (that is, breach of non-fiduciary duty), but not for breach of fiduciary duty. In *Mothew,* the solicitor had information from one client which he failed to pass on to the other, leaving him in breach of duty to the lender. But Millett L.J. said it was not a breach of *fiduciary* duty. The solicitor was acting for both clients with the consent of each. There was no allegation that the failure to pass on the information to the lender was in order to obtain an advantage for the borrower. On the lender's pleaded case the fact that the defendant was acting for the borrower played no part in his failure to report the true state of affairs to the lender. So this was not a disloyal fiduciary, but an incompetent one.

In his judgment in *Mothew,* Millett L.J. considered the rules applicable to fiduciaries which did impact on their fiduciary duties. He put to one side the different rule where a fiduciary deals with his principal:

"In this survey I have left out of account the situation where the fiduciary deals with his principal. In such a case he must prove affirmatively that the transaction is fair and that in the course of the negotiations he made full disclosure of all facts material to the transaction. Every inadvertent failure to disclose will entitle the principal to rescind the transaction. The rule is the same whether the fiduciary is acting on his own behalf or on behalf of another".

He then went on to look at the fiduciary who acts for two clients. He said that a fiduciary who acts for two principals with potentially conflicting interests without the informed consent of both is in breach of the obligation of undivided loyalty[22]; he puts himself in a position where his duty to one principal may conflict with his duty to the other. This amounts to an *automatic* breach of fiduciary duty on the part of the professional, and is sometimes described as the "double employment" rule. As Lord Millett subsequently put it in *Bolkiah*[23]:

---

[22] *Clark Boyce v Mouat* [1994] 1 A.C. 428, PC; *Boulting v Assn of Cinematograph Television and Allied Technicians* [1963] 2 Q.B. 606 at 636 per Upjohn J.; *Haslam v Hier-Evans* [1902] 1 Ch. 765.
[23] [1999] 2 A.C. 222 at 234.

"... a fiduciary cannot act at the same time both for and against the same client, and his firm is in no better position. A man cannot without the consent of both clients act for one client while his partner is acting for another in the opposite interest. His disqualification has nothing to do with the confidentiality of client information. It is based on the inescapable conflict of interest which is inherent in the situation".

Thus the rule which prohibits a fiduciary from acting for two principals with potentially conflicting interests is prophylactic. It is prophylactic because it prevents the fiduciary from being in a position where a conflict of two inconsistent duties arises:

"The key element that separates fiduciary duties from other duties not peculiar to fiduciaries is that fiduciary duties provide this enhanced likelihood of faithful adherence to duty by protecting the fiduciary from influences that are likely to interfere with proper performance of the fiduciary's non-fiduciary duties. The presence of such influences carries with it a risk that the fiduciary may be tempted not to perform properly his non-fiduciary duties. Removing the influences therefore increases the likelihood of a fiduciary performing his non-fiduciary duties faithfully. Thus the concept of fiduciary "loyalty" encapsulates a subsidiary and prophylactic form of protection for non-fiduciary duties which is designed to enhance the chance that those non-fiduciary duties will be properly performed".[24]

2–008 Once it is established that there is a potential conflict between the two duties, the fiduciary can only act with informed consent. If there is no consent, acting is a breach of fiduciary duty. But if he does obtain informed consent there will still be two circumstances in which he is at risk of a finding of breach of fiduciary duty.

The first circumstance is what Millett L.J. called the "no inhibition principle" which arises if he intentionally prefers the interests of one client to the other. If, having obtained consent, he does something which *in fact* prefers the interests of one to the other, he will be in breach of duty, but that will not be a breach of the duty of loyalty: he will be in breach of his duty of reasonable care and skill, but his failing is not a matter of loyalty and thus not a matter of breach of fiduciary duty. That was the error of the first instance judge in *Mothew:* the solicitor was acting for two clients, and preferred the interest of one to the other, in that he failed to make the required disclosure as to the second borrowing to the lender. But in the absence of any pleaded allegation that the failure was *intended* to prefer one to the other, the breach was a breach of his instructions and not a breach of fiduciary duty. Millett

---

[24] Conaglan, *Fiduciary Loyalty* (2010) pp.61–62.

L.J. pointed out that by preferring the interests of one client to the other, there would be a breach of non-fiduciary duty:

> "he must act in good faith in the interests of each and must not act with the intention of furthering the interests of one principal to the prejudice of those of the other[25]. I shall call this "the duty of good faith." But it goes further than this. He must not allow the performance of his obligations to one principal to be influenced by his relationship with the other. He must serve each as faithfully and loyally as if he were his only principal. Conduct which is a breach of this duty need not be dishonest but it must be intentional. An unconscious omission which happens to benefit one principal at the expense of the other does not constitute a breach of fiduciary duty, though it may constitute a breach of the duty of care and skill. This is because the principle which is in play is that the fiduciary must not be inhibited by the existence of his other employment from serving the interests of his principal as faithfully and effectively as if he were the only employer. I shall call this the "no inhibition" principle. Unless the fiduciary is inhibited or believes (whether rightly or wrongly) that he is inhibited in the performance of his duties to one principal by reason of his employment by the other, his failure to act is not attributable to the double employment".

So preferring the interests of one client with conflicting interests to another is only a breach of non-fiduciary duty unless it is deliberate, because it is only if it is deliberate that the duty of loyalty is engaged.

The other circumstance where informed consent will not save the fiduciary from a claim for breach of fiduciary duty is the case of what Millett L.J. called (somewhat confusingly) "actual conflict". An "actual conflict" of duty is where the fiduciary cannot fulfil his obligations to one principal without failing in his obligations to the other. Thus it may be that the professional is in breach of the duty to act with reasonable skill and diligence, in which case there is a breach of duty but (particularly given that there has already been informed consent) no breach of fiduciary duty.

The "double employment" rule and its consequences are discussed in detail in Ch.3.

E. Fiduciary obligations and non-fiduciary obligations

The analysis in *Mothew* highlights the importance of drawing a distinction between the *fiduciary* duties owed by the professional and the *non-fiduciary* duties owed by the same professional. The duty of confidentiality

2–009

---

[25] See Finn, *Fiduciary Obligations*, p.48.

is in a slightly different position from other duties and needs to be treated separately.[26] The duty of confidentiality aside, the fiduciary will owe each of the two sets of duties. For example, the professional owes a duty to act with reasonable care and skill but breach of that duty has nothing to do with fiduciary duty. This is a "non-fiduciary" duty. Breach of that duty by a fiduciary does not involve a breach of fiduciary duty. By contrast, fiduciary duty is concerned with the duty of loyalty. As we will see, equity imposes fiduciary duties as a prophylactic to prevent a professional from undertaking an obligation which jeopardizes the existing obligation of loyalty and thus to prevent breach of non-fiduciary duties by a fiduciary. In the analysis which follows, in this chapter and the next, the distinction between fiduciary and non-fiduciary duties is important.

F. Fiduciary duties are proscriptive not prescriptive

2–010   In *Breen v Williams*[27] Mrs Breen sought to obtain medical records from her doctor. She alleged that by reason of his fiduciary duty, the doctor had a positive duty to reveal the records to his patient. The High Court of Australia declined to hold that the doctor owed a fiduciary obligation at all to the patient, a view that has always been accepted in this jurisdiction.[28] But the High Court went on to say that fiduciary duties were *proscriptive* not *prescriptive*; in other words, they identified what a fiduciary may not do (no conflict, no profit) rather than what the fiduciary should do. The point was put by Gaudron and McHugh L.J.J.[29]:

> "The law of fiduciary duty rests not so much on morality or conscience as on the acceptance of the twin implications of the biblical injunction that "no man can serve two masters." Duty and self-interest, like God and mammon, make inconsistent calls on the faithful. Equity solves the problem in a practical way by insisting that fiduciaries give undivided loyalty to the persons whom they serve".

The High Court of Australia reaffirmed the proscriptive nature of fiduciary duties in *Pilmer v Duke Group Ltd*.[30] By contrast, Canada has never accepted this view of fiduciary obligations, but has always treated them as prescriptive,[31] imposing positive obligations on the fiduciary.

The Court of Appeal, consisting of Lord Woolf M.R., Millett and

---

[26] See 2–012.
[27] [1996] 186 C.L.R. 71.
[28] See *R. v Mid Glamorgan FHSA Ex p. Martin* (1993) *The Times*, June 2.
[29] At 108.
[30] [2001] 207 C.L.R. 165.
[31] *Breen* considered and declined to follow the decision of the Canadian Supreme Court in *McInerny v McDonald* 1992 2S.C.R. 138

Mummery L.J.J., adopted the proscriptive view in *AG v Blake*.[32] George Blake, British secret agent turned Russian spy, sought to publish his autobiography revealing details of his time as a British secret agent. The argument was put that Blake was in breach of contract and fiduciary duty to the Crown in failing to submit the material for clearance. The Court of Appeal[33] rejected the analysis:

> "His wrongdoing did not lie in failing to obtain clearance, but in his submitting the manuscript without it. In the second place, equity is proscriptive not prescriptive: see *Breen v Williams*. It tells the fiduciary what he must not do. It does not tell him what he ought to do".

Millett L.J. was party to the judgment of the court in *Blake*. This passage is in accord with *Mothew* (albeit *Breen* is not cited) as well as what Lord Millett has written extra-judicially, citing *Breen* in support of his views.[34]

G. Proscriptive and prescriptive duties: Item Software

2–011

A recent important decision of the Court of Appeal has been seen as confusing the analysis of fiduciary duties as it appears to treat fiduciary duties as prescriptive and not merely proscriptive. In *Item Software v Fassihi*,[35] Mr Fassihi, the sales director of Item Software, encouraged a client to take a hard line in negotiations with Item so that when negotiations broke down, he could take the contract with the client through his own company. Negotiations did break down, and the client terminated its relationship with Item, but Fassihi did not win the contract. He made no profit for which he had to account, but the question whether Item had suffered loss depended on whether Fassihi had a duty to disclose his own misconduct, thereby giving Item an opportunity to take a different stance in negotiations. The Court of Appeal, with Arden L.J. giving the leading judgment, held that as a director Fassihi had an obligation to disclose his own misconduct to the company as part of his duty of good faith to the company; there was no basis on which Mr Fassihi could have come to the conclusion that it was not in Item's interests to know of his breach of duty.

This decision is controversial because it appears to do what English law has otherwise declined to do, namely treat fiduciary duties as prescriptive rather than proscriptive, and to impose positive obligations on fiduciaries.

---

[32] [1998] Ch 439, 454.
[33] Lord Woolf M.R. gave the judgment of the court.
[34] "What distinguishes the role of equity from that of the common law is that equity is proscriptive not prescriptive. It forbids the fiduciary to act for himself. It does not tell him what to do for his principal. And if, in breach of his fiduciary duty, he does act for himself, he is treated as if he had acted for his principal."
[35] [2005] 2 B.C.L.C. 91.

In the Victoria Supreme Court in Australia, the decision in *Item Software* was not followed and criticised by Hollingsworth J. in *P&V Industries Pty Ltd v Porto*.[36] The judge referred to *Breen v Williams*[37] and said:

> "... the no conflict and no profit rules encompass the whole content of fiduciary obligations and the duty of loyalty imposed on a fiduciary is promoted by prohibiting disloyalty rather than by prescribing some positive duty".

The judge said that *Item Software* did not represent the law of Australia and he doubted whether it represented the law of England.

There is no doubt that *Item Software* has led to controversy. But it is suggested that this decision should not be regarded as affecting the general principles relating to fiduciary duties under English law, or casting doubt upon the principle that such duties are proscriptive not prescriptive. *Breen* was not cited to the Court of Appeal in *Fassihi*.[38] The conclusion reached by the court could readily have been reached by another route[39]: in *British Midland Tool Ltd v Midland International Tooling Ltd*[40] Hart J. held that a director's duty to act so as to promote the best interests of the company prima facie included a duty "to inform the company of any activity, actual or threatened, which damages those interests". Such a duty would apply "whether or not the activity in itself would constitute a breach by anyone of the relevant duty owed to the company."[41] The decision in *Fassihi* is referable to the director's duty to act in the best interests of the company. Moreover, under the Companies Act 2006 the statutory restatement of directors' duties[42] imposes positive duties on directors which are likely to give rise to a similar result.

H. Confidential information giving rise to a fiduciary relationship

2–012   The obligation of confidentiality survives the termination of the retainer. The obligation of confidence, whether owed to an existing or former client, is often described as a fiduciary obligation.[43] Breach of the obliga-

---

[36] [2006] 14 V.R. 1.
[37] 1996 186 C.L.R. 71 see 2–010 above.
[38] Indeed, Arden L.J. recorded that counsel had been unable to refer the court to any relevant Commonwealth authority [30].
[39] See generally the discussion in an excellent new book *Fiduciary Duties, Directors and Employees*, Stafford and Ritchie (2008).
[40] [2003] 2 B.C.L.C. 523 [89].
[41] Followed in *Shepherds Investments Ltd v Walters* 2006 EWHC 836 (Ch) para 106, Etherton J.
[42] Discussed at 18–001 below.
[43] See Lord Millett, "Equity's Place In The Law Of Commerce" (1998) L.Q.R. 214; see also

tion of confidentiality gives rise to equitable remedies such as an account of profits. In *Arklow Investments Ltd v Maclean*[44] the Privy Council left open[45] the question whether the obligation not to misuse confidential information was properly classed as a fiduciary duty. What was important was the content of the duty, not its label. Whether or not it was properly characterised as a fiduciary obligation, the obligation not to misuse confidential information did not carry with it an obligation of loyalty. To that extent it is important to distinguish it from the usual type of fiduciary obligation.

It is thus preferable to regard the professional as owing two distinct types of fiduciary duty. The central fiduciary obligation of loyalty will normally terminate with the retainer, subject to exceptional circumstances considered below[46] when at least some form of fiduciary obligation may survive the termination of the retainer. The obligation of confidentiality survives the retainer but to the extent that it can be described as a fiduciary obligation, it does not in itself carry with it an obligation of loyalty.[47]

2. Existence of a fiduciary relationship: problem areas

A. Joint ventures

An area where there has been controversy as to whether the agreement gives rise to a fiduciary relationship has often been joint venture agreements. The answer will vary from case to case, because it is necessary to examine the facts to see whether the parties undertook to each other obligations of undivided loyalty or whether one party accepts an obligation to act for the other. Thus the High Court of Australia declined to find a fiduciary relationship as between parties to an ordinary commercial distributorship in *Hospital Products Ltd v United States Surgical Corp*.[48] In the famous case *Lac Minerals Ltd v International Corona Resources Ltd*[49] the Supreme Court of Canada declined by a bare majority to find a fiduciary relationship between parties to a mining joint venture. But the line has not always here been consistently drawn.[50]

2–013

Att-Gen v Blake [1998] Ch. 439 at 454 (the Court of Appeal judgment was varied by the House of Lords on other grounds: [2001] 1 A.C. 268); *Lac Minerals Ltd v International Corona Resources Ltd* [1990] F.S.R. 441; (1989) 61 D.L.R. 14.
[44] [2000] 1 W.L.R. 594 at 600.
[45] At 600E.
[46] 2–020.
[47] See also *Indata v ACL* [1998] F.S.R. 248, CA.
[48] (1984) 156 C.L.R. 41, HCA.
[49] [1990] F.S.R. 441; [1989] 2 S.C.R. 574.
[50] See, e.g. *Norberg v Wynrib* [1992] 2 S.C.R. 226 at 312, S.C.C., *Hanson v Lorenz & Jones*

The Privy Council decision in *Arklow Investments Ltd v Maclean*[51] is significant for two reasons. Firstly, the claimants argued that an obligation not to use confidential information gave rise to a fiduciary obligation; secondly, they sought to allege a fiduciary obligation from a negotiation preliminary to a joint venture. The claimants provided confidential information to merchant bankers with a view to the latter providing assistance in obtaining finance for a project involving the purchase and development of an island off the coast of New Zealand. The bankers made an offer which was not accepted and the claimants sought finance elsewhere. The bankers then withdrew their offer and negotiated arrangements with others leading to the acquisition of the island by them. The trial judge in New Zealand found that the bankers owed a fiduciary obligation to the claimants. The New Zealand Court of Appeal reversed the decision and this was upheld by the Privy Council. The Privy Council held that the bankers had not expressly or impliedly undertaken any obligation to act and had no authority to do so, and since there had been no informal arrangement or continuing course of conduct between them, there was no mutuality which could give rise to the undertaking of a fiduciary duty of loyalty to the claimants not to promote or become involved in a competitive acquisition of the island. The only obligation which in fact arose was an obligation not to misuse confidential information, but the claimants had failed to prove misuse. The Privy Council left open the question whether the obligation not to misuse confidential information was properly described as a form of fiduciary duty but made clear that this was a matter of semantics: a confidentiality obligation did not in any event of itself carry with it the fiduciary obligation of loyalty.[52]

In recent English cases where the issue was whether a fiduciary relationship arose between the parties to a joint venture, whether the court has found a fiduciary relationship has proved fact specific and depends on the terms of the venture and whether one party can be said to act for another.[53] In *Murad v Al Saraj*[54] Etherton J. found a fiduciary relationship because one party relied on the other acting for it. The judge cited *United Dominions Corporation v Brian Pty*[55] where the court said:

[1986] N.L.J. Rep. 1088, CA (solicitor did not have to account for profits made in joint venture with client).

[51] [2000] 1 W.L.R. 594, PC.

[52] The action for breach of confidence is separate to the action for breach of fiduciary duty but the authorities are not clear as to whether they are concurrently available in the sense that the claimant may choose between them: see *Lac Minerals Ltd v International Corona Ltd* (1989) 61 D.L.R. (4th) 14 at 35–36 per Sopinka J.; *Indata Equipment Supplies Ltd v ACL Ltd* [1998] 1 B.C.L.C. 412; *Moorgate Tobacco Co Ltd v Philip Morris Ltd* (1984) 156 C.L.R. 414 at 436–438.

[53] Thus in *Donnelly v Weybridge Construction (No 2)* [2006] EWHC 2678 TCC Ramsey J. the court found that a joint venture to develop and sells flats involved fiduciary obligations where two of the individuals were acting for others in the consortium.

[54] [2004] EWHC 1235, see also [2005] EWCA 959 but the case went to the Court of Appeal only on the issue of remedies.

[55] (1985) 157 C.L.R. 1.

"In particular a fiduciary relationship may, and ordinarily will, exist between prospective parties who have embarked upon the conduct of the partnership business or venture before the precise terms of any agreement have been settled. Indeed, in such circumstances, the mutual confidence and trust which underlie most consensual fiduciary relationships are likely to be more readily apparent than in the case where mutual rights and obligations have been expressly defined in some formal agreement. Likewise, the relationship between prospective partners or participants in a proposed partnership to carry out a single undertaking will ordinarily be fiduciary if the prospective partners have reached an informal arrangement to assume such a relationship and have proceeded to take steps to be involved in its establishment or implementation".

Thus in *Sintra Homes Ltd v Beard*[56] two individuals operating a joint venture as a quasi-partnership each with confidence in the other to act in their respective best interests were held to owe fiduciary obligations to the other. A case on the other side of the line was *Button v Phelps*[57] where the issue was whether a fiduciary obligation should be superimposed on contractual obligations in relation to a rival bid. The judge recognised that a joint venture would often impose fiduciary obligations on participants but held no such obligation arose on the facts. Similarly, in *Sinclair Investment Holdings v Versailles Trade Finance*[58] Rimer J. declined to find a fiduciary duty in what he described as a "sales pitch" for an investment. One rather different case is the Australian case *Wimmera Industrial Minerals Pty v Iluka Midwest*[59] where the court declined to treat a scientist who did work for the claimant culminating in the grant of a patent as a fiduciary by considering the terms of his contract and finding no obligation of undivided loyalty. The only relevant obligation was held to be an obligation not to misuse confidential information.[60]

B. Employees

The question whether and when employees owe fiduciary obligations was considered by Elias J. in *University of Nottingham v*   2–014

---

[56] [2007] EWHC 3071, Ch D. Judge Behrens.
[57] [2006] EWHC 53 Deputy Judge Robert Englehart Q.C.
[58] [2007] EWHC 915 at [77]–[94].
[59] [2002] F.C.A. 653, Fed Ct of Australia.
[60] See also *Noranda Australia Ltd v Lachlan Resources* (1988) 13 N.S.W.L.R. 1. The parties to a joint venture provided in their contract that their relationship "shall be fiduciary in nature". This did not have the effect that every term was a fiduciary obligation, merely those terms relevant to the duty of each party to act in the mutual interest of both.

Fishel.[61] Dr Fishel was a lecturer at the university who did unauthorized outside work which he did not disclose to his employers. The judge held that he was in breach of duty in so doing but as he held the university suffered no loss, the issue was whether he was in breach of a fiduciary obligation so as to give rise to a liability to account for profits. Elias J. said that it was wrong to define an employee relationship either as being or not as being a fiduciary relationship; in the normal course, the mere fact of an employee relationship did not give rise to a fiduciary obligation. In an employment relationship, fiduciary duties could only result from specific contractual obligations which the employee had undertaken where he had placed himself in a position where he was obliged to act solely in the interests of his employer. In such circumstances, those fiduciary obligations were in any event circumscribed by the contractual terms. Thus every errand boy who takes a bribe is obliged to account for it even though the errand boy would not otherwise be regarded as a fiduciary.[62]

Elias J. said that the conflict of interest and duty principle was not engaged by Dr Fishel's unauthorized work abroad. Whilst doing the work was a breach of contract, it did not conflict with any interest of the university. He contrasted *Industrial Developments Ltd v Cooley*[63] where the employee's conflict arose because he took for himself a contract where it was his duty to obtain such contracts for the company. However, by contrast, where Dr Fishel was paid for work done by other embryologists for whom he was responsible, and by accepting work for them for which he was benefiting, he did put himself into a position of conflict between duty and interest, because his duty to the university was to direct the embryologists to work in the interests of the university and his own interest was served by directing them to work abroad. Thus in relation to the work of the embryologists, the university was entitled to an account of profits from Dr Fishel but not from his own work abroad.

C. Shadow directors

2–015   Another area of the law in which there is controversy as to whether fiduciary duties are owed is shadow directors, persons on whose directions or instructions the directors are accustomed to act. The opportunity to resolve the position was ducked by the Companies Act 2006, which provides that

---

[61] [2000] I.C.R. 1462.
[62] Following this decision, in *Cobbetts LLP v Hodge*, [2009] EWHC 786 (Ch) Floyd J. held that a salaried partner of a firm of solicitors was not on the facts to be treated as a true partner, but nevertheless owed fiduciary duties to the firm as employee. Mr Hodge was required to seek investors for the firm's client in its attempt to raise capital. In anticipation of leaving the law firm, he negotiated a right to purchase shares in the client's placement at par. Floyd J. held that he held them on trust for the law firm.
[63] [1972] 1 W.L.R. 443

in this regard the previous law is to apply without resolving the dispute as to what it was.[64] There are authorities both ways.[65]

D. Commercial contracts

Where the parties have a commercial relationship governed by contractual obligations, the court will be reluctant to impose fiduciary obligations on top of the contract merely because in the course of performing its contractual obligations one party acts for the other. The contested cases where the courts have declined to impose fiduciary relationships, or been hesitant to do so, are largely commercial relationships where one party was seeking to rely on the particular nature of what would otherwise be a normal commercial relationship between contracting parties so as to impose fiduciary obligations on the other. Thus in *Re Goldcorp*[66] Lord Mustill said that the fact in a commercial relationship between two parties one may act for the other through the medium of a contract does not mean that the court can impose fiduciary obligations on the contract. It has been said: "Fiduciary duties should not be superimposed on ... common law duties to improve the nature of the remedy"[67] and that there is an "undesirability of extending fiduciary duties to commercial relationships and the anomaly of imposing those duties where the parties are at arms' length from one another".[68]

2–016

E. Auditors and others

The special obligations of an auditor are probably inconsistent with a duty of loyalty, and although the point has never been authoritatively determined in this jurisdiction, it is doubtful whether the auditor owes a fiduciary obligation.[69] However, the accountant who advises as well as audits will owe a fiduciary obligation in respect of his advice. Similarly, the expert instructed to prepare a report for exchange in litigation conducted under the CPR owes duties principally to the court and it can hardly be right that he owes a duty of loyalty to the client who instructs him. There is some

2–017

---

[64] See Companies Act 2006 s.170(5).
[65] In *Yukong v Rendberg (No 2)* Toulson J. held that shadow directors owed fiduciary duties. But in *Ultraframe v Fielding 2005* EWHC (Ch) 1638, para.1284, Lewison J. held that as shadow directors did not agree to act for anyone, they did not owe fiduciary duties. The decision has been criticised: see Prentice, *Directors' Fiduciary Duties*, 2006 L.Q.R. 558
[66] [1995] 1 A.C. 74, 98.
[67] *Norberg v Wynrib* [1992] 2 S.C.R. 226 at 312, Supreme Court of Canada per Sopinka J.
[68] *Hospital Products Ltd v United States Surgical Corp.* (1984) 156 C.L.R. 41 at 149, HCA per Dawson J.
[69] See para.17–008.

authority that an architect does not owe a fiduciary obligation[70] but it may depend on the terms of the retainer.

3. Fiduciary problems before, during and after the retainer

2–018   Lord Millett in *Bolkiah* said that the fiduciary obligation came to an end when the retainer came to an end. In the usual case, that is correct. However, life is not always that simple. The remainder of this chapter deals with issues as to the precise identity of the person to whom fiduciary duties are owed, the circumstances in which duties may be held to be owed after the termination of the retainer, and also prior to the beginning of the retainer.

A. Fiduciary obligations and the terms of the retainer

2–019   The content of the fiduciary obligation is not always the same. In *Henderson v Merrett Syndicates Ltd*[71] Lord Browne-Wilkinson warned:

> "... the phrase 'fiduciary duties' is a dangerous one, giving rise to a mistaken assumption that all fiduciaries owe the same duties in all circumstances. This is not the case".[72]

The fiduciary obligations which would otherwise arise must accommodate themselves within the terms of the contract, which may vary or exclude them. The dictum of Mason J. in the High Court of Australia in *Hospital Products v United States Surgical Corporation*[73] is often cited:

> "That contractual and fiduciary relationships may co-exist between the same parties has never been doubted. Indeed, the existence of a basic contractual relationship has in many situations provided a foundation for the erection of a fiduciary relationship. In these situations it is the contractual foundation which is all important because it is the contract that regulates the basic rights and liabilities of the parties. The fiduciary relationship, if it is to exist at all, must accommodate itself to the terms of the contract so that it is consistent with, and conforms to, them. The fiduciary relationship cannot be superimposed upon the contract in such a way as to alter the operation which the contract was intended to have according to its true construction".[74]

---

[70] *Western Home Counties Developments Ltd v Stone Toms & Partners*, March 19, 1984, CA.
[71] [1995] 2 A.C. 145 at 206.
[72] See para.4–016 below, *Kelly v Cooper* [1993] A.C. 205.
[73] (1984) 156 C.L.R. 41 at 97, HCA. This passage was cited with approval by the Privy Council in *Kelly v Cooper*.
[74] See also in *Canada Carlingwood Motors v Nissan Canada* (2001) 52 O.R. (3d) 242.

The precise scope of the obligations owed, whether they are fiduciary obligations, or non-fiduciary obligations, is thus dependent on the scope of the retainer. First, it means that the fiduciary obligations may be limited by the express or implied terms of the retainer,[75] and thus it is necessary to consider what conflicts have been expressly or impliedly recognised or accepted by the client at the outset. Fiduciary duties cannot be inconsistent with the contractual duties, and the fiduciary duties may be limited or cut down by the terms of the retainer, or the terms on which the professional accepts instructions[76] or makes disclosure, as will be seen.[77]

B. Fiduciary obligations continuing despite the termination of the retainer

We have already seen that confidentiality obligations continue after the termination of a retainer. To the extent that they can be described as fiduciary obligations[78] they are a special form of fiduciary obligation and can be left out of account in the present analysis as they do not carry with them an obligation of loyalty.

2–020

Lord Millett's speech in *Bolkiah* recognises that the fiduciary relationship comes to an end with the termination of the retainer. There is no reason why the professional should be loyal to his former client. Thereafter the professional has no obligation to defend and advance the interests of his former client,[79] although he has a continuing duty to preserve the confidentiality of information imparted during its subsistence. So too in *Att-Gen v Blake*[80] Lord Woolf M.R., giving the judgment of the Court of Appeal, said:

> "we do not recognise the concept of a fiduciary obligation which continues notwithstanding the determination of the particular relationship which gives rise to it. Equity does not demand a duty of undivided loyalty from a former employee to his former employer . . . these duties only last as long as the relationship which gives rise to them".[81]

---

[75] The Federal Court of Australia recently considered the validity of an attempt to contract out of a fiduciary relationship. *Australian Securities and Investments Commission v Citigroup Global Markets Australia Pty Ltd (No 4)* 2007 FCA 963. The case is discussed in detail at 00.
[76] See, e.g. *Wimmera Industrial Minerals Pty v Iluka Midwest* [2002] F.C.A. 653, Fed Ct of Australia.
[77] See Ch.4, *Kelly v Cooper* [1993] A.C. 205, PC.
[78] See 2–012.
[79] Lord Millett in *Bolkiah* [1999] 2 A.C. 222 at 235.
[80] [1998] Ch. 439 at 453.
[81] The Court of Appeal judgment was varied by the House of Lords on other grounds: [2001] 1 A.C. 268.

This statement represents the conventional view: in order to rely on a fiduciary relationship, there must be the continued existence of an underlying relationship involving duties: once that underlying relationship has been terminated, the basis for the imposition of non-fiduciary duties is gone; the termination means that there are no longer any non-fiduciary duties owed and thus nothing that needs protection.

C. Terminating the retainer to act against the client

2–021   As a matter of fiduciary law, where a fiduciary has sought to circumvent the fiduciary doctrine's protection, for example by retiring from his position, there are circumstances where equity will intervene:

> "Fiduciary doctrine is alive to the possibility of fiduciaries seeking to skirt around its protective principles and does what it can to prevent such tactics from being effective. However, these mechanisms for preventing the avoidance of fiduciary doctrine's protection do not contradict the need for non-fiduciary duties to exist in order that fiduciary duties make sense".[82]

Thus a fiduciary may not retire from a fiduciary relationship in order to purchase property if that would not have been permitted while the relationship still subsisted,[83] and a trustee may not arrange a transaction and then resign in order to put the transaction into effect if the transaction could not have been entered into while the trustee remained in post.[84] In *Industrial Developments v Cooley*[85] Mr Cooley lied about his health to gain his release from his directorship, thereby not disclosing that he was in fact seeking to take up a lucrative contract with one of his employer's customers; the company's consent to his early release was thus ineffective.

But where the fiduciary does not resign with a view to exploiting an otherwise impermissible opportunity, fiduciary doctrine does not intervene. As Buckley J. stated in *Re Boles and British Land Co's Contract*[86]:

> "If he retired with a view to becoming a purchaser so as to put himself in a position to do what would otherwise be a breach of trust, that will not do. But if he has retired and there is nothing to show that at the time of the retirement there was any idea of a sale . . . is there anything to prevent him from becoming a purchaser? I think not".

---

[82] Conaglen, *Fiduciary Loyalty*, p.188.
[83] *Ex p. James* (1803) 8 Ves. 337, 352.
[84] *Spring v Pride* (1864) 4 De G.J. and S. 395.
[85] [1972] 1 W.L.R. 442.
[86] [1902] 1 Ch. 244, 246.

The question arises whether this principle has any application in the law of conflict of interests: if a fiduciary terminates the retainer in order to act for another client, is there a breach of fiduciary duty which the court will protect by injunction? 2-022

Such caselaw as exists only suggests a limited prohibition on this ground. In *Boles* the trustee sought to purchase the trust property. In *Cooley* the corporate opportunity was presented to Cooley in his capacity as employee.[87] The fiduciary in each case was seeking to take off his fiduciary hat and do as non-fiduciary what had not been open to him when the fiduciary opportunity had been presented to him as fiduciary. Cases such as *Cooley* deal with the circumstance where the fiduciary has received information, a benefit or an opportunity as a result of the fiduciary position which he seeks to "cash in" after the termination of the relationship. Thus a director who resigns will be liable for breach of fiduciary duty:

> "if, after his resignation, he uses for his own benefit property of the company or information which he has acquired while a director".[88]

Further, it has been said about a trustee that the no conflict principle is relevant because:

> "the fact that he retires in order to effect that purpose means that the decision to effect that purpose has been taken during the period of his trusteeship when he was actually performing the duties of a trustee".[89]

There is no English caselaw which supports a widening of the principle beyond the fiduciary who seeks to take advantage of an opportunity presented to him in one capacity by acting in a different capacity, such as for his own account. *Bolkiah* provides no support for a wider principle. The problem arose expressly in *Young v Robson Rhodes*,[90] but the point was not argued.[91] It was a case where an injunction was treated as a disproportionate remedy.

---

[87] There are a number of cases where employees have been prevented from taking up maturing business opportunities presented to them in the course of their employment: see *Foster Bryant Surveying Ltd v Bryant* [2007] EWCA Civ 200, where the judgments in the Court of Appeal bring together the caselaw.
[88] *Ultraframe (UK) Ltd v Fielding* [2005] EWHC 1638, (Ch) [1309], Lewison J.
[89] *Gould v O'Carroll* [1964] N.S.W.R. 803, 805.
[90] [1999] 3 All E.R. 524, Laddie J.
[91] Robson Rhodes, accountants, were in the process of merging with Pannell Kerr Forster ("PKF"). Robson Rhodes were retained to provide forensic accounting services and expert evidence in an action brought by Lloyds names against the auditors of the syndicate in question, who were PKF. Robson Rhodes told the names they would have to cease acting because of the merger. The names sought an injunction to delay the merger until after conclusion of the trial, on the basis that if the merger went ahead the confidential information of the names could not be protected. The judge found that Robson Rhodes' refusal to act further for the names was a repudiatory breach of the retainer agreed by Robson Rhodes, for which they

In *Bloomsbury International Ltd v Holyoake*[92] it was argued, with reference to the caselaw referred to above, that Deloittes were not entitled to terminate a retainer to the firm's client Mr Holyoake so that three of their partners could act as company administrators seeking freeze and search orders against him. Floyd J. rejected the argument, holding[93] that cases such as *Boles*:

> "are cases where a fiduciary is taking advantage of an opportunity which came to him in his capacity as such. In the normal case, such as the termination of a solicitor's retainer, the only continuing duty will be a duty in relation to confidential information".

The *Boles* principle thus may be relevant to a variety of "cashing in " cases where the second retainer gives effect to an opportunity obtained as a result of the first retainer and which conflicts with it. In the usual conflict case, where there are two retainers, the second retainer has nothing to do with "cashing in" an opportunity derived from the first retainer and thus the principle does not apply. But it is possible to think of conflicts of interest examples where even on this more restricted principle, there may be an issue. What about the solicitor who seeks to take an existing client, or existing piece of litigation, of his firm with him when he leaves the firm to his new firm, or act for the client himself? Is that not the same as *Cooley?* It has been said that:

> "the extension ought to be limited to situations in which there is a real risk that the fiduciary might have been attempting to circumvent the protection offered by fiduciary doctrine".[94]

It might be material to the analysis whether the retainer was terminated by consent or by unilateral act of the fiduciary. If the fiduciary was entitled to terminate the retainer without breach of duty, it will be much harder to complain under this ground than if he terminated it unilaterally. If he had no right to do so, but did so with the consent of the client, it might be said that the client's consent to early termination was vitiated by non-disclosure of the (on this hypothesis improper) purpose of the termination.

There is Australian authority which suggests that a fiduciary duty may continue after the retainer to prevent the lawyer acting against the client in the same or related matter, even when there is no confidential information,

---

would be liable in damages, but despite this declined to injunct the merger, holding that the information barrier offered by Robson Rhodes and various undertakings he required were adequate to protect the names from disclosure of their confidential information.
[92] [2010] EWHC 1150 (Ch).
[93] At [48].
[94] Conaglen, *Fiduciary Loyalty* (2010) p.192

and should preclude in such circumstances the professional from terminating the retainer in order to act for the other client. The controversial Australian judgment of Brooking J.A. in the Victoria Court of Appeal in *Spincode Pty Ltd v Look Software Pty Ltd*[95] is discussed in detail elsewhere,[96] is in this respect inconsistent with *Bolkiah,* and cannot be assumed to represent the law in England. But Brooking J.A. made the very point set out above; namely, that equity will prevent a fiduciary from avoiding disqualification as a purchaser of trust property by retiring from his fiduciary office, and that a trustee who retires after making arrangements for the impugned transaction cannot escape.[97] Brooking J.A.'s thesis, persuasive in many respects, was that the court historically had a much wider jurisdiction.[98] A first instance decision in Ontario, *Toddglen Construction Ltd v Concord Adex Developments Corp*[99] also goes further and holds as a matter of principle that a law firm cannot be permitted to terminate one retainer in order to avoid the rule on existing client conflicts and to sue what would otherwise be an existing client,[100] although the reasoning in the decision is limited and it does not address fiduciary rules.

D. The fiduciary duty extending to the related company: Conway

2–023
The fiduciary relationship may exceptionally be owed to an entity other than the party to an existing retainer. In *Conway v Ratiu*[101] Mr Conway had been retained to act as solicitor for a company, Regent, which had sought to acquire a development property through a subsidiary Pristbrook. Pristbrook duly acquired and resold the development through Mr Conway. Sometime later, another property came on the market, which Regent were interested in acquiring. It transpired that Mr Conway was also interested in acquiring this latter property personally, and after an enquiry from Regent as to whether Mr Conway would agree to act for them on the purchase, Mr Conway then, unbeknown to them, contacted the vendor to increase his own offer. When they discovered this, Regent wrote to the vendor's agents complaining about this conduct and stated that Mr Conway had misused information he had acquired as solicitor for Regent when acting in relation

---

[95] [2001] V.S.C.A. 248.
[96] See 5–004. Brooking J.A. took the view that there had been inadequate citation of authority in Bolkiah and said that it had failed to consider important issues, in particular the traditional supervisory jurisdiction of the court over solicitors.
[97] *Wright v Morgan* [1926] A.C. 788; *Holder v Holder* [1968] Ch. 353 at 398; see also *Re Regina and Speid* (1983) 43 O.R. (2d) 596 at 600.
[98] Discussed at 5–004.
[99] 18 November 2003, [2003] Can. L.II 9525.
[100] It was not argued that the termination of the retainer in that case was a breach of contract.
[101] 2005 [EWCA] Civ 1302, 14 November 2005.

to the earlier transactions, in an attempt to prevent Mr Conway from bidding against them. Mr Conway sued the individuals who had written the letter and Regent for libel, alleging that their letter to the vendor's agents had put him out of the running for the property. The judge directed the jury that Mr Conway's client had been Pristbrook alone, and thus at the time of the attempt to purchase the second property he owed no fiduciary duty to Regent. After an 18-day trial, the jury held that the defendants had written the letter activated by malice and awarded substantial damages to Mr Conway. This was overturned by the Court of Appeal, who held there was no evidence of malice to go to the jury, but in any event held that the judge had wrongly directed the jury on the question of whether Mr Conway owed a fiduciary duty to Regent. Auld L.J.[102] pointed out that although a solicitor's fiduciary duty to his client is normally engendered by the retainer, it is distinct from the contractual obligations created by the retainer and arises out of the relationship of trust and confidence which comes into being as a result. Whether the fiduciary relationship outlives the contractual relationship is fact-sensitive:

> "There is, it seems to me, a powerful argument of principle, in this intensely personal context of considerations of trust, confidence and loyalty, for lifting the corporate veil where the facts require it to include those in or behind the company who are in reality the persons whose trust in and reliance upon the fiduciary may be confounded".

Auld L.J. was concerned to point out that in a case where a fiduciary relationship arises out of a contractual relationship, it does not matter whether the person to whom the duty is owed entered into the contract directly or through an agent or through a nominee company. What matters is whether a relationship of trust and confidence has come into being. Because a fiduciary relationship does not depend on the existence of contractual relations, there may be circumstances in which a duty of that kind may not only arise between the fiduciary and the client but also between the fiduciary and a third person who is closely connected to the client[103]. The passage cited above was explained by Moore-Bick L.J. in *Diamantis v JP Morgan Chase Bank*[104]:

> "The importance of this passage lies in the recognition that, in a case where a fiduciary relationship arises out of a contractual relationship, it

---

[102] At [77]–[78].
[103] See [2005] EWCA Civ 1612 per Moore Bick L.J. at [33]–[37] considering and distinguishing *Conway*. Moore-Bick L.J. treated the factual position in *Diamantis* as inconsistent with an assumption of fiduciary obligations for anyone other than the contracting party: see [36]–[37].
[104] [2005] EWCA Civ 1612, per Moore Bick L.J. at [33]–[37] considering and distinguishing *Conway*.

does not matter whether the person to whom the duty is owed entered into the contract directly or through an agent or through a nominee company. What matters is whether a relationship of trust and confidence has come into being: see [80]. As I understand it, Auld L.J. was seeking to emphasise in these passages that because a fiduciary relationship does not depend on the existence of contractual relations, there may be circumstances in which a duty of that kind may arise not only between the fiduciary and the client but also between the fiduciary and a third person who is closely connected with the client".

Conway is a somewhat unusual and exceptional case. The Court of Appeal were perhaps keen to find a legitimate basis on which to overturn what might be seen as an eccentric jury award. There seems to be a suggestion that the court may be more willing to pierce the corporate veil and to find a fiduciary relationship in existence between an individual and third party not privy to any formal legal relationship where trust and confidence is involved.[105] But what is the principle here which enables one to know whether or not the fiduciary relationship exists where the contractual one does not? 2–024

In *Conway* the principle is put by Auld L.J. broadly and in a way to which exception may be taken. It is all very well saying that the fiduciary relationship is fact-specific. That must not be used as an excuse for reaching decisions which have no principle to govern them. Great care is needed to ensure that the exceptions do not become the rule here. Where the professional has a continuing relationship with the client, but there is no retainer in place, the professional is not doing work for the client, and thus not charging the client. Moreover, there are many circumstances where the professional acts for a company knowing that one individual makes the relevant decisions, and from the professional's perspective "is" the company. But in general the circumstances in which the court can override the corporate veil are very limited,[106] and will always occur at the behest of the other party-not, as here, at the behest of the party who has himself established the corporate veil. If the professional is held in consequence to owe a fiduciary duty to the individual as well as the company, the ramifications are considerable. There may be a conflict between the interests of the company and that of the individual. Certainly advice given to the individual as to his interests might be very different from advice given to the company. The professional may have a conflict in relation to the individual which would not arise if its duty was to the company. The professional would have to know far more about the individual than was necessary if the obligation was merely to the company. And what about an exclusion or limitation clause in the retainer? Would it

---

[105] See *JD Wetherspoon v Van de Berg Co* [2009] EWHC Ch. 639, Peter Smith J., relying on *Conway* for this purpose.
[106] Cf. *Trustor AB v Smallbone* [2001] 1 W.L.R. 1177.

apply in the case of a claim by the individual for breach of fiduciary duty? Would notice to the company be notice to the individual? How does the professional know where he stands? It is suggested that *Conway* is treated as a case on its own facts and the statement of principle set out by Auld L.J. is treated cautiously.

E. Terminating the retainer to take free of fiduciary obligations: discussion

2–025 The usual advice to a professional who has a conflict between two existing clients is to terminate the retainer for one of them. Even if the retainer may not lawfully be terminated, the client may consent. Even if he does not consent, the client is probably unlikely to do anything about it.

But there are a number of potential risks in such a course. Firstly, a claim for damages for wrongful termination of the retainer. In *Young v Robson Rhodes*[107] the professional was not entitled to bring to an end his retainer, and doing so led to a claim for damages. Where a solicitor is retained to act in litigation, the law implies an entire contract to conduct the action to the end.[108] The solicitor cannot terminate that retainer without reasonable notice and for good cause but the client can.[109] Where an expert is retained to assist in litigation, and in the absence of an express retainer, the terms of the retainer may differ according to the facts but in *Robson Rhodes* Laddie J. held that there was by implication an entire retainer to assist the names at least to judgment in their actions against the accountancy firm due to merge with the defendants. Whether a professional can bring his retainer to an end without breach of contract in the absence of express terms will depend on the circumstances. For example, an accountant who was retained to assist in resolving a tax dispute with the Revenue might not be at liberty to withdraw half way through the negotiations because to do so would cause the client unwarranted extra expense and inconvenience. He could do so on reasonable notice and for good cause. The good cause might be unpaid bills or a conflict arising. But it would not be good cause that a new client with a conflicting interest wanted to instruct him.

Where the professional withdraws in breach of his retainer, the client's remedy will not be for specific performance of the retainer. That is because the law will not require an individual to perform personal services against his will. This is a principle which has stood since Mlle Wagner sought to

---

[107] [1999] 3 All E.R. 524; See 2–022 above.
[108] In *Perotti v Collyer Bristow* [2003] EWHC 25 Ch Lindsay J. at [137] cast doubt on the old principle of an "entire retainer" (he said it did not apply to administration actions so he need not decide the question).
[109] *Underwood Son & Piper v Lewis* [1894] 2 Q.B. 306 at 309–312 per Lord Esher M.R. cited by Laddie J. at 532.

abandon her engagement to sing at Drury Lane for Mr Lumley in favour of a better opportunity to sing for Mr Gye at Covent Garden. An injunction requiring her to sing at Drury Lane was refused but a negative injunction restraining her from singing at Covent Garden in breach of contract was granted, not being an injunction requiring personal services.[110]

A possible claim for damages for wrongful termination of the retainer will often not be a particularly grave concern. If it occurs, it is likely to be limited to the additional cost of new lawyers reading in. But the second potential problem might be an application by the former client on the basis that the professional terminated the engagement to act in conflict with the client, a possibility discussed above. A variant on the same theme is that whilst a client may be no more entitled to specific performance than was Mr Lumley against Mrs Wagner, it should be remembered that Mrs Wagner was restrained by negative injunction from singing at Covent Garden. The client may not therefore be able to injunct the professional from terminating the retainer, but may be able to object to him terminating it in breach of contract to accept a conflicting instruction. And even if the client agrees to the early termination, he may still be able to complain on the basis that the solicitor failed to make full disclosure before he agreed early termination.

F. Close-out letters to terminate the retainer

The professional may provide services accepted by the client after the termination of the retainer. Other cases may arise when it is not easy to determine whether the retainer has in fact been terminated; for example, when a transaction is essentially complete, it may be a moot point whether it has been "closed-out" so that the lawyer has no continuing obligations. Other examples are the barrister who has complied with his instructions to advise and does not know whether the case continues or has settled, or whether he is likely to be retained to act any further.[111] The solicitor who is on a panel of firms for a particular client, being available for work as a preferred supplier, is another problem case.

2–026

"Close-out" letters are increasingly popular in other jurisdictions[112] but have not really taken off in England. They are useful as objective evidence of the termination of the retainer to demonstrate that the client is no longer an existing client for conflicts purposes. But they are not very attractive marketing tools. Most professionals try to maintain the client relationship

---

[110] *Lumley v Wagner* [1852] 1 De G.M. & G. 604; *Lumley v Gye* [1853] 2 El. & Bl. 216. See more recently boxing promoter Frank Warren's attempt to restrain a breach of contract by a young boxer signed to him: *Warren v Mendy* [1989] 1 W.L.R. 853.
[111] See 16–003 below.
[112] In the United States the Attorneys' Liability Assurance Society suggests that lawyers use "close-out" letters at the end of transactions to establish that the client does not have the status of a continuing client.

at the end of a retainer. Making clear to the client that the job is at an end and the relationship, at least in respect of the particular retainer, is complete is often not seen as inspired marketing.

G. Transactions with the former client after the retainer

2–027   In *Longstaff v Birtles*[113] a former client entered into partnership with his solicitor. The solicitor did not tell him to seek independent advice. Reversing the judge, the Court of Appeal held that the relationship of trust and confidence survived after the end of the solicitor-client retainer. The client continued to believe the defendant was also acting as his solicitor and it was found that the solicitor did nothing to disabuse him. The Court of Appeal reasoning is somewhat limited, and the court was plainly influenced by the merits, allowing an amendment in the course of argument to plead breach of fiduciary duty in a case up till then put solely in negligence. However, the court made it clear that it was not deciding the case on the basis of undue influence. Mummery L.J., in holding that the claimant was entitled to equitable compensation, said that there was a relationship of trust and confidence between solicitor and client, that relationship continued even though there was no retainer, and the opportunity appeared in the course of that relationship. The fiduciary relationship could, and here did, continue after the end of the retainer. Mummery L.J. recognised that the nature of the fiduciary relationship could not be the same after the termination of the retainer. He said:

> "A solicitor proposing either to buy property from, or to sell property to, a client is under a duty to cause the client to obtain independent advice. That duty may endure beyond the relationship of solicitor and client . . . The source of the duty is not the retainer itself, but all the circumstances (including the retainer) creating a relationship of trust and confidence, from which flow obligations of loyalty and transparency . . .".

Having concluded, as did Mummery LJ, that the solicitors owed no non-fiduciary duty, it is difficult to see a legitimate basis on which the solicitors were held to owe a fiduciary duty or that there was any conflict between duty and interest. The decision has been trenchantly criticised, ". . . the court's reasoning in *Longstaff v Birtles* was incoherent and reveals it to be another instance of hard cases making bad law".[114]

---

[113] [2001] Lloyd's P.N. 826, CA. See *Richards v Law Society* [2009] EWHC 2087 (Admin) where *Longstaff* was applied.
[114] Conaglen, *Fiduciary Loyalty* p.193. Conaglen points out that the *Longstaff* decision was commended in *Conway v Ratiu* by Auld L.J. at [75] as "an authoritative illustration of the readiness of the courts, regardless of the precise issue involved, to draw back the corporate

To the extent that the decision in *Longstaff* can be supported, it may be seen as analogous to undue influence cases decided on similar principles. In *McMaster v Byrne*[115] the client had retained a solicitor to act in relation to his business affairs generally. All retainers had come to an end, but the Privy Council held that the solicitor's failure to disclose all material facts in relation to the grant of an option to the solicitor by the client justified the setting aside of the transaction.[116] As there was no continuing retainer under which the solicitor owed the client any obligations, it is difficult to justify the decision other than on grounds of undue influence, where the influence held by the solicitor over the client imposes fiduciary obligations in any dealings between the two. Solicitors are presumed to have influence over their clients and the doctrine of undue influence may apply after the end of the retainer; the influence does not necessarily cease merely because the contract has come to an end. So too *Demerara Bauxite v Hubbard*.[117] There the formal relationship of solicitor and client had terminated prior to the transaction with the client, who had no independent advice in respect of the grant of an option to purchase to the solicitor himself. Even though the retainer had terminated, the Privy Council applied the rules of fiduciary relationships. *Demerara Bauxite* and *McMaster* are usually seen as undue influence cases, as examples where the court treats with grave suspicion any gift or sale by a client to his solicitor. The presumption of undue influence as between client and solicitor where the client transacts business with the solicitor personally will apply even if the relationship of client and solicitor has technically ceased.

What if the professional has a continuing professional relationship with the client, even though there is no current retainer? The solicitor who is on a panel of favoured contractors, or the barrister who has completed work on his instructions but has the anticipation of being retained for the trial are possible examples. However, the idea of a general retainer seems meaningless, and if there are no non-fiduciary obligations it is difficult to see what legitimate basis there is for imposing fiduciary obligations, save in a case of undue influence.

H. Revealing discreditable matters about the client after the retainer has concluded

Another respect in which it may be argued that a form of fiduciary obligation continues after the termination of the retainer is in revealing

2–028

---

veil to do justice when commonsense and reality demand it" but that as no corporations were involved in *Longstaff*, the reference to the corporate veil is difficult to understand.

[115] [1952] 1 All E.R. 1362.

[116] Compare the position in respect of partnerships, where the fiduciary duties of partners to each other continue after dissolution until the winding up of the partnership: *Don King Productions Inc v Frank Warren* [2000] Ch. 291, CA.

[117] [1923] A.C. 673.

discreditable matters about the client. In the Ontario case *Stewart v Canadian Broadcasting Commission*[118] the Q.C. who acted for a defendant in the sentencing and appeal stages of his criminal trial took part years later in a television programme featuring the case. The claimant had been tried and imprisoned as a result of his driving which had led to the death of a pedestrian. The case had become notorious. The Q.C. was criticised for exaggerating in the programme the period of time during which the pedestrian had been dragged under the car screaming. The claim was not based on confidential information because the facts were in the public domain. Macdonald J. held that although the retainer had come to an end long ago the defendant owed a continuing fiduciary duty which meant that he was not entitled to attract business to himself by seeking publicity about the case that was adverse to the former client.

Would such a decision be followed in England, and is it permissible under English law for a fiduciary to make public facts adverse to the client after termination of the retainer? Where the relevant facts are confidential, no problem arises because the remedy lies in breach of confidence. But in cases such as *Stewart*, the facts were in the public domain.

The recent House of Lords decision in *Hilton v Barker Booth & Eastwood*[119] is considered in detail below.[120] But an analogous issue arose. The same law firm acted for two parties on opposite sides of the same transaction through different individuals within the firm. One party was not told that the other had just been released from prison for dishonesty offences. Again, the information was in the public domain. There was an obligation on the firm to the innocent party to inform him of this fact highly material to the retainer. But why was the information confidential to the other party if it was in the public domain? Lord Walker[121] dealt with this by stating that the issue was not really about confidentiality; it would be a breach of fiduciary duty to reveal discreditable facts about a client without the consent of the client even if those facts were in the public domain. Academic criticism of his analysis is discussed at 6–013. However, if the information was not confidential, does it follow that once the retainer had ended, the solicitor would be free to reveal the discreditable information about his former client? So does it mean that there may be a fiduciary duty which continues after the end of the retainer limited to not disclosing discreditable material about the former client even if it is in the public domain?[122]

This presents an issue on which there is no English authority. So long as the retainer continues, of course the professional cannot reveal discreditable

---

[118] [1997] 150 D.L.R. (4d) 24. See also *Allison v Clayhills* (1907) 97 L.T. 709.
[119] [2005] 1 All E.R. 651.
[120] See 6–010.
[121] At [34].
[122] This may not be necessary if the criticism is correct of what Lord Walker says and there is a breach of confidence in revealing such discreditable information even when the information is in the public domain: see 6–013.

information about a client; to do so would be disloyal. Once the retainer is at an end, it may be deeply unattractive for a professional to give the press all sorts of discreditable information about the ex-client, even if that information is potentially available to the press as being in the public domain. But it is hard to extend the fiduciary obligation so as to impose a continuing obligation on the professional in relation to this sort of non-confidential material without giving rise to undesirable ramifications.

It is suggested that there is no analytical basis on which the professional is prevented from revealing non-confidential matters about a former client. There is no non-fiduciary obligation at this stage which binds the professional. So the argument is the same as before: other than in a case of undue influence, how can there be any fiduciary obligation at a time when there is no non-fiduciary obligation?

A contrary argument[123] relies on the Court of Appeal decision in *Schering v Falkman*.[124] Schering manufactured a drug which was alleged to cause birth defects and hired a public relations consultancy, who hired the defendant, a professional broadcaster, to provide media training. The defendant obtained information from Schering for that purpose but subsequently sought to make a documentary about the drug and the allegations made. Schering applied for an injunction to restrain publication, but the defendant argued that he was using material in the public domain. The majority of the Court of Appeal granted the injunction. Templeman L.J. said:

2–029

> "... when [the defendant] agreed for reward to take part in the training programme and received information from Scherings, he became under a duty not to use that information and impliedly promised Scherings that he would not use that information for the very purpose which Scherings sought to avoid, namely bad publicity in the future including publicity which Scherings reasonably regarded as bad publicity".

Whilst not a case involving fiduciaries or solicitors, the parallels are obvious. It is said that this case supports the proposition that a fiduciary may not even after termination of a retainer reveal discreditable matters about his former client.

However, *Schering* is a comparatively old case which predates important authority on the ability of a person who has revealed confidential information to protect it after it has been published in the media, such as *Spycatcher*.[125] The statements by the majority are difficult to reconcile with more recent authority.[126] The statement of principle set out above by

---

[123] See Flenley and Leech, *Solicitors' Negligence and Liability* (2nd ed) para 6.24.
[124] [1982] Q.B. 1.
[125] *AG v Guardian Newspapers* 1990 1 A.C. 109.
[126] For example Shaw L.J.: "It is not the law that where confidentiality exists it is terminated or

Templeman L.J. is surely expressed far too widely. There was in fact no direct retainer between Schering and the defendant at all (the defendant was engaged by the public relations firm). But even if there had been (and therefore a stronger case for the claimant), can it really be the case that the receipt of confidential information carries with it a promise never to use information received for a purpose adverse to the interests of the person providing it, even though the retainer has long since terminated and at a time when the material is not confidential and can be accessed by anyone? How can this square with the principle that a fiduciary may act against a former client so long as there is no risk of misuse of confidential information? Is he obliged to avoid using any publicly available material which was transmitted during the course of the retainer?

It is suggested that a duty which outlives the retainer not to disclose or make use of material adverse to the former client is inconsistent with both the general law on fiduciaries and would run a coach and horses through the law on conflicts of interest. It would mean that it would often be impossible to act against former clients even when there was no confidential information issue. However, it is relevant, when faced with the argument that information disclosed during the retainer is now in the public domain and thus can freely be disclosed, to bear in mind that merely because information can be accessed by members of the public does not necessarily mean that it has ceased to be confidential. Public accessibility of information may often mean that it is not confidential, but it does not automatically follow: it is a matter of degree and may depend on how readily it is accessible and how well-known the information is.[127]

I. Identifying the client to whom the fiduciary obligation is owed

2–030   In seeking to examine the ambit of the fiduciary relationship, it is relevant to know precisely who is the client. In drafting a client care letter, the professional will wish to identify the client carefully. Who will be liable for the bills of the professional? To whom does the firm owe duties? What if the vehicle company for which the professional will ultimately act has not yet been set up: in many types of transaction the vehicle for the transaction will pay the professional fees of the transaction but technically cannot instruct the professionals from the outset as it has not been incorporated.

It will be apparent from the analysis above[128] that there will be circumstances where the professional may owe a fiduciary obligation to a company other than the specific client under the retainer. But such circumstances will

---

eroded by adventitious publicity." That statement certainly does not represent the modern law.
[127] See generally Toulson and Phipps, *Confidentiality* (2nd edn) 3-106 to 3-131.
[128] 2–023.

be exceptional. Whilst it is important to keep in mind cases such as *Conway v Ratiu*[129] where there may be a fiduciary obligation owed to another company in the group, in most cases, the point is straightforward. But problems still arise even in run-of-the-mill cases. Where the client is a company, is there any bar on acting against another company in the group? If the client is a partnership, what about acting for an individual member of the partnership? And if the client is an unincorporated association such as a club, can the professional act for one of its members at the same time?

The first issue in such a case is probably to examine the respective interests in order to determine whether an actual or potential conflict exists between the two interests. The solicitor instructed in litigation by Company A may find that the fiduciary obligation of loyalty makes it practically impossible to accept instructions to act against its subsidiary. But where one litigation is an employment tribunal and the other is an application to the Companies Court there may be no problem at all.

Is there an existing client conflict where different group companies are involved? In principle, the issue should be determined by an examination on the facts as to whether it would be disloyal to the client to act against its parent or subsidiary. Where for example a professional acts for a subsidiary and seeks to act against the parent, it will be necessary to consider whether the subsidiary is interested in the action against the parent to the extent that acting against the parent would be disloyal to the subsidiary given the nature and ambit of the retainer. If the parent is the target of an acquisition, it might be possible to treat the subsidiary as an asset of the parent which will not necessary take a position as to the acquisition. But if the subsidiary opposes the acquisition, perhaps because it is concerned as to redundancies, or has contracts which can be determined on a change of control, the position may be different. And, of course, the nature of the retainer for the subsidiary and its ambit will also be important.[130] It may be easier to find that there is a conflict acting for subsidiary against parent than acting for parent against subsidiary, as the parent may often have an interest in a transaction affecting the asset value of its subsidiary but the converse may not necessarily follow.

There is no reason why terms and conditions of engagement should not deal with these issues at the outset of a relationship. The professional who deals in an area where there are partnerships or unincorporated associations such as members clubs should regard this as particularly important. Without consent, there are difficulties. The partnership is not a legal entity, although it has certain statutory rights and obligations under the Partnership Act 1890 and certain procedural rights in court. The unincorporated association is equally not a legal entity but a collection of individuals who will

2–031

---

[129] See 2–023 above.
[130] Other existing client conflict problems in connection with takeovers are considered at para.4–012 below.

usually sue and be sued in a representative capacity. The professional will thus technically owe a fiduciary duty to each member. The converse is the case with group companies or companies in the same common ownership. As the legal personality is different, there is no legal bar and thus no breach of fiduciary duty in acting for both. But there may be all sorts of practical problems which make it inexpedient to act in opposite interests.

J. Commencement of the fiduciary relationship: beauty parades

2–032   This is another point not confined to lawyers. What if the professional is invited to attend a beauty parade but fails to get the work? Will he thereby be precluded subsequently from acting for the other side? If so, is this a good way of conflicting out the competition? In attending a beauty parade, the professional will probably discuss the matter in relatively broad terms with the client and perhaps give some very preliminary advice. He may be told some limited confidential information. If he is careful, he will only have agreed to attend the beauty parade on terms that he is not thereby precluded from acting for any other party. But if you are trying to make a good impression to secure the retainer, it is often not the best time to set out terms of business explaining that if you do not get the work you may act for the other side.

The decision of the Court of Appeal in *Davies v Davies*[131] is of little legal interest but is an interesting illustration of this issue. A wife about to commence messy divorce proceedings consulted a well-known family solicitor, Mr Tooth, who gave some very preliminary advice at an initial meeting.[132] In the event, she used a different solicitor. Mr Tooth subsequently acted for the husband. When asked to cease acting, he said he had no recollection of meeting the wife at all and had opened no file. The wife brought proceedings for an injunction, but before the hearing sought to withdraw the application on the basis that it was in practical terms too late for Mr Tooth to be required to withdraw. The husband's solicitors refused to agree that the application be discontinued on terms that there be no order for costs and the judge had to rule merely on costs, regarding it as necessary to form a view on what decision he would have reached on the substantive issue. He found against Mr Tooth's firm. The Court of Appeal dismissed the appeal.

In such circumstances, it seems to be far-fetched to think that the professional can be treated as a fiduciary at this early stage. Certainly *Davies v Davies*[133] does not suggest that he does.[134] But it does illustrate that the

---

[131] [2000] 1 F.L.R. 39, CA.
[132] The judgments do not describe it as a beauty parade but it seems to come to the same thing.
[133] [2000] 1 F.L.R. 39, CA.
[134] See also to the same effect *Arklow Investments Ltd v Maclean* [2000] 1 W.L.R. 594, PC.

professional may at a very early stage learn confidential information which, if he is not careful, may preclude him from accepting subsequent instructions from others. It is said that on occasion clients have deliberately asked professionals to attend beauty parades for the specific purpose of seeking to conflict them from acting for the other side. What about the situation where advice is given at a beauty parade and then the professional *does* get the job? Does that mean that, in retrospect the court will hold that the fiduciary duty came into existence at the time of the initial meeting? This seems unlikely—even if the professional is bound by an obligation of confidentiality in relation to what he has been told, it seems wrong to backdate the fiduciary obligation to a time before he was instructed. Does it matter if the professional subsequently includes the initial meeting in his bill? The answer may differ from case to case.

CHAPTER 3

The Double Employment rule

3–001   If there is a conflict between the interests of two clients, then if the professional acts for both without informed consent, there will be an automatic breach of fiduciary duty. This chapter looks in detail at what is referred to as "the double employment rule" as articulated by Millett L.J. in *Mothew* and identifies its boundaries as applied both to client conflicts and personal conflicts.

1. Breach of the double employment rule

A. The absolute bar on acting without consent

3–002   We have seen how in *Mothew* Millett L.J. said:

> "A fiduciary who acts for two principals with potentially conflicting interests without the informed consent of both is in breach of the obligation of undivided loyalty; he puts himself in a position where his duty to one principal may conflict with his duty to the other: see *Clark Boyce v Mouat* . . . and the cases there cited. This is sometimes described as the double employment rule".[1]

And in *Bolkiah*, Lord Millett said:

> "A fiduciary cannot act at the same time both for and against the same client, and his firm is in no better position. A man cannot without the consent of both clients act for one client while his partner is acting

---

[1] [1998] Ch. 1 at 18.

for another in the opposite interest. His disqualification has nothing to do with the confidentiality of client information. It is based on the inescapable conflict of interest which is inherent in the situation".[2]

In *Mothew* Millett L.J. said that a breach of the double employment rule automatically constitutes a breach of fiduciary duty.[3] The absolute ban on acting at the same time for different clients in opposing interests without informed consent is based on the problem of owing conflicting duties of loyalty.[4] Where the professional acts for clients with competing interests at the same time, the requirement to keep confidential information obtained from the client is one facet of the obligation of a fiduciary. But what distinguishes existing and former client conflicts is that in the latter case confidential information is the basis of the conflict, and the only basis.[5] Lord Millett in *Bolkiah* makes clear that the absolute rule against acting which applies in the absence of informed consent is a disqualification based on the "inescapable conflict of interest which is inherent in the situation" namely the difficulty of the professional defending and advancing the interest of a client when he is acting in another matter against that same client. Because the basis of the problem in existing client conflicts is conflict not confidential information, Lord Millett seems to have had in mind that information barriers could never apply to protect the fiduciary in existing client conflicts, unless both clients had given their informed consent to the professional acting by means of an information barrier.[6]

B. "Actual" and "potential" conflicts: confusion of terminology

The Millett formulation as to the applicability of the double employment rule focuses on "potentially" conflicting interests of the two existing clients. Different expressions are used: the double employment rule applies where there are "potentially conflicting interests." The Solicitors Regulation Authority rule prevents a solicitor acting where there is a "conflict or significant risk" of conflict. Millett L.J. said that even where there was client consent, a fiduciary could not act where there was an "actual conflict" between

3–003

---

[2] [1999] 2 A.C. 222 at 234.
[3] [1998] Ch. 1 at 19.
[4] For some recent Commonwealth cases, particularly in New Zealand, where the court has found breaches of the double employment rule, see *Farrington v Rowe McBride* [1985] 1 N.Z.L.R. 83, NZCA; *Davey v Woolley Harvey Dale & Dingwall* (1982) 33 D.L.R. (3rd) 647; *Haira v Burbey* [1995] 3 N.Z.L.R. 396 at 408; *Day v Mead* [1987] 2 N.Z.L.R. 443.
[5] See Lord Millett in *Bolkiah* at 235.
[6] Later in his speech, Lord Millett looks at former client conflicts at 237–238, and makes it clear that in appropriate circumstances information barriers may there be permissible. The contrast is apparent.

the interests of two clients. These expressions have caused confusion. What is the difference between these various expressions and simply stating that a professional may not act where there is a conflict between the interests of two clients?

C. Viewing the matter prospectively

3–004　　The confusion of terminology is exacerbated by the problem that a decision whether to act inevitably involves looking at what may happen in future. When instructions are received by the professional, the decision whether to act will involve looking prospectively at the issues likely to arise and the content of the retainer. It will often be unclear what precisely will be involved, and whether the retainer will conflict with another existing retainer.

Where the interests arise in the same or a related matter, there will rarely be any doubt about the answer. The lender and borrower obviously have interests which conflict with each other. Sometimes it is more difficult: co-defendants who are making common cause against the plaintiff will have conflicting interests with one another if they are alternative defendants, or if there is any realistic chance that one will claim contribution or an indemnity from the other. It will be possible to see that the two clients have interests that might in some circumstances differ, but are the chances of this arising sufficient for the problem to arise? Professionals will often act for clients whose interests are unlikely to conflict where from the outset there is a merely remote possibility that a conflict will arise. The decision will inevitably need to be kept under review as events unfold. The professional will make a judgment on the information available at the outset, no doubt bearing in mind that whilst the second client may understand the professional declining instructions, termination of the retainer part way through on grounds of conflict of interest may not encourage the client to instruct him on future matters. Ultimately it can only be a question of judgment on the facts available.

D. "Actual" conflict

3–005　　Millett L.J. refers in *Mothew* to the concept of an "actual" conflict. An actual conflict involves an actual (and not prospective) clash of obligations where the professional cannot fulfil his obligations to one client without being in breach of duty to the other. Where counsel acts for two clients and in cross-examination wants on behalf of one to ask a question and on behalf of the other wants not to ask the same question, an actual conflict arises which no consent can cure. Another actual conflict is where the two clients agree to the professional acting, but the duty of the professional to one requires him not to disclose certain information to the other, but his duty to the second requires him to disclose the same information.

Lord Millett refers to what he describes as an "actual" conflict arising when the professional is acting with informed consent of both parties. This form of conflict can be described as a non-waivable conflict, a concept discussed at 3–017. So in many cases, in accordance with the *Mothew* analysis[7], it cannot be said that the conflict of interest here involves breach of any *fiduciary* obligation. The professional's failure to perform his duty may not involve any lack of loyalty. But he may be in breach of *non-fiduciary* obligations because he cannot fulfil obligations to both parties, such as the obligation of skill and care.

Thus an "actual" conflict, in the sense referred to in *Mothew*, arises in circumstances where the professional is acting with informed consent, but simply cannot perform his duty to both clients simultaneously. Sometimes this will be a breach of a fiduciary obligation, where it is deliberate and thus disloyal, but more often will involve a breach of a non-fiduciary obligation which arises because he is unable to act for each client as if that client were his only client without being in breach of duty to the other.

Definitions of conflict of interest usually refer to the taking on of two inconsistent fiduciary relationships. What is notable here is that the reason the professional is unable to act for both, in the "actual" conflict case, when he is acting with the informed consent of both parties, is not the breach of any fiduciary obligation of loyalty, but the inability of the professional to serve the client's interests in relation to the retainer in the same way as if the client were his only client. Thus ironically here the inability to act derives from the clash of non-fiduciary obligations.

E. "Potentially conflicting interests"

In order to determine what is meant by this expression used by Millett L.J. in *Mothew*, it is necessary to understand the significance of the form of protection given by fiduciary rules. Because fiduciary obligations are prophylactic, they prevent a professional from undertaking an obligation which jeopardizes the existing obligation of loyalty. The obligation of the fiduciary is that he must not place himself in a position where his duty and his interest may conflict. As the purpose of fiduciary doctrine is to encourage fiduciaries to avoid such situations altogether, that purpose would be undermined if a fiduciary were permitted to argue, as a defence to a claim for breach of fiduciary duty, that he ought to be exonerated because no loss had been suffered by his conduct. Allowing fiduciaries as a defence to claims of fiduciary duty to argue that they had duly performed their non-fiduciary

3–006

---

[7] See 2–007 above.

duties opens up the possibility of fiduciaries acting in a way that will conceal breaches of fiduciary duty, in order to avoid fiduciary liability.[8] So in *Parker v McKenna*[9]:

> "this Court . . . is not entitled, in my judgment, to receive evidence, or suggestion, or argument as to whether the principal did or did not suffer any injury in fact by reason of the dealing of the agent; for the safety of mankind requires that no agent in fact shall be able to put his principal to the danger of such an inquiry as that".

The point can be seen clearly from *Aberdeen Railway v Blaikie*.[10] There a director of a railway company entered into a contract to purchase chairs whilst also being principal in the vendor firm. The railway company was entitled to avoid the contract. What is significant about the decision is that it was held unnecessary to show that the director had breached his non-fiduciary duty by failing to get the chairs at the best price. To show this would have provided no defence. This is because the purpose of fiduciary rules is not to focus on circumstances where there is a breach of the non-fiduciary duty but where there is a risk of this occurring. Fiduciary doctrine protects against the risk of breach by taking away the temptation by prohibiting the fiduciary from acting in such situations. Thus it is unnecessary to show that the fiduciary has in fact breached his non-fiduciary duty.

So when Millett L.J. states in *Mothew* that:

> "a fiduciary who acts for two principals with potentially conflicting interests without the informed consent of both is in breach of the obligation of undivided loyalty; he puts himself in a position where his duty to one principal may conflict with his duty to the other"[11]

his reference to "potentially conflicting interests" picks up the *Aberdeen Railway* principle: there is an automatic breach of fiduciary duty where the two fiduciary obligations owed by the professional conflict, and the professional cannot be heard to say that the client would (as in *Aberdeen Railway*) still have obtained the chairs at the same price.

F. Reconciling the expressions

3–007

The confusions of terminology can, it is suggested, be reconciled as follows. Lord Millett's use of "potentially conflicting interests" does no more

---

[8] Conaglen, *Fiduciary Loyalty* p.74.
[9] [1874] L.R. 10 Ch App 96.
[10] [1854] 1 Macq 461.
[11] [1998] Ch. 1 at 18.

than reflect the prophylactic nature of fiduciary obligations, namely that the risk of breach must be avoided. It concerns the situation where a situation of conflict exists between competing fiduciary obligations. To state, as Millett L.J. does, that to act where there are potentially conflicting interests is an automatic breach of fiduciary duty merely reflects the *Aberdeen Railway* principle that it is no answer to the charge of breach of duty that the fiduciary may show that the conflict did not in fact affect his conduct or harm the interests of the client. The agent who acts for vendor and purchaser on a sale is in breach of duty to each client and it is no answer for him to show that the sale was at a price that was fair to vendor and fair to purchaser. In other words, it is no answer to the allegation of breach of fiduciary duty to contend that the client was not in the event harmed: it is the potential for harm which prevents the professional from acting.

It is suggested that a less confusing expression might be "situation of conflict". It is an automatic breach of fiduciary duty to act for two clients at the same time in a situation of conflict.

What creates a problem here is that the expression "potentially conflicting interests" is readily confused with what is ultimately no more than an evidential issue—a decision whether to act involves looking prospectively at the issues likely to arise in fulfilling the two retainers. A factual enquiry is necessary which is not engaged by any of these expressions: how great is the risk of conflict? This is a separate issue from "potential" or "actual" conflict and is particularly important when an injunction is sought. It might be described by asking: has a situation of conflict arisen at all.

By contrast, the expression "actual conflict" as used by Millett L.J. arises only in circumstances where the professional is acting with informed consent, where the professional simply cannot fulfil his obligation to both clients and to fulfil his obligations to each in the same way as if each were his only client. Where an actual conflict occurs, the professional simply cannot perform his obligations to both clients. It is not generally concerned with breach of fiduciary duty but breach of non-fiduciary duty.

The SRA rule speaks of "significant risk of conflict". This is not a term of art and it is probably difficult to give the term a precise meaning. Presumably it means "viewing the matter prospectively", does it appear that there is a significant risk that if the matter proceeds there will be a clash of fiduciary obligations (such as to give rise to what Millett L.J. describes as "potentially conflicting interests")?

G. Level of risk of a situation of conflict arising

Where an application is made for an injunction to restrain the professional from acting, the court is being asked to grant what amounts to a quia timet injunction, albeit that the test to be adopted is different from the usual

3–008

quia timet injunction. So the court does need to consider how likely it must be for the conflict to arise. As explained above, this is an evidential issue. A formulation appears from *Boulting v Association of Cinematograph, Television and Allied Technicians*[12] where it was said by the Court of Appeal that the conflict rule:

> "must be applied realistically to a state of affairs which discloses a real conflict of duty and interest and not to some theoretical or rhetorical conflict".

In determining whether to grant an injunction, the court will need to make an assessment of the likelihood of conflict. The possibilities are to injunct, not to injunct, or to adopt a "wait and see" approach. The balance of convenience will involve consideration of the disadvantages which may arise from each of these alternatives.

H. Wait and see?

3–009
In one sense the "wait-and-see" approach is always available—if an injunction is refused but evidence subsequently materialises, a second application can always be made. The "wait and see" approach is impractical and unlikely to be satisfactory in most cases. But there are cases where a different approach may be required. In *Re Baron Holding Investments Ltd*[13] the two shareholders and sole directors of a company which had been wound up sought to prevent Kanter Jules, who were solicitors to the two principal creditors of the company and had acted for those creditors in the litigation against the company which had given rise to the winding up order, from acting for the liquidator. The application was not made by an existing or former client; on the contrary, the persons applying for an injunction were persons against whom Kanter Jules were acting, both previously in the litigation against the company (when at that time there was a strong community of interest between the company and its sole directors and shareholders) and as solicitors for the liquidator, who was seeking to bring misfeasance proceedings against the directors. The judge said that on the particular facts the employment of Kanter Jules was in his view "a natural choice". Reference to the "double employment" rule begged the question: where there was simply a potential or possibility of actual conflict, it did not follow that the double employment rule had been broken, merely that it might be broken. The court in such cases could exercise its discre-

---

[12] [1963] 2 Q.B. 606 at 638.
[13] [2000] 1 B.C.L.C. 272, Pumfrey J., the judge who decided *Bolkiah* at first instance. On October 26, 1999, Chadwick L.J. refused leave to appeal: his reasons are reported on Lexis under the case name *Halstuk v Venvil*.

tion. One particular matter to take into account in the particular case was the advantage in the solicitors acting because the dual position complained of gave them a background knowledge not shared by other solicitors who might be instructed.[14] One possibility, rather than require the expense of instruction of new solicitors now, was to adopt a wait-and-see approach, and only require the appointment of new solicitors if a conflict did actually arise in practice. Whether that was a convenient course would depend on all the circumstances of the case: it would not always be necessary for the court to take steps to deal with it unless and until the actual conflict arises.

Although this sounds like an exercise of discretion, what the court was really focusing on was the balance of convenience. In a quia timet injunction, the extent of the risk of harm (i.e. whether a conflict would in fact prejudice the claimant) is part of the balance of convenience. But the case is an unusual one. It is only in cases such as this, where the solicitors are solicitors to a liquidator, that one can readily speak of the advantages in the solicitors with previous knowledge of the affairs of the company acting. That will not usually be a relevant factor. That leads to there being more of an issue of balance here than in most cases. And the issue was whether the risk of conflict was such as to bar solicitors from acting, which itself involved a judgment as to the risk and the advantages and disadvantages of reaching a decision there and then.

The conventional approach to "wait and see" arguments at the interlocutory injunction stage is to give them short shrift. An example of this was *Marks and Spencer Group Plc v Freshfields Bruckhaus Deringer*.[15] On an application for an injunction to restrain Freshfields from acting against M&S as an existing client on a takeover, Freshfields argued that as the M&S board had not yet considered the takeover bid, it was not yet clear whether the bid would be hostile or friendly, and it was therefore premature to grant relief. The argument was roundly rejected. It is usually impractical for the court to adopt this sort of approach. In any event, even if the takeover is friendly, there is an adverse interest which requires separate legal advice in the same way as two parties negotiating on opposite sides but both seeking to conclude a deal.

3–010

---

[14] This is not an advantage in the sense that they had learnt confidential information they could use; it is an advantage because they knew the background and would not have to spend time and costs acquainting themselves with the background. An analogy is the cases on jurisdictional disputes. Where substantial related litigation has already taken place in one jurisdiction, the lawyers and experts in that jurisdiction may have built up an expertise which is a factor in favour of the second set of litigation being determined in the same forum: see *The Spiliada* [1987] A.C. 460.

[15] June 2, 2004, Lawrence Collins J., CA [2004] EWCA 741, discussed at 3–012 below.

2. What sort of conflict engages the double employment rule?

A. Conflict with the business interests of the other client

3–011   In *Bolkiah* Lord Millett said:

> "The large accountancy firms commonly carry out the audit of clients who are in competition with one another. The identity of their audit clients is publicly acknowledged. Their clients are taken to consent to their auditors acting for competing clients, though they must of course keep confidential the information obtained from their respective clients. This was the basis on which the Privy Council decided *Kelly v Cooper* in relation to estate agents".[16]

This is a difficult passage. It appears to assume that were it not for special features such as the knowledge of audit clients as to the activities of their auditors, auditors would be precluded from acting as auditors for competing clients. In *Bolkiah* Lord Millett treats this as something which would not be permissible were it not for the inferred consent which arises from it being public knowledge that the accountancy firms do so act.[17] Why should there be any difficulty in most cases in complying with the fiduciary obligation to defend and advance the interests of one audit client[18] merely because the accountants have carried out (or are carrying out) an audit for a competing company? The obligation of the fiduciary to advance the interests of the client is related to the retainer, namely the audit; it is not a generalised obligation.[19] Where is the difficulty in the auditor performing his fiduciary obligations to A at their most rigorous and still performing the audit for competitor B? There is on the face of it no conflict between acting as auditor for Tesco and Sainsburys. The mere fact that the auditor acts for two clients who have competing businesses could not give rise to a conflict of interest in any normal case. It cannot be the case that a solicitor who acts for one record company cannot act for another record company without mutual consent because the clients are in competition. The true analysis is that it is

---

[16] [1999] 2 A.C. 222 at 235.
[17] In other words, he treats this as a *Kelly* case: see para.4–016.
[18] There is another point here; it is unlikely that an accountant acting as auditor (as opposed to giving advice) owes a fiduciary duty. It was assumed by Lord Millett that the accountant would owe such an obligation; the point is discussed at para.17–008.
[19] See para.2–019. So merely because the auditor has seen the budget for company A in the course of the audit, there is no reason why he should be under any duty to disclose that confidential information pursuant to his fiduciary obligations to competitor B whom he is also auditing because even though B would dearly like to have that information, it has nothing to do with the interest of company B in respect of the audit. It might be that this would be a good reason for the accountant not accepting wider obligations such as a litigation support role for B.

B. Acting against the client on unrelated matters

In another passage in *Bolkiah*, Lord Millett said: 3–012

"... a fiduciary cannot act at the same time both for and against the same client, and his firm is in no better position. A man cannot without the consent of both clients act for one client while his partner is acting for another in the opposite interest".[20]

If taken literally, this would preclude a professional from ever accepting instructions for and against the same client at the same time, notwithstanding that the two instructions might be wholly unrelated: one might be one an employment dispute and the other in respect of a landlord and tenant matter. Or it would preclude a lawyer from prosecuting and defending criminal cases at the same time. The City of London Law Society, in their Review of Conflict Rules[21] took the view that Lord Millett could not have meant this literally and should be taken to be referring to opposite interests in the same matter.

In *Marks and Spencer Group Plc v Freshfields Bruckhaus Deringer*[22] Marks and Spencer successfully obtained an injunction to prevent Freshfields acting against them on a takeover bid. Freshfields had acted and continued to act for M&S on certain retainers. Freshfields argued, following the comments of the City of London Law Society,[23] that Lord Millett's comment should be read as limited to where the conflict related to the same matter. This was rejected by both Lawrence Collins J. and the Court of Appeal.[24] Both courts accepted obiter that there had to be "some reasonable relationship" between the matters. The courts both rejected the suggestion that the principle was limited to where the matter was the same. That view had to be correct: given that the principle is based on a duty of loyalty, there was

---

[20] [1999] 2 A.C. 222 at 234.
[21] July 2000, at para.4.2: "... we are not aware of any other similar finding or dicta at law ... if this is the law we would urge strongly that it be changed."
[22] June 2, 2004, Unreported, Lawrence Collins J. The Court of Appeal heard the appeal on June 3 at the same time as an application for leave to appeal and gave full reasons for refusing leave on the same day: June 3, 2004, Unreported.
[23] *Review of Conflict Rules*, July 2000, para.4.2.
[24] In each case citing the first edition of this book, which Pill L.J. referred to as "the leading textbook on the subject".

no logic in confining it to the same matter.²⁵ But it was always hard to imagine that Lord Millett meant what he said literally, and it was always unlikely that he intended to say that the double employment matter prevented a professional acting on opposite sides in unrelated matters. There had surely to be as a matter of common sense some limitation on the principle otherwise the criminal lawyer would be unable to defend whilst acting on a current prosecution. It was always probable that Lord Millett had in mind the case where there was some relationship between the two matters such as to bring the principle of conflict into play. Thus whilst it is necessary to exercise some caution before placing too much reliance on these dicta in *M&S*, a case where the judgments were given in circumstances of considerable urgency, and although there is room for much debate about what precisely is meant by "some reasonable relationship" the test seems appropriate. Ultimately, the analysis must focus on whether there is a conflict between the two fiduciary relationships. If there is no reasonable relationship between the matters, it is difficult to see how there will be a breach of fiduciary duty.

3–013 The SRA conflict rule applies in relation to "the same or related matters."²⁶ Solicitors are therefore now routinely considering whether the matters are related. So what started life as a dictum in *M&S* appears to be accepted as the law. It is thus now clear that the double employment rule is not limited to where the matter is the same.²⁷ Further, it seems tolerably clear that it will only apply where there is "some reasonable relationship" between the matters but the meaning of that expression involves consideration as to whether there is a clash between the two fiduciary obligations.²⁸ This is hardly an unexpected result. If there is no reasonable relationship between the matters, then there is no conflict, and the obligation of loyalty which is a hallmark of the fiduciary relationship is not breached. So it might

---

²⁵ To this extent it seems clear that the City of London Law Society expressed the rule too narrowly.
²⁶ See the SRA definition of conflict of interest: referred to at 15–004.
²⁷ The dissenting judgment of Waller L.J. in *Bolkiah* in the Court of Appeal [1999] 1 B.C.L.C. 139 traces the historic rule against acting for opposite parties as first arising in circumstances where the attorney for the plaintiff ceases to be the advocate of the plaintiff and thereupon becomes the advocate for the defendant: *Earl Cholmondeley v Lord Clinton* (1815) 19 Ves. Jun. 261 at 276 per Lord Eldon L.C., see para.5–004 below. See also the formulation of Scrutton L.J. in *Fullwood v Hurley* [1928] 1 K.B. 498 at 50D not limited to "same matter" conflicts. There are by contrast many authorities which define or express the principle with reference to the "same matter" but in general such authorities are not focusing on the particular issue: see *North and South Trust v Berkeley* [1971] 1 W.L.R. 471; *Moody v Cox and Hatt* [1917] 2 Ch. 71; *Farrington v Rowe McBride & Partners* [1985] 1 N.Z.L.R. 83; *Harrods v Lemon* [1931] 2 K.B. 157; *Clark Boyce v Mouat* [1994] 1 A.C. 428. The distinction was drawn by Finn in "Fiduciary Law and the Modern Commercial World" in *Commercial Aspects of Trusts and Fiduciary Obligations* (McKendrick ed., 1992).
²⁸ See the Singapore High Court decision in *Vorobiev Nikolay v Lush John Frederick Peters* [2010] SGHC 290 which after reviewing ethical rules in the US and UK held that matters would be related if they involved the same asset or liability or the same transaction or legal dispute.

be said that the result follows from analysis of the nature of the fiduciary relationship, and the fact that its ambit is defined by the retainer.

In the Supreme Court of Victoria in *Australian Liquor Marketers Pty Ltd v Tasman Liquor Traders Pty Ltd*,[29] a firm acting in a preference action in Queensland for recovery of a small debt on behalf of a client was also instructed in proceedings in Victoria against the same client where it was alleged that the client had repudiated a business sale agreement. Habersberger J. said that in the case before him the two sets of proceedings were "truly unrelated" and refused to restrain the firm from acting in the Victoria proceedings. There is one Australian case where a solicitor was restrained from acting for and against the same client on unrelated matters. That was the decision of Mandie J. in *Westend Entertainment Centre Pty Ltd v Equity Trustee Ltd*[30] where in one set of proceedings the solicitors were acting for a client who was making serious allegations against the client who the solicitors were acting for in the other proceedings and had acted for over six years. One can see that where serious allegations are made through solicitors against a client whom they are acting for in other proceedings and have known over a lengthy period it is not hard to imagine that there will be valid ground for objection and a potential conflict between the fiduciary obligations. But there are two specific reasons for thinking that this decision would not be followed here. Firstly, the Australian courts have perhaps sometimes taken a broader view than in England of what constitutes confidential information[31] and an extended acquaintance with the client would easily lead to a claim that there was a risk of misuse even in an unrelated matter. Secondly, the court has a supervisory jurisdiction over solicitors for conflict purposes in Australia which is not invoked in England which entitles the Australian courts to stop solicitors from acting where their representation would appear inappropriate to a reasonable man.

C. Acting on unrelated matters in Canada: Neil

The position in Canada has changed in consequence of the Supreme Court of Canada decision in *R v Neil*.[32] In that case Binnie J. went out of his way (the statement of principle was obiter) to identify a much more wide-ranging prohibition: 3–014

---

[29] [2002] V.S.C. 324.
[30] [1999] V.S.C. 514, also in the Supreme Court of Victoria.
[31] See para.7–012; the Australian courts have on occasion regarded as confidential information what they refer to as "the getting to know you factors".
[32] [2002] 3 S.C.R. 631. See the discussion of *Neil* in the Canadian Advocates' Quarterly (2003) 218 by Paul M Perell (now Judge Perell). Judge Perell, who has been the foremost authority on conflicts of interest in Canada since his 1995 book "*Conflicts of interest in the legal profession*", gave generous assistance in the publication of this book.

"... it is the firm not just the individual lawyer, that owes a fiduciary duty to its clients, and a bright line is required. The bright line is provided by the general rule that a lawyer may not represent one client whose interests are directly adverse to the immediate interests of another current client—*even if the two mandates are unrelated*[33]—unless both clients consent after receiving full disclosure (and preferably independent legal advice) and the lawyer reasonably believes that he or she is able to represent each client without adversely affecting the other".[34]

The judgment contains a number of one-sided comments directed at lawyers: fiduciary principles were "the price paid for professionalism"; "Business development strategies have to adapt to legal principles rather than the other way round"; "Loyalty includes putting the client's business ahead of the lawyer's business." But there is an absence of consideration in this important Canadian judgment of the contrary public interest. There is a public interest in the client being able to use the law firm of choice, unless there are compelling reasons to prohibit it. A competitive market place encourages clients to shop around for law firms, rather than restrict them because the law firms best equipped to act are unnecessarily prevented from acting. The theory of conflicts expounded betrays what may be regarded as an old-world view of individual lawyers acting for individual clients, and does not properly recognise the size of large commercial law firms and their ability to set up effective information barriers. As Canada has both provincial and federal systems, and law firms operate in different provinces, one might have thought that it was unduly restrictive to prohibit a law firm in Vancouver from acting against the multinational client in an unrelated matter in Toronto. It means that the law firm that acts for a bank collecting a debt from a private customer in one province cannot act against that bank in major inter-bank litigation in another province thousands of miles away. Such a rule encourages "plaintiffs lawyers" and "defendants lawyers"—a firm that acts for insurer clients would find it almost impossible to act for plaintiffs without running into difficulty. There are many public policy reasons to discourage such a practice.

It is dangerous to comment adversely on rules in foreign legal systems without a full understanding of the context in which they are made. Moreover, conflicts rules are often influenced by Bar rules on conflicts, which are different in the USA and Canada to this jurisdiction. However, it is not easy to understand why such a restrictive rule is necessary or beneficial.

3–015 Speaking extra-judicially Binnie J. has sought to justify his view as follows:

---

[33] The italics are in the original judgment.
[34] At para. 29.

"Let us suppose that a lawyer is retained by a worker to claim compensation for serious injuries suffered in an industrial accident. Could the same lawyer turn around and act for a mortgage company seeking to dispossess the same incapacitated worker from his home for failure to keep payments up to date? The retainers would be factually unrelated. Would acceptance of a retainer to act simultaneously for and against the worker in these unrelated matters be satisfactory? If not, what is the principled basis for the objection? This is not to say that all "unrelated mandates" create problems. But there has to be a principle for those that do".[35]

A number of comments may be made in relation to this stimulating justification. Firstly, where a professional deals with an individual client on a matter of obvious importance for the client, the knowledge he obtains from the client may well preclude him from acting against the client on a seemingly unrelated matter. The information which will be obtained from the client about his financial situation which will be relevant to the personal injuries retainer will probably also be relevant to the possession claim, or to its enforcement, giving rise to an obligation on the part of the lawyer to disclose the information to his mortgage company client. And if the industrial injury was relevant to the reasons for not keeping payments up on the house, the retainers are not unconnected but overlap. Indeed, whenever the lawyer accepts a retainer which affects the vital interests of an individual litigant, the range of personal information which the lawyer will learn about the individual in the course of that retainer will usually be relevant in some way or other to a retainer to act against the litigant, perhaps on questions of ability to enforce a judgment. Thus under English conflicts rules in the example given, it seems highly unlikely that the lawyer could act on both sides.

The reason that Binnie J.'s example resonates is that there seems something uncomfortable about the lawyer at the same time being instructed on the one hand to defend and on the other hand to attack the same person's vital interests. If that is thought uncomfortable, it might be thought equally uncomfortable that the lawyer completes the personal injury retainer on the Monday and starts acting for the mortgage company to repossess the house the following day, although in the absence of confidential information no principle of law in England or Canada prevents the lawyer from acting in such circumstances. But the underlying assumption in Justice Binnie's example is that conflicts are all about individual lawyers acting for and against individual clients. It might be said that this old-world view should not be allowed to dictate conflicts policy in modern business. The vivid example

---

[35] "*Sondage après Sondage . . . A Few Thoughts About Conflicts of Interest*", an edited version of remarks by Justice Ian Binnie at a panel discussion at Les Journées Strasbourgeoises in Strasbourg, France on July 4, 2008.

resonates rather less if one replaces "the lawyer" with "the law firm". In practice, most conflicts problems arise in big professional firms with large numbers of professionals with corporate clients, or where firms dominate a niche market where it is hard to avoid acting for and against the same entity. His example assumes the same individual lawyer acts for and against the same individual litigant. Life, at least in the law of conflicts of interest, is rarely that simple. Why are there no references in Binnie J.'s comments to the importance of freedom of choice for the client and the importance of competition? [36] Binnie J.'s comments can be contrasted with the English approach:

> "We start with the proposition that it is desirable that a litigant should be free to instruct the lawyer of his choice. This is particularly true if the lawyer is already acting for the client and the client wishes the lawyer to continue to act in a related matter".[37]

D. The double employment rule today

3–016   In the vast majority of cases it is unthinkable that a professional should be able to act for two parties with conflicting interests in related matters without the informed consent of both. But it is too easy to characterise the issue in black and white terms. Increasingly it is a shade of grey. Elsewhere this book considers in detail some of the problems of conflicts of interest faced by financial conglomerates and multi-disciplinary partnerships. The major firms of accountants typically have hundreds of partners and thousands of qualified staff in this jurisdiction alone, quite apart from their relationships with branches of the worldwide organisation abroad or associated firms. The equitable rules as originally formulated simply did not contemplate this kind of structure. What has happened is that it is in practical terms often impossible for these bodies to comply strictly with the equitable rules. It is for consideration whether a more relaxed regulatory environment, with greater acceptance of information barriers, would be beneficial.

---

[36] Binnie J.'s comments in *Neil* were obiter, but his view has been adopted in Canada ever since *Neil* was decided. There is a view in Canada that the Binnie view is too restrictive: see the Canadian Bar Association Task Force on *Current Client Conflicts* report proposing a more nuanced position. "Canada is diverging from the rest of the Commonwealth in the area of conflicts": see Simon Chester of Heenan Blaikie LLP, Slaw magazine 23.8.10. Mr Chester has published extensively on conflicts of evidence in Canada (see e.g. "*The Conflicts Revolution*" (2006))and gave valuable assistance in the publication of this book.
[37] Lord Phillips C.J. in *Virgin Media Communications v BSkyB* [2008] EWCA Civ 612 at [20].

3. Non-waivable conflicts and professional embarrassment

A. The terms explained

If there is a conflict between existing clients, then the professional cannot act without consent. He can usually act with consent. In *Clark Boyce v Mouat*,[38] in the Privy Council Lord Jauncey said:

3–017

> "There is no general rule of law to the effect that a solicitor should never act for both parties in a transaction where their interests may conflict. Rather is the position that he may act provided that he has obtained the informed consent of both to his acting. Informed consent means consent given in the knowledge that there is a conflict between the parties and that as a result the solicitor may be disabled from disclosing to each party the full knowledge which he possesses as to the transaction or may be disabled from giving advice to one party which conflicts with the interests of the other. If the parties are content to proceed upon this basis the solicitor may properly act".[39]

So if the professional seeks to act for two existing clients with conflicting interests, he must first ensure not merely that the clients consent, but also that such consent is informed. Issues of consent are considered in Chapter 4. But there are circumstances in which the professional cannot act even with consent. We have already seen the expression used "actual conflict" to describe a situation where the lawyer's duty to one client requires him to follow one course, and his duty to a second client requires him to do the precise opposite. These circumstances are sometimes referred to as "non-waivable" conflicts.

The principle which governs here is that a professional who acts for two clients with competing interests must be able to act for each as if that were his only client. The professional must not act so as to further the interests of one principal to the prejudice of those of the other. He must not allow the performance of his obligations to one principal to be influenced by his relationship with the other. He must serve each faithfully and loyally as if he were his only principal: the fiduciary must not be inhibited by the existence of his other employment from serving the interests of his principal as faithfully and effectively as if he were the only employer. The "non-waivable" conflict, and the related expression "professional embarrassment" derive from this principle.

3–018

A non-waivable conflict arises where the lawyer is professionally embarrassed. The term "professional embarrassment" is often used and often not

---

[38] [1994] 1 A.C. 428, PC, discussed at para.4–008 below.
[39] [1994] 1 A.C. 428.

understood. It arises in a variety of circumstances where a lawyer cannot perform his duty to his client, and thus involves a form of non-waivable conflict. So if, for example, in *Clark Boyce v Mouat*[40] Mrs Mouat had asked the solicitor, who had concluded that what would otherwise have amounted to a conflict of interest did not prevent him from accepting an execution-only retainer, whether he thought the transaction was a good deal for her to enter into, the solicitor would have been professionally embarrassed by what he knew from his other retainer and unable to give a fair answer.

An example is where both parties agree that the same lawyer should act on a deal. Both parties agree to waive the obligation on the lawyer to pass information learned from one to the other. Client A tells the lawyer he would prefer a particular clause to be incorporated but will not insist on it. Client B resists the introduction of the clause and asks the lawyer for advice on whether he should maintain his position. How can the lawyer advise? The consent does not help him. He simply cannot perform his duty to both sides. The knowledge he has obtained from A means that he is embarrassed in performing his professional duty to B (and possibly to A).

3–019 What Millett L.J. in *Mothew* described as an "actual" conflict is relevant here.[41] Even if the professional is properly acting after obtaining the necessary consent, the fiduciary must take care not to find himself in a position where there is an actual conflict of duty so that he cannot fulfil his obligations to one client without failing in his obligations to the other.[42] If he does, he may have no alternative but to cease to act for one and probably both. This is the situation where the professional acts for two clients and in cross-examination wants on behalf of one client to ask a particular question and on behalf of the other client wants not to ask the same question. The problem may arise similarly where there is an obligation to one client to disclose information and an obligation to the other client not to disclose the same information. An "actual" conflict is where any course of action will involve the professional not doing his duty to one of the two clients. In such a situation, consent is irrelevant.

3–020 Sometimes the professional is embarrassed in situations which are not connected to existing client conflicts. An example is where the lawyer receives in error a letter from the other side's lawyers intended for their client "we agree that you should be willing to pay up to £1m to settle this case." Having read it, the lawyer appreciates the letter was sent in error and agrees not to use or disclose the information contained in it. His client then receives an offer for £800,000 and wants advice as to what to do. How can he give that advice?

Professional embarrassment, therefore, arises where the professional is

---

[40] [1994] 1 A.C. 428 see para.4–008.
[41] See 3–005 above.
[42] *Moody v Cox and Hatt* [1917] 2 Ch. 71; *Commonwealth Bank of Australia v Smith* [1991] 102 A.L.R. 453.

unable to fulfil his obligation to a client by reason either of his obligations to another client, or an obligation of confidence. In the examples given above, the first gives rise to professional embarrassment because of the obligation to another client, the second because of an obligation of confidence albeit not owed to a client.

Two particular points are relevant to professional embarrassment. The first is that the problem is not resolved by client consent, as the first example demonstrates.

The second is that it can be distinguished from other types of conflicts because it affects the particular professional, rather than the firm. What embarrasses the professional is the information he already possesses and which he cannot shut out of his mind. Another member of the firm who does not have the same information in his mind is not embarrassed in the same way. In the example of the £800,000 offer, another member of the firm who had not seen the prior letter sent in error would not be embarrassed.

In general,[43] it is permissible for a professional to act for two parties with adverse interests with the informed consent of both clients.[44] So it is possible to envisage circumstances where a firm could act with consent for two clients with competing interests but an individual could not personally be involved in both retainers. So long as the client agreed, and the same individual was not involved in both retainers, and the knowledge obtained from one retainer was not available to the individuals on the other retainer, there would in principle be no problem. But where the same individual was involved, it can be seen that the individual would be in an impossible position—he would be professionally embarrassed.

B. The "No inhibition" principle

In *Mothew*, Millett L.J. said that a fiduciary must be able to act for each client as if each were his only client. Even if a fiduciary had the informed consent of both clients, he was in breach of fiduciary duty if he intentionally furthered the interests of one client to the prejudice of the other. Dishonesty was not a prerequisite, but intention was, before there was a breach of fiduciary duty under this ground. An innocent breach of duty to one client would not be a breach of fiduciary duty. The principle that a fiduciary must not be inhibited from serving the interests of each client as though that client were his only principal was referred to by him as the "no inhibition" principle.

3–021

This is another confusing expression. On one level, the "no inhibition" principle is nothing more than a form of professional embarrassment not

---

[43] And subject to professional rules such as the SRA conflicts rules.
[44] See *Clark Boyce v Mouat* [1994] 1 A.C. 428.

cured by consent. A acts for two clients with consent. He feels inhibited by his relationship with one from pleading fraud against him. But whether or not the client against whom fraud is to be pleaded is an existing client, a former client, or simply a client with whom he maintains a personal relationship even if no retainer, if consciously or subconsciously he is in danger of "pulling his punches" then he should not act against him, because he cannot do his duty for the other client in the same way as if that were his only client. Again, consent will not resolve the problem.

What Millett L.J. had in mind went further. In not pleading fraud in the example above, there is likely to be a breach of the non-fiduciary duty to act in the best interests of each client, but not normally a breach of fiduciary duty. However, where the action is intentional, what Millett L.J. refers to as the no inhibition principle comes into play and a breach of fiduciary duty occurs. If the professional holds back, intentionally preferring the interests of one to the other, he is in breach of fiduciary duty. There is a breach of fiduciary duty because what he is doing is disloyal.

4. Personal conflicts and the professional

3–022   The court's view of personal conflicts can be seen in *Spector v Ageda*[45] where a solicitor sought to enforce a mortgage against the defendant, who was her client and to whom she had lent money:

> "The solicitor must be remarkable indeed if he can feel assured of holding the scales evenly between himself and his client. Even if in fact he can and does, to demonstrate to conviction that he has done so will usually be beyond possibility in a case where anything to his client's detriment has occurred. Not only must his duty be discharged but it must manifestly and undoubtedly be seen to have been discharged. I abstain from any categorical negative: the circumstances of life are of such infinite variety. But I can at least say that in all ordinary circumstances a solicitor ought to refuse to act for a person in a transaction to which the solicitor is himself a party with an adverse interest; and even if he is pressed to act after his refusal, he should persist in that refusal. Nobody can insist on an unwilling solicitor acting for him, at all events when there is a conflict of interest".[46]

What constitutes a conflict of interest for this purpose? In the vast majority of cases, the answer is obvious. But it is worth bearing in mind that the professional often encounters conflicts of interest that are not perceived as

---

[45] [1973] Ch. 30.
[46] [1973] Ch. 30 at 47, per Megarry J.

conflicts at all. The estate agent asked to advise the vendor whether to press for another £20,000 on the purchase price knows that by so doing the sale of £1,000,000 may be lost. If there is no sale, he obtains no commission, but the extra £20,000 presents only a minimal personal advantage. So too the lawyer asked to advise on a settlement who knows that he will be deprived of large fees if the case settles. In *Dennard v PricewaterhouseCoopers LLP*[47] it was argued that the defendants faced a conflict of interest because they had an expectation of future work from one party to a valuation they were independently conducting and it was thus in their interests to value at a low price. Vos J. said the allegation (which had no factual foundation) was effectively one of corruption. He said:

> "Major accountancy firms, like major legal firms, frequently attract business by acting against their prospective client. They do that by impressing that prospective client with their professionalism and competence, not by showing that they are willing to act against the interests of their own client. If the prospective client once thought that its prospective adviser had a propensity to act in breach of fiduciary duty, it would, if well advised, run in the other direction".[48]

In *Moody v Cox*[49] the Court of Appeal proceeded on the basis that there was no distinction between the case of the solicitor who acts for two clients with conflicting interests in the purchase of property and the solicitor who acts for a client whose interest conflicted with his own personal interest in the property purchase. Lord Cozens-Hardy M.R. said:

> "A man may have a duty on one side and an interest on another. A solicitor who puts himself in that position takes upon himself a grievous responsibility. A solicitor may have a duty on one side and a duty on the other, namely, a duty to his client as solicitor on the one side and a duty to his beneficiaries on the other; but if he chooses to put himself in that position it does not lie in his mouth to say to the client 'I have not discharged that which the law says is my duty towards you, my client, because I owe a duty to the beneficiaries on the other side'. The answer is that if a solicitor involves himself in that dilemma it is his own fault. He ought before putting himself in that position to inform the client of his conflicting duties, and either obtain from that client an agreement that he should not perform his full duties of disclosure or say which would be much better 'I cannot accept this business'. I think it would be the worst thing to say that a solicitor can escape from the obligations, imposed upon him as solicitor, of disclosure if he can prove that it is

---

[47] [2010] EWHC 812 (Ch).
[48] [215].
[49] [1917] 2 Ch. 71, CA.

not a case of duty on one side and of interest on the other, but a case of duty on both sides and therefore impossible to perform. I do not desire to draw any distinction between the simple case where he has one client who is selling his own property to him and a case like the present, where he has a client and as trustee is selling to that client".

3–023   There are comments in a number of authorities that it makes no difference whether the court is dealing with personal conflicts or client conflicts.[50] Sometimes the courts have treated existing client conflicts as conflicts between the interest of the existing client and the personal interests of the professional in obtaining a second set of fees.[51]

However, when the fiduciary deals with his principal, there is an additional hurdle to be overcome which is not applicable in the usual case of conflicts involving two clients. The fiduciary must not only prove that he made full disclosure but also must show that the transaction is fair; otherwise it may be rescinded. A recent case which highlights the harsher attitude of the courts to this sort of conflict is *Johnson v EBS Pensioner Trustees Ltd*.[52] O'Shea borrowed money from clients of Churchers solicitors and guaranteed the loan. The contract of loan and guarantee were executed by Churchers partners on behalf of their clients. Churchers did not disclose their own service charge on the loan interest to O'Shea. The judge held that the non-disclosure by the firm of their service charge had prevented the client from negotiating a lower charge, but had held that cases involving purchase by a fiduciary from his client were limited to sales or purchases of property and leases and thus were of no application. The Court of Appeal disagreed, and said that where there is a relationship of trust and confidence, there must be full disclosure and proof by the fiduciary that the transaction was a fair one. It did not matter whether in acting for both sides the solicitor was acting for himself or clients and the rule of fair dealing applied across the board and not merely where there was a purchase of property or a lease. It was not an answer to a claim for breach of the fiduciary duty of full disclosure that the client would have entered into the transaction anyway.[53]

3–024   Conflicts involving professionals today are usually concerned with the conflict between client and client. But the older authorities on fiduciaries are mostly concerned with the historic problem of conflict between client and

---

[50] See *Fullwood v Hurley* [1928] 1 K.B. 498 at 502, per Scrutton L.J. where the test for conflicts between two clients was treated as the same as for personal conflicts, and Scrutton L.J. referred to the need for the "fullest disclosure", and *Farrington v Rowe McBride & Partners* [1985] 1 N.Z.L.R. 83 at 90, to same effect, cited in *Clark Boyce* at 436. See also *Moody v Cox and Hatt* [1917] 2 Ch. 71 at 81–82; *Australia Beach Petroleum v Abbott Tout Russell* [1999] N.S.W.C.A. 408; *Maguire v Makaronis* (1997) 188 C.L.R. 449; *Breen v Williams* (1996) 186 C.L.R. 71; *Haywood v Toadnight* [1927] V.L.R. 512.
[51] This is how it was put by Lightman J. in *Re Solicitors (A Firm)* [1997] Ch. 1 at 11 and by Pumfrey J. at first instance in *Bolkiah* [1999] 1 B.C.L.C. 1 at 10.
[52] [2002] Lloyd's P.N. 309, CA.
[53] See *Brickenden v London Loan and Savings Co* [1934] 3 D.L.R. 465, PC.

professional, where the professional has a personal interest in the transaction. He is thus doing something which equity has traditionally abhorred, namely competing with the client himself. There are circumstances where the professional has to deal with a personal conflict outside the examples of egregious behaviour in the old cases. The most obvious is where in a financial conglomerate the client is on one side of a transaction and on the other the firm is dealing off its own book. And the conflicts faced by directors of companies are usually personal conflicts and thus different from the problems faced by professionals.

But even if the rules are similar, the approach of the court in applying the rules may sometimes be a little more relaxed in client conflicts and this has on occasion been recognised by the courts.[54] Equity has always enforced rigorous rules to prevent trustees benefiting from the trust. Often it is the existence of the trust which has revealed or enabled the opportunity which the trustee wishes to take advantage of to the detriment or disadvantage of the client. That is not the case where the professional wishes to act for two clients. There is something distasteful about a trustee competing with the trust, seeking to further his own interest at the expense of the trust. There is nothing inherently distasteful in quite the same way in acting for two clients with potentially competing interests at the same time. For example, the driving force behind the client conflict issue may be the new client who wants the professional to act for him; the professional can properly say: "Unless you can resolve the point with the other client, I leave it to the court to decide what is proper".

Where the professional deals with his principal, the basis of the court's intervention may at times be as a result of a fiduciary obligation arising from undue influence. The courts have at times set aside transactions between professional and former client as cases where the professional relationship gives rise to a presumption of undue influence[55] extending beyond the duration of the retainer. Thus in *Demerara Bauxite v Hubbard*,[56] the formal relationship of solicitor and client had terminated prior to the transaction with the client, who had no independent advice in respect of the grant of an option to purchase to the solicitor himself. Even though the retainer had terminated, the Privy Council applied the rules of fiduciary relationships. Similarly in *McMaster v Byrne*[57] the client had retained a solicitor to act in relation to his business affairs generally. All retainers had come to an end, but the Privy Council held that the solicitor's failure to disclose all material

3–025

---

[54] In *Nationwide Building Soc v Balmer Radmore* [1999] Lloyd's Rep. P.N. 241 at 260 Blackburne J. pointed out that the cases before him were not cases of personal conflict, thereby suggesting that the position might have been different if they had been. However, it seems he was concerned with potential remedies. The best illustration of a more flexible attitude is *Clark Boyce v Mouat* [1994] 1 A.C. 428 discussed at para.3–017.
[55] See *Chitty on Contracts*, 30th edn, Vol. 1, para. 7–069.
[56] [1923] A.C. 673.
[57] [1952] 1 All E.R. 1362.

facts in relation to the grant of an option to the solicitor by the client justified the setting aside of the transaction.[58]

One practical difference between the personal conflict and the client conflict is that in client conflict cases, the court is considering whether to prevent the professional from acting. It is not usually focusing on the damages or other financial consequences of the professional wrongfully acting. It is thus usually looking at the matter prospectively: will a conflict arise, and if so what should be done about it. There is bound to be an element of pragmatism about the result, which may involve looking at the likelihood of a problem developing and elements of proportionality in the result given the extent of the problem. But where the issue is competition between professional and client, although it is possible that the court will be considering an injunction,[59] more often what concerns the court is whether to require the fiduciary after the event to disgorge profit made out of the transaction.

3–026 It is wrong to think that all personal conflicts are regarded equally distastefully. Where, for example, a financial services conglomerate deals off its own book, there may be a personal conflict with a client who has asked for an order to be executed. As will be apparent, in such organisations, conflicts are in practice impossible to avoid and there will normally be no issue of moral stigma. There seems no need for the courts to regard such cases with severity. But in general, whatever the principles it is likely that there are circumstances in which the court may be willing to treat a client conflict more flexibly. Another possible difference between the application of the rules as between personal and client conflicts is that the possibility of permitting a personal conflict by exclusion clauses, disclosure clauses or duty defining clauses in advance is likely to be one the courts will find deeply unattractive. And the duty of disclosure might be applied slightly differently: the court will need to consider whether the professional has made full disclosure to the client, as without such disclosure there can be no question of the fiduciary competing with the client. The old cases[60] on disclosure are strict. It is easy in most cases to find some fact which was not disclosed which might have been and which might have been material. The books are full of cases of fiduciaries without moral turpitude who had personal conflicts thought they had made full disclosure but where the courts held otherwise.[61] The approach to disclosure may be less strict in cases of existing client conflicts.[62]

---

[58] Compare the position in respect of partnerships, where the fiduciary duties of partners to each other continue after dissolution until the winding up of the partnership: *Don King Productions Inc v Frank Warren* [2000] Ch. 291, CA.
[59] Perhaps to restrain the fiduciary from competing.
[60] See para.4–013.
[61] See for example *Phipps v Boardman* [1967] 2 A.C. 46.
[62] See, e.g. *Clark Boyce v Mouat* [1994] 1 A.C. 428 discussed at para.4–008.

CHAPTER 4

Managing Conflicts by Contract

The double employment rule discussed in the last chapter has the effect that, without consent, a professional may not act for two clients at the same time in a situation of conflict. There are some situations, referred to as non-waivable conflicts,[1] where the professional may not act even with consent. But in principle, and subject to professional rules, a client may consent to the professional acting in a situation of conflict. This chapter looks at conflicts problems which derive from the retainer itself, and the extent to which client consent may free the professional to act in what would otherwise be a situation of conflict, as well as what is meant by "informed consent".

4–001

1. The retainer

A. Ambit of the retainer

The starting point is to consider the retainer. In determining whether and to what extent there is a conflict of interest, the court will not operate in a vacuum. What has the professional undertaken to do? It will always be important to identify the retainer. The retainer defines the obligations of the professional. It is impossible to ascertain whether there is a conflict without considering the ambit of the retainer. The narrower the ambit of the retainer, the easier it will be for the professional to act without conflict.

4–002

Now the solicitor is under a regulatory obligation to explain to the client his responsibilities.[2] In the absence of express terms of the retainer, the duty of the professional will be to advise his client in terms appropriate to

---

[1] See 3–017.
[2] SRA 2011 Code Chapter 1.

the client's understanding and experience.[3] The extent of any duty of care thus depends on what the professional is instructed to do.[4] In *Carradine Properties Ltd v DJ Freeman & Co*[5] Donaldson L.J. said:

> "the precise scope of that duty will depend, inter alia, upon the extent to which the client appears to need advice. An inexperienced client will need and will be entitled to expect the solicitor to take a much broader view of the scope of his retainer and of his duties than will be the case with an experienced client".[6]

Careful identification of the terms of the retainer is at the heart of consideration of conflicts.[7] In cases which turn on the terms of the obligation to disclose information learned through one client to another client, the terms of the retainer are crucial. The central issue may well be whether and to what extent the solicitor has accepted an obligation to advise. In *Clark Boyce v Mouat*[8] it was because Mrs Mouat made it clear that she did not want advice on the merits of the transaction but merely wanted the conveyance effected that the Privy Council held there was informed consent to the professional acting for both son and mother despite their different interests and no conflict. The line of cases where the solicitor acts both for mortgage lender and borrower emphasise that the mortgage lender typically does not require advice on the merits of the transaction, and thus define the duty of the solicitor in narrow terms, thereby protecting the solicitor from many of the problems which arise from knowledge he has learned from his borrower client.

4–003   Thus in *National Home Loans v Giffen Couch & Archer*,[9] the Court of Appeal considered the extent of the obligations of the solicitors who had been instructed by the borrower simply "to act on the remortgage" and by the lender "in the preparation of a mortgage with any other appropriate documents in accordance with the notes for guidance and the documents provided". The approach of the court was to consider, in accordance with *Carradine Properties*, what in all the circumstances of the case the duty of the solicitor could reasonably be expected to be, taking into account in the

---

[3] *County Personnel v Pulver* [1987] 1 W.L.R. 916 at 922, per Bingham L.J.
[4] However, what matters is the work undertaken by the professional, as opposed to the work the subject of any original retainer. It follows that where the work done exceeds the work the professional originally agreed to do, his obligations relate to the work he has actually carried out: see *Beach Petroleum v Abbott Tout Russell* [1999] N.S.W.C.A. 408; *Birtchnell v The Equity Trustees Executors and Agency Co Ltd* (1929) 42 C.L.R. 437; *Australian Breeders Cooperative Society v Jones* (1997) 150 A.L.R. 488.
[5] (1982) 126 S.J. 157.
[6] Cited with approval in *Virgin Management v De Morgan Group* [1996] E.G.C.S. 16, and *National Home Loans v Giffen Couch & Archer* [1997] 3 All E.R. 808 at 813.
[7] See, e.g. *Jewo Ferrous BV v Lewis Moore*, unreported, October 19, 2000, CA.
[8] [1994] 1 A.C. 428. See 4–008.
[9] [1997] 3 All E.R. 808; see para.6–005.

case of the lender the experience of the lender in giving instructions. The court did not merely seek to construe the words of the retainer.[10] In cases where the terms of the retainer say little, as in *Giffen Couch & Archer*, such an approach by the court is understandable. It is also apparent from the *Giffen Couch & Archer* case that the court was much less likely to be sympathetic to an experienced client. So where the solicitor is dealing with an experienced client such as a mortgage lender, the court will have little difficulty in accepting that the terms of the instructions give rise to a limited retainer. That means that the professional will need to ensure that he has set out the basis and terms of the retainer in writing, and has given thought to the obligations he is willing to undertake.

The professional may therefore agree to accept instructions under a relatively narrow retainer in order to avoid the conflicts problems which would arise if the retainer was more broadly defined. In principle, there is no objection to using this as a means of managing potential conflicts. However, this may not be so straightforward when dealing with individual or non-commercial clients. Here the professional will need to take much more care. If the client is inexperienced, it is much less like to be acceptable for the professional to get away with a retainer which puts the client in a position where he obtains less advice than he reasonably needs. And on a very narrow retainer, the professional has huge problems when the client says "what do you think of this idea", which is unsatisfactory.[11]

B. Strother: construing the retainer

Another recent decision of the Supreme Court of Canada *Strother v 3464920 Canada Inc*[12] focuses on the importance of the retainer in determining breach of fiduciary duties.[13] Monarch produced films with the benefit of a tax-efficient investment scheme. The law firm Davis & Co acted for Monarch through its partner Strother. Davis and Strother were retained by Monarch on terms which prohibited them acting for other clients on similar work. That retainer ended at the end of 1997 and was not renewed when legislative changes were generally believed to have defeated the tax benefits of the scheme, and was replaced by a much more limited 1998 retainer. An ex-employee of Monarch, Darc, approached Strother, suggested a revised tax scheme and invited him to join with him in a company called Sentinel developing the new scheme on terms that they share profits. Strother became

4–004

---

[10] Although in fact the conclusion reached was in accordance with the wording of the instructions.
[11] The reason that the issue as to whether the auditor owes duties of a fiduciary has not been decided in this jurisdiction is no doubt because auditors tend not just to perform audits; they normally give advice as well; see para.17–008.
[12] See *R. v Neil* (2003) 218 D.L.R. (4th) 671, discussed at 3–014.
[13] *Strother v 3464920 Canada Inc* [2007] S.C.C. 24.

involved in Sentinel in 1998, although he initially doubted whether the new scheme could work and did not mention it to his partners at Davis. In October 1998 a favourable tax ruling was obtained, Strother resigned from Davis and went to work for Sentinel, where he made large amounts of money from marketing tax schemes when he had originally told Monarch the opportunities no longer existed. Monarch sued Davis and Strother for breach of fiduciary duty. As they could not show loss,[14] they sued Strother (and Davis vicariously) for disgorgement of $32m profits Strother had made through Sentinel and Davis for disgorgement of $9m legal fees it received from acting for Sentinel.

4–005
The judgment of the 5-4 majority in the Supreme Court of Canada has been heavily criticised[15] and is difficult to follow. The minority, following the trial judge, held that the 1997 Monarch retainer was at an end, the 1998 retainer did no more than require general clean-up and corporate services, Strother was only to provide advice if specifically engaged to do so,[16] and thus there was no conflict or breach of duty. The majority founded liability on a broad construction of the retainer which smacks of public policy rather than contractual construction,[17] and which seems to require the lawyer to do things for a client he has not undertaken to do. Binnie J. continuing a moral theme he had first embarked upon in *R. v Neil*[18] referring to lawyers as being "professional advisers, not used car salesmen or pawnbrokers."[19]

The principle on which the decision is based is uncontroversial: examine the contract of retainer and determine what the lawyer has agreed to do. In the light of that, firstly consider whether the lawyer has accepted a retainer which conflicts with that duty and secondly consider whether he has an

---

[14] They had exited the market.
[15] [2008] L.Q.R. 21 Edelman "Unanticipated fiduciary liability".
[16] [123].
[17] Binnie J. for the majority treated the 1998 retainer as wider: relying on conversations Strother had with Monarch representatives that alternative tax-assisted business opportunities might in future be explored, he treated the retainer as extending to considering and advising on tax-assisted business opportunities. If this was indeed the ambit of the retainer, which may be regarded as highly surprising, then surely Davis and Strother were in breach of fiduciary duty in accepting a retainer from a competing client, namely Sentinel. However, the majority held that there was no such breach because the interests of Monarch and Sentinel were potentially aligned in relation to such opportunities (also highly surprising as Monarch and Sentinel were potential competitors in relation to the marketing of such schemes), and the breach was merely that of Strother by virtue of his undisclosed personal interest in Sentinel, and thus in pursuing the new scheme, which conflicted with his obligation to give further advice to Monarch regarding the new scheme. Although Davis and Strother were found not liable in breach of fiduciary duty, they were held liable vicariously to disgorge Strother's profits based on the court's interpretation of the British Columbia Partnership Act, so the victory was pyrrhic.
[18] Binnie J.'s judgment in *R. v Neil* 2003 3 S.C.R. 631 holds that in Canada a lawyer cannot act against an existing client even on an unrelated matter: see 3–014.
[19] [42].

undisclosed personal interest which conflicts with that retainer.[20] It is the application of that principle which is problematic. Is the notion that the lawyer is obliged as a professional to go beyond what the client has asked him to do and to refuse another retainer which does not conflict with what the existing client has asked him to do? There seems an implicit requirement in the decision that the lawyer will advise the client on matters he believes will be of relevance to the client's business, which is not satisfactory as a substitute for construing the retainer. What are the client's obligations to pay the lawyer in such circumstances? How does either party have certainty as to what their respective obligations are? How does the lawyer know what other obligations his firm may take on?

C. Joint instructions under the retainer

Is it possible for the professional to accept joint instructions? This will not be an appropriate or possible solution in most cases. But the professional may in some cases be able to consider whether to accept joint instructions. Of course, this will require informed consent of both clients, and clear understanding as to such matters as whether they are both responsible for all the fees incurred by the professional.[21]

4–006

It is important to appreciate the effect of taking on joint clients. There can be no confidence between two joint clients in respect of the matters the subject of the retainer. Where the relationship is such that privilege may be claimed, which is principally where the professional is a lawyer (but not exclusively, as is apparent from *Bolkiah* where it was accepted that some of the documents of the accountants attracted litigation privilege), then as between joint clients one cannot assert privilege against the other even though the privilege can be claimed against the rest of the world,[22] even if the joint clients subsequently fall out.[23] Thus the privilege can only be waived jointly and not by one party.[24]

---

[20] See the minority judgment of McLachlin C.J. at [132]–[134].
[21] See *Farrer v Copley Singletons* [1998] P.N.L.R. 22, CA. Acting for several plaintiffs a solicitor had a duty to keep each informed of difficulties and, where necessary, to obtain instructions from each. The solicitor could only act on instructions from one if the one had actual or ostensible authority.
[22] Where a solicitor accepts joint instructions, it will be a serious breach of duty to withhold information from one of the two clients: *Perry v Edwin Coe, Independent*, April 1, 1994.
[23] *Phipson on Evidence* (17th edn, 2009), para.24–01.
[24] *Rochefoucauld v Boustead* (1896) 65 L.J. Ch. 794; *Re Konigsberg* [1989] 1 W.L.R. 1257. See now the formulation of the Court of Appeal in *TSB Bank v Robert Irving and Burns* [1999] Lloyd's Rep. I.R. 528. There the Court of Appeal analysed the position where solicitors and counsel acting for insurer and insured in litigation as a joint retainer to the lawyers which gave rise to a waiver of privilege between the two parties. The court held that the waiver of privilege between these parties was not effective where there was an actual conflict between them. Whilst the court reached the right result in this curious case, the route is not free from difficulty: see para.15–018 below.

The professional who accepts joint instructions to act for two clients will find it difficult subsequently to act for one against the other. The precise legal basis on which such representation is barred may not be straightforward. Where the retainer is joint, there can be no privilege or confidentiality between joint clients.[25] So if, as between the clients, there are no confidences in the matters relevant to the retainer, why should the lawyer not subsequently act for one against the other?[26] Technically, where there has been a joint retainer, the issue as to whether the lawyer can act for one party on a subsequent instruction is a former client conflict. Where there is no relationship between the matters, there is no reason why a problem should arise. Where the matters are related, it is likely to be unattractive for the lawyer to act for one against the other of joint clients and a court faced with an injunction application is likely to be unsympathetic to the lawyer. But if there is no existing client conflict, and there is no confidential information between the joint clients, it is hard to explain what the problem is.

4–007 This is an area where the position is clearer in Australia. There, as explained below,[27] the court is not limited to the existing and former client principles set out in *Bolkiah*. There is a further ground, founded in the court's inherent supervisory jurisdiction over solicitors, which enables the court to restrain a solicitor from acting where the reasonable well-informed observer would consider that the administration of justice was affected by the lawyer continuing to act. It is easy to see that this situation fits neatly into that jurisdiction. In a recent New Zealand case, the court injuncted the solicitor from acting for one former joint client against the other[28] based on similar principles.

2. Consent as a defence to conflict

A. Clark Boyce v Mouat

4–008 In other jurisdictions there is an absolute bar on professionals, or at least lawyers, acting at the same time for two clients in competing interests. Indeed, in certain US jurisdictions, the law has been taken further so that

---

[25] For joint privilege, see *Phipson* 17th edn, (2009) Ch.24; Hollander, *Documentary Evidence* 10th edn, 2009, para.15–01. In general there will be no basis for a claim for privilege based on common interest if at the time of the communication there was a conflict of interest between the parties.
[26] There are cases where one of the parties who jointly instruct the solicitor consults him confidentially on matters in dispute between the two of them suggesting that privilege can be claimed in these circumstances: see, e.g. *Harris v Harris* (1931) P. 10, but this is unlikely to be a happy state of affairs.
[27] See 5–004.
[28] *Raats v Gascoigne Wicks* [2006] N.Z.H.C. 598.

even in the case of former client conflicts, where a lawyer has acted for one side, his partner will be barred from acting in an opposing interest if this would give rise to a possible perception of impropriety, irrespective of the substance of the matter.[29] The Privy Council held in *Clark Boyce v Mouat* that was not the law in this jurisdiction.[30]

In *Clark Boyce v Mouat*,[31] Mrs Mouat agreed to mortgage her home as security for a loan being made to her son. The son's usual solicitors declined to act in the conveyancing transaction and Clark Boyce were asked to act for Mrs Mouat and son. The solicitors explained the transaction to Mrs Mouat and advised her to obtain independent advice (on three occasions), which she declined to do, and on that basis acted both for her and the son. The son subsequently became bankrupt, and Mrs Mouat sued the solicitors, contending that they were in breach of fiduciary duty in not refusing to act for her, failing to disclose to her that the son's usual solicitors had refused to act, and failing to advise her not to sign the mortgage. The Privy Council, allowing the appeal from the New Zealand Court of Appeal, said that there was no general rule of law to the effect that a solicitor should never act for both parties in a transaction where their interests may conflict; on the contrary, he may act provided he has the informed consent of both to his acting.

Lord Jauncey pointed out that the first step in the analysis is to determine the extent of the retainer. In determining whether the professional has obtained informed consent, the Privy Council pointed out that it is essential to determine precisely what services are required of him by the parties. The services of the solicitor were here sought in order to effect the conveyance, not to give advice as to the wisdom of the transaction. It was an execution-only retainer. Once the solicitor had advised Mrs Mouat to obtain independent advice, there was no duty to decline to act, and advice as to the wisdom of the transaction was never sought or required:

> "when a client in full command of his faculties and apparently aware of what he is doing seeks the assistance of a solicitor in the carrying out of a particular transaction, that solicitor is under no duty whether before or after accepting those instructions to go beyond those instructions by proferring unsought advice on the wisdom of the transaction".

Lord Jauncey set out the general principle:

> "There is no general rule of law to the effect that a solicitor should never act for both parties in a transaction where their interests may

---

[29] As recognised in *Supasave Retail v Coward Chance* [1991] 1 All E.R. 668 at 674, per Browne-Wilkinson V.C.
[30] Technically they held that this was not the law in New Zealand; the principle stated in *Clark Boyce* was however approved in *Bolkiah*.
[31] [1994] 1 A.C. 428, PC.

conflict. Rather is the position that he may act provided that he has obtained the informed consent of both to his acting".

This is an important decision, because it makes clear that informed consent permits a fiduciary to act in circumstances of conflict. Of course, there are circumstances in which, as we have seen,[32] even informed consent will not solve the problem, as is recognised by Lord Jauncey.[33]

B. Clark Boyce: discussion

4–009   The case is authority for the principle that there is no general rule of law precluding a solicitor from acting for both parties in a transaction where their interests may conflict, so long as he has obtained informed consent. The Privy Council held that the refusal of Mrs Mouat's family solicitor to act was not material information, particularly as nothing sinister was seen in the refusal. Lord Jauncey focused on the terms of the retainer. There is a distinction between the professional who is instructed to advise on the wisdom of the transaction, and the retainer where the professional is required to perfect title. As we will see[34] this distinction is particularly significant in cases where a mortgage lender complains of a failure by the solicitor who acts both for lender and borrower to pass on information learned from the borrower, perhaps during a different retainer. Mrs Mouat had made it clear she did not want advice on the wisdom of the transaction.

Where one is dealing with professional mortgage lenders, the position may be straightforward. The mortgage lender instructs the solicitor to perfect title. The solicitor will probably never meet the mortgage lender in the course of the transaction, and probably there will be little contact even by telephone. There is nothing problematic in defining the duty of the solicitor in such standard-form transactions narrowly: if the mortgage lender seeks a full service from the solicitor, it can say so or decline to instruct the borrower's solicitor. So to say that the mortgage lender does not seek advice as to the wisdom of the transaction is fair enough. But it is necessary to be much more careful when the context does not involve professional mortgage lenders but mother and son. The professional is entitled to make far less assumptions as to the knowledge and understanding of the client. If he accepts the dual retainer in these circumstances, he is much more at risk if things go wrong, when the mother has failed to understand the basis on

---

[32] See 3–017, in relation to non-waivable conflicts.
[33] Citing at 274d Richardson J. in *Farrington v Row McBride & Partners* [1985] 1 N.Z.L.R. 83, 90 where that judge indicated that there would be some circumstances where the solicitor could not act fairly and adequately for both clients even when acting with informed consent.
[34] See Ch.6.

which the solicitor accepted the instructions. And it is all very well saying that Mrs Mouat did not require him to advise on the wisdom of the transaction. But the solicitor who accepts instructions in such circumstances will quickly come unstuck when something unexpected happens in the course of acting and the client says "what should I do now?".

The decision in *Clark Boyce*, which predated *Mothew* and *Bolkiah*, has been referred to with approval in other important conflict cases. It remains the leading authority for the proposition that there is no rule of law prohibiting a professional from acting on both sides of a transaction with informed consent so long as he is able to fulfil his duty to each party. So far so good. However, it is suggested that whilst the decision in *Clark Boyce* may be justified on the facts, there are number of passages in Lord Jauncey's opinion which cannot readily be reconciled with principles established in other cases.

4–010

Firstly, Lord Jauncey seems to suggest that the double employment rule only arises where the professional is instructed for different parties in respect of the same transaction. But the double employment rule is not and cannot be so limited.[35]

Lord Jauncey's formulation of informed consent is also problematic. Informed consent meant:

". . . consent given in the knowledge that there is a conflict between the parties and that as a result the solicitor may be disabled from disclosing to each party the full knowledge which he possesses as to the transaction or may be disabled from giving advice to one party which conflicts with the interests of the other. If the parties are content to proceed upon this basis the solicitor may properly act".[36]

This is not a happy passage. Where informed consent is sought, the client may well not appreciate that these are the consequences unless this is clearly spelled out to him. In *Clark Boyce* there is no suggestion that either of these matters were explained to Mrs Mouat. She was told that there was a conflict of interest, and advised to obtain independent legal advice, and said she did not think it was necessary to see another lawyer. So how can she have been taken to realise that this was the consequence of the solicitor acting for her? Lord Jauncey appears to assume that informed consent carries with it an agreement by the client to waive the duty of disclosure of all matters relevant to the retainer (which may be important where the professional has taken on a conflicting retainer). The solicitor who has obtained informed consent to acting in a position of conflict cannot assume that the client has waived the duty of disclosure of all matters relevant to the retainer unless this has been expressly spelled out and agreed, or unless it is so obvious

---

[35] See para.3–012 above and *Marks & Spencer v Freshfields* [2004] EWCA Civ 741.
[36] [1993] 4 All E.R. 268 at 273h.

from the circumstances that it must follow by implication from what has been agreed. This passage might be taken to that there is a further requirement in obtaining informed consent, namely that the client would need to agree that the solicitor may be disabled from disclosing to each party the full knowledge which he possesses as to the transaction or may be disabled from giving advice to one party which conflicts with the interests of the other; however, this seems unlikely as if such a requirement arose, then it is hard to see how it could possibly have been satisfied in respect of Mrs Mouat.

4–011   It seems that the Privy Council may have relied upon the judge's finding that Mrs Mouat stated she did not think it was necessary to see another lawyer. The solicitor "formed the impression that she had made her decision and that was the end of the matter", but that could not have involved consent to consequences which had not been explained to Mrs Mouat. And if there had been a failure to make full disclosure it is settled law that it is no defence to show that disclosure would not have affected the beneficiary's decision whether to proceed.[37]

Finally, where one is dealing with relatives, issues of possible undue influence between them usually need consideration. So any formulation in this context requires a word of caution in that regard. Lord Jauncey has been criticised for expressing in unequivocal terms what might usefully have been tempered by reference to undue influence cases.[38]

It is suggested that it is be dangerous to seek to derive principles from *Clark Boyce* which go beyond the principle that there is no rule of law precluding a professional ever from acting on two sides of the same transaction.

C. Does client consent permit acting on opposite sides in litigation or on a takeover?

4–012   Consider the position in contested litigation where a law firm seeks to act on both sides with consent, or a contested takeover. Leaving aside any professional rules which explicitly forbade this, could it be done? If the same lawyers were involved, there would be professional embarrassment problems. But why should not the same firm act with information barriers if the clients consented? The law firm in question might be the firm of

---

[37] *Boardman v Phipps* [1967] 2 A.C. 46; *Regal (Hastings) Ltd v Gulliver* [1967] 2 A.C. 134; *Brickenden v London Loan & Savings* [1934] 3 D.L.R. 465 at 469, PC; *Glennie v McDougall & Cowan Holdings Ltd* [1935] 2 D.L.R. 561 at 579; *Farrington v Rowe McBride & Partners* [1985] 1 N.Z.L.R. 83 at 93; *Estate Realties v Wignall* [1991] 3 N.Z.L.R. 482. It may however be relevant to any claim for damages for breach of fiduciary duty: see *Target Holdings v Redferns* [1996] A.C. 421; *Bristol & West Building Soc v Mothew* [1998] Ch. 1.
[38] See e.g. the passage in the Court of Appeal judgment in *Kenyon-Brown v Desmond Banks* [2000] P.N.L.R. 266 at 344 per Mance L.J.; there is no reference to *Clark Boyce* in the *Kenyon-Brown* judgment in the House of Lords at [2002] 2 A.C. 773.

choice of both sides. The SRA recently carried out an investigation into the conduct of one of the magic circle firms which acted on both sides on a friendly takeover. The law firm had comprehensive signed consents from both clients who each had inhouse lawyers and independent financial advisers who approved the arrangement. Ultimately, the SRA backed off disciplinary proceedings.

English professional rules now[39] prohibit solicitors from doing this.[40] And it may seem highly unlikely that a company involved in a contested takeover would wish to use the other side's advisers. A lawyer discussing an arrangement of this sort would be obliged to flag up to the clients that in a takeover with publicity it would be unlikely to be in the client's interests to be seen to be using the same advisers as the other side. The lawyers face risks too: the more hostile the relationship, the greater the risk that one party might subsequently seek to challenge the informed nature of the consent. But it is suggested that the effect of *Clark Boyce v Mouat* [41] is that the "firm within a firm" principle which enables firms to act in adverse interests with consent provides no common law basis for stating that such a course would be improper. In principle, and subject to professional rules, the same firm is entitled to act with consent for both parties on opposite sides. It can be seen from *Bolkiah* that Lord Millett had in mind that this was permissible:

"...a fiduciary cannot act at the same time both for and against the same client, and his firm is in no better position. A man cannot without the consent of both clients act for one client while his partner is acting for another in the opposite interest...."

This passage makes clear that a fiduciary may with consent act for one client when his partner acts in the opposite interest. To the same effect, Scrutton L.J. said in *Fulwood v Hurley*[42] that informed consent will permit a fiduciary to act in the opposite interest (and not just where there is what is referred to as a potential conflict):

"No agent who has accepted an employment from one principal can in law accept an engagement inconsistent with his duty to the first principal from a second principal unless he makes the fullest disclosure to each principal of his interest and obtains the consent of each principal to the double employment".

---

[39] But not at the time of the previous example.
[40] See 15–004.
[41] [1994] 1 A.C. 428 discussed at 4–016 below.
[42] (1928) 1 K.B. 498 at 502.

And similarly in *Clarke Boyce v Mouat*[43], "Informed consent means consent given in the knowledge that there is a conflict between the parties..."

It has been argued that to act in such circumstances could not be in the best interest of one or both clients and thus to do so would involve a breach of the core obligation of a lawyer. As explained above, there may often be good reasons for the solicitor not to accept both retainers even with consent, and whether it is professionally permissible will depend upon the express provisions of the regulatory rules. But the circumstances would have to be truly extreme before acting with the consent of both parties in circumstances not prohibited by the common law could be regarded as behaviour likely to diminish the trust the public place in the lawyer or the legal profession.

3. Informed consent

A. The caselaw

4–013   If a professional seeks client consent, how much information will he need to give the client before the consent is treated as effective? This is a potentially problematic issue. The cases show that the disclosure must be full and complete. If consent is to be effective, the cases make clear that there must be full disclosure of all material facts, it being insufficient to disclose merely that the fiduciary has an interest or put the client on enquiry.[44] Thus it is said the full nature and extent of the professional's interest must be disclosed.[45] Indeed, the concern that the professional may use his position to gain an advantage at the expense of the client is so great that the extent of the obligation of disclosure in such circumstances has always been treated as extremely strict.

On this basis, any facts which might affect the client's decision whether or not to proceed must be disclosed,[46] which may include any effect which the professional's interest will have on the client's legal rights.[47] The onus

---

[43] [1992] 4 All E.R. 268, 273.
[44] *New Zealand Netherlands Society "Oranje" Incorp v Kuys* [1973] 1 W.L.R. 1126 at 1131–1132, PC; *Dunne v English* (1874) L.R. 18 Eq. 524 at 533; *Tufton v Sperni* [1952] 2 T.L.R. 516; *Tate v Williamson* (1866) L.R. 1 Eq. 528 at 536–537; *Demerara Bauxite Co v Hubbard* [1923] A.C. 673.
[45] *Rothschild v Brookman* (1831) 2 Dow & Cl. 188; *Bagnall v Carlton* (1877) L.R. 6 Ch. D. 371; *Liquidators of Imperial Mercantile Credit Assn. v Coleman and Knight* (1873) 6 L.R. H.L. 189; *Emma Silver Mining v Grant* (1879) L.R. 11 Ch. D. 918; *Gluckstein v Barnes* [1900] A.C. 240; *Bartram and Sons v Lloyd* (1904) 90 T.L.R. 357.
[46] *New Zealand Netherlands Society "Oranje" Incorp v Kuys* [1973] 1 W.L.R. 1126; *Moody v Cox* [1917] 2 Ch. 71 at 80; *Demerara Bauxite v Hubbard* [1923] A.C. 673; *McMaster v Byrne* [1952] 1 All E.R. 1362 at 1367.
[47] e.g. *Boulting v Assn of Cinematograph Television and Allied Technicians* [1963] 2 Q.B. 606 at 636.

of proving adequate disclosure rests on the professional.[48] Partial disclosure is inadequate.[49] Thus where the professional proposes to sell his property to the client he must disclose not merely his interest as vendor but also if the property was purchased recently, the price at which it was acquired and any profit resulting from the sale.[50] It is no defence to show that the client would not or could not have proceeded with the relevant transaction[51] or that disclosure would not have affected the beneficiary's decision whether to proceed.[52]

Although much will depend on the precise facts, such as the knowledge and expertise of the client, and whether he is experienced and familiar with transactions on the relevant market,[53] where the professional has a personal conflict, acting for the client may prove to be a potential minefield. The obligation will be treated as one of uberrimae fidei, utmost good faith.[54]

B. Informed consent: discussion

The problem with the caselaw is that these cases are almost all cases where there is a conflict between the personal interest of the professional and his client's interest. It is in precisely this sort of case that the courts take a hard line. The cases suggest that the burden of disclosure is exceedingly difficult to satisfy. There is almost always scope for alleging that something was not disclosed which might have been if the court is unimpressed by the transaction. But it is interesting to contrast the approach adopted in these authorities with the much more generous approach to the solicitor on the facts in *Clark Boyce*. One might have thought that it would have been easy to make out a case that Mrs Mouat had not been made aware by the solicitor of everything she needed to know in order to give informed consent to him acting for her son as well as herself.

4–014

---

[48] *Rothschild v Brookman* (1831) 2 Dow & Cl. 188; *Dunne v English* [1874] L.R. 18 Eq. 524; *Williams v Scott* [1900] A.C. 499 at 508; *FHR European Ventures LLP v Mankarious*, 2011(Ch), Simon J.
[49] *Bartram and Sons v Lloyd* [1904] 90 T.L.R. 357; *Gluckstein v Barnes* [1900] A.C. 240; *Peek v Gurney* (1873) L.R. 6 H.L. 377; *Arkwright v Newbold* (1881) L.R. 17 Ch. D. 301 at 318.
[50] *Driscoll v Bromley* (1837) 1 Jur. 238; *Kuhlirz v Lambert Brothers Ltd* [1913] 108 L.T. 565 at 568; cf. *Regier v Campbell Stuart* [1939] Ch. 766.
[51] *Boardman v Phipps* [1967] 2 A.C. 46; *Regal (Hastings) Ltd v Gulliver* [1967] 2 A.C. 134.
[52] *Brickenden v London Loan & Savings* [1934] 3 D.L.R. 465 at 469, PC; *Glennie v McDougall & Cowan Holdings Ltd* [1935] 2 D.L.R. 561 at 579; *Farrington v Rowe McBride & Partners* [1985] 1 N.Z.L.R. 83 at 93; *Estate Realties v Wignall* [1991] 3 N.Z.L.R. 482. It may however be relevant to any claim for damages for breach of fiduciary duty: see *Target Holdings v Redferns* [1996] A.C. 421; *Bristol & West Building Soc v Mothew* [1998] Ch. 1.
[53] *Sachs v Spielmann* [1889] 5 T.L.R. 487 at 488; *Lord Norreys v Hodgson* [1897] 13 T.L.R. 421 at 422; *Baring v Stanton* (1876) L.R. 3 Ch. D. 502 at 505; *Stubbs v Slater* [1910] 1 Ch. 632 at 642, 648.
[54] Compare the authorities in insurance contracts on the duty of disclosure to the assured, which is the principal area of law where contracts are treated as uberrimae fidei.

In practice, a client who complains that a professional has acted in a position of conflict may not find it very difficult to overcome a consent defence. The professional asked for consent several months ago and the client gave it. Was the particular problem which has now arisen and has given rise to the complaint mentioned when consent was sought? If not, then why not? If it was known to the professional at the time the consent was sought and not mentioned, the client can complain that full disclosure was not made. If the particular problem had not arisen when consent was sought, then the client will say that circumstances have changed from those which obtained when consent was given, and thus the consent cannot apply in the changed circumstances.

A difficulty which will often arise is: what can the professional tell the client about his other client in order to seek consent? Plainly, he cannot reveal confidential information. The fact that he has been instructed by the other client may be confidential in itself. Certainly, if both clients are competing for the same asset, or business opportunity, it would be quite wrong to disclose anything about one to the other. It may well be a serious breach of confidence merely to disclose the existence of a competing bidder. In some circumstances it will be feasible to ask one client whether you can disclose their existence to the other. But the less you can tell one about the other, the less likely the consent will be effective as informed.

One purpose for the professional of obtaining consent is risk management. Most clients who consent to a solicitor acting in a position of potential client will not subsequently complain for the simple reason that they were asked to give their blessing to the professional acting and know they did so. That is not a legal issue, but a practical one.

4. Undue influence as a restriction on consent

4–015

Undue influence arises in conflicts in two separate respects. Firstly, there are cases where the professional has to consider whether an issue of undue influence may arise between his client and himself. This will only normally arise where the client makes a will in favour of the professional, or there is a personal conflict.[55]

What is more likely is that the professional faces a claim for negligence or breach of fiduciary duty in respect of his acting for two clients between whom there was a conflict, and it is contended that the consent given by one client to the professional acting for both was vitiated by undue influence between the two clients. This will arise most commonly in cases involving husband and wife where the wife gives a legal charge or guarantee.

---

[55] *Demerara Bauxite v Hubbard* [1923] A.C. 673, *McMaster v Byrne* [1952] 1 All E.R. 1362, see 2–027 above.

It is therefore important to be aware as to the circumstances in which a solicitor may be treated as being on notice of undue influence between husband and wife. This area of the law was reviewed by the House of Lords in a series of consolidated appeals in *Royal Bank of Scotland v Etridge (No.2)*.[56] There the House of Lords held that a transaction that is not readily explicable by the relationship of husband and wife remains one of the two elements necessary to give rise to a rebuttable evidential presumption of undue influence, shifting the evidential burden of proof from the party who is alleging undue influence to the party who is denying it.

Etridge was principally concerned with the obligation on banks to satisfy themselves that wives signing away assets in support of their spouse were properly advised. To this end the House of Lords sought to draw a distinction between the circumstances which gave rise to a presumption of undue influence and circumstances which satisfied a lesser requirement, namely whilst not giving rise to a presumption of undue influence in themselves, put a bank on inquiry so that it became obliged to take reasonable steps to satisfy itself that that the wife has taken independent legal advice.[57] In the ordinary course, a wife's guarantee of her husband's business debts was consistent with a normal relationship between spouses and did not without more give rise to a presumption of undue influence. Thus some special circumstances which went beyond that were necessary before the presumption of undue influence arose. However, the lower test of the bank being put on enquiry (which means that the bank must satisfy itself that the wife has had independent legal advice) comes into play where a wife offers to stand surety for her husband's debts, but not where money is being advanced, or has been advanced, to husband and wife jointly, unless the loan is being made for the husband's purposes. Where the wife becomes surety for the debts of herself and her husband, a bank lending money would be on inquiry because as between husband and wife the shareholding interests and the identity of the directors are not a reliable guide to the identity of the persons who actually have the conduct of the company's business.[58]

This formulation principally affects the position of the bank lending money. However, it is relevant to a solicitor's duty because he will need to be alert to the possibility of a conflict between husband and wife. The formulation of the House of Lords will mean that the solicitor who acts for husband and wife is less at risk from a claim that he should have appreciated there was a possibility of undue influence than before. It means that the solicitor is less likely to be faced with the sort of professional negligence actions such as *Kenyon-Brown v Desmond Banks & Co*,[59] which was one

---

[56] [2002] 2 A.C. 773.
[57] [2002] 2 A.C. 733 para.44.
[58] [2002] 2 A.C. 733 para.49.
[59] [2002] 2 A.C. 733 para.352.

of the consolidated appeals heard at the same time as *Etridge*. The solicitor had regularly acted for Mr Kenyon-Brown and two of his companies, in which Mrs Kenyon-Brown had an interest. He also acted less frequently for Mrs Kenyon-Brown in the course of their marriage. Mr Kenyon-Brown borrowed money against a second mortgage on the matrimonial home given by both husband and wife. When the bank required to be assured that the wife had taken legal advice, the solicitor advised the wife whilst at the same time acting for the husband. Thereafter, when indebtedness to the bank grew, the bank required a second mortgage of the holiday home. Again advice was given to both, the solicitor seeing husband and wife together. But in respect of the holiday home, Mrs Kenyon-Brown had in fact gone along with the second mortgage because her husband had (unbeknown to the solicitor) incorrectly told her she would be bankrupted if she did not agree, and the court found she agreed as the result of the undue influence of her husband. The Court of Appeal had held that in these circumstances the solicitor was on notice that there might be undue influence and was negligent in failing to investigate the background and motivation behind Mrs Kenyon-Brown's wish to execute the second mortgage on the holiday home. In allowing the appeal Lord Scott said[60]:

> "A solicitor does not have reason to suspect undue influence simply because he knows a wife has trust and confidence in her husband and is proposing to give a charge over her property to support his financial position. That she is willing to do so is consistent with a normal relationship between spouses".

It followed that although a solicitor who does have reason to suspect undue influence is placed under a duty to the client to try and protect her[61] there was no special duty in the present case.

5. Deemed consent

A. The Kelly decision

4–016   In *Kelly v Cooper*,[62] a certain H. Ross Perot was interested in purchasing property in Bermuda. The same estate agent acted for the sellers of two

---

[60] [2002] 2 A.C. 733 para.373.
[61] *Bank of Montreal v Stuart* [1911] A.C. 120 at 138.
[62] [1993] A.C. 205; Nolan [1994] C.L.J. 34. Ian Brown, "Divided Loyalties in the Law of Agency" (1993) 109 L.Q.R. 206 at 209. See to much the same effect Reynolds, "Agency" [1994] J.B.L. 144 at 149: "the rather brusque reasoning, and the citation of two cases on commercial distributors, seems to deny fiduciary obligations at all and leave everything to express and even implied terms of the contract. Variable as the degree of fiduciary liability

adjoining houses, Vertigo and Caliban. Mr Perot agreed to purchase Vertigo and shortly thereafter agreed to purchase Caliban as well. The owner of Caliban did not know of the purchaser's interest in, and proposed purchase of, Vertigo until after completion of his own sale. He sued the estate agent, refusing to pay the commission and claiming damages on the basis that the agent had a fiduciary obligation to inform him of the Vertigo purchase. The argument was that a purchaser who particularly wanted a pair of houses could expect to pay a premium on the value of two single houses; if he had known the purchaser wanted to buy the pair of houses, that could have enabled him to negotiate the price upwards and was material information for him to be told by the agent.

The Privy Council accepted that the information was material and that this fiduciary duty would, in the normal case, lead to an obligation to disclose the information. But the Privy Council held that there was no breach of duty by the estate agent. Whilst in general terms an agent must not act for competing principals, it is the business of estate agents to act for numerous principals. Where properties are of a similar description, there will be a conflict of interest between the principals each of whom will be concerned to attract potential purchasers to their property rather than that of another. Estate agents must be free to act for competing principals otherwise they will be unable to perform their function.[63] In the light of this rationale, the Privy Council held that the term of the contract between agent and client contained implied terms that the agent would be entitled to sell competing properties and to keep confidential the information obtained from each of his principals. It followed that the implied terms which governed the retainer in contract also shaped the fiduciary obligations owed by the estate agent to the client. The fiduciary obligations were subject to the same limitation as arose by virtue of the implied terms in contract.[64] Fiduciary obligations did not exist in a vacuum; they could vary according to the terms of the retainer.

B. Kelly: discussion

As with *Clark Boyce,* the *Kelly* case was decided prior to *Mothew* and *Bolkiah,* in a court missing Lord Millett at a time when English conflicts law was at a more formative stage, and some of the statements in the decision are difficult to reconcile with subsequent authorities and principles. Moreover, it is unfortunate that *Kelly* came to the Privy Council as an

4–017

---

is, such reasoning cannot be appropriate to agency law in general. And it would be most unfortunate if it was taken as a carte blanche for persons acting in potentially inconsistent capacities in the area of financial services."
[63] Lord Browne-Wilkinson, who gave the Opinion of the Board, at 214. Lord Browne-Wilkinson also was party to the *Bolkiah* decision.
[64] At 215.

appeal from a Bermuda decision where the plaintiff was a litigant in person who had declined to give evidence. It looks as though the issues at the trial were far from well-defined in consequence and one suspects that some of the points that might have been taken had the action been fought afresh were no longer available by the time the matter was heard by the Privy Council.

In *Kelly*, the interests of the two purchasers were perhaps more complementary than conflicting; if Mr Perot was interested in both houses, it was in the interest of both vendors to sell the pair to him. If he had already purchased or agreed to purchase one of the two houses, there was no conflict between the interests of the two vendors because a second sale would not have affected the first sale. The conflict issue was a disclosure of information issue, in that without the consent of the owner of Vertigo, the agent could not properly reveal Mr Perot's interest and agreement to buy Vertigo to the vendor of Caliban. That led to the potential conflict, if it led to a position where the agent was not at liberty to give to the vendor of Caliban all the information within his knowledge material to whether and on what terms he accepted Mr Perot's offer.

Lord Browne-Wilkinson expressed the analysis as implied terms of the contract between agent and the vendor. There is no explanation in the judgment as to the basis of the implication, and no reference in the note of counsel's argument in the law reports to an argument based on implied terms. The implied term in *Kelly* is not consistent with trade custom (being derived from the vendor's knowledge of the means of estate agents doing business). The difficulty with the implied term analysis seems have been apparent to Lord Millett in *Bolkiah* when he "explained" the *Kelly* decision. In his speech in *Bolkiah* he treated the analysis as one of consent or deemed consent. In *Bolkiah* there is no reference in respect of *Kelly* to any implied term. Lord Browne-Wilkinson, who delivered the opinion of the Privy Council in *Kelly*, agreed with the speech of Lord Millett in *Bolkiah* without delivering a separate speech. So one may take it that he agreed with his analysis. Lord Millett said:

> "The large accountancy firms commonly carry out the audit of clients who are in competition with one another. The identity of their audit clients is publicly acknowledged. Their clients are taken to consent to their auditors acting for competing clients though they must of course keep confidential the information obtained from their respective clients. This was the basis on which the Privy Council decided *Kelly v Cooper* in relation to estate agents".[65]

4–018　There was in fact no consent by the vendor of Caliban to the agent acting for the purchaser of Vertigo. There was certainly no consent to the agent

---

[65] The first part of this paragraph is discussed at para.3–011 above.

withholding from him material about the interest of the purchaser in both properties. The vendor was not given the necessary facts on which to make a decision whether to consent. He could not give informed consent, because he did not know information was being withheld or what it was. It is far from clear that if he had been asked to consent he would have done so.

The basis of the decision is the knowledge of the vendor of Caliban that estate agents and in particular the defendant estate agent acted in the course of their business for principals of competing properties. But this is problematic. It is one thing to know that an agent is acting in a particular way. That knowledge is not the same as consenting to it. What happens in the *Kelly* type case if the client happens not to have even the basic knowledge required for the principle to take effect? Certainly, Lord Browne-Wilkinson was at pains to point out the importance of knowledge in *Kelly*,[66] and if the client is under a misapprehension as to the nature of the business of the professional the position would be different.[67] It also means that the term will not be implied (or the consent deemed to have been given) where the vendor does not have such knowledge, which leads to curious and artificial distinctions. It would mean that a vendor who was resident abroad (and thus had no knowledge as to how Bermudan agents operated) would not be subject to the same implied term or give the same consent. In some cases, the client may have no idea whether or not the agent has any competing clients (particular if he is an agent slightly out of his normal locality). There will be cases where an inexperienced customer or perhaps a foreign client will not be aware of even the most basic practices. It seems curious in such circumstances to think that *Kelly* might have been differently decided in the case of a different client.

The Privy Council formulation also throws up a serious problem even on its own facts. When the agent informed Ms Kelly of Mr Perot's first offer, Ms Kelly is recorded as having asked the agent if she thought that Mr Perot would increase the offer.[68] How could the agent, given her obligation as a fiduciary, give a proper answer to this question without revealing her knowledge of Mr Perot's prior offer on Caliban? This conundrum will always present a problem for the professional who acts for two clients. Whether he proceeds on the basis of the sort of implied or deemed consent found in Kelly, or is able to rely upon a limited retainer and thus a limited duty as in Clark Boyce, he will come to grief when the client asks the unexpected "what do you think?" Both the approach adopted in *Kelly* and the alternative formulation in *Bolkiah* are unsatisfactory in many cases where there is not really an underlying conflict between the interests of the two clients, but only a conflict between the fiduciary's obligation loyally to

---

[66] At 214, 215.
[67] If the client had asked the agent whether he took on other properties in the area and the agent said he did not, there would be no reason to imply the terms in *Kelly*.
[68] At 211c.

4–019

deploy all the information he has for the benefit of client A and his duty to keep confidential the information disclosed to him by client B. It will be seen that the courts are continuing to have difficulties in grappling with this problem.[69]

Although *Kelly* was concerned with estate agents, the Privy Council made it clear that the position would be even clearer in respect of stockbrokers who cannot be contractually bound to disclose to any one of their private clients inside information disclosed by the brokers in confidence by a company for which they also act.[70] And according to Lord Millett, it may also apply to auditors, although that passage is somewhat problematic.[71]

Kelly was recently considered by the Supreme Court of New Zealand in *Stevens v Premium Real Estate Ltd*[72]. Premium acted as real estate agents for the vendors of property in a sale to an individual with whom they had an ongoing relationship. As they misled the vendors as to what they said about the vendor, principally that he was buying to sell on rather than as his own residence, the court was able to decide the case on a narrow ground. However, the majority also held that the agents were obliged to disclose information within their knowledge relating to the purchaser likely to be material to the vendor. Whilst recognising that real estate agents will normally act for multiple clients, and will be expected to do so by their clients, in the instant case the information they had about the purchaser could not be described as confidential and thus there was no reason for the usual obligation of an agent to disclose information to be modified. But even if the information was confidential, which was the position in *Kelly*, the majority doubted[73] whether that should lead to a different view as to the obligation of the agent: either the agent should obtain a release from one party or the other in relation to the disclosure or non-disclosure of the information, or cease to act. [74] The majority referred to the "controversial" decision in *Kelly*, held that it was unnecessary to decide whether it should be followed in New Zealand, but suggested that it was not easy to reconcile with established agency law. The comments of the New Zealand Court of Appeal are very much more consistent with other authority than those of the Privy Council in *Kelly*.

---

[69] See Ch.6.
[70] At 214.
[71] See 3–011.
[72] [2009] N.Z.S.C. 15.
[73] [77].
[74] Elias C.J. gave a separate judgment, and suggested that if the usual duties of agents were applied to real estate agents that might be unfairly onerous and that a lower duty might apply; however it was unnecessary to decide the point as the case could be decided on a narrower ground given the misleading information provided by Premium: [27]–[28]

C. Inferred consent, knowledge and unconscionability

Kelly cannot really be explained as a consent case. There is nothing which could be regarded as a contractual agreement. It seems artificial to say in circumstances where the client did not know about the particular conflict, signed no agreement authorising it and objected strongly to it, that he has consented. However, that was the approach of the Privy Council in *Kelly* in treating it as affecting the implied terms of the agreement as well as the fiduciary obligations. It might be suggested that a client who does business with a professional without enquiring as to the nature of the business of the professional should be taken to accept and consent to the professional carrying on business in the manner that other professionals in the same business carry on business and that in these circumstances there would be less room for divergence in the terms to be implied.[75] However, there is not much support in the authorities for such a proposition.[76]

4–020

Kelly is better explained as a "deemed consent" case. There will be cases when it would be wrong to state that the client had expressly consented, but where it cannot be right that he is entitled to complain that the professional acts for more than one client at the same time.

This form of inferred or implied consent arises where the client instructs the professional knowing facts which, in the circumstances, preclude him from complaining that the professional has accepted instructions for a competing client. Consideration of the facts of *Bolkiah* makes the point clear. KPMG were auditors and longstanding accountants of the BIA. When Prince Jefri first instructed KPMG, he knew this. Prince Jefri must have appreciated, therefore, that if a dispute arose between him and his brother, the Sultan would have instructed KPMG on behalf of the BIA. The majority of the Court of Appeal regarded this as relevant to the balancing exercise as to whether to grant the injunction as equitable relief. However, in the House of Lords, Lord Millett said there was no balancing exercise; the point was, as Lord Millett put it, in the circumstances did Prince Jefri give inferred

---

[75] The argument would be that in the absence of enquiry as to the nature of the business of the professional, the officious bystander would assume that the implied terms of the contract would reflect an assumption that the professional was carrying on business in the same essential manner as like professionals.

[76] There are some authorities in the context of stockbrokers that the rules of the Stock Exchange will be incorporated into contracts with those dealing with stockbrokers: *Duncan v Hill* (1873) L.R. 8 Ex. 242 at 248; *Perry v Barnett* (1885) 15 Q.B.D. 338; *Harker v Edwards* (1888) 57 L.J.Q.B. 147; *Smith v Reynolds* (1892) 66 L.T. 808; *Cunliffe-Owen v Teather and Greenwood* [1967] 1 W.L.R. 1421 at 1442; but these are probably based on principles of trade custom rather than on outsiders being required to be bound by such terms. That was the view of the Law Commission in its 1992 Consultative Paper No.124 "Fiduciary Duties and Regulatory Rules". In *Wilkie v Scottish Aviation Ltd* (1956) S.C. 198 it was said "if a person employs a professional man to perform some service and makes no inquiry as to the basis on which the professional man is to be remunerated, it is not unreasonable that he should pay for the services on the usual and customary basis", but this seems to go beyond any usual basis for implication of implied terms.

consent to KPMG acting in the circumstances which arose by instructing them himself with knowledge of their position as auditors and accountants for BIA. On the facts, the House of Lords held that Prince Jefri did give inferred consent to KPMG accepting instructions from BIA on matters that, whilst not a part of their role as auditors, arose out of their role as auditors. That consent did not, however, extend to the further and separate assignment which was the subject of the complaint which was "a very different matter".[77]

4–021   The principle in issue here comes into play through the combination of two factors. First, the knowledge of the client. Secondly, the instruction of the professional with that knowledge. Where the client instructs the professional with knowledge which makes it unconscionable or inequitable for him to be heard to complain about the double employment, the court will treat the matter as one of inferred, implied or deemed consent. In other words (although Lord Millett did not express himself in such terms) it would have been inequitable or unconscionable in the circumstances, for Prince Jefri to complain about KPMG acting in matters which arose out of their role as auditors, but not inequitable for him to complain of KPMG acting in different matters.

So what is the legal principle here? Although it is similar to estoppel, it may be difficult to describe it as estoppel because there is no representation and no convention. It is suggested that the issue is whether it is unconscionable or inequitable for the client to complain in the light of the instruction of the professional with the knowledge that puts in play the unconscionability or inequity. An analogy might be unilateral mistake rectification. If A settles a claim at $100,000 and B agrees knowing that A meant £100,000, A's remedy is not merely rescission of the $100,000 contract but rectification to make the contract one for £100,000. It will be no answer for B to say that he would never have considered settling for £100,000 because it would, given his conduct, be unconscionable for him so to contend.[78] In each case, the combination of knowledge and conduct with that knowledge makes it unconscionable for the defendant to put forward a particular contention. Such a formulation provides a more satisfactory case-based solution to the problem. Once it is appreciated that the issue is whether the client is precluded from complaining, and thus is taken to have consented, it is apparent that knowledge is crucial, and it will be an answer to show that the client did not in fact have the requisite knowledge even though everyone else did. All this does is to emphasise the importance for the professional in having careful terms and conditions in place which set out from the outset the circumstances in which the agent will act for more than one party.

---

[77] [1999] 2 A.C. 222 at 237.
[78] *Commission for the New Towns v Cooper (GB) Ltd* [1995] 2 All E.R. 929, CA per Stuart Smith L.J. with whom Farquharson L.J. agreed.

6. Varying the terms by trade custom

Trade custom is of importance where the relevant parties are in the same business, as will often be the case in transactions involving financial conglomerates. In such cases, trade custom may not only involve antique practices, incorporating them into any relevant contract, but will also incorporate the basic rules on which the business is conducted, including the code of conduct of the profession.

4–022

Trade custom may provide a reason for implication of terms which cut down the fiduciary obligations which would otherwise arise, but this is likely to apply only where client and professional are members of the same trade. Terms may be implied by trade usage where both parties are members of the same trade because the officious bystander would assume that the parties intended to contract with reference to the customs and usages of the trade whether they mentioned them expressly or not. Trade custom may be incorporated into the terms of any contract whether oral or written unless the custom is inconsistent with the express or implied terms of the contract. The custom must be strictly proved; it must be so notorious that everybody in the trade enters into a contract with that usage as an implied term. It must be uniform and have as much certainty as the written contract itself.[79] In trade usage cases, what must be proved is that the custom or practice should be established as a practice having binding effect.[80] A course of conduct observed by a particular class of people may give rise to a custom as may a course of conduct within a particular industry or service.[81] If it is notorious, then it will be treated as an implied term even though the parties or one of them are not aware of it,[82] although the fact that one or both parties are unaware of it may be evidence that the custom cannot be notorious at all. The trade custom must also be reasonable to be binding.[83] Thus the courts have said that the practice of Lloyds brokers acting for both underwriters and assured in respect of claims, though well-established, would not

---

[79] *Nelson v Dahl* [1879] 12 Ch. 568 at 575, Jessel M.R.; see also *Clark v Smallfield* [1861] 4 L.T. 405 per Cockburn C.J.; *Gibson v Small* [1853] 4 H.L. Cas. 333 at 397, per Parke B.; *Wilkins v Wood* [1848] 17 L.J.Q.B. 319 at 320, per Lord Denman C.J.; *Smith v Wilson* (1832) 3 B. & Ad. 728; *Moult v Halliday* [1898] 1 Q.B. 125 at 129, per Channell J.
[80] Rather than a practice followed in a particular commercial community frequently or even habitually as a matter of convenience or commercial exigency: see *General Reinsurance Corp v Forsakringsaktiebolaget Fennia Patria* [1983] Q.B. 856 at 874, per Slade L.J.
[81] In *Robinson v Mollett* (1875) L.R. 7 H.L. 802 the custom of the London tallow market was accepted even though it was peculiar to that market and did not exist on the Liverpool tallow market.
[82] *Grissell v Bristowe* (1868) L.R. 3 C.P. 112 at 128, per Bovill C.J. reversed on the facts (1868) L.R. 4 C.P. 36; *Buckle v Knoop* (1867) L.R. 2 Exch. 125 at 129, per Kelly C.B. affmd (1867) L.R. 2 Exch. 333.
[83] In *Robinson v Mollett* (1875) L.R. 7 H.L. 802 the existence of a custom permitting a tallow broker to deal off his own book was accepted but was held not enforceable as incompatible with the broker's position as an agent.

be upheld on grounds of unreasonableness.[84] There seems no reason why, in an appropriate case the court should not uphold as reasonable a trade custom which limits or modifies fiduciary duties. The parties can so agree by acceptance of terms of engagement of the other. There is no distinction in principle between agreement in accepting terms of engagement and implied agreement by trade custom, and there is Australian authority to support this proposition.[85]

7. Exclusion and restriction of duties by contract

A. Types of clauses which restrict and exclude

4-023   One may divide up clauses which exclude or restrict liability into three types:

(a) *Exclusion clauses*: clauses which seek to exclude or limit liability for breach of duty.
(b) *Duty defining clauses*: clauses which seek to redefine the relationship between fiduciary and beneficiary, thus preventing the accrual of certain fiduciary obligations and rights or delimiting them.
(c) *Disclosure clauses and conflict waiver clauses*: clauses which purport to make generalised advanced disclosures of material interests which the fiduciary may have or of possible conflicts of interest and duty which may arise during the course of the fiduciary relationship. These can be treated together with conflict waiver clauses: it is not necessary that the client is stated to be agreeing to waive conflicts in particular cases or generally. But this category is a generic title for those clauses which disclose the intention of the professional to act in specified circumstances for competing clients.

These clauses serve similar purposes and should be treated as different animals of the same species, rather than different animals. The recent *Citigroup* case focuses on their efficacy.

B. Citigroup—excluding the fiduciary relationship

4-024   The decision of Jacobson J. in the Australian Federal Court in *Australian Securities and Investments Commission v Citigroup Global Markets*

---

[84] *North and South Trust Co v Berkeley* [1971] 1 W.L.R. 470 at 482 and *Anglo-African Merchants v Bayley* [1970] 1 Q.B. 311.
[85] *Jones v Canavan* [1972] 2 N.S.W.L.R. 236.

Australia Pty Ltd[86] considers the legitimacy of excluding fiduciary duties in the retainer letter. The somewhat bizarre facts involved a chapter of accidents. Toll was planning a hostile takeover of Patrick. Toll agreed to retain Citigroup's private side advisory services in addition to its financial and market services. The engagement letter for Citigroup's role as adviser provided that Citigroup be retained solely "as an independent contractor, and not in any other capacity including a fiduciary." It also stated that Citigroup may be providing "financial or other services to other parties with conflicting interests." In fact, Citigroup's public side proprietary trading department worked behind information barriers trading in the securities market on its own account to build up its own capital base. A Citigroup analyst was asked whether a takeover bid for Patrick was likely. He refused to comment. This led to market participants, including Citigroup public side, purchasing Patrick shares in anticipation of a bid, pushing up the price, and thus reducing Toll's room for manoeuvre as a prospective acquirer. One Citigroup trader acquired $6m of Patrick shares. The private side decided to intervene at this stage and, after some discussion as to what course to adopt, simply took the trader aside and told him without explanation "don't buy any more." The trader, apparently thinking that his colleagues were warning him to divest himself of the shares in the light of a likely price fall, divested himself of all his Patrick shares. The market saw this as a further sign Citigroup was preparing a bid on Toll's behalf and the Patrick share price continued to rise. Toll acquired Patrick for $1.8bn more than anticipated. Regulatory proceedings were commenced by the Australian Securities and Investments Commission ("ASIC") in the Federal Court against Citigroup.

Jacobson J. held that there was no existing fiduciary obligation owed by Citigroup until conclusion of the retainer, and thus there was no objection to the clause in the retainer excluding a fiduciary relationship. Thus, although he said that if there had been a fiduciary obligation, he would have held that there was no informed consent because full disclosure was not given as to Citigroup's public and private side arrangements before the retainer was concluded, the action failed.

C. Restrictions on excluding duty in the light of Citigroup

This raises the question in acute form: what restrictions if any are there on a professional excluding his duties. Can a solicitor exclude the fiduciary obligation?

4–025

The starting point is that, as discussed above,[87] a professional will not normally owe fiduciary duties prior to the commencement of the retainer.

---

[86] [2007] F.C.A. 963.
[87] See 2–020.

Nor, it is suggested, will a solicitor owe fiduciary duties in relation to an attempt to vary the terms of a retainer, unless the proposed variation is in substance an attempt to obtain informed consent for something that would be impermissible as a breach of fiduciary duty under the existing retainer.

Moreover, it is common for a solicitor to include in the retainer an exclusion of the duty to disclose confidential information learned in the course of acting for another client. Is such an exclusion valid? It is suggested that it probably is unobjectionable to include such a term in the retainer letter.[88] But if a proposal is made to an existing client in the course of acting to the effect that such a term be agreed, then it seems likely that will be precisely the situation where a fiduciary obligation does arise, and full disclosure must be given so that the consent may be informed.

Does that mean that a solicitor is free, as was Citigroup, to exclude the fiduciary obligation? This seems unlikely. Firstly, this may well involve a breach by the solicitor of a regulatory obligation. The SRA are unlikely to consider that the agreement of a retainer which excludes all liability or which has the effect that the client does not receive the advice that he needs fulfils the solicitor's regulatory obligations.

Secondly, there are circumstances in which the court will not enforce a clause which is inconsistent with the relationship between the parties. In the case of trustees, there are authorities which suggest that there is a minimum core level of duty which cannot be exempted. If a person described as a trustee is exempted from all duties, he is not a trustee. Historically there were restrictions in a trustee's power to exclude liability for wilful default[89] and it is not clear to what extent the authorities on trustees and beneficiaries are relevant to fiduciaries.[90] But a similar principle applies in other areas of the law too. As a matter of contract law, an exemption clause which is so broad and general in scope that to apply it literally would create an absurdity or defeat the main purpose of the contract will be construed so as to be

---

[88] In the 2011 SRA Code, IB (4.4) it is contemplated that the client may consent to non-disclosure or a different form of disclosure.

[89] s.30(1) of the Trustee Act 1925, now repealed by s.40 of the Trustee Act 2000 in relation to trusts entered into after the legislation came into force, provided that a trustee "shall be answerable and accountable only for his own acts, receipts, neglects or defaults ... not for any other loss unless the same happens through his own wilful default." In *Re Vickery* (1931) 1 Ch. 572 at 583-584 Maugham J. held that wilful default did not include gross negligence or conduct short of reckless indifference. This has been criticised; Jones, "Delegation by Trustees: A reappraisal" [1959] 22 M.L.R. 381, 390-393; Stannard; "Wilful Default" [1979] Conv. 345. It is said *Re Vickery* is inconsistent with a line of cases supporting the proposition that trustees cannot be exempted from liability for breach of trust arising from gross negligence or bad faith: *Williams v Hogg* (1861) 5 L.T. 467 at 470; *Pass v Dundas* (1880) 43 L.T. 665; *Wyman v Paterson* [1900] A.C. 271 at 281, 287. There is modern commonwealth authority for the proposition that a trustee cannot be relieved in the trust instrument for loss resulting from his gross negligence: *Re Poche* [1984] 6 D.L.R. (4d) 40 at 55.

[90] In *Re City Equitable Fire Insurance Co* [1925] Ch. 407 at 523-524, a distinction is drawn between trustees and other fiduciaries.

consistent with the main purpose of the contract.[91] This may mean that its literal meaning may not be given effect.[92] In this regard, the different obligations of investment bankers and solicitors may not lead to the same result.

D. Efficacy problems

The following issues may also arise in construing terms of a retainer which exempt or restrict liability:

4–026

(a) *Excluding fraud and deliberate breach*: Fiduciaries like all contracting parties may not exclude themselves from liability for their own fraud.[93] Whether for this purpose fraud includes equitable fraud or deliberate breach of duty is unclear.[94]

(b) *Use of rules of construction*: The rules of construction which limit the ability of a party to exempt liability will also be employed in respect of the construction of clauses exempting a professional from what would otherwise be a breach of duty. Thus clauses are construed *contra proferentem*. There is a presumption that general words will not exclude liability for certain very serious breaches which can only be displaced by clear words.[95] Clear words must be used to exclude liability for negligence unless the clause is wide enough to comprehend negligence and is not susceptible of being interpreted as exempting the contracting party from other forms of liability.[96]

(c) *Unfair Contract Terms Act 1977*: Where it applies, UCTA either prohibits clauses which exclude or restrict liability or subjects them to a reasonableness test. It does not apply to contracts of insurance or to any contract so far as it relates to the creation or

---

[91] See *Chitty on Contracts*, 30th edn. (2008), Vol. 1, para 14–007.
[92] See also Reynolds, "The Law of Agency in Relation to Intermediaries" in *The Regulation of Financial and Capital Markets* (Singapore, 1991), relying on *Robinson v Mollett* (1874) L.R. 7 H.L. 802.
[93] *S. Pearson & Son Ltd v Dublin Corporation* [1907] A.C. 351 at 353, 362. The position may be different if what is in issue is the fraud of one of the servants or agents of the firm rather than one of the partners. Fraud also gives rise to difficult issues as to whether the knowledge of the fraudulent person can be treated as the knowledge of the firm.
[94] Compare the authorities on loss of privilege on grounds that the lawyer was instructed in contemplation of fraud, where the authorities have gradually extended the principle into all sorts of unconscionable conduct: *Barclays Bank v Eustice* [1995] 1 W.L.R. 1238. It was suggested by the Law Commission Consultation Paper No.124, "Fiduciary Duties and Regulatory Rules" (1992) that it would be odd if a court permitted a fiduciary to contract out of unconscionable behaviour or deliberate breach of duty.
[95] See, e.g. *Suisse Atlantique v NV Rotterdamsche Kolen Centrale* [1967] 1 A.C. 361 at 435.
[96] *Canada Steamship v R.* [1952] A.C. 192; *Smith v South Wales Switchgear* [1978] 1 W.L.R. 165.

transfer of securities or any right or interest in securities.[97] The wording of UCTA is geared to exclusions or restrictions of breach of contract, contractual performance and contractual obligations, and thus it may be argued UCTA has no application in respect of the exclusion or restriction of duties which are not contractual in nature but purely fiduciary.[98] Sections 2(2) and 3 of UCTA, which relate to exclusions of liability arising in contract and from negligence falling short of death or personal injury apply to "business liability"[99] which will apply to professionals. They apply where one contracting party deals as consumer[100] or on the other's standard terms of business. Section 2(2) provides that provisions in any contract term or notice which exclude or restrict liability for negligence or exclude the duty giving rise to liability in negligence resulting in loss or injury short of death or personal injury are invalid insofar as the clause does not satisfy the requirement of reasonableness. Section 3 affects provisions whereby one party to the contract seeks as against the other to:

"when himself in breach of contract, exclude or restrict any liability of his in respect of the breach; or

(b) claim to be entitled—
    (i) to render a contractual performance substantially different from that which was reasonably expected of him, or
    (ii) in respect of the whole or any part of his contractual obligation, to render no performance at all".

Similarly, where s.3 applies, the clause will be invalid in so far as it does not satisfy the requirement of reasonableness.

(d) *Unfair Terms in Consumer Contracts Regulations 1999*: The 1999 Regulations give effect to Council Directive 93/13. The 1994 Regulations applied to all relevant contracts made after July 1995 but were revoked and replaced by the 1999 Regulations.[101] The 1999 Regulations apply to pretty well all consumer contracts.[102] In contracts to which the regulations apply, a contractual term which has not been individually negotiated shall be regarded as unfair if,

---

[97] Sch.1, paras 1(a) and (e); see *Micklefield v SAC Technology* [1991] 1 All E.R. 275 at 281.
[98] But see *Smith v Eric S Bush* [1990] 1 A.C. 831, which in analogous circumstances rejects this approach.
[99] Defined in s.1(4).
[100] Defined in s.12.
[101] The main difference is that injunctive relief could under the 1994 Regulations only be obtained by the Director General of Fair Trading but under the 1999 Regulations a number of "qualifying bodies" may apply to the court.
[102] See the discussion in *Chitty on Contracts* 30th edn. (2008) on the 1999 Regulations at 15–044. Another reason for the change from the 1994 to the 1999 Regulations was to increase the ambit of contracts to which the Regulations apply but this has not been achieved in a particularly clear manner.

contrary to the requirement of good faith, it causes a significant imbalance in the parties' rights and obligations arising under the contract, to the detriment of the consumer. Such terms are not binding on the consumer.

E. Duty defining clauses

The professional may be able to satisfy himself that the task he is retained to carry out on behalf of one client is sufficiently narrow that it does not conflict with the obligations owed to another client. This was done successfully in *Clark Boyce v Mouat*.[103] This may be by means of a duty-defining clause, or by less formal means. However, where a limited retainer means that a client does not receive the advice that is required, there are potential regulatory problems for the professional and the court may well look for means of putting the professional in breach of duty. And the limited retainer may have the effect that the client asks the professional questions or seeks advice which go beyond the limited retainer; the court might treat the limited retainer as having been extended by conduct.

4–027

There is very little authority on the attitude of the courts to contractual attempts by a professional to limit his responsibility by defining his duty narrowly. The extent of the duties of a professional depends upon the terms and limits of the retainer and any duty of care to be implied must be related to what he is instructed to do.[104] In *Carradine Properties Ltd v DJ Freeman & Co*[105] Donaldson L.J. said:

> "The precise scope of that duty will depend inter alia upon the extent to which the client appears to need advice. An inexperienced client will need and be entitled to expect a solicitor to take a much broader view of the scope of his retainer and his duties than will be the case with an experienced client".

However, subject to the issues canvassed above, there is no reason in principle why the court should not generally give effect to duty-defining clauses, limiting the retainer, showing no partnership or agency relationship is created, or that a particular duty is excluded.[106] There is some authority

---

[103] See para.4–008 above.
[104] In relation to solicitors, per Oliver J. in *Midland Bank Trust Co v Hett Stubbs & Kemp* (1979) Ch. 384 at 402.
[105] (1982) 126 S.J. 157.
[106] See *Jirna v Mister Donut of Canada* [1975] 1 S.C.R. 2; *Molchan v Omega Oil and Gas* [1988] 1 S.C.R. 348. On this basis clear clauses could abrogate the no profit rules (*Dale v IRC* [1954] A.C. 11 at 27; *Space Investments v Canadian Imperial Bank of Commerce Trust Co* [1986] 1 W.L.R. 1072 at 1074) the self-dealing rule (*Movitex v*

that the strict construction rule does not apply to duty-defining clauses.[107] It may be a nice point in any particular case whether a duty-defining clause is in fact treated as an exclusion clause for the purposes of UCTA.[108]

F. Disclosure clauses and conflicts waiver clauses

4–028   Again, there is a considerable overlap with the prior sections. A professional may obtain informed consent either to conflicts already in existence or to potential future conflicts. There may be a difference between the two cases. Where there is an existing conflict the facts will be known to the professional but not to the client. The professional must be wary of the court subsequently taking the view that the facts disclosed were insufficient for the client to understand the true nature and extent of the conflict, and thus hold that his consent was not an informed consent.[109] Where there is a potential future conflict the professional will normally not know in advance the precise facts which will give rise to the conflict and thus the disclosure or permission which he seeks to give himself in advance will of necessity be in general terms. Here the concern is that the disclosure will be insufficient for the client to understand exactly what he is letting himself in for, and to exactly what conflicts with what consequences he is consenting.

Bulfield [1988] B.C.L.C. 104 at 120) or the disclosure of all relevant information to the customer.
[107] *The Angelia* [1973] 1 W.L.R. 210 at 231, disapproved on another point in *The Nema* [1982] A.C. 724.
[108] In some cases the courts have been unwilling to accept the argument that the clause is only duty defining, and that in consequence it avoids UCTA: see *Phillips Products v Hyland* [1987] 1 W.L.R. 659; *Harris v Wyre Forest DC, Smith v Eric S. Bush* [1990] 1 A.C. 831; *Thompson v T. Lohan (Plant Hire)* [1987] 1 W.L.R. 649; *McGrath v Shah* (1989) 57 P. & C.R. 452; but contra *GH Renton & Co v Palmyra Trading Corp of Panama* [1957] A.C. 149; *The Angelia* [1973] 1 W.L.R. 210.
[109] See the comments on the extent of the duty of disclosure at para.4–002 above.

CHAPTER 5

Perception of impropriety as a test for conflicts

This chapter looks at circumstances in which the classic *Bolkiah* test may be inapplicable.

1. The supervisory jurisdiction over solicitors

A. The court's supervisory role over solicitors and officers of the court

5–001 As we have seen, in *Bolkiah* Lord Millett based the court's jurisdiction to restrain a professional from acting in conflicts cases on the double employment rule in the case of existing client conflicts and confidential information in the case of former client conflicts. These are treated as the only basis of relief. Thus Lord Millett said:

> "It follows that in the case of a former client there is no basis for granting relief if there is no risk of the disclosure or misuse of confidential information".[1]

Other jurisdictions, in particular Australia, have suggested that there is a long standing English common law supervisory jurisdiction which may be exercised over solicitors as officers of the court, and have taken the view that the jurisdiction implicitly survives *Bolkiah* because it could not have been Lord Millett's intention to abolish that jurisdiction *sub silentio*. The

---

[1] [1999] 2 A.C. 222 at 236.

test applied is whether a fair-minded, reasonably informed member of the public would conclude that the proper administration of justice requires that a legal practitioner should be prevented from acting. That jurisdiction has been used to fill what has been seen as a lacuna in the *Bolkiah* principle.

The *Bolkiah* principles are concerned with actual impropriety, not perception of impropriety. In existing client conflicts, the issue is whether there is a potential breach of the fiduciary obligation of loyalty. In former client conflicts, the issue is whether there is a risk of misuse of confidential information. It is no part of the *Bolkiah* investigation to consider whether there is a perception of impropriety. By contrast, in judicial conflicts, appearance and perception is everything. What the supervisory jurisdiction does is to give the court a basis for requiring the solicitor not to act where there is a legitimate basis for concern which falls outside the existing client conflict rule and there is no confidential information relevant. The perception of impropriety test is seen as providing a safeguard where the *Bolkiah* test does not give a remedy. It is at heart the test applied to judicial conflicts[2] although obviously its application is very different. As will be seen, there are already areas where the English court applies this test, or something close to it, to lawyers, although they are exceptional rather than the norm.

5-002 The structure of this chapter will involve examining the Commonwealth jurisprudence which applies and gives effect to this test, then reviewing those areas in which English law already applies, or may apply, a similar test, before reviewing how such a principle could stand with *Bolkiah*.

B. Perception of impropriety before Bolkiah

5-003 The "perception of impropriety" test had some supporters in Commonwealth cases prior to *Bolkiah*. In *Black v Taylor*[3] the New Zealand Court of Appeal refused to permit a solicitor who had for decades acted as solicitor or counsel to members of the Taylor family from acting for the other side, founding itself on the inherent jurisdiction of the court to control its own processes and so prevent a practitioner from acting in relation to litigation in a way which would cause reasonable members of the community to lose confidence in the judicial system. In giving judgment Richardson J. referred to Canadian decisions[4] on whether an appearance of impropriety could justify restraining a practitioner from acting in litigation. In the leading Canadian case, the decision of the Canadian Supreme Court

---

[2] See 11-011.
[3] [1993] 3 N.Z.L.R. 403; see also *Kooky Garments Ltd v Charlton* [1994] N.Z.L.R. 587.
[4] In particular *Everingham v Ontario* (1992) 88 D.L.R. (4th) 755.

in *MacDonald Estate v Martin*,[5] there was an element of appearance of impropriety in the test:

> "The test must be such that the public represented by the reasonably informed person would be satisfied that no use of confidential information would occur".[6]

In Australia, in *Grimwade v Meagher*[7] Mandie J. restrained counsel from acting in a proceeding in order to ensure the due administration of justice and to protect the integrity of the judicial process and in order not only that justice be done but be manifestly and undoubtedly be seen to be done.[8] He considered that a fair-minded reasonably informed member of the public would conclude that the proper administration of justice required that counsel concerned be prevented from appearing in the action because of real risks of lack of objectivity and of conflict of interest and duty. Perception was also relied upon in *D&J Construction Pty Ltd v Head*[9] when Bryson J. said "the spectacle or the appearance that a lawyer can readily change sides is very subversive of the appearance that justice is being done." In *Oceanic v HIH*[10] Austin J. said:

> "In the realm of conflicts of interest and conflicts of duty, the solicitor's duty to the court may not be much different from his or her fiduciary duties to former or present clients. However, the duty to the court tends to be expressed in such a way as to emphasise the public interest in preserving confidence in the administration of justice and therefore in the appearance as well as the reality of independence, and the court's practical approach to its supervisory discretions".[11]

---

[5] (1990) 77 D.L.R. (4d) 249.

[6] At 267. Although Lord Millett cannot be taken as approving this sentence, he made it clear that in general the court was adopting a modified version of the test set out in *MacDonald Estate*.

[7] [1995] 1 V.R. 446.

[8] Australian authority which has focused on public policy as the basis for a decision to require a lawyer not to act includes *Spincode Pty Ltd v Look Software Pty Ltd* [2001] V.S.C.A. 248, see para.5–006 below; *Sent v John Fairfax Publication Pty Ltd* [2002] V.S.C. 429, Nettle J.; *Wan v McDonald* (1991) 33 F.C.R. 491 at 512; *Murray v Macquarie Bank* (1991) 33 F.C.R. 46 at 49; *D&J Constructions Pty Ltd v Clayton Utz* (1987) 9 N.S.W.L.R. 118 at 124-125; *Caruso v Tartaglia* [2002] V.S.C. 91; *Uncle Toby's Co Pty Ltd v Trevor Jones Steel Fabrications Pty Ltd*, Unreported, October 12, 1995; *Lincoln v Holmesglen Institute of TAFE* [1999] F.C.A. 601; *Grey v Alexander* [2000] Australian and New Zealand Conveyancing Reports 386.

[9] (1987) 9 N.S.W.L.R. 118 at 123.

[10] [1999] N.S.W.S.C. 292. The case was decided after *Bolkiah* but argued before *Bolkiah*, so does not refer to it.

[11] At para.48; see *Freuhauf Finance Corp Ltd v Feez Ruthning* [1991] 1 Qd. 558; *Kooky Garments Ltd v Charlton* [1994] 1 N.Z.L.R. 587.

C. Spincode

5-004   In *Spincode Pty Ltd v Look Software Pty Ltd*[12] Brooking J.A. in the Victoria Court of Appeal considered that in *Bolkiah* the citation of authority was inadequate and that the House of Lords had not conducted a sufficiently full review of the caselaw. Although his analysis of *Bolkiah* was obiter (he held in the case before him that there was no reason to doubt the correctness of the judge's view that there was no real risk of misuse of confidential information[13]) his lengthy review makes compelling reading.

Brooking J.A. pointed out that the starting point was the decision of Lord Eldon L.C. in *Earl Cholmondeley v Lord Clinton*.[14] Seymour and Montriou had acted as solicitors for Lord Clinton in the plaintiff's action to recover grant estates in Devon and Cornwall. They dissolved their partnership and Montriou told Lord Clinton he had been appointed as the plaintiff's solicitor. There was evidence that Montriou had acquired confidential information about the estates. Sir Samuel Romilly, for Lord Clinton, said in argument that there were two heads of jurisdiction: irreparable injury that supports an injunction and in addition the general jurisdiction over an officer of the court. Lord Eldon, after consulting all the judges, laid it down that a solicitor, not having been discharged from the relationship of solicitor and client was not at liberty to become solicitor for the opposite party in the same cause. Lord Eldon's brief reasons say nothing about confidential information. Subsequent authorities differ as to whether the decision was in fact based on confidential information[15] but suggest the basis of the decision was that the court would restrain a solicitor from acting for the other side where he had brought the retainer to an end by his own act.[16] In *Rakusen v Ellis Munday and Clarke*,[17] which was considered in some detail in *Bolkiah*, different views were expressed as to the basis of Lord Eldon's decision.[18] However, whatever the basis of *Earl Cholmondeley v Lord Clinton*, Brooking J.A. said since it was established in *Davies v Clough* in

---

[12] [2001] V.S.C.A., 248.
[13] "[I]t would be enough to say that the decision below can be supported, on the most narrow view of the law, as resting on confidential information and its possible misuse. But I take the opportunity of considering the wider question."
[14] (1815) 19 Ves. Jun. 261, 34 E.R. 515.
[15] Lord Eldon referred to the decision in *Beer v Ward* [1821] Jac. 77 at 82 37 E.R. 779 but made no reference to confidential information; however, in *Bricheno v Thorp* [1821] Jac. 300 at 301, 37 E.R. 864 he did suggest confidential information was the basis.
[16] *Johnson v Marriott* (1833) 2 C. & M. 183, 149 E.R. 725; *Griffiths v Griffiths* (1843) 2 Hare 587, 67 E.R. 242.
[17] [1912] 1 Ch. 831.
[18] Cozens Hardy M.R. said Lord Eldon proceeded on the footing that the solicitor could not by discharging himself in the middle of the suit deprive the client of the right which he had by contract of retainer to the services of that solicitor, Fletcher Moulton L.J. referred to the explanations by Lord Eldon of the decision in subsequent cases (themselves inconclusive) and Buckley L.J. treated the decision as dependent on confidential information.

1837[19] it has not been doubted that the court has jurisdiction to restrain solicitors from acting which arose both from risk of irreparable injury and from the court's general jurisdiction over officers of the court. In *Davies v Clough* Shadwell V.C. said:

> "The cases ... appear to afford this general principle, namely, that all Courts may exercise an authority over their own officers as to the propriety of their behaviour; for applications have been repeatedly made to restrain solicitors who had acted for one side from acting on the other, and those applications have failed or succeeded upon their own particular grounds, but never because the Court had no jurisdiction".

So too in *Rakusen*[20] all members of the court spoke of the court's jurisdiction over solicitors. Brooking J.A. recognised that the foundation of Lord Eldon's decision in *Cholmondeley v Clinton* remained a matter of debate. However, Brooking J.A. referred to the court's inherent jurisdiction to remove solicitors as officers of the court without the need for proof of misuse of confidential information as being well-established and drew attention to Commonwealth authorities putting forward an "appearance of impropriety" test, thereby giving support for a jurisdiction over officers of the court not merely based on misuse of confidential information.[21] It had been said that his special position as an officer of the court and the public policy involved in his role meant that his fiduciary obligation could not be treated as at an end merely by the termination of the retainer.[22]

Basing himself on the views of Professor Finn,[23] Brooking J.A. drew attention to the public policy impact if a solicitor was permitted to change sides in the same or a related matter,[24] because of the entitlement of the client to the undivided loyalty of the fiduciary who has been retained. He referred to certain Australian authority which supported a view that the court would

5–005

---

[19] (1837) 8 Sim. 262, 59 E.R. 105.
[20] [1912] 1 Ch. 831.
[21] See 5–003 above.
[22] *Carindale Country Club Estate Pty Ltd v Astill* (1993) 115 A.L.R. 112, FCA. See *Wan v McDonald* (1991) 33 F.C.R. 491 at 512; *Murray v Macquarie Bank* (1991) 33 F.C.R. 46 at 49; *D&J Constructions Pty Ltd v Head* (1987) 9 N.S.W.L.R. 118 at 124–125.
[23] Professor Finn has written extensively on fiduciary duties and conflicts of interest since his book "Fiduciary Obligations" was published in 1977. His influential 1992 article "Fiduciary Law and the Modern Commercial World", published in *Commercial Aspects of Trusts and Fiduciary Obligations* (McKendrick ed.) is particularly interesting for the depth of his analysis on conflicts of interest at a time when the case law both in England and Australia was far less developed than it is now. Finn's terminology is confusing given terms now used because he distinguishes "same matter conflicts" (conflicts between two existing clients in respect of the same matter) and "former client conflicts" (acting on the other side in a same or related matter from a previous retainer) from "separate matter conflicts" (where confidential information from the first retainer is or may be relevant).
[24] See Finn, Fiduciary Obligations (1977); Finn, "Fiduciary Law and the Modern Commercial World", in *Commercial Aspects of Trusts and Fiduciary Obligations* (McKendrick ed., 1992); *Wan v McDonald* (1991) 33 F.C.R. 491 at 513.

for such reason restrain a solicitor from acting on the other side in the same or a related matter irrespective of confidential information issues,[25] Brooking J.A. concluded that Australian law had diverged from English and confidential information was not the sole basis for restraining a solicitor.[26]

D. The supervisory jurisdiction in Australia since Spincode

5–006   Brooking J.A.'s remarks in *Spincode* were obiter. As for the other two judges in the court, Ormiston J.A. decided the case narrowly ("If I had had the luxury of further time to consider them, I may have reached agreement with Brooking J.A. on each of these aspects, but the case came on urgently and was given an expedited hearing") as did Chernov J.A. ("It is not necessary to decide for the purposes of this appeal whether there is an absolute obligation on solicitors not to act against their former clients in the same or substantially the same proceeding, although if I may say so with respect, the learned judgment of Brooking J.A. makes a compelling case for such a view"). The judgment of Brooking J.A. has given rise to much debate in Australia. The weight of authority for a while appeared to be against it.[27] But it now appears to be broadly accepted that there is a parallel jurisdiction to prevent a solicitor from acting pursuant to the court's supervisory jurisdiction.[28] The test to be applied is as follows:

> "... whether a fair-minded, reasonably informed member of the public would conclude that the proper administration of justice requires that a legal practitioner should be prevented from acting, in the interests of the protection of the integrity of the judicial process and the due administration of justice including the appearance of justice".[29]

Why is a supervisory jurisdiction necessary? Is it not sufficient that lawyers may be restrained where there is an existing client conflict or risk of misuse

---

[25] *Macquarie Bank Ltd v Myer* [1994] 1 V.R. 350; *Holdsworth v MR Anderson & Associates Pty Ltd*, Unreported, August 26, 1994, *McVeigh v Linen House Pty Ltd* [1999] 3 V.R. 394.
[26] See also *Flanagan v Pioneer Building Society Ltd* [2002] Q.S.C. 346, para.10 (no obligation of loyalty prevents a solicitor from acting for a former client's opponent in the same or any other matter provided the solicitor did not discharge the client for the purpose of representing the opponent).
[27] Young C.J. followed *Bolkiah* in preference to *Spincode* in *Belan v Casey* [2002] N.S.W.S.C. 58. In *Sent v Fairfax Publication Pty Ltd* [2002] V.S.C. 429 Nettle J. said that if it were necessary (although it does not seem that it was necessary on the case before him), he would follow *Spincode*. In *British and American Tobacco Australia Services Ltd v Blanch* [2004] N.S.W.S.C. 7 Young C.J. in the New South Wales Supreme Court said, whilst following Bolkiah and not Spincode, that there may be some exceptional cases where equity might give relief to a former client against his solicitor who sought to act against him even where the plaintiff could not demonstrate potential misuse of confidential information.
[28] See *Kallinicos v Hunt* [2005] N.S.W.S.C. 1181, and *Asia Pacific Telcom v Optus Network* [2005] N.S.W.S.C. 550, which provide a full citation of cases.
[29] *Kallinicos v Hunt* [2005] N.S.W.S.C. 1181 at para 76.

of confidential information? It is interesting to look at cases in which the Australian courts have made use of this jurisdiction. In *Geelong School Supplies Pty v Dean*[30] a solicitor who had acted for joint venture companies and interests of certain directors was likely to be a material witness at the forthcoming trial of disputes between various interest-holders in the joint venture. Because of his personal involvement, the court took the view that he was unlikely to be in a position to give objective advice, and was injuncted from acting. In *Kallinicos v Hunt*[31] the solicitor who had previously acted for the plaintiff had personal involvement in the transactions which were the subject of the proceeding such as to render it likely that he would be a material witness, and that his conduct would be challenged. It was said that it affected the proper administration of justice for him to be permitted to act. There was no confidential information issue. In *Adam 12 Holdings Pty Ltd v Eat and Drink Pty Ltd*[32] it was far less clear that the solicitor's conduct would be challenged in court, but it was a possibility, and in addition the solicitor had at the relevant time acted for the opposite party. The court held that an informed member of the public would conclude that the solicitor's independent objectivity had been compromised by conflicts between loyalty to his client on the one hand, and his role as a witness and his personal interest in the outcome referable to the possible challenge to his own conduct on the other.[33] In *Surfing Hardware International Holdings v William McCausland (No 3)*[34] the solicitor was not retained but confidential information was imparted to him in anticipation of a possible retainer. Because the solicitor had not been retained, the court applied the test of whether the fair-minded observer would think that the administration of justice required the solicitor not to act, and held, on the basis of undertakings given, to allow the firm to act. It seems unnecessary in this last case to rely on the inherent jurisdiction, as the case could readily have been decided on confidential information principles. Most recently, in *Cleveland Investments Global v Evans*[35] Ward J. held that a lawyer who was retained by the company and accepted instructions to act in relation to a claim made against the company should not be entitled to act against the company in relation to the same time, notwithstanding that the company was unable to identify any relevant confidential information received by the lawyer.

Recent New Zealand authority takes a similar approach. In *Raats v Gascoigne Wicks*[36] Gendall J. followed *Black v Taylor*[37] and emphasised the

---

[30] [2006] F.C.A. 1404.
[31] [2005] N.S.W.S.C. 1181.
[32] [2006] V.S.C. 152.
[33] See also *Styles v O'Brien* [2007] Tas. S.C. 67, where the court applied *Spincode* and *Kallinicos* but thought the complaint without merit on the facts.
[34] [2007] N.S.W.I.R. Comm 64.
[35] [2010] N.S.W.S.C. 567.
[36] [2006] N.Z.H.C. 598.
[37] [1993] 3 N.Z.L.R. 403.

importance of justice being seen to be done and said "it is not just situations of obvious conflict but also the likelihood of perceived conflict to which a practitioner must be alive".[38] There a solicitor was enjoined from acting for one client for whom he had previously acted pursuant to joint instructions against the other, notwithstanding that the joint nature of the instruction prevented there being confidential information between the two. The application was based on the inherent jurisdiction because there was no existing client conflict and, in the circumstances, no risk of misuse of confidential information.

5–007   In Canada, the courts have paid particular regard to the duty of loyalty, with the consequence that a lawyer may not act at the same time for and against the same client even on unrelated matters.[39] A first instance decision in Ontario, *Toddglen Construction Ltd v Concord Adex Developments Corp*[40] goes further and holds as a matter of principle that a law firm cannot be permitted to terminate one retainer in order to avoid the rule on existing client conflicts and to sue what would otherwise be an existing client.[41] The Canadian jurisprudence thus goes well beyond *Bolkiah* in the protection it offers the client or former client.

Thus the cases in which this jurisdiction has arisen are cases outside the norm: where the lawyer has had a longstanding professional relationship with one party but then seeks to act on the other side, where the lawyer will or may be a material witness, or where he is acting against one of two former joint clients on a matter related to the joint retainer.[42]

2. Cases where the English court has adopted an appearance of impropriety test

5–008   In judicial conflicts, the courts have adopted a test which focuses on the perception of impropriety or bias.[43] Where this test is applied, the issue is not whether there is actual impropriety but how the matter would appear to a well-informed fair-minded observer. This test is influenced by art.6 of the European Convention on Human Rights and has been justified with reference to the proper administration of justice. It is therefore more appropriate in circumstances where propriety and appearance are important. This section considers circumstances in which the English courts have applied a similar or analogous test for persons who do not have judicial functions.

---

[38] At [30].
[39] *R. v Neil* (2003) 218 D.L.R. (4th) 671, discussed at 3–014.
[40] November 18, 2003; [2003] Can.LII 9525.
[41] It was not argued that the termination of the retainer in that case was a breach of contract.
[42] Other Australian cases based on the supervisory jurisdiction over solicitors are discussed below within the specific categories discussed.
[43] See Ch.11.

One word of caution is necessary here. There can be said to be a public interest in taking a strict view of the obligations of lawyers because of the importance of the administration of justice. The perception of impropriety is an important part of the public interest justification in every case. Thus one must be careful not to overplay the importance of citations which emphasise "perception" in their reasoning, as the majority are decisions which are in no sense inconsistent with *Bolkiah* principles. But it is wrong to think that the perception of impropriety approach is never applied in this jurisdiction outside the field of judicial conflicts. It has been applied where the nature of the proceedings, and the role of the lawyers, differs from the usual adversarial standpoint, where the lawyer's role is closer to public servant than merely advocate promoting a cause. In such circumstances, although the cases are not always consistent, the courts treat the issue as something close to a judicial conflict and apply a test analogous to the appearance of bias test which applies in that context.

A. The Geveran principle

This line of cases deals with relations between counsel and one of the parties. In *Skjevesland v Geveran Trading Company*[44] the Court of Appeal considered an application to set aside an order on the grounds that counsel should not have acted in consequence of a limited prior acquaintance with the respondent's wife. There was no issue as to confidential information. The Court of Appeal accepted that the circumstances in which an advocate may be restrained by the court from acting as an advocate in litigation were likely to be very exceptional, but recognised that there had been cases in which this might be appropriate even though there was no confidential information in issue: examples were when a pupil barrister met the accused and discussed his case with him then subsequently sat behind the prosecutor,[45] when a husband and wife or other cohabiting partners appeared as advocates against each other in a contested criminal matter,[46] or when the solicitor for the local authority in care proceedings cohabited with the solicitor for the family.[47] Where the trial judge considered that the basis of objection was such as to lead to a real risk that any order of the court will be set aside on appeal, he should accede to an order restraining an advocate from acting.

5–009

Arden L.J., giving the judgment of the court, made clear that this was a highly exceptional course. Such an objection could readily be made for tactical purposes and would cause inconvenience and delay in the proceedings

5–010

---

[44] [2003] 1 All E.R. 1, discussed at 16–009.
[45] *R. v Smith (Winston)* (1975) 61 Cr. App. R. 128, CA (conviction quashed).
[46] *R. v Batt* [1996] Crim. L.R. 910, CA.
[47] *Re L (children) (care proceedings: cohabiting solicitors)* [2001] 1 W.L.R. 100, Wilson J.

as well as undermining the cab-rank rule which applied to barristers. All the circumstances needed to be considered: the nature of the connection, the nature of the proceedings, the extent to which there were relevant conflicts of fact and any special factor affecting the role of the advocate (such as whether he is prosecuting counsel, counsel for a local authority in care proceedings or an amicus curiae). The Court of Appeal was at pains not to limit the circumstances in which this issue might arise. But it did not appear to think that this sort of complaint would often be justified.

B. Family cases

5–011   In England in *T&A (Children)*[48] the Court of Appeal rejected the argument that the *Bolkiah* test did not apply to family proceedings. The solicitor for the guardian ad litem had previously acted for the father in criminal proceedings. The court refused to injunct the solicitor from acting for the guardian. There was no issue as to confidential information and the family court would follow *Bolkiah*. Ward L.J. said that in family cases there was a need to tread carefully but the rule was the same. But a different approach was taken in *Re L*,[49] a case in which the solicitor with the conduct of care proceedings on behalf of a local authority was cohabiting with the solicitor acting for the parents. Wilson J. dismissed the application to preclude the solicitor for the local authority from continuing to act based on confidential information, but allowed it on the basis of apprehension of bias. He said that the power of the local authority in care proceedings placed a premium on the local authority being seen to act impartially. Wilson J. pointed out that whereas civil litigation and criminal trials comprised a confined investigation of past events, the inquiry in care proceedings goes wider and involves an important investigation into all matters relevant to the future life of the child. In that inquiry, the local authority is the arm of the state and has a role of crucial importance. The local authority had to be seen to act impartially and there was a reasonable apprehension that its approach would be coloured by favour towards one party if the solicitor for that party was cohabiting with the solicitor for the local authority having charge of the proceedings. The cohabitation without more grounded apprehension of bias. *In Geveran Trading Company v Skjevesland*[50] the Court of Appeal referred to this case as an example of exceptional circumstances in which a person can be prevented from acting even without confidential information.[51]

Australian authority also supports a more sensitive approach in family

---

[48] [2000] Lloyd's Rep. P.N. 452, CA.
[49] [2001] 1 W.L.R. 100.
[50] [2003] 1 All E.R. 1.
[51] Per Arden L.J., at para.41.

cases. In *Mullins v Rothschild*[52] Cox C.J. in the Tasmanian Supreme Court referred to a line of Australian authority suggesting that particular care was required on solicitors changing sides in the context of family court disputes because of the particular sensitivities there involved and to ensure justice was seen to be done. Frederico J. had said *In the Marriage of Thevenaz*[53] that the court should intervene even if the risk was more theoretical than practical. So too in *Macmillan v Macmillan*[54] the Full Court of the Australian Family Court referred to the "particular sensitivities" necessary in such proceedings. In *Mullins* an attempt was unsuccessfully made to extend this line of authorities into the field of crime, where a solicitor who had previously acted for the defendant to a criminal prosecution was now employed by the office of the prosecutor when the defendant was charged with new offences.

C. Criminal trials

Another area in which bias principles have been applied to others than decision-makers is in criminal prosecutions.[55] In *R. v Smith (Winston)*[56] a pupil barrister met the accused and discussed his case with him and then appeared behind prosecuting counsel at the trial. The Court of Appeal accepted that no confidential information had been divulged but set aside the conviction because it was impossible to say that justice had been seen to be done. Similarly in *R. v Batt*[57] the Court of Appeal considered that it was generally undesirable for a husband or wife or other cohabiting partners to appear as advocates against each other in a contested criminal matter because:

5–012

> "to do so may give rise to the apprehension, however unjustified that may be in any given case, such as the present, that the proper conduct of the case may have been in some way affected by that person or relationship".

It can readily be seen that particular issues arise in criminal trials, and a prosecutor in particular can be expected to behave towards the defendant in a way which would not be required of an advocate in most civil proceedings. Here too the Australian courts have acted similarly. In *Ismail Zai v State of Western Australia,*[58] decided by the Court of Appeal of Western Australia, a

---

[52] [2001] T.A.S.S.C. 76.
[53] [1986] F.L.C. 91–748.
[54] [2000] F.L.C. 93–048.
[55] See also *Mullins v Rothschild* [2001] T.A.S.S.C. 76, Cox C.J., see para.5–011 above.
[56] [1975] 61 Cr. App. R. 128.
[57] [1996] Crim. L.R. 910.
[58] [2007] W.A.S.C.A. 150.

prosecutor had previously represented the appellant in an unrelated matter. The appellant sought to have his conviction quashed on the basis that the prosecutor should not have taken the case. The court dismissed the appeal, stressing that the inherent supervisory jurisdiction of the court was an exceptional one and should be exercised with circumspection and caution, citing *Geveran Trading Company v Skjevesland*[59] as one of the authorities in support of this proposition. The court referred to Australian authority where prosecutors had been restrained from acting where a fair-minded person would conclude that they might not discharge their obligations with appropriate fairness and detachment. In this category were a case in which the prosecutor had made public comments in breach of Bar rules[60] and a case where a prosecutor was not permitted to prosecute a defendant whom he had defended on a rape charge seventeen years before.[61] *Grimwade v Meagher*[62] was a case where a prosecutor had acted against a defendant in two trials, the first aborted and leading to a conviction overturned on appeal in which the court was critical of the conduct of the prosecution case. The prosecutor was injuncted from acting against the defendant in related civil proceedings, the judge considering that a fair-minded observer would consider there was a real risk the lawyer could not act with that objectivity and detachment which the court expects of counsel appearing before it, and that the lawyer could be unable to distinguish or avoid a conflict between his own personal interests (the justification of the conduct of the prosecution) and his duty to his clients in the civil action.

D. Experts

5–013   The position of the expert in court has changed significantly since the CPR came into force in England in 1999. The rules have sought to stress the expert's primary duty to the court rather than his appointor. So the expert wears a number of hats. He may receive confidential information from his appointor which he is not at liberty to disclose. He will prepare drafts of his report which will normally be privileged in the hands of his appointor, and may see other privileged documents. Yet his primary duty is to the court, and he must sign a statement in his report recognising that obligation and the effect of it.[63] Thus he is treated differently from factual witnesses, for example as to whether an expert can be summoned to attend and give evidence on a witness summons if he is or becomes unwilling to do so otherwise: whilst the rule is that in theory an expert

---

[59] [2003] 1 All E.R. 1.
[60] *MG v The Queen* N.S.W.C.C.A. 57.
[61] *R. v Robinson* May 15, 1995, Unreported, Supreme Court of Western Australia.
[62] [1995] 1 V.R. 446.
[63] See CPR r.35.3, PD 35 and *The Ikarian Reefer* [1993] 2 Lloyd's Rep. 68 at 81.

is a compellable witness, that principle is sometimes treated as more theoretical than real.[64]

Since the CPR, the court has asserted much more control over the use of experts and has insisted that experts who do not display the necessary objectivity should not be permitted to give evidence. There are a number of recent cases in which the court refused to permit a party to call an apparently partisan expert as witness. In *Stevens v Gullis*[65] Lord Woolf M.R. said that the expert had shown he had no concept of the CPR requirements and the judge had had no alternative but to bar him from giving evidence in third party proceedings. Having reached that conclusion, the Court of Appeal then barred the same expert from giving evidence in the main proceedings notwithstanding that the parties had consented that he should: it was wrong to impose an inappropriate expert on the judge by consent.[66]

But it does not follow that the test is in any way the same as for judges. In *Field v Leeds CC*[67] Lord Woolf M.R. said that the fact an expert was employed by a party did not automatically disqualify him; it was a matter for the court whether he had the necessary impartiality. In *Admiral Management Services Ltd v Para-Protect Europe Ltd*[68] the court said that a properly qualified expert who understands that his primary duty is to the court is not necessarily disqualified from giving evidence by the fact that he is employed by one of the parties. In *Liverpool Roman Catholic Archdiocesan Trustees Inc v Goldberg (No.3)*[69] Evans-Lombe J. excluded evidence from a Q.C. who was in the same chambers as the defendant who was a friend and colleague and said his "personal sympathies" were with the defendant. This was disapproved by the Court of Appeal in *R. Ex p. Factortame v Secretary of State for Transport (No.2)*.[70] Lord Phillips M.R. said the test for an expert was not to be treated as though it were the same as a test for apparent bias in a judicial tribunal. If an expert had some form of interest in the outcome, that should be made known as soon as possible so the court could decide whether it was appropriate for him to give evidence.

CPR r.35.7 provides for the court to direct that evidence may be given by a single joint expert, and provides that the court has power to choose

5–014

---

[64] *R. v King* [1983] 1 W.L.R. 411; see *Seyfang v Searle* [1973] Q.B. 148 at 152, *Lively v City of Munich* [1976] 1 W.L.R. 1004, *Harmony Shipping v Davis* [1979] 3 All E.R. 177; *Society of Lloyds v Clementson (No.2), The Times*, February 29, 1996; *Burton v Chemical Vessel Services* [1984] C.L.Y. 1525; the court will not permit a party to get out of payment obligations to his expert by serving a witness summons on an expert whose bill has not been paid: *Brown v Bennett, The Times*, November 2, 2000.
[65] [2000] 1 All E.R. 527, CA.
[66] See also *Breeze v Ahmad Storey* [2005] EWCA Civ 223; *Storey v Dorset Community NHS Trust*, Unreported, November 11, 1999; *Anglo Group v Winther Brown & Co*, 72 Con.L.R. 118; *SPE International v Professional Preparation Contractors Ltd* [2002] EWHC 881.
[67] *Independent*, November 16, 1999, CA.
[68] [2002] EWHC 233; [2002] 1 W.L.R. 2722.
[69] [2001] 1 W.L.R. 2337.
[70] [2002] 4 All E.R. 97 at 118, para.69.

that expert. Here the joint expert is not a decision-maker but it is suggested that a test at least closer to the *Magill*[71] test applicable to judicial conflicts will apply in these circumstances, because the court will usually hear from the expert without any party calling any other expert evidence. Thus the joint expert must not attend on one of the parties in the absence of the other.[72]

5–015   The recent decision of Mann J. in *Meat Corporation of Namibia Ltd v Dawn Meats (UK) Ltd*[73] differentiates the position of experts from the *Bolkiah* test. The expert agreed in principle to act for the claimants, then after receiving some preliminary instructions, and without acting on them, decided at that time that that her other commitments precluded her acting as an expert and she withdrew. Subsequently she was instructed by the defendants, and accepted instructions. It was accepted that she had received some confidential information from the claimants. The claimants said she had been told of offers made by the defendants, the reasoning behind the offers, tactics concerning mediation, and the claimant solicitor's view of the litigation. Mann J. distinguished the case from the *Bolkiah* line of authorities. This was not a case where the expert had agreed to do anything; the information was provided in the course of enquiries as to whether the expert would act. It was different from where a solicitor received information in the course of acting for a client. The judge said that the information was "fundamentally uninteresting" and the expert had undertaken not to discuss it. Thus whilst there was no real risk of disclosure, applying the *Bolkiah* test, the judge went on to cite *Harmony Shipping Co SA v Saudi Europe Line Ltd*[74] where a handwriting expert who had fulfilled brief instructions to advise on a document, unwittingly gave advice to the other side, then, realising what had occurred, declined to act for either side, but the party instructing him second served him with a subpoena. Declining to set it aside, Lord Denning M.R. said:

> "The reason is because the Court has a right to every man's evidence. Its primary duty is to ascertain the truth. Neither one side nor the other can debar the Court from ascertaining the truth either by seeing a witness beforehand or by purchasing his evidence or by making communication to him".

Mann J. said that whilst the *Harmony Shipping* case was not directly on point, its thrust was contrary to the application of the *Bolkiah* principle to recusing expert witnesses merely because they are in receipt of confidential

---

[71] *Porter v Magill* [2002] 2 A.C. 357, see 11–011.
[72] *Peet v Mid Kent Healthcare NHS Trust* [2002] 1 W.L.R. 210; *Smith v Stephens*, Unreported, May 15, 2001.
[73] [2011] EWHC 474 (Ch).
[74] [1979] 1 W.L.R. 1380.

information. There the expert was required to give evidence notwithstanding that he had previously acted for one party.

The *Meat Corporation* case is an interesting and unusual example of the courts treating experts differently from advisers. The litigation expert does not owe a fiduciary duty of loyalty to his appointer; it would be inconsistent with the role of the expert to owe such a duty. This book has always argued that the special *Bolkiah* test should be inapplicable where there has been no prior fiduciary relationship.

It was argued in *Meat Corporation* that the expert had effectively contractually bound herself not to act for the defendant.[75] The judge did not find in the defendant's favour on the facts on this point, but if he had, this would have raised the interesting question whether the court would have given effect to such an agreement. In *Harmony Shipping v Davis*[76] Lord Denning M.R. said that there was no property in a witness—otherwise it would be possible to instruct all the experts in a small field and neutralise them all from acting on the other side. In *Harmony Shipping* the court said that if on their proper construction the terms of the consultancy agreement with the expert disabled him subsequently from acting as expert against his former clients, those terms would be unenforceable as contrary to public policy. There, as in *Meat Corporation,* the court refused relief on confidentiality undertakings being given. The English court has also said that it would be contrary to the public interest for an expert to contract that he will not act as an expert witness for the other party.[77]

The Australian case of *Wimmera Industrial Minerals Pty v Iluka Midwest*[78] was less one-sided and raises issues as to whether on the facts the expert will owe the obligations of a fiduciary where his involvement goes beyond merely being an expert in litigation. The plaintiffs to a patent dispute sought to restrain the other party from conferring with or using an expert in subsequent litigation because the expert worked for them in a fiduciary capacity in work culminating in the grant of the patents in suit. The court looked at the expert's contract with the plaintiffs and found no undivided loyalty clause (he had worked as a consultant for the plaintiffs whilst at the same time working for others), and held that he had not been subject to a fiduciary obligation but merely an obligation of confidence.[79]

---

[75] [33].
[76] [1979] 3 All E.R. 177.
[77] *Lilly Icos v Pfizer Ltd* [2000] Intell Prop Digest, Nov 23089. In *EuroAfrica Shipping Lines v Zegluga Polska*, Unreported, December 16, 2003, Tomlinson J. an application was made to stop a Polish lawyer acting as an expert on Polish law because his firm had previously acted for the other party. In the light of uncontradicted evidence that the lawyer in question had no knowledge of the client, the judge dismissed the application.
[78] [2002] F.C.A. 653, Fed Ct Australia.
[79] See e.g. *Hospital Products v US Surgical Corporation* (1984) 156 C.L.R. 41.

E. Liquidators and insolvency practitioners

5–016　　Cases involving liquidators or insolvency practitioners are discussed in chapter 17. In general they have been decided on ordinary principles relating to existing client conflicts of interest. However, insolvency office holders have some quasi-judicial functions and must not only be independent, but be seen to be independent.[80] On this basis, it has been said that "It may also be right to remove a liquidator where the circumstances are such that, through no fault of his own, he is perceived to be—even though he may not be—biased in favour of, say, one or more of the creditors".[81] Similarly a petition to wind up a company has been granted in part on the ground that "in a case in which there is evidence to suggest that assets have been transferred for inadequate value to an associated company, the independent trade creditors should ordinarily be entitled to have the company's affairs investigated by a liquidator who is not merely independent but who can be seen to be independent".[82]

There are a number of Australian cases to similar effect.[83]

In *Bloomsbury International Ltd v Holyoake*[84] partners of Deloittes were appointed administrators of companies by the court. They then, in that capacity, sued the chief executive of the companies for fraud. They obtained a freezing order and search order against him and a number of his personal companies. In fact, Holyoake was a tax client of Deloittes and Deloittes, who had advised him on the tax structure of his assets, had set up his personal companies for him. There was no suggestion that the administrators themselves had received any confidential information, and the information barriers within Deloittes were conspicuously solid. Holyoake sought an order that the court appoint an additional administrator to deal with the part of the administration which related to the proceedings against him on

---

[80] *Re Gordon & Breach Science Publishers Ltd* [1995] 2 B.C.L.C. 189, [1995] BCC 261.
[81] Per Neuberger J. in *AMP Enterprises v Hoffman* [2003] 1 B.C.L.C. 319.
[82] In *Re Palmer Marine Services Ltd* [1986] 1 W.L.R. 573 at 579, per Hoffmann J.
[83] In the South Australian case *Pradhan v Eastside Day Surgery Pty*, [1999] S.A.S.C. 256. G when a partner at Grant Thornton was receiver and manager of a company, then joined Arthur Anderson, whereupon one of his partners became liquidator of the company. It was argued there was a conflict because it is the liquidator's duty is to scrutinise the decisions of the receiver. The court said that the liquidator must be seen to be independent. The Full Court of the Supreme Court of South Australia recognised that if disputed evidence that G had given the applicant confidential advice as to his personal position was proved it would be inappropriate for the liquidator to continue to act. In *Re Club Superstores Australia Pty Ltd* [1993] A.C.S.R. 730 at 734–735 the liquidator was removed because before being appointed liquidator he had given specific advice to a director of the company regarding his own personal affairs including advice as to possible exposure to liability to the liquidator. By contrast, in *Advanced Housing Pty Ltd v Newcastle Classic Devts Pty* [1994] 14 A.C.S.R. 230 at 233–234 it was said to be permissible for the liquidator to have prior involvement with the company if that was not likely to impede him from acting impartially and not likely to give rise to reasonable apprehension on part of a creditor that the liquidator might be so impeded or inhibited.
[84] [2010] EWHC 1150, Ch. Floyd J.

grounds of a conflict of interest. Shortly before the hearing of the application, Deloittes terminated the retainer with Holyoake on notice. Floyd J. held that as there was no real risk of disclosure of confidential information, and the retainer was now at an end, there was no reason to appoint a new administrator.

Bloomsbury differs from almost all cases involving insolvency practitioners in that it was brought by the defendant, not the creditors. There are numerous authorities which emphasise the importance that insolvency practitioners both are, and are seen to be, independent.[85] But in each of these cases the issue was whether the insolvency practitioner was perceived as likely to prefer the interests of one creditor to other creditors. In general, the defendant to litigation brought by the insolvency practitioner should have no choice as to his claimant. Thus in D*eloitte & Touche AG v Johnson*[86] the Privy Council refused an application by a defendant to proceedings brought by the liquidator, holding that the defendant had no legitimate interest in complaining of a conflict of interest which, on analysis, only affected the creditors, because the defendant did not rely on any interest or duty owed to him. The only similar case unearthed by counsel was in the Polly Peck insolvency, where an additional administrator was appointed at the behest of the administrators, partners of Coopers & Lybrand, because Mr Asil Nadir was a client of the firm and it seemed likely they would need to sue him.[87] In *Bloomsbury* the defendant certainly had an interest to protect, and had a right not to be sued by a person whose firm had a fiduciary relationship with him, at least for the duration of that fiduciary relationship. The case was argued on the basis that there was an appearance of bias, although the judge did not find it necessary to consider whether that basis of the application added anything.

F. Other cases

Although art.6 only applies to decision-makers (and thus to judges, juries and tribunals but not to the categories referred to above) it is possible to envisage other types of case where the court will adopt a test close to the perception of impropriety test. An amicus, or friend of the court, is a possible example where the court will apply a test closer to that applicable for judicial conflicts. In *Skjevesland v Geveran Trading Corporation*[88] the

5–017

---

[85] *Re Gordon & Breach* [1995] 2 B.C.L.C. 189, 199, per Robert Walker J., *AMP Enterprises v Hoffmann* [2003] 1 B.C.L.C. 319 at [24][25], per Neuberger J; *Re Lowerstoft* 1986 B.C.L.C. 81, 84, per Hoffmann J., *Re Palmer Marine Surveys* [1986] B.C.L.C. 106, 111, per Hoffmann J.; *Doffman v Isaacs*, September 13, 2011, Unreported, Proudman J.
[86] [2000] 1 B.C.L.C. 485 PC.
[87] The actual decision of Morritt J. on 25 October 1990 is Unreported and seems untraceable but it is referred to in *Re Maxwell Communication Corp* [1992] B.C.C. 372, 374–5.
[88] [2003] 1 All E.R. 1.

Court of Appeal recognised that there were exceptional cases of various types where the court would restrain an advocate from appearing even in the absence of confidential information.

3. Does the court in this jurisdiction retain an inherent jurisdiction to prevent solicitors from acting?

5–018   The starting point is that Lord Millett's speech in *Bolkiah* is the basis of the law on conflicts of interest in this jurisdiction. Lord Millett says nothing about the court's inherent jurisdiction over solicitors and makes clear that the test in relation to conflicts of interest is based simply on existing client conflicts and misuse of confidential information. It is tempting to take the view, therefore, that there is no room in this jurisdiction for this additional jurisdiction. However, the position is far from straightforward.

In *Bolkiah*, it does not appear that *Cholmondeley v Clinton* was cited in the House of Lords.[89] In his judgment in the Court of Appeal, Waller L.J. made reference to it, treating it as laying down a rule at the time it was decided to the effect that a solicitor could not give up one party and then act for the other in any circumstances, although Waller L.J. did not suggest that such a rule was still the law. It was argued for *Prince Jefri*, with reference to Commonwealth and US as well as English authority,[90] that a solicitor must not accept a retainer to act adversely to a former client in a matter closely related to the work he did for that client, irrespective of confidential information, although counsel appear to have resiled from that position in the course of argument.[91] Lord Millett expressly rejected a rule which precluded a solicitor (without consent) from acting on a retainer adverse to a former client on a related matter, notwithstanding citation of authority which supported such a rule, and thus must be taken to have rejected the views expressed in the writings of Professor Finn which had also supported such a principle: "it follows that in the case of a former client there is no basis for granting relief if there is no risk of the disclosure or misuse of confidential information".[92]

Having said that, it is apparent from the analysis in this chapter that

---

[89] However, *Rakusen*, which did refer to it, and which considers the basis of the court's jurisdiction, was considered in detail.
[90] *D&J Constructions Pty v Head* (1987) 9 N.S.W.L.R. 118; *Mallesons Stephen Jacques v KPMG Peat Marwick* [1990] 4 W.A.R. 357; *Carindale Country Club Estate Pty Ltd v Astill* (1993) 115 A.L.R. 112, *Russell McVeagh McKenzie Bartleet v Tower Corporation*, [1998] 3 N.Z.L.R. 641; *Weglarz v Bruck* (1984) 470 N.E.2d 21; *Tekni-Plex Inc v Meyer and Landis* (1995) 632 N.Y.S.2d 565; *Solow v WR Grace & Co* (1993) 597 N.Y.S.2d 361; *United States Ex rel Cherry Hill Convalescent Centre Inc v Healthcare Rehab System Inc* (1997) 994 F. Supp. 244.
[91] [1999] 2 A.C. 222 at 234.
[92] [1999] 2 A.C. 222 at 236.

English law does already recognise that the *Bolkiah* principle is not applicable in all cases and there is an exceptional principle where the courts will grant relief to prevent a lawyer acting notwithstanding that there is no existing client conflict and there is no risk of misuse of confidential information. *Geveran* makes clear that the circumstances in which that will arise, albeit exceptional, are not limited. So it is not right to take Lord Millett's dictum as definitive. There is a range of cases, many of which are discussed in *Geveran*, which cannot be explained on *Bolkiah* principles, and where in this jurisdiction a test very similar to the fair-minded observer test is already applied. The cases tend to occur where the administration of justice requires advocates to be seen to have an element of impartiality. Family cases and prosecutors are examples where there is authority already. Other cases do not (or do not necessarily) involve solicitors: insolvency practitioners are examples.

Firstly, whilst the Australian and New Zealand courts have followed *Bolkiah*, both those respected jurisdictions have recognised that the *Bolkiah* principles are insufficient to cover all cases and a residual power is required for cases where the legitimate concern as to the lawyer acting is not resolved by an application of *Bolkiah* principles. The decisions to that effect cannot be lightly disregarded. 5–019

Secondly, there is English common law authority that the court has traditionally exercised a supervisory jurisdiction over solicitors. Lord Millett neither refers to this, nor were any of the authorities cited to him. Can it have been his intention to do away with a jurisdiction exercised historically by the court over its officers?

Thirdly, *Bolkiah* was about forensic accountants, not solicitors. So there would have been no basis on which the court's jurisdiction over solicitors was relevant to the determination. It is true that Lord Millett's speech goes further than was necessary for the decision, and what he says, which seems inconsistent with the exercise of such a jurisdiction, is important authority. Moreover, he treated the position of forensic accounts as the same as that of solicitors so far as material to the decision. But in a case concerned with forensic accountants it is perhaps not surprising that neither counsel nor the court were focusing on the historic supervisory jurisdiction of the court over solicitors.

Fourthly, in the vast majority of cases, it is unnecessary to invoke the jurisdiction over solicitors to deal with the issue before the court. The rules on existing client conflicts and confidential information are normally sufficient to protect litigants. So it is only in exceptional cases which do not fall within these categories that it may be appropriate to look at the additional jurisdiction. *Bolkiah* was a confidential information case, so (quite apart from it being concerned with accountants) the problem did not arise.

Commonwealth jurisprudence recognises such a jurisdiction and gives effect to it where the fair-minded observer would think that the administration of justice required the solicitor not to act. The Australian courts have not limited the jurisdiction to the types of case identified above but treated 5–020 it as giving rise to a broad-based power. They have sought to use the jurisdiction in cases where the solicitor is likely to be a material witness at the trial. Here the rationale appears to be, at least in part, that the fair-minded observer would think the solicitor's personal interest in justifying his position could conflict with his professional duty to do his best for his client. A second type of case where the jurisdiction may be exercised is where the solicitor has previously acted for the other side in a related matter but the party complaining is not able to point to the risk of misuse of confidential information. An example is where the solicitor acts for joint clients (where there can be no confidential information or privilege between the clients) and now seeks to act for one of the two former clients against the other. A third type of case is where the solicitor previously acted on a related matter but not for the same party—for example, where the solicitor previously acted for a subsidiary and is now asked to act against the parent. Cases where the solicitor has "changed sides" are particularly suitable for a wider jurisdiction than *Bolkiah* provides.

The danger with such a jurisdiction is that it is easy for it to become unprincipled. If a lawyer is to be injuncted, not because he is likely to have a clash of fiduciary duties, nor because there is a risk of disclosure of confidential information, but because an observer might consider that it would affect the administration of justice if he were permitted to act, one needs to ask the question: why would the observer so think if there was no risk of breach of fiduciary duty or disclosure of confidential information? Where one is dealing with decision-makers, such as judges or juries, then public perception is vital, which is why the test is based on apprehension of bias rather than bias itself. Where the advocates can be seen to be particularly closely identified with the judicial process, as is the position of the prosecutor in a criminal trial, then it is easy to understand the extension of the principle. But outside this, care must be taken if a test is based on perception rather than reality.

In *Winters v Mishcon de Reya*[93] Henderson J. reviewed the equivalent passage in the previous edition of this book, and was asked to hold that even when a confidential information case failed, the English court had a residual inherent jurisdiction to prevent a solicitor from acting. He said[94] that he was prepared to accept without deciding that such a jurisdiction existed but would not exercise it on the facts in any event, in relation to what appears to have been a hopeless case.

5–021
In conclusion, it is clear that *Bolkiah* provides an inadequate foundation on which to decide all cases. It is unsatisfactory that at present those rare cases where there is a legitimate problem with the lawyer, or other professional, acting but which cannot be decided as falling within *Bolkiah* principles have no guiding principle which determines them. Moreover, it can

---

[93] [2008] EWHC 2419 Ch.
[94] [94].

legitimately be argued that an extension of the *Bolkiah* jurisdiction in the manner done in Australia would be beneficial, so long as the jurisdiction is kept on a firm footing and not allowed to be used as a substitute for proper analysis of the alleged conflict. Cases where the solicitor has previously acted on a related matter are particularly suitable and inadequately covered in the *Bolkiah* test.

CHAPTER 6

The Obligation to Disclose Information

1. The obligation to transmit information learned from one client to another

A. The obligation to disclose information relevant to the retainer

6–001   The professional is instructed for client A and client B. He learns some information in the course of acting for B which would obviously be of interest to A. When does he have an obligation to pass it on to A?

The obligation to disclose information has long been seen as a fundamental part of the professional's obligation to a client. *Moody v Cox and Hatt*[1] involved the sale of a public house and cottages from the defendants, who were also solicitors and acted both for the claimant and as solicitors for the trust. Cox conducted the negotiations on behalf of the trust but failed to reveal the existence of certain valuations which would affect the price. Scrutton L.J said in *Moody v Cox & Hatt*[2]:

> "... it is said that he could not disclose that information consistently with his duty to his other clients, the cestuis que trust. It may be that a solicitor who tries to act for both parties puts himself in such a position that he must be liable to one or the other whatever he does. The case has been put of a solicitor acting for vendor and purchaser who knows of a flaw in the title by reason of his acting for the vendor, and who, if he

---

[1] [1917] 2 Ch. 71.
[2] [1917] 2 Ch. 71 at 91.

discloses that flaw in the title which he knows as acting for the vendor, may be liable to an action by his vendor, and who, if he does not disclose the flaw in the title, may be liable to an action by the purchaser for not doing his duty as solicitor for him. It will be his fault for mixing himself up with a transaction in which he has two entirely inconsistent interests . . .".

Similarly in *Spector v Ageda*[3] Megarry J. stated:

"A solicitor must put at his client's disposal not only his skill but also his knowledge, so far as is relevant; and if he is unwilling to reveal his knowledge to his client, he should not act for him. What he cannot do is act for the client and at the same time withhold from him any relevant knowledge that he has".

So too the Law Commission:

6–002

"A customer is entitled to a duty of loyalty from a firm, which requires it to put at its customer's disposal all information in its possession which is relevant to the discharge of the obligations that it has assumed".[4]

In *Boyce v Rendells*[5] Lawton L.J. accepted the following proposition:

". . . if, in the course of taking instructions a professional man like a land agent or a solicitor learns of facts which reveal to him as a professional man the existence of obvious risks, then he should do more than merely advise within the strict limits of his retainer. He should call attention to and advise upon the risks".

There is plenty of other authority to the same effect. The position was expressed similarly by Donaldson J. in *North & South Trust v Berkeley*.[6] Professor Finn referred to *Spector v Ageda* as authority for the proposition that an adviser cannot justify a failure to make relevant information available to a client because that information is subject to a duty of secrecy to a third party.[7] The decision in *Kelly v Cooper*[8] was premised on the finding that the agent would under the general law have had a duty to disclose Mr Perot's interest in Vertigo to the owner of Caliban. When Lord Millett in *Bolkiah* sought to explain *Kelly v Cooper*, he says nothing which casts

---

[3] [1973] Ch. 30 at 48.
[4] Law Commission Consultation Paper No.124, "Fiduciary Duties and Regulatory Rules" (1992), p.161.
[5] (1983) 268 E.G. 268 at 272.
[6] [1971] 1 W.L.R. 470.
[7] *Commercial Aspects of Trusts and Fiduciary Obligations* (McKendrick ed., 1992), p.31.
[8] See para.4–016 above.

B. Is the obligation to disclose information part of the fiduciary obligation of a professional?

6–003   The approach of Millett L.J. in *Mothew* was to differentiate between the fiduciary and non-fiduciary duties of the professional, and only to hold that a professional was in breach of fiduciary duty where his conduct engaged the core fiduciary obligation of loyalty. Thus obligations such as of reasonable skill and care may be breached by a fiduciary but without incurring liability for breach of fiduciary duty.

We have also seen that fiduciary duties are proscriptive not prescriptive. Thus in *Breen v Williams*[9] Mrs Breen sought to obtain medical records from her doctor. She alleged that by reason of his fiduciary duty, the doctor had a positive duty to reveal the records to his patient. The High Court of Australia, whilst declining to hold that the doctor owed a fiduciary obligation at all to the patient, (a view that has always been accepted in this jurisdiction)[10] went on to say that fiduciary duties were proscriptive not prescriptive; in other words, they identified what a fiduciary may not do (no conflict, no profit) rather than what the fiduciary should do. The point was put by Gaudron and McHugh L.J.J.[11]:

> "The law of fiduciary duty rests not so much on morality or conscience as on the acceptance of the twin implications of the biblical injunction that "no man can serve two masters." Duty and self-interest, like God and mammon, make inconsistent calls on the faithful. Equity solves the problem in a practical way by insisting that fiduciaries give undivided loyalty to the persons whom they serve".[12]

English authority is consistent with the Australian approach.[13]

It might be said that a positive obligation to disclose is a prescriptive duty, and thus cannot be regarded as a fiduciary duty. But certainly there are authorities which treat the duty as a fiduciary one. The point has usually

---

[9] [1996] 186 C.L.R. 71, see 2–010
[10] See *R. v Mid Glamorgan FHSA Ex p. Martin*, (1993), *Times*, 2 June.
[11] At 108.
[12] The High Court of Australia reaffirmed the proscriptive nature of fiduciary duties in *Pilmer v Duke Group Ltd*, [2001] 207 C.L.R. 165.
[13] See 2–011, *AG v Blake* [1998] Ch. 439, 454 CA (not discussed in HL) and Lord Millett writing in *Equity's Place in the Law of Commerce* 1998 14 L.Q.R. 214. Canada has never accepted this view of fiduciary obligations, but has always treated them as prescriptive. *Breen* considered and declined to follow the decision of the Canadian Supreme Court in *McInerny v McDonald* [1992] 2 S.C.R. 138.

arisen in the context as to whether a senior employee or a director has an obligation to disclose his own misconduct. This point, and the decision of the Court of Appeal in *Item Software v Fassihi*[14] is discussed at 2–011. The assumption here is that to the extent there is a disclosure obligation, it arises as an attribute of a fiduciary obligation.[15]

The explanation seems to be that whether the duty is prescriptive or proscriptive may depend on how it is fashioned. It can best be regarded not as a *disclosure* obligation but as a negative obligation not to *withold*: it would be disloyal to hold back or keep from the client any information which is relevant to the retainer.

It is thus suggested that in the normal course, a breach of the disclosure obligation is a failure to comply with an obligation of loyalty. The professional who acts for a client but nevertheless holds back information known to him is disloyal to his client. But it may also be an express or implied term of the retainer: it may be that if the professional unintentionally withheld information, then there would be no breach of fiduciary duty, but there might be a breach of a contractual obligation.

2. The mortgage lending cases

A. Mortgage Express

A line of mortgage lending cases in the 1990s caused many to question the ambit of the duty to disclose information. Increasingly, these cases are seen as turning on the particular circumstances of mortgage lending, where the solicitor, who may be a solicitor who has acted previously for the borrower in relation to his family affairs, and thus may have particular knowledge of the borrower, acts for borrower and lender with the consent of both, under closely-defined rules set by mortgage lenders.

6–004

In *Mortgage Express Ltd v Bowerman & Partners*[16] the solicitor acting for mortgage lender and borrower became aware that the vendor was himself purchasing the property at a price significantly lower than the valuation before simultaneously selling it on to the purchaser. He was held in breach of duty in not communicating the information to the mortgage lender. Here the solicitor had the implied authority of the borrower to pass on the information to the mortgage lender: the information appeared on the borrower's documents of title and a solicitor has the implied authority of his client to communicate all documents of title to the mortgagee's solicitor.[17] Sir

---

[14] [2005] 2 B.C.L.C. 91.
[15] See also *University of Nottingham v Fishel* [2000] I.C.R. 1462 discussed at 2–014.
[16] [1996] 2 All E.R. 836 at 842.
[17] [1996] 2 All E.R. 836 at 845, per Millett L.J.

Thomas Bingham M.R. said that when a solicitor acting for purchaser and lender receives information common to both, the question whether he should pass it on to one client or the other or both or neither depends on the relevant interest of each client which the solicitor is engaged to serve.[18] Here the solicitor was not engaged to advise the mortgage lender on the commercial merits of the transaction. His obligation was to investigate and perfect title. But anything which had a material bearing on the valuation of the lender's security or some other ingredient of the lending decision was something the lender needed to be advised on. So far so good. But Sir Thomas Bingham M.R. expressed the principle in what suggests only a limited obligation:

> "A client cannot expect a solicitor to undertake work he has not asked him to do and will not wish to pay him for such work, but if in the course of doing the work he is instructed to do the solicitor comes into possession of information which is not confidential and which is clearly of potential significance to the client. I think that the client could reasonably expect the solicitor to pass it on, and feel understandably aggrieved if he did not".[19]

He concluded:

> "... if in the course of investigating title, the solicitor discovers facts which a reasonably competent solicitor would realise might have a material bearing on the valuation of the lender's security or some other ingredient of the lending decision, then it is his duty to point this out".

Millett L.J. decided the appeal on the narrower ground that the information was material and the solicitor had implied authority to communicate it, so he was in breach of duty. Schiemann L.J. agreed with both judgments.[20]

B. Duties specific to mortgage lending

6–005   There have been a number of authorities on the precise obligation of disclosure which lies on the solicitor for the borrower. In general, they turn

---

[18] [1996] 2 All E.R. 836 at 841.
[19] [1996] 2 All E.R. 836, per Bingham M.R. at 842; Schiemann L.J. agreed with Bingham M.R.; Millett L.J. did not find it necessary to deal with the point.
[20] In the subsequent case of *Bristol & West Building Society v May May Merrimans* [1996] 2 All E.R. 801 Chadwick J. drew attention to two features on the facts relevant to the decision in *Mortgage Express*. First, the instruction to the solicitor provided "these instructions are not intended to be exhaustive and in no way limit the normal duties of a solicitor when acting for a mortgagee". Secondly, the valuation report disclosing the mortgage lender's valuation on which the lender was relying was enclosed with the initial letter of instructions.

on the terms of the precise instructions of the mortgage lender. In *Mortgage Express* the instructions to the solicitor from the mortgage lender were open-ended in relation to the duty of disclosure. But in most cases, there are specific instructions from the mortgage lender. In *National Home Loans v Giffen Couch & Archer*[21] the Court of Appeal held that when a solicitor in the course of acting for both borrower and lender in a remortgage transaction, discovered information casting doubt on the borrower's ability to repay the loan, he was not under a duty to report that information to the lender unless his instructions required him to do so. Peter Gibson L.J. pointed out that the experienced mortgage lender had provided instructions as to the particular matters on which it wanted to be informed[22]; in such circumstances there was limited room for a duty to inform as to any other matters. The Court of Appeal drew a distinction between the obligations of the solicitor relating to perfecting security, which was the basis of the retainer, and obligations going to the worth of the personal covenant, which were not part of the retainer.[23]

Giffen Couch & Archer considers *Mortgage Express* in some detail, and suggests that when Bingham M.R. said that if in the course of investigating title, the solicitor discovers facts which a reasonably competent solicitor would realise might have a material bearing on the valuation of the lender's security, then there is a duty to disclose, but that when the facts have a material bearing on "some other ingredient of the lending decision" Bingham M.R. went too far in suggesting that the solicitor owes a duty to point this out. Thus in *Birmingham Midshires Mortgage Services Ltd v David Parry*[24] the Court of Appeal treated *Giffen Couch & Archer* as authority for the proposition that it is not normally part of a solicitor's duty to make a report or to supply information about a borrower's financial position. There is also material in *Giffen Couch & Archer* which suggests that in the usual mortgage lending case, the clear instructions as to the disclosure required by the mortgage lender may operate as an implied exclusion of the duty to disclose other information. But these points seem confined to the narrow issue of mortgage lending.[25]

---

[21] [1997] 3 All E.R. 808.
[22] Although Peter Gibson L.J. refers to the obligation of the solicitor to "advise" the lender, the expression is used in the sense of "inform" the lender of matters the lender had required to be informed on: the retainer was again not a retainer to give advice on the transaction.
[23] The same distinction was drawn in *Maes Finance v Sharp & Partners*, July 27, 1999, H.H.J. Bowsher Q.C.
[24] [1997] E.G.C.S. 150.
[25] The best analysis of the law in relation to the duty of disclosure in mortgage lending is in Flenley & Leech, *Solicitors' Negligence and Liability* 2nd edn, 10.45ff.

C. A wider principle?

6–006 The more significant question for a work on conflicts of interest is whether anything in these cases undermines the principle that a solicitor is obliged to disclose all information within his knowledge relevant to the retainer, whether learned in the course of acting or otherwise, and if so, whether the principle applies outside mortgage lending.

Mortgage Express has certainly been seen as giving rise to such a principle. But if Bingham M.R. was suggesting in *Mortgage Express* that a solicitor's usual obligation does not include an obligation to pass on information learned other than in the course of acting on the retainer, he cited no authority to that effect.[26] The law reports record judgment being given the day after the argument commenced.[27] Sir Thomas Bingham M.R. appears to have been dealing with the argument that a solicitor fulfils his duty in an execution-only case merely by effecting execution. Unless therefore the information affects the execution, why should the solicitor have any wider obligation to pass on information to the lender when he can fulfil his execution obligations without that? Seen this way, Bingham M.R.'s comments are not a limiting principle, as they have often been interpreted; they are an expansionary principle. What he is saying is that even in an execution-only transaction there is an obligation which goes beyond the execution. It is clear that this is what he has in mind because of the word "but":

> "A client cannot expect a solicitor to undertake work he has not asked him to do and will not wish to pay him for such work, but[28] if in the course of doing the work he is instructed to do the solicitor comes into possession of information which is not confidential and which is clearly of potential significance to the client, I think that the client could reasonably expect the solicitor to pass it on and feel understandably aggrieved if he did not".

6–007 It was a series of subsequent decisions which led to the view that *Mortgage Express* was authority for a wider principle. Chadwick J. in *Bristol & West*

---

[26] He referred to two authorities but said he did not derive much assistance from them. He cited *Scholes v Brook* (1891) 63 L.T. 837 but as he recognised that took the matter little further. No reference is made to *Kelly v Cooper* ([1993] A.C. 205, see para.6–004 above) in the judgments in Mortgage Express. There the Privy Council held that the information was material (at 213) and although it cannot be said that they decided that there would have been an obligation of disclosure in a case where the terms they implied on the facts before them were not present, that certainly appears the premise on which they proceeded, referring to Bowstead on *Agency* as putting forward the proposition that "an agent is in general under a duty to keep his principal informed about matters which are of his concern" (which expresses the point widely) and *North and South Trust v Berkeley* [1971] 1 W.L.R. 470.
[27] So either the argument continued over the second day and judgment was extempore or it was reserved only overnight.
[28] Authors' italics.

Building Society v Baden Barnes Groves[29] understood what Bingham M.R. had said much more widely:

> "Where solicitors are instructed to act for a lender in circumstances in which they are already the solicitors of the borrower, it is likely that those solicitors will know much more about the borrower's affairs than solicitors acting solely for the lender would ever know or discover in the course of carrying out the work which the lender had instructed them to do. To take two simple examples the borrower's solicitors may well know, through having acted for the borrower over the course of years, that the borrower is committed to make payments to a former wife under a matrimonial order; or may well know that the borrower has entered into arrangements to satisfy his creditors by instalment payments short of a formal voluntary arrangement. Both matters would undoubtedly be information which any reasonably competent solicitor would realise might be of significance to a building society as a prospective lender. Indeed, they are facts that a building society might be expected to attempt to ascertain by the questions put to the prospective borrower on an application form. But those matters are not matters which a solicitor acting solely for the lender would be likely to ascertain in the course of doing the work which, as solicitor for the lender, he was instructed to do: namely, the work of investigating title to the property to be mortgaged and of ensuring that on completion, the lender obtained a good title as mortgagor.
>
> The question, therefore, is whether a solicitor who is instructed by both the building society and the borrower in a lending transaction is under an obligation to disclose to the building society all the information relevant to the lending risk which the solicitor has; including information obtained as a result of acting for the borrower in other transactions unrelated to the transaction in which he is instructed by the lender".

This was a case therefore where it was alleged that the solicitor learned of information during a different retainer for the borrower. Chadwick J. struck out the pleading. He said about *Mortgage Express*:

> "In my view, the words 'if in the course of doing the work he is instructed to do' reflect an important and significant qualification to the solicitor's duty to disclose information relevant to the lending risk. A solicitor is obliged to disclose information which comes into his possession in the course of doing the work which the lender has instructed him to do; but he is not obliged to disclose information which has come

---

[29] [2000] Lloyd's Rep. P.N. 788.

into his possession independently of any work which the lender has instructed him to do including, for example, information which has come into his possession as a result of earlier transactions in which he has been retained by the borrower.

... To impose on a solicitor the obligation to inform the building society of everything that he knows including matters which he knows as a result of acting for the borrower in the past which could affect the lending decision which the society has to make would, in my view, be oppressive and unrealistic. Such an obligation would, in most circumstances, require a solicitor who had acted for the borrower in earlier transactions to decline instructions from the lender on the ground that the obligation would put him in a position in which he could not fulfil his duties of confidentiality to the borrower client. But, if limited to information which the solicitor has acquired in the course of doing what he was instructed to do, the obligation is not oppressive or unrealistic".

He also pointed out:

"The question, as it seems to me, is not whether this information was information which might be of significance to the lender, but whether it was information which the solicitor was under a duty to disclose".

It is significant that leave to appeal from the *Baden Barnes Groves* decision was refused by Millett L.J.[30]

Chadwick J. reached a similar conclusion in *Bristol & West Building Society v May May Merrimans*.[31] He recognised there must be an obligation to disclose even in the execution-only retainer, but where the information did not fall within the terms of the retainer he treated the obligation as going no further than material non-confidential information learned in the course of the retainer.[32] However, in seeking to determine how far Chadwick J. was intending to take the law in these decisions, it is noticeable that in the following passage Chadwick J. reaffirmed the classic principle:

"The scope of the fiduciary duty owed by a solicitor to a lender for whom he acts must be defined by the terms of the retainer; but that duty cannot be cut down (in the absence of an express term in that retainer)

---

[30] February 26, 1997. His reasons are cited in the judgment of Blackburne J. in *Nationwide v Balmer Radmore* [1999] Lloyd's Rep. P.N. 241 at 263.
[31] [1996] 2 All E.R. 801.
[32] He pointed out that where (as in *Mortgage Express*) the solicitor was in possession of a valuation report, what was material to be disclosed (as having a material bearing on the valuation of the lender's security or some other ingredient of the lending decision) might be different, as the solicitor would not usually be aware of the valuation on which the lender had relied.

by the fact that the solicitor, to the knowledge of the lender, acts also for the borrower. A solicitor who acts for two parties in the same transaction is not released from his obligations to the one by the fact that, in performing those obligations, he may be in breach of his obligations to the other. The solicitor who puts himself in the position in which he cannot advance the interests of one client without failing in his duty to another has only himself to blame".[33]

In *Darlington v O'Rourke James Scourfield & McCarthy*[34] the Court of Appeal struck out a writ which alleged an obligation on the solicitors to advise the mortgage lenders of any information which would or might affect the decision to lend or the terms on which the loan would be made. The information was in fact obtained in the course of a different retainer. The Court of Appeal held that (quite apart from a separate limitation problem) the obligation was too widely pleaded. Sir Iain Glidewell said that where a solicitor acting for purchaser and lender receives information common to both, the question whether he should pass it on to one client or the other or both or neither entirely depends on the relevant interest of each client which the solicitor is engaged to serve.[35] This decision, which appears to be an extempore judgment, can be explained on the same basis as previous cases, namely that if the solicitor was able properly to carry out his retainer without disclosing the information, then the solicitor's obligation to disclose was limited in the way set out above. However, there is a passage in the judgment of Sir Iain Glidewell[36] which can be read as supporting a principle that a solicitor acting for borrower and lender is always obliged not to disclose information learned during a retainer for the borrower on a separate transaction, which it is suggested is either poorly expressed or put too widely.

6–008

In *Nationwide Building Society v Balmer Radmore*[37] Blackburne J., basing himself on the above cases, summarised the principles where the lender instructs the solicitor on its standard terms, which the judge considered. When it comes to providing information necessary to enable the documentation required by the lender to be completed, the consent of the borrower to the solicitor acting for the lender will usually give the solicitor implied authority to disclose all matters to which the lender's instructions relate, including matters enabling the solicitor to complete the report on title and make whatever disclosures necessary to enable the solicitor to comply with the society's instructions. In a case of doubt in the last-mentioned case, the solicitor should seek express consent before disclosing and if it is not forthcoming he must cease to act. In addition to the obligation which

---

[33] At 815, citing *Moody v Cox and Hatt* [1917] 2 Ch. 71.
[34] [1999] Lloyd's Rep. P.N. 33.
[35] [1999] Lloyd's Rep. P.N. 33 at 36.
[36] [1999] Lloyd's Rep. P.N. 33 at 37; Waller and Nourse L.JJ. agreed with Sir Iain Glidewell.
[37] [1999] Lloyd's Rep. P.N. 241 at 259–261.

arises from the terms of the retainer, a solicitor retained by a lender[38] is generally obliged to report to it information obtained by him in the course of investigating title or preparing for completion which was not confidential and which a solicitor of ordinary competence would have regarded as information which might cause the lender to doubt either the correctness of the valuation or the bona fides of the borrower. There is no obligation which arises by virtue of the retainer by the lender to disclose to the lender information learnt otherwise than in the course of acting.

D. The present position

6–009   In *Hilton v Barker Booth & Eastwood*[39] it was suggested in argument that there were special rules for lender/borrower cases. In the House of Lords, Lord Walker said that it was neither necessary or helpful to embark on a survey of the recent mortgage lending cases, many of which he said turned on special features of the mortgage lender's instructions to the solicitor.[40] Lord Walker referred to *Mortgage Express*, but cited the judgment of Millett L.J., and did not refer to the judgment of Bingham M.R.

It is suggested that there are several possible views of the mortgage lending cases referred to above. The first is that the restricted duty of disclosure which some of the cases referred to above posit, simply cannot stand with the House of Lords decision in *Barker Booth & Eastwood*.

The second view is that in any case where the mortgage lender expressly sets out the disclosure required by the borrower's solicitor, any further duty of disclosure has been impliedly excluded. Thus in *National Home Loans v Giffen Couch & Archer*[41] Peter Gibson L.J. pointed out that because the experienced mortgage lender had provided instructions as to the particular matters on which it wanted to be informed, there was limited room for any further duty of disclosure.[42]

A third view might be that there are special rules in mortgage lending cases. In such cases the retainer is an execution-only retainer; there is no obligation on the solicitor to advise. The lender will be an institutional client, which may be relevant to the degree of sophistication of the client and thus the obligations of the solicitor accordingly. These are consent cases, where both lender and borrower consent to the solicitor acting for both. The solicitor has the implied authority of the borrower to pass certain

---

[38] The judge was considering the case where the lender instructs the solicitor on its standard terms, which the judge considered.
[39] [2005]. 1 W.L.R. 567, see 6–010
[40] At [45].
[41] [1997] 3 All E.R. 808.
[42] Although Peter Gibson L.J. refers to the obligation of the solicitor to "advise" the lender, the expression is used in the sense of "inform" the lender of matters the lender had required to be informed on: the retainer was again not a retainer to give advice on the transaction.

information over to the lender. In mortgage lending the terms on which the solicitor is instructed are generally standard in form. Here as elsewhere the retainer must be examined with care to determine what the obligations of the solicitor are. Where the information which comes to the solicitor in the course of doing the work he is instructed to do falls within the retainer, or is material to the task he is retained to do, he must disclose it or cease to act. Where it falls outside the retainer, but is nevertheless material to the interests of the client in the transaction, an open-ended obligation to disclose is likely to cause practical problems in mortgage-lending where there are significant practical advantages in the solicitor being able to act for both lender and borrower. So the practical problems inherent in an open-ended obligation can be mitigated by restricting the disclosure obligation. It has subsequently been said that this principle (or rather, these limitations on the principle) is necessary, otherwise the obligation would be "oppressive or unrealistic"[43] or that "life would be impossible on any other basis".[44]

Whichever of these views prevails, it seems increasingly clear that nothing in the mortgage-lending cases affects the law on conflicts of interest more generally, which is not a position that seemed clear a few years ago. It is suggested that there probably is no separate rule for mortgage-lending cases, but the use of express instructions by mortgage lenders may in practice be treated as impliedly excluding the duty of wider disclosure.

3. Barker Booth and Eastwood

A. The decision

In *Hilton v Barker Booth and Eastwood*,[45] the House of Lords considered the effect of the duty to disclose. Issues of conflicts sufficiently rarely are heard by the House of Lords that the case requires detailed analysis.

6–010

The defendants ("BBE"), were retained by a Mr Bromage to act for him in criminal proceedings for company management offences. Mr Gorman was the solicitor. Mr Bromage was sentenced to nine months imprisonment and made bankrupt. On his release, he sought to acquire land for development of flats with Mr Hilton and instructed BBE together with Mr Hilton. After Mr Gorman had advised both on three occasions, he told Mr Hilton he could not continue to act for both and suggested that Mr Hilton instruct a junior employee of BBE, Mr Scott, which he did. There were three contracts: a contract for the sale of the land to Mr Hilton, a contract for the purchase of the flats when built from Mr Hilton to Mr Bromage and a third contract

---

[43] Chadwick J. in *Baden Barnes Groves* [2000] Lloyd's Rep. P.N. 788.
[44] Millett L.J. refusing leave to appeal in *Baden Barnes Groves*, February 26, 1997.
[45] [2005] 1 W.L.R. 567.

(of which Mr Hilton was unaware) for the resale of the flats by Mr Bromage to a third party at a profit. Mr Hilton bought the land, the third party disappeared, Mr Bromage could not fund the purchase from Mr Hilton and the contract between Mr Hilton and Mr Bromage was rescinded with Mr Hilton making a huge loss. He sued BBE, complaining that BBE had failed to tell him of Mr Bromage's conviction and bankruptcy; had he known, he said he would not have dealt with him. The judge said that BBE could not reveal the confidential information of their client Mr Bromage but were in breach of duty in that they should have ceased to act for Mr Hilton because of the conflict. He then said that if that had happened, Mr Hilton would not have learnt of the conviction or bankruptcy from the new solicitor (as he would not have known about it) so although there was a breach of duty there was no loss.

The Court of Appeal dismissed the appeal.[46] Morritt V.C., giving the leading judgment, held that the duty of a solicitor to his client does not include disclosing or deploying the confidential information of another client or former client even when the information is actually known to the solicitor and is relevant to the services performed for the new client. The court then held that there was an implied limitation in the retainer of BBE by Mr Hilton which excluded from the solicitor's duty of disclosure any information which they were legally obliged to treat as confidential. Morritt V.C. then went on to agree with the judge that once faced with the problem of not being able to disclose, the solicitor was obliged to cease to act. He agreed with the judge that if that had happened, the client would have instructed a new solicitor, and as there was no reason to believe a new solicitor would have been aware of the bankruptcy or conviction, there was no loss.

The House of Lords allowed the appeal. Lord Walker held that the case was determined by the principle in *Moody v Cox*[47]:

> "... if a solicitor is unwise enough to undertake irreconcilable duties it is his own fault, and he cannot use his discomfiture as a reason why his duty to either client should be taken to have been modified".[48]

It followed that the solicitor's relevant obligation was to disclose to Mr Hilton the conviction of Mr Bromage, and he also had an obligation to Mr Bromage not to disclose that fact. The duty, therefore, to Mr Hilton was not (as had been held by the lower courts) merely a duty to cease acting. As the judge had found as a fact that if Mr Hilton had been aware of Mr Bromage's antecedents he would have had nothing to do with the business deal, damages were substantial rather than nominal.

---

[46] [2002] Lloyd's P.N. 500.
[47] [1917] 2 Ch. 71.
[48] At [46].

B. Confidentiality

The first question for consideration is whether BBE's knowledge of the conviction and bankruptcy were in fact confidential. This information represented the result of the proceedings in which Mr Gorman had initially been instructed, and was a matter of public record. How could the fact of the conviction and the fact of the judgment be confidential? Solicitors send to the legal press details of recent cases in which they have acted all the time. So long as what has happened is in open court, surely there is no breach of confidentiality?[49] In the Court of Appeal Morritt V.C.[50] records that it was accepted that disclosure of the conviction and bankruptcy would have involved a breach of duty to Mr Bromage "notwithstanding that his conviction and bankruptcy were matters of public record and so not confidential in any strict legal sense".

6–011

In the House of Lords, Lord Walker said that confidentiality was not really relevant to the issues in the case. He said that to disclose discreditable facts about a client without the client's informed consent was likely to be a breach of duty, even if the facts are in the public domain. He treated references in the Court of Appeal judgments to confidential information in this "looser" sense. It was conceded that disclosure of Mr Bromage's past would have been a breach of duty, and that concession was not withdrawn.

6–012

There is in general no difficulty in treating the disclosure of discreditable facts about one's client as being a breach of fiduciary duty of loyalty so long as the retainer, and fiduciary duty, continues. As there was an existing retainer for Mr Bromage, this would have caused no difficulty were it not for the fact that breach of fiduciary duty was never pleaded against the solicitors,[51] a problem which Lord Walker slipped over with an ease not shared by subsequent commentators, although it is right to say that the concession BBE were not at liberty to disclose information about Mr Bromage's past to Mr Hilton was not withdrawn in the House of Lords. As a matter of fiduciary duty, it is right that the solicitors were under an obligation not to reveal discreditable information about Mr Bromage to Mr Hilton, even if it was publicly available information. But what would have been the position if the retainer to Mr Bromage had ended?[52] The solicitor does not usually owe a fiduciary duty to a former client.

6–013

---

[49] Compare the Ontario case of *Stewart v Canadian Broadcasting Commission* [1997] 150 D.L.R. (4d) 24 where a Q.C. was found to be in breach of a continuing fiduciary duty when he participated for purposes of personal publicity in a TV programme about a notorious criminal case where he had acted for Mr Stewart several years before. The decision was not based on confidential information as the facts were in the public domain. It is debatable whether the English court would reach a similar decision: see para.2–028.
[50] At [11].
[51] See [30].
[52] See the discussion on this point at 2–028.

Given the concession, the analysis of Lord Walker can be said to be strictly obiter. There is a detailed criticism of his analysis on this point in *Toulson and Phipps on Confidentiality*.[53] They refer to cases in which the court has protected the identity of a person previously convicted in open court of a grave crime which has received national publicity.[54] They state:

> "It is hard to see why a court should not be able to protect information which is not as a matter of practicality readily accessible and has been received in circumstances which a reasonable person would regard as confidential ... if the law of confidentiality is circumscribed so that it cannot apply to information imparted in confidence about anything which has occurred in open court or is contained in a record theoretically available to the public, regardless of how secret or accessible it may be in practical terms, then the defendants' duty of non-disclosure could only be explained on some other basis ... it is suggested that this is an over narrow view of the law".

The authors suggest that whether information is or once was a matter of public record is simply a factor in determining whether it is so generally accessible that it would not be just to require the party against whom a duty of confidentiality is alleged to treat it as confidential.

C. Moody v Cox

6–014   The main issue in *Barker Booth & Eastwood* involved a reaffirmation by the House of Lords of the principle in *Moody v Cox*.[55] If a professional takes on two conflicting retainers, he cannot pray in aid one as a defence to performance of his retainer in the other. The decision ought to cause no surprise; in truth it was the decision of the Court of Appeal that was out of line with established authority. What causes difficulty in analysing the House of Lords decision, and Lord Walker's speech, is that the case was not properly pleaded or argued below, and came to the House of Lords with no pleading of breach of fiduciary duty, and a series of concessions not clearly linked to legal principles. Thus an analysis that would better fit into an analysis of breach of fiduciary duty appears in a breach of contract claim, with Lord Walker suggesting that the analysis was valid without a claim for breach of fiduciary duty.

---

[53] 2nd edn, 2006 para 3–149.
[54] *Venables v News Group Newspapers Ltd* [2001] Fam. 430, *X (formerly Mary Bell) v O'Brien* [2003] EWHC 1101.
[55] [1917] 2 Ch. 71.

4. Disclosure of information problems after Barker Booth & Eastwood

A. Can an implied term precluding disclosure ever be appropriate?

Where informed consent is given, it will often be important to ask the client expressly to waive the duty of disclosure so far as it relates to information learned as a result of the other retainer.[56]

6–015

Lord Jauncey said in *Clark Boyce v Mouat*[57]:

> "Informed consent means consent given in the knowledge that there is a conflict between the parties and that as a result the solicitor may be disabled from disclosing to each party the full knowledge which he possesses as to the transaction or may be disabled from giving advice to one party which conflicts with the interests of the other. If the parties are content to proceed upon this basis the solicitor may properly act".

This runs together two issues that are essentially separate—was there informed consent to acting notwithstanding potential conflict, and was there a waiver of the disclosure duty. One can be effective without agreement on the other. Insofar as Lord Jauncey can be read as suggesting that the giving of informed consent carries with it an automatic waiver of the duty to disclose information learned in the course of the other retainer, or that one cannot be effective without the other, this goes too far.[58]

However, there will be cases where it may be appropriate to imply a term into a retainer to the effect that the solicitor will not disclose information learned in the course of acting for another client, and such a term may be implied even where the terms of the retainer would otherwise require the disclosure of the information. Where the clients have given informed consent to an existing client conflict, the circumstances may be such that it is obvious the clients were agreeing that the solicitor would withhold from one client what he had learned in confidence from the other. It will surely depend on the knowledge of the two clients, all the circumstances, and what is explained or understood by then as to the consequences of the consent. Similarly, in the mortgage lending case *National Home Loans v Giffen Couch & Archer*[59] Peter Gibson L.J. pointed out that because the experienced mortgage lender had provided instructions as to the particular

---

[56] This is contemplated by the SRA 2011 Code IB (4.4).
[57] [1994] 1 A.C. 428. see 4–008.
[58] See 4–010 above.
[59] [1997] 3 All E.R. 808.

matters on which it wanted to be informed, there was limited room for any further duty of disclosure.⁶⁰

If the clients are sophisticated, or if this consequence has been explained to the two clients, then it can be said that their knowledge or consent to this situation precludes them from complaining that they have not been told the information in question, as in *Kelly v Cooper*.⁶¹ The analysis we have suggested as applicable to such cases is that there will be an inferred or deemed consent to the non-disclosure of information where the combination of the knowledge of the client and the decision to instruct the professional with that knowledge means that it is unconscionable or inequitable for the client to complain about non-disclosure of information communicated in confidence to the solicitor by the other client. That gives rise to a deemed or inferred consent to the non-disclosure, which we suggest at Ch. 4 is a form of waiver by election.

6–016 Where there is a former client conflict, and the obligation is to disclose information learned in the course of the prior retainer, the *Kelly v Cooper* analysis is much more difficult to justify. The client will often know that the solicitor will previously have accepted past retainers where he will have obtained confidential information which he will be duty bound to keep confidential and not to use for the benefit of his new client. There is an argument that the position should be the same as in *Kelly v Cooper*: the new client could be treated as consenting to the solicitor not revealing the confidential information to him. He is deemed to consent by virtue of his instructing the professional with the necessary knowledge about prior retainers. Sir Mark Waller, in a review of the first edition of this book, suggested that the "deemed knowledge" approach may be the correct analysis here.⁶² But caution may be required. Precisely what knowledge does the client have about past retainers of the solicitor? It is surely to be expected that the knowledge of prior retainers would need to be specific and relevant before it could be said that the combination of that knowledge and the instruction of the professional with that knowledge rendered it unconscionable or inequitable for the client to complain about non-disclosure of relevant information to him. If the new client is not in fact being asked to consent to anything, why in the normal case should he be treated as giving consent to something he never agreed to and may have refused to agree? Why in such circumstances should he be treated as though he had given a consent that he was never asked to give? Why should it be unfair for him to hold the professional to the normal obligations of a fiduciary?

The starting point is always to define the retainer, as this will determine

---

⁶⁰ Although Peter Gibson L.J. refers to the obligation of the solicitor to "advise" the lender, the expression is used in the sense of "inform" the lender of matters the lender had required to be informed on: the retainer was again not a retainer to give advice on the transaction.
⁶¹ See paras 4–016.
⁶² (2001) 117 L.Q.R. 335.

the extent of the duty of disclosure; the retainer may be easy to define in the standard-form mortgage lending case. It will be harder where the solicitor is not acting for an institution to define the retainer as narrowly as has been done in mortgage lending cases. It is always the case that if the solicitor does not or cannot get information necessary to answer truthfully and accurately the requests for information from the lender, he cannot act. In lender cases, when it comes to providing information necessary to enable the documentation required by the lender to be completed, the consent of the borrower to the solicitor acting for the lender will usually give the solicitor implied authority to disclose all matters to which the lender's instructions relate, including matters enabling the solicitor to complete the report on title and make whatever disclosures necessary to enable the solicitor to comply with the society's instructions. In a case of doubt in the last-mentioned case, the solicitor should seek express consent before disclosing and if it is not forthcoming he must cease to act.

B. Information barriers in the mind?[63]

6–017 Even where there is no obligation to pass on confidential information learned in the course of another retainer, the problem does not end there. Once the professional has learnt the information, how can he unlearn it or ignore it? If in the course of his earlier retainer to a client he has learnt that the client has county court judgments against him, when acting for a mortgage lender to that client, how can he in good faith exercise a judgment whether or not to search for county court judgments against the borrower when he knows what the answer will be? He cannot forget what he has learnt. Does he try to operate an information barrier in his mind? Even if he does not have to disclose it, what is the position as regards using the information for purposes of making decisions and giving advice? Are they obliged to use the information themselves for these purposes? Or should they put it out of mind?

The problem is vividly illustrated by the curious decision in *Omega Trust v Wright Son and Pepper (No.2)*[64] where the defendant solicitors ("WSP") had acted for a Mr Sharif. He had financial difficulties and did not pay WSP's fees. WSP were later asked to act for the claimant lender, who was about to lend money to a company controlled by Mr Sharif, with a guarantee from Mr Sharif himself. At almost the same time, Mr Sharif agreed to discharge the old fees by instalments and instructed WSP to act for him on some other transactions. On October 16, 1991, a bankruptcy petition was presented against Mr Sharif and the loan was completed on October 28.

---

[63] The equivalent section in a previous edition was headed "Chinese Walls of the Mind". It has to be said, this is a case where the use of the old expression is rather more pithy.
[64] [1998] P.N.L.R. 337.

The loan was never repaid. The claimant alleged that WSP was liable, firstly, by failing to disclose the information they had about Mr Sharif's finances; and secondly, by failing to conduct a bankruptcy search.

Douglas Brown J. applied the *Baden Barnes Groves* principle and held that the solicitors were not obliged to disclose to the lender the confidential information they possessed about Mr Sharif's poor payment record. On expert evidence, he held that the lender's solicitor has no general duty to conduct a bankruptcy search on a guarantor and so he dismissed the first head of claim. However, he also held that WSP were negligent for not conducting a bankruptcy search because they should have used the confidential information that WSP had about Mr Sharif's financial circumstances and reached the conclusion in the light of that such a search was necessary. In other words, whilst the information could not be disclosed to the lender it should have been used by the solicitor in deciding whether to make a bankruptcy search as part of the fulfilment of the retainer to the lender.

6–018 This is plainly not a satisfactory resolution of the problem. The adviser has information which he cannot disclose, but which according to this decision he ought to act upon in the service of his client. What if he is later asked to justify the expense of the bankruptcy search? Does the solicitor have to say to his own client that he cannot explain it, because he did it for confidential reasons? If information is confidential to client B, it cannot be right that the adviser should deploy it in the service of client A, especially in a way inimical to the interests of Client B. That is to misunderstand what confidentiality is about. In a case such as *Omega Trust v Wright Son and Pepper (No.2)* if the solicitor must make a judgment which he cannot do given the information he has obtained from his other retainer, he is professionally embarrassed and must cease to act.

Although the analysis in *Omega Trust v Wright Son and Pepper (No.2)* is open to criticism, it may be that the result can be justified. Rather like the situation in *Hilton v Barker Booth & Eastwood*, the solicitor should not have continued to act for both parties. However, having so continued, he is in a position where a breach of duty to at least one client is inevitable. It may have been correct to spell out the consequences of professional embarrassment by finding that to fail to use the confidential information of the guarantor for the benefit of the lender (to decide that the circumstances did require a bankruptcy search) was a breach of duty to the lender, even though it would also have been a breach of duty to the guarantor had the solicitor done so.

C. The obligation to disclose and the obligation to advise

6–019 The authorities do not deal with the situation where the lender asks specific questions of the solicitor or where the giving of more general advice is part of the retainer ("how secure is this loan?" "what is this borrower like?"). In mortgage lending, where the solicitor's role is execution-only this will generally not arise. Acting for individuals is rarely so simple. Once the obligation ceases to be an execution-only retainer it seems fraught with problems.

Remember that in *Kelly v Cooper* when the agent informed Ms Kelly of Mr Perot's first offer, Ms Kelly is recorded as having asked the agent if she thought that Mr Perot would increase the offer.[65] How could the agent, given her obligation as a fiduciary, give a proper answer to this question without revealing her knowledge of Mr Perot's prior offer on Caliban? Plainly the professional cannot be a party to the borrower providing information to the lender which he knows to be untrue or misleading. If the client asks "do you know of any reason why we should not enter into this transaction" the solicitor cannot possibly say "no" when the answer is "I cannot tell you because the relevant information was acquired pursuant to a previous retainer". Even worse, he cannot give that answer without revealing, in breach of duty to the borrower, that some information, probably discreditable to the borrower, exists. How can he give advice at all?

Wright Son & Pepper (No.2) highlights a similar issue. How can the solicitor exercise his discretion whether to search for county court judgments against one client whilst acting for another, when he already knows through acting in the past for the second client that there are a series of such judgments. He may thus in existing client cases where there is consent sometimes find himself in breach of what Millett L.J. referred to as the "no inhibition" principle, or where there is a former client equally unable to act without being professionally embarrassed. Even in the *Kelly* type case, which might be thought a very much easier case from the perspective of the professional, the professional may face real embarrassment. What if the second client says to him "what do you think of the offer"? He has not disclosed that he is acting for the next door property owner. Indeed, he cannot do so without consent. So how does he answer the question? If he says "it seems a good offer" when he means "it seems a good offer taking into account your property alone and remembering that I may have information I cannot tell you which might lead me to take a different view", is his answer not potentially misleading?

If one takes the example of a retainer for litigation, the retainer will relate to the litigation in hand, but litigation may carry with it the possibility of wide-ranging cross-examination as to credit which may go far beyond the issue before the court. Surely it cannot be the case that in such circumstances the solicitor can keep to himself valuable information learned outside the course of acting notwithstanding that it would be relevant to cross-examination?

On this issue, unusually, there has been little debate in the Australian

6–020

---

[65] [1993] A.C. 205 at 211c.

courts. The traditional *Spector v Ageda* view has usually been followed without much discussion. Thus in *British American Tobacco Australia Services Ltd v Blanch*[66] Young C.J. said "it is Mr Blanch's duty to make available to [his clients] all knowledge and information he has about BATAS which might assist in the case". The New South Wales Court of Appeal in *O'Reilly v Law Society*[67] said that a solicitor owed to his client the duty to tell him of everything which he knows which will be of assistance to the client in relation to the matters within the retainer. Within such limits, the solicitor must do what he can to further the client's interests.[68] The one decision which does look at the duty of disclosure is *Rexstraw v Johnson*[69] where the New South Wales Court of Appeal recently followed *Mortgage Express*. But it does not seem to have been necessary to consider the issues set out in this chapter.

D. The fraud exception

6–021   There is one exception where the professional must even in mortgage lending clearly disclose information which he has gained otherwise than in connection with or in the course of acting in the instant transaction. That is where he has information which indicates or strongly suggests that the client is intending in the instant transaction to defraud the lender. Then, if the solicitor continues to act for the lender, he is obliged to disclose the information to alert the lender to the intended deception.[70] This was said[71] to be no more than an illustration of the principle that there is no confidence in iniquity (and thus the information would not have been confidential from disclosure) but this does not seem right: if the recent cases represent the law,[72] the solicitor would have no obligation to disclose the information simply because he did not obtain it in the course of his retainer for the lender, and it would be irrelevant whether the information was confidential or not. Thus this must be regarded as a public policy exception to the general rule.[73]

---

[66] [2004] N.S.W.S.C. 70.
[67] (1988) 24 N.S.W.L.R. 204.
[68] The court relied upon Lord Westbury L.C. in *Tyrrell v Bank of London* (1862) 10 H.L.C. 26, at 39–40, 11 E.R. 934 at 939–940 and *Law Society of New South Wales v Harvey* [1976] 2 N.S.W.L.R. 154.
[69] [2003] N.S.W.C.A. 87.
[70] This was held in *Nationwide v Balmer Radmore* [1999] Lloyd's Rep. P.N. 241 at 263–64, following *Darlington v O'Rourke James Scourfield & McCarthy* [1999] Lloyd's Rep. P.N. 33 at 37.
[71] Blackburne J. in *Nationwide v Balmer Radmore* [1999] Lloyd's Rep. P.N. 241 at 264.
[72] Blackburne J. was dealing with a lender/borrower case, so he was making the observation in circumstances where the law was that the obligation to disclose did not extend beyond information learned in the course of the retainer.
[73] What happens if the solicitor ceases to act rather than pass on the information? Does this solve the problem? Once he has begun to act, it may be said that the obligation to disclose

5. Attribution of knowledge

A. Attribution within the firm

To date we have focused on the position where the knowledge is in the mind of a single individual: the problem of the "information barrier in the mind". What is the position when the relevant knowledge is split between different individuals in the firm?   6–022

Is the knowledge of one team within the firm to be attributed to the other? If one follows the fiduciary rules to their logical conclusion, it might be thought that such a conclusion followed. The client instructs the firm, not the individual professional. The individual professional is not a party to the contract. The rule on existing client conflicts impacts on the firm rather than the individual. So surely the knowledge of the individual must be the knowledge of the firm? Both *Moody v Cox*[74] and *Spector v Ageda*[75] suggest that a solicitor is under an obligation to put not just his or her skill and knowledge at the client's disposal but also that of the entire firm. That would seem to suggest an obligation to disclose to each client knowledge relevant to his affairs that may be possessed by any of its partners or staff. Alternatively, it might be said that for the purpose of conflicts of interest a firm, or any particular solicitor within a firm, is fixed with the knowledge of all the partners or staff in the firm.

It would indeed be absurd if this were the law. Such a rule would place a ridiculous burden on a huge multi-disciplinary partnership, to trawl all parts of the firm to try to find out whether anyone knows anything, which may have been information imparted in confidence in acting for the old client to a partner or associate in a completely different part of the firm, perhaps in another part of the country, which it may be in the interests of the new client to learn. Life would be impossible in a large accountancy firm with hundreds of partners where one part of the firm learns information about one client in the course of acting for another in different circumstances through a different department or office. It is one thing to say that the firm is to be treated as a single entity for purposes of conflicts, in that as an entity the firm cannot act at the same time for two clients with different interests. It is quite another to suggest that the knowledge of one partner obtained in the course of acting for one client is to be treated as the knowledge of the firm for the purpose of defining the obligations of the firm acting for a different client through a different partner.

The Australian and Canadian courts have considered this issue. In the   6–023

---

arose before he ceased to act, and thus he is in breach of duty even though he has ceased to act. The point may arise for consideration, but it seems to be assumed in most of the authorities where the issue arises that ceasing to act without more is good enough.

[74] [1917] 2 Ch. 71.
[75] [1973] Ch. 30.

Western Australia case *Mallesons v KPMG Peat Marwick*[76] in 1990 Ipp J. said that it had long been an accepted tenet of partnership law that the knowledge of one partner is to be imputed as the knowledge of the other. He cited *Davies v Clough*[77] as well as Australian authority[78] and suggested that Canadian law was to the same effect.[79] He referred to Professor Finn; "a person who engages the services of a partner acting as such engages the service of the whole firm and not merely of the persons who actually render the service".[80] By 1997 the same judge had changed his mind. He reviewed the issue in *Unioil v Deloitte Touche Tohmatsu*.[81] He pointed out that the law in Canada had changed since he relied upon it in his judgment in *Mallesons*. Since then in *MacDonald Estate v Martin*[82] the Supreme Court of Canada had rejected his previous view; he cited Sopinka J. who said that the assumption that the knowledge of one member of the firm is the knowledge of all[83] was "unrealistic in the era of the mega-firm" and had held[84] that there should be a rebuttable presumption that the knowledge of one partner is to be regarded as the knowledge of his or her partner. The Canadian Supreme Court thus in *MacDonald Estate* applied two rebuttable presumptions: first, confidential information will have been communicated by the former client in the course of the retainer and second, lawyers who work together share confidences. In other words, if the confidential information of the client was transmitted to the firm, it will be assumed that the solicitor acting for the new client is aware of it unless the contrary is shown. Ipp J. adopted the view taken by the Canadian Supreme Court: if a presumption is rebuttable it may be rebutted by evidence sufficient to justify an information barrier.[85] In respect of the statement of principle of Megarry J. in *Spector v Ageda*,[86] Ipp J. said:

---

[76] [1990] 4 W.A.R. 357.
[77] (1837) 8 Sim. 263, 59 E.R. 105. See Andrew Mitchell "Whose Side Are You on Anyway? Former Client Conflicts of Interest" (1998) 26 Australian Business Law Review 418 at 429, where he suggests that the presumption of imputed knowledge can be traced to *Davies v Clough* and says that the presumption has been justified by the danger of inadvertent disclosures of confidence inherent in everyday exchange of ideas and discussion of problems amongst law partners and by a concern to avoid even the appearance of impropriety. A review of the first edition of this book by Andrew Mitchell and Tania Voon appeared in the Melbourne University Law Review at (2002) 26 M.U.L.R. 241.
[78] *In the Marriage of A and B* (1990) 13 Fam. L.R. 798; *In the Marriage of Magro* (1989) 93 F.L.R. 365; *D&J Construction Pty Ltd v Head* (1987) 9 N.S.W.L.R. 118.
[79] *Davey v Woolley Hames Dale & Dingwall* (1983) 133 D.L.R. (3d) 647.
[80] "Conflicts of Interest and Professionals" published by the New Zealand Legal Research Foundation.
[81] (1997) 17 W.A.R. 98.
[82] (1990) 77 D.L.R. (4th) 249.
[83] (1990) 77 D.L.R. (4th) 249 at 268.
[84] (1990) 77 D.L.R. (4th) 249 at 269.
[85] *MacDonald Estate* took the view that the burden was on the lawyer to show that "all reasonable measures have been taken to ensure that no disclosure will occur". Lord Millett considers that test, and modifies it, in *Bolkiah*: see para.1–011.
[86] [1972] Ch. 30.

"while the remarks ... ordinarily apply to situations where the solicitor possessing the knowledge is in fact personally doing the work for the client, it does not necessarily follow that they will always apply to a solicitor who possesses knowledge that may be helpful to a client of his firm, for whom he, personally, is not doing any work, but who is being represented by one of his partners".[87]

The point was recognised by Staughton L.J. in his dissenting judgment in *Re Solicitors*.[88] There the majority of the Court of Appeal regarded the possibility of leakage of confidential information as a reason for injuncting solicitors from acting in connection with litigation where they had previously acted for a party with conflicting interests in related litigation. Staughton L.J. said that there was no support in the authorities for the proposition that a large firm of many partners is obliged to disclose to each client knowledge relevant to his affairs that may be possessed by any of its partners or staff. He regarded such an obligation, when applied to a large firm, as impractical and would not hold it to be the law. To hold otherwise would put upon a large firm an intolerable obligation to seek out and obtain any information which another member of the firm might in the past have obtained. In his judgment in the Court of Appeal in *Bolkiah*,[89] Waller L.J. treated *Cholmondeley v Clinton*[90] as the foundation for the nineteenth-century view that there was an irrebuttable presumption that knowledge would be imparted to all other members of the firm thereby leading to automatic disqualification, but suggested, relying on *Re a Firm of Solicitors*[91] that such a view did not represent current English law.

It seems to follow logically that if the attribution of knowledge rule were taken to its logical conclusion, information barriers could not exist. If the knowledge of any member of the firm were attributed to the firm, then information learned by one partner from one client would be subject to an obligation of disclosure by a different partner acting for a different client even though the second partner had no knowledge of it and there was an information barrier in place in the firm.

Lord Millett's speech in the House of Lords in *Bolkiah* seems largely to have resolved the issue so far as this jurisdiction is concerned.[92] Because existing client conflicts are concerned with conflict not confidentiality,

---

[87] [1972] Ch. 30 at 110.
[88] [1992] Q.B. 959 at 972. The point was not dealt with by the majority. Parts at least of the majority judgment now cannot stand with *Bolkiah*, as indicated by Timothy Walker J. in *Re Solicitors* [2000] 1 Lloyd's Rep. 31.
[89] [1999] 1 B.C.L.C. 1 at 39 at 40.
[90] (1815) 19 Ves. Jun. 261 at 276; 34 E.R. 515 at 520, Lord Eldon L.C. see para.5–004.
[91] [1992] Q.B. 959.
[92] *Bolkiah* was followed in Australia on this point in *Bureau Interprofessionel des Vins de Bourgogne v Red Earth Nominees Pty Ltd (t/a Taltarni Vineyards)* [2002] F.C.A. 588, Ryan J. at [34].

attribution of knowledge does not feature as an issue in such cases: if there is an existing client conflict the firm cannot act at all without the consent of both clients. The attribution of knowledge problem arises when there is a former client conflict issue. Lord Millett[93] cited *MacDonald Estate v Martin*[94] where Sopinka J. referred to rebuttable presumptions, but Lord Millett rejected the "rebuttable presumption" approach. But his formulation was not substantially different. Lord Millett said that in England the burden of proof is on the former client to show (i) the firm is in possession of information confidential to the former client and to the disclosure of which he has not consented and (ii) the information is or may be relevant to the new matter in which the interest of the other client is or may be adverse to his own. The burden was not a heavy one: the first may readily be inferred, the latter will often be obvious. Once that burden has been satisfied, the evidential burden shifted to the professional and it was for the professional to show there was no real risk of disclosure to the persons acting for the new client. He said:

> "But given the basis on which the jurisdiction is exercised, there is no cause to impute or attribute the knowledge of one partner to his fellow partners. Whether a particular individual is in possession of confidential information is a question of fact which must be proved or inferred from the circumstances of the case".

The rule is a pragmatic rule intended to cater for the practical difficulty of ascertaining within a large organisation whether any of hundreds of individuals has any knowledge which might be relevant. An obligation to that effect would be almost impossible to comply with. And it is plain that where there is risk of misuse of confidential information there is scope for information barriers to protect the confidential information of the former client.

B. Rules of attribution and their place in the law of conflicts

6–024　Once it is recognised that *Bolkiah* expressly legitimises information barriers, it is apparent that traditional rules on attribution of knowledge have little place in an analysis of the law of conflicts of interest. Attribution of knowledge is generally irrelevant in existing client conflicts, because the professional cannot act at all without consent, and can only set up an information barrier if the clients have consented. And it is apparent that attribution of knowledge in former client conflicts has to be understood in the light

---

[93] [1999] 2 A.C. 222 at 235.
[94] (1990) 77 D.L.R. (4th) 249.

of information barriers being permitted even without client consent. So it could not be the case that the knowledge of one person in the firm removed from the retainer is attributed to those involved in the retainer.

So far as partnerships are concerned, s.16 of the Partnership Act 1890 provides: 6–025

> "Notice to any partner who habitually acts in the partnership business of any matter relating to partnership affairs operates as notice to the firm, except in the case of a fraud on the firm committed by or with the consent of that partner".

It is apparent from the above that this is not to be treated as attributing knowledge of one partner to another for conflicts purposes. In the Scottish case *Campbell v McCreath*[95] Lord Stott rejected an argument that this meant anything known by one partner could be treated as known by all partners of the firm.[96] He said the section was concerned with the relationship between partner and firm. It was not concerned with imputing knowledge as to the affairs of third party clients to other partners within the firm. *Campbell v McCreath* was not cited in another Scottish case: *Zurich GSG v Gray & Kellas*[97] in which Lord Brodie reached a sensible ultimate conclusion by way of the unsatisfactory reasoning that:

> "In my opinion the effect of section 16 is to do with imputed or deemed knowledge. It has nothing to do with actual knowledge. At least one partner, acting in the partnership business must, at least at one moment in time, have actual knowledge of the relevant fact. Once that is the case knowledge of the fact is imputed to the firm by virtue of section 16 but that is as far as it goes. There is nothing in the language of section 16 to suggest that the other partners are taken actually to know what in fact they do not know".[98]

Ipp J. in the Western Australia case *Unioil International v Deloitte Touche Tohmatsu*,[99] following *Campbell*, said that the confidential information of a client was not to be attributed to other partners of the firm because the

---

[95] [1975] S.C. 81 at 85.
[96] But see the Canadian decision *Davey v Woolley Hames Dale & Dingwall* (1983) 133 D.L.R. (3d) 647 stating that it was "an accepted tenet of partnership law that the knowledge of one partner is to be imputed as the knowledge of the other". This decision must now be read subject to the Canadian Supreme Court decision *MacDonald Estate v Martin*, see para.6–023.
[97] [2007] C.S.O.H. 91.
[98] This is unsatisfactory because the last two sentences are self-contradictory. If knowledge is attributed to the firm (for a given purpose), what that means it that (for that purpose) the other partners are taken to know. It is of no relevance to say that they are not taken "actually" to know.
[99] (1997) 17 W.A.R. 98 at 108.

partner was bound to maintain solicitor-client confidentiality, and thus there could be no obligation to make disclosure to fellow partners.[100]

The reasoning does not seem satisfactory in either of these cases, although the result is. The section of the Partnership Act seems to have been drafted to facilitate proof in actions against partnerships, by preventing partners from setting up their own personal lack of notice where the notice has been given to one of their number acting within the business of the partnership.[101] The section probably has two consequences. Firstly, if a firm claims the benefit of a transaction entered into by a partner or is otherwise bound by his acts, it cannot use its own ignorance of what a partner knew to place itself in a more favourable position than could have been achieved by that partner if he had been acting on his own account.[102] Secondly, when it is necessary to prove that a firm has notice of some fact, all that is required is to show that notice was given to one of its partners who habitually acts in the partnership business. So the section seems not to have the effect of automatically rendering the knowledge of one partner the knowledge of the others for all purposes.

Where the legal entity is a company rather than a partnership, s.16 is inapplicable but the *Bolkiah* principle will still apply. In relation to companies, imputation of knowledge is generally a matter of agency law. In *El Ajou v Dollar Land Holdings*[103] Hoffmann L.J. explained that whether the knowledge of an agent would be imputed to a company may depend on the actual or apparent authority of the agent to receive the communications in question, the terms of the contract in respect of which the agent was engaged, whether the agent had a duty to communicate the information to the principal, or whether the principal was under a duty to investigate or make disclosure of the matters that came to the agent's knowledge. In respect of companies, in *Meridian Global v Securities Commission*[104] Lord Hoffmann, speaking for the Privy Council, explained that the primary rules for attribution of knowledge in respect of a company would be found in the company's constitution, typically the articles. There are also primary rules of attribution implied by company law. Lord Hoffmann said these rules, together with the rules applicable as a result of the law of agency and the rules of law relating to attribution of knowledge[105] (estoppel and ostensible

---

[100] See also *Northumberland Insurance v Alexander* [1984] 8 A.C.L.R. 882 at 905.
[101] See Sir Mark Waller's review of the first edition of this book at 117 L.Q.R. 335. The review contains a stimulating analysis of the issues involved in attribution of knowledge for purposes of conflicts of interest.
[102] *Collinson v Lister* (1855) 7 De G.M. & G. 634; *Oppenheimer v Frazer & Wyatt* (1907) 2 K.B. 50.
[103] [1994] 2 All E.R. 685, CA.
[104] 2 A.C. 500.
[105] There are also a number of express statutory provisions which provide their own rules for attribution of knowledge: see Law of Property Act 1925, s.199(1)(ii)(b): purchaser deemed to have the knowledge of his counsel, solicitor or other agent which the latter acquires in the particular transaction in which he is acting for the purchaser; Trustee Act 1925, s.28:

authority in contract and vicarious liability in tort), would answer many of the issues as to attribution of knowledge in respect of the company.[106] It is important to remember that each company in the same group is a separate legal entity and thus the knowledge of one company within the group will not be attributed to another company within the group.[107]

There is old authority which suggests that there may in some circumstances be an automatic attribution of knowledge, although it has never been applied in relation to conflicts of interest. In *Harrods v Lemon*[108] information known by a trading company's estate agency department and its building construction department, which were physically separated, were pooled and treated as one, and in *Lloyds Bank v EB Savory & Co*[109] the House of Lords held that information possessed by one branch of a bank was treated as possessed by another branch of the bank with the consequence that the bank was held in breach of duty to its customer. However, more recently, it has been held that *Lloyds Bank v Savory* is not authority for the proposition that "all aspects of a bank's knowledge about a customer are assumed to be accumulate in every employee of a bank, so that a bank cannot rely on any division of knowledge between department and department".[110]

---

trustee or personal representative who acts for more than one trust or estate will not be deemed to have notice of matters acquired from dealing for one trust or estate when dealing with the affairs of another trust or estate; Companies Act 2006, s.40: in favour of any person dealing with a company in good faith the power of the board of directors should be deemed to be free of any limitation under the company's constitution. Good faith is defined at s.40(2)(b) to provide that a person shall not be treated as acting in bad faith by reason only of his knowing that an act is beyond the powers of the directors under the company's constitution.

[106] There is an exception in the case of fraud: where the agent is acting in fraud of his principal in the transaction in question, his state of mind will not be imputed to the principal, at least in cases where the concealment of the relevant knowledge from the principal was part of the fraud: *Re Hampshire Land* [1896] 2 Ch. 743; *Bowstead and Reynolds on Agency*, 19th edn., para.8–213; *PCW Syndicates v PCW Reinsurers* [1996] 1 Lloyd's Rep 241; *Group Josi Re v Walbrook* [1996] 1 Lloyd's Rep. 345; *Arab Bank v Zurich Bank* [1999] 1 Lloyd's Rep. 262; see also *Armstrong v Strain* [1952] 1 K.B. 232 (court not willing to pool knowledge of agent and principal so as to find that a fraudulent misrepresentation had been made by agent in connection with the sale of property).

[107] And equally the documents of one group company will not be treated as in the control of another group company: *Lonrho v Shell Petroleum* [1980] 1 W.L.R. 627, HL.

[108] [1931] 2 K.B. 157.

[109] [1933] A.C. 201; see also *Standard Investments v Canadian Imperial Bank of Commerce* (1986) 22 D.L.R. (4d) 410.

[110] *Architects of Wine Ltd v Barclays Bank Plc* [2007] 2 Lloyd's Rep 471 at para. 10, per Rix L.J. See also *Malhi v Abbey Life* [1994] C.L.C. 615, [1996] IRLR 237 where the insured had a life assurance policy and applied for another one from the same company. He was refused because of certain information which had not been disclosed when the first policy was taken out. The company continued to accept premiums on the first policy, but the Court of Appeal held that it had not waived its right to avoid the first policy for non-disclosure because the knowledge of the agent was not to be imputed to the company for all purposes.

CHAPTER 7

Information barriers

1. When information barriers become relevant

A. Information barriers and Chinese Walls

7–001   Where a firm has learned confidential information in the course of acting for a former client, it may in some circumstances be permitted to act for a new client even though the confidential information is relevant to the new retainer if it acts through different individuals in the firm and where the confidential information obtained by those acting for the former client is protected from disclosure to those acting for the new client.

"Chinese Wall" has in the past been the expression used to refer to an information barrier within the firm which is intended to ensure that information available to or known by certain members of the firm is not available to other members of the firm. The origin of the expression is somewhat obscure. It seems to have become popular following the 1929 US stock market crash when the US government legislated informational separation between investment bankers and brokerage firms to limit conflicts of interest. There are several schools of thought. One is that it refers to the Great Wall of China—as a strong barrier. Another is that it derives from "Chinese whispers".[1] A third relates back to the Chinese standing screens which allow for the temporary installation of a wall in a room lacking the permanent architectural features.[2]

---

[1] "The Chinese used to make walls out of paper through which you could whisper and therefore the name is a flagrant indication of what goes on": J. Quarrell, "Modern Trusts in Legal Education", [1991] 5 Trusts Law International 99, 103–4.
[2] It is said that F.D. Roosevelt used the expression in 1927. In 1934 T.S. Eliot said "After the erection of the Chinese Wall of Milton, blank verse has suffered not only arrest but also retrogression" (whatever that meant). There are a number of obscure early uses of the expression which seems to have come into common usage by 1980. Contrast the informa-

In recent years, the phrase has fallen out of favour.[3] It might be said that it should be no more unacceptable than an English muffin or French fries. However, use of nationalities appears more permissible in food than in other spheres. There was a brief flirtation with the expression "ethical walls" but it seems now that the expression of preference is "information barriers", and that term will be adopted hereafter.

According to Lord Millett in *Bolkiah*[4] an effective information barrier produces "a modern equivalent of the circumstances which prevailed in *Rakusen*'s case". In *Rakusen v Ellis Munday & Clarke*[5] a small firm of solicitors had two partners who carried on what amounted to separate practices, each with his own clients, without knowledge of the other's clients and with the exclusive services of some of the clerks. When a client who had consulted one partner found that the opposing party in litigation had consulted the other partner (who had never met the first client and was not aware his partner had been consulted), the Court of Appeal refused to grant an injunction, holding there was no risk of misuse of confidential information.[6] The effect of an information barrier is, therefore, to treat different parts of the same firm for this purpose as though they were separate entities.

7–002

B. The need for information barriers in former client conflicts

In former client conflicts, the obligation is to protect the old client's confidentiality. The information barrier presupposes that the professional holds, in documents or in his mind or the mind of his employees or agents, confidential information of the former client. This will not always be common ground.[7] As Lord Millett made clear, the obligation is to keep the information confidential, not merely to take all reasonable steps to do so. The duty to preserve confidentiality is unqualified. It is a duty not merely not to communicate it to a third party, but a duty not to make any use of it or cause any use to be made of it by others, otherwise than for the client's

7–003

---

tion barrier referred to by Gillard J. in *Yunghanns v Elfic Ltd*, Unreported, July 3, 1998, Supreme Court of Victoria at p.28 as "A Dutch dyke; a good barrier to water but involving the ever present risk of seepage leading to a leak."

[3] See *Peat Marwick Mitchell & Co v Superior Court* 200 Cal. App. 272, 293-4 (1988) Low J. for a Californian judge's criticisms of the use of the expression.

[4] [1999] 2 A.C. 222 at 238.

[5] [1912] 1 Ch. 831.

[6] This was always seen as the leading English case until *Bolkiah*. The test set out by the Court of Appeal in *Rakusen* was long criticised and was not adopted in *Bolkiah*; partly this was because all three members of the Court of Appeal in *Rakusen* expressed themselves in slightly different terms, and partly because the test which it was thought had been adopted by the Court of Appeal "reasonable probability of mischief" was thought too generous to the professional.

[7] Thus in *Re Solicitors (A Firm)* [1995] 3 All E.R. 482, Lightman J., the solicitors' defence was that they did not hold any relevant confidential information of the former client ("there is no evidence that anything confidential was ever communicated to the . . . partner").

benefit. The former client cannot be protected completely from accidental or inadvertent disclosure. But he is entitled to prevent his former solicitor from exposing him to any foreseeable risk, which includes the increased risk of the use of the information to his prejudice arising from the acceptance of instructions to act for another client with an adverse interest[8] in a matter to which the information is or may be relevant. In *Bolkiah*, Lord Millett said that the court should intervene to prevent the professional from acting unless satisfied there was no risk of disclosure. The risk must be a real one, not merely fanciful or theoretical. But it need not be substantial. In applying this test, the House of Lords chose the most onerous of the various tests previously applied.[9] Lord Millett said that the court should restrain the firm from acting unless satisfied on the basis of clear and convincing evidence that effective measures have been taken to ensure no disclosure will occur.[10]

7–004 A distinction should be drawn between confidential information held by other members of the firm and information learned from the former client by the individual who proposes to act on the second retainer. If the same individual holds confidential information for the former client as intends to act for the new client, unless there is consent the court will not normally permit him to act. The difficulty of acting in such circumstances without inhibition or professional embarrassment means that it is better not to act at all.[11]

C. Adverse interest

7–005 In his speech in *Bolkiah* Lord Millett identified the circumstances in which the court would intervene in former client conflicts to circumstances where it can be shown:

> "(i) that the solicitor is in possession of information which is confidential to him and to the disclosure of which he has not consented and (ii) that the information is or may be relevant to the new matter in which the interest of the other client is or may be adverse to his own".

---

[8] See 7–005 for a discussion as to whether this is a limiting factor.
[9] The test applied was that applied in *Re Solicitors (A Firm)* [1997] Ch. 1 at 9, Lightman J., in *Carindale Country Club Estate Pty Ltd v Astill* (1993) 115 A.L.R. 112, Drummond J. and applied by Pumfrey J. in *Bolkiah* at first instance. An alternative test, a "reasonable probability of real mischief" appears from *Rakusen v Ellis Munday & Clarke* [1912] 1 Ch. 831, CA, criticised in New Zealand in *National Mutual Holdings Pty Ltd v Sentry Corp* [1989] 22 F.C.R. 209, and abandoned in Canada: *MacDonald Estate v Martin* (1990) 77 D.L.R. (4th) 249.
[10] This sentence was an amended form of the test adopted by Sopinka J. in *MacDonald Estate v Martin* (1990) 77 D.L.R. (4th) 249 at 269 in the Supreme Court of Canada. In fact the amendment substantially changes the meaning, "effective" replacing "all reasonable" in the original.
[11] See the formulations in *Re Solicitors (A Firm)* [1995] 3 All E.R. 482 at 489 and *Re Solicitors (A Firm)* [1992] Q.B. 959 both of which envisage that in such circumstances the professional cannot act at all.

The reference to "adverse interest" is confusing because it suggests that the court may only intervene in such circumstances. The confusion has been exacerbated because the expression has been incorporated into SRA regulatory rules. But it is not correct. The professional will not be able to act where there is an information conflict, notwithstanding that the confidential information was not obtained from a party who now has an adverse interest: where the conflict is simply that the firm holds relevant information which it would be obliged to disclose to the new client but it cannot do so because of its obligation to the former client, the firm will be unable to carry out its duty to its new client without breaching its duty to its old client. In such circumstances it does not matter whether the former client has an adverse interest or any interest at all.

D. Mergers and changes of firm

Mergers often cause problems. In considering whether to merge, consideration of potential conflicts is always a key issue. If it becomes necessary to cease action for large numbers of the clients of one firm or the other, the merger will not exploit synergies; on the contrary, it will mean that the new firm is able to handle far fewer clients. Where the individual firms merge, or one takes over the other, then the new firm will not be able to accept retainers for clients whose retainers conflict, without informed consent. Where there are existing clients with continuing retainers, the attempt to terminate the retainer may not be straightforward. This was the problem in *Young v Robson Rhodes*,[12] albeit an accountants' not a solicitors' case, where the accountants who unilaterally terminated a retainer to act as expert witnesses in litigation because they were about to merge with the defendants to that very litigation faced an action for damages for wrongful termination of the retainer.[13] Mergers are likely to give rise to broader problems where the two firms acted regularly for separate clients in the same business sector who regularly cross swords in business, transactions or litigation with each other. Sometimes this will be merely a commercial conflict, where it becomes practically rather than legally impossible to continue to act. On other occasions there will be confidential information problems which make it impossible to act for either even with an information barrier.

7–006

The former client conflict may arise on a merger in two situations. First, where one retainer is terminated on the merger, or secondly, where one of the firms was at the time of the merger in possession of confidential information relevant to the retainer which continues after the merger. In these

7–007

---

[12] [1999] 3 All E.R. 524, discussed in detail at para.2–022.
[13] In *Robson Rhodes* the retainer was determined in anticipation of the merger and Laddie J. held that was an unlawful termination. But when the firm ceases to exist, might that not be good reason for the determination of the retainer.

instances the new firm will not actually have ever owed a fiduciary duty to the former client—it is the old firm or some of its partners which owed that duty. But nevertheless some of the individuals within the merged firm will be in possession of relevant confidential information and the firm will only be able to act if it is able to set up an effective information barrier.

The issue is the same where a single individual moves firms. If only one person has moved firms, it may not be very difficult to ensure that that person has no involvement and is kept away from the action. It may thus be possible to show no real risk that confidential information will be disclosed. However, what might have been seen as a relatively straightforward case where precisely this occurred, *Koch Shipping v Richards Butler*,[14] led to an injunction granted at first instance notwithstanding wide-ranging undertakings being given by both individual solicitor and new firm, and although the Court of Appeal subsequently allowed the appeal and discharged the injunction, this suggests that the position may not always be straightforward even in this sort of case.[15] If there are a series of individuals who have left the old firm, it may be harder to satisfy the court. *In Re Solicitors (A Firm)*[16] the solicitor who moved firms acted for the former-firm former client and the new firm client, which is a more difficult position, but he persuaded the judge that his only involvement at his prior firm was to exchange a few pleasantries on the stairs with the general counsel, and was not in possession of confidential information of the former client at all, at least so far as he was aware. Thus he succeeded in showing there was no real risk of disclosure of confidential information.[17]

It does not make a difference whether the solicitor who moves is a partner or an employee because the issue on former client conflicts is confidentiality not fiduciary obligation.

2. Confidential information

A. What is confidential information?

7–008   There is an obligation not to disclose or misuse the confidential information of the client, whether the issue is an existing client conflict or a former client conflict. In the latter case, the confidential information obligation is

---

[14] [2002] Lloyd's Rep. P.N. 604, see para.7–017.
[15] For a recent Australian case where one individual joining a firm held confidential information learned from a former-firm client see *Bureau Interprofessionel Des Vins de Bourgogne v Red Earth Nominees Pty Ltd (T/a Taltarni Vineyards)* [2002] F.C.A. 588, Ryan J.
[16] [1995] 3 All E.R. 482, Lightman J. Not everything that Lightman J. said can stand with *Bolkiah* but the test adopted by Lightman J. was expressly adopted by Lord Millett in *Bolkiah*.
[17] See also *Halewood International v Addleshaw Booth & Co* [2000] Lloyd's Rep. P.N. 298.

the only obligation that remains. So what is confidential information in this context? In general, for there to be a breach of confidence, the relevant information must have the necessary quality of confidence, must have been imparted in circumstances importing an obligation of confidence and there must be an unauthorised use of that information to the detriment of the party communicating it.[18] In the normal course communications between solicitor and client will be presumed confidential[19] and there is no reason why any different rule should apply in respect of other professionals.[20] The presumption in favour of solicitor/client communications being confidential thus suggests confidential information is treated more widely in these circumstances than, for example, after the termination of employment when an employee wishes to use the confidential information of his former employer for his own purposes.[21]

There is little authority in this jurisdiction which expressly considers what constitutes confidential information for the purpose of conflicts. In principle, there should be no difference as to what is confidential for this purpose and what is confidential in English law for other purposes. Because the question only becomes significant where the information is relevant to the second retainer, there should not usually be much difficulty in determining whether it is confidential. If it is communicated in the course of the retainer, is not in the public domain, and is relevant to the second retainer, it is likely to be easy to show that it is confidential.

In *Re Solicitors (A Firm)*[22] Lightman J. said[23]: 7–009

"Confidential information passing between solicitor and client and otherwise acquired by a solicitor on behalf of his client may, like any other confidential information communicated to anyone else, subsequently cease to be confidential. Confidential documents and information may become common knowledge or at least known to an opponent in the course of a trial. Some information may be memorable and some eminently forgettable. Common sense requires recognition that not all confidential information acquired by a solicitor will remain in the mind of the solicitor or be susceptible of being triggered as a recollection after the lapse of a period of time. For the purpose of the law imposing constraints upon solicitors acting against the interests of former clients, the law is concerned with the protection of information which (a) was originally communicated in confidence, (b) at the date of the later proposed

---

[18] *Coco v AN Clark (Engineers) Ltd* [1969] R.P.C. 41 at 47, Megarry J.; *Att-Gen v Guardian Newspapers (No.2)* [1988] 3 All E.R. 545 at 648–49 per Lord Griffiths.
[19] *Minter v Priest* [1930] A.C. 558 at 581, per Lord Atkin.
[20] A solicitor has a professional obligation to keep the affairs of his client confidential. Most professions have similar rules.
[21] See, e.g. *Faccenda Chicken Ltd v Fowler* [1987] Ch. 117.
[22] [1997] Ch. 1.
[23] At 9-10.

retainer is still confidential and may reasonably be considered remembered or capable, on the memory being triggered, of being recalled and (c) relevant to the subject matter of the subsequent proposed retainer. I shall refer to information that satisfies these three qualifications as 'relevant confidential information'".

Lightman J. thus drew a distinction between "memorable" and "eminently forgettable" information. This goes to the distinction between the casual conversation on the one hand and the formal memorandum which was prepared by lawyers and was an important document. This is not the first time such a distinction has been drawn.[24] But this issue is not really concerned with whether information is confidential; it may be in the most casual conversation that the most important information is conveyed. It is concerned with whether a professional is likely to remember information imparted in a casual conversation, which goes to whether a remedy should be granted.

B. Identifying the confidential information

7–010 The authorities, both in this jurisdiction and in particular in Australia, have focused on the extent it is necessary to define the confidential information in question with particularity. In England, the starting point is that where a party seeks to prevent the disclosure of confidential information, it will usually be incumbent on him to identify precisely what the confidential information in question is. This is often difficult in a conflict of interest case, where the claimant may have good grounds for suspicion but little concrete evidence or recollection as to what confidential information may have been provided to the professional. Sometimes relief will be refused simply on the ground that the lack of particularity is a fatal deficiency, other cases are less strict. An example of the harsh approach is that adopted by Lightman J. in *Mannesmann v Goldman Sachs*.[25] The claimants sought to identify the confidential information on which they sought to rely. The judge said that the information relied upon could not be categorised as confidential information, but even if it were, by referring to it in open court it had lost any confidentiality it might once have possessed and thus could not be relied upon.

Lord Millett said in *Bolkiah*[26] that the burden was on the claimant to show that the solicitor is in possession of information which is confidential

---

[24] See *KPMG v White & Case*, November 18, 1996, Unreported, Harman J. The application was based on a ten minute call involving a partner in Stephenson Harwood who said she could not remember the conversation at all.
[25] Unreported, November 18, 1999, see paras 19–016.
[26] [1999] 2 A.C. 222 at 235.

to him and to the disclosure of which he has not consented and that the information is or may be relevant to the new matter in which the interest of the other client is or may be adverse to his own. But he then said:

> "although the burden of proof is on the plaintiff, it is not a heavy one. The former may readily be inferred; the latter will often be obvious".

So it may be possible to infer that confidential information has been disclosed. In *Macartney Ball v Druces and Attlee*[27] the Court of Appeal refused permission to appeal from the grant of an injunction by Burton J. restraining solicitors from acting notwithstanding that the judge had failed to specify the confidential information in question. The Court of Appeal treated the judge as having concluded by virtue of the closeness of the connection that the solicitors must have been in possession of relevant confidential information. And in *Re Solicitors*[28] Timothy Walker J. regarded the failure to specify the confidential information in question as relevant but not decisive.

In Australia the caselaw shows a similar tension between principle and practice. The importance of particularity was emphasised in *Carindale Country Club Estate Pty Ltd v Astill*[29] where Drummond J. said that it was a basic requirement that before material will be recognised as having the character of confidential information, the information in question must be identified with precision and not merely in global terms.[30] The judge said that the requirement is insisted upon even though it may necessitate disclosing to the court the very information the confidentiality of which it is sought to preserve by the action. The requirement had its foundation in the need for the court to be able to frame a clear injunction, should relief against misuse of confidential information be granted.[31] The judge said:

7–011

> "The more general the description of the information which a plaintiff seeks to protect, the more difficult it is for the court to satisfy itself that information so described was imparted or received or retained by a defendant in circumstances which give rise to an obligation of confidence".[32]

So too in New Zealand in *GBR Invt Ltd v Keung HC Christchurch*[33] Associate Judge Bell said that the applicant "must be able to identify with specificity the confidential information, and not merely in global terms".

---

[27] Unreported, February 8, 2002.
[28] [2000] 1 Lloyd's Rep. 31.
[29] (1993) 115 A.L.R. 112.
[30] For a case in which the Australian court held that the description of confidential information was inadequate, see *Belan v Casey* [2002] N.S.W.S.C. 58, Young C.J.
[31] See *Oceanic v HIH* [1999] N.S.W.S.C. 292, Austin J. at para.43.
[32] Citing *Independent Management Resources Pty Ltd v Brown* [1987] V.R. 605, 609.
[33] [2010] N.Z.H.C. 411.

However, the Australian courts have also said that that principle needed to be applied with flexibility. The next section looks at Australian authority which may be regarded as watering down what is regarded as confidential information for this purpose.

C. "The getting to know you" factors as confidential information

7–012   You know from the prior retainer that the managing director buckles under pressure and likes to settle his cases. Is that confidential information? There is a line of Australian cases which have treated as confidential information what has been referred to in Australia as the "getting to know you" factors. This expression (which seems unlikely to catch on in this jurisdiction) is derived from *Yunghanns v Elfic Pty Ltd*[34] where Gillard J. said:

> "The degree of particularity of the confidential information must depend on all the circumstances. Often, it cannot be identified for fear of disclosure. In considering this factor it must be borne in mind that a solicitor makes notes, forms views and opinions of clients and observes things that the client may have forgotten or overlooked. In some cases, the circumstances of the retainer and the nature of the legal work will be sufficient to establish the nature of the confidential information. In this regard, the relationship between solicitor and client may be such that the solicitor learns a great deal about his client, his strengths, his weaknesses, his honesty or lack thereof, his reaction to crisis, pressures or tension, his attitude to litigation and settling cases and his tactics. These are factors which I would call the 'getting to know you' factors. The overall opinion formed by a solicitor of his client as a result of his contact may in the circumstances amount to confidential information that should not be disclosed or used against the client".

In *British American Tobacco Australia Services Ltd v Blanch*[35] Young C.J. proceeded on a similar basis. He said that for the purpose of conflicts of interest cases, confidential information was not the same as between employer and employee, and:

> "... the relationship between solicitor and client may be such that the solicitor learns a great deal about his client, his strengths, his weaknesses, his honesty or lack thereof, his reaction to crisis, pressure or tension".

---

[34] 1998 Butterworths Cases 9803497.
[35] [2004] N.S.W.S.C. 70.

Thus in *Blanch*, it was said that matters involving the client's forensic tactics and strategies would come under this head; if an insurer told his solicitor that it would always accept 75 per cent of a claim for instant cash, that would come within the category of confidential information.[36]

On the basis of these cases, it was suggested in previous editions of this book that Austalia took a broader view of what constitutes confidential information than the English courts. This view has been criticised[37] on the ground that in *Yunghanns* Gillard J. said the matters in question were "relevant to and essential background to" the matter in which the firm was now seeking to act and there was a risk that the confidential information would be used contrary to the interests of the second client. But this is not quite the point. The question is not whether "the getting to know you factors" can be used against the client but whether their somewhat nebulous nature means that they cannot be treated as having the necessary attributes of confidential information.

If the chief executive buckles under pressure, and tends to settle his cases, that information may be known to a wide range of people. It will probably be known as much to opponents as colleagues. Can this really properly be described as confidential information? Another example may be the professional who acts for insurers and learns of their views on settlement. If he simply forms the view that they are litigation-averse then it is unlikely that this will be regarded as confidential information. But if they have specific formal policies as to settlement of litigation, those policies will almost certainly constitute confidential information.

7–013
It may be, however, that there is notwithstanding this, little difference between English and Australian law here. A couple of recent citations from Australian cases suggest that the "getting to know you" factors are not generally understood to constitute confidential information. In *Mintel International Group Ltd v Mintel (Australia) Pty Ltd*,[38] Heerey J. said:

> "There are many bodies such as Commonwealth and State government entities, banks, insurers, media companies and many others which are constantly engaged in litigation. Counsel retained to act on behalf of such bodies inevitably acquire information, not confidential information in the strict sense, but experience as to the corporate culture of the clients, their internal policies, the way they deal with litigation, tactics, the personalities of important decision-makers and so forth. I do not

---

[36] Citing *PhotoCure v Queen's University at Kingston* [2002] I.P.R. 56, Goldberg J., FCA. So too in *Sent v Fairfax Publication Pty Ltd* [2002] V.S.C. 429 Nettle J. said that he thought that there was likely to have been disclosure of "getting to know you factors" and relied upon that in support of his decision to grant an injunction.
[37] Goubran, "Conflicts of Duty—The Perennial Lawyers' Tale—A Comparative Study of the Law in England and Australia" (2006), 30 Melb. U.L. Review 88, 109, an interesting article which explores the comparisons between conflicts law in the two jurisdictions.
[38] [2000] F.C.A. 1410.

accept that general experience of that kind would impose what presumably on the respondent's argument would be lifeline restraints on counsel from acting against such a body".

In *Ismail-Zai v State of Western Australia*[39] Steytler P. said:

"If these so-called "getting to know you" factors, to the extent that they involve knowledge of the client rather than of anything imparted in confidence by the client concerning his or her affairs, can constitute confidential information (a proposition that seems to me, with respect, to be questionable) they will only rarely do so".

3. Features of an information barrier

A. A high test

7–014   It is not just in this jurisdiction that the courts have recognised that there is a heavy burden on the firm which seeks to show as a result of information barriers that there is no real risk of misuse of confidential information. In Western Australia in *Newman v Phillips Fox*[40] Steytler J. observed[41] that ordinarily information moved within a firm of solicitors. It was possible that an information barrier could be erected to prevent this, but there was very great difficulty for a firm to convince a court that the wall would be effective. He pointed out that walls or information barriers of that kind have "not often found favour with the courts". In *MacDonald Estate v Martin*[42] in the Supreme Court of Canada, Sopinka J. put it in similar terms, starting with rebuttable presumptions that confidential information will have been communicated by the former client in the course of the retainer, and that lawyers share confidences. And in *Pradhan v Eastside Day Surgery Pty*[43] Bleby J. said in the Full Court of South Australia that it would only be "in a very rare case if at all" that an information barrier would satisfy the "no real risk" test and that any such arrangement was likely to be almost impossible in a relatively small firm. As Wootten J. put it in the New South Wales Supreme Court in *Thompson v Mikkelsen*[44]:

"A client is entitled to assume that his solicitor will be in a position to approach the matter concerned with nothing in mind but the protection

---

[39] [2007] W.A.S.C.A. 150.
[40] (1999) 21 W.A.R. 309.
[41] (1999) 21 W.A.R. 309 at 324.
[42] (1990) 77 D.L.R. (4th) 249.
[43] (1999) S.A.S.C. 256.
[44] Unreported, October 3, 1974, N.S.W. Supreme Court, quoted in *Unioil* (1997) 17 W.A.R. 98 at 105.

of his client's interests against those of the other party. He should not have to depend on a person who has conflicting allegiances and who may be tempted either consciously or unconsciously to favour the other client or simply to seek a resolution of the matter in a way which is least embarrassing to himself".

B. Structural and ad hoc information barriers

In *Bolkiah*, Lord Millett borrowed a distinction derived from the rules made for the financial services industry. He distinguished a structural information barrier, one which is part of the established fabric of the firm, from an ad hoc information barrier, which is established for a particular case or to manage a particular conflict. Where one partner works in the John O'Groats office and another in Land's End, there is a structural information barrier. The likelihood of careless talk in such circumstances was inherently significantly less than where the individuals are separated for the very purpose of permitting the firm to act for the new client notwithstanding the potential conflict.

7–015

Lord Millett said that an effective information barrier:

"needs to be an established part of the organisational structure of the firm, not created ad hoc and dependent on the acceptance of evidence sworn for the purpose by members of staff engaged on the relevant work".

Lord Millett's speech in *Bolkiah* can be read as outlawing ad hoc information barriers altogether[45] as stating that ad hoc information barriers could never be adequate to control the flow of information, where the people involved were accustomed to working together on different projects as part of the same team or department. This was always an extreme view, particularly as Lord Millett makes it clear that there is no rule of law that information barriers or other arrangements of a similar kind are insufficient to eliminate the risk.[46] In *Young v Robson Rhodes*,[47] Laddie J. made clear that this was not to be treated as an absolute rule and Lord Millett should not be read as so stating:

7–016

"The crucial question is "will the barriers work?" If they do, it does not matter whether they were created before the problem arose or are erected afterwards. It seems to me that all Lord Millett was saying was that Chinese Walls which become part of the fabric of the institution

---

[45] [1999] 2 A.C. 222 at 238–9.
[46] At 237.
[47] [1999] 3 All E.R. 524, see para.2–22.

are more likely to work than those artificially put in place to meet a one-off problem".

In fact, as Lord Millett talked about producing "a modern equivalent of the circumstances which prevailed in *Rakusen*'s case", it is surely a question of fact in every case whether that result has been achieved. It is now clear that there is no absolute rule[48]—indeed there is no rule of law which requires there to be a information barriers at all to show that there is no real risk of misuse. In an age of computers and instantaneous communications, a black and white distinction between structural and ad hoc walls is itself misleading. The John O'Groats partner will be on the same computer network as his Lands End partner even if they are hundreds of miles apart. It may be necessary to ensure that the Lands End partner does not receive emails which would normally be copied to him.

C. Caselaw on information barriers

7–017   A significant recent English decision on the adequacy of information barriers is the Court of Appeal decision in *Koch Shipping v Richards Butler*.[49] Ms Peaston acted for Koch whilst a partner of Jackson Parton. She then moved to Richards Butler, who acted against Koch in an arbitration relating to the vessel Atlas M. Koch sought an injunction to restrain Richards Butler from continuing to act. Undertakings were offered by Ms Peaston including an undertaking not to communicate (at all) with any person working on the Atlas M arbitration. She was located on the tenth floor of Richards Butler's building, whereas the Atlas M casehandlers were on the eleventh floor, so there was a degree of physical separation, which Richards Butler agreed to continue. Undertakings were also given by Richards Butler and the Atlas M casehandlers. Andrew Smith J. nevertheless granted an injunction restraining Richards Butler from continuing to act because the risk of inadvertent disclosure was not fanciful.[50] This decision caused shock waves when it was first reported: if these undertakings were insufficient, how could effective information barriers ever be built? The Court of Appeal allowed the appeal. They placed significance on the fact that only one individual was here involved, which materially affected the risk of inadvertent disclosure.[51] Tuckey L.J. said[52]:

---

[48] See *Koch Shipping v Richards Butler* [2002] Lloyd's P.N. 604 at 607, 609 and *Halewood International v Addleshaw Booth & Co* [2000] Lloyd's Rep. P.N. 298, per Neuberger J.
[49] [2002] Lloyd's P.N. 604.
[50] [2002] Lloyd's Rep. P.N. 201.
[51] For a recent Australian case where one individual joining a firm held confidential information learned from a former-firm client see *Bureau Interprofessionel Des Vins de Bourgogne v Red Earth Nominees Pty Ltd (T/a Taltarni Vineyards)* [2002] F.C.A. 588, Ryan J.
[52] At para.53.

"I think there is a danger inherent in the intensity of the adversarial process of courts being persuaded that a risk exists when, if one stands back a little, that risk is no more than fanciful or theoretical. I advocate a robust view with this in mind, so as to ensure that the line is sensibly drawn".

Another post-*Bolkiah* decision on information barriers is *Re Solicitors*.[53] That was a case where a shipping Protection and Indemnity club sought an injunction to restrain solicitors from acting against them because they had acted for them in related proceedings. In refusing an injunction, the judge took into account the weakness of the link between the proceedings which he described as "somewhat tenuous". Timothy Walker J. accepted that it was to be inferred that confidential information had been imparted during the previous relationship but took into account in favour of the solicitors that it had not proved possible to specify what any of the information was. What really impressed the judge, however, was the apparent strength of the information barriers, which arose between the admiralty department on the one hand and the insurance and reinsurance department on the other hand of the firm in question. The barrier existed long before the conflict issue arose. The relevant personnel worked in different buildings and had never visited each other's offices. The judge said that the club was left with the argument that mistakes do occur, which was in the circumstances an inadequate basis for an injunction. The judge was pressed with citations from the previous case of *Re Solicitors (A Firm)*[54] to the effect that it was doubtful to what extent impregnable information barriers could ever be created and it was only in very special cases that an attempt should be made to do so.[55] He said that to the extent that this authority provided a different approach, it should not be followed since *Bolkiah*.[56]

---

[53] [2000] 1 Lloyd's Rep. 31.
[54] [1992] Q.B. 959.
[55] A comment made in the context of solicitors by Parker L.J. and echoed by Sir David Croom-Johnson.
[56] Another relevant decision is that of Neuberger J. in *Halewood International v Addleshaw Booth & Co* [2000] Lloyd's Rep. P.N. 298. A solicitor involved in proceedings to protect the claimants' trade mark switched firms to the defendants, who were instructed on the other side in passing off proceedings relating to the same brand. An injunction to restrain the defendants from acting was refused on undertakings being given, including undertakings that the individual would not work on the case and would work in a different building to those working on the litigation. The judgment is largely an application of principles in other cases. The court took the view that the individual did learn relevant confidential information but took into account the fact that the claimant was unable to specify what it was with any precision. It is plain that whilst the judge paid more than lip service to the claimant's concerns, he thought they were overstated and there was unlikely to be a problem. The moving of the individual to a different building is another form of ad hoc Chinese Wall, but it is wrong to suggest that Lord Millett intended to suggest in *Bolkiah* that this could never be effective and the judge here certainly did not take such a view.

The most recent English authority[57] on information barriers is the decision of the Court of Appeal in *Gus Consulting v Leboeuf Lamb Greene and Macrae*.[58] Six members of Debevoise & Plimpton, including Arthur Marriott Q.C., who had the conduct of an arbitration, moved to Leboeuf Lamb Greene and Macrae ("LLGM"), where they took over conduct of the arbitration through LLGM. LLGM had previously acted for the other party to the arbitration and in consequence held relevant confidential information. The judge declined to grant an injunction, taking into account the undertakings given in relation to information barriers and the fact that the advice given to the party complaining was some time before and not in relation to matters of central relevance in the arbitration. Mummery L.J. shared the judge's reservations about LLGM's decision to act in the arbitration[59] but saw no error in the judge's analysis[60]:

> "Each case turns on a careful judicial analysis and assessment of the quality of the evidence about the effectiveness of the precautions taken to protect the confidentiality of the former client's information from the risk of disclosure and misuse. If there is clear and convincing evidence that the precautions taken will provide effective protection, there will be no real risk to justify the grant of an injunction".

D. Elements of an information barrier

7–018 The purpose of an information barrier is to limit information to some parts of the firm or company and to provide an information barrier preventing information reaching other parts. The most common features are as follows:

(a) The physical separation of the various departments including details such as dining arrangements: where the relevant individuals work in different office buildings or in separate sections of the same office building, the room for leaks is diminished. There will be no problem in one receiving faxes intended for another,[61] they will not be able to gossip to each other at lunch.

---

[57] In *Re Z* [2009] EWHC 3621 (Fam) Bodey J. granted relief precluding a small firm of solicitors for acting through an assistant solicitor for a wife when the senior partner had acted for the husband when the couple had contemplated divorce nine years earlier. The senior partner had then briefly become a personal friend of the husband. The small firm was too small to make it realistic for the assistant to act through an effective information barrier. This was a clear case with little legal analysis relevant to this book.
[58] [2006] EWCA Civ 683.
[59] Which suggests support for a wider inherent jurisdiction over solicitors acting: see 5–018
[60] At [31].
[61] Although if what is in issue is a former client conflict, only those acting for the new client are likely to be receiving faxes.

(b) An information barrier which is part of the natural division of the operations of the firm or company (such as between the London and Leeds offices, or between different departments) will be more effective than an ad hoc division created by the needs of the particular conflict.
(c) An educational programme, normally recurring, to emphasise the importance of not improperly or inadvertently divulging confidential information.
(d) Strict and carefully defined procedures for dealing with a situation where it is felt the wall should be crossed and the maintaining of proper records where this occurs.
(e) Monitoring by compliance officers of the effectiveness of the wall.
(f) Disciplinary sanctions where there has been a breach of the wall.

It is easy to see that in some cases it should be possible to maintain an effective information barrier whereas in others it will be much more difficult. Some pointers are as follows:

(a) Where there are different offices of a partnership or firm, for example regional offices, it should be relatively easy to keep information confidential so that it is not shared between offices.
(b) The most likely means of breaching a geographical wall will be by electronic mail or communication which is oblivious of geographical boundaries.
(c) The number of people working on the different projects may be important. Where it is a couple of people in the firm that worked for the old client, it will be much easier to maintain the security of the wall than where there are a large number of individuals. In *Bolkiah*, 168 KPMG personnel worked on the project for Prince Jefri, the former client. It is easy to see why the House of Lords were anxious as to leaks. This was a point emphasised by the Court of Appeal in *Koch Shipping v Richards Butler*.[62]
(d) Whilst it will be a point against the efficacy of an information barrier that the number of individuals concerned is large, because there will be a greater potential for leaks, by contrast it will be significantly harder to persuade a court that an information barrier is adequate where the firm is very small. Where the firm consists only of a small number of individuals, it will be particularly difficult to show that there is no risk of leaks. In *Pradhan v Eastside Day Surgery Pty Ltd*[63] Bleby J. in the Full Court of South Australia said that in a small firm it was likely to be almost

---

[62] [2002] Lloyd's Rep. P.N. 604, CA, see para.7–017.
[63] [1999] S.A.S.C. 256.

impossible to have an information barrier which will satisfy the "no real risk" test.[64]

(e) The nature of the confidential information may be important. Is it the sort of information where a chance remark at lunch could give the game away? For example, an exercise where assets are being traced might be regarded as in this category, or where there are allegations of fraud or serious wrongdoing. There might be less of a concern where the matter related to a dispute as to quantum of damages. Exactly what has or might the client have done by way of making a clean breast of matters to his adviser? Is the information likely to be privileged from production in litigation or would it be information that would have to be disclosed anyway?

(f) There is no English case which places emphasis on an educational programme to emphasise the importance of not improperly or inadvertently divulging confidential information, although there is Australian authority where this was the principal reason given for regarding the proposed information barrier as inadequate. In *Newman v Phillips Fox*[65] Steytler J. regarded the ad hoc wall there proposed as inadequate: it was not accompanied by an educational programme or procedures and there were no record keeping or disciplinary sanctions proposed.

7–019　Some of the features of information barriers which have been discussed in US cases are as follows[66]:

(a) *Prohibited access to documents.* Some courts have required documents related to the matter in question to be maintained in a separate, often locked, location within the firm, with keys provided only to those permitted access. This procedure has been adapted to computerised files through password restrictions.

(b) *Segregation of the tainted lawyer.* Courts have on occasion required a tainted lawyer to relocate his or her personal office within a firm, and to prohibit the lawyer from visiting certain floors or areas of a firm's office.

(c) *Making one or more lawyers directly responsible to the court for ensuring compliance.* Some courts go so far as to require periodic reports by lawyers working on the matter in question to the effect that all information barrier procedures have been adhered to.

(d) *Firm notice.* Most courts require that the firm send a memorandum

---

[64] The 2011 SRA Code of Conduct also regards this as important: see Note 2 to Ch. 4.
[65] (1999) 21 W.A.R. 309.
[66] Many of these are discussed in *Petroleum Wholesale Inc v Marshall* 751 S.W. 2d 295, Texas Ct App (1988).

to all lawyers (or all personnel) informing the entire firm that no one should discuss the case with the tainted lawyer.
(e) *Prohibition of fee sharing.* This can prove to be the most difficult requirement to implement as a practical matter, in the sense that compensation in many large firms is set, at least in part, at the end of each year, with the compensation committee taking all factors of a lawyer's performance into account. Documenting the fact that a lawyer was not permitted to share in any part of a fee from a given matter in such circumstances simply cannot be proved.[67]
(f) *Affidavits by tainted lawyers.* Many courts require the tainted lawyer to execute affidavits stating that they have not and will not engage in communications regarding their prior representation or the current representation with any other member or staff of the firm.
(g) *Logging of all meetings.* Some courts have forbidden informal meetings regarding the matter in question, requiring instead that all meetings be held in closed conference rooms, and the names of those in attendance be documented.

In determining whether the information barrier proposed is adequate, it is relevant to note that the US courts have taken into account the following:

(a) *Nature of the work done for the previous client.* The more limited the scope and duration of the previous representation, the more likely an information barrier will be considered adequate.
(b) *Early creation of the wall.* Where an effective wall has been implemented as soon as the potential conflict has been identified, there is a higher likelihood that the court will permit a wall.
(c) *Period of time between representations.* The longer the time between the previous representation and the present representation, the more likely it is the court will approve of the use of screening procedures.
(d) *Firm size.* Logically large firms are more capable of creating and maintaining an effective information barrier because they can better physically separate lawyers on the two sides of the wall, and often have separate departments or practice groups which reduces the likelihood of "hall talk" between lawyers in different groups.
(e) *Specialities involved.* Where the tainted lawyer works in a different area of the law than those working on the present matter, courts are more likely to approve of a wall.
(f) *Number of tainted lawyers.* Courts are understandably sceptical of

---

[67] Nevertheless, this factor is required and is regarded as extremely important by the courts and the bar itself. See ABA Comm of Ethics and Professional Responsibility Formal Op. 342 (1975).

the effectiveness of a wall that is to be applied to a large number of lawyers.

(g) *Position of the tainted lawyer.* Whether the tainted lawyer is, or was at the time of the prior representation, a junior associate as opposed to a senior partner is frequently taken into account by courts. The less authority the lawyer had, the less likely a court will find that he is likely to have had broad knowledge of client confidences.

E. Information barriers: unnecessarily restrictive rules?

7–020 Where the claimant is able to show that the firm is in possession of relevant confidential information, it is never easy for the lawyer to satisfy the court that an information barrier will adequately protect the interests of the client. To an extent, the courts have taken a stricter line than might have been expected since *Bolkiah*. That a well-respected judge could have granted an injunction notwithstanding the protections and undertakings offered at first instance in *Koch Shipping v Richards Butler*[68] surprised many practitioners. Certainly, the decision was reversed on appeal, but the case provides no comfort to those advising on the efficacy of information barriers at the creation stage.

An interesting contrast, albeit in a slightly different context, which suggests a more flexible approach is the Court of Appeal decision on judicial conflicts, *Locabail (UK) v Bayfield Properties*.[69] In one of the cases, the judge was a solicitor who discovered part way through the hearing that clients of his firm had an interest in the failure of one of the defendants in the issues before the court. Yet that interest would apparently, under Law Society regulatory rules, have prevented the judge's firm from acting for that defendant. The Court of Appeal said that as the judge only discovered this half way through the trial, disclosed what he knew and no one doubted what he had said to be accurate, no one could sensibly suggest this could affect his mind.

Large firms today are well equipped to maintain information barriers, and are accustomed to doing so. Where the firm consists of hundreds of partners and an even greater number of employees, the position is very far removed from the small businesses of old. There is much to be said for a more relaxed position on information barriers and increased acceptance of their use and utility. There is a public interest in clients being able to use their lawyer of choice wherever possible. If on large transactions or in niche market areas the small group of firms with the relevant experience are too

---

[68] [2002] Lloyd's Rep. P.N. 201, reversed at 604.
[69] [2000] 1 All E.R. 65, CA, considered in detail at 13–003.

readily conflicted, the clients suffer and there is a lack of market competition. It is precisely in these circumstances that conflicts problems are at their most acute. If too few professionals are available to act because of conflicts, market competition suffers. Lawyers tend to become "claimant lawyers" or "defendant lawyers" or focus on a smaller retinue of clients if the conflict rules are too strict. Of course the client is entitled to have his confidential information protected, but experience shows that many allegations of conflict are either tactical or simply misguided. A more relaxed environment and less strict rules would, it is suggested, serve the public interest rather than damage it. However neither the law nor the professional rules are obviously moving in that direction. Other jurisdictions are hardly setting more relaxed rules either: in Canada the law has recently changed so that a lawyer cannot act against an existing client even on an unrelated matter.[70]

As we have seen, English case law has suggested a marked reluctance to accept that information barriers will be effective. But there has been very little authority since *Koch Shipping* in 2002. The increasing sophistication of legal services over the last generation has meant that law firms and other professionals are increasingly accustomed to use information barriers as a matter of everyday practice, and that clients are equally increasingly accustomed to seeing them. There is, it is suggested, a real difference from the position ten years ago. Ten more years of information barriers have led to a greater acknowledgment in business of their necessity. There seems more of an emphasis on the importance of a client being entitled to have the services of his lawyer of choice unless there is good reason to the contrary.[71] It is suggested that the English courts may now take a more relaxed view of information barriers than they did in the few years after *Bolkiah*. They certainly should do so.

---

[70] See 3–014.
[71] See for example Lord Phillips C.J. in *Virgin Media Communications v BSkyB* [2008] EWCA Civ 612 at [20]: "We start with the proposition that it is desirable that a litigant should be free to instruct the lawyer of his choice. This is particularly true if the lawyer is already acting for the client and the client wishes the lawyer to continue to act in a related matter".

CHAPTER 8

Litigating conflicts

8–001 This chapter considers the remedies available in cases of conflicts of interest, and the tactics which may require consideration in such litigation.

1. Injunction

A. Interim and final injunctions

8–002 The most effective weapon in most cases is to apply for an injunction to restrain the professional from acting. An injunction may be either interim or final. A final injunction ultimately determines the rights of the parties. Final injunctions are in general granted after trial, after disclosure of documents and exchange of any witness and expert reports. An interim injunction is a temporary order which determines the rights of the parties on an interim basis until the court can hold a full trial. Of necessity, the court will take into account whether it is more convenient to grant an interim injunction than not.

In the normal interim injunction case, the claimant merely needs to show a "serious issue to be tried" a low threshold which merely requires showing that the claim is more than frivolous or vexatious. Once that is satisfied, then the court considers the "balance of convenience"—whether it is more convenient to grant an injunction or not to grant an injunction pending trial. The court will weigh the respective disadvantage to both sides of the grant or failure to grant an injunction pending trial, bearing in mind such factors as the adequacy of the claimant's cross-undertaking in damages, the possibility of a speedy trial, the adequacy of damages as a remedy instead of an injunction, and maintenance of the status quo. These principles are derived from Lord Diplock's speech in *American Cyanamid v Ethicon*[1].

---

[1] [1975] A.C. 396, HL.

However, in the case of a conflict application, this is all a bit unrealistic. The premise in the normal application for an interim injunction is that the court is "holding the ring" pending a full trial. But conflict applications almost never, at least in this jurisdiction, go beyond the interim application.

In the typical conflict application, the real remedy will be an injunction. At the early stage there will be no valid claim for damages at all. Damages are in any event a wholly inadequate remedy in a case where the client is concerned about conflict. Nor is it realistic to regard an interim injunction as "holding the ring". The client needs to be represented in the period between interim injunction and trial. It is wholly unsatisfactory for the position to be uncertain as to whether the client will be obliged to secure a new set of advisers. If a new firm becomes involved, that will need to take effect once and for all. Moreover, the costs of a full trial may look disproportionate in such circumstances. That has a number of consequences on the application for an interim injunction. The interim application is in effect in any normal case the final application. It means that the matter is decided without disclosure, and that there is no cross-examination or oral evidence.

There is not usually time to have a full trial. In *Bolkiah*, the writ against the accountants was issued at the end of August 1998. The hearing before Pumfrey J. took place on September 15, before the Court of Appeal on September 29 with judgment on October 19, and before the House of Lords on November 9–12, announcing their decision on November 18 and giving full reasons on December 18. Moreover, everyone will usually want the court to determine the matter once and for all. Even if the client is supportive of the professional's defence (or perhaps has encouraged it) the client will not want the position to lie unresolved. The potential costs incurred in taking the matter to trial will not be incurred. The claimant has the advantage that he does not have to give a cross-undertaking as to damages. In the usual injunction case, the injunction will determine the case: there are usually no damages because the grant of an injunction has prevented damage from being suffered.

It is open to the parties to agree to treat the interim hearing as the final hearing, essentially dispensing with cross-examination and disclosure. But even if the parties have not agreed that the hearing of the interim injunction will be the trial of the action, the court will recognise that the conclusion it reaches is likely in practice to be final, and thus will have in mind a more rigorous analysis of the strength of the claimants' case than would be appropriate for a normal interim injunction.[2] But in fact, perusal of the authorities in this area show very little reference to the balance of convenience at all. The authorities appear to pay little regard to the more conventional factors relevant to grant of an interim injunction.

---

[2] *Cayne v Global Natural Resources Plc* [1984] 1 All E.R. 225, CA; *NWL Ltd v Woods* [1979] 1 W.L.R. 1294, HL; *Lawrence David v Ashton* [1989] I.R.L.R. 22, CA; *Lansing Linde v Kerr* [1991] 1 All E.R. 418.

In a case where, unusually, the balance of convenience does feature, the balance is unlikely to be in favour of the professional, whose interests will be protectable through an undertaking in damages. In such circumstances the court may think the balance of convenience favours either the claimant client or former client (who is concerned about disclosure of his confidential information) or the existing client, who is unlikely to be a party to the action, but might assist the professional by putting in evidence as to why it is important to him to retain the services of his chosen professional. It is possible that the client might even want to intervene as a party for this purpose, although risks of being liable in costs may make this unattractive. In a case such as *Bolkiah* one can see that if BIA had explained all the reasons why it was cheaper and more effective for KPMG to act rather than some other accountants, it would have been relevant evidence, whether at trial or at an interim hearing. If BIA had done so as a party to the litigation, the court could not help but be influenced.

Although in some sorts of case without notice injunctions may be obtained, it is unlikely that it will be appropriate in normal cases to seek an injunction without giving notice. In some types of case, such as asset-freezing injunctions or search orders, where secrecy is crucial, in the first instance the order will be sought without giving notice to the defendant. There is no reason to make an application for an injunction without giving notice to the professional in any normal case. It is possible to conceive of cases where the urgency is so great that it may be appropriate to apply without notice, but such cases will be few and far between.

B. A different test in conflict cases

8-003 Where the basis for the claim is an existing client conflict, the burden of proof lies on the client to establish the conflict or risk of conflict. Where the basis is a former client conflict, Lord Millett saw the position as giving rise to a two-stage burden of proof. It is for the former client to establish that the firm is in possession of information which was imparted in confidence and that the firm is proposing to act for another party with an interest adverse to his in a matter to which the information is or may be relevant.[3] If that first burden is satisfied, the burden shifts to the professional. He must show that there is no real risk of misuse. It is a high burden. The first stage burden is different from that adopted in Canada, where in *MacDonald Estates v Martin*[4] the Supreme Court of Canada applied a rebuttable presumption that confidential information will have been communicated by the former client in the course of the retainer. Lord Millett set out the position in this jurisdiction[5]:

---

[3] [1999] 2 A.C. 222 at 237.
[4] [1990] 77 D.L.R. (4th) 249.
[5] [1999] 2 A.C. 222 at 237.

> "There is no rule of law that Chinese Walls or other arrangements of a similar kind are insufficient to eliminate the risk. But the starting point must be that, unless special measures are taken, information moves within a firm. In *MacDonald Estates v Martin* Sopinka J. said that the court should restrain the firm from acting for the second client 'unless satisfied on the basis of clear and convincing evidence that all reasonable measures have been taken to ensure that no disclosure will occur.' With the substitution of the word 'effective' for the words 'all reasonable' I would respectfully adopt that formulation".

It is also relevant to have in mind the comment of Lord Phillips C.J. in *Virgin Media Communications v BSkyB*[6]:

> "We start with the proposition that it is desirable that a litigant should be free to instruct the lawyer of his choice. This is particularly true if the lawyer is already acting for the client and the client wishes the lawyer to continue to act in a related matter".

There is a second respect where the order made in a *Bolkiah* case is different. In other cases, the court may simply grant an injunction to prevent misuse of information. But in these cases, the usual remedy is an injunction to restrain the professional from acting.

C. When does the special Bolkiah test apply?

In any normal injunction or confidential information case, the burden is on the applicant. Proving actual misuse of confidential information, or proving a sufficiently serious risk such as to justify grant of a quia timet injunction may often be difficult in conflict cases. But the *Bolkiah* test is easier to satisfy. All the applicant has to do is put forward an adequate case on possession by the professional of relevant confidential information. Then it is for the professional to show there is no real risk of disclosure. The test is therefore much easier for the applicant to satisfy in a conflict case.

8–004

So when exactly does the *Bolkiah* test apply? This is a really important point. One question is whether the lower threshold for the claimant under *Bolkiah* can apply to an application to restrain a professional in the absence of a prior fiduciary relationship with the party objecting.[7] The previous receipt of relevant confidential information may be largely sufficient to satisfy the *Bolkiah* test, but may leave the applicant well short if a higher test

---

[6] [2008] EWCA Civ 612 at [20].
[7] In the Australian case *D&J Constructions Pty Ltd v Head* (1987) 9 N.S.W.L.R. 118, 123 Bryson J., there is a suggestion that an application by a client rather than a non-client may be afforded wider protection by the law.

is applied of threatened misuse. Where the professional has previously acted for a related party, the confidential information in question is not the confidential information of the former client but that of a related party, such as a parent. However, in such cases, the party whose confidential information in issue will usually be a claimant, or the claimant, brought in as a party to the action in order to protect his confidential information, so the issue will probably not arise.[8]

8–005
The real issue is whether the test applies to the range of cases where the claimant is not a party who was in a prior fiduciary relationship with the professional. The circumstances discussed in Ch. 9 are particularly in point. This book has always taken the view that the lower threshold test under *Bolkiah* should only apply where there is or was a "true" fiduciary relationship. The expression "true" fiduciary relationship is used to distinguish circumstances where the only prior relationship is an obligation of confidentiality, as opposed to a prior retainer. In *British Sky Broadcasting Group Plc v Virgin Media Communications Ltd*[9] the Court of Appeal cited without disapproval a decision of the New Zealand Court of Appeal in which a professional was injuncted from acting on the other side to a party in a second action because it had received relevant confidential information from that party in the course of a mediation. The issues arising are discussed at 9–005. It is submitted that the justification for applying the *Bolkiah* test is the public policy importance of protecting former clients from concerns as to their confidential information being used or disclosed against their interests. There is no justification for applying that exceptional rule in the absence of a prior fiduciary relationship and the courts should not extend the *Bolkiah* test.

In *Meat Corporation of Namibia Ltd v Dawn Meats (UK) Ltd*[10] Mann J. held that the *Bolkiah* test did not apply to an application by the claimant to recuse a litigation expert who had agreed to act for the claimant and received limited confidential information before declining to act and subsequently agreeing to act for the other side. He pointed out that the accountants in *Bolkiah* were engaged to provide services. The expert had done nothing but agree in principle to act as expert. Although Mann J. then went on to review authority on the position of experts, the distinction he drew with the *Bolkiah* line of authority supports the point made above.

The applicability of the *Bolkiah* test was considered in a different context by the Hong Kong Court of Final Appeal in *PCCW HKT Telephone Ltd v Aitken*.[11] An employer sought to restrain a former employee who had in the course of employment acquired confidential and privileged information not merely from using that confidential information but from being

---

[8] See 7–005.
[9] [2008] EWCA Civ 612.
[10] [2011] EWHC 474 Ch, considered in detail at 5–015 above.
[11] [2009] HKCU 198. Lord Hoffmann was part of the court.

employed by a business rival, whose interests were adverse to those of the first employer. The wider injunction was refused. Lord Hoffmann said[12]:

> "The principle applied in the *Rakusen* and *Prince Jefri* cases is a branch of the law of confidence, not the law of privilege. It is a special remedy against solicitors and the like which the courts have devised to protect the confidentiality of communications between solicitor and client, or between either of them and third parties, for the purpose of enabling the solicitor to advise or otherwise act for the client. As Lord Millett said[13], the basis of the court's jurisdiction is the protection of confidential information. It is true that one of the reasons why the law of confidence provides this special remedy against solicitors is the reason which justifies LPP,[14] the policy of encouraging free communication between client and solicitor in the interests of justice. But that does not enable one to transfer features of the law of privilege into the law of confidence".[15]

The Hong Kong Court of Final Appeal, in declining to grant the order sought, pointed out that where an ordinary employee was involved, issues of restraint of trade were important. The principles applicable to solicitors could not be imported here. So although the case is different, there is a recognition that there are special rules to protect the clients of professionals.

D. Wider injunctions

There is the possibility that an injunction may be even wider than merely restraining the professional from acting, on the basis that no other relief can properly protect the old client. These are exceptional cases.[16] In *Young v Robson Rhodes*[17] it was argued that where an expert's firm merged with the potential defendants in the litigation in respect of which he was providing litigation support services and expert evidence, the only effective means of protecting the claimant's confidential information was to injunct the merger until the conclusion of the litigation. Such a conclusion was logical but extreme and one can understand how the court was enthusiastic to find a way round the problem.

8–006

The theoretical possibility exists that an injunction may not be limited to the lawyer. If there is evidence that there has already been a leak of information, or that as a result of the inappropriate representation the client

---

[12] At [61].
[13] *Bolkiah* at p.234.
[14] Legal professional privilege.
[15] See also Ribeiro P.J. at [39].
[16] They are sometimes tactically useful if the proposed remedy is a serious one; they tend to cause panic in the professional's office!
[17] See para.2–022 above.

has obtained an unfair advantage, the court could injunct the client from proceeding with a takeover bid or other transaction adverse to the former client's interest. The closest that the court has come to such a conclusion is *United Pan-Europe Communications NV v Deutsche Bank AG*[18] where the Court of Appeal granted an injunction restraining a party from disposing of shares acquired after a takeover bid which had arguably been successful as a result of misuse of confidential information. The Court of Appeal thought it was arguable that at trial the successful bidder would treated as holding the shares on constructive trust. So the client might be injunted from proceeding with a deal or bid and then sues the lawyer for not recusing himself at the outset or for scuppering the bid by improperly disclosing confidential information to him. No doubt such cases would indeed be extreme.

2. Remedies other than injunction

A. Rescission

8–007   A possible remedy which does not arise in many cases is rescission of the underlying contract. Where what is in issue is conflict between professional and two clients, this will not often arise. It is much more common in the case of personal conflicts where the books are full of old cases where courts of equity set aside transactions involving breaches of fiduciary duties.

A recent case in which rescission was refused was *Johnson v EBS Pensioner Trustees Ltd.*[19] Where money was borrowed from solicitors' clients, a different client guaranteed the loan, the guarantee being executed by the solicitors themselves who did not disclose their own service charge on the loan interest. The Court of Appeal held that whilst the remedy of rescission of the guarantee was in principle available, as a matter of discretion they declined to grant such a remedy as it would amount to an unjustified windfall. They ordered an account of monies paid by way of the service charge as a remedy.

The cases in which rescission may be a relevant remedy in client conflicts will be rare. There may be undue influence cases in which it will be argued that because the wife or other person under undue influence was not properly advised,[20] the underlying transaction may be set aside and that may lead to a consequential claim against the lawyer. Alternatively, the fact that the underlying transaction was not set aside may lead to a claim by the person under undue influence for whom the professional acted against the professional. An application may be made to set aside the contract with the professional. This is not usually done but where, for example,

---

[18] [2000] 2 B.C.L.C. 461.
[19] [2002] Lloyd's P.N. Rep. 309, CA, see para.3–023.
[20] See para.4–015.

the professional was in breach of duty in agreeing to act at all, it might be possible to set aside that contract. This might have advantages in terms of recovering monies paid or taking free of unpleasant exclusion clauses. In most cases the disadvantages will probably outweigh the advantages. The client suing usually wants to keep the professional to his obligations, not to nullify them. The issues involved have not really been explored in any cases, but the possibility is simply put forward as one to consider in an appropriate case.

B. Financial remedies: damages compared to account of profits

8–008
Where an injunction is not an available remedy it will be necessary to consider whether a claim can be made for compensation. This involves consideration of two separate sets of remedies: damages claims at common law, and equitable compensation. Equitable remedies are likely to be more potent in some cases than common law claims for damages. Damages claims are based on compensation for loss suffered by the client. This may involve wasted costs in hiring a second set of professionals. In some circumstances it may be possible to contend that a failure to pass on relevant information has meant that a disadvantageous deal was struck which has caused loss, although causation may be difficult. But in most cases proving substantial damage will be difficult. Equitable remedies normally arise where the claim is for breach of fiduciary duty. Equitable remedies may involve constructive trusts and account of profits. So if a claim in equity can be made good, it is usually worth relying on the equitable claim. But whether by way of equitable compensation or damages, breach of duty will not always lead to a financial claim, as the court may well conclude that breach of the double employment rule was not causative of any loss.[21]

It will therefore be important to consider whether the breaches of duty by the professional are breaches of non-fiduciary duties (such as duties of care and skill) or of fiduciary duties as the remedies will be different. As we have seen,[22] in some conflict cases, the breaches will not be breaches of fiduciary duty. Thus in *University of Nottingham v Fishel*[23] Dr Fishel was a lecturer at the university who did unauthorized outside work which he did not disclose to his employers. The judge held that he was in breach of duty in so doing but as the university suffered no loss, the issue was whether he was in breach of a fiduciary obligation so as to give rise to a liability to account for profits. Elias J. said that the conflict of interest and duty principle was not

---

[21] *Bristol & West Building Society v Daniels* [1997] P.N.L.R. 323; *Bristol & West Building Society v Fancy & Jackson* [1997] 4 All E.R. 582 at 614.
[22] See 2–009.
[23] 2000 I.C.R. 1462, discussed at 2–014.

engaged by Dr Fishel's unauthorized work abroad. Whilst doing the work was a breach of contract, it did not conflict with any interest of the university. However, by contrast, where Dr Fishel was paid for work done by other embryologists for whom he was responsible, and by accepting work for them for which he was benefiting, he did put himself into a position of conflict between duty and interest, because his duty to the university was to direct the embryologists to work in the interests of the university and his own interest was served by directing them to work abroad. Thus in relation to the work of the embryologists, the university was entitled to an account of profits from Dr Fishel but not from his own work abroad.

Although there is a semantic debate as to whether a claim for misuse of confidential information is a fiduciary obligation,[24] for purposes of remedies it gives rise to equitable remedies in the same way as breach of fiduciary duty.

C. Damages

8–009   If an injunction is refused, the old client can sue in damages. Common law damages are available for breach of the professional's duties in contract and tort. The cause of action will be breach of contract or negligence.

What sort of damage is likely to be recoverable, if any? By way of example, in *Young v Robson Rhodes*[25] the judge held that the accountants were in breach of their retainer in terminating it. The retainer to act in the litigation carried with it implied obligations not to terminate it prior to the end of the litigation without cause. So the claimant was entitled to damages. The wasted costs involved in getting another expert who would have to duplicate much of the work would be the likely damage. Perhaps there would also be some damage if the claimant had to spend his own time briefing the new firm of accountants, although that probably would not be a substantial expense. The damages there were recoverable because of the wrongful early termination of the retainer. One can see that in other cases the old client may have to change advisers and be able to claim the additional costs of so doing from the professional. But this will not be a head of damages in former client cases and even in cases involving existing client conflicts; there will not be many circumstances where this sort of damage arises. Otherwise it may be difficult to show damage. The misuse of confidential information is hard to quantify in damages.

One possibility is a claim for damages on the basis that the breach of duty by the professional has resulted in the transaction on which the professional was advising being completed when it would not have otherwise been

---

[24] See 2–012.
[25] [1999] 3 All E.R. 524, see para.8–006 above.

completed, or at a less advantageous price. The professional might be at risk in respect of such a claim where the contention is that he has, by reason of his conflict of interest, failed to pass on some important information or give some particular piece of advice. Thus in *Kelly v Cooper*[26] it was alleged, unsuccessfully, that had the estate agent communicated the vendor's interest in buying the pair of adjoining properties, the price for the second of the "pair" would have been enhanced and the vendor would have been able to obtain a better price. In cases involving mortgage lenders, an issue has often been whether the professional was obliged to disclose information to the lender whilst also acting for the borrower. Causation of loss will always be a serious problem for any claimant. In some circumstances it may be that the court will have to assess the loss of a chance.[27]

Whether substantial damages could be obtained may depend on the characterisation of the breach. In *Hilton v Barker Booth & Eastwood*,[28] discussed at 6–010, the solicitors acted for two clients in a situation of conflict of interest. The lower courts treated the breach as the failure to cease acting, and thus awarded nominal damages on the basis that if other solicitors had acted there would have been no disclosure of the criminal convictions and dubious past of the other client. The House of Lords treated the breach as the failure to disclose the criminal convictions and dubious past which the solicitors were obliged to do as a result of having taken on the improper dual retainer, and thus remitted the case for assessment of damages on that basis.

D. Claims for equitable compensation

If the compensation claim is made in equity, the claim may be for equitable compensation rather than damages. An equitable claim may also give rise to an entitlement to an account of profits, which is considered below. Since the decision of the House of Lords in *Target Holdings v Redferns*[29] a claim for equitable compensation requires establishing a causal connection between the breach of trust and the loss suffered, as in a common law claim. But there are potential advantages in a claim for equitable compensation. Equitable compensation is to be determined at trial in the light of all the circumstances then known. As Lord Browne-Wilkinson put it[30]:

8–010

---

[26] [1993] A.C. 205, see para.4–016.
[27] Where the chance depends on the action of some third party, a percentage figure based on the chance may be appropriate; see *Allied Maples Group v Simmons & Simmons* [1995] 1 W.L.R. 1602.
[28] [2005] 1 All E.R. 651 HL.
[29] [1996] A.C. 421.
[30] At 439. It is striking how many of the important cases in this area feature leading judgments or speeches by Lord Millett or Lord Browne-Wilkinson.

"The quantum is fixed at the date of judgment at which date, according to the circumstances then pertaining, the compensation is assessed at the figure then necessary to put the trust estate or the beneficiary back into the position it would have been in had there been no breach".

Equitable compensation for breach of trust is designed to make good a loss in fact suffered by the beneficiaries and which, using hindsight and common sense can be seen to have been caused by the breach.[31] The traditional obligation of the defaulting trustee is to effect restitution to the estate. As restitution in specie may not always be possible, equity awards compensation in place of compensation in specie, by analogy for breach of fiduciary duty, for the purpose of restoring to the estate that which was lost through the breach.[32] In many cases equitable compensation will not differ in substance from common law damages. The principal differences appear to be as follows[33]:

(a) Equitable compensation looks at the position at the time of judgment[34] whereas common law damages usually look at the position at date of breach;
(b) The defence of contributory negligence does not apply to a claim for breach of fiduciary duty;[35]
(c) The traditional view is that the victim is under no duty to mitigate his loss in cases of breach of fiduciary duty.[36] In practice, it is always open to the court to refuse the claim on the basis that the loss has not been caused by the breach;[37]

---

[31] Lord Browne-Wilkinson in *Target v Redferns* [1996] A.C. 421 at 439.
[32] *Canson Enterprises v Broughton & Co* (1991) 85 D.L.R. (4th) 129 at 157 and 163, per McLachlin J. who was in the minority in the Supreme Court of Canada but her judgment was approved by Lord Browne-Wilkinson in *Target*.
[33] It cannot be said the law is very certain here. For the present it is best to use Lord Browne-Wilkinson in *Target* as the starting point and regard anything else as open to doubt. There is an excellent discussion of the principles in Flenley and Leech, *Solicitors' Negligence and Liability*, 2nd edn. (2008), pp.194–215. In *Swindle v Harrison* [1997] 4 All E.R. 705 at 731, Mummery L.J. said that the remedies in equity were more "elastic".
[34] Lord Browne-Wilkinson in *Target v Redferns* [1996] A.C. 421 at 437.
[35] The defence is statutory and the Law Reform (Contributory Negligence) Act 1945 is inapplicable to claims in breach of fiduciary duty. In *Nationwide Building Society v Balmer Radmore* [1999] Lloyd's Rep. P.N. 241 at 281, Blackburne J. refused to reduce equitable compensation on a basis analogous to contributory negligence, at least in cases of intentional breach of duty within the second and third categories identified by Millett L.J. in *Mothew*: see para.2–007.
[36] *Canson Enterprises v Broughton & Co* (1991) 85 D.L.R. (4th) 129 at 162, per McLachlin J. who was in the minority in the Supreme Court of Canada but her judgment was approved by Lord Browne-Wilkinson in *Target*.
[37] See Blackburne J. in *Nationwide Building Society v Balmer Radmore* [1999] Lloyd's Rep. P.N. 241 at 282.

(d) The common law rules limiting damages claims on grounds of remoteness do not apply in the same way;[38]
(e) There appear to be less rigorous tests required to establish causation in cases of breach of fiduciary duty.[39]

E. Account of profits

An alternative measure of compensation in cases of breach of fiduciary duty is an account of profits. Where breach of fiduciary duty is alleged and there is some reason to believe that the professional has or will make a profit from his breach, this may be claimed. It should be claimed in the alternative to damages and an election made between remedies at trial.[40] As explained above, it is important to consider whether the obligation breached is a fiduciary or non-fiduciary obligation.

8–011

Where the professional should never have acted for both clients at all, it may be said that the second set of fees represents the profits he has made as a result of his breach of fiduciary duty. Although there does not appear to be any decided case which establishes such fees are recoverable as an account of profits, in principle there seems no reason why they should not be recoverable. However, it seems to follow logically that each of the two clients should be able to claim such fees as an account of profits where the professional is in breach of fiduciary duty in failing to decline to act. Does that mean that both clients can claim all the fees so that the professional has to pay them back twice over?

Where the complaint is confidential information, such a claim will be much more difficult. Here the fees earned by the professional will normally not derive from the confidential information but from acting. So there is unlikely to be any causative link between fees earned and alleged misuse of confidential information.

Other advantages of making a claim for an account of profits, which will normally be regarded as a proprietary remedy, are that it will be traceable into mixed assets and in a case of insolvency the monies may be not generally available to creditors. In *Att-Gen v Blake*[41] the Court of Appeal

---

[38] *Canson Enterprises v Broughton & Co* (1991) 85 D.L.R. (4th) 129 at 162, per McLachlin J.; *Guerin v R.* (1984) 13 D.L.R. (4th) 321, Supreme Court of Canada.
[39] *Canson Enterprises v Broughton & Co* (1991) 85 D.L.R. (4th) 129 at 162, per McLachlin J.; *Caffrey v Darby* (1801) 6 Ves. 488, 31 E.R. 1159; *Clough v Bond* (1838) 3 My. & Cr. 490. These authorities were approved by Lord Browne-Wilkinson in *Target* at 434.
[40] That is when an election should be made: see *United Australia v Barclays Bank* [1941] A.C. 1. In cases where a default or summary judgment is obtained, it is permissible to put off the time for election until additional information is available: see *Island Records Ltd v Tring International Plc* [1996] 1 W.L.R. 1256; *Wienerworld v Vision Video*, July 24, 1997.
[41] [1998] Ch. 439. The decision of the Court of Appeal was varied by the House of Lords on other grounds [2001] 1 A.C. 268.

recognised for the first time that there might be circumstances where damages proved an inappropriate and inadequate remedy and where an account of profits might be appropriate as a remedy for breach of contract. The mere fact that the professional's breach of his contract with the claimant has enabled him to enter into a more profitable contract with someone else was not such a circumstance,[42] although a case where a man had obtained a profit by doing the very thing he contracted not to do could be an appropriate case for imposing an account of profits as a remedy.[43]

F. Contributory negligence

8–012   The defence of contributory negligence is available to reduce damages which would otherwise be claimable in contract or tort. Being a statutory defence under the Law Reform (Contributory) Negligence Act 1945, contributory negligence only applies where the statute so provides. Commonwealth authority has suggested that equitable compensation for breach of fiduciary duty may be reduced in a manner analogous to contributory negligence.[44] In *Nationwide Building Society v Balmer Radmore*[45] the judge was dealing with breaches of fiduciary duty which, in their nature, could not be regarded as unconscious breaches of an obligation of loyalty. He held that contributory negligence had never been applied to intentional torts and thus could not be applied here, whether by analogy or otherwise. The judge expressed no view in cases where the breach could be regarded as unintentional.[46]

G. Depriving the professional of remuneration

8–013   One possibility is to refuse to pay the professional's bill, on the basis that he was in breach of duty. This argument failed in *Kelly v Cooper*.[47] The Privy Council said that a fiduciary who commits an honest mistake, and is although acting in good faith in breach of duty, does not lose his right to

---

[42] Per Lord Woolf M.R., citing *Teacher v Calder* [1899] A.C. 451.
[43] In *Att-Gen v Blake*, Blake had promised not to disclose official information when employed by the Crown without lawful authority. His fiduciary obligation not to disclose lasted until the information was in the public domain but his contractual obligation was without limit. Because much of the information was in the public domain, the fiduciary obligation could not be relied on but the contractual obligation could. It remains to be seen to what extent a general principle will be allowed to develop from this decision.
[44] *Day v Mead* [1987] 2 N.Z.L.R. 443, NZCA; *Canson Enterprises v Broughton & Co* (1991) 85 D.L.R. (4th) 129, S.C.C..
[45] [1999] Lloyd's Rep. P.N. 241 at 281, Blackburne J.
[46] For a citation of the relevant Commonwealth articles, see [1999] Lloyd's Rep. P.N. 241 at 281.
[47] [1993] 1 A.C. 205.

commission or to fees.⁴⁸ The position is different where he acts in bad faith where he will usually not be able to claim his fees.⁴⁹ Where the professional fails to perform a single entire retainer without good reason, he may be unable to recover his fees.⁵⁰ If his breach of duty is such that there is in effect a failure to perform, again he may have difficulty recovering his fees at all. And it may be that a claim for an account of profits can in effect lead to the professional being deprived of his fees.⁵¹

3. Litigation issues

A. Inspection of the solicitors' file

There may be cases in which the court wishes to inspect the solicitors' file in order to determine the application. This will not be a course adopted in many cases. It is for the claimant to establish the communication of confidential information and the important documents can be exhibited to witness statements. Inspection of the file by the court may either be impractical or not take the matter further. Some judges are much more attracted to this sort of route than others. The benefit may be forensic—offering to show the judge the relevant material in the file as a sign of good faith. In *Bogle v Coutts*⁵² Farrer & Co had acted for Bogle in matrimonial proceedings and in the early stages of negotiations with Coutts, but then retained the files by virtue of a lien for unpaid fees. The claimant was refused an injunction to restrain the firm acting for Coutts; all the solicitors who had acted for the claimant had now left the firm and the files were in storage. Peter Smith J. refused an injunction after requiring production of the files to examine whether they contained relevant confidential information.

8–014

---

⁴⁸ Relying on *Keppel v Wheeler* [1927] 1 K.B. 577; see also *Robinson Scammell & Co v Ansell* [1985] 2 E.G.L.R. 41; *Eric Stansfield v South East Nursing Home Services Ltd* [1986] 1 E.G.L.R. 29.
⁴⁹ The cases to this effect are cases of the professional making a profit in a situation where his duty to the client and self-interest conflict or deliberately acting against the interests of the client: *Andrews v Ramsay* [1903] 2 K.B. 635; *Hippisley v Knee Bros* [1905] 1 K.B. 1.
⁵⁰ Whether the retainer is a single entire contract so that the professional is entitled to nothing unless he effects substantial performance will depend on the terms of the retainer. In *Heywood v Wellers* [1976] Q.B. 446 the Court of Appeal not merely refused to permit a claim for fees but allowed the dissatisfied client to reclaim that already paid; that was a case where the solicitor handled the client's affairs incompetently.
⁵¹ See para.8–011 above.
⁵² [2003] EWHC 1865, Ch.D, Peter Smith J.

B. The role of the court in identifying conflicts in relation to those appearing before it

8–015　Can the court take the conflict point of its own volition or is it purely a matter for the affected party? If the matter is one purely of contract, then the court has no separate function, other than to supervise and give effect to the contractual position. Cases where the tribunal has a conflict of its own raise quite different considerations and are dealt with in Ch.11. In this category there may be cases where someone who is involved with the administration of justice has a conflict.[53] Interesting conflict questions under this head may arise when the court appoints an expert under CPR r.35.7. Where the court has involvement itself in the process, such as supervising the winding up of a company, the position may again be different. But in the usual case, whilst the court may alert a party to the fact that there is a potential conflict and ask whether he wishes to take the point, or at least to consider his position, because the conflict can be waived, it is for the party affected not the court to take the point. Thus in *Hood Sailmakers v Berthom Boat*[54] the Court of Appeal were unimpressed with the conduct of the County Court judge who had taken it upon himself to take the point that solicitors for one party had a conflict which he considered embarrassed them, despite the fact that none of the parties were objecting and the matter had been ventilated in correspondence.

C. Evidence in the application—who can see it?

8–016　In order to make out a ground for the application, the claimant will need to explain to the court the basis for concern. That is likely to involve an explanation as to what the confidential information in question is. Sometimes it will be possible to do this in general terms. But often it will be necessary for the information to be rather more specific. If so, then it is being referred to in a witness statement which will be seen by a professional currently acting for the client. It will often be inappropriate for that individual to see the information if he continues to act. If the injunction application fails, then the professional will continue acting. Yet there will often be a converse problem: the professional who is currently acting may recognise the problem and decide it is better not to see the evidence lest this encourages the court to prevent him from continuing to act. But in such a case, how is the evidence to be answered? It is the professional acting for the client who is likely to be in the best position to rebut the evidence. There is no easy answer here. The party serving the evidence might serve a

---

[53] Such as the prosecutor in *R. v Dunstable Mags Court Ex p. Cox* (1986) N.L.J. 310, who was a solicitor who had previously advised the defendant on the charge he was prosecuting.
[54] *Independent*, May 10, 1999, CA.

redacted version and offer to provide unredacted versions only on an undertaking that the unredacted material be not shown to the individuals currently acting. But this still does not resolve the problem that the individuals acting would be best placed to answer the unredacted material. There is no authority on point, so any application to court will need to be dealt with on principles similar to those applicable to other similar confidential material.

D. Waiver

Because judicial conflicts impact on art.6, waiver issues in judicial conflicts involve different principles. In the context of professional conflicts, it is necessary to consider what is meant by waiver. The first type of waiver is consent, or what is regarded as deemed or inferred consent. This has already been considered in detail.[55] Sometimes waiver will be something short of consent; it is most likely to consist of conduct which disentitles a party from seeking remedies in court. It may be delay in exercising remedies, and thus argued to disentitle the claimant from obtaining an injunction. Sometimes, where for example the risk of misuse of confidential information is not great, delay or conduct which is said to amount to some sort of waiver might tip the balance against an injunction. But it will be a rare case when waiver is likely to provide a defence: if it is inappropriate for a lawyer to continue to act, it may still be inappropriate for the lawyer to act notwithstanding that the point could and should have been taken earlier. There are Australian cases in which waiver features. There is a citation of authority in *Colonial Portfolio v Nissen*[56] where Rolfe J. would have refused an injunction on this ground had he not decided there was no real risk of misuse of confidential information. Notwithstanding steps being taken in relation to proposals to resolve the litigation, no objection was taken initially to object to the other side's solicitors acting. The claimants made it clear that they did not intend to take a point on a conflict of interest in consequence of which the other side continued to instruct their solicitors. Rolfe J. treated it as a case of acquiescence.[57]

8–017

E. Offensive tactics

In the position of the claimant, it is important to act quickly. Delay may not be fatal, but it leaves the judge and other side with the impression that you are not serious. Do not disclose the confidential information in question

8–018

---

[55] See para.4–020.
[56] [2000] N.S.W.S.C. 1047.
[57] Referring to *Orr v Ford* (1989) 167 C.L.R. 340 and *South Blackwater Coal Limited v McCullough Robertson*, Unreported, May 8, 1997, Muir J. Supreme Court of Queensland.

in open documents or open court, or you may find that the court holds it is in consequence lost its confidence.[58] It is important to try to identify with precision exactly what sort of confidential information was transmitted in what circumstances to the adviser. This may not be easy. Often the confidential information will be relatively nebulous—at least that which can be recalled. If the client cannot recall what he has told the adviser that was confidential, the court may take the view that the adviser probably will not remember it either.[59]

Where the professional is still working on the disputed retainer, disclosure of confidential material to those involved will be problematic, as the mischief which it is sought to protect against will occur. So the information can be served in confidential exhibits only provided to those on the other side who are not involved in the retainer and who undertake not to show it to anyone inappropriate.

When undertakings are offered by the defendants, and details of the information barrier set out, the claimant will try to show potential weaknesses. Where the wall is an ad hoc wall it will obviously be easier to criticise. Where it is an organisational wall, it may be more difficult. The judge will probably not be impressed by suggestions that something might go wrong, unless possible problems can be identified. The client will only have the information in the affidavit about the wall which will probably not alert him to the potential weaknesses. If there is time, a list of searching questions about the wall should be drafted and sent to the adviser in order to try to elicit the information to flush out potential weaknesses. The adviser seeking to show that his practices are all above-board will be unwilling to refuse to answer.

F. Defensive tactics

8–019

When the other side first complain about the adviser acting, it is easy to produce a curt, irritated reply. The complaint may well be perceived as purely tactical and an irritant, at least at the outset. But curt, uninterested responses look unattractive in the glare of the courtroom[60] and may get the adviser off to a bad start in the litigation that follows. Much better to write a straightforward letter seeking to reassure the enquirer.

The cases where the adviser has been successful in fending off the challenge are often those where the adviser is able to say "I cannot recall any

---

[58] *Mannesmann AG v Goldman Sachs International*, 18 November, 1999, Lightman J.
[59] *Halewood International v Addleshaw Booth & Co* [2000] Lloyd's Rep. P.N. 298, para.7–017 above.
[60] The accountants in *Bolkiah* were criticised for their initial response and although the House of Lords did not decide the matter on that basis they might have had a stronger hand to play if they had responded differently.

information which I received from my former client which was confidential". Where it is apparent that genuinely relevant confidential information has been disclosed, the court will be unlikely to accept this-after all, memories can be jogged and what has been forgotten may revive in the memory when prompted by a review of other related matters. The court is more likely to accept such statements as adequate where it is doubtful whether relevant confidential information was disclosed, or where it seems apparent the information was peripheral or very limited.[61]

The adviser will need to set out in detail in evidence of the information barrier which is operated and the efforts which are made to keep it intact. Information barriers rarely survive scrutiny unless they have been established at the outset of the job. He should consider carefully the undertakings which can properly be given.

---

[61] As in *Re Solicitors* [2000] 1 Lloyd's Rep. 31, Timothy Walker J., see para.7–010 above.

CHAPTER 9

The Duty to the Other Side

1. A professional's duty to the other side?

A. Assumption of duty

9–001　This far, the concern has been with the duty to the client or the former client. There are circumstances when problems will arise without a second retainer, such as when a solicitor moves from one firm to another and has confidential information of a client of the old firm and that client is in dispute with a client of the new firm. But the concept of a duty to the adversary is rather different.

In general, the idea of an obligation to the adversary is anathema to a jurisdiction based on fiduciary obligations of loyalty. Most of the attempts to invoke such a duty have failed. The lawyer owes no duty to those who are not his clients. He is no guardian of their interests and indeed what he does for his client may be hostile and injurious to his opponents. So in the ordinary course of adversarial litigation the lawyer owes no duty to his lay client's adversary.[1]

In England, the traditional view that no duty can be owed to the other side is represented by the decision of Sir Donald Nicholls V-C in *Gran*

---

[1] Brooke L.J. in *Connolly-Martin v Davis* [1999] Lloyd's P.N. 790 at 795, citing *Orchard v South Eastern Electricity Board* [1987] 1 Q.B. 565 at 571, 581; *Business Computers International Ltd v Registrar of Companies* [1988] 1 Ch. 229 at 239; *Al-Kandari v Brown* [1988] 1 Q.B. 665 at 672, 675; *White v Jones* [1995] 2 A.C. 207 at 256; *Elguzouli-Daf v Commissioner of Police* [1995] Q.B. 335 at 348, 352. See now *Thames Trains Ltd v Adams* [2006] EWHC 3291, Nelson J. (solicitor under no duty in settlement discussions to mention to other solicitor that she had just made a faxed offer of settlement on terms inconsistent with and which undermined the terms of the discussion she was having where it was obvious the other solicitor had not been shown the fax.)

Gelato v Richcliff.² The purchaser of an underlease relied upon an answer to pre-contractual inquiries given by the vendor's solicitor which turned out to be wrong through the fault of the solicitor, not the vendor. The purchaser had an action in misrepresentation against the vendor who was responsible for the answer of his solicitor as his agent, but it was not clear whether the vendor had sufficient means to satisfy the claim, so the purchaser also sued the solicitor. The Vice-Chancellor was not impressed by the argument that if a duty was owed to the purchaser, it would place the solicitor in a position of conflict: he said the duty to both sides was the same: to give an accurate answer.³ The Vice-Chancellor founded his decision that no duty of care arose on the fact that the solicitor answered only as agent for the vendor, so the purchaser had a remedy against the vendor and did not need one against the solicitor.

As the Vice-Chancellor recognised in *Gran Gelato*, there are some exceptions, for example where a lawyer undertakes a responsibility to the other side, such as where he holds his client's passport as an officer of the court,⁴ where he could be in breach of a duty of care to the other side.⁵

9–002

There are New Zealand cases which have gone further⁶: a solicitor who provided a certificate to a lender that an instrument was fully binding on his client and there were no other charges on his yacht assumed a responsibility to the other side.⁷ The New Zealand statute⁸ which provides that an agreement to contract out of the Matrimonial Property Act is only effective if witnessed by a solicitor who certifies that the effect and implications have been explained has given rise to two decisions. In *Connell v Odlum*⁹ the solicitor who negligently gave the certification when in fact he had not given the necessary advice to the wife was held liable to the husband after the pre-nuptial agreement was declared void. Thomas J., giving the leading judgment of the New Zealand Court of Appeal, stressed that the solicitor stepped outside his role as his client's solicitor and accepted with the act of certification a direct responsibility to the other party to the agreement. The solicitors had:

---

² [1992] Ch 560.
³ Query how realistic this is where several answers are possible within the bounds of strict accuracy, which may give very different impressions.
⁴ *Al-Kandari v Brown* [1988] 1 Q.B. 665 at 672, 675.
⁵ *Batten v Wedgwood* (1886) 31 Ch. D. 346; *Welsh v Chief Constable of Merseyside Police* as explained in *Elguzouli-Daf v Commissioner of Police* [1995] Q.B. 335 at 348, 350, 352.
⁶ In *Primosso Holdings v Ampers* [2004] 3 N.Z.L.R. 521, the New Zealand Court of Appeal held that it was arguable that a solicitor who becomes aware that he is being used by a borrower to facilitate a fraud on the lender owes a duty of care to the lender to cease acting for the borrower.
⁷ *Allied Finance v Haddow* [1983] N.Z.L.R. 22.
⁸ The Property (Relationships) Act 1976, s.21F and s.21(6) (c).
⁹ [1993] N.Z.L.R. 257.

"undertaken a duty which is 'separate and different' from their professional duty to their client and one which they must contemplate will be relied upon by the other party to the agreement".[10]

Odlum was heavily relied on in *Radisich v Templeton*.[11] This related to a divorce rather than pre-nuptial settlement but the same statutory provision was relevant. At the end of a mediation both counsel signed a Heads of Agreement for the disposition of matrimonial property reflecting the agreement between the spouses but no certificate was signed, so the agreement was again void. The husband sued both his counsel and the wife's counsel for negligence, in the case of the wife's counsel for failing to procure the necessary certificate. Randerson J. struck out the claim. What gave rise to the duty in *Odlum* was the representation contained in the certificate by counsel. Without the certificate, there was no reason to impose a duty on the wife's counsel; it was reasonable to expect that the husband's counsel would be able to advise him as to the effect of the absence of the certificate.

In *McCullagh v Lane Fox*,[12] the issue was whether a vendor's estate agent owed a duty of care to a prospective purchaser in relation to a representation as to the area of land being purchased. The Court of Appeal unanimously held that the agent had effectively disclaimed liability and the majority (Nourse L.J. and Sir Christopher Slade) also held that on the facts no duty of care would have arisen in any event. But Hobhouse L.J. criticised the reasoning in *Gran Gelato* and held that, if it was correct at all, it was "confined to a special rule applicable to solicitors in conveyancing transactions". The special rule did not apply to estate agents, who were thus subject to ordinary principles of duties of care. Nourse L.J. commented that any analogy between an estate agent and a solicitor should be approached with caution.

Although the decision in *Gran Gelato* was referred to with apparent approval by Lord Goff in *White v Jones*, its reasoning is weak, it has been doubted elsewhere in the common law world,[13] and has to an extent been undermined or, at best, restricted in its scope, by later authority. The fact that the defendant acts pursuant to a contract with a third party (e.g. a vendor) who themselves contracts with the claimant was held to be no bar to a direct duty of care being owed the claimant in *Henderson v Merrett*.[14]

In *Dean v Allin & Watts*,[15] the Court of Appeal held that a solicitor acting for a borrower owed a duty of care to the lender properly to put in

---

[10] [1993] N.Z.L.R. 257 at 270.
[11] [2009] N.Z.H.C. 654.
[12] (1995) 49 Con. L.R. 124; [1996] 1 E.G.L.R. 35.
[13] Doubts have been expressed in Ireland in *Doran v Delaney* [1998] 2 I.R. 61 and in New South Wales in *Bebonis v Angelos* [2003] N.S.W.C.A. 13 and *Votraint v Commonwealth* [2005] N.S.W.C.A. 249.
[14] [1995] 2 A.C. 145.
[15] [2001] Lloyd's Rep. P.N. 605.

place the agreed security, even though that would (in the event of default) be to the detriment of his own client and the benefit of the other side.[16] The leading judgment was given by Lightman J. who saw the result as an extension of the principle in *White v Jones*[17] that a solicitor may owe a duty to the persons whom his client's instruction were intended to benefit. Lightman J. said that a conflict would preclude a duty of care to a non-client save where "special circumstances of a particular case" require a different conclusion.[18] Robert Walker L.J. agreed but preferred to see the case as an example of the kind of exceptional case contemplated in *Gran Gelato*, rather than a manifestation of any principle from *White v Jones*. The judgment of Sedley L.J. did not directly comment on this debate.

In England the trend of authorities is towards judging the issue of a duty of care to another party in a transaction on its own merits and away from the quick application of a general rule that the professional cannot owe a duty to his client's adversary. It may be that a helpful question to ask in a given case is whether the claimant was, for the particular purpose of the duty alleged, truly the adversary of the client, or just another person relying on the professional for the same purpose as the client. In the former case, no duty can arise because of the conflict of interest inherent in the situation; in the latter it may or may not arise depending on the usual tests.[19]

9–003

B. Confidence as the basis for duty to the other side

There will also be cases where the lawyer for one party to litigation learns of confidential information of the adversary—in a mediation, or without prejudice discussions. And he will see documents on discovery which he cannot use for any purpose outside the action. Then he is asked to act in another case against the same defendant and where this confidential information is material. Does he have a problem? If he acts, surely he will be misusing his opponent's confidential information?

9–004

Two situations may be distinguished here. One is where the professional learns confidential information under an obligation of confidentiality to the other side. Examples are a without prejudice discussion, or a mediation. The second is where the information is learned in the course of litigation where there is an implied or express obligation not to use it for other purposes.

---

[16] It is important, though, that the borrower had instructed the solicitor to perfect the security, so the legitimate interest that the solicitor was employed by the borrower to serve did not in fact conflict with the interest of the lender.
[17] [1995] 2 A.C. 207.
[18] [33] See also *Brownie Mills v Shrimpton* 1999 P.N.L.R. (N.Z.C.A.), *Jaison Property Development Co Ltd v Swinhoe* [2010] EWHC 2467 (QB), at [108], Simon Picken Q.C.
[19] This analysis is consistent with the approach of Lord Hoffmann and Lord Mance in *Customs and Excise Commissioners v Barclays Bank* [2007] 1 A.C. 181 at paras [40] and [106]–[109] respectively.

The first situation differs from that which usually applies in that there is no fiduciary relationship between the parties. It is true that the obligation of confidentiality is a form of fiduciary obligation[20] but it is different from the usual form of fiduciary obligation and does not of itself encompass a duty of loyalty. Whilst it will always be possible for someone who has imparted information to a professional on the other side under circumstances of confidentiality to bring an action for misuse of confidential information, the higher test there applicable[21] is likely to make it difficult to injunct the professional from acting for his new client.

The decision of the Court of Appeal in *British Sky Broadcasting Group Plc v Virgin Media Communications Ltd*[22] is important in this analysis. There were three sets of proceedings between the parties: High Court proceedings based on breaches of competition law, an investigation carried out by Ofcom in the light of allegations made by Virgin, and applications made by each of the parties to the Competition Appeal Tribunal ("the CAT proceedings") for review of the Competition Commission's investigation of the acquisition by Sky of an interest in ITV. Sky instructed different lawyers in the CAT proceedings from the High Court proceedings but Virgin instructed the same lawyers in all three proceedings. Sky contended that lawyers who had seen their sensitive documents in the High Court proceedings, where CPR 31.22 provides a collateral undertaking prohibiting use of the documents for purposes outside the action in which they were disclosed without leave of the court, would be influenced by their knowledge of those documents in the advice they gave in the CAT proceedings, and thus sought an order in the High Court proceedings restricting access to those sensitive documents to lawyers not acting in the CAT proceedings, the effect of which would be to make it impossible for those lawyers to act in the High Court proceedings.

The Court of Appeal, chaired by Lord Phillips C.J., held that the duty not to make ulterior use of disclosed documents was not the same as an obligation of confidentiality. The court was entitled to give permission for use of the documents, but the significance of the decision is in its treatment of a line of authorities referred to in previous editions of this book. Lord Phillips relied on the judgment of Giles A.S.P. in the Federal Court of Canada in *Merck v Interpharm*,[23] where the Ontario court declined to remove a solicitor from one action because he had been party to his clients obtaining documentation on a search order, when the defendant was the same in both actions and it was asserted the solicitor could not fulfil his duties to the second client without using documents he was obliged not to use other

---

[20] See *Arklow v Maclean* [2000] 1 W.L.R. 594.
[21] Making good a claim for misuse of confidential information as opposed to the "real risk of disclosure" test: see 8–003 above.
[22] [2008] EWCA Civ 612. The decision in the *BSkyB* case was announced just as the last edition of this book went to press and thus the decision was referred to, but the Court of Appeal's reasons were not published until after the book's publication date.
[23] (1992) 44 C.P.R. (3d) 440, affirmed (1993) 46 C.P.R. (3d) 513.

than for the purposes of the action.[24] Giles A.S.P. said that the undertaking would be most impractical if it resulted in an ability to remove from a case any solicitor who bound by such an undertaking:

> "The implied undertaking is not of sufficient public interest when balanced against the right of a party to choose his own solicitors and the public interest in the efficient administration of justice to require the court to disqualify any solicitor who might wrongly deploy information subject to the undertaking".

Lord Phillips said[25] that "in a rare case" the fact that documents have been disclosed to solicitors acting for a party in one sent of proceedings might conceivably preclude those solicitors from acting for a different party in another set of proceedings, but not when the parties were the same.

Where the first action has proceeded to trial already, the problem may have wholly or mostly ceased to arise because the collateral undertaking has ceased to apply when the documents are in the trial bundle or used in open court.[26] There is authority that the collateral undertaking is an obligation which arises under the rules of court (which derive from statutory authority) and breach of the collateral undertaking in court proceedings does not give rise to any common law remedy for breach of confidence.[27] There is authority that where a breach of the collateral undertaking is in issue, the usual remedy will be an injunction preventing misuse rather than an injunction restraining the solicitors from continuing to act.[28]

Lord Phillips contrasted with this the position where an express obligation of confidentiality had been entered into, even if it was an obligation to the other side. It was not necessary for the purposes of the decision in the case to do more than draw a distinction between such cases and the case before the court, and the two decisions referred to were not discussed in detail. However, one was expressly stated by Lord Phillips to have been correctly decided and the second referred to without criticism, notwithstanding that the passage from a previous edition of this book criticising those decisions was put before the court.

9–005

One was *Adex International (Ireland) Ltd v IBM UK Ltd*,[29] where Judge Hallgarten Q.C. in the Central London County Court Business List granted

---

[24] See also *The Attorney General of Canada v The Information Commissioner of Canada* [2002] F.C.T. 128.
[25] [30].
[26] CPR rr.31.22; *Barings Plc v Coopers & Lybrand* [2000] 1 W.L.R. 2353.
[27] *Apple Corps Ltd v Apple Computer Inc* [1992] 1 C.M.L.R. 969; *Derby v Weldon (No.2)*; Unreported, October 19, 1988.
[28] *Re Schuppan* [1996] 2 All E.R. 664 at 670, Robert Walker J.; *Re a Firm of Solicitors* [1995] 3 All E.R. 482 at 492, citing *English and American Insurance Company Ltd v Herbert Smith* [1988] F.S.R. 232 and *Goddard v Nationwide Building Society* [1987] Q.B. 670.
[29] Unreported, November 17, 2000.

an injunction restraining a solicitor from acting in a second action for claimants suing the same defendants as the solicitor had acted against in the first action. The first action had settled and the terms of the settlement were confidential. The judge held that the solicitor would not be able to put out of his mind the confidential settlement figure, which would be material to the advice he gave in the second action. Although the reasoning in the decision is limited, Lord Phillips went out of his way to say it had been correctly decided.[30]

The other case referred to where the lawyers sought to act on a second action against the same defendants was the decision of the New Zealand Court of Appeal in *Carter Holt Harvey Forests Ltd v Sunnex Logging Ltd*.[31] The complaint was that the lawyers had signed a comprehensive confidentiality agreement when participating in a mediation at which the first action was settled. The New Zealand Court of Appeal held that the lawyers were in possession of confidential information and that disclosure of that information could prejudice the defendants if they acted against the defendants in the second action. The confidential information included the terms of settlement. The court granted an injunction.[32] Blanchard J. said:

> "There is an inherent incompatibility between lawyers' participation in a confidential mediation and their desire to act for other clients in parallel litigation. The dilemma cannot satisfactorily be resolved by means of an undertaking to observe the obligations of confidentiality... the lawyer cannot screen out what was gleaned from the mediation and what was acquired elsewhere".[33]

9–006 These decisions suggest a disturbing trend. The first point is the applicability of the *Bolkiah* threshold test to circumstances where there was no prior professional (and therefore fiduciary) relationship between professional and claimant seeking the injunction.[34] *Carter Holt* simply applies the *Bolkiah*[35] test to this situation. However, although *Bolkiah* is dealing with misuse of confidential information, it provides a special and onerous rule because the

---

[30] [22].
[31] [2001] 3 N.Z.L.R. 343.
[32] Since then a first instance decision in New Zealand seems to have gone even further. In *South Island Commercial (2004) Ltd v Kiwi Green Island Club Ltd* [2008] NZSC 2032 granted an injunction preventing counsel from acting in a second set of proceedings against a party when he had attended a confidential mediation in the first proceedings against the same party and there had been an overlap of issues between the proceedings. French J.'s decision surprisingly does not seek to identify the confidential information disclosed in the first mediation relevant to the second action at all, but merely focuses on the degree of overlap between the proceedings.
[33] at [30].
[34] Discussed at 8–003 above.
[35] Or the local equivalent, *Russell McVeigh McKenzie Bartlett v Tower Corporation* [1998] 3 N.Z.L.R. 641.

lawyer has accepted a fiduciary obligation of loyalty to his former client which calls for special protection. The contractual obligation of confidentiality accepted by the lawyers to the other party is in a very different category as it is not based on any such underlying obligation.[36] As such, there is no need of special protection and the general law of confidentiality should apply.

Secondly, in such circumstances it is for consideration whether in any individual case the appropriate remedy is an injunction, rather than lesser relief such as has been applied in cases on the collateral undertaking. It is suggested that there is no public policy justification for extreme measures such as the grant of an injunction which prevents the lawyer from acting for another client. If there is to be a remedy at all, it should surely be possible to accept undertakings relating to misuse of information disclosed.

Thirdly, in normal circumstances a professional attending a confidential mediation is surely only rarely likely to learn any confidential information from the other side which would assist in separate proceedings acting for another claimant against the same defendant. Of course it depends: if the professional learnt from the first information the extent of the insurance cover of the defendant that could well be highly material information which would preclude him acting against the same defendant in proceedings with a different claimant. But the New Zealand Court of Appeal seems to have taken a very generous view in favour of the defendants of the likely importance of the confidential information in the second action. They were persuaded that matters such as the price at which the clients would be willing to settle the first action and the terms of the eventual settlement, covered by the confidentiality agreement, were of sufficient importance as confidential information to justify an injunction against the lawyers acting in the second action. Yet it must be doubtful whether this was genuinely relevant to the second action, leaving aside whether an injunction would be a proportionate remedy to protect this sort of information save in an unusual case.

Fourthly, the New Zealand Court of Appeal did not seem to think the case before them in any way exceptional. On the contrary, it seems to have thought that it would be more exceptional to permit a party who had attended a mediation subsequently to act for another party in related litigation against the same defendant than to restrain them from doing so.[37] Surely this cannot be right? This is no mean incentive not to mediate disputes!

Fifthly, the effect of *Carter Holt* is that it becomes relatively easy to prevent a party from retaining the legal representative of choice even at the behest of an adverse party. It is suggested that courts should be very

---

[36] Although the obligation of confidentiality is sometimes referred to as a fiduciary obligation, it is of a very different nature to the usual fiduciary obligation: see 2–013.

[37] This certainly seems the effect of the subsequent decision in *South Island Commercial (2004) Ltd v Kiwi Green Island Club Ltd* [2008] N.Z.H.C. 2032.

reluctant to accede to such applications. In *BSkyB* Lord Phillips recognised that it was desirable that a litigant should be free to instruct the lawyer of his choice. In *Tricontinental Corporation Ltd v Holding Redlich*[38] Mandie J. said in the Supreme Court of Victoria:

> "It is a serious matter to prevent a party from retaining the legal representative of its choice, particularly upon the application not of a former client but of an adverse party".

9–007   So where does the decision in *BSkyB* leave the position? Firstly, the Court of Appeal did not consider whether the lower threshold test applied in *Bolkiah* was applicable in cases where the professional never undertook a fiduciary obligation to the person seeking the injunction. The point did not arise in *Adex*. It is submitted there is no possible justification for applying the lower threshold in such circumstances.[39]

Secondly, it is right that there will be circumstances in which confidential information disclosed by the other side in the course of a confidential mediation does prevent the recipient from acting on the other side in a subsequent action. The example given above as to insurance cover would be such a case. The analysis is certainly different where the information disclosed in the first action was disclosed to the lawyers under an express confidentiality provision as against reliance on the weaker collateral undertaking. *BSkyB* does not really go much beyond that. And Lord Phillips did make clear that the court's starting point was always that it was desirable that a litigant should be free to instruct the lawyer of his choice. So the points made above remain up for decision in any future case. But it is fair to say that those seeking to obtain such injunctions may gather some support from obiter comments by Lord Phillips C.J. in *BSkyB*. By contrast, dicta in the Hong Kong Court of Final Appeal *PCCW HKT Telephone Ltd v Aitken*,[40] discussed in detail at 8–005, may provide some support for treating *Bolkiah* as laying down special principles applicable to professional and their former clients.

There is another possible argument against granting an injunction which may be of some relevance in borderline cases. In certain situations the courts have recognised the legitimate advantage to a client in being able to instruct a lawyer who is familiar with the subject-matter of the dispute. This has been recognised where a solicitor who has acted for the principal creditor of a company is asked to act for the liquidator[41] and in the very different context of determining whether England is the appropriate forum

---

[38] Unreported, December 22, 1994, Supreme Court of Victoria, Mandie J.
[39] See most recently *Stiedl v Enyo Law LLP* [2011] EWHC 2649 (Comm), Beatson J. especially at [39]. What Beatson J. says is consistent with the view taken by this book, but it does not look as though Beatson J. had the authorities referred to in this chapter cited to him.
[40] [2009] H.K.C.U. 198. Lord Hoffmann was in the court.
[41] *Re Baron Holding Investments Ltd* [2000] 1 B.C.L.C. 272, 9–009.

on a jurisdiction dispute.⁴² It is hard to give it much weight in the usual case where the lawyer seeks to accept a second retainer, but it might be a more persuasive discretionary argument in favour of the lawyer continuing where the lawyer has never accepted a retainer for the other side and the client seeks to instruct him because of his knowledge of the subject-matter.

It is hoped that the English courts will take a robust line where the claimant seeks an injunction to prevent a lawyer acting against him in these circumstances. There are public policy reasons for ensuring that the defendant is not easily able to take out his opponent's lawyer of choice. Although the mediation in *Carter Holt* involved signed confidentiality agreements of wide scope, Blanchard J. doubted whether it mattered whether there were signed agreements because of the obligation of confidentiality implicit in the mediation.⁴³ Mediations are regular occurrences in litigation and offers are invariably made. It seems in principle no different from a "without prejudice" meeting. This is a very dangerous precedent.

9–008

And how does this apply to arbitrations? Where the proceedings are by way of arbitration rather than court, there is no collateral obligation, but an implied obligation of confidentiality to the other party which is of a similar nature.⁴⁴ So does this mean that the collateral undertaking analysis does not apply, but instead the court will look at the confidentiality analysis? Here there is a real issue, particularly as there is no hearing in open court which provides for a termination of the undertaking.

2. Solicitors for liquidators

There is a line of cases where applications are made to injunct solicitors from acting for liquidators which has similarities to the foregoing analysis. Here application is made to prevent solicitors from acting for a liquidator because of a previous allegedly conflicting retainer. What makes these cases different from other conflict applications is that the applicant is not the former client but the party sued or to be sued by the liquidator.

9–009

In *Re Baron Holding Investments Ltd*,⁴⁵ the two shareholders and sole directors of a company which had been wound up sought to prevent Kanter Jules, who were solicitors to the two principal creditors of the company and

---

⁴² *The Spiliada* [1987] A.C. 460, HL. The fact that the London lawyers and experts had been involved in a related action which settled after 21 weeks of trial in the commercial court was regarded as a relevant factor in favour of English jurisdiction; this is generally referred to in the jurisdiction context as "the Cambridgeshire factor" after the name of the vessel involved in that first trial.
⁴³ [2001] 3 N.Z.L.R. 343 at para.24.
⁴⁴ *Ali Shipping Corp v Shipyard Trogir* [1998] 2 All E.R. 136, CA.
⁴⁵ [2000] 1 B.C.L.C. 272, Pumfrey J. On October 26, 1999, Chadwick L.J. refused leave to appeal: his reasons for refusing to do so are reported on Lexis under the case name *Halstuk v Venvil*.

had acted for those creditors in the litigation against the company which had given rise to the winding up order from acting for the liquidator. It was argued that there were conflicts inherent in these solicitors acting for these two clients whose interests conflicted. The persons applying for an injunction were persons against whom Kanter Jules were acting, both previously in the litigation against the company (when at that time there was a strong community of interest between the company and its sole directors and shareholders) and as solicitors for the liquidator, who was seeking to bring misfeasance proceedings against the directors. The judge refused an injunction on the facts. But one particular matter to take into account was the advantage in the solicitors acting because the dual position complained of gave them a background knowledge not shared by other solicitors who might be instructed. This is not a factor which will arise in most conflict cases. Pumfrey J. placed reliance on two pre-*Bolkiah* authorities which adopted a similar approach. One was the decision of Robert Walker J. in *Re Schuppan*[46] where the trustee in bankruptcy had instructed the petitioning creditors' solicitors even though the petitioning creditor was the object of potential claims by the trustee himself; the other case was *Re Maxwell Communications Plc*,[47] where Hoffmann J. considered whether auditors of a subsidiary should be appointed administrators of the company although their audit might have to be investigated in due course. In *Hornan v Latif*[48] Pumfrey J. distinguished *Baron*, saying that such cases were concerned with the steps to be taken when there is a risk of conflict of interest for the solicitor acting for the petitioning creditor and liquidator and how the problem can be accommodated without depriving the liquidator of the advantages of employing a solicitor who is well informed regarding the affairs of the company, unless it was necessary to do so.

---

[46] [1996] 2 All E.R. 664.
[47] [1992] B.C.L.C. 465; see also *Re Polly Peck International Plc* [1991] B.C.C. 503.
[48] [2003] 2 B.C.L.C. 186, Pumfrey J.; there was litigation by a liquidator as to ownership of property. The respondents sought to remove the solicitor for the liquidator. He was formerly a partner of the solicitors who acted in related litigation for the company on behalf of one faction, and his firm's bill was the largest proof accepted by liquidator. It was said he would be a witness, had a financial interest in the liquidation and had confidential information he was not free to use, so his firm should be removed as solicitor for the liquidator. It was said that whilst acting for the company he received confidential information for one of the factions and that party was defendant to action by the liquidator.

CHAPTER 10

Blowing the whistle on the client

A. The legislation

Part 7 of the Proceeds of Crime Act 2002 ("POCA") came into force on February 24, 2003. POCA was enacted to put into effect the United Kingdom's obligations under the EU Second Money Laundering Directive.[1] The Money Laundering Regulations 2003 ("the Regulations")[2] came into force on March 1, 2004. Since then there have been amendments to the legislation first under the Serious Organised Crime and Police Act 2005, and most recently under the Money Laundering Regulations 2007,[3] making amendments designed to give effect to the EU Third Money Laundering Directive, which also covers anti-terrorist measures. The power to amend primary legislation by regulations arises because the regulations give effect to UK treaty obligations to enact EU directives.[4]

Two words of caution are appropriate at the outset. Firstly, it is essential to look at an up to date version of POCA, in the light of the various amendments to its provisions. Secondly, authority considering provisions which have now been amended needs to be treated with great caution, in particular the first decision under POCA, *P v P*,[5] which suffers from the dual problems of being based on the old statutory wording and in any event being largely wrong even based on the wording it interprets[6].

The professional will be accustomed to subjugating his duties to his client to his duties to the court or his professional obligations. But efforts

10–001

---

[1] Directive 2001/97/EC.
[2] SI 2003/3075. See Appendix B.
[3] In force December 15, 2007.
[4] S.2(2) European Communities Act 1972.
[5] [2003] 4 All E.R. 843.
[6] As held in *Bowman v Fells* [2005] 4 All E.R. 609.

to prevent money laundering and otherwise to trace proceeds of crime have led to fresh obligations which provide a new conflict between obligations to the client and regulatory duties. Now the professional who suspects that his client may be involved in money laundering or otherwise in criminal activity is obliged to act as whistleblower.

10–002　The structure of Pt 7 of POCA is to provide that certain actions or inactions which involve money laundering are criminal offences unless the action or inaction have been sanctioned by an appropriate disclosure to the National Criminal Intelligence Service ("NCIS"). "Criminal property" is defined as a person's benefit from criminal conduct or it represents such a benefit, and the alleged offender knows or suspects that it constitutes or represents such a benefit.[7] So where the professional suspects that the client's property is in whole or part the proceeds of crime, the transfer of such property to and from a firm's client account potentially falls within the criminal offence under s.327. Advising on tax planning or how the client should deal with funds which are suspected to be the proceeds of crime will involve becoming concerned in an arrangement which facilitates the acquisition, retention, use or control of criminal property and is a criminal offence under s.328. If the money is in the client account, it may involve the criminal offence of possession of criminal property within s.329.

Where a person carries on a business in the regulated sector significant additional obligations arise. Firstly, the Regulations require in relation to the carrying on of a business in the regulated sector the maintenance of appropriate procedures for client identification, record keeping and staff training.[8] Thus any business which carries out work which is likely to fall within the definition of the regulated sector will need to comply. Failure to comply is a criminal offence. The businesses most likely to be affected are accountants, bankers, auditors, tax advisers, art dealers, estate agents and solicitors.

The same definition as used for the applicability of the Regulations is used to determine the applicability of the additional obligations under POCA.[9] POCA ss.327–329 provide that positive acts, even if committed in good faith by a professional not personally involved in money laundering, may constitute criminal offences if prior disclosure is not made. However, where the information comes to the professional in the course of a business in the regulated sector, s.330 applies, which provides that suspicion that another person, who may be a client, is carrying on money laundering, will itself give rise to a criminal offence unless disclosure is made and consent given. Thus, so long as the information comes to the professional in the course of a business in the regulated sector, there may be a criminal offence committed by inaction as well as action. Section 330 provides:

---

[7] s.340(3).
[8] s.3 of the Regulations.
[9] See POCA Sch. 9.

"(1) A person commits an offence if the conditions in subsections (2) to (4) are satisfied.
(2) The first condition is that he—
   (a) knows or suspects, or
   (b) has reasonable grounds for knowing or suspecting, that another person is engaged in money laundering.
(3) The second condition is that the information or other matter—
   (a) on which his knowledge or suspicion is based, or
   (b) which gives reasonable grounds for such knowledge or suspicion, came to him in the course of a business in the regulated sector.
(3A) The third condition is—
   (a) that he can identify the other person mentioned in subsection (2) or the whereabouts of any of the laundered property, or
   (b) that he believes, or it is reasonable to expect him to believe, that the information or other matter mentioned in subsection (3) will or may assist in identifying that other person or the whereabouts of any of the laundered property
(4) The fourth condition is that he does not make the required disclosure to—
   (a) a nominated officer, or—
   (b) a person authorized for the purpose of this Part by the Director General of SOCA as soon as is practicable after the information or other matter mentioned in subsection (3) comes to him.
(5) The required disclosure is a disclosure of—
   (a) the identity of the other person mentioned in subsection (2), if he knows it
   (b) the whereabouts of the laundered property, so far as he knows it, and
   (c) the information or other matter mentioned in subsection (3).
(5A) The laundered property is the property forming the subject-matter of the money laundering that he knows, or suspects, or has reasonable grounds for knowing or suspecting, that other person to be engaged in."

Lawyers, accountants, insolvency practitioners and other professionals will thus be within these sections, at least in many cases, by the definition of "business within the regulated sector".[10] The starting point for a professional is thus whether the Regulations apply in respect of any par-

---

[10] See Sch. 9 of POCA.

ticular type of business. If they do, then the obligation to maintain appropriate procedures under the Regulations applies, and the obligations of disclosure under s.330 apply too in relation to that type of business. The provisions will apply to those involved in giving financial advice, banks, accountants and others concerned in dealing with clients' money. Section 330 will only apply when the Regulations apply. In such circumstances the criminal offence in issue will not merely be a failure to report; the professional will commit a criminal offence if he simply fails to establish the necessary procedures under the Regulations.

10–003　　Under s.330 the obligation to disclose arises where there is suspicion of money laundering. Money laundering sounds very grand. It suggests drug money, or other scams involving money passed through accounts in Switzerland or other similarly friendly jurisdictions. But the ambit of this legislation includes very much more mundane activity. Money laundering is defined[11] as committing or assisting in offences under ss.327, 328 and 329 so it is a much wider definition than the words would at first blush suggest. So where s.330 applies there is an obligation to make disclosure where there is suspicion that the client or the other side's client is involved in what amounts to dealing with monies acquired through criminal conduct. The section also applies where there are reasonable grounds for suspicion which seems to cover the case where the professional should have suspected but in fact did not.

The Regulations cover accountancy, tax and audit services and a variety of forms of business. The Regulations provide that they apply to auditors, insolvency practitioners, external accountants and tax advisers and independent legal professionals.[12] The definition of "independent legal professional"[13] is:

> "a firm or sole practitioner who by way of business provides legal or notarial services to other persons, when participating in financial or real property transactions concerning—
> (a) The buying and selling of real property or business entities
> (b) The managing of client money, securities or other assets
> (c) The opening or management of bank, savings or securities accounts
> (d) The organisation of contributions necessary for the creation, operation or management of companies or
> (e) The creation, operation or management of trusts, companies or similar structures."

---

[11] s.340.
[12] reg. 3(1)(c) and (d).
[13] reg. 3(9).

POCA Sch. 9 para. 1(1)(n) copies this definition into "a business in the regulated sector", to the extent that the business consists of the above. Where Sch. 9 applies, the additional s.330 obligations apply.

10–004 The Regulations do not appear to apply where the lawyer is ascertaining and advising upon the legal position of a client once a transaction has taken place, nor where the lawyer is representing a client in legal proceedings which culminate in a settlement or order of the court. The Regulations will however cover much non-contentious or advisory work in relation to financial or real property transactions. Being based on an EU Directive, the Regulations must be construed purposively in accordance with the aims of that Directive. Any doubts as to the meaning of the Regulations can thus be resolved by referring to the Directive.[14] Of course, even if the transaction or retainer falls outside this definition, s.327–329 may still apply and require the professional to make a disclosure to NCIS. Section 328 provides for a wider obligation:

"(1) A person commits an offence if he enters into or becomes concerned in an arrangement which he knows or suspects facilitates (by whatever means) the acquisition, retention, use or control of criminal property by or on behalf of another person.
(2) But a person does not commit such an offence if—
   (a) he makes an authorised disclosure under section 338 and (if the disclosure is made before he does the act mentioned in subsection (1)) he has the appropriate consent;
   (b) he intended to make such a disclosure but had a reasonable excuse for not doing so;
   (c) the act he does is done in carrying out a function he has relating to the enforcement of any provision of this Act or of any other enactment relating to criminal conduct or benefit from criminal conduct."

10–005 Section 340 defines criminal conduct broadly. Conduct carried out overseas is criminal conduct if it would constitute an offence in any part of the United Kingdom if it occurred there. By s.340 property is "criminal property" if it constitutes a person's benefit from criminal conduct[15] or represents such a benefit in whole or part and whether directly or indirectly and the alleged offender knows or suspects that it constitutes or represents such a benefit.

---

[14] Recitals 16 and 17 together with the definition of "institutions" from which the definition of "relevant business" is taken, make the position clear.
[15] See under prior legislation *R. v Causey* [1991] 1 W.L.R. 1551 as to whether property represents proceeds of crime.

B. Bowman v Fells

10–006
The first case on Pt 7 of POCA was *P v P*. In *P v P*[16] counsel acting for a wife in family litigation sought directions on what was intended to be an ex parte basis, as to their obligations where the husband's assets arguably included the proceeds of tax evasion. The concern was that the husband had been involved in tax evasion, and that in consequence part of the matrimonial assets might fall within the very wide definition of criminal property. Thus the concern was that the lawyers, in consequence of their involvement in the litigation, might be involved in the "acquisition, retention, use or control of criminal property" and thus under an obligation to report by virtue of s.328. Dame Elizabeth Butler-Sloss P. heard submissions from a range of interested parties, but all assumed that merely acting for parties to family division proceedings and advising on a settlement was sufficient to bring s.328 into play.

This always seemed an unlikely reading of s.328.[17] The Court of Appeal heard a test case on POCA in *Bowman v Fells*,[18] with representations from the Bar Council and Law Society as well as NCIS and the parties to the litigation. The court held that s.328 was not intended to cover or affect the ordinary conduct of litigation by legal professionals. That included any step taken by them in the litigation from the issue of proceedings, the securing of injunctive relief or a freezing order up to its final disposal by judgment or consensual resolution of issues by the parties. In any event, the court held that s.328 could not have the effect of overriding legal professional privilege.

Section 330 (6) provides a privilege defence for an independent legal adviser. Such an adviser does not commit an offence:

> "(a) if he knows either of the things mentioned in subsection (5)(a) and (b), he knows the thing because of information or other matter that came to him in privileged circumstances, or
> (b) the information or other matter mentioned in subsection (3) came to him in privileged circumstances."

There is a defence of reasonable excuse for not making prior disclosure. It is not clear how far that will go. Is urgency of an application to court a good reason not to make disclosure? It may be, but sometimes urgent applications are planned some time in advance, so it may be difficult to be certain this will provide a defence in any given case.

---

[16] [2003] 4 All E.R. 843.
[17] See the criticisms of *P v P* in the 2nd edition of this book at para. 8–10.
[18] [2005] 4 All E.R. 609.

C. Tipping off

There are "tipping off" offences under s.333A and there is also an offence of prejudicing an investigation under s.342.[19] Section 333A provides something close to a strict liability offence of tipping off once a disclosure has been made where the information on which the disclosure is based came to the person in the course of a business in the regulated sector. Section 333A removes the privilege defence within the regulated sector unless the tipping off is to the adviser's client for the purpose of dissuading the client from engaging in money laundering.[20] The change arises as a result of art.28 of the EU Third Money Laundering Directive. Whilst the privilege exception to the disclosure obligation in s.330 (6) is necessary in order to ensure that lawyers are not under an obligation to use material obtained in privileged circumstances to make a disclosure, the same issue does not arise under the tipping-off provision: preventing a lawyer carrying on business within the regulated sector from tipping off his client as to the fact that a disclosure has been made, or as to the existence of an investigation, does not infringe legal professional privilege. There is a legal professional privilege exemption under s.342,[21] which is a section not restricted to the regulated sector.

10–007

---

[19] s.333 previously applied to disclosures within the regulated sector sections and gave rise to issues as to when a professional could tell his client he was about to make a disclosure or had made a disclosure. In *P v P* Butler-Sloss P. suggested that good practice required that the professional wait seven days after disclosure before notifying the client: [2003] 4 All E.R. 843 at [67] but that raised serious questions as to whether not telling the client promptly where s.333 did not prohibit it might involve a breach of fiduciary duty to the client.
[20] s.333D(2). S.33 has been repealed.
[21] s.342 (3) (c) and (4).

CHAPTER 11

Judicial Conflicts: Bias and apparent bias

11–001 This chapter and those which follow deal with what is largely a discrete area: when should a conflict of interest lead the tribunal to recuse itself. Although most of the decisions relate to judges, they also apply to other bodies rendering judicial or quasi-judicial decisions including juries, and disciplinary or other tribunals. What first gave this a topical flavour was the decision of the House of Lords in *R. v Bow Street Metropolitan Stipendiary Magistrate Ex p. Pinochet Ugarte (No.2)*.[1] The public interest generated by that decision led to a number of applications for judges or tribunals to recuse themselves on grounds which would not previously been thought to have merit. Since the coming into force of the Human Rights Act 1998 the courts have needed also to consider art.6.[2] Clarity as to the test to be applied when a judge is asked to recuse himself since the decision of the House of Lords in *Porter v Magill*[3] has not stopped the flow of cases.

There is a steady stream of new cases in this area. Many of them are simply applications of the general principle. But there is no doubt that over the last decade the courts have become vastly more sensitive about apprehension of judicial bias, and whilst the test may not have changed since *Porter v Magill*[4] was decided, it is being applied to situations where no one would have thought a problem arose a few years ago.

---

[1] [2000] 1 A.C. 119, HL. This will henceforth be referred to as "Pinochet".
[2] Considered below at para.11–005.
[3] [2002] 2 A.C. 357.
[4] [2002] 2 A.C. 357.

1. Bias, apparent bias and the impartial tribunal

A. Actual bias

Any judge[5] who allows any judicial decision to be influenced by partiality or prejudice deprives the litigant of the important right to a fair trial and thus violates one of the most fundamental principles underlying the administration of justice.[6] Actual bias as a ground for disqualification is very rare. It is in practice very difficult to prove actual bias because of:

11–002

(a) the undesirability of investigating the state of mind of a judge, juror or magistrate, especially given the confidential nature of the judicial process;
(b) the difficulty of proving actual bias;
(c) the fact that the judicial officer may not be conscious of any bias;
(d) the public interest in maintaining confidence in the integrity of the administration of justice requires that the appearance of bias should be avoided and thus makes it unnecessary to allege actual bias.

However, the practical reason why bias is not proved is simply that it is not necessary to allege actual bias (other than in the *Dimes* sense discussed below), and it simply raises the temperature, so in practice it is almost never done. Whilst judgments often commence by stating that actual bias was not alleged, this appears in judgments largely as a sop to the decision-maker whose conduct is being impugned.

B. Direct pecuniary or proprietary interest: The Dimes principle

Lord Hoffmann was not the first holder of high judicial office to encounter a problem. In 1852, orders and decrees made by no less a person than the Lord Chancellor, Lord Cottenham, were set aside on the ground that he had had at the relevant time a substantial shareholding in the respondent company in *Dimes v The Proprietors of the Grand Junction Canal*.[7] Lord Campbell said[8]:

11–003

---

[5] It is convenient to use the word judge as shorthand but the principles are generally equally applicable to magistrates, arbitrators, regulatory tribunals and other makers of judicial or quasi-judicial decisions.
[6] *R. v Inner West London Coroner Ex p. Dallaglio* [1994] 4 All E.R. 139 at 161, per Bingham M.R.
[7] (1853) 3 H.L. Cas. 759.
[8] At 793.

"No one can suppose that Lord Cottenham could be, in the remotest degree, influenced by the interest that he had in this concern; but, my Lords, it is of the last importance that the maxim that no man is to be judge in his own cause should be held sacred. And that is not to be confined to a cause in which he is a party, but applies to a cause in which he has an interest. Since I have had the honour to be Chief Justice of the Court of Queen's Bench, we have again and again set aside proceedings in inferior tribunals because of an individual, who had an interest in a cause, took a part in the decision. And it will have a most salutary influence on these tribunals when it is known that this High Court of last resort, in a case in which the Lord Chancellor of England had an interest, considered that his decree was on that account a decree not according to law, and was set aside. This will be a lesson to all inferior tribunals to take care not only that in their decrees they are not influenced by their personal interest, but to avoid the appearance of labouring under such an influence".

In the context of automatic disqualification, the issue is not whether the judge has some link with a party involved in a cause before the judge but whether the outcome of that cause could realistically affect the judge's interest.[9] Thus if the judge holds a relatively small number of shares in a large company and the sums involved in the litigation could not realistically affect the value or the dividend, that will not be the case. In *Locabail (UK) Ltd v Bayfield Properties*,[10] the special Court of Appeal consisting of the Lord Chief Justice, the Master of the Rolls, and the Vice Chancellor convened to establish guidelines for judicial conflicts in the light of *Pinochet*, spoke of a de minimis exception,[11] but any doubt should be resolved in favour of disqualification. Where the interest derived from the interest of a spouse, partner or other family member the link must be so close and direct as to render the interest of the other person for all practical purposes indistinguishable from an interest of the judge himself.[12] The right to object in an

---

[9] [2000] Q.B. 451.
[10] [2000] Q.B. 451.
[11] *BTR Industries South Africa (Pty) Ltd v Metal and Allied Workers' Union* (1992) (3) S.A. 673 at 694; *R. v Inner West London Coroner Ex p. Dallaglio* [1994] 4 All E.R. 139 at 162; *Auckland Casino v Casino Control Authority* [1995] 1 N.Z.L.R. 142 at 148; *Clenae Pty Ltd v Australia and New Zealand Banking Group* (1999) V.S.C.A. 35 (Supreme Court of Victoria) but cf. *R. v Rand* (1866) L.R. 1 Q.B. 230 at 232, Blackburn J. *and R. v Camborne Justices Ex p. Pearce* [1955] 1 Q.B. 41, which suggest that any pecuniary interest however small is sufficient; this must now be regarded as disapproved. The Court of Appeal reaffirmed in *Weatherill v Lloyds TSB Bank Plc*, Unreported, July 26, 2000, CA, that a de minimis pecuniary interest was not a ground for recusal.
[12] See *Jones v Das Legal Expenses Insurance Co* [2004] I.R.L.R. 218.CA. The tribunal chairman disclosed that her husband was a barrister in chambers handling DAS work. A claim based on economic interest failed; neither husband nor wife had an economic interest in DAS—the interest was in their own well-being. This was really an apparent bias case but that failed on the facts too.

automatic disqualification case may be waived but the waiver must be clear and unequivocal, and made with full knowledge of the relevant facts.[13]

C. Extension of the Dimes principle to non-pecuniary interests

This principle relates to pecuniary or proprietary interests. In *Pinochet* the House of Lords made clear that it extended to a limited class of non-financial interests. The House of Lords was asked to determine difficult and controversial issues under international law relevant to whether the extradition warrant issued against the former Chilean dictator Senor Pinochet should be set aside. The human rights organisation Amnesty International successfully sought leave to be joined to the hearing to support the extradition. Lord Hoffmann, one of the law lords who sat on the appeal was a director and chairman of Amnesty International Charity Limited, a related charity with the same objects. The House of Lords held that the *Dimes* principle extended to circumstances where the matter at issue was not money or economic advantage but the promotion of the cause, the rationale disqualifying the judge applied just as much if the judge's decision will lead to the promotion of a cause in which the judge is involved together with one of the parties. Thus the House of Lords set aside their own decision.

In *Pinochet* the House of Lords held that the principle of automatic disqualification applied as Lord Hoffmann was judge in his own cause, applying the Latin maxim *nemo debet esse iudex in propria causa*. As Lord Campbell said in *Dimes*, the principle was not to be confined to a cause in which he is a party, but applies to a cause in which he has an interest.[14] Although Lord Hoffmann had no personal interest in the case, he was director of a part of a movement working towards the same goals with an interest in the proceedings' outcome. As we will see, if a person is treated as judge in his own cause, the tribunal cannot be treated as independent (which also impacts on art.6 rights) and there is *automatic* disqualification.

The *Pinochet* case thus involved a very limited extension of the *Dimes* principle. It was said[15] that it might apply also where the interest of the judge in the subject-matter of the proceedings arising from his strong commitment to some cause or belief or his association with a person or body involved in the proceedings could shake public confidence in the administration of justice as much as a shareholding in a company involved in the litigation. But the courts are likely to hesitate long before creating any other special category of automatic disqualification because this would create

[13] *Locabail* [2000] Q.B. 451.
[14] (1852) 3 HL 759, 793.
[15] By Lord Hutton.

uncertainty as to the parameters of the category.[16] It is notable that in *Meerabux v AG of Belize*[17] Lord Hope, giving the Privy Council's opinion said that the decision in *Pinochet* to extend the *Dimes* principle to cover the interest Lord Hoffmann had "appears in retrospect to have been a highly technical one".[18] The court in *Locabail* made the point that any extension of the automatic disqualification rule would limit the power of the judge and any reviewing court to take account of the facts and circumstances of a particular case, and would have the potential to cause delay and increased cost in the final disposal of the proceedings, and thus there should be no extension of the automatic disqualification rule unless required to give effect to these underlying principles.

2. Article 6 requirements

A. Provisions of art.6

11–005   The starting point is to consider the ECtHR jurisprudence because, since the Human Rights Act, the English courts are obliged to comply. Article 6(1) provides that in the determination of civil rights and obligations, everyone is entitled to a fair and public hearing within a reasonable time by an independent and impartial tribunal established by law. In *Porter v Magill*[19] Lord Hope said[20] that the rights to a fair hearing, to a public hearing and to a hearing within a reasonable time are separate and distinct rights from the right to a hearing before an independent and impartial tribunal established by law. It was no answer to a complaint that the tribunal was not independent or was not impartial to show that it conducted a fair hearing.[21]

Article 6 provides for a serious of separate but related rights:

(a) a fair hearing
(b) a public hearing
(c) within a reasonable time
(d) by an independent tribunal

---

[16] *R. v Gough* [1993] A.C. 646 at 673, per Lord Woolf. This does not seem a particularly convincing reason. Lord Goff agreed at 664; the High Court of Australia took a similar view in *Webb v R.* (1994) 181 C.L.R. 41 at 75, per Deane J.
[17] [2005] 2 A.C. 513.
[18] At [21]. The comment is all the more striking because Lord Hoffmann himself was part of the board (and thus must be treated as having concurred in the opinion). *Meerabux* is discussed at 11–021. However, in *R (on the application of Darsho Kaur) v Institute of Legal Executives Appeal Tribunal* [2011] EWCA Civ 116, Rix L.J. treated this comment as relevant to whether the *Dimes* principle should be treated as a separate principle or merely part of the law of apparent bias. *Pinochet* was decided prior to *Porter v Magill*.
[19] [2002] 2 A.C. 357.
[20] [2002] 2 A.C. 357 at para.87.
[21] *Millar v Dickson*, (2001) S.L.T. 988.

(e) by an impartial tribunal
(f) established by law.

The right to determination by an independent and impartial tribunal is thus guaranteed by art.6(1). There is a close relationship between the concept of independence and that of impartiality.[22] In both cases, the tribunal must not only be independent and free from bias—it must not appear in an objective sense to lack these qualities. Bias means a predisposition or prejudice against one party's case or evidence on an issue for reasons unconnected with the merits of the issue.[23]

B. Independent tribunal

The ECtHR has explained that whether a judicial tribunal is independent primarily depends on its "manner of appointment of its members and their term of office, the existence of guarantees against outside pressures and whether it presents an appearance of independence".[24] In one sense, the "independent tribunal" requirement reflects the automatic disqualification where the *Dimes* principle is infringed, and to that extent the two principles overlap. In cases such as *Pinochet,* the *Dimes* principle was held to be engaged and thus the court could not be regarded as an independent tribunal. But, as we will see, art.6 has also led to tribunals being held not to be independent in circumstances where the *Dimes* principle would not have been regarded as infringed and the courts have not fully worked out the relationship between the two. The problem has particularly arisen also in disciplinary tribunals, where a tribunal member has also had an involvement in the prosecution process or is part of the executive of the prosecuting authority. Such cases are considered at 12–008 below.

11–006

C. Prior legislative involvement

This principle has led to recusal where the judge has had a prior role in the legislation under challenge. In *McGonnell v United Kingdom*,[25] McGonnell made a planning application to the relevant Guernsey tribunal, which he lost, and appealed. The appeal tribunal, which was presided over by Sir Graham Dorey, dismissed the appeal. The basis of refusal was that the tribunal was bound to take into account Guernsey Detailed Development Plan 6, which was a statement of policy approved by the Guernsey authorities.

11–007

---

[22] *Findlay v United Kingdom* (1997) 24 E.H.R.R. 221 at 244–5, para.73.
[23] *R v Inner West London Coroner Ex p. Dallaglio* [1994] 4 All E.R. 139 at 151.
[24] *Bryan v UK* (1995) 21 E.H.R.R. 342, para.37.
[25] [2000] 2 P.L.R. 69, ECtHR.

Sir Graham Dorey, as Bailiff, had legislative and executive functions which involved presiding over the process of approval of Detailed Development Plan 6. There was no allegation of actual bias against Sir Graham. The ECtHR held that in view of his legislative and executive role Sir Graham did not have the appearance of independence or the required objective impartiality, and held there was a breach of art.6.[26] In *Davidson v Scottish Ministers*[27] the House of Lords held that where a judge who had participated in the drafting or promotion of legislation during the parliamentary process was called on to rule judicially on the effect of legislation, there was a risk of apparent bias. But it is not enough that he was a member of government; there must be some nexus between the issue before the court and the role of the judge whilst he was a minister.[28]

D. Security of tenure

11–008   Another area where this principle has been important is in relation to security of tenure of judges. In *Starrs and Chalmers v Procurator Fiscal*[29] the Scottish Court of Session upheld a claim that trial before a Deputy Sheriff contravened the right to a fair trial under art.6. Large numbers of Scottish criminal cases were heard by deputy sheriffs appointed for one year at a time. The amount of work offered to them during that period, whether they were reappointed for another year, and whether they were eventually offered a permanent appointment, all depended on the exercise of discretion by the Lord Advocate under the policies of the day. The Court of Session concluded that there was a real risk that a well-informed observer would think that when deciding cases a temporary sheriff might be influenced by his hopes and fears as to his personal advancement, either in relation to appointment on a temporary basis or the prospects of a permanent appointment. For the executive to decide who sits on the bench is consistent with judicial independence only if it is supported by adequate guarantees that the appointed judge enjoys security of tenure. In relation to temporary sheriffs, the court held there were no such guarantees. Temporary judges carrying short-term appointments and no security of tenure included tribunal members, assistant recorders and deputy high court judges. Even if a judge has security of tenure and is only removable from office for good cause, such as misconduct, Lord Prosser said that the determination of whether such good

---

[26] Compare *Panton v Minister of Finance*, Unreported, July 12, 2001, PC, where the Privy Council rejected the argument that the Jamaica Court of Appeal hearing the case was not an independent and impartial tribunal because the President of the court had certified when previously Attorney-General that an act whose constitutionality was now challenged was constitutional. In fact the president had played no significant part in the passing of the legislation.
[27] *The Times*, July 16, 2004, HL [2004] U.K.H.L. 34.
[28] *R (Ewing) v Secretary of State for Justice* [2008] EWHC 3416, (Admin), Beatson J.
[29] November 16, 1999, Court of Session.

cause exists cannot be left in the hands of a member of the executive branch of government on whom the judge should not be dependent. This case led to a review of the terms of appointment in England of part-time judges. The position of "assistant recorder" was abolished, and the terms of appointment of recorders were amended so as to give increased security of tenure. More recently, in *Kearney v HM Advocate*[30] the Privy Council held that the system for appointment of temporary judges in Scotland did pass muster as to manner of appointment and security of tenure. The issue was whether lack of security of tenure leads to an apprehension of bias because the fair-minded observer would be concerned that the temporary judge would have an inclination to be over-deferential to those who had power to terminate or renew his appointment. There was no single test that was decisive; all the circumstances had to be taken into account.[31]

E. Separation of functions

Whether the tribunal could be regarded as independent for the purposes of art.6 was in issue in *R. (on the Application of Alconbury Developments Ltd) v Secretary of State for the Environment, Transport and the Regions*.[32] The impugned powers were the processes by which the Secretary of State called in applications for planning permission, recovered appeals against refusals of planning permission, and made orders in respect of compulsory acquisition of land. Decisions made under those processes were subject to judicial review or statutory appeal but there was no provision for appeal on the facts or the merits. The complaint was that in each of these cases whenever a decision was taken by the Secretary of State, the Secretary of State's role in the making of policy meant he had such an interest in the making of policy that he could not be regarded as an independent and impartial tribunal. The Divisional Court thus held that the system did not comply with art.6. The House of Lords accepted that the Secretary of State could not be regarded himself as an independent or impartial tribunal for this purpose, but the issue was whether there was sufficient judicial control over the actions of the Secretary of State to ensure determination by an independent tribunal subsequently. ECtHR jurisprudence did not require such control to constitute a rehearing by way of appeal on the merits. What was required was that there should be a review of the legality of the decisions and the procedure followed. The judicial review jurisdiction of the High Court constituted such a review.[33]

11–009

---

[30] [2006] HRLR 15 PC.
[31] See *Kearney* at [51] to [53], per Lord Hope, see also *Save Guana Cay Reef Association Ltd v R* [2009] UKPC 44 at [51], per Lord Walker.
[32] [2003] 2 A.C. 295, HL.
[33] *Albert v Belgium* (1983) 5 E.H.R.R. 533 at para.29; *Bryan v UK* (1995) 21 E.H.R.R. 342; *Chapman v UK* (2001) 10 B.H.R.C. 48.

Another topical issue is whether a senior employee or executive can sit on a jury or tribunal on a prosecution brought by the body of which he is employee or executive. There is a discussion of recent caselaw on the point in relation to disciplinary tribunals at 12–008 below. In *R v LL*[34] the Court of Appeal heard an appeal where it transpired that one juror was a CPS employee with general administrative duties, another was a serving police officer in an administrative and non-operational role and a third was a former police officer who had retired. The Court of Appeal dismissed the appeal in relation to the two police officers, but decided that the CPS employee, not being a temporary employee of the CPS, was of sufficient seniority and long-service to render the tribunal not independent.

In recent years many decision-making bodies have taken steps to separate their functions from the executive as well as making their own decision-making entirely independent from the prosecution process. It has often been seen as important that the tribunal meets at a venue separate from that where its prosecutors work. The new Supreme Court carried on its business in a building separate from its predecessors in order to emphasise its complete separation and independence from its predecessors who were part of the House of Lords. The Financial Services and Markets Tribunal, which hears appeals from the Regulatory Disputes Committee, sits across London from the Regulatory Disputes Committee itself, which although having a measure of independence would not fulfil the art.6 criteria of independence.

However, in the constant scrutiny of tribunals from the executive, not everyone has been held to have the necessary independence. In *Brooke v Parole Board*[35] the Parole Board's relationship with the ministry, including its sponsorship of confidential meetings and the lack of security of its appointees, were held by the Divisional Court not to meet the level of independence required for the tribunal.

3. Apparent bias

A. ECtHR jurisprudence

11–010   The ECtHR said in *Hauschildt v Denmark*[36] that the impartiality of the tribunal was to be determined:

> "according to a subjective test, that is on the basis of a personal conviction of a particular judge in a particular case, and also according to an

---

[34] [2011] EWCA Crim 65.
[35] [2007] EWHC 2036, Admin.
[36] (1989) 12 E.H.R.R. 266.

objective test, that is ascertaining whether the judge offered guarantees sufficient to exclude any legitimate doubt in this respect".[37]

The subjective element of the test was said to involve whether it can be shown on the facts that a member of the tribunal acted with personal bias against the applicant,[38] whilst the objective element involves an objective test of impartiality. The ECtHR has emphasised the importance of appearances because what is at stake is the confidence which the courts in a democratic society must inspire in the public and, above all, as far as criminal proceedings are concerned, in the accused.[39] In deciding whether in a given case there is a legitimate reason to fear that a particular judge lacks impartiality, what is decisive is whether the concerns of the party making the complaint can be objectively justified.[40]

B. From Gough to Magill

In 1863, in *Di Sora v Phillips*,[41] Lord Westbury L.C. recused himself from sitting on appeal on the grounds that he had been counsel in the case. Lord Wensleydale[42] expressed the view that he was wrong to do so, but Lords Chelmsford and Cranworth thought he had exercised a very wise discretion. Matters have moved on a little since then. But the combination of ECtHR jurisprudence and criticism from abroad as to the test previously applied has led to a shift in the test in England.

11–011

In *R. v Gough*[43] one of the jury was the next door neighbour of the brother of the defendant charged with robbery. The brother was also charged but discharged at the committal stage and the defendant indicted on a single charge of conspiracy with his brother to commit robbery. Although the brother was referred to during the evidence, it was only after the defendant had been sentenced to 15 years imprisonment and the brother started shouting in court that the juror realised he was the man next door. The bias principle applied as much to a juryman as to any other decision-maker. The House of Lords held that the test was whether there was "real danger or possibility of bias" and as the juror did not know about the connection until after the verdict there was no possibility

---

[37] *Hauschildt v Denmark* (1989) 12 E.H.R.R. 266.
[38] *Piersack v Belgium* (1982) 5 E.H.R.R. 169; *De Cubber v Belgium* (1984) 7 E.H.R.R. 236; *Langborger v Sweden* (1990) 12 E.H.R.R. 416.
[39] *Fey v Austria* (1993) 16 E.H.R.R. 387; *Sramek v Austria* (1984) 7 E.H.R.R. 351.
[40] *Hauschildt v Denmark* (1989) 12 E.H.R.R. 266, para.48; *Fey v Austria* (1993) 16 E.H.R.R. 387, para.30; *Campbell and Fell v UK* (1984) 7 E.H.R.R. 165, para.85; *Gregory v UK* (1997) 25 E.H.R.R. 577, para.45.
[41] (1863) H.L.C. 624, 11 E.R. 1168.
[42] At 1175.
[43] [1993] A.C. 646.

that it could have affected her decision.⁴⁴ It was a matter for the court to decide how much weight to place on the statement of the person against whom bias was alleged as to the relevant facts, but the court would not cross-examine or seek disclosure from the judge or decision-maker and would not pay attention to any statement by the judge concerning the impact of any knowledge on his mind or his decision.

Once the Human Rights Act came into force, it was for consideration whether the *Gough* test was consistent with the ECtHR jurisprudence. The *Gough* test had not in any event found universal favour, and had not been accepted in Australia or certain other jurisdictions⁴⁵; other tests had found favour at different times and in other jurisdictions.⁴⁶

The *Gough* test was first modified by the Court of Appeal in *Re Medicaments and Related Classes of Goods (No.2)*.⁴⁷ The *Medicaments* case illustrated the problem with the *Gough* test. The Restrictive Practices Court heard a lengthy reference by a trade association, the tribunal consisting of Lightman J. and two specialist lay members. During the hearing, the economist lay member applied for a job with the economic consultancy firm of which the principal witness for the Director General of Fair Trading (who was a party) was a director. A few days later, on the advice of the judge, she sent a personal statement to the parties stating that she had not recalled the witness was a director,⁴⁸ and informing the consultancy that in consequence her application could not be pursued until after the conclusion of the trial, and attached a letter from the consultancy to the effect that they did not have any relevant vacancies. The Restrictive Practices Court dismissed an application that they recuse themselves as the member had not been aware of the potential conflict when she made her application and once it was clear she had no prospect of obtaining a job with the firm the potential for conflict fell away.

The Court of Appeal pointed out that the *Gough* test ran into difficulty when the issue was whether the tribunal's own evidence as to what it knew should be accepted. As Lord Phillips M.R. put it⁴⁹:

---

⁴⁴ Of course, the court is not bound to accept the statement of the person accused of bias.
⁴⁵ Scotland: *Doherty v McGlennan* (1997) S.L.T. 444; Australia: *Webb v R.* (1994) 181 C.L.R. 41; South Africa: *Moch v Nedtravel (Pty) Ltd* (1996) (3) S.A. 1.
⁴⁶ Reasonable suspicion or apprehension of bias: *Law v Chartered Institute of Patent Agents* [1919] 2 Ch. 276 at 290; *R. v Sussex Justices Ex p. McCarthy* [1924] 1 K.B. 256 at 259; *Metropolitan Properties v Lannon* [1969] 1 Q.B. 577 at 599, 602, 606; *R. v Liverpool City Justices Ex p. Topping* [1983] 1 W.L.R. 119 at 123; *R. v Mulvihill* [1990] 1 W.L.R. 438 at 444; in Scotland see *Bradford v McLeod* (1986) S.L.T. 244; in Australia see *R. v Watson Ex p. Armstrong* (1976) 136 C.L.R. 248; in South Africa *BTR Industries South Africa (Pty) v Metal & Allied Workers' Union* (1992) (3) S.A. 673 at 694. Real danger or likelihood of bias: *R. v Rand* (1866) L.R. 1 Q.B. 230 at 233; *R. v Sunderland Justices* [1901] 2 K.B. 357 at 371; *R. v Camborne Justices Ex p. Pearce* [1955] 1 Q.B. 41, 51; *R. v Barnsley Licensing Justices Ex p. Barnsley and District Licensed Victuallers' Association* [1960] 2 Q.B. 167 at 186; *R. v Spencer* [1987] A.C. 128.
⁴⁷ [2001] 1 W.L.R. 700.
⁴⁸ Notwithstanding that he had the unusual name Zoltan Biro.
⁴⁹ At para.67.

"What is the court to do when, although inclined to accept a statement about what the judge under review knew at any material time, it recognises the possibility of doubt and the likelihood of public scepticism? It is invidious for the reviewing court to question the word of the judge in such circumstances, but less so to say that the objective onlooker might have difficulty in accepting it".

Lord Phillips M.R. drew attention to the criticism made of the *Gough* test by the High Court of Australia in *Webb v R*.[50]: a test based on "real danger" rather than focused on the perception of a fair-minded and informed onlooker may be unfairly damaging to the reputation of the decision-maker who will often not have been a party to the appellate decision and whose subjective thought processes may not have been investigated by the appellate court. Lord Phillips M.R. said that the problem with the "real danger" test was particularly acute when a judge is invited to recuse himself. In such a situation it is invidious to expect a judge to rule on the danger that he may actually be influenced by partiality. The Court of Appeal, applying ECtHR jurisprudence, held that a test based on the fair-minded and informed observer should be applied. They held that the observer's concern that the economist's wish to work for the consultancy demonstrated partiality would be augmented by a concern that she might still have hopes of doing so. As she would have discussed the economic issues with the other members of the tribunal, all three members were required to stand down.

The test adopted in *Medicaments* was approved with minor modification by the House of Lords in *Porter v Magill*.[51] Lord Hope, referring[52] to the criticism of the *Gough* test in *Webb v R*.[53] said that the *Gough* test had been criticised on the ground that it tended to emphasise the court's view of the facts and to place inadequate emphasis on the public perception of the irregular incident. The test was reformulated as follows[54]:

"The court must first ascertain all the circumstances which have a bearing on the suggestion that the judge was biased. It must then ask whether those circumstances would lead a fair-minded and informed observer to conclude whether there was a real possibility . . . that the tribunal was biased".

Lord Hope said that this test was consistent with the ECtHR jurisprudence, that which is applied in most Commonwealth jurisdictions, and

---

[50] (1994) 181 C.L.R. 41 at 71–2, Deane J.
[51] [2002] 2 A.C. 357.
[52] At para.102.
[53] (1994) 181 C.L.R. 41 at 50, HCA.
[54] At para.102.

Scotland. The test is of general application and applies in all cases save where there is automatic disqualification under *Dimes*. The test is now applied to all applications based on apparent bias.

4. Features of the Magill test

A. Dealing with an allegation of bias

11–012   Guidance was given by the Court of Appeal in *Jones v DAS Legal Expenses Insurance Co Ltd* [55] as to dealing with an application based on apparent bias. The court said that where a judge becomes aware of circumstances which might give rise to an appearance of bias the following steps should be taken:

> (i) if there is a real as opposed to fanciful chance of objection being taken by the fair-minded spectator, the judge should ascertain whether another judge is available as it is better to transfer than risk a complaint of bias. The judge should then clarify what his interest is relevant to the conflict so the full facts can be put before the parties
> (ii) time should be taken to prepare carefully the explanation given to the parties
> (iii) the explanation should be recorded
> (iv) the explanation should be punctilious in setting out all matters known to him. An explanation should be given as to why the problem had only arisen so late in the day. The parties should be told whether it would be possible to move the case to another judge that day
> (v) the options open to the parties should be explained in detail
> (vi) the parties should be told that they will be given time before electing.

In *Mireskandari v Law Society*[56] the judge had given directions in relation to the hearing of a late application that he recuse himself from sitting in a case, but declined to defer the giving of directions for the substantive hearing of the case in the meantime lest this cause delay. The Court of Appeal upheld the ruling, but Lord Clarke M.R. counselled caution on the part of a judge in making such orders lest they subsequently be set aside if the recusal application succeeded.

---

[55] [2004] I.R.L.R. 218.
[56] [2009] EWCA Civ 864.

B. Identifying the relevant circumstances

Caselaw has emphasised the importance of the first part of the *Magill* test—the court must ascertain all the circumstances which have a bearing on the suggestion that the judge was biased. This is relevant both for the tribunal deciding whether it should stand down and for the appellate body reviewing a refusal to stand down. Identification of the relevant circumstances is essential, firstly in order to determine whether the complainant has received full information about the facts relevant to bias, and thus whether there was an informed waiver, and secondly, because an appellate tribunal cannot determine whether the allegation of potential bias is well-founded without carefully identifying the material facts or circumstances. In *L-H (Children)*[57] Patten L.J. said[58]:

11–013

> "Where a judge is faced with an application that he should recuse himself of the ground of apparent bias it is in my judgment incumbent on him to explain in sufficient detail the scale and content of the professional or other relationship which is challenged on the application. The parties are not in the position of being able to cross-examine the judge about it and he is likely to be the only source of the relevant information. Without this, it becomes difficult if not impossible properly to apply the informed bystander test".

In *Smith v Kvaerner Cementation*[59] the Court of Appeal considered that the litigant had not been furnished with all the necessary material by the judge in order to make an informed decision as to whether to waive the right to ask the judge to stand down. Other cases have drawn attention to the issue being very fact-sensitive.[60]

C. The attributes of the fair-minded and informed observer

What is the fair-minded observer and what are his attributes? The issue is not as straightforward as it sounds. What degree of expertise or knowledge is assumed for the hypothetical observer? It has been suggested that the court has at times only paid lip service to the concept of the fair-minded and informed observer.[61] So it is said that there have been instances where the notional observer has been deemed to have knowledge of technical procedural rules,[62] or would understand aspects of the law relating to mis-

11–014

---

[57] [2010] EWCA Civ 1118.
[58] [21].
[59] [2006] 3 All E.R. 593; See 11–020.
[60] See *Man O'War v Auckland City Council* [2002] U.K.P.C. 28; see 13–020.
[61] See Atrill, "Who is the fair-minded observer? Bias after Magill" [2003] C.L.J. 279.
[62] *Taylor v Williamson, The Times*, August 9, 2002 where the Court of Appeal rejected a

representation, causation and security for costs,[63] or would understand that judges frequently state an opinion at the outset that may strongly favour one side but often change their minds after hearing oral argument.[64] The temptation to imbue the observer with technical knowledge is difficult to resist.[65]

The House of Lords have looked at the attributes of the fair-minded and informed observer more than once. In *Gillies v Secretary of State for Work and Pensions*,[66] the House of Lords held that the fair-minded and informed observer would think there was nothing wrong in a lay member of a disability appeal tribunal being a medically qualified practitioner who had provided reports to the Benefits Agency in disability allowance cases. Lord Hope said about the fair-minded and impartial observer[67]:

> "The fair-minded and informed observer can be assumed to have access to all the facts that are capable of being known by members of the public generally, bearing in mind that it is the appearance that these facts give rise to that matters, not what is in the mind of the particular judge or tribunal member who is under scrutiny. It is to be assumed, as Kirby J. put it in *Johnson v Johnson*[68] that the observer is neither complacent nor unduly sensitive or suspicious when he examines the facts that he can look at. It is to be assumed that he is able to distinguish between what is relevant and what is irrelevant, and that he is able when exercising his judgment to decide what weight should be given to the facts that are relevant".

In *National Assembly for Wales v Condron*[69] Richards L.J. said:

> "The court must look at all the circumstances as they appear from the material before it not just at the facts known to the objectors or available to to the hypothetical observer at the time of the decision".

Most recently, the House of Lords looked at the fair-minded observer again in *Helow v Secretary of State for the Home Department*.[70] This is an important decision. The Lord Ordinary in Scotland refused permission to

---

submission that a judge who delivered a preliminary judgment expressed to be subject to alteration before hearing final submissions from counsel might have appeared to have closed his mind; "the informed observer would know that the judgment sent to the parties was not a final judgment in the full sense", per Clarke L.J.

[63] *Hart v Relentless Records*, The Times, October 8, 2002.
[64] *Sengupta v Holmes*, The Times, August 19, 2002; *London Borough of Southwark v Jiminez*, April 8, 2003, CA.
[65] The Canadian courts have had similar problems: see *R. v Lippe* [1991] 2 S.C.R. 114 at 152.
[66] [2006] 1 All E.R. 731, HL.
[67] At [17].
[68] [2000] 5 L.R.C. 223, 243.
[69] [2006] EWCA Civ 1573 at [50].
[70] [2008] 1W.L.R. 2416.

appeal an asylum applicant's notice of removal. The Lord Ordinary was a member of the International Association of Jewish Lawyers and Jurists and a founder member of the Scottish branch. The Association had in the past expressed strong views against the Palestine Liberation Organisation, an organisation with which the applicant had been involved. Lord Hope said that the gender-neutral fair-minded and informed observer had attributes which many of us might struggle to attain:

> "The observer who is fair-minded is the sort of person who always reserves judgment on every point until she[71] has seen and fully understood both sides of the argument. She is not unduly sensitive or suspicious . . . Her approach must not be confused with that of the person who has brought the complaint. The "real possibility" test ensures that there is this measure of detachment. The assumptions that the complainer makes are not to be attributed to the observer unless they can be justified objectively. But she is not complacent either. She knows that fairness requires that a judge must be, and must be seen to be, unbiased. She knows the judges, like anybody else, have their weaknesses. She will not shrink from the conclusion, if it can be justified objectively, that things that they have said or done or associations that they have formed may make it difficult for them to judge the case before them impartially.
>
> Then there is the attribute that the observer is "informed". It makes the point that, before she takes a balanced approach to any information she is given, she will take the trouble to inform herself on all matters that are relevant. She is the sort of person who takes the trouble to read the text of an article as well as the headlines. She is able to put whatever she has read or seen into its overall social, political or geographical context. She is fair-minded, so she will appreciate that the context forms an important part of the material which she must consider before passing judgment".[72]

Lord Hope said that if there had been evidence that the Lord Ordinary had associated herself with any of the more-fervently pro-Israeli statements made by members of her organisation, he would have had no difficulty in holding that the test for apparent bias was made out. But merely because the Lord Ordinary was a member of the organisation would not satisfy the fair-minded observer that the test of apparent bias was made out. The fair-minded observer would read the balanced articles published in the association's magazine as well as the extreme ones.

This judgment is helpful in explaining the attributes of the fair-minded observer and will serve to solve many of the inconsistencies which have

11–015

---

[71] The applicant and judge were both female, hence the use of "she".
[72] [2]-[3].

arisen in applying the test. Thus in *Virdi v Law Society*[73] the Court of Appeal considered whether the Solicitors Disciplinary panel were affected by apparent bias because the clerk employed by the SRA retired with the panel. The court reviewed it from the position of the fair-minded observer who, as they put it, has no inappropriate knowledge and is imbued with commonsense. Stanley Burnton L.J. pointed out that if someone had challenged the procedure and the tribunal had explained exactly what the role of the clerk was, the fair-minded observer would not have regarded there as being any cause for complaint. So if the true facts did not give reason to complain, the applicant could hardly be in a better position by not asking for the full facts to be explained.[74]

It is hoped that *Helow* will mean that there is greater consistency of approach in future. In the past sometimes only lip service has been paid to the concept. In *Paul v Deputy Coroner of the Queen's Household*[75] the issue arose as to whether the coroner appointed to hear the inquest on Princess Diana should sit in the title of Coroner of the Queen's Household. The court held that, given the allegations being made about the royal family, it would be inappropriate for the coroner to sit in that capacity as the title itself gave rise to the appearance of bias. Even though the same individual would sit as coroner if the coroner's title was changed, it was preferable not to sit in that capacity. It is entirely understandable that in a case with so much sensitivity and media interest the court should strive to reach such a conclusion. But the observer who had the characteristics identified by Lord Hope would surely take the view that an apprehension of bias in such circumstances was ridiculous.

D. Apparent bias not a matter of discretion

11–016   It is wrong to treat recusal for apparent bias as a matter where the court has discretion. Either the claim is made out, or it is not. No doubt as a matter of pragmatism the judge is more likely to take a cautious view in asking a juror to stand down at the start of the trial (where there will be no delay or prejudice to the conduct of the trial) than where the problem arises part way into a long trial, but the principles are no different. In *Re Medicaments*[76] the application was made near the end of a case which had

---

[73] [2010] EWCA Civ 100.
[74] *Burcombe v R [2010] EWCA Crim 2818* is a rather different sort of example. The court jury officer was imprisoned after choosing a jury from (among others) her family members by forging documents. On the appeal from a trial where she had done this, the issue was whether there was improper contact between the jury officer and the jurors such as to render the jury subject to apparent bias. However, the Court of Appeal said that the submission involved mere speculation.
[75] [2007] EWHC 408, Admin.
[76] [2001] 1 W.L.R. 700, see 11–011.

been proceeding for many months, and it was a matter of huge inconvenience to the parties that it became necessary to start again with a fresh tribunal.[77]

In *Morrison v AWG*[78] the Court of Appeal disagreed with the attempt by the judge prior to the start of a long trial to make arrangements to avoid having to recuse himself because of his acquaintance with a non-central witness. The Court of Appeal stressed that the inconvenience, cost and delay of the judge recusing himself did not weigh in the balance where the overriding principle of judicial impartiality was properly invoked. The safe course was for the judge to recuse himself prior to the commencement of the trial rather than possibly suffer the disaster of having to abandon the trial during the hearing.

E. Contamination

11–017 The "contamination" principle is relevant where the decision-making tribunal is of more than one person. If it appears in the course of a hearing, or thereafter, that one member is subject to apparent bias, and should be removed, should the tribunal as a whole be removed? This problem affects juries, arbitral tribunals, disciplinary tribunals, and the Court of Appeal amongst others.

The *Medicaments* case has already been referred to.[79] There the person subject to apparent bias was a specialist economist member, on whom the other members of the tribunal would rely on matters of economics. The hearing was well-advanced when the problem arose, so the tribunal would have discussed the issues together many times. The whole tribunal was regarded as contaminated, notwithstanding the presence of a judge on the panel.

Contamination principles were explored in detail in *Competition Commission v BAA Ltd*.[80] The Competition Commission had carried out a market investigation into anti-competitive practices in the supply of airport services and in March 2009 reported, adopting a package of remedies including divestment by market operators. After a preliminary report by the Commission, an organisation which was advised by one of the commission members made an offer for Gatwick airport. When this was drawn to the attention of the commission member, he stood down immediately, was quarantined, and was not a party to the final report. The Competition Appeal Tribunal upheld BAA's contention of apparent bias and quashed the report, on the basis that the member was subject to

---

[77] See [99]-[100].
[78] [2006] EWCA Civ 8, discussed at 13–021.
[79] See 11–011.
[80] [2010] EWCA Civ 1097.

apparent bias throughout the period of his participation on the commission from October 2007 until he stood down in early 2009, with the result that the investigation, its deliberations, thinking and conclusions were affected by apparent bias. On appeal to the Court of Appeal, the court did not agree on the facts that the member's interests gave rise to apparent bias until December 2008. The relevant period was thus much shorter, particularly as the member was quarantined from 20 January 2009 prior to his standing down.

The Court of Appeal regarded the relevant principle as set out by Andrew Smith J. in *ASM Shipping Ltd v Harris*[81]:

> "I am unable to accept that there is an invariable rule, or it is necessarily the case, that where one member of a tribunal is tainted by apparent bias, the whole tribunal is affected second hand by apparent bias, and therefore should recuse themselves, or should be excluded, from the proceedings. After all, it is common practice where a juror has to be discharged . . . for the judge to consider whether there is a risk of "contamination" of other jurors and if there is no reason to think that there is, to continue the trial with the remaining jurors".

Having made clear that the question of contamination was fact-specific, the Court of Appeal considered whether the presence of the member on the commission during what was now seven weeks (rather than eighteen months) of apparent bias contaminated the rest of the commission. Maurice Kay L.J.[82] said that as the commission had reached provisional views by then, the idea that the commission member would have prevented his colleagues from changing their minds over that short period was "moving into the reaches of fantasy", and the fair-minded observer would have taken the same view.

F. Waiver

11–018   In *Hakansson v Sweden*[83] the ECtHR held that a waiver of art.6 rights must be made in an unequivocal manner and must not run counter to any important public interest.[84]

If appropriate disclosure has been made, a party who has made no objection to the judge hearing or continuing to hear the case cannot thereafter

---

[81] [2007] EWHC 1513 Comm at [44].
[82] At [36].
[83] (1991) 13 E.H.R.R. 1 at 16, para.66.
[84] The Commission has expressly held that the right to an impartial tribunal can be waived: *D v Ireland*, App. No.11489/85; 51 D.R. 117 (1986) although when the issue was before the ECtHR the point was not decided: *Pfeifer & Plankl v Austria* (1991) 19 E.H.R.R. 389.

complain of the matter disclosed as giving rise to a real danger of bias. It would be unjust to the other party and undermine both the reality and appearance of justice to allow him to do so.[85] A judge has no obligation to disclose what he does not know, nor is he bound to fill any gaps in his knowledge which if filled might provide stronger grounds for objection.[86] There is no doubt that waiver must be clear and unequivocal and made with full knowledge of all the facts relevant to the decision whether to waive or not.[87] In *Millar v Dickson*[88] Lord Bingham said:

> "In most litigious situations the expression "waiver" is used to describe voluntary, informed and unequivocal election by a party not to raise a right or raise an objection which it is open to that party to claim or raise. In the context of entitlement to a fair hearing by an independent and impartial tribunal, such is in my opinion the meaning to be given to the expression".[89]

When a litigant complains afterwards that the judge should have recused himself, the first question is: why did you not complain at the time? Of course, if the appellant did not know all the facts at the time, waiver does not arise. In *Jones v DAS Legal Expenses Insurance*[90] the court stated that full knowledge of the facts was necessary for waiver to operate:

11–019

> "Waiver would never operate if "full facts" meant each and every detail of factual information which diligent digging can produce. Full facts relevant to the decision to be taken must be confined to the essential facts. What is important is that the litigant should understand the nature of the case rather than the detail. It is sufficient if there is disclosed to him all he <u>needs</u> to know which is invariably different from what he <u>wants</u> to know".[91]

It is incumbent upon the objector to make his objection with reasonable promptness but he must be given "a fair opportunity to reach an unpressured decision".[92] What an informed potential objector must not do is to wait and see if the outcome of the proceedings is favourable or unfavourable before raising his objection.

---

[85] *Locabail* [2000] 1 All E.R. 65; *Shrager v Basil Dighton* [1924] 1 K.B. 274 at 293; *R. v Essex Justices Ex p. Perkins* [1927] 2 K.B. 475 at 489; *Pinochet* [1999] 2 W.L.R. 272 at 285; *Auckland Casino v Casino Control Authority* [1995] 1 N.Z.L.R. 142 at 150–51.
[86] *Locabail* [2000] Q.B. 451.
[87] *R. v Bow Street Mag exp Ex p. Pinochet* 2000 1 A.C. 119, 137, *Locabail (UK) Ltd v Bayfield Properties* [2000] Q.B. 451, 475.
[88] [2002] 1 W.L.R. 1615, PC.
[89] See also *Sumukan v Commonwealth Secretariat* [2007] EWCA Civ 1148.
[90] [2004] I.R.L.R. 218; see 11–012 above.
[91] At [36].
[92] *Smith v Kvaerner Cementation* [2006] EWCA Civ 242, at [29].

The burden of proof is on the person making the objection to show by evidence his unawareness of the essential facts. Although this was established in *R v Kent Justices* in 1880[93] not much attention has been given to the burden of proof in this context until its importance was stressed by the Court of Appeal in *Competition Commission v BAA Ltd*[94] where it was said that the *Kent Justices* case and authorities that followed it[95] remain influential in Australia.[96] Maurice Kay L.J. in *BAA* said it remained a salutary rule because objectors ought not to be allowed "to have their cake and eat it, to approbate and reprobate".[97] It is thus important in an application made after the event to lead evidence of "unawareness",[98] providing positive evidence that the applicant was not aware of the problem at the time it arose.

11–020 However, the decision of the Court of Appeal in *Smith v Kvaerner Cementation*[99] shows the Court of Appeal treating waiver as a difficult defence to make out. In *Kvaerner*, the recorder sitting as deputy judge in a personal injury case was the head of the chambers in which both counsel practised. He disclosed out that he had acted for companies in the same group as the defendant and was acting for such companies in litigation that was still ongoing. Mr Smith was advised by counsel that he could expect an entirely fair hearing from this judge, that there was some advantage in appearing before a judge known to counsel, and that counsel did not know when the case would be heard if an objection was raised. He gave strong advice to the client to raise no objection and commended, from his own knowledge, the personal virtues of the recorder. The client accepted the advice, but said that it was only after the hearing that he began to perceive there was something wrong with the fact that the recorder had these chambers and professional connections. He felt that he had been set up. Lord Phillips C.J. said that it was important that the facts were made clear by the recorder: he should have made efforts to find out how quickly the case could be tried if it were transferred to another judge and explained to Mr Smith himself at the outset what the options were. The court was critical of the way in which counsel had given strong advice to his client not to object: counsel should have confined himself to telling his client of the judicial oath and explaining that judges are trained in considering cases objectively and disregarding any personal views they might hold and left the decision to the client.

The court referred to the guidance in *Jones v DAS Legal Expenses Insurance*[100] as to the steps to be taken by the tribunal when an allegation

---

[93] (1880) 44 J.P. 298.
[94] [2010] EWCA Civ 1097.
[95] *R. v Byles* (1911–1913) All E.R. Rep 430 at 431, *R. v Williams* [1914] 1 KB 608, 615.
[96] *R. v Magistrates Court at Lilydale Ex p. Ciccone* 1973 VR 122, *Nickelseekers Ltd v Vance* 1985 1 QdR 372, *Kempe v Bailey* [2003] 174 F.L.R. 460.
[97] At [52].
[98] See also *Baker v Quantum Clothing Group* [2009] EWCA Civ 499.
[99] [2006] 3 All E.R. 593.
[100] [2004] I.R.L.R. 218, see 11–012 above.

of bias was made, but said that it should not be treated as a set of rules which must be complied with if a waiver is to be valid. The Court of Appeal held that in the circumstances the decision to agree to the recorder continuing was not made freely and was not made with knowledge of all available information because Mr Smith was not told when the trial could take place before another judge.

It is possible to see why this course was necessary in the particular case. The court was obviously troubled by the strong advice not to object to a judge who was counsel's head of chambers, and in the cold light of day a more balanced presentation of the arguments for and against agreeing to go ahead would have been much better. The advice was dangerous in that form because counsel's personal relationship to the recorder, his head of chambers, could leave a litigant with a sense of unease—hence the suggestion that he was being "set up". But to say that the waiver was not made freely on the basis of counsel's advice is perhaps a surprising conclusion. After all, inexperienced litigants nervous about appearing in court often will need to be guided by counsel's professional view and, it is suggested, would sometimes benefit from counsel giving the client a steer. However, the comments in Lord Phillips' judgment about counsel's advice do not read as directed to the rather special facts of the case[101] but as precepts generally applicable to cases where the judge alerts the parties to a potential bias issue. And whilst it would have been much better for the judge to have made enquiries as to possible alternative arrangements and how long it would take before the case could be tried before another judge, and that is a course recommended in *Jones v DAS Legal Expenses Insurance*,[102] often that cannot be ascertained with any certainty at short notice. It is also perhaps surprising that the failure of the recorder to make these enquiries and explain the position in this regard was treated as preventing the waiver being made on full facts.

G. Regulatory authorisation

In *Meerabux v AG of Belize*[103] the Bar Association had commenced proceedings to remove a judge for misconduct in office. The chairman of the investigating tribunal was a member of the bar, and thus (in theory) both prosecutor and judge. On the basis of the constitutional procedure, a judge could not be removed other than after an investigation by the Belize Advisory Council. The chairman of that association was required under the constitutional procedure to be a member of the Bar Association. So the principle of necessity arose. Amongst the various reasons for dismissing the

11–021

---

[101] See [33].
[102] [2004] I.R.L.R. 218.
[103] [2005] 2 A.C. 513.

challenge, the Privy Council held that the framers of the constitution must be taken to have recognised that bare membership of the Bar Association should not be treated of itself as debarring a member from sitting.

In *Meerabux* the challenge was a formal one. There was no suggestion that the chairman had any special interest or involvement such as would make him an inappropriate member, or otherwise subject to apparent bias. Rules of associations establishing disciplinary tribunals may also be taken to authorise individuals to sit, so that a challenge based on their formal position would be inconsistent with the scheme of the rules. It would be different if the person in question had a particular interest beyond the formal position which gave rise to apparent bias; compare the discussion at 12–008 below.

CHAPTER 12

Juries, tribunals and other decision-makers

1. Juries

A. Dealing with the jury

Of course, the bias rule is not limited to judges. It applies to all decision-makers. The *Gough* case itself involved a juror. Problems relating to jurors showing bias bedevil criminal trials. The problems here rarely concern a conflict of interest. They are more frequently concerned with manifestation of prejudiced attitudes or views. In *R. v Connor*[1] the House of Lords reaffirmed that a court would not receive evidence as to what went on in the jury room even when allegations were made as to improper or inappropriate conduct which might be relevant to juror bias and therefore the safety of any conviction. They held[2] that the common law rule, underpinned by s.8(1) of the Contempt of Court Act 1981 which made it a contempt of court to obtain, disclose or solicit information as to deliberations of jurors, was justified on public policy grounds.

12–001

Where the complaint arises out of conduct or remarks, or expressions suggesting bias which occur outside the jury room, the judge will have a wide range of options. He may need to dismiss the individual juror, or discharge the entire jury. He may give an appropriate direction, and if necessary can ask one or all jurors questions to satisfy himself that the juror or jury can continue. He will have to consider questions of possible contamination of other jurors by the one against whom complaint is made. However, there

---

[1] [2004] 1 All E.R. 925.
[2] Notwithstanding a powerful dissent from Lord Steyn.

will be practical problems in conducting anything which amounts to a trial within a trial; it will be difficult for the judge to make findings of fact as to whether disputed remarks were made, for example.

B. ECHR caselaw

12–002 Nevertheless, the judge must take steps to deal with the position. The ECtHR has considered jury problems on three recent occasions. Unfortunately, the decisions are not consistent with each other and make difficult reading. In *Gregory v UK*[3] the jury passed the judge a note whilst considering their verdict to the effect that the jury were showing racist overtones and one of their number should be excused. After consulting counsel, the judge warned the jury to put aside any prejudice and try the case according to the evidence. The ECtHR dismissed the subsequent complaint by the defendant that he had not had a fair trial. But in *Sander v UK*[4] the ECtHR took a different view. A juror handed up a letter during the summing up indicating that two of the jurors had been making racist remarks and expressed his concern that the defendant would not receive a fair verdict. The judge told the jury to search their consciences overnight and let the court know if they felt they were not able to try the case solely on the evidence, and after receiving written assurances next morning that they would do so without racial bias, allowed the trial to proceed. This time the ECtHR held four to three that the judge had not acted in a sufficiently robust manner and had failed to provide sufficient guarantees to exclude any objectively justified or legitimate doubts about the impartiality of the court. They then refused the defendant compensation on the somewhat curious ground that there was no causal connection between the partiality of the jury and the three years the defendant had spent in jail following his conviction. The reasoning in the case is difficult. There is a powerful dissent from the British judge, Sir Nicholas Bratza, in *Sander*,[5] and it is plain that the House of Lords in *Connor* found the majority view hard to reconcile with *Gregory*. A third case, *Remli v France*[6] causes no difficulty: the ECtHR held there was a breach of art.6 where the court declined to investigate information received after the verdict as to an alleged racist remark by a juror not yet selected or empanelled.

---

[3] (1998) 25 E.H.R.R. 577.
[4] (2001) 8 B.H.R.C. 279.
[5] In *R. v Bajwa* [2007] EWCA Crim 1618, the Court of Appeal dismissed an appeal where *Sander* was relied on when the defendants claimed to have lip-read two jurors making racist remarks about them. The jurors denied the allegation, the trial had continued with all the jurors and the judge had directed the jury with great care in the circumstances
[6] (1996) 22 E.H.R.R. 253.

C. Police officers and prosecutors

In *R. v Abdroikov*[7] the House of Lords considered whether in three separate cases the presence of policemen or prosecutors on a jury might give rise to apprehension of bias. Their lordships were not unanimous as to the result of the three cases: a majority allowed two of the three appeals whilst a minority would have dismissed all of them. Because of the difference of views in the House of Lords, it is not easy to identify clear principles.[8]

12–003

In the first police officer case, the case had not turned on a contest between the evidence of police and defendant. Thus even if there had been unconscious prejudice, it would have been unlikely to work to the disadvantage of the defendant. The appeal was dismissed. By contrast, in the second police officer case, the police sergeant was the alleged victim of the crime, and he shared the same local service background as the policeman on the jury. There was an important conflict of evidence between the sergeant and the defendant. In that case the majority allowed the appeal. The majority held that the fair minded and informed observer would think there was a real and possible source of unfairness beyond the reach of standard judicial warnings and directions. Lord Bingham and Baroness Hale, for the majority, considered one important factor was whether there was a significant conflict of evidence between police officer and the defendant. If so, the instinct of the police officer might be to prefer the evidence of a brother officer. Baroness Hale thought that in that case the connection between the police and prosecution "too close for comfort" given the identity of the juror.[9]

In the case of the Crown Prosecution Service employee, Lord Bingham said[10] that justice would not be seen to be done if one discharging the very important neutral role of juror is a full-time salaried long serving employee of the prosecutor.[11] Baroness Hale said[12] that it was relevant to consider whether the employee was short-term, temporary or in a junior position. There would be no objection where the employee's connection with the organisation was peripheral, or for one employee to sit on a jury where the prosecution was brought by another person or authority. The appeal was allowed.

In *R. v Khan*[13] the Court of Appeal, presided over by Lord Phillips C.J., determined a series of appeals arising from the *Abdroikov* decision. Lord

---

[7] [2007] UKHL 37.
[8] As the Court of Appeal noted in *Khan v R.* [2008] EWCA Crim 531 at [24], per Lord Phillips C.J.
[9] [53].
[10] [27].
[11] See *Pullar v UK* [1996] 22 E.H.R.R. 391.
[12] [51].
[13] [2008] EWCA Crim 531.

Phillips distinguished between partiality towards the case of one of the parties and partiality towards a witness.[14] Each can be described as bias, but they are different in kind and can have different consequences:

> "Just because a juror feels partial to a particular witness does not mean that the juror will be partial to the case in support of which that witness is called. It may do so if the witness is so closely associated with the prosecution that partiality to the witness is equated with partiality towards the party calling the witness".

This ties in with the "too close for comfort" comment by Baroness Hale in *Abdroikov*. Lord Phillips gave as an example *Re Medicaments*[15] where an appearance of bias arose from the fact a member of the tribunal had applied for a job to the experts whose evidence was the foundation of the case of one of the parties.

12–004 Lord Phillips said there were two questions[16]:

> "Where an impartial juror is shown to have had reason to favour a particular witness, this will not necessarily result in the quashing of a conviction. It will only do so if this has rendered the trial unfair, or given it an appearance of unfairness. To decide this it is necessary to consider two questions:
> (a) would the fair-minded observer consider that partiality of the juror to the witness may have caused the jury to accept the evidence of that witness? If so
> (b) would the fair minded observer consider that this may have affected the outcome of the trial?"

Unless the answer to both questions was yes, the partiality of the juror would not have affected the safety of the verdict.

On the facts, the Court of Appeal dismissed all the appeals, applying Lord Phillips' two stage test. One of the appeals related to a CPS communications officer sitting on a jury. Lord Phillips said that in *Abdroikov* the juror was in the employment of the prosecutor, which was not the case here.

There have been a number of decisions since *Khan*[17] but the decisions have been increasingly fact-specific. It is apparent that the mere presence of a police officer on the jury is not sufficient to lead to an apprehension of bias. The analysis involves consideration of the nature of the dispute on the evidence, the closeness of the police to the evidence, and the extent to which

---

[14] [9].
[15] See 11–011.
[16] [10].
[17] *R. v Yemoh* [2009] EWCA Crim 930, *R. v Ali* [2009] EWCA Crim 1763, *R. v J.* [2009] EWCA 1638.

the fair-minded observer might have been concerned on the facts of the case as to possible partiality of the particular officer on the jury.

In *R v LL*[18] the Court of Appeal rejected an appeal relating to the presence of two police officers on the jury but allowed it in relation to a long-serving CPS employee also on the jury on the grounds that, because the prosecution was brought by the CPS, the tribunal was not in consequence independent, rather than on grounds of apparent bias. Rix L.J. questioned in *R (on the application of Darsho Kaur) v Institute of Legal Executives Appeal Tribunal*[19] whether it is necessary for there to be two separate threads behind these decisions, rather than the courts treating the independent tribunal issue as in itself giving rise to apparent bias.

If a supermarket brought a prosecution for shoplifting, or a local council brought a prosecution, the same analysis would presumably apply if one of its employees sat on the jury.

D. Jurors with strong views

In *R. v C*[20] it transpired after the trial that one of the jurors was a columnist for the Sun newspaper. He was described as an outspoken polemicist who held strong and well-publicised views on law and order, soft judges, knife crime, drugs and immigration which could be characterised as populist and tendentious. Some of his more inflammatory articles were put before the Court of Appeal. Leveson L.J. said the question of sentence (to which many of the views were relevant) was not one for the jury; the issue for them was whether the defendant was guilty. Strong and populist published views on sentencing would not normally give rise to apprehension of bias in determining whether the defendant was guilty. Leveson L.J. did say that one article written by the juror was on mercy killing, and the position might have been different if the juror was concerned in such a trial.

12–005

E. Other jury problems

A rather different problem arose in *R. v Alexander*.[21] After the end of a long trial the female jury foreman sent the prosecutor champagne and a note suggesting dinner. The Court of Appeal declined to treat this as showing apprehension of bias. They pointed out that one juror had been removed in the course of the trial as a result of complaints from other jurors and regarded this as an indication that this was an independent jury alert to

12–006

---

[18] [2011] EWCA Crim 65, discussed at 11–009.
[19] [2011] EWCA Civ 1168 at [44] discussed at 12–008.
[20] [2009] EWCA Crim 2458.
[21] Unreported, July 28, 2004, CA.

suggestions of impropriety. In *R. v Price*[22] the presence of the trial judge at a case dinner between sentence and confiscation proceedings did not create a risk of bias where all counsel were present. The Court of Appeal emphasised the importance of defence counsel being present at the dinner. The question arises whether the dinner would have caused a problem had defence counsel been unable to attend or what the position would have been had they cancelled at short notice.[23]

A novel problem arose in *R. v KS*.[24] The judge had presided with juries over nine trials arising from the same set of facts. He had ruled on public interest immunity applications and other matters where the jury had been excluded. When he discharged the jury as a result of jury tampering he ruled that he should continue the trial sitting as judge alone. The Court of Appeal held that a different judge should hear the trial. His previous involvement in the nine trials led to a risk of apparent bias when acting as a decision maker on the facts not present when he sat with a jury.

2. Disciplinary tribunals

A. Applying the apparent bias test

12–007 Whilst the test is the same for disciplinary tribunals, the court may apply the principles differently in different types of tribunal. The Court of Appeal took a robust line in relation to sporting disciplinary tribunals in *Flaherty v National Greyhound Racing Ltd*.[25] Amongst the various complaints as to one of the stewards who conducted the inquiry, it was said that the individual demonstrated apparent bias by his aggressive attitude towards the applicant, in particular when questioning him and showed apparent contempt for certain points made on behalf of the applicant in the course of the hearing. Drawing attention to the inquisitorial nature of the hearing, the Court of Appeal pointed out that it was conducted by stewards familiar with the world of greyhound racing and the conditions and venues in which it is carried on. These factors distinguished it from adversarial court proceedings. Where proceedings are adversarial the tribunal necessarily has to test the evidence and the case presented. Citing Gleeson C.J. in the Australian case *Re Refugee Tribunal Ex p. H*[26]:

---

[22] [2010] Crim L.R. 522 CA.
[23] It is common for judges to invite counsel appearing in their court on occasion to lunch with them. As this decision indicates, that is all very well if all counsel can come, but what if only some are able to do so? It might be helpful for clear rules to be set out, to prevent this sort of application.
[24] [2008] EWCA Crim 2377.
[25] [2005] EWCA Civ 1117.
[26] [2000] A.L.R. 425, at [30].

"Where, as in the present case, credibility is in issue, the person conducting inquisitorial proceedings will necessarily have to test the evidence presented—often vigorously. Moreover the need to ensure that the person who will be affected by the decision is accorded procedural fairness will often require that he or she be plainly confronted with matters which bear adversely on his or her credit or which bring his or her account into question. Similar questions by a judge in curial proceedings in which the parties are legally represented may more readily give rise to an apprehension of bias than in the case of inquisitorial proceedings".

The distinction between inquisitorial and adversarial proceedings was one reason for approaching the proceedings of a tribunal in a different manner to proceedings in court. But the court also warned against seeking to double guess regulating bodies in charge of domestic arrangements[27]:

"Sports regulating bodies ordinarily have unrivalled and practical knowledge of the particular sport that they are required to regulate. They cannot be expected to act in every detail as if they are a court of law. Provided they act lawfully and within the ambit of their powers, the courts should allow them to get on with the job they are required to do. It is important to look at the consequences of anything that appears to have gone wrong. [Counsel] submits that the judge never explained why he felt it proper to intervene in this case. He never confronted the overall question whether there had been a fair result or whether the procedural defects had produced an unfair result".[28]

B. Involvement in the prosecution or executive process

That an individual who plays a role in the prosecution function should not sit on a disciplinary tribunal on the same case seems obvious. The tribunal would not be independent and the member would be regarded as a judge in his own cause.[29] But the principle has been applied where the individual has not been personally involved in the decision to prosecute. It has been applied where the individual is either a long-serving and senior employee of the prosecutor, or has an executive role. In the case of juries, the principal authority on point is *R. v Abdroikov*.[30] The cases have partly been decided on the basis of whether the tribunal is independent[31] and partly on

12–008

---

[27] At [20].
[28] At [21].
[29] The Latin maxim, *nemo iudex in sua causa*.
[30] [2007] UKHL 37 considered at 12–003.
[31] See 11–006 above.

apparent bias, although the two principles tend to run together and it may be thought unnecessary to have two parallel principles rather than a single inclusive issue of apparent bias.[32] There is recent authority here of particular relevance to disciplinary tribunals. In *P v General Council of the Bar*[33] the Visitors of the Inns of Court[34] held that there was apparent bias where a lay member of the Professional Conduct and Complaints Committee, which determined whether to prosecute members of the Bar against whom complaints had been made, sat on the disciplinary tribunal, notwithstanding that she had personally played no part in the decision to prosecute. The Visitors, sitting on appeal from the tribunal, held that the member was, as a member of the committee which decided whether to prosecute, judge in her own cause and it mattered not what her personal role in the decision to prosecute was.[35] Thus the tribunal could not be regarded as independent within art.6, and there was an automatic disqualification. In addition, the Visitors found, for the same reason, that there was apparent bias. In the recent important case of *R (on the application of Darsho Kaur) v Institute of Legal Executives Appeal Tribunal*[36] the Court of Appeal applied these principles to the case where an ILEX council member and director of ILEX sat on the disciplinary tribunal and the council's vice president on the appeal tribunal. Neither had previously had any involvement with the case in question but both were actively involved in the governance of ILEX and responsible for its regulatory policies. In quashing the decisions Rix L.J. said[37]:

> "Participation in a prosecutorial capacity, even if not in the case in question, will disqualify or else raise concern in the mind of the fair-minded observer about the appearance of impartial justice. Even an employee of a prosecuting agency may fall within this disqualification or concern, even though not employed in a prosecutorial capacity, provided the employment is significant enough in length or importance or location. However, that would not apply to every employee. Similarly, mere membership of a prosecuting association will not disqualify, where there is no involvement in the case in question, but a more senior role in governance may possibly do so, even though again there has been no specific involvement in the case in question, at any rate where the person in that role is not excluded from concern for regulation in general".

---

[32] In *R (on the application of Darsho Kaur) v Institute of Legal Executives Appeal Tribunal* [2011] EWCA Civ 1168 Rix L.J. queried whether it was necessary to treat the principle set out in *Pinochet* as different from the *Porter v Magill* apparent bias principle.
[33] [2005] 1 W.L.R. 3019.
[34] The body which hears appeals from Bar disciplinary tribunals and is chaired by a High Court Judge.
[35] See also *Sadler v General Medical Council* [2003] 1 W.L.R. 2259, which turned on the different functions of different GMC committees and *Meerabux v Attorney General of Belize* [2005] 2AC 513, discussed at 11-021 above.
[36] [2011] EWCA Civ 1168.
[37] At [35].

Rix L.J. said[38] that although it was unnecessary to decide the point, he thought the same would apply to all ILEX council members and directors.

C. Retiring with the tribunal

There has been recent authority where clerks or similar employees retire with the tribunal. In *Virdi v Law Society*[39] the clerk, who was an employee, retired with the Solicitors' Disciplinary Panel. The Court of Appeal declined to find apparent bias. They considered what the fair-minded observer, who had no inappropriate knowledge and was imbued with commonsense, would think. As the court pointed out, if someone had challenged the procedure at the time, and the tribunal had explained the facts, the observer would have had no concerns. Similarly in *Colman v GMC*[40] Owen J. heard a challenge to a decision of the General Medical Council based on the involvement of the deputy registrar in the decision making. It was suggested that the deputy registrar fulfilled in part the role of a prosecutor. However, the court said that a prosecutor decides whether to proceed with a case then prepares and conducts it; the deputy registrar does none of those. Nor was there reason to think that the deputy registrar had influenced the panel.

12–009

D. Professional associations of tribunal members

Members of specialist tribunals will usually have separate employment. As it is their specialist expertise which enables them to sit, it is not surprising that potential conflicts arise from them combining employment with sitting on tribunals. Thus in *R. (PD) v West Midlands and NW Mental Health Review Tribunal*[41] a medical member of the mental health tribunal was employed as a consultant by the healthcare trust which was party to the proceedings. The Court of Appeal held there was no appearance of bias. There was no general rule that an employee could never sit on a tribunal that was adjudicating in proceedings in which the employer was party. Although the trust was a party to the proceedings, it was not interested in the outcome in the sense that it had an interest in wishing the application to fail. A reasonable and informed member of the public would not be so concerned at the potential reaction of the trust and the implications for his own position that it might consciously or unconsciously affect his decision. It may be said the trust is not a prosecutor in a mental health hearing

12–010

---

[38] At [47].
[39] [2010] EWCA Civ 100.
[40] [2010] EWHC 1608 QB.
[41] [2004] EWCA Civ 311; (2004) 148 S.J.L.B. 384.

in the way it might be so regarded in other forms of hearing. Similarly in *Galloway v Barnet Enfield and Haringey Mental Health NHS Trust*[42] the fact that a lay member had worked for an NHS Trust did not give rise to apparent bias in a case simply because the employer was another NHS Trust. There was a particular benefit to tribunals having lay members with relevant experience.

3. Councils and councillors

12–011 Councillors will often have to make decisions in a quasi-judicial capacity. There are a number of features particular to such decisions. First, party affiliations and policies may be relevant. Second, councillors may more than other decision-makers be prone to expressing views in advance of the decision.

Councillors are permitted in decision-making to take into account electoral and manifesto policies. They are entitled to be predisposed towards a particular outcome. But they must nevertheless determine the issues before them on their merits, and not merely vote along party lines. [43] In *Bovis Homes v New Forest DC* [44] Ouseley J. said[45]:

> "In my judgment a Council acts unlawfully where its decision-making body has predetermined the outcome of the consideration which it is obliged to give to a matter, whether by the delegation of its decision to another body, or by the adoption of an inflexible policy, or as in effect is alleged here, by the closing of its mind to the consideration and weighing of the relevant factors because of a decision already reached or because of a determination to reach a particular decision. It is seen in a corporate determination to adhere to a particular view, regardless of the relevant factors or how they could be weighed. It is to be distinguished from a legitimate predisposition to a particular view".

In *Georgiou v Enfield LBC*[46] Richards J. noted that the fair-minded and informed observer test applied both to bias and predetermination, although they were related concepts. He recognised that the test must be applied in relation to local government where the fair-minded observer is familiar with the structure of local government and in a way that makes due allow-

---

[42] [2010] EWCA Civ 1368.
[43] See *R. v Amber Valley Ex p. Jackson* 1985 1 W.L.R. 298, *R. v Waltham Forest LBC Ex p. Baxter* 1988 1 Q.B. 419.
[44] [2002] EWHC 483 (Admin), decided one month after *Porter v Magill*.
[45] [111].
[46] [2004] EWHC 779 (Admin).

ance for the need to carry on local government without undue disruption.[47] However, in *R (Island Farm Development Ltd) v Bridgend BC*[48] Collins J. protested that the approach of Richards J. ran the risk of making local government impossible, as many of the issues before the councillors will have been election issues.[49] In *National Assembly for Wales v Condron*[50] the Court of Appeal (Richards L.J. giving the leading judgment) referred to both judgments without a hint of disapproval for either. Thus Jackson J. concluded in *R (Lewis) v Redcar and Cleveland BC*[51] that the notional observer was a person cognisant of the practicalities of local government, not taking it amiss that councillors have previously expressed views on the matters for decision. The observer trusts councillors, whatever their pre-existing views, to approach decision making with an open mind. If there are additional and unusual circumstances which suggest that councillors have closed their minds before embarking on a decision, he will conclude there is a real possibility of bias.[52]

4. Coroners

In *R (Pounder) v Coroner for North and South Districts of Durham and Darlington*[53] Burnett J. considered whether a coroner who had already expressed strong views in a first inquest quashed after a judicial review application should be recused from presiding over a second inquest. The judge pointed out that a coroner has an inquisitorial function which goes beyond the powers of a judge: he decides on the scope of the inquest and which witnesses to call.[54] Treating the issue as fact sensitive, he removed the coroner in the light of the views previously expressed. He pointed out that in *Howell v Millais*[55] Clarke M.R. had said that whilst deciding a case previously against a party, or criticising the party or his lawyers would rarely give rise to apparent bias, the position might well be different if there was evidence of animosity. In the coronial context, examples were *R (Butler) v HM Coroner for the Black Country District*[56] where the coroner's correspondence was inappropriately combative, and *R. v Inner London Coroner Ex*

12–012

---

[47] [31].
[48] [2006] EWHC 2189 (Admin).
[49] [30]–[31].
[50] [2006] EWCA Civ 1573 discussed at 13–016.
[51] [2007] EWHC 3166 (Admin).
[52] [75].
[53] [2010] EWHC 2419 (Ch).
[54] He referred to two Northern Ireland decisions of Weatherup J. on whether prior views should lead a coroner to recuse himself, one going each way: *Re Hemsworth's Application* (2009) NIQB 33, *Re Ramsbottom's Application* (2009) NIQB 55.
[55] See 13–015 below.
[56] [2010] EWHC 43 Admin.

parte Dallaglio[57] where the coroner had said something seriously derogatory of an interested party.

5. Others involved in the administration of justice[58]

12–013 There is a real difference between the position of the tribunal or judge as to conflict of interest and that of the professional acting for or on behalf of one of the parties. In the one case, it is the appearance of bias and the concern is the effect on the administration of justice. In the other, what is important is conflict or confidential information. There have been some occasions where the principles applying to decision-makers have been applied to those involved in the administration of justice. There is here no art.6 issue: art.6 is limited to decision-makers. However, there have been cases where the court has applied principles analogous to those applicable to decision makers to others. These are discussed in detail at para.5–008. They include those involved in child cases, those concerned with criminal trials, experts (especially court-appointed experts) and liquidators.

---

[57] [1994] 4 All E.R. 139.
[58] The position of arbitrators is dealt with separately at Chapter 14.

CHAPTER 13

Judicial Conflicts: Applying the Principles

1. Applying the principles

A. The duty to try a case

The court in *Locabail* made clear that it was wrong for a judge to accede to applications for recusal unless he regarded them as well-founded. A judge has a duty to try any case in which he is not obliged to recuse himself. The danger of bias must be assessed in the light of the judicial oath to administer justice without fear or favour and the ability to carry out that oath by reason of their training and experience.[1] Nor should he raise conflicts issues unnecessarily. In *Taylor v Lawrence*[2] Lord Woolf C.J. said:

13–001

> "A further general comment which we would make, is that judges should be circumspect about declaring the existence of a relationship where there is no real possibility of it being regarded by a fair-minded and informed observer as raising a possibility of bias. If such a relationship is disclosed, it unnecessarily raises an implication that it could affect the judgment and approach of the judge. If this is not the position no purpose is served by mentioning the relationship. On the other hand, if the situation is one where a fair-minded and informed person might regard the judge as biased, it is important that disclosure should be

---

[1] See *President of the Republic of South Africa v South African Rugby Football Union* (1999) (7) B.C.L.R. (CC) 725 at 753; *Re JRL Ex p. CJL* (1986) 161 C.L.R. 342 at 352, HCA; *Re Ebner* (1999) F.C.A. 110, Australian Federal Court; *Clenae Pty v Australia and New Zealand Banking Group* (1999) V.S.C.A. 35, Supreme Court of Victoria.
[2] [2003] Q.B. 528, para.64.

made. If the position is borderline, disclosure should be made because then the judge can consider, having heard the submissions of the parties, whether or not he should withdraw. In other situations disclosure can unnecessarily undermine the litigant's confidence in the judge. If disclosure is made, then full disclosure must be made. This case demonstrates the danger of making partial disclosure. If there has been partial disclosure and the litigant learns that this is the position, this is naturally likely to excite suspicions in the mind of the litigant concerned even though those concerns are unjustified".

The Court of Appeal made similar comments in *Dobbs v Triodos Bank*.[3] It was important for judges to resist the temptation to stand down merely because a litigant objects as otherwise litigants will try to "judge shop" and delay cases.[4] In practice, the natural inclination of any tribunal in respect of whom an arguable claim of apparent bias is made will be to recuse themselves if another judge or tribunal can readily be found and if the recusal can be done before the hearing commences.[5]

B. Importance of the facts

13–002
In *Man O'War Station Ltd v Auckland City Council*[6] the father of the main prosecution witness was mentor, colleague and long-term employer of the member of the New Zealand Court of Appeal delivering the leading judgment. The Privy Council held that there was no appearance of bias. The decision is perhaps a little curious. Firstly, the Privy Council were faced with the position that the New Zealand court had approached the position on the basis of the *Gough* test, because it was heard before the *Magill* decision. As there had been no argument before the New Zealand court on whether *Magill* should be followed in New Zealand, and the Privy Council recognised that this was a matter on which they would defer to the New Zealand court's view, this presented a dilemma. Lord Steyn said that on the facts of the case the difference between the two tests could not arguably influence the conclusion. However, as the judgment recites in detail the extent of the social and other contacts between the judge and the witness, one might have thought it was precisely the sort of case, like *Medicaments*, where the fair-minded and well-informed observer might take a different view to that which would apply on the *Gough* test. Secondly, it looks a case very close to the line ("much was made by counsel for the appellant of the

---

[3] [2005] EWCA Civ 548.
[4] In that case, a litigant in person claimed that the judge was likely to be biased in favour of professional advocates. See also Elias J. in *Hamilton v GRB* [2007] I.R.L.R. 391, EAT.
[5] See *Jones v DAS Legal Expenses Insurance Co Ltd* [2004] I.R.L.R. 218.
[6] [2002] UKPC 28.

analogy of a judge being disqualified from sitting on a case involving the son of his brother or best friend"). Yet the Privy Council judgment dismissing the appeal does not even make reference to what would seem to be the most important issue—whether on the appeal the factual findings of the trial judge were challenged in respect of the witness in question. That stands in contrast to Lord Steyn's statement that the facts need close consideration in any such case:

> "This is a corner of the law in which the context, and the particular circumstances, are of supreme importance. In their Lordships' view an intense focus on the essential facts of the case ... convincingly shows that there was no danger or possibility of apparent bias ... disembodied analogies, stripped of their context, are not helpful. They do not answer the specific reasoning of the Court of Appeal on the particular facts of the present case".

C. Objections likely to be valid or invalid

The court in *Locabail* sought to give examples where in normal cases objections on bias grounds would be unlikely to succeed:

13–003

(a) Based on religion, ethnic or national origin, gender, age, class, means or sexual orientation of the judge.
(b) Based on the judge's social, educational, service or employment background or history nor that of any member of the judge's family.
(c) Based on the judge's previous political associations or membership of social or sporting or charitable bodies or Masonic associations.
(d) Based on the judge's previous judicial decisions.
(e) Based on the judge's extra-curricular utterances in text-books, lectures, speeches, articles, interviews, reports or responses to consultation papers.[7]
(f) Based on previous receipt of instructions to act for or against any party, solicitor or advocate engaged in a case before him.
(g) Based on membership of the same Inn, circuit, local law society or chambers.[8]

The court thought that a real danger of bias might well be thought to arise in the following circumstances:

---

[7] But see para.13–018 below.
[8] cf. *KFTCIC v Icori Estero SpA*, June 28, 1991, Internat. Arb. Report, Vol.6, #8 8/91, Paris Court of Appeal.

(a) There was personal friendship or animosity between the judge and any member of the public involved in the case.
(b) The judge was closely acquainted with any member of the public involved in the case, particularly if the credibility of that individual could be significant in the decision of the case.[9]
(c) In a case where the credibility of any individual was an issue to be decided by the judge, he had in a previous case rejected the evidence of that person in such outspoken terms as to throw doubt on his ability to approach such person's evidence with an open mind on any later occasion. However, the mere fact that a judge earlier in the same case or in a previous case had commented adversely on a party or witness, or found the evidence of a party or witness to be unreliable, would not without more found a sustainable objection.[10]
(d) If on any question at issue in the proceedings before him the judge had expressed views, particularly in the course of the hearing, in such extreme and unbalanced terms as to throw doubt on his ability to try the issue with an objective judicial mind.[11]
(e) If there were other reasons for doubting the ability of the judge to ignore extraneous considerations prejudices and predilections and bring an objective judgment to bear on the issues before him.

D. Significance of the judicial oath

13–004 The taking of the judicial oath was described by the Supreme Court of Canada in *R v S (RD)*[12] as "possibly the most significant event in the career of a judge". Sometimes the judicial oath is prayed in aid as a reason for rejecting a claim of apparent bias. In *Helow v Secretary of State for the Home Department*[13] Lord Mance played down the importance of the judicial oath as an argument to rebut an allegation of judicial apparent bias. He said that there was a presumption that the judge would be true to his oath, but that the oath was:

---

[9] There are numerous cases where the connection is with a close family member of the judge: e.g. *Perot Systems Europe v Johnson*, Unreported, May 5, 2003, where Tugendhat J. held there was a reasonable basis for apprehension of bias where the defendant had a separate dispute with Abbey National, of which the judge's brother was at the time chairman. For a case where a casual acquaintance with the defendant was insufficient see *Hampshire CC v Gillingham*, Unreported, April 5, 2000, CA.
[10] But see *Lodwick v Southwark LBC* [2004] EWCA Civ 306; (2004) 148 S.J.L.B. 385, CA where the Court of Appeal allowed an objection to the chairman of an employment tribunal on precisely that ground.
[11] *Vakauta v Kelly* (1989) 167 C.L.R. 568.
[12] [1997] 3 S.C.T. 44 [116]–[119].
[13] [2008] 1 W.L.R. 2416 HL.

"more a symbol than a guarantee of the impartiality that any professional judge is by training and experience expected to practice and display".[14]

E. Relevance of a failure to make disclosure

It is sometimes argued that the failure of the tribunal to make disclosure, or make adequate disclosure voluntarily, should be a factor in deciding whether there is apparent bias. If the fair-minded observer test is applied strictly, it seems unlikely that this will usually be relevant because the fair-minded observer looks at the actual facts objectively; the time of their disclosure is principally relevant to waiver. It would have to be a rather special case before the fair-minded observer was influenced by the time and circumstances of the disclosure in deciding whether apparent bias was made out. In *Helow v Secretary of State for the Home Department*[15] it was argued that the failure of the Lord Ordinary to disclose her membership of the Association of Jewish Lawyers and Jurists was itself a significant factor to take into account; it was said that the fair-minded observer would have seen disclosure as a badge of impartiality, that she had nothing to hide and was fully conscious of the factors which might be apprehended to influence her judgment. Lord Mance said[16] that this would be a marginal fact at best: if there was good reason to stand down, disclosure would not affect that. If there was not good reason to stand down the fair-minded observer would probably conclude that it had not crossed the judge's mind that there was an issue.

13–005

2. Objections based on expressing prior views: keeping an open mind

Of course, the types of bias application are more or less unlimited, so breaking them down into categories is somewhat invidious. However, a number of the categories tend to reappear and it is often helpful to see how the courts have treated similar types of application.

13–006

A. Expressing decided views before the case has concluded

There have been a number of applications for recusal based on the judge showing his hand before the conclusion of the proceedings. These have

13–007

---

[14] [57].
[15] [2008] 1W.L.R. 2416.
[16] [58].

often failed because it has been said that the fair-minded observer would appreciate that even strong expressions of provisional views are usually no more than that.[17] A different case was where the judge forgot that final submissions were still to come, and delivered a draft judgment to the parties in error. The judge then recalled the judgment and sought to proceed to final submissions. The Court of Appeal did not consider his memory failure disqualified him from proceeding to complete the case, notwithstanding the draft judgment.[18]

There have however been a number of instances of judges expressing more than provisional views while the case continued. This may lead to a complaint of apprehension of bias, in the sense that the judge is not prepared to listen with an open mind to evidence and arguments. In *Jiminez v London Borough of Southwark*[19] Peter Gibson L.J. said:

> "the premature expression of a concluded view or the manifesting of a closed mind by the tribunal may amount to the appearance of bias".

Thus in *Steadman-Byrne v Amjad*[20] the Court of Appeal found appearance of bias where the district judge in a small personal injury claim arising from a traffic accident heard the claimants' evidence, called counsel to his room, said he believed the claimants, that although he had not heard the defendant give evidence he did not see how he could win, that it was "flavour of the month" for insurers to prosecute claimants with "Asian sounding names", noted that the defendant worked for the police, and said that someone with a police background "always thinks they are right and find it difficult to accept they are mistaken" and invited counsel for the defendant to take instructions over the lunch break.

13–008
This sort of conduct is plainly unacceptable. But where does one draw the line? In his judgment in *Steadman-Byrne*, Sedley L.J. referred to *Hart v Relentless Records*[21] and said a judge may legitimately give assistance to the parties by telling them what is presently in the judge's mind:

> "this may properly include . . . letting the parties know before reaching the defence case that the judge did not think much of the claimant's evidence. What is not acceptable is for the judge to form, or to give the impression of having formed, a firm view in favour of one side's credibility when the other side has not yet called evidence which is intended to impugn it".[22]

---

[17] *Hart v Relentless Records*, The Times, October 8, 2002; *London Borough of Southwark v Jiminez*, April 8, 2003, CA.
[18] *Taylor v Williamson*, The Times, July 17, 2002, CA.
[19] [2003] I.C.R. 1176.
[20] [2007] EWCA Civ 1148.
[21] [2002] EWHC 1984, Ch. at [38], per Jacob J.
[22] At [10].

Sedley L.J. pointed out that it could make no difference that the judge's remarks were made in the confines of his own room. Counsel was not permitted by the rules of professional conduct to keep what was said from his client. Whilst it might be helpful to make comments with a view to encouraging settlement or narrowing the issues, it is plain that the risk of giving an impression of prejudgment will arise if it is not made clear to the parties that any views expressed are but provisional, that the tribunal's mind is not yet made up and that it remains open to persuasion.[23] Similarly in *Jiminez* Peter Gibson L.J. emphasised that a strongly expressed view could still be a provisional view.

A different type of case was *Ezsias v North Glamorgan NHS Trust*.[24] After a preliminary employment tribunal hearing on an application for a deposit to be paid by the applicant, a hearing was fixed on the respondent's application to strike out the claim. After the deposit hearing but prior to the strike out hearing the chairman promulgated a document entitled "Judgment" purporting to strike out the claim. The document was withdrawn as an error and the chairman subsequently explained that the document in fact reflected a preliminary opinion not a judgment. Accepting the explanation of the tribunal chairman, the Court of Appeal agreed with the judge that whilst the explanation could acquit the tribunal chairman of actual pre-determination, it could not displace the perception of the fair-minded informed observer that there was a real possibility that she had a concluded view or a closed mind.

B. Renewal of applications for leave to the Court of Appeal

In the Court of Appeal, a single lord justice will determine applications for leave to appeal on paper. If the single judge refuses leave, there is a right to an oral hearing. Often the oral application is listed before the lord justice who has refused leave on paper. In *Mahomed v Morris*,[25] a single lord justice had refused leave to appeal on paper and then presided at the oral renewed application for permission to appeal. The full court held that there was no need for him to recuse himself. The expression of a preliminary view did not mean he could not hear the appeal impartially. The Court of Appeal have subsequently made clear that a renewed oral hearing on permission for appeal is not intended as a separate hearing afresh but a failsafe to ensure that the decision on paper did not overlook anything.

13–009

---

[23] See *Project v Hutt* (2006) UKEAT S/0065 EAT, per Lady Smith. See also *R. v Broadhead* [2006] EWCA Crim 3062 where the Court of Appeal quashed a confiscation order where comments of the judge indicated he had made up his mind in advance.
[24] [2007] EWCA Civ 330.
[25] February 3, 2000, CA.

In *Sengupta v Holmes*[26] Laws L.J. refused leave to appeal on paper, but at the oral hearing two other lords justices gave leave. An application was made to recuse Laws L.J. from sitting on the substantive appeal. The Court of Appeal heard full argument on the issue, and reconsidered *Mahomed*, which had been decided before the HRA became law. Laws L.J., giving the leading judgment[27] said that in the usual case, where the judge hearing the paper application for leave has not himself had to resolve the case's factual merits, and has not expressed himself incontinently, there is no reason to doubt that the judge will be able to determine the appeal involving oral argument with an open mind.[28]

C. Views expressed in prior hearings in the same case

13–010   Where judges are involved in long-running cases, they may hear a series of applications. They may try preliminary issues, or liability before quantum, and make findings of fact before going on to hear other applications or try other issues in the same case. If they express themselves too strongly, it may be suggested that they cannot hear with an open mind subsequent parts of the case. But if it is possible to recuse a judge in these circumstances, it will subvert the system. In *A-B v British Coal Corporation*[29] the Court of Appeal said that if one characterised too readily a judge's conduct in managing group litigation (which may include revisiting his earlier rulings) as conduct at risk of being perceived as apparent bias, it would subvert the proactive case management role of judges expected under the Civil Procedure Rules. It will generally be wrong for a judge to be disqualified from trying further hearings merely because he has made adverse findings on preliminary issues.[30]

As with other circumstances where a judge shows his hand before the conclusion of the proceedings, the question is whether the fair-minded observer would think the judge could not retain an open mind on the subsequent issues in the case. There would have to be extreme circumstances. In *Sengupta v Holmes*[31] Laws L.J. contemplated there might be cases where the judge expresses himself in such vituperative language that the fair-minded observer would regard him as disqualified from taking a fair view of the case if he was called on to revisit it.[32]

---

[26] [2002] EWCA Civ 1104.
[27] One cannot help thinking it might have been preferable if one of the other lords justices had given the leading judgment.
[28] See also *Dwr Cymru Cyfngedig v Albion Water* [2008] EWCA Civ 97.
[29] [2006] EWCA Civ 172.
[30] *Times Newspapers v Choudry*, December 17, 1999, CA; *Bahain v Rashidian* [1985] 1 W.L.R. 1337.
[31] [2006] EWCA Civ 172, see 13–009 above.
[32] [34].

This issue was touched on in *Locabail*. If on any question at issue in the proceedings before him the judge had expressed views, particularly in the course of the hearing, in such extreme and unbalanced terms as to throw doubt on his ability to try the issue with an objective judicial mind, the judge should recuse himself.[33] In a case where the credibility of any individual was an issue to be decided by the judge, the Court of Appeal said that the judge should recuse himself if he had in a previous case rejected the evidence of that person in such outspoken terms as to throw doubt on his ability to approach such person's evidence with an open mind on any later occasion. However, the mere fact that a judge earlier in the same case or in a previous case had commented adversely on a party or witness, or found the evidence of a party or witness to be unreliable, would not without more found a sustainable objection.[34] It is apparent that evidence of animosity could also be a justification for recusing the judge.

D. Previously deciding the same point

In *Amec Capital Projects v Whitefriars City Estates*[35] the court held that there was no apprehension of bias where an adjudicator had to decide the same issue of law or construction which he had decided previously. The court recognised that given the previous decision, the adjudicator might well reach the same decision the second time. But apprehension of bias would arise where the tribunal appeared to hear the case with a closed mind.

In *Davidson v Scottish Ministers*[36] Lord Bingham said[37]:

13–011

> "Rarely, if ever, in the absence of injudicious or intemperate behaviour, can a judge's previous activity as such give rise to an appearance of bias. Over time, of course, judges acquire a track record, and experienced advocates may be able to predict with more or less accuracy how a particular judge is likely to react to a given problem. Since judges are not automata this is inevitable, and presenting a case in the way most likely to appeal to a particular tribunal is a skill of the accomplished advocate. But adherence to an opinion expressed judicially in an earlier case does not of itself denote a lack of open-mindedness; and there are few experienced judges who have not, on fresh argument applied to new facts in a later case, revised an opinion expressed in an earlier. In practice, as the cases show, problems of

---

[33] *Vakauta v Kelly* (1989) 167 C.L.R. 568.
[34] But see *Lodwick v Southwark LBC* [2004] EWCA Civ 306; (2004) 148 S.J.L.B. 385, CA where the Court of Appeal allowed an objection to the chairman of an employment tribunal on precisely that ground.
[35] [2004] EWHC 393 TCC Judge Toulmin Q.C.
[36] [2004] UKHL 34.
[37] [10].

apparent bias do not arise where a judge is expected to revisit a question on which he or she has expressed a previous judicial opinion, which must happen in any developed system..."

E. Seeing inappropriate material

13-012 The judge is asked to rule on the admissibility of without prejudice or privileged material. He rules that the material is inadmissible. Can he go on to hear the case?

Where it is feasible, it may be better to make the application for determination of whether the material is admissible before a different judge in advance of the trial. Where the material consists of a document, it will often be far-fetched to suggest that by seeing the material the judge is unable to try the case. But in other cases, such as where a Pt 36 offer to settle the case has been disclosed, the position is more finely balanced. In *Berg v IML London*[38] Stanley Burnton J. reviewed the authorities and considered that whether the tribunal should recuse itself was fact-specific. The instant case was a summary judgment application before the master where there had been reference to a without prejudice offer. Stanley Burnton J. rejected the contention that the master was obliged to recuse himself. He said that although the application was not based on apparent bias, the principles were the same. His judgment was approved by the Court of Appeal in *Garratt v Saxby*.[39]

F. Hearing wasted or non-party costs applications

13-013 An application for wasted costs, or non-party costs, should normally be heard by the judge who has heard the trial or substantive application in relation to which the satellite application for wasted or non-party costs applies. That judge is familiar with the factual material and is generally best placed to judge the satellite application. However, by definition that judge will have reached decisions in the substantive matter, possibly in trenchant terms, without having heard from the non-party or lawyer as a party in his own right. In the famous case *Re Freudiana*,[40] an unfair prejudice petition between company shareholders estimated to last four weeks took something close to a year to determine. The trial judge took the view that much of the fault lay with the way the case had been conducted by certain of the counsel in the case, and ordered that they show cause as to why they should not pay the wasted costs incurred personally. Counsel on their behalf

---

[38] [2002] 4 All E.R. 87.
[39] [2004] 1 W.L.R. 2152.
[40] [1994] NPC 89, affirmed on appeal 28 November 1995, *Times*, 4 December 1995.

attended before the judge and told him that it was their intention to argue that a reason for the delay was the way the judge, rather than counsel, had conducted the case, and that in consequence the wasted costs application could not be heard by the trial judge. Recognising that he could not hear the application himself, and that it was not feasible for another judge to get to grips with this massive piece of litigation without disproportionate expense, the trial judge dismissed the application for wasted costs which he had himself initiated.

Once again, there is no bright-line rule here. The judge should consider whether he should recuse himself from such applications.[41] Where possible, the judge should hear the satellite applications and will be the person best placed to do so. In *Thomson v Berkhamsted Collegiate School*[42] Blake J. said that the application should normally be conducted by the trial judge who could give effect to any views he had expressed as to the conduct of the non-party without constituting appearance of bias.

G. Hearing contempt applications

Where a litigant commits a contempt in the face of the court, should the judge whose court has been disrupted hear the contempt application? In *Balogh v St Albans Crown Court*[43] an irate Melford Stevenson J. sentenced a contemnor[44] to two months imprisonment for an unsuccessful attempt to pump laughing gas into the courtroom. The Court of Appeal, quashing the custodial sentence, recognised that an angry judge whose court was disrupted was not always the best person to try such an application, particularly immediately after the disruptive event has occurred. Nowadays the contemnor is given an opportunity to take legal advice, and where appropriate to apologise. In *Williamson v Official Solicitor*[45] the issue arose whether the judge whose delivery of judgment was violently disrupted by the contemnor (who had been remanded in custody and given an opportunity to take legal advice) should hear the contempt application. The Court of Appeal rejected the argument that the fair-minded observer would think there was a real possibility of bias or that such a course infringed art 6. In many cases, the judge should refer the matter to another judge to deal with,[46] but it depended on the facts and there was no rule.

13–014

---

[41] *Bahai v Rashidian* [1985] 1 W.L.R. 1337; *Symphony Group v Hodgson* [1994] Q.B. 179.
[42] [2009] EWHC 2374 Q.B.
[43] [1975] Q.B. 73.
[44] Mr Balogh was the son of a former cabinet minister. After sentencing he is remembered for having told the judge: "You are a mindless automaton; why do you not self-destruct?".
[45] Unreported, February 4, 2003.
[46] See Practice Direction (Committal Applications) para.13 (6).

H. Incautious comments

13–015   Less than temperate comments and ill-judged jokes can also lead to apprehension of bias. In *El Farargy v El Farargy*[47] the family court judge formed an adverse view of a sheikh giving evidence. He made a number of comments in his absence about whether the sheikh would return to court "at this relatively fast-free time of the year", referring to him flying off "on his magic carpet" and referred to his affidavit as being "gelatinous" as a precursor for his punch line "just like Turkish Delight". In the Court of Appeal, Ward L.J. recused the judge. The judgment blends sympathy for a judge whom he obviously knew well and respected, with a recognition that such remarks are wholly unacceptable. He suggested that where an application for recusal involves criticism of the conduct of the judge himself, it may well be appropriate for the judge to pass on the application to a colleague to determine. Ward L.J. said that he was personally all for humour in court as a means of lightening the atmosphere but care was needed with humorous remarks[48] at the expense of those involved.

Another judge came in for strong criticism from the Court of Appeal in *Howell v Millais*.[49] The applicant was a trustee and the defendants sought on an application to make the trustees personally liable for costs. The judge had personally had recent employment discussions with the firm of which the applicant was a partner which had ended acrimoniously, although the judge did not know the applicant personally. On the recusal application, the judge had acted intemperately and then cross-examined counsel about matters within his personal knowledge. The Master of the Rolls applied *Morrison v AWG*[50] and expressed great concern at the spectacle of the judge conducting a heated debate with counsel relying on matters within his personal knowledge not set out in evidence.

A more generous view was taken by the EAT where a lay member of the employment tribunal had made intemperate and discourteous gestures. In *D Ross v MicroFocus Ltd*[51] Burton J. declined to find bias; he pointed out that a judge with no personal interest was more likely to be frustrated by unmeritorious arguments raised before him than to have a closed mind.

Cases where the judge intervenes excessively raise an aspect of a fair trial, albeit may not be regarded as an apprehension of bias problem. The principles are set out in *Almeida v Opportunity Equity Partners*.[52]

---

[47] 23 November, 2007.
[48] See *Robertson v Hendrie EAT Scotland*, Unreported, February 7, 2007. A training lay tribunal member watched the proceedings as an observer. The chairman asked if there was an objection to the lay member retiring with the panel. Laughter was heard from the retiring room, the tribunal then came back and decided against the applicant. An application to recuse failed.
[49] [2007] EWCA Civ 720.
[50] [2006] EWCA Civ 8; see 13–021.
[51] November 18, 2009, EAT.
[52] [2006] UKPC 44, PC.

I. Comments outside the courtroom

In *National Assembly for Wales v Condron*[53] one of the lay members on a planning appeal was overheard making a chance remark before the hearing that he would be "going with the report of the inspector". The judge found apparent bias, but the Court of Appeal overturned the decision.[54] The judge had erred in focusing on the position as it stood at the time of the remark, rather than the evidence of the chairman of the whole process and how the relevant member had taken part in open discussion at the hearing as to the pros and cons of the inspector's decision. It was the position as it stood subsequently that was critical, not the position as it stood at the time of the remark.

13–016

J. Conversations in the absence of one or more parties

In *Taylor v Lawrence*[55] the Court of Appeal were not prepared to find apparent bias in what might be called an administrative conversation (about setting a timetable) between the judge and one party in the absence of the other. Similarly, in *R v Khyam*[56] discussions between the President of the Queen's Bench Division and the trial judge as to the reasons for the vacation of date on a major criminal trial did not preclude the president sitting on the appeal.

13–017

But where the conversation was not of an administrative nature, the position was different, as was apparent in the EAT case of *Gill v Humanware Europe Ltd*[57] where the tribunal's decision was set aside as a result of two inappropriate conversations relevant to the case between one counsel and the chairman. In *Thompson v Collins*[58] the recorder gave judgment in a boundary dispute and identified the boundary in his judgment. He ordered the parties to agree the boundary on the basis of his judgment so a line could be drawn on a plan to give effect to it. The parties failed to agree this, and the claimants' solicitor contacted the recorder by telephone at his home to explain this. The recorder stated that the best way forward was for him to hold a conference with the parties and for him to give directions for the final resolution. The Court of Appeal said the telephone call should not have taken place; the proper procedure was to correspond with the court and ask that the correspondence be placed before the judge. However, the Court of Appeal said this was no evidence at all of apparent bias.[59]

---

[53] [2006] EWCA Civ 1573.
[54] For principles particular to councillors, see 12–011.
[55] [2003] Q.B. 528.
[56] [2008] EWCA Crim 612.
[57] April 24, 2009, Judge McMullen EAT.
[58] [2009] EWCA Civ 525.
[59] One of the authors recalls a case in the Court of Appeal when the chair of the court sat next

K. Articles written by the judge

13–018   The other one of the five cases heard by the Court of Appeal and dealt with in the *Locabail*[59a] judgment which is of interest is *Timmins v Gormley*. That was a personal injury action unsuccessfully defended by insurers and heard by a recorder who was a prolific writer on personal injury matters. The court was shown four articles written in legal publications by the recorder which indicated that the recorder was a committed advocate of the cause of personal injury claimants. The articles had nothing to do with the case or the issues in the case. The court made it clear there was an established tradition for judges to write books and textbooks; there was no suggestion this was inappropriate. But the articles went beyond measured debate. They were expressed in a tone and with a trenchancy which suggested to the reasonable reader that the recorder held preconceived anti-insurer views so firmly that it would not be possible for him to try the case with an open mind.[60] The Court of Appeal ordered a retrial.[61]

This is a different sort of issue form where the judge has written articles about the point of law in issue in the case. So long as the terms of the article do not suggest that the judge would be unable to hear the arguments and keep an open mind, this should not be a reason for recusal, and this conclusion is apparent from *Locabail*[62]

3. Objections based on relationships and affiliations

A. Relationships between court, party and advocate

13–019   In *Taylor v Lawrence*[63] a five-member Court of Appeal including the Lord Chief Justice and the Master of the Rolls, heard a second appeal in the case based on judicial bias after further information had appeared as to the use made by the judge of the claimants' solicitors for the purpose of making his will. The Court of Appeal thought that the fair-minded observer would not think the judge would be influenced by the fact that he had instructed the claimants' firm of solicitors to act for himself for a purpose wholly removed from the action. They pointed out that unlike some jurisdictions

---

to leading counsel for the other side at lunch in hall the day before the appeal commenced and told him to agree with the author a means for sharing the allotted time for the appeal between the parties. Totally innocuous, in one sense—but how does one explain to one's sensitive foreign clients how this request has arisen?

[59a] See 13–003.
[60] See *Vakauta v Kelly* (1989) 167 C.L.R. 568, HCA.
[61] The Recorder subsequently resigned as a Recorder.
[62] See in the arbitration context on this point *Urbaser SA v Argentina* ICSID Case No ARB/07/27.
[63] [2003] Q.B. 528.

the judiciary here does not isolate itself from contact with the profession. The judiciary is recruited from chambers and law firms, and there is a tradition of bench and bar lunching together in the Inns of Court. Lord Woolf C.J. said[64] that this close relationship has enhanced rather than prejudiced the administration of justice. The informed observer would be aware that in the ordinary way contacts between the judiciary and the profession should not be regarded as giving rise to a possibility of bias. Judges do not live lives of cloistered isolation.

Notwithstanding the strength of the court in *Taylor,* subsequent decisions have rather undermined the tenor of Lord Woolf's comments in *Taylor*. In *Smith v Kvaerner*[65] a Court of Appeal containing the current Lord Chief Justice and Master of the Rolls expressed concerns as to part-time judges sitting in cases involving members of their chambers remunerated by conditional fee agreements,[66] lest this be construed as a financial interest in the case. This seems extreme, but in the light of these comments the Bar Standards Board has now issued guidance designed to ensure that chambers notify court listing authorities with a view to ensuring that barristers working on conditional fee arrangements do not appear in front of members of their own chambers.

In New Zealand, in *Saxmere Company Ltd v Wool Board Disestablishment Co Ltd*[67] an application to recuse a member of the Court of Appeal from sitting on an appeal was based on the fact that he had a close relationship with counsel on one side and they had a joint interest in a stud farm. The court said, dismissing the application, that when the two individuals were both Q.C.s together they would have argued cases against each other; it was ridiculous to think now that deciding a case against his friend would have affected the relationship.

Most recently, in *Mireskandari v Associated Newspapers*[68] the claimant sought disclosure of the number of occasions on which the judge who had made an order against the claimant had whilst at the Bar been instructed by the defendant newspaper owners. The court held that there was no power to order such disclosure, but Eady J. said that, following *Locabail,* in any event the fact that a judge had previously acted for a party whilst at the bar would not normally give rise to apparent bias. One would imagine that all the judges who hear defamation cases in the High Court regularly acted for the newspaper proprietors when they were at the Bar.

The relationship between the parties and tribunal members has caused problems of a different sort. In *Lawal v Northern Spirit*[69] the House of Lords outlawed the practice of counsel who served as part-time judges of the

13–020

---

[64] At para.61.
[65] Discussed in detail at 11–020.
[66] At [12].
[67] [2009] N.Z.L.R. 72.
[68] [2010] EWHC 967 (QB).
[69] [2004] 1 All E.R. 187.

Employment Appeal Tribunal appearing as counsel in front of lay members with whom they had previously sat. Disagreeing with the view of the majority of the Court of Appeal, Lord Steyn said that lay members looked to the judge for guidance on the law and could be expected to develop a fairly close relationship of trust and confidence with him. He said that similarly a recorder who in a criminal case had sat as judge with jurors might not subsequently appear as counsel in a case in which one or more of those same jurors served and to do otherwise tended to undermine public confidence in the system. *Lawal* is surely another rather surprising decision; after all, the advocate is not a party to the litigation. Would the fair-minded observer really regard the tribunal as subject to apparent bias here? In a different sphere, in *R. v Spear*[70] the House of Lords considered whether the courts-martial procedure breached art.6. They held that if a member of the panel was subordinate to one of the parties, the court would require safeguards to show the independence of the judicial figure if it was to find no bias.[71]

B. Friends and relatives of the judge

13–021   When faced with an application based on the judge's prior relationship with a material witness, the Privy Council in *Man O' War Station Ltd v Auckland City Council*[72] said that it was important to focus on the facts in detail. In *Morrison v AWG*[73] the judge was due to hear a lengthy trial and had been heavily involved in advance of the trial as managing judge. It became apparent to him that he knew one of the witnesses well. The judge raised the problem and asked whether the evidence to be given was likely to be challenged as to its truthfulness. The party calling the witness responded by indicating that the evidence to be given by the witness in question could in fact be given by other witnesses who were members of the same relevant committee, and in the light of this the judge held that it was unnecessary to recuse himself. The Court of Appeal disagreed. The trial was complex and it was difficult to predict what would arise in the course of the witness' evidence. If the replacement witnesses gave the same evidence as the initial witness and its truthfulness was challenged, the real possibility of bias remained. The Court of Appeal stressed that the inconvenience, cost and delay of the judge recusing himself did not weigh in the balance where the overriding principle of judicial impartiality was properly invoked. The safe course was for the judge to recuse himself prior to the commencement of the trial rather than possibly suffer the disaster of having to abandon the trial during the hearing.

---

[70] [2003] 1 A.C. 734.
[71] See *Sramek v Austria* (1984) 7 E.H.R.R. 351; *Belilos v Switzerland* (1988) 10 E.H.R.R. 466.
[72] [2002] UKPC 28. see 13–002 above.
[73] [2006] EWCA Civ 8.

The same judge, Evans-Lombe J., had previously been reversed by the Court of Appeal for reaching an opposite conclusion, in holding that a decision-maker's prior relationship with those involved in a hearing led to apprehension of bias: in *Flaherty v National Greyhound Council*[74] a tribunal member had had a prior social relationship within a professional context with individuals involved in the organisation responsible for the doping tests on the greyhound the subject of the appeal. Citing *Man O'War* as authority for this being an area of the law where context and particular circumstances were of supreme importance, the Court of Appeal thought it unrealistic to suggest that such prior contacts gave rise to an apprehension of bias.

C. Where judges and tribunals are likely to know the parties and witnesses

In *Grant v Teachers' Appeal Tribunal*[75] the Privy Council on an appeal from Jamaica rejected a contention of apprehension of bias where the tribunal chairman whose conduct was in issue had met the judge ten or so times in twenty years, and again stressed the importance of the facts of each case. The Privy Council's opinion, given by Lord Carswell recognises the difficulty of applying the principles in the same way when the judge is part of a relatively small community:

13–022

> "In such communities it is commonly found that many of the parties and witnesses who are concerned in cases in the courts are known, and not infrequently well known, to the judge assigned to sit. It is incumbent on the judge to apply a careful and sensitive judgment to the question whether he is a close enough friend of the person concerned to make it undesirable for him to sit on the case. If he errs on the side of caution by too much, he may make it impracticable for him to carry out his judicial duties as effectively as he should. If on the other hand, he is not ready enough to recuse himself, however unbiased and impartial his approach may in fact be, he will leave himself open to the suggestion of bias and damage the reputation of the judiciary for independence and impartiality. In this connection it is relevant to take into account the issues in the proceedings".[76]

The passage cited above recognises that the rules have to take account of local and individual issues. But this applies not merely where the judge is part of a small community. In the case of sporting tribunals, the panel will

---

[74] [2005] EWCA Civ 1117.
[75] [2006] UKPC 59.
[76] [38].

often all know the sportsman who comes before them, and all the witnesses. The rules have to be applied with commonsense.

D. Tribunals chosen because known to the parties

13–023   Sometimes the parties choose a tribunal whom they know already. Religious organisations sometimes require their members to submit disputes to a minister or community sage. Contracts, particularly in the case of small companies, often provide that in case of dispute, the company's shares shall be valued by the company's auditors. The auditors will be sufficiently familiar with the company's affairs not to need time to acquaint themselves with the company's business, and are independent of the company's shareholders. But the auditors' connections with the parties make it unlikely that they would pass the normal apparent bias test. It can be seen that in a case such as this, it would not be open to one of the parties to object to the appointment of the auditors on the grounds of their connections with the other party.

Such clauses may not in fact work well. In *Macro v Thompson (No 3)*[77] Robert Walker J. said that the expert was extremely imprudent in his dealings with the solicitor for the companies, regarding the entire episode as "a classic example of how not to conduct an articles valuation of shares in a private company". The judge recognised that the usual rules of apparent bias could not apply. However he said:

> "... when the court is considering a decision reached by an expert valuer who is not an arbitrator performing a quasi-judicial function, it is actual partiality, rather than the appearance of partiality, that is the crucial test. Otherwise auditors (like architects and actuaries) who have a long-standing professional relationship with one party (or persons associated with one party) to a contract might be unduly inhibited, in continuing to discharge their professional duty to their client, by too high an insistence on avoiding even an impression of partiality".[78]

It is plain that the apparent bias test must be applied differently in such cases, to recognise the choice of the parties. The parties have chosen the expert expressly because of those characteristics which would normally be badges of apparent bias, so they must be taken to have consented to the expert acting notwithstanding those characteristics. But there will be other features which the parties have not consented to, and it is suggested that

---

[77] [1997] 2 B.C.L.C. 36.
[78] At 65f.

there is no reason why they should be limited to actual bias.[79] The test is surely whether the tribunal demonstrates apparent bias, taking into account the characteristics of the tribunal to which the parties have consented.

E. Employment tribunals

There have been a number of apparent bias applications arising in employment tribunals. The combination of a large volume of hearings, regular non-legal representation, lay members who have separate employment which may give rise to conflicts and a level of case reporting unusual in tribunals may explain the apparent volume. It is helpful to look at *Hamilton v GRB*,[80] where the union representative was required to stand down from sitting as he had a senior position in a union with the same pay policy as the union whose policy was in issue in the case, where Elias J. sets out bias principles arising in the employment tribunal context.

13–024

Thus in *Peninsula Business Services v English*[81] the part-time legal chairman was recused from acting on a tribunal where employment consultants were a party after the law firm of which he was a partner had published an advertisement strongly critical of the use of non-qualified employment consultants. In *City & County of Swansea v Honey*[82] the employment tribunal member was a trade union representative who was involved in a separate dispute with the employer council. His trenchant criticisms of the council had gone well beyond the case which concerned him. The EAT held that there was apparent bias.

F. Affiliations of connected third parties

In *R (Compton on behalf of Community Action for Savernake Hospital) v Wiltshire Primary Care Trust*[83] Cranston J. posed the question: can bias on the part of third party consultants ever affect or taint the decision makers? As the judge made clear, in a sense that is the wrong question: the issue is whether the attitude or connections of the third party has affected or tainted the decision makers. On the facts, he rejected the contention that consultants who had been employed by a health authority to review and

13–025

---

[79] One of the authors once had a case where a solicitor was suing his law firm, and the partnership agreement provided for the arbitrator to be appointed by the Chairman of the Law Society. The Chairman of the Law Society was at the time the senior partner in the firm. The parties could not have intended that the senior partner of the defendant should choose the arbitrator.
[80] [2007] I.R.L.R. 391, EAT.
[81] EAT 27 August 2009.
[82] November 7, 2008, EAT.
[83] [2008] EWHC 1824.

consider consultation replies tainted the decision makers where a director of the consultants was the partner of a key individual in the health authority.

G. Membership of organisations

13–026
In *Helow v Secretary of State for the Home Department*[84] the House of Lords considered whether the Lord Ordinary in Scotland should have recused herself from hearing an asylum application by virtue of her membership of the International Association of Jewish Lawyers and Jurists (she was a founder member of the Scottish branch) where the Association had in the past expressed strong views against the Palestine Liberation Organisation, an organisation with which the applicant had been involved. The House of Lords dismissed the application. Whilst the views expressed by persons representing the association, or speaking at meetings of the association had on occasion been extreme, the Lord Ordinary was not an officer of the association, and had not at any stage associated herself with the extreme views expressed. Moreover, the association was not in itself an extreme organisation and many more moderate views had been expressed.

Helow is a significant decision. Their lordships held that mere membership of an association, or subscription to a journal, would not of itself normally carry with it endorsement of the more extreme views expressed by or in the organisation—although there would no doubt be organisations themselves so extreme that mere membership would carry some form of endorsement of views. It is thus relevant to consider what evidence there is as to endorsement by the judge of the views in question. And it is notable that their lordships recognised that if there had been evidence that the Lord Ordinary had associated herself with the more extreme views, it would not have been appropriate for her to sit on the appeal.

H. The solicitor judge

13–027
One of the applications heard by the Court of Appeal in *Locabail* was in relation to Lawrence Collins Q.C., a partner of the city solicitors Herbert Smith, then sitting as a Deputy High Court Judge.[85] On the eighth day of the trial the judge disclosed that he had looked at some new discovery documents overnight and it appeared from a press cutting that his firm had been involved, in circumstances he knew nothing of, in proceedings to obtain a bankruptcy order against the defendant's ex-husband, Mr Emmanuel, and to wind up a company of which the husband had been a guarantor. The

---

[84] [2008] 1 W.L.R. 2416 HL, discussed at 11–014.
[85] Lord Collins has recently retired from the Supreme Court.

defendant, Mrs Emmanuel, contended that Mr Collins was not a proper person to have been the judge in a case where the claimant Locabail sought to enforce securities obtained from Mr Emmanuel and his companies in respect of which Mrs Emmanuel was claiming equitable interests. There were issues as to waiver, as no objection had been taken when the judge made the disclosure and the Court of Appeal made the point that if it had not occurred to the defendant to object or ask for further information at the time the disclosure was made, it could hardly be said that a reasonable man would consider there was a real risk of bias. The contention that the judge should have made further enquiries as to matters he was not aware of was rejected. But the interesting point in respect of this application was that the court rejected the allegation that the facts gave rise to a real danger of bias at all. In doing so, the court accepted that under the then current version of the Law Society rules, the judge and his firm would have been precluded from acting for Mrs Emmanuel in the litigation.[86] The judge, as a partner of Herbert Smith, owed a personal fiduciary obligation to companies, albeit not parties to the litigation, but whose interests were opposed to those of Mrs Emmanuel. What is striking about the court's decision is the pragmatic approach. Given that no one doubted that Mr Collins knew nothing of his firm's involvement until he made the disclosure, the idea that he could have been thought to be less than impartial seems absurd. Yet the existence of a fiduciary relationship owed by Mr Collins as a partner in Herbert Smith to a company which had conflicting interests to those of Mrs Emmanuel presents a difficulty.[87]

I. Race and religion

In *Seer Technology Incorporation v Saddi Abbas*,[88] the defendant complained that as he was an Arab it was wrong for the hearings to take place before a Jewish judge where the claimant's solicitor was also Jewish. It is not surprising that Pumfrey J. did not think much of that as a ground for asking the judge to recuse himself.

13–028

---

[86] Rule 15.01 of the old rules, now repealed: see Ch.15. The position would not have been different under the new rules.
[87] Lord Collins' former life as a partner of city firm Herbert Smith has given rise to a number of applications for him to recuse himself based on retainers taken on by Herbert Smith. But unless he was involved in the matter personally there is no reason for this to be a ground for recusal: see, e.g. *BCCI v Ali*, December 3, 2001.
[88] February 2, 2000.

CHAPTER 14

Arbitrations

14–001   In the past, the position of arbitrators has been considered within judicial conflicts. In fact, not all of the issues are judicial conflict issues. But in any event arbitrations deserve their own chapter. Arbitration conflicts have become a hot topic. Applications are now being made to arbitrators by one party asking them to disqualify the other party's lawyers from representing their clients. Is there power to do this? What should an arbitrator do when faced with this problem?

Two particular issues are relevant for arbitrations. Firstly, when is the arbitrator "impartial" for the purpose of potential conflicts of interest. Secondly, what are the powers of arbitrators in relation to conflicts of interest on the part of the lawyers appearing in front of them.

1. The impartial arbitrator

A. Section 24 impartiality

14–002   Section 24(1) of the Arbitration Act 1996 provides:

> "A party to arbitral proceedings may (upon notice to the other parties, to the arbitrator concerned and to any other arbitrator) apply to the court to remove an arbitrator on any of the following grounds—
> (a) that circumstances exist, that give rise to justifiable doubts as to his impartiality;"

The Court of Appeal in *Locabail*,[1] then applying the *Gough* test,[2] said it also applied to arbitrators. The same was said in *Gough*[3] and in two subsequent cases involving arbitrators, *Laker Airways v FLS Aerospace*[4] and *AT&T Corp v Saudi Cable Co.*[5] It seems highly likely that the courts will now hold that the Arbitration Act test is the same as the *Magill* test. In *AT&T Corp* the arbitrator was, unbeknown to one of the parties to an ICC arbitration, a non-executive director of a competitor company which was not merely a commercial rival of that party in business, but was also a disappointed bidder for the very contract which formed the background to the dispute submitted to arbitration. The submission that the different regime under the Arbitration Act imposed different rules was expressly rejected, as was the application.[6] In *A v B*[6a] Flaux J. applied the *Porter v Magill test*; it does not seem to have been in issue that it applied.[6b]

In *Norbrook Laboratories v A Tank*[7] Colman J. held that if there was a reasonable apprehension of bias, the provisions of s.24(1) were automatically satisfied and there was no need for a separate inquiry as to whether that has caused the other party substantial injustice. Attempts to remove arbitrators for apprehension of bias have sometimes been made after unilateral communications by the arbitrator with one party. In *Norbrook* the court said that such discussions are to be deprecated and can lead to removal if they are intentional or frequent, or go beyond administrative matters.[8]

Care must be taken to make the objection before the arbitrator promptly. Section 73(1) of the Arbitration Act 1996 provides that the applicant may

---

[1] [2000] Q.B. 451. see 13–003.
[2] The test which predated that determined by the House of Lords in *Porter v Magill: see 11–011*.
[3] Where it was both obiter and prior to the 1996 Act [1993] A.C. 646 at 670.
[4] [1999] 2 Lloyd's Rep. 45, Rix J.
[5] [2000] 1 Lloyd's Rep. 22, Longmore J.; see also *Rustal Trading Ltd v Gill & Duffus SA* [2000] 1 Lloyd's Rep. 14 and *Save and Prosper Pensions Ltd v Homebase*, Unreported, March 2, 2000, Judge Rich Q.C.
[6] A recent decision of the Paris Court of Appeal SA *J&P Avax SA v Société Tecnimont SPA*, Paris Court of Appeal, 12 February 2009, Rev. Arb. 2009 186, has caused much debate in the arbitration community. A well-known arbitrator who was a partner in one of the world's largest law firms disclosed that his firm had represented the parent company of one of the parties in a concluded case in which he had never been involved. Counsel to one of the parties discovered that, subsequent to his appointment, the law firm of the arbitrator was assisting on various projects a company which had since then been acquired by the other party's parent company. The arbitrator was not aware of this. A challenge to the arbitrator was rejected by the ICC. However, the Paris Court of Appeal quashed a 400-page substantive award made by the panel after enormous expense had been incurred on the grounds of non disclosure by the arbitrator.
[6a] [2011] EWHC 2345 (Comm) discussed at 14–015.
[6b] [21].
[7] [2006] 2 Lloyd's Rep. 485; see to same effect *ASM Shipping Ltd v Bruce Harris* [2007] EWHC 1513 at [32], per Andrew Smith J.
[8] See also *Discain Project Services v Opecprime Development* [2000] B.L.R. 402, where discussions between an adjudicator and one party concerning issues of jurisdiction gave rise to apprehension of bias, *Pacific China Holdings Ltd v Grand Pacific Holdings Ltd* HCCT 5/2007 (HK Supreme Court).

not raise an objection before the court or tribunal if he continued to take part in the arbitral proceedings without objecting forthwith or within such time as is allowed by the arbitration agreement unless he shows that, at the time he took part in the proceedings, he did not know and could not with reasonable diligence have discovered the grounds for the objection. Thus in *ASM Shipping Ltd of India v TTMI Ltd of England*[9] although apparent bias was shown, the award was not set aside in consequence of s.73(1).

This raises the question whether there are non-waivable grounds which trump s.73. The position is not clear.[10] In W*eissfich v Julius*[11] the point was raised but not decided. It is suggested that there must be some circumstances, albeit limited ones, which override s.73. Some conflicts are such that it would be an affront to English public policy to enforce the award: for example, if it came to the attention of one party that the arbitrator had accepted a bribe, s.73 could hardly prevent him from challenging either the award or the continued participation of the arbitrator notwithstanding the fact that no application had been made at the time.

B. Contamination

14–003   The issue of contamination (whether the apparent bias of one arbitrator should lead to the entire tribunal being required to stand down) is considered in relation to judges more generally at 11–017.[12] While the principles are not different in relation to arbitrations, there is authority specifically in relation to arbitrations. In *ASM Shipping Ltd v Harris*[13] Andrew Smith J. emphasized that the decision would vary from case to case and that there was no rule. At a previous hearing a different judge had required one of the arbitrators, a Q.C., to stand down because he had previously as counsel appeared as advocate on an application for disclosure of documents from an individual who was a principal witness in the arbitration. The Q.C. had, until required to do so by the court, declined to stand down and stated himself satisfied that there was no reason for him to stand down. The other arbitrators had supported his position. Andrew Smith J. held that the subsequent application to court for the other arbitrators to stand down was barred by s.73 because the party had continued with the arbitration without making objection promptly. But he said that even if he was wrong on that ground, he did not consider that the fair-minded observer would have justifiable doubts as to the impartiality of the other arbitrators. The objection

---

[9] [2006] 1 Lloyd's Rep. 375.
[10] See *Russell on Arbitration* 23rd edn (2007) at para.7-128.
[11] [2006] EWCA 218.
[12] The leading case more generally is now the decision of the Court of Appeal in *BAA v Competition Commission* [2010] EWCA Civ 1097.
[13] [2008] 1 Lloyd's Rep. 61.

had been made on the ground that they had discussions with the Q.C. in the course of the reference, and further had supported the decision not to recuse himself that the Q.C. had taken prior to the court ruling. Andrew Smith J. emphasized that allegations of apparent bias must be decided on the facts and circumstances of the individual case including the nature of the issue to be decided.[14] As the Q.C. had made clear that he recalled nothing relating to the previous case which gave rise to any doubt in his mind about the propriety of the witness' conduct, and there was no suggestion to the contrary,[15] there was no real possibility that there could have been discussions between the Q.C. and the two arbitrators which might improperly influence their assessment of the witness.

C. The IBA Guidelines

In 2004 the International Bar Association published Guidelines on Conflicts of Interest in International Arbitration after appointing a Working Group of 19 experts in 14 countries. Whilst these Guidelines are not binding on international arbitrators, they are frequently relied on and are now well-known in international arbitration. The Guidelines set out at General Standard 2(b) the test of bias:

14–004

> "... if facts or circumstances exist, or have arisen since the appointment, that from a reasonable third party's point of view having knowledge of the relevant facts, give rise to justifiable doubts as to the arbitrator's impartiality or independence ..."

This is pretty well identical to the *Magill* test. In contrast to the objective test set out in General Standard 2, the Guidelines adopt what has been described as a subjective standard for the obligation of disclosure on the arbitrator. General Standard 3(a) provides for an obligation on the arbitrator to make disclosure if facts or circumstances exist that may in the eyes of the parties give rise to doubts as to the arbitrator's impartiality or independence. It also provides that disclosure should be made in case of doubt. Disclosure is not an admission of a conflict and does not auto-

---

[14] *Flaherty v National Greyhound Racing Club Ltd* [2005] EWCA Civ 1117 at para. 27, per Scott Baker L.J.
[15] The decision of the previous court to require the Q.C. to recuse himself is reported at [2006] 1 Lloyd's Rep. 375, Morison J. The fact that an arbitrator's prior involvement as advocate on the other side to a witness was capable of giving rise to apparent bias can be seen from *Rustal Trading Ltd v Gill & Duffus SA* [2000] 1 Lloyd's Rep. 14, Moore Bick J. In the *ASM* case there were disputed issues of fact as to the prior proceedings involving the witness, and Andrew Smith J. quotes in his judgment from the Q.C. suggesting angrily in correspondence that the facts had been misrepresented to or misunderstood by Morison J.

matically lead to disqualification. The explanation to General Standard 3 states:

> "In determining what facts should be disclosed, an arbitrator should take into account all circumstances known to him or her, including to the extent known the culture and the custom of the country of which the parties are domiciled or nationals."

General Standard 4 provides that if a party does not raise an express objection within 30 days of disclosure by the arbitrator or after a party learns of circumstances that could constitute a conflict of interest that party is deemed to have waived the conflict.

The Guidelines provide Red, Orange and Green lists. The Red list is in two parts: firstly, non-waivable conflicts and secondly, conflicts which may be expressly waived but only after disclosure. The Orange list is a non-exhaustive enumeration of specific situations which, depending on the facts of a given case, in the eyes of the parties may give rise to justifiable doubts as to the arbitrator's independence or impartiality. If the arbitrator makes disclosure, the parties are deemed to waive the conflict if they do not object within the 30 days provided by General Standard 4. Orange list conflicts do not automatically lead to disqualification where objection is taken, even if no disclosure was made. The Green list is a non-exhaustive list of situations which do not give rise to appearance of, or actual, conflict.

2. Power of arbitrators to disqualify lawyers

A. Application of s.33

14–005   What happens when a party applies for an order to disqualify the other side's lawyers? Should the arbitrator consider the application? Has he power to do so? There is limited authority on the issue.

The arbitrator has no power to make an order against a lawyer directly. The lawyers are not parties to the arbitration and have not entered into the arbitration agreement. So if an order is made, the order must be made against the party.

It would be difficult to say that an arbitrator had no jurisdiction to make an order debarring a party from appearing through a particular lawyer or law firm. Section 33 of the Arbitration Act 1996 provides that:

> "(1) The tribunal shall—
> (a) act fairly and impartially as between the parties, giving each party a reasonable opportunity of putting his case and dealing with that of his opponent, and
> (b) adopt procedures suitable to the circumstances of the par-

ticular case, avoiding unnecessary delay or expense, so as to provide a fair means for the resolution of the matters falling to be determined.

(2) The tribunal shall comply with that general duty in conducting the arbitration proceedings, in its decisions on matters of procedure and evidence and in the exercise of all other powers conferred on it."

In extreme cases, an arbitrator may decide that s.33 requires an order debarring a party from being represented before the tribunal by a particular lawyer. In principle, the arbitrator must have jurisdiction to do so. If the lawyer was persistently abusive, for example, or committed what would in court be regarded as a contempt of court, such an order might be appropriate, or if there was blatant evidence of misuse of confidential information so that the other side would be prejudiced if that lawyer appeared.

However, most cases are less straightforward. There are significant problems in arbitrators exercising jurisdiction in cases that are less clear cut.

14–006

Firstly, the arbitrators' powers are powers over the parties and may only be exercised in relation to the arbitration under the arbitration agreement. Thus no order for disclosure could be made against the lawyers directly, and many of the relevant documents in the control of the lawyers may not be within the control of the party to arbitration. Even if the relevant documents were in the control of the party to the arbitration, it is debatable whether arbitrators should (or can) order disclosure of documents not material to the issues in the dispute the subject-matter of the arbitration and relevant only to satellite litigation.

Secondly, whilst it seems that the arbitrators would be able to make an order debarring a party from *being represented at the hearing* by a particular lawyer, the jurisdiction of the arbitrator to require the lawyer not to provide assistance to a party to the arbitration at all in relation to the reference is much more debatable. Whether a party can be represented by a particular lawyer, or law firm, can be regarded as "procedures" of the arbitration and the arbitrators "conducting the arbitral proceedings" within s.33. But an order debarring a party from consulting with a particular lawyer or law firm in relation to the subject-matter of the arbitration may not fall within s.33 and looks more like an order made against the lawyer than the party.

There are arguments both ways as to whether such an order falls within s.33 but an order of this breadth would require considerable boldness, at the very least, on the part of the arbitrators. The arbitrators are bound to adopt procedures suitable to the circumstances of the particular case so as to provide a fair means for the resolution of the matters falling to be determined under s.33(1)(b). But is that wide enough to cover an order requiring a party not to consult with a particular lawyer or law firm? There is nothing in s.34, which covers procedural and evidential matters that would assist such an interpretation.

In normal circumstances, a party has a right to be represented by his lawyer of choice. An order debarring a particular lawyer or law firm from consulting with his client in relation to a particular matter is depriving him of a right. Moreover, there may be practical problems: where a party has a number of retainers with the same law firm, and perhaps related litigation. Such an order may raise a difficult line as to what is and is not a breach of the order. For example, where insurers or reinsurers are involved in the issues underlying the claim, could the law firm advise on these matters notwithstanding the order made by the arbitrators?

The point is an important one, because if arbitrators do not have power to make an order barring a party from consulting with a particular lawyer or law firm, the idea of the arbitrators taking jurisdiction to bar the lawyer from appearing before them may well be a largely pointless exercise. True it is that (by way of analogy) in a number of jurisdictions, only lawyers called to the local bar have a right to be heard before the local courts, and sometimes foreign counsel will draft the written submissions for the local lawyer to speak to in submissions in court, but where what is in issue is potential conflict of interest, the possibility that the allegedly tainted lawyer may continue to advise or draft may mean that a trip to court for a full injunction is still necessary to provide an effective remedy.

Thirdly, in international arbitrations, questions of conflict of interest may raise multi-jurisdictional issues of law and professional practice which the arbitrators may be ill-equipped to handle. A US party to a London arbitration represented by a US law firm complains that the English law firm on the other side previously acted for their Singapore subsidiary through their Singapore office and hold confidential information relevant to the subject-matter of the arbitration. What is the relevant law applicable to the confidential information issue, and to any questions of professional practice which arise? Is expert evidence of foreign law necessary? In some jurisdictions, such as US, the rules principally appear from local Bar rules. In other jurisdictions, such as England, the primary rules are rules of common law and the professional rules are of much more limited significance when a challenge is made. Would it be right for the arbitrators to become involved on difficult issues of this nature on a matter not relevant to the substantive issues in the arbitration? There is a real risk that the arbitrators will be asked to decide what may be a substantial piece of satellite litigation here.

Fourthly, where an application is made in court to injunct a law firm, the law firm must be guided by its own interests, as it is the law firm which will be injuncted, is liable for the costs and stands to suffer the reputational damage if it loses. Of course it will have regard to its duties to the client undertaken by accepting the retainer and the client's stance, but the decision whether to terminate the retainer in the light of challenge (which may lead to it being sued by the client for wrongly accepting the retainer) must ultimately be that of the firm. Where an application is made against the party to the arbitration, there is something of a blurring of the separate interests as the client will instruct the law firm in the arbitration to see off the challenge. The law firm must take great care in relation to potential conflicts of interest here.

The conclusion to be drawn from the above analysis is that arbitrators should be very wary of being drawn in to these issues. Whilst in particularly egregious cases the arbitrators may rely on s.33 as giving them the necessary powers, in most cases they will do much better to leave these issues to the courts rather than try to use their more limited powers to do the job themselves. 14–007

There is no doubt, however, that such applications are increasingly made to arbitrators. One reason may be that there can be good reason for the parties to consent to the issue being decided by the arbitrators. We have seen that English law firms are often reluctant to run the reputational risks of having their alleged conflicts debated in open court in the full glare of potential publicity. No such concerns arise where the matter is heard in the course of a confidential arbitration. The arbitral tribunal is already in place, and to ask the arbitrators to determine the issue may prove quicker and cheaper than if an action is commenced in the High Court. Once again, there may be tensions between the interests of the lawyers and the interests of their client, in that these advantages in agreeing that the matter should be determined by arbitrators may not always enure to the benefit of the client.

B. Disqualification of counsel: caselaw

A number of the problems flagged up above were identified by the arbitral tribunal in *Rompetrol Group NV v Romania*[16] where the tribunal were asked to "remove" a legal representative from the case and "forbid him from participating in any way" on the ground that he had previously been employed by the law firm of which one of the tribunal was a member. The tribunal dismissed the application on the facts. They pointed out that there was no provision for a challenge to the appointment by a party of counsel in ICSID rules, that absent express provision the only justification for the tribunal to award itself the power would be an overriding and undeniable need to safeguard the essential integrity of the entire arbitral process, and what would constitute such a threat was not easy to discern. They said that they could see that such a risk based on a previous relationship between counsel and arbitrator might lead to a challenge to the tribunal, but a challenge to counsel of a party's choice should not be seen as an alternative to such an application. They pointed out that in a compelling case an order by the arbitrators to prevent a particular lawyer from appearing or signing 14–008

---

[16] ICSID ruling January 14, 2010. Unlike the usual position where arbitrations are confidential, many ICSID awards are published on the ICSID website.

a pleading might be of little use if he was entitled to continue advising the client in relation to the arbitration, and an order preventing the lawyer from advising the party or interviewing witnesses has obviously stark and far-reaching consequences. Whilst not needing to reach definitive views on the arbitrators' powers under ICSID rules, the tribunal stressed the real difficulties involved in making orders disqualifying counsel.

There is US caselaw on recusal of counsel in arbitrations, particularly in New York and Pennsylvania. Although it has been described as "underdeveloped"[17] it seems better developed than elsewhere. In *Bidermann Industries Licensing Inc v Amvar NV* the New York Court of Appeals said that:

> "issues of attorney disqualification involve interpretation and application of the Code of Professional Responsibility and Disciplinary Rules, as well as the potential deprivation of counsel of the client's choosing . . . and cannot be left to the determination of arbitrators selected by the parties themselves for their expertise in the particular industries engaged in".[18]

Although not all US courts have taken the same view, this is probably the favoured approach in the US. The courts have not merely suggested that arbitrators (who may be chosen as industry experts) are not equipped to decide this sort of dispute, but that because it raises public policy issues, the courts are better equipped. And it is said that the cheap and speedy resolution of disputes by arbitration will be compromised if arbitrators decide ancillary disputes of this nature.

None of these arguments are entirely persuasive: arbitrators may not be chosen as experts on procedure or foreign law either but they are still obliged to decide such issues when they arise in the course of the reference. Arbitration is often neither cheap nor speedy at the best of times, but it may be more convenient to have ancillary matters raised in the arbitration rather than starting separate proceedings in court. It is suggested that the more powerful arguments are those canvassed above,[19] which militate in favour of arbitrators having jurisdiction to determine disqualification issues, but that unless both parties positively ask them to resolve the issue, they should in any normal case leave it to the courts.

The issue raised in *Bidermann* has not been raised before the English courts. It is suggested that it is unlikely the English courts will decide to

---

[17] See "Conflicts of Interest Affecting Counsel in International Arbitrations", by J.L. Jacobus and A.J. Hefty, Mealey's International Arbitration Report August 2005, Vol 20 no 8. The article, whilst referring to US caselaw to the effect that it is for the courts to decide such matters, suggests that the better view is to permit arbitrators to make such decisions.
[18] 173 AD2d 401, 402.
[19] See 14–006.

follow the *Bidermann* approach. It is hard to see a basis on which arbitrators applying the English Arbitration Act could be said to have no *jurisdiction* to disbar counsel from appearing, whatever the arguments suggesting they should leave well alone.

C. Enforcement issues

Where the arbitrators are asked to make a decision disqualifying counsel, it is possible that their decision may give rise to an issue at the stage of enforcement of the award.

14–009

Where England is the seat of the arbitration, or where the English court otherwise has jurisdiction over the arbitration, a challenge to the award may be made on grounds of serious irregularity. By s.68 of the Arbitration Act 1996 "serious irregularity" means an irregularity of one or more of specified kinds which the court considers has caused or will cause substantial injustice to the applicant. The specified kinds of irregularity include:

(a) failure by the tribunal to comply with s.33 (general duty of the tribunal)
(b) the tribunal exceeding its powers (otherwise than by exceeding its substantive jurisdiction: see s.67)
(c) failure by the tribunal to conduct the proceedings in accordance with the procedure agreed by the parties.

The New York Convention on Enforcement of Arbitration Awards is the international convention on enforcement of foreign arbitral awards and applies in most jurisdictions. It is incorporated into English law by s.104 of the Arbitration Act 1996. Section 2(e) provides that recognition or enforcement of the award may be refused if the person against whom it is invoked proves:

"that the composition of the arbitral tribunal or the arbitral procedure was not in accordance with the agreement of the parties or, failing such agreement, with the law of the country in which the arbitration took place."

Section 104(3) further provides that recognition or enforcement of the award may also be refused if it would be contrary to public policy to recognize or enforce the award.

Decisions either involving an arbitrator standing down or disqualifying counsel may thus give rise to challenge in the courts. Where the arbitrators disqualify counsel on grounds of counsel holding confidential information or having a conflict of interest, the issue may be whether the arbitrators have gone beyond what is submitted above to be the jurisdiction available to them.

A particular problem may arise because as English law and conflicts rules take the view that no problem arises where counsel is associated with the same chambers as the arbitrator, the basis of the entitlement of the arbitrators to disqualify counsel or stand down on this ground may be suspect.

Thus if the arbitrators disqualify counsel on this ground, the party instructing counsel could argue that as the use of counsel in these circumstances was permissible under English law and conflict rules, they were deprived of their right to use the lawyer of choice for no good reason. It is not easy to see an answer to this, unless the rules of the arbitration permitted the course adopted by the arbitrators.

What if the arbitrator rather than counsel stepped down in such circumstances? It might be argued that in such circumstances there was no justification for the arbitrator stepping down, and that therefore there was a failure by the tribunal to conduct the proceedings in accordance with the procedure agreed by the parties, so that there was a serious irregularity within s.68(2)(c). Obviously, it depends on the rules of the arbitration body, but a challenge on this ground looks more difficult. In a foreign arbitration where the New York Convention was applicable, if English law was inapplicable, there might be a ready justification in the arbitrator standing down, but under English law a party might rely on s.103(2)(e) arguing that the composition of the arbitral tribunal or the arbitral procedure was not in accordance with the agreement of the parties.

These possibilities militate further towards the arbitrators leaving decisions as to disqualification of counsel to the courts. They cannot of course do the same in relation to a decision whether an arbitrator should himself stand down.

3. Conflicts through connections between arbitrators and counsel

14–010   In contrast to other judicial conflicts, most of the conflicts issues involving arbitrations involve relationships or prior relationships between arbitrator and counsel. A particular problem arises because English counsel often share chambers with arbitrators and, as self-employed practitioners, are permitted by English bar rules to act in cases against other members of their chambers. Other conflicts arise because often English counsel themselves practice both as arbitrators and counsel.

A. Counsel in the same chambers as the arbitrator

14–011   English barristers are self-employed. They practice from chambers. Because they do not practice in partnership they are permitted to act in cases against other members of chambers and this practice has been sanctioned by the courts.[20] English barristers who sit as arbitrators, either full time or as an adjunct to their practice as barristers, will normally be members of a set of chambers. This gives rise to two sets of problems. Firstly, the possibility arises that one of the parties will be represented by counsel in the same chambers as the arbitrator. Secondly, an arbitrator who also practices as a barrister may find that he has a conflict by reason of clients whom he has acted for or advised.

English part-time judges who are barristers affiliated to chambers are not required to stand down in court proceedings if counsel appearing in front of them is a member of their chambers,[21] although the position is different if counsel is paid by a conditional fee arrangement, because in such circumstances the fact that barristers usually share chambers expenses on a pro rata basis means that the judge is regarded as having a more than minimal financial interest in the result of the proceedings.

However, these arrangements are often unfamiliar to foreign lawyers who may be uncomfortable with the position where an arbitrator appears in proceedings when counsel representing one of the parties is in the same chambers as the arbitrator. This has become an increasing problem in recent years.

Technically, so far as counsel is concerned, there is no bar on appearing in such circumstances under English conflict rules. English Bar rules do not prohibit it, and English caselaw sanctions the practice. The analysis is not the same for the arbitrator, because the test is different and the focus is on the more onerous test of apparent bias which only applies to decision makers and therefore not to counsel. There is no doubt that some arbitral tribunals take the view, when dealing with international parties, that an apparent bias issue is raised here. It would not arise under English law or conflicts rules, as there is caselaw recognising that a decision-maker would not be required to stand down in such circumstances.[22] But even where English law applies, arbitrators often remain uncomfortable where international parties are concerned.

The IBA Guidelines on Conflicts of Interest in International Arbitration[23] has a lengthy section in its Background Information issued by the Working Group on the problem of counsel being in the same chambers as an arbitrator at 4.5. The section explains in some detail the position of English barristers operating from the same chambers and states:

"While the peculiar nature of the constitution of barristers' chambers is well recognized and generally accepted in England by the legal

---

[20] *Laker Airways Inc v FLS Aerospace* [1999] 2 Lloyd's Rep. 45, see 16–008.
[21] See *Smith v Kvaerner Cementation* [2006] 3 All E.R. 593 see 11–020.
[22] *Smith v Kvaerner Cementation* [2006] 3 All E.R. 593.
[23] Published in (2004) Business Law International 433.

profession and by the courts, it is acknowledged by the Working Group that, to many who are not familiar with the workings of the English Bar, particularly in light of the content of the promotional material which many chambers now disseminate, there is an understandable perception that barristers' chambers should be treated in the same way as law firms. It is because of this perception that the Working Group decided to keep on the Orange list, and thus subject to disclosure, the situation in which the arbitrator and another arbitrator or counsel for one of the parties are members of the same barristers' chambers."

The reference to promotional materials points to the fact that many sets of chambers often present themselves, on websites and elsewhere, with a collective connotation, sometimes referring to different "teams" within chambers, referring to their collective mode of operation, the sharing of clerking facilities, and citing law directories enthusing as to their collective reputation.

The IBA Guidelines themselves put this type of conflict on their Orange List at 3.3.3:

"The arbitrator and another arbitrator or the counsel for one of the parties are members of the same barristers' chambers."

The Background Information section seeks to offer comfort to those concerned by these practices and, whilst emphasizing the importance of disclosure, seems to lean towards a view that no problem should arise. It states:

"there is a clear and obvious distinction to be drawn between barristers and law firms operating in these jurisdictions."[24]

It is notable that the situation where two members of the same chambers act as co-arbitrators is also on the Orange list.

14–012 In the *Hrvatska Elektroprivreda dd v Republic of Slovenia*[25] arbitration, considered below,[26] one of the parties notified the arbitrators that they intended to be represented by an English Q.C. associated with the same chambers as the president of the tribunal. The ruling of the panel referred to the English practice but in the light of the IBA Guidelines[27] took the view that if the Q.C. represented his clients before them, the president could not continue. On the facts, (discussed below) they made an order disqualifying the Q.C. from appearing.

---

[24] In addition to the position in England it refers to a similar situation in New Zealand.
[25] ICSID Case No ARB/05/24, May 6, 2008.
[26] 14–013.
[27] As explained above, the Guidelines alert arbitrators to the problem where counsel is in the same chambers, and require disclosure, but do not of themselves require the arbitrator to stand down. The panel seems to have been persuaded, however, without any additional grounds, that it was not possible for the president to continue in such circumstances.

This should not be an option in most cases, because as a matter of English law and conflict rules, the Q.C. has done nothing improper. So, unless the rules of the arbitral panel say differently, there will only be two options: do nothing, or stand down the arbitrator. As explained above, this should not technically be necessary in an English law arbitration, as under English law there is no apparent bias, but, as in the *Hrvatska* arbitration, many international arbitrators will not feel comfortable here.

However this in itself creates problems. Counsel may be instructed at a late stage. If the effect of instructing counsel associated with the same chambers as the arbitrator is that the arbitrator must stand down, this is very unsatisfactory. It leaves open the possibility of arbitrator-shopping. For example, an arbitrator has made a number of negative comments against a party in the course of an interlocutory hearing and that party takes the view that he has shown a hostility to them. Can the party require the arbitrator to stand down by instructing new counsel in the arbitrator's chambers?

There is no simple solution to the problem. English arbitrators associated with chambers might at least ensure that their chambers websites and publicity material provide a separation (or separate website) as between the arbitrators and the advocates in chambers. However that might be seen as merely cosmetic and in any event a number of the members of chambers will combine advocacy with sitting as arbitrators. Another possibility is that the parties could reach an enforceable agreement at the commencement of the arbitration that they will not instruct counsel in the same chambers as the arbitrators they have chosen, although reaching such an agreement will not always be practical.

B. Conflicts between counsel and arbitrators: caselaw

As arbitrations are confidential, decisions are not in the usual course publicly available. One that has become publicly available is the ICSID ruling in *Hrvatska Elektroprivreda dd v Republic of Slovenia*.[28] When the respondent sent to the arbitrators a list of attendees at the hearing, they included an English Q.C. The president of the tribunal was a door tenant at the Q.C.'s chambers, although he had never had any personal relationship with the Q.C.

14–013

The issue of arbitrators being associated with the same chambers as advocates in the case has created problems, and is discussed above. However, in the light of the opposition of the claimant, the panel decided that the president could not continue to sit if the Q.C. remained in the case. Neither of the parties wanted the president to change and the panel referred in their judgment to the principle under ICSID rules of "the immutability

---

[28] ICSID Case No ARB/05/24, May 6, 2008.

of properly constituted tribunals". The panel took the view that they had power under ICSID arbitration rules to deal with any issues necessary for the conduct of matters falling within the jurisdiction of the arbitration, and thus ruled that the continued participation of the Q.C. in the case would be inappropriate and improper.

So the tribunal took the view that their procedural powers did give them power to order that the Q.C. not participate further in the case. The panel took the view that the president could not continue to act in these circumstances because the connection with the Q.C. would give rise to apparent bias. Logically, therefore, he would have to stand down. But in the light of the desire of all parties that the arbitral tribunal continue as constituted, the alternative consequence, that they make an order barring the Q.C., produced a satisfactory result. The argument of the party instructing the Q.C. was that there was no need for either arbitrator or Q.C. to stand down; if one of these courses was held to be required, they do not seem to have suggested that it was the arbitrator that should stand down.

Whilst this decision is support (at least in ICSID cases) for the power of arbitrators to bar counsel from representing clients before them, it looks very much a one-off decision (and was so treated by the panel in *Rompetrol*) and leaves most questions unanswered. Could the Q.C. go on assisting and advising the party and could the arbitrators stop him from doing so?[29] The respondent seems to have made it easy for the panel by saying that they did not want to replace the president. In a normal case, where the party wants to stick with its lawyers, the logical consequence is that the arbitrator will need to be replaced as the lawyer has done nothing wrong, yet under the different test of apparent bias which applies to decision-makers, it is (if anyone) the arbitrator and not the lawyer who has a problem. And the tribunal, pointing out that the claimant had helpfully accepted that the withdrawal of the Q.C. (whatever was encompassed by that) would "eliminate the problem entirely" tantalisingly commented:

> "The position could be different if a party objects, on reasonable grounds, that its opponent's case has been irretrievably infused with decisive strategic contributions from the counsel in question in memorials and other important written submissions embodying that party's position, with the consequence that withdrawal of counsel would not be a complete and satisfactory solution."

It is not clear what the panel thought would be an appropriate solution in a case where that arose.

14–014 A more conventional conflict arose in another ICSID case.[30] The respond-

---

[29] The order made was that the Q.C. "may not participate further as counsel in this case".
[30] Not identified deliberately as it has not been published in the ICSID website.

ent objected that the lead lawyer for the claimant had represented him in related proceedings. The tribunal ruled on the disqualification issue. It concluded, as did the *Hrvatska* tribunal, that it had power to disqualify counsel from acting as counsel before it, but did not have "deontological responsibilities or jurisdiction over the parties' legal representatives in their own capacities". The tribunal declined to consider local Bar ethical rules put before it but considered "what general principles are plainly indispensible for the fair conduct of the proceedings". The tribunal declined to rely on presumptions as to whether the lawyer had received relevant confidential information in the previous retainer, considered whether there was evidence that he had, and concluded that there was no such evidence.

A recent LCIA award[31] considered a challenge to a Q.C. appointed as arbitrator by the non-appointing party. Three Lloyds syndicates were respondents. The Q.C. disclosed at the outset that as a barrister specializing in insurance disputes he would in the normal course act for and against Lloyds syndicates and often would not be aware of the identity of the particular syndicate. The Q.C. was pressed into making a series of further more detailed disclosures in the course of which he disclosed that over the couple of months since his initial appointment, he had been instructed in one case against (among other syndicates) a respondent syndicate and on another case where the reinsurers included a respondent syndicate and had had two new sets of instructions from the solicitors who appointed him. He also disclosed that in the last five years about 11% of his instructions (including some substantial cases) derived from the solicitors who had appointed him. The LCIA set up a special panel to review whether to uphold the objection and duly ruled so to do. They were very critical of the fact that the Q.C. had not voluntarily disclosed either of the two post-appointment sets of instructions involving respondents nor the fact that he had received two new sets of instructions from the solicitors that appointed him. They cited the Swiss Supreme Court decision in *Hitachi Ltd SMS v Schloemann Siemag Aktiengesellschaft*[32] which held that the independence of the arbitrator might be questioned if he or she draws an important part of his or her revenues from an ongoing relationship with the counsel of the appointing party. They criticized the disclosures by the Q.C. as being "by and large general, selective and incomplete".

It was not unusual that the Q.C. had acted (or was acting) for and against one of the respondent syndicates: most insurance and reinsurance disputes concerning the Lloyds market involve a number of syndicates. Nor was it surprising that 11% of his instructions over the previous five year period came from his appointors and that he had accepted two sets of instructions from them since his initial appointment. What was surprising, and

---

[31] LCIA Ref 81160, August 28, 2009 reported at Arbitration International, Vol 27, Issue 3 p.442.
[32] June 30, 1994.

disturbing, was that the LCIA panel thought that the 11% figure was sufficient to give rise to apparent bias. An application of the *Porter v Magill* test would have been very unlikely to have disqualified the Q.C. on the ground that he received regular instructions from his appointors, although if he was acting for and against one of the respondent syndicates, he owed a fiduciary duty in each particular case in relation to that party which was inconsistent with his acting as an arbitrator in relation to that party without consent.

Just as this edition was about to go to press, Flaux J. decided *A v B*.[33] The sole arbitrator in an LCIA arbitration was a Q.C. who had previously acted for clients instructed by each of the sets of solicitors involved in the arbitration. A case in which he had been instructed by the defendants' solicitors had been stayed at the time of his appointment but unexpectedly became active after his appointment and the arbitrator advised and was to be instructed on the trial as counsel. The arbitrator inadvertently failed to disclose that instruction until just before delivering his award. The LCIA appointed one of the members of its Court to rule on the challenge to the award, which was rejected. Flaux J., hearing the matter de novo on an application to set aside the award, rejected the apparent bias claim, rejected the contention that the situation fell within the IBA Red List and held that the application did not satisfy the *Magill* test, which he held applied to arbitrators. Nor did the failure of the arbitrator to make prompt disclosure provide an alternative argument under s.68 of the Arbitration Act: either the disclosure would have given rise to a successful challenge or, if not, the failure to make disclosure could not put the defendants in a better position. Flaux J. recognised that apparent bias might arise if the arbitrator received as barrister a substantial proportion of his instructions as counsel from one of the solicitors' firms instructed in the arbitration, but in indicating what he meant by "substantial proportion" he said "say 60%"[34] which, although not intended as a precise ruling, presents a very striking contrast with the 11% figure which was regarded as sufficient for apparent bias to arise in the LCIA award referred to at footnote 31 above.

C. Counsel and arbitrators: discussion

14–015 There is no doubt that the arbitration community are sensitive to the views of foreign clients who do not understand and are not comfortable with the English rule that there is no conflict between counsel acting against each other in the same chambers. If they take the view that arbitration organisations should make rules forbidding this, then that is for them to decide. What is less satisfactory is the failure to grapple with the juridical

---

[33] [2011] EWHC 2345 (Comm).
[34] [62].

basis for such an exception. The IBA rules do not require disqualification on such a ground. Nor does *Porter v Magill*. An inexperienced litigant before the English courts might have all sorts of legitimate concerns from the fact that the part-time judge was in the same chambers as opposing counsel, but the fair-minded observer who knew the facts would be taken to know that there was no reason to be concerned.[35] So as a matter of English law and practice, the foreign client who is concerned about the arbitrator being connected with the same chambers as counsel should have no better right to object. Yet that is not how it seems to be perceived amongst the arbitration community.

The international arbitration community may take the view that in order to maintain confidence in the process of international arbitration, it is unsatisfactory that counsel and arbitrator are connected in this way. But the proper means of doing this is for bodies such as the ICC, ICSID or LCIA to develop arbitration rules which make the position clear rather than purporting to apply English law in a way which is incorrect.

---

[35] See 16–008.

CHAPTER 15

Solicitors

15–001　Most of the conflicts cases involve lawyers. It is therefore inevitable that much of the part of this book relating to the general law deals with issues or cases that relate to lawyers. It is difficult to keep the principles of general application separate from those which apply to lawyers, particularly as the cases tend not to make clear whether the points are points of general principle or points which apply specifically to lawyers.

1. The Code of Conduct

A. New rules in force

15–002　The last edition of this book referred in detail to the new rules which had come into force as the Code of Conduct for solicitors. Now the rules have changed again. On July 1, 2007, the new Solicitors' Code of Conduct 2007 came into force, incorporating the new conflict rules that were already in force.[1] From August 2011, the SRA[2] commences its phased implementation, with the key implementation date being October 6, 2011. The new rules involve Outcomes Focused Regulation.

B. Status of the new rules in court

15–003　The Code of Conduct 2011 is made under the powers given to the Law Society[3] by s.31 of the Solicitors Act 1974, which gives the Law Society

---

[1] Only the rule numbers changed.
[2] Solicitors' Regulation Authority, the regulatory body for solicitors.
[3] The Law Society is an Approved Regulator for the purpose of the Legal Services Act 2007, and the SRA is its regulatory arm.

power to make rules, and s.9 and 9A of the Administration of Justice Act 1985, in the case of LLPs. Since the Legal Services Act 2007, the rules require the approval of the Legal Services Board.[4] The rules take effect in the same way as statutory instrument.[5]

In *Swain v Law Society*[6] the House of Lords held that rules made under Pt II of the Solicitors Act 1974, which gives the Law Society powers (including s.31) to make rules in the public interest, had effect as subordinate legislation under the Act. What the Law Society does under those powers gives rise to public law remedies. In *Swain* Lord Diplock did not decide whether rules made under those statutory powers would give rise to a private law cause of action but recognised that they might well do so. Whether secondary legislation gives rise to a claim for breach of statutory duty depends on whether the person making the claim is the person for whose benefit the legislation is enacted and whether Parliament intended that there would be a private law remedy for breach.[7] The legislation is plainly for the benefit of the client, but s.31(2) of the Act states:

> "If any solicitor fails to comply with rules made under this section, any person may make a complaint in respect of that failure to the [Solicitors' Disciplinary] Tribunal."

It could be argued that the express reference to a tribunal remedy was an indication that breach of rules made under s.31 was not intended to provide private law remedies for breach. If that were the case, a client seeking to sue or obtain an injunction for breach would need to rely on common law remedies, and the Code could not be relied upon for that purpose. The issue as to whether a private litigant can sue a solicitor for breach of statutory duty as a result of breach of the code of conduct has not yet been decided.[8] But there is an argument that clients should be entitled to rely upon the rules against the solicitor in this way. Another possibility is that it may be an implied term of the contract of retainer that the solicitor will comply with the legal requirements of his profession,[9] which will have the effect of incorporating the rules into the contract of retainer.[10]

---

[4] See para.19 of Sch. 4 of the Legal Services Act 2007.
[5] See *Swain v Law Society* [1983] 1 A.C. 598, per Lord Diplock, making clear that this was the effect of rules made by the Law Society under the Solicitors Act 1974.
[6] [1983] 1 A.C. 598.
[7] See the discussion in *Clerk & Lindsell on Torts* 20th edn, para.9—11ff.
[8] See Arden L.J. in *Garbett v Edwards* [2005] EWCA Civ 1206 at [37] although this does not determine the position now.
[9] But it may be argued that such an implied term does not fulfil the criteria of necessity and thus should not be incorporated into the contract: see Flenley & Leech, *Solicitors Negligence and Liability*, 2nd edn (2008) at 2.15. The authors take the view that a breach of the Code may well be the starting point in proving negligence or breach of duty, see, e.g. *Omega Trust Co Ltd v Wright Son & Pepper (No 2)* [1998] P.N.L.R. 337, 347D–E, but does not of necessity involve breach of duty. It is for consideration whether that analysis applies to the conflicts rules.
[10] In *Johnson v Bingley Dyson and Finney* [1995] P.N.L.R. 392 it was argued that it was an

That leaves the residual question: do the rules become the exclusive basis on which solicitors act, or is the common law still relevant? Whilst as time goes on, the professional rules may become the principal basis on which the conduct of solicitors is regulated by the courts, there seems no basis for the rules altering the common law. If for some reason the rules provide lesser obligations than the common law, the courts are likely to remain vigilant to protect the rights of litigants. Moreover, it will be apparent from reading this book that the rules do not cover all areas of a solicitor's obligations relating to conflicts. So it is important not to treat the rules as the exclusive source of a solicitor's obligation.

Outcomes focused regulation involves less emphasis on detailed rules, and greater emphasis on high-level principles and required outcomes. As the SRA say:

> "Outcomes-focused regulation focuses on the high-level principles and outcomes that should drive the provision of legal services for consumers. It will see the current detailed and prescriptive rulebook replaced with a targeted, risk-based approach concentrating on the standards of service to consumers. There will be greater flexibility for firms in how they achieve outcomes (standards of service) for clients."

Whatever view one may take about outcomes focused regulation, in conflicts of interest one needs clear and precise rules. Not surprisingly, therefore, the new SRA rules on conflicts of interest follow much the same scheme as their predecessors. The substance of the rules is similar to the former rr. 3 and 4 of the SRA Code of Conduct 2007. The extensive (and very helpful) guidance has gone, and there are some general sections as to desired outcomes to fit the scheme of the new Code.

The structure of the new rules is to set out rules, then to set out Outcomes which must be achieved ("you have effective systems in place to enable you to identify and assess potential conflicts of interest"). The Outcomes include specific prohibitions on acting and exceptions where the solicitor may act. There are then "Indicative Behaviours" listed. Acting in the ways specified may tend to show the solicitor has achieved the outcomes and complied with the principles set out in the Code, and the converse: acting in other specified ways may tend to show that the solicitor has not achieved the outcomes and thus not complied with the principles. The definitions section is more extensive than before but there is no Guidance.

---

implied term of the contract of retainer that the solicitor will comply with the professional rules in place (then the Guide to the Professional Conduct of Solicitors, which admittedly had a different status, not being by way of statutory instrument). The point was not decided.

2. SRA Code of Conduct Ch.3: Conflicts of interest

A. The Conflict of Interest Rule

The Code treats the Confidentiality and Disclosure Rule (Ch. 4) separately from Conflicts of Interest (Ch. 3). Chapter 3 distinguishes client conflicts from "own interest" conflicts:

15–004

> "You can never act where there is a conflict, or a significant risk of conflict, between you and your client.
>
> If there is a conflict, or a significant risk of a conflict, between two or more current clients, you must not act for all or both of them unless the matter falls within the scope of the limited exceptions set out at Outcomes 3.6 and 3.7. In deciding whether to act in these limited circumstances, the overriding consideration will be the best interests of each of the clients concerned and, in particular, whether the benefits to the clients of you acting for all or both of the clients outweigh the risks."

The definition of "conflict of interest" largely replicates the old definition. It means any situation where:

> "(a) You owe separate duties to act in the best interest of two or more clients in relation to the same or related matters, and those duties conflict, or there is a significant risk that those duties may conflict; or
>
> (b) Your duty to act in the best interests of any client in relation to a matter conflicts, or there is a significant risk that it may conflict, with your own interests in relation to that or a related matter."[11]

The effect of this is (subject to the exceptions set out) to restrict existing client conflicts to the same or related matters. This is significant. Ever since Lord Millett in *Bolkiah* said without qualification that a man may not act on a matter where he or his partner already acts in an adverse interest unless both clients consent, it has been for consideration whether there is any limitation on the principle. The point is discussed at para.3–012 above. In *Marks & Spencer Plc v Freshfields*[12] both Lawrence Collins J. and the Court of Appeal, the latter giving full reasons for refusing leave to appeal, rejected the argument that Lord Millett's comments were limited to where

---

[11] The only difference is that the old definition made clear that a related matter would always include any other matter which involves the same asset or liability.

[12] June 2, 2004, Lawrence Collins J.; June 3, 2004, CA giving full reasons for refusing leave to appeal.

the matter was the same (which could never have been right, given that the principle is based on competing fiduciary obligations), but accepted obiter that there must be "some reasonable relationship" between the matters.[13] By contrast, in Canada, a lawyer may not act for and against the same client at the same time even on unrelated matters.[14]

When are two matters related? It seems the test will simply be that there is sufficient relationship between the two matters that one may sensibly regard the fiduciary obligations to the two clients as being in conflict.[15] In other words, it reflects the common law, and is intended to make clear that the Canadian ban on acting on other sides in unrelated matters does not apply here.

Outcomes (3.6) and (3.7) provide for specified exceptions to the prohibition where there is an existing client conflict and both clients give informed consent to the solicitor or the firm acting. This continues to be significantly more restrictive than the common law. At common law, a solicitor can act for two parties who have adverse interests with the informed consent of both, so long as he can perform his duty to each client as if that were his only client. Chapter 3 prohibits a solicitor from acting even with informed consent unless one of the two relatively limited exceptions is applicable. To this extent, therefore, the solicitor is being prevented from doing something permitted at common law with client consent.

B. The common interest exception

15–005

The first exception is where there is a common interest. Where all the clients have given informed consent in writing, the solicitor may act if the clients have "a substantially common interest in relation to that matter or a particular aspect of it." One might construe this narrowly or broadly, but the expression is now a defined term:

> "a situation where there is a clear common purpose in relation to any matter or a particular aspect of it between the clients and a strong consensus on how it is to be achieved and the client conflict is peripheral to this common purpose."

---

[13] Both courts approached the point on the basis that there had to be some limitation on what Lord Millett said but recognised that what he said could not be read as limited to same matter conflicts. They did not need to decide the precise limit of the principle. The judgments were extempore and the matter was heard as a matter of great urgency. So it is necessary to be careful not to place too much weight on the precise expression adopted by the courts here.
[14] *R. v Neil* [2002] S.C.C. 70, per Binnie J. at [29] see 3–014 above.
[15] See the Singapore High Court decision in *Vorobiev Nikolay v Lush John Frederick Peters* [2010] SGHC 290 which after reviewing ethical rules in the US and UK held that matters would be related if they involved the same asset or liability or the same transaction or legal dispute.

The common purpose exception is likely to arise where more than one individual or entity instructs the solicitor jointly, whether because they are family members, business partners or joint venturers. An issue arises where their interests differ. Rather than the trouble and expense of instructing a new firm, it might be better for different solicitors in the firm to protect the respective interests of the two parties. It would be in the clients' interests because it would be cost efficient. In niche areas, it would be in the client's interests that both clients could call on the expertise of the firm. There would normally be an agreement that the solicitor would not be required to pass information learned from one to the other.[16]

Other circumstances where there may be a common purpose will be in relation to sophisticated users of legal services—different tiers of lenders entering into a financing structure where there is already an agreed or commonly understood structure. More often, this will fall within the other exception[17] where the clients are competing for the same asset. In one sense, two parties to a proposed transaction who want to reach agreement could always be said to have a "common purpose" to reach agreement, but this is not what the exception has in mind. It is only likely to be possible to come within this exception if the structure has already been agreed, for example where joint venture companies are bidding for a project but then need to enter into an agreement between themselves in circumstances where they have already agreed or understand the basic terms and structure.

Negative indicative behaviour IB (3.11) relates to the situation when the clients' interests in the end result are not the same, although this seems confusing as in such a situation surely the absolute ban on acting save where the exception applies is determinative? IB (3.12) refers to where it is unreasonable to act for both because of unequal bargaining power. It is notable that IB (3.6) (only acting where the clients are sophisticated users of legal services) is directed merely at the "same objective" exception, which seems to indicate that it does not provide a restriction on this exception.

C. Competing for the same objective

The other exception where the solicitor may act with the informed written consent of both clients is if the clients are competing for the same objective. This is defined as follows: 15–006

> "any situation in which two or more clients are competing for an "objective" which, if attained by one client, will make that "objective" unattainable to the other client or clients and "objective" means . . . an

---

[16] See Chapter 6 and *Hilton v Barker Booth & Eastwood* [2005] 1 W.L.R. 567.
[17] Discussed at 15–006 below.

asset contract or business opportunity which one or more clients are seeking to acquire or recover through a liquidation (or some other form of insolvency process) or by means of an auction or tender process or a bid or offer which is not public."

Thus the objective need not necessarily be something physical: it can include a contract or a business opportunity, it will include acting on insolvencies so that a firm can act for more than one creditor, acting for competing bidders, or those involved with the funding of bidders, for a business being sold by auction, or acting for competing tenderers submitting tenders to perform a contract.

This exception will probably cover more cases than the "common purpose" exception. It will certainly be more important for city firms as it is geared towards sophisticated users of legal services. Whereas the common purpose exception will usually arise where the firm is acting for parties on the same side already and will enable the firm to act when on specific issues the clients' interests diverge, the same objective exception will usually arise where the firm would otherwise be unable to accept the second retainer because it has an existing retainer for a different party whose interest conflicts. It is used where the firm wants to act for more than one party bidding against each other, or more commonly where it acts for one party to the proposed deal and to another party who is a financier or a financial adviser where there may be said to be some adverse interest.

Indicative behaviour IB(3.6) refers to only acting under this exception where the clients are sophisticated users of legal services. This is significant.

D. Other Ch. 3 requirements

15–007 a) **Reasonableness** In relation to both exceptions, there is a requirement of reasonableness. As so long as he can serve the interests of each client as if each was his only client, the solicitor would always be able to act at law, it could be said that it was usually reasonable for the solicitor to do what, apart from the rule, was permissible at law. This is of particular importance where the clients are not sophisticated users of legal services.

15–008 b) **Informed consent** Where relying on either of the exceptions, there is a requirement of informed consent. The requirement is worded differently in the two cases. In relation to common interest, there is simply an informed consent requirement. The solicitor must draw all the relevant issues to the attention of the clients and have a reasonable belief that the clients understand the relevant issues.

In relation to competing for the same objective, the clients must confirm in writing that they want the solicitor to act in the knowledge that the solicitor acts or may act for one or more other clients who are competing for the same objective. The different wording probably reflects that the SRA do not contemplate that the competing for the same objective exception will apply other than in relation to sophisticated users of legal services, and there will be circumstances where confidentiality prevents full disclosure. However, in some cases the confidentiality of the second retainer may make this provision difficult to comply with. Will it be sufficient to obtain client consent in general terms at the outset of the retainer, for example in standard terms and conditions? If so, the requirement that the client has confirmed in writing means that sending a client the terms and conditions will not be adequate-at the very least the client must have signed the terms. The prudent course seems to be both to rely on signed standard terms covering the point in general terms and a more specific discussion to the extent that confidentiality permits at the time when the issue arises.

3. SRA Code of Conduct Ch.4: The Confidentiality and Disclosure Rule

A. The Confidentiality and Disclosure Rule

Chapter 4 provides for the duty of confidentiality: 15–009

"The duty of confidentiality to all clients must be reconciled with the duty of disclosure to clients. This duty of disclosure is limited to information of which you are aware which is material to your client's matter. Where you cannot reconcile these two duties, then the protection of confidential information is paramount. You should not continue to act for a client for whom you cannot disclose material information, except in very limited circumstances, where safeguards are in place."

The SRA continues to state that the duty of confidentiality takes precedence over the duty of disclosure: see O(4.3), which is not consistent with the decision of the House of Lords in *Hilton v Barker Booth & Eastwood*.[18] If the duties clash, the solicitor must cease to act. Of course the obligation of confidentiality is of fundamental importance, but it is not clear why the SRA continues to assert a precedence between these obligations. Indicative behaviour IB (4.4) recognises that the client may agree to contract out of the duty of disclosure. The client must give informed consent to non-disclosure or a different standard of disclosure.

---

[18] [2005] 1 W.L.R. 567 see 6–010.

B. Information barriers

15-010   The 2007 Code of Conduct originally prohibited acting with information barriers without client consent save where the solicitor was already acting or in a matter related thereto. Those restrictions, which were significantly more onerous than the common law, were seen as unnecessary, and the rules were liberalised. Outcome O(4.4) requires that:

> "you do not act for A in a matter where A has an interest adverse to B, and B is a client for whom you hold confidential information which is material to A in that matter, unless the confidential information can be protected by the use of safeguards, and
> (a) You reasonably believe that A is aware of, and understands, the relevant issues and gives informed consent;
> (b) either
>   (i) B gives informed consent and you agree with B the safeguards to protect B's information; or
>   (ii) Where this is not possible, you put in place effective safeguards including information barriers which comply with the common law; and
> (c) It is reasonable in all the circumstances to act for A with such safeguards in place."

The definition of "client" includes former clients. In this provision, B is the former client. So in order for the solicitor to act for A, A must give informed consent to the solicitor acting notwithstanding holding confidential information of a former client. Either the former client must also give informed consent, or "where this is not possible" information barriers are put in place. Under the previous Code, it was made clear that the former client had to be asked for consent if at all possible.[19] The words "where this is not possible" suggest the position remains the same.

Indicative Behaviour IB (4.5) refers to not acting for a client for whom the solicitor holds confidential information "unless the confidential information can be protected". Note 2 to Ch. 4 states that it may be difficult to implement effective safeguards and information barriers where the clients are not sophisticated users of legal services.[20] The same note also points out that it may be difficult to maintain effective information barriers where the physical structure or layout of the firm means that it will be difficult to preserve confidentiality.

So the rule now requires informed consent of the new client, and permits

---

[19] 2007 Rule 4 Guidance para.37 "You should always seek consent when you can reasonably do so."
[20] Surely the efficacy of information barriers is dependent on the systems operated by the law firm, rather than the nature of the client? This is difficult to understand.

acting without the consent of the former client with information barriers, but requires the solicitor to seek the consent of the former client if possible.

As previously, this Outcome applies where client A has an "interest adverse" to former client B. But the problem of the solicitor holding relevant confidential information does not depend on whether there is an adverse interest between new and former client. "Adverse interest" must mean adverse legal interest, not commercial interest. The problem most commonly arises in acting for group companies. The solicitor acts for company B. He then seeks to act for company A. Where the other party to the transaction, or the litigation, is a different company in B's group, there will be no adverse interest between A and B. Yet the confidential information amassed whilst the solicitor acted for B may be highly material to the matter in which the solicitor acts for A. The absence of a conflict between the clients may be relevant to the question whether there is in fact a real risk of disclosure or misuse of the confidential information of the first client,[21] but that is as far as it goes. The SRA can fairly complain that the words "adverse interest" are derived from Lord Millett in *Bolkiah*,[22] but neither Lord Millett nor the SRA recognise that there will be circumstances where the solicitor holds confidential information for a former client who does not have an adverse interest yet still must decline to act. The solicitor may, for example, not be able to act because he owes the new client an obligation to disclose relevant information of the former client and owes the former client, who has no adverse interest to the new client, a duty not to disclose the same information. It does not matter whether the former client has an adverse interest or any interest at all. It still presents a problem.[23]

The new Code omits the parts of its predecessor which suggested principles for information barriers. It is perhaps useful to repeat what the old Guidance said in this regard[24]:

15–011

"(a) that the client who or which might be interested in the confidential information acknowledges in writing that the information held by the firm will not be given to them:
(b) that all members of the firm who hold the relevant confidential information ("the restricted group") are identified and have no involvement with or for the other client;
(c) that no member of the restricted group is managed or supervised in relation to that matter by someone from outside of the restricted group;
(d) that all members of the restricted group confirm at the start of

---

[21] See Toulson and Phipps, *Confidentiality* 2nd edn, 16–010.
[22] Discussed at 7–005.
[23] The issue was previously flagged up in the r.4 Guidance para.30 but there now seems no reference to it in the Indicative Behaviours or Outcomes.
[24] Para.45.

the engagement that they understand that they possess or might come to possess information which is confidential, and that they must not discuss it with any other member of the firm unless that person is, or becomes a member of the restricted group, and that this obligation shall be regarded by everyone as an ongoing one;

(e) that each member of the restricted group confirms when the barrier is established that they have not done anything which would amount to a breach of the information barrier; and

(f) that only members of the restricted group have access to documents containing the confidential information."

The 2007 Code Guidance also stated that the following arrangements may also be appropriate, and might in particular be necessary where acting in circumstances where the former client has not consented:

"(g) that the restricted group is physically separated from those acting for the other client, for example, by being in a separate building, on a separate floor or in a segregated part of the offices, and that some form of "access restriction" be put in place to ensure physical segregation;

(h) that confidential information on computer systems is protected by use of separate computer networks or through use of password protection or similar means;

(i) that the firm issues a statement that it will treat any inadvertent breach of the information barrier as a serious disciplinary offence;

(j) that each member of the restricted group gives a written statement at the start of the engagement that they understand the terms of the information barrier and will comply with them;

(k) that the firm undertakes that it will do nothing which would or might prevent or hinder any member of the restricted group from complying with the information barrier;

(l) that the firm identifies a specific partner or other appropriate person within the restricted group' with overall responsibility for the information barrier;

(m) that the firm provides formal and regular training for members of the firm on duties of confidentiality and responsibility under information barriers or will ensure that such training is provided prior to the engagement being undertaken; and

(n) that the firm implements a system for the opening of post, receipt of faxes and misattribution of email which will ensure that confidential information is not disclosed to anyone outside the restricted group.

"Member" in the context of this note, applies to principals and all staff members, including secretaries but does not apply to any staff member (not having any involvement on behalf of any relevant client) whose duties include the maintenance of computer systems or conflict/compliance procedures and who is subject to a general obligation of confidentiality in relation to all information to which he or she may have access in the course of his or her duties."

4. The new rules—discussion

The SRA rules have changed significantly since this book was first published. In 2004 the long-discredited Guide to the Professional Conduct of Solicitors, containing a curious farrago of rules and advice, many of which were inconsistent with the law, was repealed. Our initial instinct was to query the need for rules which were significantly more restrictive than the common law, although the profession ultimately appeared to welcome a prescriptive set of rules. Such drafting problems as appeared at the outset were largely ironed out over time. The information barrier rules were in due course liberalised so that, at least in relation to dealing with sophisticated clients, they ceased to be significantly and unjustifiably restrictive in circumstances where no consent to acting was forthcoming from the former client.

15–012

Whilst one can debate whether the new approach is as useful as the old code with its detailed and helpful Guidance, there is not much in the new Code to which one can seriously object. The conflict of interest rules on acting with client consent remain more restrictive than the law, for reasons which are not obvious, at least in relation to sophisticated clients (although the SRA did consult on the issue), but this is of much less significance than the restriction in relation to information barriers which the SRA has now got rid of.

In the last edition, we expressed concern that the framing of the Code would suggest to solicitors that this is a comprehensive Code setting out the solicitor's obligations in relation to conflicts of interest. Certainly that is not an obvious issue in the more laconic outcomes-focused 2011 Code. Some of the examples where the Code does not resolve all issues are given above, such as where a solicitor with confidential information may not act even if there is no "adverse interest". Other examples are where the circumstances are such that a wider test than that applied in *Bolkiah* applies[25] or where the solicitor holds relevant information subject to a duty of confidence owed to someone other than a client.[26] The less prescriptive outcome-focused 2011 Code may be preferable to its predecessor in this regard.

---

[25] See 7–005.
[26] See 8–003.

5. EU and Cross-border practice

15–013   The section of the 2007 Code which deals with cross-border practice does not appear in the new Code. Instead, each individual section contains a reference to overseas practice. In relation to Chs 3 and 4, it is merely stated that the outcomes in these chapters apply to overseas practice. So an English solicitor practising outside the UK has to comply with the Code in relation to conflicts.

Until the 2007 Code came into force, those involved in cross-border activity had to comply with the Law Society rules of conduct together with the CCBE Code of Conduct for Lawyers in the European Community (adopted on October 28, 1988, as interpreted by art.1 (the preamble) thereof and the Explanatory Memorandum and Commentary thereon prepared by the CCBE's Deontology Working Party and dated May 1989). The CCBE Code obligations are not dealt with separately now in the Code.

CCBE r.3.2.1 states:

> "A lawyer may not advise, represent or act on behalf of two or more clients in the same matter if there is a conflict, or a significant risk of a conflict, between the interests of those clients."

The other relevant provisions are 3.2.2 and 3.2.3:

> "3.2.2 A lawyer must cease to act for both clients when a conflict of interest arises between those clients and also whenever there is a risk of a breach of confidence or where his independence may be impaired
> 3.2.3 A lawyer must also refrain from acting for a new client if there is a risk of a breach of confidences entrusted to the lawyer by a former client or if the knowledge which the lawyer possesses of the affairs of the former client would give an undue advantage to the new client."

In precluding a lawyer from acting for either client in circumstances where the Code would permit the solicitor continuing to act for one client, the CCBE Code appears more restrictive here. Those drafting the Code do not seem to have considered that this needed to be covered. If the solicitor acting on cross-border work complies with Code Ch.3, and continues acting for one of two clients, might he find himself in breach of the CCBE Code?

6. Particular conflicts problems affecting solicitors outside the Code

This section considers problems specific to solicitors outside the Code.

A. A higher test for lawyers?

Both at first instance and in the Court of Appeal in *Bolkiah* it was originally argued on behalf of the accountants that the cases placed a higher burden on solicitors than on other professionals. The argument was based on privilege and the lawyer's role in the administration of justice. It was also said that solicitors have different obligations as to passing on information to other professionals; this proposition, which seems not to have been given importance in the Court of Appeal, is factually very suspect.[27]

15–014

From time to time other arguments have been used to justify the court's entitlement to demand the highest ethical standards from lawyers: the need for the public to have confidence in the integrity of the legal profession, the need to protect the client from the possible subsequent embarrassment of the solicitor when acting in a potential conflict situation which might oblige the solicitor to withdraw from the case and perhaps cause expense to the client, the ease with which information can unwittingly be communicated, the difficulty of accurately identifying what information is of importance because this will often only be determined subsequently by the evolution of future unforeseen events, and the fact that a client in order to prove breach of confidence may be forced to forfeit lawyer/client privilege.[28] It may also be said that one of the features about litigation is that the parties are directly hostile to each other, in that one is seeking to succeed against the other.[29] Lawyers are not always retained to conduct litigation, but the importance of the administration of justice provides sufficient justification to apply such rules to lawyers even when they are not conducting litigation.

In *Bolkiah,* some at least of the information which the accountants had was subject to litigation privilege. The accountants were not acting as auditors but providing litigation support services. The attempt to draw a distinction between lawyers and forensic accountants met no success on the facts of the case, and was abandoned in the course of argument in the House of Lords. In *Bolkiah*, the lower courts merely rejected the argument that in the instant case there was a difference.[30] In the House of Lords Lord Millett said:

---

[27] See the cases on the obligation of the solicitor to pass on information: Ch.6.
[28] This collection of arguments was assembled by the Law Commission Paper No.124, at 4.5.11.
[29] In *Re Solicitors (A Firm)* [1992] Q.B. 959 at 972, in his dissenting judgment Staughton L.J. said that the reason for the absolute bar in the double employment rule without consent of the client is the inherent conflict in the same firm being paid by both sides "to win". This may well be an inadequate and inaccurate explanation of the principle but it does provide a vivid pointer as to the difference between acting in litigation and in other matters.
[30] Waller L.J. in his dissenting judgment in the Court of Appeal at [1999] B.C.L.C. 46 said that he thought that if the defendants had been solicitors rather than accountants he had little doubt that an injunction would have been granted. This was because he thought the case for an injunction was stronger than in *Re Solicitors (A Firm)* [1992] 1 All E.R. 353.

"The duties of an accountant cannot be greater than those of a solicitor, and may be less, for information relating to his client's affairs which is in the possession of a solicitor is usually privileged as well as confidential. In the present case, however, some of the information obtained by KPMG is likely to have attracted litigation privilege, though not solicitor-client privilege, and it is conceded by KPMG that an accountant who provides litigation support services of the kind which they provided to Prince Jefri must be treated for present purposes in the same way as a solicitor".[31]

15–015 The citations in the authorities may emphasise the special position of lawyers, but there is nothing to indicate how this may enable a more relaxed approach to be taken elsewhere. Could the test for former client conflicts be lower than the "no real risk of disclosure"? Might the court take a more relaxed view of information barriers outside the legal profession? What can be gleaned from *Bolkiah* is that harsh rules are to be applied to lawyers and others involved in litigation. It seems likely that the *Bolkiah* rules will be applied to all those who accept fiduciary obligations in the context of the administration of justice. But what is the position beyond these situations? *Bolkiah* in fact leaves open the question whether the rules may on occasion differ for other professions. Certainly *Kelly v Cooper*[32] gives at least some support for a more relaxed view of conflicts for estate agents and stockbrokers. Where privilege does not arise, and where there is no issue as to the administration of justice, and where what is in issue is a fiduciary relationship which may be "less intense" than that between lawyer and client, or no fiduciary obligation at all, it may be that the courts would be prepared to adopt a more relaxed view.

In considering this issue, it is necessary to distinguish once again existing and former client conflicts. In the case of existing client conflicts, where the professional owes a fiduciary obligation of loyalty, there is no reason why the "double employment" rule and the analysis of Millett L.J. in *Mothew* should apply differently to other professionals. What may however be said is that although the same underlying principles apply in the case of all professionals, their application will depend upon the different obligations, tasks and manner of business of different types of profession. It is possible to see from cases such as *Kelly* that the courts will take cognisance of the manner of operating of different professions and seek to take the special factors into account in reaching their decision. It is not the rules, therefore, that are different but the way they operate. The better way of dealing with the point, therefore, is not to hold that one set of professionals inherently has a higher duty than another, but that the circumstances of the employment of

---

[31] [1999] 2 A.C. 222 at 234.
[32] [1993] A.C. 205, see para.4–016.

particular professionals will dictate the terms on which they are retained, as in *Kelly* in the case of estate agents.[33]

Outside the administration of justice, the justification for the harsher *Bolkiah* rule is the voluntary undertaking by the professional of a fiduciary relationship. It may well be that the courts will not impose *Bolkiah* principles where there is no pre-existing fiduciary relationship. To date, the courts have only relied on *Bolkiah* in this jurisdiction in respect of lawyers and forensic accountants, but there is equally no case where the court has declined to apply *Bolkiah* to another sort of professional. It is important to have in mind that Lord Millett in *Bolkiah* established rules for information barriers with reference to the procedures adopted by financial institutions in London and elsewhere.[34] So it might be said to be anomalous to adopt a different rule for conflicts in financial institutions, although the point remains open.[35] Elsewhere, it remains to be seen whether the courts will adopt a softer approach.

As has been seen,[36] in one respect other jurisdictions have adopted a higher test for lawyers and it is for consideration whether, and in what circumstances the English courts will do the same. That relates to the court's supervisory jurisdiction over solicitors, where Australian and New Zealand courts have held that the court has jurisdiction to prohibit lawyers from acting where the reasonable informed observer would consider that the proper administration of justice was affected. There has been no suggestion that this rule, based on old common law authority relating to the special position of a lawyer, could be applied to other professions.

15–016

B. Termination of the retainer

One issue which arises for solicitors in seeking to determine whether they can act or continue to act is whether a client can properly be regarded as an existing or former client, and if an existing client, whether it will be possible to terminate the retainer. It was a matter of importance in *Young v Robson Rhodes*.[37] The retainer and its terms will usually be set out or evidenced by a written document from the solicitor.[38] But the document may not provide the crucial information as to the extent of the retainer. In the absence of any

15–017

---

[33] This is how the point was dealt with by Waller L.J. in the Court of Appeal [1999] B.C.L.C. 1 at 45.
[34] [1999] 2 A.C. 222 at 238.
[35] See para.19–003.
[36] See Ch.5.
[37] [1999] 3 All E.R. 524, Laddie J. see para.8–006.
[38] In the 2007 Code Rule 2.01 (2) provided that the solicitor must not cease acting for a client except for good reason and on reasonable notice. Now Outcome O(1.3) simply requires the solicitor when deciding whether to terminate instructions, to comply with the law and the Code.

agreement to the contrary, the general rule is that when the client retains a solicitor, the solicitor contracts to finish the business for which he is retained.[39] This applies both to contentious[40] and non-contentious business.[41] However, it may be varied either by particular circumstances or by agreement.[42]

The client may terminate the retainer at any time and for any reason. The solicitor's right to determine the retainer may depend on whether the retainer is treated as an entire contract. Where the retainer is to sue a third party for breach of contract or to convey property, the retainer will normally be an entire contract, a single job. If the solicitor is employed to do non-contentious work for the client over a period of time on the basis that bills are to be rendered and paid as matters proceed, and the client obtains benefit from each item of work completed, the contract is not an entire contract.[43] If the contract is not entire the solicitor may terminate the retainer where the client fails to perform his part of the bargain.[44] The solicitor may terminate for good cause and on reasonable notice. The retainer may also terminate by operation of law, for example where the solicitor becomes bankrupt or mad.

Where the contract is entire, the solicitor must not terminate the retainer except for good reason and on reasonable notice. The solicitor who terminates the retainer wrongfully cannot sue for his fees.[45] "Good reason" appears to include the following:

(a) Where the solicitor is asked to do something dishonourable;[46]
(b) Where the solicitor cannot continue to act without being in breach of the rules of conduct, such as in a case where there is a conflict of interest;[47]

---

[39] *Warmington v McMurray* [1936] 2 All E.R. 745, affmd [1937] 1 All E.R. 562, CA. In *Perotti v Collyer Bristow* [2003] EWHC 25 (Ch) at [137] where Lindsay J. expressed scepticism as to whether the traditional view as to the solicitor's contract of retainer was an "entire" contract still was applicable in the modern world. It proved unnecessary to decide the point as a result of authority to the effect that administration actions (which were the subject of the case) did not give rise to entire contracts.

[40] *Underwood Son & Piper v Lewis* [1894] 2 Q.B. 306, CA; *Young v Robson Rhodes* [1999] 3 All E.R. 524.

[41] *Warmington v McMurray* [1936] 2 All E.R. 745, affmd [1937] 1 All E.R. 562, CA.

[42] Although it is common to employ a solicitor over an indefinite period, the retainer in each case in the absence of special agreement is limited to the particular business in respect of which he is employed and there is no such thing as a general relationship of solicitor and client of a standing and permanent character for all occasions and all purposes: *Saffron Walden BS v Rayner* [1880] 14 Ch. D. 406, CA; *Midland Bank v Hett Stubbs & Kemp* [1979] Ch. 384 at 402, Oliver J., cited by Hoffmann J. in *Re a Solicitor*, March 31, 1987. See most recently *Minkin v Cawdery, Kaye, Fireman & Taylor* [2010] EWHC 177 (QB).

[43] *JH Milner & Son v Percy Bilton* [1966] 1 W.L.R. 1582. "There is no such thing as a general retainer imposing a duty to consider all aspects of the client's interests whenever the solicitor is consulted": *Regent Leisuretime Ltd v Skerrett* [2007] P.N.L.R. 9 at [34], per Peter Gibson L.J.

[44] *Re Hall and Barker* [1878] 9 Ch. D. 538.

[45] *Wild v Simpson* [1919] 2 K.B. 544.

[46] *Underwood Son & Piper v Lewis* [1894] 2 Q.B. 306, CA.

[47] This will sometimes be a ground, but in other cases the court will take the view that the

(c) Where the solicitor is unable despite diligent effort to obtain instructions from the client;
(d) Where there is a serious breakdown in confidence between solicitor and client, such as may arise in some circumstances where the client refuses to follow advice;
(e) Where the client refuses to pay an interim bill in a contentious matter;[48]
(f) Where the work for which the retainer is given is protracted and there is a natural break in the proceedings it is possible to terminate the retainer at such a break.[49]

C. Acting for insured where the insurer pays the bill

Wherever the client is insured, the solicitor will need to take care to bear in mind that his client is the insured even though the bill is paid by the insurer and, in many cases, the solicitor will have his professional relationship with the insurer rather than the insured. Thus in *Groom v Crocker*[50] a solicitor acting for an insured but instructed by insurers was held in breach of duty to the insured when he served a defence admitting liability contrary to the wishes of the insured. The solicitor admitted liability because insurers gained a financial advantage by reason of an agreement sharing liability with a third party if the defendant rather than the claimant (who they also insured) was liable.

15–018

The decision of the Court of Appeal in *TSB Bank v Robert Irving and Burns*[51] is as dramatic an example as is imaginable and a number of lessons can be derived from it. TSB sued the defendant firm of valuers for negligently valuing property. Counsel accepted instructions for the valuers through insurers and solicitors nominated by insurers. The valuers' insurers instructed counsel to advise whether they could avoid the policy taken out

---

solicitor has got himself into the mess and will not help him to get out of it. The court did not regard the conflict problems of Robson Rhodes on their merger as good reason in *Young v Robson Rhodes* [1999] 3 All E.R. 524, but, treating the principles as the same in accountants cases where the accountant was instructed for the purpose of giving expert evidence, held them liable to pay damages for wrongful termination of the retainer.

[48] Solicitors Act 1974, s.65(2). If the contract is not entire, this reason may be relied on in wider circumstances: see, e.g. *Robins v Goldingham* (1872) L.R. 13 Eq. 440.
[49] See *Re Hall and Barker* [1878] 9 Ch. D. 538. But this ground will not always be appropriate. If the retainer is to conduct proceedings it seems unlikely that it will be open to the solicitor unilaterally to terminate the retainer after the trial of liability before the trial of quantum, for example.
[50] [1939] 1 K.B. 194, CA. The decision is mainly noteworthy because the court held that the solicitor owed duties to his client in contract but not in tort and thus the client could not claim damages for injury to his reputation or feelings. The rule that a solicitor only owes duties in contract not tort has long since been disapproved: see *Midland Bank v Hett Stubbs & Kemp* [1979] Ch. 384.
[51] [1999] Lloyd's Rep. I.R. 528.

by the valuers; counsel advised "with regret" there was no basis for doing so.[52] When the expert evidence indicated that it would be difficult to defend the claim, counsel was instructed to reconsider the avoidance issue and to see the individual who had made the valuation on behalf of the valuers in conference. Both counsel and solicitors intended that the conference should be an opportunity to cross-examine the individual valuer with a view to eliciting answers from the valuer which would give insurers a basis on which to avoid cover. Not being aware of this purpose, the valuer gave unguarded answers in conference which enabled insurers to avoid cover as planned. The Court of Appeal were as unimpressed with the turn of events as was the judge.[53] The decision struck out those parts of the defence of insurers to the valuers' claim for an indemnity under the policy which were based on what was said by the individual valuer in conference and injuncted insurers from relying on that material, on the ground that the implied waiver of privilege as between valuer and insurer for the joint purpose of instructing counsel did not extend to circumstances in which there had been an actual conflict of interest between them. The usual rule between two parties who jointly instruct lawyers or instructed them pursuant to a common interest was that the communications with the lawyers were privileged against the rest of the world but the parties waived privilege against one another. Where there was in fact an actual conflict of interest between the parties which had arisen, the waiver of privilege did not apply so one party could not rely on the privileged material against the other. The precise grounds of the decision, whilst laudable in the result, are not free from difficulty.[54]

Those who regularly act for insurers must be vigilant as to potential conflicts.[55] The New South Wales Supreme Court recently reaffirmed in *Oceanic v HIH*[56] that a solicitor owes a fiduciary obligation to his client even when instructed by someone else such as an insurer to act for the client. Whilst *TSB* is a particularly striking example, there will often be a

---

[52] The judge said "the fact that [counsel] should regret the conclusion that the defendant had insurance cover in respect of TSB's claim indicates to me that he had overlooked that the defendant was his client."

[53] "I was surprised to learn from [the solicitor] that even now neither she nor such colleagues at [the solicitors' firm] as she has consulted on the point, acknowledge any error."

[54] Speaking of a limited waiver of privilege in this context is somewhat confusing. The real point is surely that one person who jointly instructs a solicitor cannot claim privilege against the other because although the communications were confidential against the rest of the world, they were not confidential as between the two parties. Analysed this way, it is hard to justify the grounds for the decision. Surely the better argument is that this was a form of equitable fraud on the valuer, and the court will restrain the use of evidence obtained by unconscionable conduct: see *Calcraft v Guest* [1898] 1 Q.B. 759. This ground was additionally relied upon by the judge but not the Court of Appeal.

[55] There is an interesting Australian article on the problems in acting as a lawyer for insurer and insured, and identifying some of the pitfalls: Tony Scotford, Geoff Masel Lecture, Walking the Tightrope at *www.aila.com.au/speakersPapers/downloads/06-09-07_Geoff_Masel_Lecture.pdf*

[56] [1999] N.S.W.S.C. 292, Austin J. at para.39.

potential conflict where the insurer wishes to keep open the possibility of avoiding cover. If evidence emerges which may provide the insurer with a ground for refusing to pay the insured, the solicitor will need immediately to inform both insurer and insured, and if such a term is not an express term of the insurance contract, it will be implied. Whether or not this is properly to be treated as a contractual term, the solicitor who tries to act for insurer and insured at the same time when there are issues as to avoidance but fails to obtain the informed consent of the insured is in breach of the double employment rule and potentially liable for breach of fiduciary duty. Even if he has obtained informed consent, this may be one of the cases within the *Mothew* categorisation where he cannot act even with informed consent.

Another area of potential conflict is where the potential claim or liability is greater than the insurance cover. On a claim for £5m with insurance of £2m, the insured will want to pay £2m to settle in order to avoid the risk of personal bankruptcy if the full claim succeeds. The insurer may prefer to take the 50 per cent chance of the defence succeeding in full. There is a mass of US authority in this area, virtually none in this jurisdiction. The insurer will owe an obligation of good faith to the insured. The solicitor must be aware of the potential for conflict and recognise that he has duties of loyalty to the assured as well as insurer, even though it is the insurer that provides him with regular instructions. This is a much narrower form of conflict than that previously discussed and it may well be that the matter can be dealt with on the basis of both insurer and insured consenting to the discrete point of settlement being dealt with by the parties taking separate advice on the point.

15–019

In the case of legal expenses insurance business, regulations[57] provide that an insurance company carrying on such business must adopt at least one of three specified arrangements designed to avoid conflicting interests with parts of its own business concerned with other classes of insurance. One of these arrangements is that the insurer shall "in the policy, afford the insured the right to entrust the defence of his interests, from the moment that he has the right to claim from the insurer under the policy, to a lawyer of his choice."

---

[57] Giving effect to EC Directive 87/344, SI 1990/1159, especially reg.5.

CHAPTER 16

Barristers

A. Differences between barristers and solicitors relevant to conflicts

16–001 By contrast to solicitors, there are not many cases which deal with conflicts of interest relating to members of the Bar. This may partly reflect the much smaller number of barristers than solicitors. However, one reason why the law relating to claims against barristers is generally under-developed in England is because until recently the barrister had immunity against negligence suits, at least in respect of court work.[1] There are a number of relevant differences here between barristers and solicitors which mean that the barrister's position is slightly different to that of a solicitor in respect of conflicts.

Firstly, the barrister traditionally enters into no contract with either solicitor or lay client. He owes a duty of care to the lay client in tort. This is changing. Annexe G2 of the Bar Code of Conduct provides that in the absence of express agreement to the contrary, the barrister carries out work pursuant to terms of work which are not contractually binding. Recently the Bar Standards Board has indicated its intention to abolish these terms and barristers will in future deal on terms which are binding in contract.

Secondly, the barrister is bound by the "cab-rank" rule which requires him to accept instructions within his area of expertise save in limited circumstances (which, of course, include situations where there is a conflict of interest). The solicitor is free to refuse instructions, and thus may do so where he perceives there is a "commercial" conflict. The barrister has no such option.[2]

---

[1] Until the decision of the House of Lords in *Hall v Simons* [2000] 3 W.L.R. 543. Until *Saif Ali v Mitchell* [1980] A.C. 198 the barrister had complete immunity.
[2] Rule 11.04 of the 2007 SRA Code of Conduct provided that a solicitor must not refuse

Thirdly, barristers practice as sole practitioners within chambers; they do not form partnerships. This will not remain true in future. The Legal Services Act 2007 facilitates a range of alternative business structures between lawyers and other lawyers and between lawyers and non-lawyers. The Bar Standards Board has already indicated that it proposes to permit barristers practise in partnership and in LLPs and companies in future. The Bar Code of Conduct is also presently subject to a comprehensive review by the Bar's Regulator, the Bar Standards Board.

The Code of Conduct[3] seeks to reflect the law and to say as little as possible by way of gloss. It provides that a barrister must in any field in which he professes to practise in relation to work appropriate to his experience and seniority accept instructions[4] subject to exceptions. Paragraph 603 provides:

16–002

> "A barrister must not accept any instructions if to do so would cause him to be professionally embarrassed and for this purpose a barrister will be professionally embarrassed:
> ... (d) if the matter is one in which he has reason to believe that he is likely to be a witness or in which whether by reason of any connection with the client or with the Court or a member of it or otherwise it will be difficult for him to maintain professional independence or the administration of justice might be or appear to be prejudiced;
> (e) if there is or appears to be a conflict or risk of conflict either between the interests of the barrister and some other person or between the interests of any one or more clients (unless all relevant persons consent to the barrister accepting the instructions)
> (f) if there is a risk that information confidential to another client or former client might be communicated to or used for the benefit of anyone other than that client or former client without their consent."

Paragraph 606.1 provides:

> "A barrister (whether he is instructed on his own or with another advocate) must in the case of all instructions consider whether consistently

---

instructions to act as an advocate on the grounds that the nature of the case, the conduct opinions or beliefs of the client or the source of any financial support are objectionable to the solicitor. This has not been re-enacted in the 2011 Code, although there is an obligation not to discriminate unlawfully when accepting or refusing instructions to act referred to at IB(2.5)

[3] The new Code of Conduct is likely to come into force in 2012. The text reflects the correct Code.
[4] 8th edn, 2000, para.602.

with the proper and efficient administration of justice and having regard to:

... (d) his relationship with the client;

the best interests of the client would be served by instructing or continuing to instruct him in that matter."

Paragraph 607 states:

"If at any time in any matter a barrister considers that it would be in the best interests of any client to have different representation, he must immediately so advise the client."[5]

B. The barrister's fiduciary duty

16–003   It is surprisingly difficult to identify an authority which holds in terms that a barrister owes a fiduciary obligation of loyalty to the client.[6] Perhaps barristers do not often nowadays seek to buy property from their clients.[7] Although the barrister does not handle client money, it seems clear that the barrister does owe a fiduciary duty to the client, and no one seems to have doubted it. The Code of Conduct imposes what amounts to a fiduciary obligation on the barrister at para.303(a) by providing that a barrister:

"must promote and protect fearlessly and by all proper and lawful means the lay client's best interests and do so without regard to his own interests or to any consequences to himself or to any other person (including the professional client or other intermediary or another barrister);"

The professional obligations of the barrister and his duty to the court[8] require him to exercise a measure of discretion in the manner in which

---

[5] See also para.608 which provides for withdrawal from a case and return of instructions in terms which mirror the previous rules.
[6] In *Szarfer v Chodos* (1986) 54 O.R. (2d) 663, confirmed on appeal (1988) 66 O.R. (2d) 250, the defendant was engaged by the claimant to represent him in an employment matter. In the course of the retainer he learned confidential information about the claimant's impotence and other reasons why the claimant's marriage was failing. The lawyer exploited this information to commence a sexual relationship with the claimant's wife. The Ontario court held the lawyer liable for breach of fiduciary duty. Pattenden in her excellent book *The Law of Professional-Client Confidentiality* (2003) at 5.72 points out that the English courts have generally restricted breach of fiduciary duty to taking advantage of some property interest of the defendant.
[7] In *Carter v Palmer* (1839) 1 Dr. & Wal. 722, affmd (1841) 8 Cl. & Fin. 657, HL, a barrister who used information obtained whilst employed as a barrister to acquire charges on his former client's land cheaply was held to be a trustee of those charges for his client.
[8] Code of Conduct para.302.

he presents his client's case, even if the client has contrary views.⁹ This is another hallmark of a relationship of trust and confidence. The existence of a duty to the court does not affect the existence of a fiduciary obligation-it merely subjugates the duty to the client to that owed to the court.¹⁰

The barrister who has previously acted for a particular client may be unable to act against that client in subsequent litigation where he is in possession of confidential information¹¹; here the principles are not special to barristers but those of general application. But a more difficult question is to determine when a barrister has a conflict of interest (or existing client conflict). The problem arises because barristers are usually instructed by solicitors in respect of specific pieces of work in litigation, and although there may be and will often be an expectation of being asked to carry out further work as counsel involved in the litigation, there is no question of a retainer in the way that arises for solicitors. If, therefore, a barrister has settled a defence but is asked to act for the other side in circumstances where there is a potential conflict of interest, but no confidential information problem, are the rules applicable to those of existing or former client conflicts? The issue is when the barrister continues to owe a fiduciary obligation to the client which goes beyond the obligation to keep the confidences of the client. The barrister is not instructed to see the job through in the way that a solicitor is in the normal retainer. The barrister who has completed the piece of work he was asked to carry out has no expectation of being asked to act further, and may not be kept aware of proceedings, or, for example, whether the litigation has settled. The better view seems to be that the barrister only owes a fiduciary obligation so long as he has instructions, and the fiduciary obligation to the lay client comes to an end on completion of those instructions and revives only when further instructions are delivered.

Notwithstanding *Bolkiah*, we have seen that there are circumstances in which a solicitor's fiduciary duty does not come to an end for all purposes on termination of the retainer.¹² It is unclear whether similar principles could be applied to barristers—for example when a barrister who is not in receipt of instructions or relevant confidential information bids against the client for a property.

16–004

Another related issue is the extent of the barrister's obligation to put all

---

⁹ For example, he may be under a professional obligation to decline to take points which the client wants him to take.

¹⁰ However, a barrister who is head of chambers does not owe a fiduciary duty to the other members of chambers: *Appleby v Cowley*, *The Times*, April 14, 1982. If barristers owed fiduciary obligations to other members of chambers it would be very difficult for them to appear in cases against each other.

¹¹ In *China Light & Power Co Ltd v Ford* [1996] H.K.L.R. 57, the barrister retained confidential papers belonging to a client after his retainer was terminated and used them to institute proceedings on his own behalf in the United States. The Hong Kong court found him liable for breach of confidence.

¹² See para.2–020.

his knowledge at the disposal of the client.[13] If he learns something relevant to the client's matter, is he obliged to disclose it to the client? If he has instructions, then para.303(a) of the Code will give rise to such an obligation. If he does not have extant instructions, he can hardly owe such an obligation.

C. Conflict between client and professional client

16–005   The barrister is instructed by the solicitor. The solicitor, not the client,[14] is responsible for payment of counsel's fees. Thus in one sense the barrister may regard the solicitor, his professional client, as the client. But it is the client to whom the barrister will owe a duty of care. As explained above, on general principle it must be that a barrister owes a fiduciary duty to the client. There will be a conflict on occasion between the barrister's client and his professional client. This will usually arise where there is reason to believe that the solicitor has been negligent. In such circumstances, the barrister's duty is to the client, not the solicitor. He must advise the client that the solicitor may have been negligent and will be in breach of duty if he fails so to do. In *Moy v Pettman Smith*[15] a barrister advised against settlement because although the offer was worth taking on the evidence admitted to date, the case would improve if an application to lead further evidence succeeded. If the application to lead further evidence failed, there would be a case that the solicitors were negligent. The barrister said that she took into account in giving advice what she said was a duty to her professional client as well as the client. The Court of Appeal were very clear that no such duty existed; the duty was owed to the lay client. In *Moy* the position was straightforward because the alleged duty to the solicitor would have conflicted with the duty to the client. But that leaves open the question where there is no such conflict. Conditional fee cases are good examples.[16] If the barrister is negligent and in consequence the lay client's claim fails, the solicitor will suffer loss. Can he sue counsel? Or conversely, if the solicitor's negligence leads to a claim being dismissed when counsel has a conditional fee? It is suggested that the courts would be highly unlikely to countenance imposition of such duties. When the barrister undertakes to act or advise,

---

[13] See generally Ch.6
[14] The expression is sometimes used "lay client" but this can be confusing as the lay client may be a professional. Thus the expression "client" is used here and "professional client" refers to the solicitor.
[15] [2002] Lloyd's Rep. P.N. 513. The appeal was allowed in the House of Lords but this point did not arise, [2005] 1 W.L.R. 581.
[16] In *Hussain v Cuddy Woods & Cochrane* [2001] Lloyd's Rep. P.N. 134, in dismissing a claim for negligence against a barrister who advised settlement which was said to be negligent advice, the Court of Appeal refused to draw any inference from the conditional nature of the fee structure which was said to lead to an inference that the barrister had a financial interest to advise in favour of settlement.

he is not undertaking to look after the solicitor's interests; on the contrary, he is undertaking to protect the client's interests even if that involves telling the client that the solicitor has been negligent. Imposition of a duty of care to a solicitor, in any normal situation, would be inconsistent with such an obligation. Nor is it necessary to impose a duty to the professional client in any normal situation. If the solicitor reasonably relies on counsel's advice, he will have a defence to a claim by the client against himself for negligence. However *Moy* is the only authority.

D. Barristers and conflicts

In the past, there were very few instances of conflicts of interest involving barristers. Things are changing. In the same way that conflicts complaints against solicitors are on the increase, so too it is perceived that there may be tactical benefit in offsiding the other side's first choice counsel. In the case of solicitors' conflicts, it will generally be the firm that decides whether to fight a complaint.[17] In the case of a barrister, he will have to reach a decision himself. That may give rise to practical problems in litigation: in a case against a firm of solicitors, where there is confidential material which the claimant wishes to put before the court, which cannot be shown to the individual solicitor who continues to act because he will be obliged by his continuing obligations to show it to his client, the problem can be resolved by the material being shown not merely to those acting for the firm, but also to the management team within the firm so long as the individuals have no involvement in the disputed retainer. But this cannot be done in the same way with counsel who is a sole practitioner, and there are problems in permitting the court to see material which is not shown to the other party to litigation. The courts have not yet had to grapple with this issue.

16–006

E. Retainers

Bar Standards Board guidance points out that the expression "retainer" is used in different senses. However, it is improper for a barrister to enter into an arrangement with a client which prevents the barrister from acting against the client in any matter as to do so would subvert the Bar's cab rank rule. There is no professional difficulty in a barrister being retained on a particular matter before he is required to carry out specific work (the purpose being to prevent the other side from retaining the barrister) but fees may only be charged[18] by the barrister "for any work undertaken by him."

16–007

---

[17] Although the individual solicitor runs the risk of disciplinary action being taken by the SRA against him personally, so it cannot be entirely the firm's decision.
[18] Code para.405.

Whilst a payment may be agreed on account of work anticipated to be done, even if non-refundable if the case settles (for example, where the barrister agrees to keep his diary free for the purpose), a fee not related to work done or anticipated to be done may not be charged for retaining the barrister.

F. Sharing chambers and facilities

16–008 Many foreign lawyers and professionals are surprised that barristers who share chambers are not inhibited from arguing cases against other members of the same chambers with whom they share expenses and facilities,[19] sometimes appearing in front of judges who were themselves former members of the same chambers.[20] In *Laker Airways Inc v FLS Aerospace*[21] Rix J. considered a challenge to a Q.C. acting as arbitrator[22] in a dispute where another member of his chambers was instructed as counsel to appear in front of him. In refusing the challenge,[23] the judge pointed out[24] that barristers were self-employed and not merely as a matter of form. Practising barristers are prohibited by the rules of their profession from entering partnerships or accepting employment precisely in order to maintain the position where they can appear against or in front of each other. If it were otherwise, public access to the bar would be severely limited, particularly in matters involving specialist expertise, and this would be a severe limitation on the administration of justice in this country. The applicant relied on *Bolkiah* and it was suggested that the sharing of facilities, information and clerking were likely to be inadequate to provide a sufficient information barrier under the stringent test set by the House of Lords. The judge said the position was not comparable, because barristers were independent self-employed practitioners. On the contrary, for that reason the burden would lie on the applicant to show that the particular circumstances were such that there was a real risk of breach of confidentiality.[25]

Nevertheless, many would say that the Bar might be more sensitive to the concerns of those who are troubled by what often seems, at least to outsiders, to be a relatively cavalier view of conflicts. The fear that professional confidences will be made light of over chambers tea or in the circuit

---

[19] A barrister is vicariously liable for his clerk, at least so far as wasted costs are concerned: *R. v Rodney* [1997] P.N.L.R. 489.
[20] Or who remain existing members of chambers sitting as Recorders.
[21] [1999] 2 Lloyd's Rep. 45.
[22] In relation to the position of arbitrators sitting in cases where members of their chambers are instructed, see 14–010.
[23] Strictly, this was a case of a potential judicial conflict. But the remarks of the judge are important in the context of the point under consideration here.
[24] [1999] 2 Lloyd's Rep. 45 at 52.
[25] He went on to hold that even if the *Bolkiah* test was applicable, he was not satisfied that there was a real risk of disclosure. See generally Kendall, "Barristers, Independence and Disclosure", (1992) 8(3) Arbitration International 287.

mess is one that often should not be ignored. The following is typical of a commonly held view:

> "The reality is that barristers in chambers share clerical and secretarial staff, premises, and, often, a computer network. Professional, informal and social contact may well be more likely between barristers in a small set of chambers, than between solicitors or forensic accountants in a large, departmentalised firm".[26]

Allegations as to chambers gossip led to an unsuccessful attempt to remove counsel in *Pavel v Sony*.[27] It became apparent in the course of acrimonious patent proceedings that Robin Jacob Q.C., leader of the Sony team prior to his appointment as a High Court Judge, had discussed certain aspects of the case with a close colleague in chambers, Hugh Laddie Q.C. (also subsequently a High Court Judge). When Mr Laddie appeared for Pavel's patent attorneys opposing Sony's application for a wasted costs order and on issues as to maintenance of the action, Sony objected. Mr Laddie said he could remember nothing of any such conversations.[28] The Court of Appeal said that it seemed on the evidence there must have been conversation of a social and superficial kind but there was no reason to believe anything had been communicated which was in the nature of a professional confidence.

The court also took the view that in any ordinary case the decision should be left to the individual member of the bar concerned. It is hard to imagine that the court would express itself in quite the same way in the climate which pervades today; the way the judgments of the court are expressed makes it apparent how far sensitivity about conflicts has moved on in recent years.

G. Barristers and personal relationships

In *Skjevesland v General Trading Co*[29] the Court of Appeal heard an appeal from an unsuccessful attempt to set aside a bankruptcy petition. The hearing had been contested, involved cross-examination of witnesses, and lasted five days. The debtor's wife learned at a late stage of the hearing the name of counsel for the petitioning creditor. The debtor then sought to apply for a retrial on the grounds that his wife had been acquainted with

16–009

---

[26] O'Sullivan, "Conflicts of Interest and Chinese Walls", (2000) 16 Prof Neg 88, 99.
[27] Unreported, April 12, 1995.
[28] "Mr Carman urged Mr Laddie to take advice on his position, perhaps from the Chairman of the Bar. Mr Laddie replied that he had no need to take independent advice; that he was a grown up; that he had discussed the matter with his junior and his solicitors and was satisfied that he was not embarrassed."
[29] [2003] 1 All E.R. 1., See also 5–009.

counsel for the petitioner in the past: he might have consciously or unconsciously obtained information about the debtor's family relevant to an issue in the case. It was argued that might give rise in the mind of a lay observer to the view that justice might not be done or be seen to be done, thus undermining public confidence in the administration of justice. The case was hopeless on the facts, but the Court of Appeal heard it in order to give guidance as to the circumstances in which an advocate should decline instructions in the absence of any issue as to confidential information. The Court of Appeal accepted that the circumstances in which an advocate may be restrained by the court from acting as an advocate in litigation were likely to be very exceptional, but recognised that there had been cases in which this might be appropriate even though there was no confidential information in issue: examples were when a pupil barrister met the accused and discussed his case with him then sat behind the prosecutor,[30] when a husband and wife or other cohabiting partners appeared as advocates against each other in a contested criminal matter,[31] or when the solicitor for the local authority in care proceedings cohabited with the solicitor for the family.[32] Where the trial judge considered that the basis of objection was such as to lead to a real risk that any order of the court will be set aside on appeal, he should accede to an order restraining an advocate from acting.

Arden L.J., giving the judgment of the court, made clear that this was a highly exceptional course. Such an objection could readily be made for tactical purposes and would cause inconvenience and delay in the proceedings as well as undermining the cab-rank rule. All the circumstances needed to be considered: the nature of the connection, the nature of the proceedings, the extent to which there were relevant conflicts of fact and any special factor affecting the role of the advocate (such as whether he is prosecuting counsel, counsel for a local authority in care proceedings or an amicus). If counsel was aware of circumstances which might reasonably lead to objection, even if he considers he is not professionally embarrassed within the meaning of the Code of Conduct and can continue to act, he should draw it to the attention of his client and it may be necessary to inform the other side, as part of the duty of the parties to co-operate in procedural matters[33] so that if there is an objection it can be adjudicated upon promptly and without causing an adjournment of the substantive hearing.

The Court of Appeal was at pains not to limit the circumstances in which this issue might arise. It may be inappropriate for counsel to have to call a friend a liar, for example—although the concern is likely to be much greater where there is cross-examination. It could be suggested that the litigant has a right to be protected too: art.6 requires every party to have a reasonable

---

[30] *R. v Smith (Winston)* (1975) 61 Cr. App. R. 128, CA (conviction quashed).
[31] *R. v Batt* [1996] Crim. L.R. 910, CA.
[32] *Re L (children) (care proceedings: cohabiting solicitors)* [2001] 1 W.L.R. 100, Wilson J.
[33] CPR r.1.3.

opportunity of presenting his case to the court under conditions which do not place him at a substantial disadvantage[34]; in this regard appearances are important as well as sensitivity to the fair administration of justice.[35] The Court of Appeal in *Skjevesland* did not appear to think that this sort of complaint would often be justified.

---

[34] *De Haes v Belgium* (1998) 25 E.H.R.R. 1 at 56-7, para.53.
[35] *Bulut v Austria* (1997) 24 E.H.R.R. 84 at 103-4, para.47.

CHAPTER 17

Accountants

1. The business of accountants

17–001 Professional accountants act for their clients in a wide variety of different roles. Major functions often carried out by accountants include all of the following:

(a) Bookkeeping and preparation of accounts;
(b) Auditing;
(c) Reviewing accounting information falling short of an audit;
(d) Advising a business on financial and management issues, including acting as management consultant;
(e) Advising on taxation and tax planning;
(f) Acting as agent for the client in dealings with tax authorities;
(g) Corporate finance services, e.g. carrying out due diligence work in respect of a proposed corporate takeover or organising the supply of data by a target company;
(h) Investigating third parties' financial affairs, e.g. investigating a borrower's finances at the instigation of a lender;
(i) Litigation support work including financial investigations for forensic purposes and acting as expert witness;
(j) Insolvency work, including acting as trustee in bankruptcy, administrator, liquidator, receiver or administrative receiver;
(k) Expert valuer, particularly of shares or businesses;
(l) Giving investment advice;
(m) Acting as company director or as trustee.

As well as facing conflicts of interest in the same way as a solicitor might where a former client's interests are at odds with those of a new client,[1] accountants frequently face conflicts of interest by virtue of the variety of their functions. It is a commonplace in the financial press to complain that auditors' independence is compromised by their high fees for other work for the company, particularly management consultancy.[2] Accountants frequently find themselves challenged over investment advice given without the same care and attention to conflicts as the accountant might apply to his other roles. A particularly troublesome area is the appointment of an accountant in an insolvency role when the same firm has in the recent past acted as adviser to the insolvent person.

Most controversial of all is the role of the accountant as auditor. This is a peculiarly awkward function because the auditor is required to hold the ring between different organs of a single legal person the company. The auditor is supposed to act as watchdog[3] for the shareholders over the directors, but in practice his reappointment depends upon the directors. Particularly in large companies, the directors' proposal as to appointment of auditors is invariably rubber stamped by the shareholders in general meeting. The auditor takes regularly recurring fees from the company for looking into the affairs of that company; but if the auditor's findings are unwelcome to management, then the auditor may lose the opportunity to continue to audit the company and earn further fees.

The court expects accountants to be aware of the possibility of conflicts of interest. Judges may adopt a strict approach to individuals who are qualified as accountants even where they are acting in another capacity.[4]

17–002

---

[1] As Vos J. put it in *Dennard v PricewaterhouseCoopers* [2010] EWHC 812 (Ch), [215], "Major accountancy firms, like major legal firms frequently attract business by acting against their prospective client. They do that by impressing the prospective client with their professionalism and competence, not by showing that they are willing to act against the interests of their own client."
[2] For judicial discussion of this issue in general terms, see *Wong Kok Chin v Singapore Society of Accountants* [1990] 1 M.L.J. 456.
[3] He is a watchdog but not a bloodhound as famously stated by Lopes L.J. in *Re Kingston Cotton Mill Company (No.2)* [1896] 2 Ch. 279.
[4] An example is *Body v Bellbourne Group Ltd*, July 28, 1998, Lexis, in which a company director who happened to be an accountant was held to have been properly dismissed as a result of putting his own interest above that of the company. Although the same decision may well have been reached had the defendant director not been an accountant, Judge David Smith Q.C. (sitting as a deputy judge of the Queen's Bench Division) said of the defendant: "He was a chartered accountant. He must have been fully aware of the need to be punctilious in the use of company money when there might be a conflict of interest." Other dismissal cases in the context of public bodies with particular regulations concerning conflicts of interest include *Sparkes v Enterprise Newfoundland*, June 16, 1994, Lexis and *Cote v Revenue Board*, February 8, 1999, Lexis. However, a company director was permitted to receive fees for accountancy services where the conflict of interest had been waived by the majority shareholder in *Flame Bar-B-Q v Hoar's Estate* (1978) 22 N.B.R. (2d) 595, 39 A.P.R. 595. A different type of case is the rather stern decision of Hogg J., in the Ontario Court (General Division) in the case of *Begin v McInnis*, March 11, 1991, Lexis that an accountant sitting as a local councillor was in breach of a statute prohibiting conflicts of interest when he voted as a councillor on a proposal that might financially benefit one of his accountancy clients, the rationale being that any benefit to a client is bound indirectly to benefit the accountant.

In some cases, judges have emphasised the role of the standards set by professional bodies. Indeed it seems that an accountant will generally be judged by the court by a standard at least as high as that of his own Institute.[5]

2. Professional standards

17–003
The Institute of Chartered Accountants of England & Wales' Code of Ethics adopts a conceptual framework approach, setting out fundamental principles and then giving guidance as to examples of situations which may arise and safeguards that may be adopted, rather than listing detailed rules. The analysis in the Code largely proceeds in terms of "threats" to compliance with the fundamental principles and "safeguards" to eliminate or minimise the threats. The fundamental principles include "Objectivity" meaning that the accountant "should not allow bias, conflict of interest or undue influence of others to override professional or business judgments".

The Code of Ethics includes a separate statement on conflicts of interest.[6] A test suggested for accountants to apply is whether a reasonable and informed observer would perceive that the accountant's objectivity is likely to be impaired. This formulation suggests a degree of flexibility available to the accountant with a self-interest conflict that is unlikely to be afforded by the court. The formulation is not necessarily wrong but is an unhelpful restatement of the fundamental question whether there is a conflict between the accountant's interest and his duty. Wherever there is an objective conflict between the interests of the accountant and those of his client, the court will invariably hold that the accountant's ability to give objective advice is liable to impaired.[7] Unlike its predecessor (statement 1.205 revised October 1, 2002), the Code of Ethics fails to point out that where informed consent is not obtained to the accountant acting despite a self-interest conflict, he must cease to do so. Instead, the Code again suggests a level of flexibility which is not available in law, stating "Where a conflict of interest poses a threat to one or more of the fundamental principles, including objectivity, confidentiality or professional behaviour, that cannot be eliminated *or reduced to an acceptable level through the application of safeguards*,[8] the professional accountant in public practice should conclude that it is not

---

[5] Professional guidance as to ethical standards was relied upon by the Court in *Breda v Breda* (1997) 29 O.T.C. 223 and *Re Hurt* (1988) 80 A.L.R. 236.
[6] s.220.
[7] In the solicitor's case of *Boardman v Phipps* [1967] 2 A.C. 46, the solicitor gave excellent advice which benefited his client, but remained liable in equity to account for his own profits because he had a personal interest in it.
[8] This phrase or cognates is repeated frequently in the Code. It should be relied upon only with close attention to whether it actually applies in a given situation.

appropriate to accept a specific engagement or that resignation from one or more conflicting engagements is required."[9]

Both existing and former client conflicts are treated by the Code as being largely concerned with confidential information.[10] This is appropriate insofar as accountants are not playing a fiduciary role, but it may be misleading where they are doing so.[11]

Auditors in England must comply with the Auditing Practices Board Ethical Standard 1: "Integrity, Objectivity and Independence" (revised December 2010). This follows the same approach as the ICAEW's Code of Ethics, identifying at a high level of generality principles (integrity, objectivity and independence) and requiring auditors to identify threats to those principles and apply safeguards to minimise those threats. Other APB standards set out more detailed guidance which is generally more flexible and less prescriptive than the previous set of rules.

17–004

3. Investment advice and personal conflicts

Where an accountant advises on investments, which he may do in pursuance of a retainer to give tax planning advice, he must be careful to make full disclosure before advising his client to invest in ways that benefit the accountant.[12] The accountant with a real self-interest will fall within the personal conflict line of cases and may find it very difficult to persuade a court that any disclaimer or disclosure is sufficient.

17–005

Thus, in *Madhani v Pirani*[13] the defendant accountant recommended an investment in an hotel project. The defendant told his client, a psychiatrist, that he was heading up the project and that he would indirectly benefit from the client's investment. However, the defendant did not supply the details of his relevant interests, nor disclose that the company in which the investment was to be made was in serious financial trouble. The defendant was liable for breach of fiduciary duty and for breach of implied contractual terms both for the non-disclosures and for failing to ensure or recommend that the plaintiff receive independent advice.

---

[9] s.220.5, emphasis supplied.
[10] See s.220.4A of the Code: "Where a conflict of interest arises, the preservation of confidentiality, and the perception thereof will be of paramount importance. Therefore firms should deploy safeguards, which generally will take the form of information barriers." The first sentence is an over-generalisation of *Bolkiah*. The second sentence suggests a professional body in a state of denial about the decision in *Bolkiah*.
[11] As discussed earlier in this work, existing client conflicts are not solely, or even principally, concerned with confidential information, but are about clashes between contradictory fiduciary duties.
[12] See *Hodgkinson v Simms* (1994) 97 B.C.L.R. 1 for a lengthy discussion of the applicable principles in a factually straightforward accountant's case.
[13] British Columbia Supreme Court, October 16, 1997, Lexis.

The accountant made greater efforts to make proper disclosure in *Zivadinovich v Mehta*,[14] but was still found liable. There the defendant accountant usually helped the plaintiff with tax returns. The defendant mentioned to the plaintiff that he was a principal in a real estate scheme from which he was hoping to get spectacular returns. The first instance judge found that the accountant may well have told the plaintiff that the investment was too risky for somebody in the plaintiff's position. The plaintiff invested and lost all his money. Both Pitt J. at first instance and the Ontario Court of Appeal relied strongly upon the implicit trust placed by the plaintiff in the accountant's judgment and advice. The Court of Appeal said "[i]t is also fair to say that accountants, even more so than lawyers perhaps because of their alleged fiscal conservatism are considered by lay people as having good judgment in matters of finance". Pitt J. considered that the accountant should have provided, but did not provide, to the plaintiff every piece of information that he had concerning the investment. Pitt J. also held that the accountant should have insisted upon him receiving independent advice before accepting his investment. The Ontario Court of Appeal upheld the decision on the basis of the accountant's "non-disclosures about the speculative nature of the investment and his own interest in it", though it is not clear that non-disclosures of these particular facts were actually found by the trial judge.

4. Existing client conflicts

17–006

The rules as to existing client conflicts are in principle no different for accountants than for other professionals. Such recent authority as exists in relation to accountants suggests a tough line.

One relatively hard case is the Australian decision, *Australian Breeders Co-operative Society v Jones*.[15] The defendant accountant acted for the promoter of a bloodstock investment syndicate scheme and also acted for the syndicate. He told the investors in the scheme that he could not discuss with them anything related to the price or value of the horses which were being sold to the syndicate by the promoter because of the accountant's conflict of interest. However, the accountant did not tell the investors that he knew and was not disclosing to them a highly material fact, namely that the promoter had purchased the horses for a much lower price than that for which he was proposing to sell them to the syndicate. Because of this omission, the investors' consent to the accountant acting for the syndicate despite his conflict of interest was held not to have been informed consent. Furthermore, the accountant played a role in selecting an independent bloodstock valuer

---

[14] (1997) 25 O.T.C. 198, affmd (1999) 117 O. A.C. 328.
[15] (1997) 150 A.L.R. 488.

for the syndicate and in so doing was held to have extended his retainer so as to negate any disclaimer of advising on valuation.

In *Berry Taylor v Coleman*[16] the defendant accountant acted for a client who required increased capital for their business and who advised the client's parents-in-law that further lending to the business would be a good investment was liable for negligent misstatement. The Court of Appeal held that the plaintiffs' reliance upon the accountant's statement was reasonable, even though the plaintiffs had been told by a legal executive working for solicitors acting for the plaintiffs that the defendant would be acting in the interests of his own clients and that the plaintiffs ought to take independent advice on the advisability of the investment.

Even where the issue is not investments, a strict view has usually been taken of accountants who seek to act for clients with conflicting interests. An example is the Scottish case of *Mitchell or Anderson v Messrs Pringle and Watt*[17] which concerned a family company. The defenders were auditors and accountants to the company and to each of the shareholders. The pursuer was one of the family shareholders who was considering selling her shares to the company itself. The pursuer went to the defenders for advice as to the value of the shares. The court held that the defenders should have advised the pursuer to seek independent advice elsewhere because of their obvious conflict of interest as the company's auditors and because they had already advised the company on the value of the shares, which information they could not disclose to the pursuer.[18]

17–007

On the other hand, a more pragmatic approach was taken in *Dennard v PricewaterhouseCoopers*[19] to an allegation that an accountant had a personal interest in attracting future work from the party on the other side of a deal to a current client. It was held there that:

> "What matters is the perverse incentive. Thus, if the facts give rise only to the indication that the professionals will do a particularly good job for their client in order to impress them [the other party] and obtain future work, no question of conflict will arise. A corrupt and contra-intuitive motive will not be inferred without a factual premise for that inference. But if there are some facts that give rise to the inference that the professionals actually have a perverse incentive to achieve a result that may be at odds with the interests of their client, a conflict may be held to exist".

---

[16] Unreported, July 19, 1996, CA.
[17] May 3, 1991, Court of Session, Outer House, Lexis.
[18] The pursuer was not awarded any damages because her pleaded claim was for loss caused by the valuation being negligently low, which it was held not to have been.
[19] [2010] EWHC 812 (Ch). Permission to appeal was refused at [2010] EWCA Civ 1437.

5. Does an auditor owe fiduciary duties?

17–008   The nature and purpose of the auditor's statutory duties were considered at length in the speeches in the House of Lords in *Caparo v Dickman*.[20] However, the conclusion from that case can be stated quite shortly. The statutory auditor is concerned with providing information to the shareholders of the company as a body for the purpose of the exercise of their stewardship of the company in general meeting. For this purpose, the shareholders are more or less indistinguishable from the company itself. The information provided is whether the accounts give a true and fair view of the financial affairs of the company. The close relationship between the auditor and the company as a legal person is emphasised by the fact that an auditor will for many purposes be an officer of the company despite having no role in its management.[21]

It has often been assumed that an auditor, like other officers of the company, generally owes fiduciary duties to the company.[22] Cases against auditors are often pleaded on the footing that the ordinary run of auditor's duties is fiduciary. Most notably, this may have been the assumption of Lord Millett in *Bolkiah* when he said:

> "It is otherwise where the court's intervention is sought by an existing client, for a fiduciary cannot act at the same time both for and against the same client, and his firm is in no better position. A man cannot without the consent of both clients act for one client while his partner is acting for another in the opposite interest. His disqualification has nothing to do with the confidentiality of client information. It is based on the inescapable conflict of interest which is inherent in the situation ... this is not to say that such consent is not sometimes forthcoming, or that in some situations it may not be inferred. There is a clear distinction between the position of a solicitor and an auditor. The large accountancy firms commonly carry out the audit of clients who are in competition with one another. The identity of their audit clients is publicly acknowledged. Their clients are taken to consent to their auditors

---

[20] [1990] 2 A.C. 605. A string of decisions of the Court of Appeal in recent years have eaten away at the result of *Caparo* by keeping open the potential for accountants to owe duties of care to a wider class of claimants than just the company itself. Even so, the House of Lords' analysis of the functions of an auditor qua auditor remains definitive.

[21] *Mutual Reinsurance Company Ltd v Peat Marwick* [1997] 1 Lloyd's Rep. 253 and see also *Joint Liquidators of Sasea Finance v KPMG* [1998] B.C.C. 216 and, in Hong Kong, *New China Hong Kong Group v Ernst & Young* [2003] HKCU 457. For a context in which an auditor is not an officer, see *Aquachem Ltd v Delphis Bank Ltd* [2008] UKPC 7.

[22] For an early example, see per Branson J. in *Cooper v Luxor* [1939] 1 All E.R. 623 at 629. The position of the auditor was mentioned without use of the term "fiduciary" in the Court of Appeal [1939] 4 All E.R. 411, but was not referred to in the House of Lords [1941] A.C. 108.

acting for competing clients, though they must of course keep confidential the information obtained from their respective clients. This was the basis on which the Privy Council decided *Kelly v Cooper* in relation to estate agents".

However, there should be recalled Lord Millett's own strictures in *Mothew*. The expression "fiduciary duty" is properly confined to those duties which are peculiar to fiduciaries and the breach of which attracts legal consequences differing from those consequent upon the breach of other duties.[23]

This principle was applied by the Supreme Court of South Australia in *State of South Australia v Peat Marwick Mitchell & Co*[24] in which Olsson J. struck out a Statement of Claim which alleged that an auditor owed a fiduciary duty to carry out his work with care and skill. Olsson J. at times suggests that an auditor may not be a fiduciary at all.[25] In *Pilmer v Duke Group Ltd (in liquidation)*[26] the High Court of Australia held that an accountant carrying out a valuation of shares pursuant to a statutory requirement for an independent valuation in the context of a takeover bid did not owe fiduciary duties in addition to the ordinary common law duties. Although this case did not concern the audit function, there is no reason in principle to distinguish between the accountant in *Pilmer v Duke* who gave an opinion on the reasonableness and fairness of the price to be paid for shares and an auditor who gives his opinion on the truth and fairness of a set of accounts.

17–009

There is considerable attraction in the view that an auditor may not generally be a fiduciary. As Lord Millett points out in the passage cited above from *Bolkiah*, the auditor is not expected to obtain specific consent before acting for competing clients. The auditor more often than not has other commercial dealings with his client, e.g. the sale of taxation or consultancy advice. In these dealings, the client would not expect full disclosure of all facts material to the transaction, nor even of the auditor's profit margin. Of course, the auditor may not sell (or otherwise disclose) the client's confidential information, but this can be explained on the basis that the information is known to be confidential, without recourse to the fiduciary notion of secret profits.

The dearth of reported decisions which depend upon whether an auditor is a fiduciary suggests that the point is not especially troublesome in practice. This may be because practical problems of this sort rarely arise for the

---

[23] [1998] Ch. 1.
[24] (1997) 24 A.C.S.R. 231.
[25] A similar view in respect of an accountant conducting a review short of an audit was tentatively expressed by Himel J. in the Ontario Court of Justice in *Ontario Ltd v Proulx* (1998) 73 O.T.C. 347.
[26] [2001] 2 B.C.L.C. 773.

auditor *qua* auditor. It is when the auditor expands his role to give advice as to management or tax planning, or to conduct negotiations with taxation authorities or investigations in support of litigation, that he enters the fiduciary realm. This is because it is in these activities that loyalty, which Millett L.J. in *Mothew* called the distinguishing obligation of the fiduciary, is implicitly required, and it is here that problems of conflicts of interest usually arise. The auditor *qua* auditor is required to be competent, but there is no call for him to be loyal.

17–010   The foregoing analysis may be supported by dicta in the Canadian case of *Drabinsky v KPMG*,[27] in which the Ontario Divisional Court upheld a decision to restrain the claimant's accountant and tax adviser from continuing to act upon instructions from a new client to investigate alleged wrongdoing by the claimant (i.e. a *Bolkiah*-like injunction). The issue on appeal was whether the motions judge below had been correct to treat as arguable pleaded allegations of breach of fiduciary duty. The court observed that in a case where the accountant was a company auditor, it may be that the only fiduciary duty would be one of confidentiality, but in this case it was at least arguable that wider fiduciary duties were owed because of the long-standing advisory relationship.

Drabinsky was followed on this point in *Re YBM Magnex International Inc*.[28] In that case, a special purpose corporation established by Ernst & Young was the court appointed receiver of a company which was involved in disputes against the applicants, who were themselves audit clients of Ernst & Young. The receiver had put in place measures to protect the confidential information of the applicants, who had at first accepted its appointment. However, they later became disillusioned with some of the decisions made by the receiver and applied for its removal. Paperny J. in the Alberta Court of Queen's Bench, in rejecting the application on various grounds, relied upon a distinction between (i) the audit function of accountants which gave rise only to narrow fiduciary duties of confidentiality[29]; and (ii) other functions, especially involvement in litigation, which could involve wider fiduciary obligations including loyalty.

Drabinsky was also followed in *Re Canada Post Corp* in which it was held that an accountant was not prevented from giving expert evidence by his firm's role as auditor of the adverse party in the litigation where the expert evidence was unrelated to the audit engagement.[30]

---

[27] (1999) 56 C.L.A.S. 382; 87 A.C.W.S. 3d 1233. For other aspects of the case see Perell's article at (2001) 24 Advocates' Quarterly 109.
[28] (2000) 275 A.R. 352 at paras 48 to 62.
[29] We would respectfully query why confidentiality is not sufficiently protected by the general law, without recourse to the notion of a narrow fiduciary obligation in that regard.
[30] (2000) 89 L.A.C. (4th) 124.

6. Former client conflicts

In recent years, accountants have been particularly concerned with conflicts between the interests of former clients and new clients. The governing principle here is that the former client is not taken to have consented to run any risk that his confidential information may be passed to new clients with conflicting interests.[31] It follows that (absent express consent from the former client) the accountant will often be barred from acting for a new client on a project antipathetic to the interest of the former client.[32]

17–011

The landmark case of *Bolkiah*,[33] and the important following case of *Young v Robson Rhodes*, have been discussed in earlier chapters of this work. They emphasise two important areas where the modern practice of large accountancy firms is raising new problems. In both *Bolkiah* and *Young v Robson Rhodes*, the background was the involvement of the accountants in litigation support and other forensic investigatory work. Litigation and disputes where litigation is in prospect raise starker conflicts than, say, the conflict of the commercial interests of two clients who happen to operate in the same sector. Clients who are already involved in litigation are more ready to go to court to protect their interests from potential conflicts.

The *Robson Rhodes* case also raised the spectre of the effect of mergers upon the accountancy profession. Conflicts of interest are inevitably a danger where two firms merge because two firms which on one day are able to represent clients with directly conflicting interests on the next day become a single firm. "A fiduciary cannot act at the same time both for and against the same client, and his firm is in no better position."[34] The decision of Laddie J. in *Young v Robson Rhodes* suggests a somewhat more pragmatic approach than the House of Lords adopted in Bolkiah in circumstances where the consequences of a strict approach would have been much more severe upon the accountants involved.

Where two merged firms have acted in opposite interests, the new firm cannot continue to act for both. Thus one of the opposed clients becomes a former client of the merged firm. The problem then is that the new firm finds itself acting in a particular interest, which may be seen to conflict with the firm's duty of confidentiality to the former client of a predecessor firm. An example is the case of *Ernst & Young Inc v Royal Trust Corp of*

17–012

---

[31] *Bolkiah* [1999] 2 A.C. 222.
[32] For example, where two partners fell out, the partnership accountant could not safely continue to act for one partner in *Michel v Lafrentz* (1997) 199 A.R. 81, and the same applied to spouses in a matrimonial dispute where the accountant previously acted in the business interests of both spouses in *Breda v Breda* (1997) 29 O.T.C. 223; 10 O.F.L.R. 208; 70 A.C.W.S. (3d) 362.
[33] Applied in Australia to an accountant in an insolvency context in *Pradhan v Eastside Day Surgery Pty Ltd* [1999] S.A.S.C. 256 at paras 48 to 51.
[34] Per Lord Millett in *Bolkiah*.

Canada,[35] in which the Alberta Queen's Bench, anticipating the House of Lords in *Bolkiah*, applied the earlier Canadian solicitor's case, *McDonald Estate v Martin*[36] to accountants. Ernst & Young were receiver/manager of a company and in that capacity brought an action against the defendant. The defendant complained that during part of the period of time relevant to the action it had been audited by a firm that had since become part of Ernst & Young by merger and that, in consequence, it was likely that Ernst & Young held relevant confidential information belonging to the defendant. Ritter J. concluded:

> "that an accounting firm which has been the auditor of a defendant should not sue that defendant where that accounting firm might have obtained information which might assist the accounting firm during the course of the audit".

He ordered that new plaintiffs be substituted for Ernst & Young. It seems that what was objectionable was not merely the naming of the accountants as plaintiffs, but the fact that the former auditors would have conduct of the action as receivers. Given the small number of accounting firms which between them now have the conduct of virtually all large company audits and insolvencies, the ramifications of this type of decision could be highly significant. In one respect, however, Ritter J.'s conclusion may be too widely stated. As stated, it would seem to bar even an action for unpaid auditor's fees where the auditor had relevant information derived from the audit. It may be acceptable for the accountant to use information obtained in the course of his engagement in a dispute between the accountant himself and the former client, though unacceptable for the same information to be at the disposal of some other client who might use it in a dispute against the former client.

In *Akai Holdings v RSM Robson Rhodes LLP*,[37] two firms which were about to merge had been retained as expert witnesses on opposite sides of substantial litigation. The court refused an injunction requiring the firm to continue to act for one of the clients, the claimant, on the ground that a contract for services would not be enforced by injunction. However, an injunction was granted restraining the merger save on terms that the firms gave undertakings that they would cease to act for the other client and would protect the claimant client's confidential information.

---

[35] (1997) 71 A.C.W.S. 3d 1079.
[36] (1990) 77 D.L.R. (4th) 249; [1990] 1 W.W.R. 705.
[37] [2007] EWHC 1641(Ch).

7. Accountants as insolvency practitioners

Accountants are frequently called upon to act as office-holders in insolvency. In this situation, they may be required to act impartially, as officers of the court, as between the stakeholders in the insolvent company (or individual) including at least the various creditors, secured and unsecured, shareholders and sometimes even directors and employees. It is an essential requirement that the office-holder is independent and, like a judge, seen to be independent. A reasonable perception of bias by a liquidator or manager towards one stakeholder or against another will usually disqualify the accountant from office.[38] However, insolvency work generates possible conflicts of interest more frequently than other areas of accountants' practice. In a world in which there is a very small, and dwindling, number of firms (or international groups of firms) of accountants with the ability to handle complex multi-national insolvencies it is inevitable in such cases that some association can be found between any such firm and a group of creditors or an entity in the insolvent group or an entity against which the insolvent company may wish to make a claim.[39]

17–013

The courts have usually taken a pragmatic view of these circumstances, by placing considerable emphasis on the stage at which the application to remove (or appoint) the office holder is made and upon the efficacy of possible solutions short of removal (or non-appointment). The cases may be divided into broad categories. In the first category, the accountant takes office as receiver at the behest of a creditor of the company[40] and that creditor's interest may conflict with the company's interest as perceived by the shareholders or directors, especially where there is a suggestion that the company may have a claim to make against the appointing creditor. In the second category are cases where the same firm takes office in several companies, often within a former group of companies, whose interests conflict with each other. Then, in the third category, is the case where the accountant who takes an insolvency office has had a previous involvement in the affairs of the company perhaps as auditor or as investigating accountant.[41]

---

[38] See *Advanced Housing Pty Ltd (in liquidation) v Newcastle Classic Developments Pty Ltd* (1994) 14 A.C.S.R. 230 for a clear statement of the general principle.

[39] The endemic nature of conflicts of interest in large international insolvencies was recognised by Sir Andrew Morritt VC in *Re Barings Plc* [2001] 2 B.C.L.C. 159; [2002] B.P.I.R. 85 when he said (at para.51): "Indeed the time may be approaching when, to deal with the conflicts faced by all the major firms of insolvency practitioners in liquidations such as this, serious consideration will have to be given to leaving the official receiver as the liquidator and authorising him to employ as his agents insolvency practitioners of his choice and to requiring him to monitor their costs and expenses." See also *Sisu Capital Fund v Tucker* [2006] B.P.I.R. 154 at paras 94 to 97 commenting on this dictum.

[40] The same issues of conflict do not arise where the receiver is appointed by the court, because he has no special duty to any particular creditor.

[41] In the classic case on this type of problem, *In re Sir John Moore Gold Mining Company*

A. The receiver appointed by a creditor and the interests of the company: the controversy over Newhart Developments

17-014   The leading English case in relation to the first category is *Newhart Developments Ltd v Co-operative Commercial Bank Ltd*.[42] In *Newhart Developments* the defendant bank appointed a receiver under a floating charge. The receiver had power to carry on the business of the company and specifically to take proceedings in the company's name.[43] This action, however, was commenced in the company's name by the directors without the concurrence of the receiver. The company claimed that the bank had been in breach of contract when it withdrew financial support for the company's activities. The Court of Appeal refused an application by the bank to set aside the writ made on the grounds that such an action could not be brought without the consent of the receiver. The Court of Appeal held that since the directors had indemnified the company against any adverse costs orders that might be made in the action, the bank's interests as creditor were not prejudiced by the company's involvement in the action, so that it did not constitute an interference with the receiver. Shaw L.J. noted that if the receiver had to decide whether or not to pursue the action against the bank, his appointor, he "would find himself faced with a very great conflict of interest" and Stephenson L.J. similarly thought that the result of the case saved the receiver from an unenviable position.

In England, *Newhart Developments* was doubted by Sir Nicolas Browne-Wilkinson V.C. in *Tudor Grange Holdings Ltd v Citibank NA*.[44] Although holding himself to be bound by the decision in *Newhart Developments*, the then Vice-Chancellor had "substantial doubts" whether it was correctly decided and limited its application to cases where the directors did indemnify the company for any costs liability. He drew attention to the difficulties that could occur if both the directors and the receiver had power to bring proceedings on the same cause of action and the question of who would have conduct of any counterclaim brought by the bank in a *Newhart Developments* situation. Sir Nicolas Browne-Wilkinson preferred to resolve the receiver's potential conflict of interest by requiring the receiver to apply to the Court for directions under s.35 of the Insolvency Act 1986.

In *Regent Leisuretime Ltd v Natwest Finance*,[45] *Newhart Developments* was cited for the proposition that during a receivership the directors retained power to commence proceedings, with the consequence that their knowledge of facts relevant to a potential claim of the company was to be attrib-

---

(1879) 12 Ch. D. 325, the liquidator had been the company secretary; and the contributory who petitioned successfully for his removal as liquidator believed that the company ought to sue its former officers, including the secretary/liquidator himself.
[42] [1978] Q.B. 814; [1978] 2 All E.R. 896.
[43] In modern terminology this was an administrative receivership.
[44] [1992] Ch. 53; [1991] 4 All E.R. 1.
[45] [2003] EWCA Civ 391 at [77] and [78].

uted to the company for limitation purposes. The Court of Appeal accepted the consequence on the facts of the case, but might be taken as indicating approval of *Tudor Grange* rather than *Newhart Developments*, by saying this:

> "It may be that, in practical terms, the receivership would have prevented the directors from commencing proceedings in the name of the Company so long as it lasted (see *Tudor Grange Holdings Ltd v Citibank NA*), but it does not follow that knowledge acquired by the Company's directors that the Company had a claim in fraud against the Bank is not to be treated as knowledge acquired by the Company for the purposes of section 32(1) of the 1980 Act".[46]

On the other hand, the Court of Appeal in *GE Capital Commercial Finance v Sutton*[47] followed *Newhart Developments*, in holding that an action (commenced by directors on behalf of a company in administrative receivership) was properly constituted (or, more precisely, that the solicitors conducting it had due authority from the company) where it did not threaten the interests of the debenture holder as such, that is, its interest in the assets subject to the charge.[48] The Court of Appeal commented that it was probably a necessary feature of such cases, where the charge was over all the assets of the company, that the directors would have to find outside funds to finance the action without the costs falling on the charged assets.

17–015

There has been a similar division of opinion in Scotland, where *Newhart Developments* has been adopted as the law in one case,[49] and Sir Nicolas Browne-Wilkinson's substantial doubts adopted in another.[50] In the Irish High Court case of *Lascomme Ltd v United Dominions Trust (Ireland) Ltd*,[51] Keane J. discussed the two English cases and came down on the side of the Court of Appeal in *Newhart Developments*. He pointed out that if the receiver had to decide whether to seek directions as to a potential action against his appointor, even to make that decision would expose the receiver to a conflict of interest. In *Lascomme*, unlike in the English cases, the directors did not offer an indemnity for any costs suffered by the company, but Keane J. still allowed the action to go ahead. In his view, the defendant bank's remedy was to apply for security for costs, which would be in the discretion of the court.

---

[46] [2003] EWCA Civ 391 at [105], per Jonathan Parker L.J. with whom Schiemann and Keene L.JJ. agreed.
[47] [2004] EWCA Civ 315, [2004] 2 B.C.L.C. 662 at [44] to [51].
[48] Although the judgment of the Court of Appeal does not discuss *Tudor Grange*, it is clear from the first instance judgment of McCombe J. [2003] EWHC 1648, QB that *Tudor Grange* was cited.
[49] *Shanks v Central Regional Council* [1987] S.L.T. 410.
[50] *Independent Pension Trustee Ltd v Law Construction Co Ltd* [1997] S.L.T. 1105.
[51] [1993] 3 I.R. 412; [1994] 1 I.R.L.M. 227.

Elsewhere in the Commonwealth, *Newhart Developments* has generally been followed. The New Zealand Court of Appeal adopted it in *Paramount Acceptance Co Ltd v Souster*,[52] and it was referred to without apparent doubt by the Privy Council in *Downsview Nominees v First City Corporation*.[53] *Newhart Developments* has often been applied in Canada.[54] In Australia, not only has *Newhart Developments* been accepted,[55] but Sir Nicolas Browne-Wilkinson's doubts have been rejected.[56] However, in Australia, unlike in Ireland, the Federal Court will restrain the directors' action if an indemnity for costs is not provided,[57] and in appropriate cases, security may be required to back the indemnity.[58] An indemnity for the costs will be required only if the receiver decides as a matter of commercial judgment to call for it, so that, in contrast to the views expressed in *Tudor Grange*, a failure to give an indemnity at the outset will not (in Australia) necessarily invalidate the action.[59]

17–016   It is submitted that the position reached by the Australian courts is a satisfactory resolution of the issues, which is consistent with the decision of the Court of Appeal in *Newhart Developments* and which is distinctly preferable to the uncertainty which might have been engendered in England following the oblique reference to *Newhart Developments* and *Tudor Grange* by the Court of Appeal in *Regent Leisuretime*. The position is perhaps clearer in England since the Court of Appeal's decision in *GE Capital v Sutton*, but it could be improved still further if the appellate courts take a future opportunity to deal directly with the dicta in *Tudor Grange*.

B. Office-holders of related companies with conflicts between the different companies

17–017   The second category of insolvency conflict is represented in England by a pair of contrasting first instance cases of the same vintage: *Re Arrows Ltd*[60] and *Re Wallace Smith & Co Ltd*.[61]

In *Re Arrows*, two partners in Ernst & Young had been appointed provi-

---

[52] [1981] 2 N.Z.L.R. 38.
[53] [1993] A.C. 295.
[54] See *Levy-Russell Ltd v Tecmotiv Inc* (1994) 54 C.P.R. 3d 161 and the authorities there cited.
[55] See *Australia & New Zealand Banking Group Ltd v P De Burgh Day*, May 6, 1994, Supreme Court of Victoria, Lexis; *Deangrove Pty Ltd (Receivers and Managers Appointed) v Commonwealth Bank of Australia* (2001) 108 F.C.R. 77; [2001] F.C.A. 173; *Gartner v Ernst & Young* [2003] F.C.A. 152.
[56] *Re Geneva Finance Ltd* (1992) 7 A.C.S.R. 415; 7 W.A.R. 496.
[57] *Re Charmae Investments Pty Ltd*, November 12, 1990, Lexis.
[58] *Deangrove Pty Ltd (Receivers and Managers Appointed) v Commonwealth Bank of Australia* (2001) 108 F.C.R. 77; [2001] F.C.A. 173.
[59] *Gartner v Ernst & Young* [2003] F.C.A. 152.
[60] [1992] B.C.C. 121.
[61] [1992] B.C.L.C. 970.

sional liquidators of Arrows Ltd and different partners in the same firm had been appointed by the court as receivers of some 80 associated companies. Arrows Ltd applied to the court to remove its provisional liquidators on the ground that because there were disputes between the 80 companies on the one hand and Arrows Ltd on the other, Ernst & Young should not control both. Hoffmann J. noted that there were considerable practical advantages to having the same firm involved in both sets of insolvencies and that the firm had already done a considerable amount of work that any new provisional liquidator would have to duplicate. Some of the conflicts had been resolved by the appointment of debenture holders' receivers to some of the 80 companies, in whose favour the court-appointed receivers stepped aside. In other cases, the accountants had applied for directions and the Vice-Chancellor had authorised the receivers to commence proceedings and the provisional liquidators to defend them. Accordingly, Hoffmann J. took the view that conflicts that had arisen to date had been satisfactorily dealt with and that any conflicts arising in the future should be considered on a pragmatic basis as they arose. He therefore dismissed the application.

In the *Wallace Smith* case, Edward Nugee Q.C. sitting as a deputy judge of the Companies Court dismissed a petition by the joint liquidators of an English company to wind up a Canadian company in the same group. There was a substantial on-going dispute between the two companies being litigated in Canada. Among other reasons for dismissing the petition, the court considered the conflict of interest that would arise because the joint liquidators expected to be appointed liquidators of the Canadian company if the order was made. The court in this case held that the liquidators if appointed to both companies "would be subject to an acute conflict of duties, and the conflict would be hardly less acute for anyone else who is a member of KPMG Peat Marwick McLintock or any firm associated with it". Mr Nugee Q.C. said that in *Re Arrows* Hoffmann J. had given "serious consideration to the possibility of removing Ernst & Young and appointing a different firm, but concluded there were very considerable practical disadvantages in this course". Wallace Smith was different because "here there is not merely a potential conflict of interest but substantial litigation on foot" between the two companies.

The reasoning in neither case is wholly satisfactory. In *Wallace Smith* it is hard to see why the potential conflict of interest was a bar to a winding up order being made, even though it may be right to say that it should have been a bar to KPMG being appointed liquidator. However, there were several other reasons for which the petition was dismissed, which may have been more cogent. Furthermore, the ground of distinction from *Re Arrows* relied upon by the judge is unconvincing because the conflicts were actual and not just potential in *Re Arrows* as well. A different ground of distinction might, however, be significant: namely, that in *Wallace Smith* the issue was as to a new appointment rather than the removal of an established office holder. A pragmatic approach would suggest that a refusal

17–018

to appoint should require less overwhelming grounds than a decision to remove.

If the approach in *Re Arrows* was applied to all cases, it could have the consequence that a firm in liquidation has no right to insist that its controlling will (the insolvency office-holder) does not labour under the most severe conflict of interest, namely conducting litigation against another corporation controlled by the same will. (This was not the case in *Re Arrows* itself because of the replacement of the provisional liquidator by receivers in some of the 80 companies.) A direction by the court that authorises the accountants to take and defend the proceedings is not sufficient to remove all such conflict because the nature of litigation is that difficult decisions arise at every turn which cannot all be resolved by consensual applications for directions.

A different approach to the problem was suggested by Needham J. in the Supreme Court of New South Wales in *Re Nickel Mines Ltd*,[62] which was not cited in the English cases.[63] Needham J. recognised that it is usually sensible for the same liquidator to be appointed to related companies. However, where a conflict of interest actually arises, the liquidator ought to apply to the court for a discharge from one of his competing positions. Thus, potentially conflicting interests will not be sufficient to require the liquidator to step down, but actual conflicts will be.[64] Where the interests of two companies might strictly be said to conflict, but there is no actual dispute as to the outcome of their transactions, this will be treated for present purposes as a potential conflict, or perhaps as no conflict at all.[65]

17-019
Re Nickel Mines Ltd was cited in the High Court of Hong Kong in *Re Perak Pioneer Ltd (No.2)*,[66] where the principle that it is undesirable for the same person to act as provisional liquidator for two companies in litigation with each other was accepted, but the case of court-appointed special manager was distinguished on the basis of the latter's limited powers compared to liquidators.

It seems that the approach adopted in *Re Nickel Mines Ltd* and summarised above is the position that the English courts will adopt, as it is entirely consistent with the useful discussion of the English authorities by Warren J. in *Sisu Capital Fund v Tucker* [2006] B.P.I.R. 154 at paras 98 to 113, where the difference between *Re Arrows Ltd* and *Re Wallace Smith*

---

[62] (1978) 3 A.C.L.R. 686.
[63] And see also in Australia *Re Bruton Pty Ltd* (1990) 2 A.C.S.R. 277 and *Re Nida Pty Ltd* (1993) 10 A.C.S.R. 195.
[64] And see *Dreiberg v Bettles and Carter* (2007) N.S.W.S.C. 1204 in which similar reasoning was applied to the question whether liquidators of a company should also be appointed as trustee of a trust where there was a merely potential conflict between the trust and the company.
[65] This appears to be the view of the Court of Appeal in *Katz v McNally* [1997] 2 B.C.L.C. 579 at 583–4.
[66] [1985] 2 H.K.C. 430, and see also in Hong Kong *Re Luen Cheong Tai Construction Co Ltd* [2002] 1354 H.K.C.U. 1.

& Co Ltd was treated as being due to the difference between potential and actual conflicts.

In a case where an actual conflict arose, though short of litigation, the Privy Council has said that liquidators ought to apply to the court for directions. In *Parmalat Capital Finance v Food Holdings Ltd*,[67] the Board was critical of joint liquidators who had sought to deal with a negotiation between two group companies by adopting a role playing approach, with each of the two joint liquidators negotiating for one of the companies. However, on the facts of the case, the Privy Council stopped short of removing the liquidators or ordering further investigation.

C. Office-holder previously involved in advising company or other interested parties

The third category of insolvency cases are those where the accountant has previously been involved with a company, including by investigating it, is then appointed as an officer-holder in an insolvency procedure.[68] Unsurprisingly, an accountant who advises or investigates a company on terms that he will not later accept such an appointment is bound by those terms, which will be enforced by injunction.[69] Similarly, there is no objection to an accountant specifying by way of an engagement letter upon accepting instructions for the company that he might later accept appointment as an insolvency office-holder.[70] In most cases, however, where there is no engagement letter, or it does not refer to this issue, the answer to this kind of conflict is not quite so short.

17–020

The fundamental conflict here is often between the interests of the insolvent company or its creditors and the possible interest of the accountant or auditor in supporting the competence of his own previous work and the correctness of the conclusions he previously reached.[71] The Institute for Chartered Accountants of England and Wales in the Code of Ethics section for Insolvency Practitioners[72] requires an insolvency practitioner to consider how to deal with the potential conflict of interest that may arise where a "significant relationship" has existed with the entity or someone connected with the entity. No hard and fast guidance is given, though numerous factors are set out in ss.400.44 which might indicate the significance of a

---

[67] [2008] UKPC 23; [2009] 1 B.C.L.C. 30.
[68] This situation is not unusual in England: *Sisu Capital Fund v Tucker* [2006] BPIR 154 at paragraph 114.
[69] *Sheppard & Cooper Ltd v TSB Bank Plc* [1997] 2 B.C.L.C. 222.
[70] As suggested by David Richards J. in *Wade v Poppleton & Appleby* [2003] EWCH 3159, Ch. at [155].
[71] The risk can also be manifested as a concern that the accountant as office holder may not be impartial as between the competing interests of different creditors, shareholders etc.
[72] s.400.31.

relationship including that "It is likely that greater threats will arise (or may be seen to arise) where work has been carried out within the previous three years." The statement also provides that when practices merge, they become subject to common constraints on accepting new appointments to clients of any of the former practices. However, existing appointments which are rendered in apparent breach of the guidance by reason of the merger need not be determined automatically.

This statement reflects the law as it is developing in the common law jurisdictions. Its thrust is similar to the professional regulations approved by the Federal Court of Australia in *Re Hurt*.[73]

17–021   In *Re Maxwell Communication Corporation Plc*,[74] the directors of the company petitioned for the appointment of administrators, seeking the appointment of partners in the firm of Touche Ross, who had prepared a report under r.2.2 of the Insolvency Rules 1986. A group of banks who were unsecured creditors of the company agreed that administrators should be appointed, but sought the appointment of partners in Price Waterhouse who had investigated the affairs of the company on behalf of the group of creditors for some 18 days, during which Price Waterhouse had spent 7,000 person hours on the investigation. The directors argued that Price Waterhouse had a conflict of interest because they had audited a US corporation which was a joint venture between a subsidiary of the company concerned and another company. There was no evidence that the audit was open to criticism but it was said to be possible that it would have to be investigated. Hoffmann J. held that this was "no more at the moment than a mere distant possibility". He appointed Price Waterhouse on the ground that they had a substantial head start in terms of knowledge of the company as a result of their investigative role. As to the potential conflict, Hoffmann J. held that it could be dealt with as and when it arose, perhaps by the appointment of an additional administrator from another firm to deal with any matters in respect of which Price Waterhouse would be embarrassed.[75]

The Australian authorities[76] were usefully reviewed by Santow J. in *Advance Housing Pty Ltd (in liquidation) v Newcastle Classic Developments Pty Ltd*.[77] In that case, the liquidator was a member of Ernst & Young, which had acted as accountants for the company. In that capacity Ernst & Young had received payments totalling $20,000 which the defendant said ought to be investigated as unfair preferences. The test to be applied was whether there was a real, not merely theoretical possibility of conflict. Removal of a liquidator was to be judged by the same standard as appoint-

---

[73] (1988) 80 A.L.R. 236.
[74] [1992] B.C.L.C. 465; [1992] B.C.C. 372.
[75] As was done in *Re Polly Peck International Plc* [1991] B.C.C. 503.
[76] Including *Re Club Superstores Australia Pty Ltd* (1993) 10 A.C.S.R. 730.
[77] (1994) 14 A.C.S.R. 230.

ment. The court was satisfied that there was a reasonable case that the payments should be investigated and accordingly held that there was an inherent conflict of interest for the liquidator. The court did not actually order the liquidator's resignation, but gave him the opportunity to retire in the light of the judgment.

In the *Advance Housing* case, the defendant's standing to complain of the liquidator's conflict of interest was assumed on the basis that the defendant claimed to be a creditor of the plaintiff company. Santow J. also stated that there may be a broader category of "person aggrieved" who can apply to remove a liquidator. However, in *Deloitte & Touche v Johnson*, the Privy Council has held that only a creditor has sufficient standing to make such an application. Lord Millett delivering the advice of the Board said:

> "The rule is that a fiduciary may not without the informed consent of his principal place himself in a position where his interest may conflict with his duty to the principal. The danger is that his interest may affect him in the discharge of his duty to the prejudice of his principal. The only persons with a legitimate interest in complaining of a breach of the rule are the persons to whom the duty is owed; and they may waive the breach".[78]

In a case in England, partners in the defendant firm of accountants were instructed to advise an insolvent company and its owners and three days later accepted appointment from a creditor of the company as administrative receivers. David Richards J. held that there was no breach of fiduciary duty because:

17–022

> "once the Bank had decided to appoint receivers, there was nothing further which they could do or were required to do. Their acceptance of the appointment did not affect or undermine the work which they had previously done or in any other way create a conflict with the performance of their duties".[79]

The decision of Hamilton J. sitting in the Equity Division of the Supreme Court of New South Wales in *Domino Hire Pty Ltd v Pioneer Park Pty Ltd (in liquidation)*[80] illustrates the need for caution in cases where an accountant is asked to move directly from investigating on behalf of a creditor to acting as office-holder. In this case a liquidator was removed from office because of a possible conflict of interest arising from the liquidator having previously investigated the company on behalf of a major secured creditor. It is significant that in this case there were other factors in addition to the

---

[78] [1999] 1 W.L.R. 1605 at 1612.
[79] *Wade v Poppleton & Appleby* [2004] 1 B.C.L.C. 674 at [150], David Richards J.
[80] December 15, 1999, Lexis.

liquidator's former role as investigating accountant which suggested a lack of impartiality between creditors.

In one Canadian case, the accountant failed to disclose his firm's earlier involvement with relevant companies upon accepting appointment by the court as receiver and manager. The accountant was not only removed but also deprived of his fees.[81] By contrast, in another Canadian case, where the accountant was (through an affiliate) auditor to several creditors, but the position had been disclosed at the outset, an application by the audit client creditors to remove him as receiver and manager was dismissed.[82]

In England, in Re Maxwell Communication Corporation Plc, discussed above, it does not seem to have been argued that Price Waterhouse's role as investigators on behalf of a group of creditors of itself led to any risk that they would not be, and be seen to be, impartial as administrators.

17–023   As recognised by the ICAEW Code of Ethics for Insolvency Practitioners, the position of the liquidator is less clear when a conflict arises by reason of a merger of accountants' firms that affects a liquidation already on foot. An example of this is the Canadian case of Scarth v Northland Bank (liquidator of)[83] in which the liquidation had been proceeding for over ten years and was almost complete when the liquidator's firm merged with the company's former auditors. The company's directors applied to remove the liquidator on the ground of conflict of interest because, the directors argued, the liquidator should consider suing the auditors. However, the liquidator had already considered and rejected pursuing an action against the auditors before the merger took place, and all the other creditors supported the liquidator's continuance in office to complete the winding up. The court refused the directors' application to remove the liquidator.

Similarly, where an accountant who had previously advised a director of a company in liquidation joined a firm, a partner in which was acting as liquidator to the company and actively investigating suing the director, the Supreme Court of South Australia would not remove the liquidator on the grounds of lack of independence, but did refer for trial the possibility of his removal because of the risk of disclosure of the director's confidential information, following Bolkiah.[84] A similar approach, but with a different result, was applied in the English case of Bloomsbury International v Holyoake,[85] where it was held that if an administrator still owed fiduciary duties to a former director of the company who had been their client, then it would have been improper for them to commence proceedings in the name of the company against that client, but that since the retainer for the former director had ceased by the time of the application, any defect had been cured. As

---

[81] Canadian Co-operative Leasing Services v Price Waterhouse (1992) 128 N.B.R. (2nd) 1.
[82] Re YBM Magnex International Inc (2000) 275 A.R. 352.
[83] December 6, 1996, Manitoba Queen's Bench, Lexis.
[84] Pradhan v Eastside Day Surgery Pty Ltd [1999] S.A.S.C. 256.
[85] [2010] EWHC 1150 (Ch).

to confidential information, applying Bolkiah, it was held that there was no real risk of the former director's information passing from those in the firm who had advised him to the administrators.

In a Hong Kong case, *Re Orient Power Holdings*,[86] an accountant was appointed liquidator despite also serving as receiver and manager of the same company under a debenture. In that case, some unusual measures, including the appointment of three joint liquidators so that the one who was also receiver would be in the minority, were adopted to manage the potential conflicts of interest.

---

[86] [2008] H.K.C.U. 200.

CHAPTER 18

Directors

A. The Companies Act 2006

18–001 The company director, whether executive or non-executive, will owe fiduciary duties to the company. It has been said that a director is not a trustee but owes duties similar to those of a trustee.[1] In 1999 the Law Commission[2] summarised the fiduciary obligations of a company director as encompassing the following heads: duty of loyalty, duty to act for proper purpose, no fetters on discretion, the no-conflict and no-profit rules, the duty to act in accordance with the company's constitution and the duty to deal fairly as between different classes of shareholders.[3] The director also has statutory obligations of disclosure in certain cases. In the case of the company director the possibility of a personal conflict is likely to be relevant more often than where the conflict faces a professional.

Now English company law is governed by the Companies Act 2006, the longest statute ever to appear on the statute book. The Act is in some respects a codification of existing common law and statute, and in other respects goes well beyond a codification exercise.

Chapter 2 of Pt 10 of the Act is headed General Duties of Directors. For the first time, the Act seeks to codify duties which in the past have been derived from caselaw. Sections 171–177 set out the duties of directors. Section 170(2) states that a person who ceases to be a director continues to be subject to the duty to avoid conflicts of interest as regards the exploitation of any property information or opportunity of which he became aware at a time when he was a director and to the duty not to accept benefits from

---

[1] *Re Lands Allotment Co* [1894] 1 Ch. 616 at 631, per Lindley L.J.
[2] Company Directors: Regulating Conflicts of Interest and Formulating a Statement of Duties, 1999, Law Comm. No.261.For a recent restatement of directors' duties prior to the Companies Act 2006 see *Foster Bryant Surveying v Bryant 2007* EWCA 200.
[3] At 11.4.

third parties as regards things done or omitted to be done by him before he ceased to be a director.

For purposes of conflicts of interest, the key sections are s.172 (duty to promote the success of the company) and s.175 (duty to avoid conflicts of interest). Other relevant sections are s.173 (duty to exercise independent judgment, which is not infringed by the director acting in accordance with an agreement duly entered into by the company that restricts the future exercise of discretion by its directors), s.174 (duty to exercise reasonable care, skill and diligence), s.176 (duty not to accept benefits from third parties) and s.177 and s.182 (duty to declare an interest in existing or proposed transaction or arrangement with the company). Failure to disclose an interest under s.182 is a criminal offence.[4] Sections 188, 228 and 237 provide statutory control over directors' service contracts. Section 190 requires substantial property transactions with directors to be approved in advance by the company in general meeting. Sections 197–214 set out restrictions on loans, quasi loans and credit transactions being entered into with directors. Section 228 requires companies to keep a copy of service contracts available for inspection by members. Section 237 requires any indemnity provision for the benefit of the directors similarly to be available for inspection.

It is for consideration how far the statutory duties under the Act can be regarded as supplementing the equitable fiduciary duties owed by directors, and how far they can be treated as supplanting them. Equitable fiduciary duties normally give rise to different, and wider, remedies than statutory provisions (such as an account of profits). Section 178 states that:

"(1) The consequences of breach (or threatened breach) of sections 171 to 177 are the same as would apply if the corresponding common law or equitable principles applied.
(2) The duties in those sections (with the exception of section 174 (duty to exercise reasonable care, skill, and diligence) are accordingly, enforceable in the same way as any other fiduciary duty owed to a company by its directors."

Section 170 provides as follows:

"(3) The general duties are based on certain common law rules and equitable principles as they apply in relation to directors and have effect in place of those rules and principles as regards the duties owed to a company by a director.
(4) The general duties shall be interpreted and applied in the same way as common law rules or equitable principles, and regard shall be had

---

[4] s.183. It may be debatable whether breach of ss.177 and 182 gives rise to civil remedies: see Stafford and Ritchie, *Fiduciary Duties: Director's and Employees* (2008 Jordans) para 2.60

to the corresponding common law rules and equitable principles in interpreting and applying the general duties."

It seems, therefore, that it is permissible for existing caselaw to be used to interpret these duties.

B. Promoting the success of the company

18-002   Section 172 provides for a newly-expressed duty to promote the success of the company. That duty must be exercised for the benefit of its members as a whole, having regard to the likely consequences of any decision in the long term, the interests of the company's employees, the need to foster the company's business relationships with suppliers, customers and others, the impact of the company's operations on the community and the environment, the desirability of the company maintaining a reputation for high standards of business conduct and the need to act fairly as between members of the company.

18-003   The duty to promote the success of the company means that a director must place the interests of the company as a whole above the interests of the members or a class of them.[5] One issue is whether s.172 answers the thorny question whether a director has an obligation to the company to disclose his own misconduct. A director has been said generally not to have an obligation to disclose his own misconduct. This is the result of the famous, or perhaps notorious, decision of the House of Lords in *Bell v Lever Bros*.[6] It has been held that the director does have an obligation to disclose misconduct of other employees[7] notwithstanding that the effect of this may be the disclosure of his own wrongdoing. But recently in *Item Software (UK) Ltd v Fassihi*,[8] a case under the old law, Arden L.J. suggested that the duty of a director to disclose his own misconduct was not a separate and independent duty but part of his fundamental duty to act in good faith in what he considers to be the best interests of the company.[9] Whether as a consequence of *Item Software* or as a result of s.172, or both, the effect is probably to

---

[5] See *Re BSB Holdings Ltd* (No 2) 1996 1 B.C.L.C. 155, 251 Arden J.
[6] [1932] A.C. 161.
[7] *Horcal v Gatland* [1984] I.R.L.R. 288, CA; *Sybron v Rochem* [1984] Ch. 112, CA; *Swain v. West (Butchers)* [1936] 3 All E.R. 261, CA.
[8] [2005] 2 B.C.L.C. 91, discussed in relation to fiduciary duties at 2–011.
[9] [41]. Arden L.J. said it was unnecessary to consider to what extent an employee as distinct from a fiduciary had a duty to disclose his own wrongdoing. At [46] Arden L.J. said that *Bell v Lever Brothers* [1932] A.C. 161 "is not authority for the proposition that there are no circumstances in which an employee can have a duty to disclose his wrongdoing." It was unnecessary to decide whether *Bell* applied when there had been fraudulent concealment by the employee. See also *British Midland Tool Ltd v Midland International Tooling Ltd* [2003] EWHC 466.

reverse for this purpose the decision in *Bell v Lever Bros*,[10] which has long been regarded as ripe for reconsideration, and to provide a statutory underpinning for a duty on a director to disclose his own misconduct. It is hard to see how a director could be promoting the success of the company as required by s.172 by concealing his own misconduct.

C. Statutory duty to avoid conflicts of interest

Section 175 provides for a duty to avoid conflicts of interest: 18–004

"(1) A director of a company must avoid a situation in which he has, or can have, a direct or indirect interest that conflicts, or possibly may conflict, with the interests of the company.
(2) This applies in particular to the exploitation of any property, information or opportunity (and it is immaterial whether the company could take advantage of the property, information or opportunity).
(3) This duty does not apply to a conflict of interest arising in relation to a transaction or arrangement with the company.
(4) This duty is not infringed-
   (a) if the situation cannot reasonably be regarded as likely to give rise to a conflict of interest; or
   (b) if the matter has been authorised by the directors."

Section 175 (5)–(6) provide for the circumstances in which an authorisation by the directors may be effective.

D. Engaging in competing businesses

Section 175(1) requires a director to avoid a situation in which he has, or can have, a direct or indirect interest that conflicts or possibly may conflict with the interests of the company. This applies equally to conflicts of interest and duty: s.175 (7). Avoiding conflicts of interest has always been part of the fiduciary duty of a director. A famous illustration is *Industrial Development Consultants v Cooley*.[11] The director resigned as managing director and director to take up in his own name a valuable contract which had previously been sought by the company but where the company's approach had been rejected. He obtained the contract. He was held accountable to the company for all the profit he made on the contract because he had allowed his interest and duty to conflict and had 18–005

---

[10] [1932] A.C. 161.
[11] [1972] 2 All E.R. 162, Roskill J.; contrast this with *Island Export Finance v Umunna* [1986] B.C.L.C. 460.

failed to disclose to the company information obtained before resigning. This was despite the fact that the judge held that there was only a 10 per cent chance that the company could have obtained the contract itself. The reasoning was that he had misappropriated the company's property, namely information, but the case can be seen as a director liable to account for profits where he had let his personal interest conflict with that of the company. Moreover, the prophylactic nature of fiduciary encourages compliance by preventing the director from contending that the company would not have been awarded the contract. Section 170(2) provides for the continuation after termination of the duties under s.175 and s.176 in relation to property, information, opportunities or things done before ceasing to be a director.

The combined effect of s.172 and s.175 may alter the common law position and prohibit directors from accepting competing appointments without the informed consent of the company. The increasingly obsolete *Mashanoland* decision had historically suggested that a director of one company might be a director of a competing company unless prohibited by contract.[12] But if the director is provided with confidential information whilst a director of company A, how can he promote the success of competitor company B, of which he is also a director, unless he discloses it to company A? Where the director is an executive, the obligations under his service contract will probably prevent him from taking on a competing company directorship. The position is less clear where the director is a non-executive, but the courts may well use these sections as a basis for finally getting rid of the old *Mashonaland* rule.

E. Disclosing interest in transactions

18–006   Section 177 requires a director to declare an interest in a proposed transaction or arrangement with the company. Section 182 requires a director to declare his interest in an existing transaction or arrangement. If he has declared his interest prior to the transaction being entered into, he need not

---

[12] The decision of Chitty J. in *London & Mashonaland Exploration Co Ltd v New Mashonaland Exploration Co Ltd* [1891] W.N. 165 which was endorsed by Lord Blanesburgh (with whom Lord Atkin and Lord Thankerton agreed) in *Bell v Lever Bros Ltd* [1932] A.C. 161 has been taken as establishing that a director is not necessarily precluded from engaging in a competing business. But more recent authority suggested that this view was increasingly obsolete. There is criticism of the traditional approach in *Item Software (UK) Ltd v Fassihi* [2004] EWCA Civ 1244, per Arden L.J. obiter at [63] In *Plus Group Ltd v Pyke* [2002] 2 B.C.L.C. 201, Sedley L.J. whilst recognising that this was binding on the court, sought to restrict its effect, at [84]–[90], making clear that there was no warrant for treating the decision as a licence for directors to put themselves into situations where their duty and interest conflict. Brooke and Jonathan Parker L.JJ. did not find it necessary to deal with the *Mashonaland* case, although Brooke L.J. did speak of it as "rather startling" at [72]. See *Bhullar v Bhullar* [2003] 2 B.C.L.C. 241, and *Prentice and Payne* (2004) 120 L.Q.R. 198.

make a s.182 declaration. Unlike s.177, a failure to declare an interest under s.182 is a criminal offence. Unlike s.177, a declaration under s.182 must be made in a prescribed manner: at a meeting of the directors, by notice in writing, or by general notice. If a director enters into a transaction or arrangement with the company without declaring his interest, he will be under an immediate s.182 obligation with criminal sanctions.

If a director complies with s.177, the company can decide on an informed basis whether to proceed with the proposed transaction. Section 180 indicates that this declaration replaces the need for the approval of the company's members under the equitable rules, although any additional requirements imposed by the articles will still have to be met. If these requirements have been complied with, the transaction cannot be impugned. If s.177 is not complied with, the director will be in breach of initially s.177 and then s.182. Equitable remedies may be pursued against the defaulting director for breach of statutory duty (see s.178)[13] and rescission sought where appropriate (depending on third party rights).

F. Nominee directors

The nominee director, the director nominated by a parent, shareholder or creditor company, will often face acute conflicts of interest. The nominee will usually be appointed to the board of a company to serve the interests of another company. For example, he may be appointed at the request of and perhaps as a condition of further support from, a debenture holder; the purpose of his appointment will be to oversee the business to protect the interests of the debenture holder.

18–007

There is no special creature of nominee director under English law. The duties owed by nominee directors are no different from those owed by any other director. Section 173 restates this position, by requiring the director of a company to exercise independent judgment.[14] The nominee director, therefore, has a real problem. If he simply follows the wishes of his appointor, he runs of the risk of conflict, as his obligation is to act in the interests of the company to which he is appointed.[15] Where there is an insolvency, he

---

[13] It has been queried whether civil remedies apply to breaches of s.177 and s.182 because although s.178(1) provides that the consequences of breach of ss171–177 are the same as would apply if the corresponding common law rule or equitable principle applied, and s.178(2) provides that the duties in those sections are enforceable in the same way as any other fiduciary duty owed to a company by its directors, there was no pre-2006 equivalent of s.177: Stafford and Ritchie, *Fiduciary Duties: Directors and Employees* (2008 Jordans) para 2.60. However, the specific reference to s.177 in s.178 suggests that it was intended that civil law remedies would apply to breach of s.177.

[14] However, s.173(2) permits a director to act in accordance with a duly completed contract which restricts the exercise of a discretion, and in a way authorised by the company's constitution.

[15] It has been said that "the Courts in Australia and New Zealand have adopted a less

must act in the interests of the creditors as a whole rather than the interests of his appointor. Thus an agreement executed by a director to act at all times in accordance with the instructions of his principal is likely to be unenforceable. In *Kuwait Asia Bank EC v National Mutual Life Nominees*[16] the Privy Council held that on the liquidation of a money-broking company, directors appointed by a bank which was beneficially interested in the company were bound in the performance of their duties as directors to ignore the interests and wishes of the bank and could not plead any instruction from the bank as an excuse for any breaches of their duties to the company.[17]

G. Interests of the group

18–008   A similar problem arises where the company forms part of a group. Directors of a company within the group may when taking decisions have regard to the interests of the group as a whole but must not prejudice the company for the benefit of the group. Thus in a conflict between the interests of group and subsidiary, the directors of the subsidiary must protect its interests. Again, this follows from s.173. In *Charterhouse Corporation v Lloyds Bank*[18] the test was said to be:

> "the proper test ... in the absence of actual separate consideration must be whether an intelligent and honest man in the position of a director of the company concerned could ... have reasonably believed that the transactions were for the benefit of the company."[19]

In the instant case, it was held that the collapse of the parent would have been a disaster for the subsidiary, and thus the directors of the subsidiary were not in breach of duty in agreeing to give security for a debt owed by parent to bank notwithstanding that the directors had given no separate consideration to the position of the subsidiary.

H. Joint venture companies

18–009   This is another common situation where the director will face conflict between the interests of the company and those of the appointee and risk breaching s.173. Here it is particularly stark because there will often be a

---

uncompromising approach in an effort to recognise the reality of commercial activity": *Dairy Containers v NZI Bank* [1995] 2 N.Z.L.R. 8 at 96, and cf. the cases there cited.

[16] [1991] 1 A.C. 187, PC.
[17] See also *Boulting v ACTAT* [1963] 2 Q.B. 606; *Re Broadcasting Station 2 GB Pty* (1964–65) N.S.W.R. 1648.
[18] [1969] 2 All E.R. 1185.
[19] *Charterbridge Corporation v Lloyds Bank* [1970] Ch 62.

significant overlap between the business of the shareholder and that of the joint venture company.[20] Thus in *Scottish Co-operative Society v Meyer*[21] three directors appointed under the articles of a joint venture company by the Co-op failed to inform the joint venture company that its business was being misappropriated by the covert efforts of the majority shareholder. This led to a successful application by the minority shareholder for the purchase of its shares under a minority shareholder's petition. Lord Denning said that once the interests conflicted, the nominee directors were placed in an impossible position. There is the further problem that if the nominee directors take a decision which is in the interests of their appointor, when challenged they may have real difficulty in persuading a court that they had in mind the interests of the joint venture.[22]

Another problem area is confidential information. The nominee director is not as of right entitled to pass on confidential information of the company to his appointor. The articles of the joint venture company may deal with the problem. Otherwise, the director should obtain express permission, ideally in blanket terms.[23] In practice, joint venture companies contain constitutions or are set up by shareholder agreements which reserve major decisions for determination by the shareholders or provide for shareholder veto rights, to avoid conflicts problems.

---

[20] For example, where the joint venture arrangements envisage that the joint venture will be supplied by the shareholders.
[21] [1959] A.C. 324.
[22] *Lee Panavision v Lee Lighting, The Times,* June 25, 1991, CA; *Howard Smith v Ampol Petroleum* [1974] A.C. 821 at 834. The position is really no different to conflicts problems elsewhere: the director who faces an actual conflict of interest simply cannot objectively reach a decision and should not try, any more than the professional should (compare Millett L.J. in *Bristol & West Building Soc v Mothew* [1998] Ch. 1).
[23] He might be able to satisfy himself that in certain circumstances it is in the interests of the joint venture company for him to do so. But this is fraught with problems where there is any possibility of conflict.

CHAPTER 19

Conflicts in the City

1. The regime under the Financial Services and Markets Act 2000

A. The Financial Services and Markets Act 2000

19–001　The new environment in the city after "Big Bang" in 1986 led to concern that because large organisations were being set up to effect "one-stop shopping" for financial services, additional conflicts problems arose. The principal regulatory statute was then the Financial Services Act 1986. Now the Financial Services and Markets Act 2000 ("FSMA") and the Financial Services Authority ("FSA"), has replaced the 1986 Act.

FSA Rule SYSC, 10[1] deals with conflicts of interest. SYSC, r.10.1 deals with conflicts of interest generally and SYSC, r.10.2 deals specifically with what FSA still refer to, somewhat surprisingly, as Chinese Walls. SYSC, r.10.1.3 requires identification of conflicts of interest. SYSC, r.10.1.4 identifies types of situation to be regarded as conflicts of interest. SYSC, r.10.1.6 requires maintenance of records of conflicts and r.10.1.7 requires maintenance and operation of effective organisational and administrative arrangements with a view to taking all reasonable steps to prevent conflicts of interest for constituting or giving rise to a material risk of damage to the interests of the client. There are also provisions relating to disclosure of conflicts, establishment and implementation of a conflicts policy. SYSC, r.10.1.12 requires that a conflicts policy pay special attention to:

---

[1] SYSC stands for Senior Management Arrangements Systems and Controls. The FSA Conduct of Business Rules were amended from November 1, 2007 in order to take into account the EU MIFID directive which came into force on that date.

"the activities of investment research and advice, proprietary trading, portfolio management and corporate finance business, including underwriting or selling in an offering of securities and advising on mergers and acquisitions. In particular, such special attention is appropriate where the firm or a person directly or indirectly linked by control to the firm performs a combination of two or more of those activities".[2]

Section 147 of FSMA enables rules to be made by the FSA about the disclosure and use of information held by an authorised person. The FSA Conduct of Business rules are made under s.147. Section 147 is the successor of s.48(2)(h) of the 1986 Act. Section 48(2)(h) did not make clear whether the SIB rules made under its powers would override common law duties. Thus under the 1986 Act it was never decided whether SIB r.36 (which authorised information barriers) merely constituted a defence to regulatory criticism or action, or whether it could be deployed as a defence to a claim for breach of a common law legal or equitable obligation. Now SYSC, r.10.2.2 provides that:

"(1) When a firm establishes and maintains a Chinese Wall (that is, an arrangement that requires information held by a person in the course of carrying on one part of its business to be withheld from, or not to be used for, persons with or for whom it acts in the course of carrying on another part of its business) it may:
(a) withhold or not use the information held; and
(b) for that purpose, permit persons employed in the first part of its business to withhold the information held from those employed in that other part of the business;
but only to the extent that the business of one of those parts involves the carrying on of regulated activities, ancillary activities or, in the case of MiFID business, the provision of ancillary services.
(2) Information may also be withheld or not used by a firm when this is required by an established arrangement maintained between different parts of the business (of any kind) in the same group. This provision does not affect any requirement to transmit or use information that may arise apart from the rules in COBS.
(3) For the purpose of this rule, "maintains" includes taking reasonable steps to ensure that the arrangements remain effective and are adequately monitored, and must be interpreted accordingly."

The other relevant SYSC rule is 10.2.4 which relates to attribution of knowledge:

19–002

---

[2] See art.26 of MIFID implementing directive. SYSC, r.10.1.15 deals specifically with corporate finance conflicts policies.

"When any of the rules of COBS or CASS apply to a firm that acts with knowledge, the firm will not be taken to act with knowledge for the purposes of that rule if none of the relevant individuals involved on behalf of the firm acts with that knowledge as a result of arrangements established under SYSC 10.2.2."

For SYSC, r.10.2.4 to apply, it requires the establishment and maintenance of the information barrier. This must be an arrangement requiring information held by a person in the course of carrying on one part of the firm's business to be withheld from persons employed in other parts of the business or between different parts of the business in the same group. The establishment and maintenance of the information barrier has the effect that it will provide a justification for not using information which the firm might otherwise be obliged to use and from withholding that information. SYSC, r.10.2.5 reinforces this and provides that:

"When a firm manages a conflict of interest using the arrangements in SYSC 10.2.2 which take the form of a Chinese wall, individuals on the other side of the wall will not be regarded as being in possession of knowledge denied to them as a result of the Chinese wall."

B. Effect of SYSC, r.10

19–003   The first question is whether SYSC, r.10.2 is limited to information barriers which are part of the structure of the firm, or whether it includes information barriers which are ad hoc in nature. Where information barriers are set up in regulated firms, it is more likely that the recurring conflicts which occur will necessitate information barriers as part of the established structure of the firm, and there may be much less call for the one-off ad hoc information barriers which can be necessary in law firms. However, it is suggested that SYSC, r.10.2 has moved away from the old Financial Services Act wording under SIB r.36 which appeared merely to relate to structural information barriers:

"36. Chinese Walls
  1. Where a firm maintains an established arrangement which requires information obtained by the firm in the course of carrying on one part of its business of any kind to be withheld in certain circumstances from persons with whom it deals in the course of carrying on another part of its business of any kind, then in those circumstances:
      (a) that information may be so withheld; and
      (b) for that purpose, persons employed in the first part may withhold information from those employed in the second;

but only to the extent that the business of one of those parts involves investment business or associated business."

In his speech in *Bolkiah*, Lord Millett drew attention to SIB r.36 (then in force) as the basis for the distinction between information barriers which were part of the established structure of a firm and those which were merely ad hoc. But it is striking that the words "established arrangement" are missing from SYSC, r.10.2.2. It is true that SYSC, r.10.2.2(3) speaks of maintaining the wall by effective monitoring, but that needs to be done for an ad hoc information barrier too. Whilst no doubt the principal concern of SYSC, r.10.2.2 is structural information barriers, that no longer seems to be the only type contemplated.

The next question is the effect of SYSC, r.10.2. Under the old FSA regime, there was a long-running debate never tested in the courts as to whether SIB r.36 merely provided a defence to regulatory action or statutory offences and torts, or whether it had effect beyond that as a defence to a common law or equitable claim for breach of fiduciary duty.[3] It was perhaps surprising that the opportunity was not taken in s.147 to make the position clear.[4] The government view in drafting the legislation seems to have been that it goes further than providing a defence to statutory or regulatory action. Lord Millett's use in *Bolkiah* of the SIB rules on information barriers as a foundation for his distinction between structural and ad hoc information barriers seems to have given those drafting FSMA confidence that s.147 (and thus rules made under it) overrode legal or equitable obligations. That was certainly the intention of the government, and in introducing the bill the minister said that the provisions were aimed specifically at displacing the fiduciary duties that would otherwise arise[5] and insisted that nothing else was needed to achieve that result.

19–004

It is suggested that the position is much less clear than the government appears to have thought. Section 147 is part of the regulatory scheme applicable to firms authorised by the FSA. There is a body of authority to the effect that it is presumed statutes do not alter the common law where statutes accord power to public bodies.[6] The argument that s.147 does not affect the general law is based on the two sets of rules operating in different spheres: s.147 affects regulatory obligations only. It certainly does not indi-

---

[3] See the 1st edition of this book at para.11–03.
[4] The Law Commission took the tentative view that Rule 36 was intra vires and did affect the general law although not everyone agreed with this. The Law Commission recommended that there should be an amendment to FSA s.48(2)(h) to give statutory protection to a firm operating an established information barrier which complies with regulatory rules: see Fiduciary Duties and Regulatory Rules 1995 No.236.
[5] Hansard, HL cols 1405–9 (May 9, 2000); Hansard, HL col.421 (May 18, 2000).
[6] *Mixnam's Properties v Chertsey UDC* [1965] A.C. 735 at 750–52; *Torquay Local Board v Bridle* (1882) 47 J.P. 183; *Colman v Mills* [1897] 1 Q.B. 396; *White v Morley* [1899] 2 Q.B. 34 at 39; *Powell v May* [1946] K.B. 330.

cate that it affects the general law. It seems difficult to read s.147 as encompassing a radical alteration of fiduciary duties. SYSC, r.10.2.2 applies to firms that conduct designated investment business. There is nothing to suggest that it restricts the rights of others.[7] On the contrary, the SYSC, r.10.2.3 guidance under the heading "Effect of rules" makes clear that compliance with r.10.2.2 will provide a defence to proceedings under s.397 (Misleading statements and practices), s.118 (Market abuse), FSA Enforcement action, or an action for damages under s.150 (Breach of statutory duty), but there is no suggestion that it provides a defence to common law or equitable claims. Moreover SYSC, r.10.2.2(2) provides expressly that "this provision does not affect any requirement to transmit or use information that may arise apart from the rules in COBS." So, even if s.147 gave the FSA the power to exclude common law and equitable claims where the firm has acted in compliance with COBS rules, it may be that the rule made under its powers does not go as far.[8]

So what practical difference does it make whether SYSC, r.10.2.2 is limited to regulatory action? Recent authorities on transmission of information[9] will have the effect that information received on one side of an information barrier from one client is unlikely to be treated as being information which other parts of the firm are obliged to pass on to a different client even without SYSC, r.10.2.5. But it is suggested there are some respects in which compliance with SYSC, r.10.2.2 may not provide protection.

If a firm complies with SYSC, r.10.2.2 it might seem difficult to obtain an injunction restraining it from acting in a given case, but the width and lack of specificity in SYSC, r.10.2.2 leaves the firm open to the charge that although an information barrier has been set up and falls within the wording of SYSC, r.10.2.2, it is insufficiently robust to prevent the possibility of leakage of information. For example, an ad hoc information barrier may fall within SYSC, r.10.2.2 but not satisfy a court applying what Lord Millett said in *Bolkiah*. As SYSC, r.10.2.2 gives no guidance as to what is sufficient, it leaves the issue open for argument. And if the efficacy of an information barrier can be challenged in this way, surely a claim for breach of fiduciary duty can at least in principle be levelled at the firm?

19–005 Another area for challenge relates to existing client conflicts. SYSC, r.10.2.2 appears to relate as much to existing client conflicts as it does to former client conflicts. Although the term "information barrier" is usu-

---

[7] There is no case law on this point but as to the effect of the COB rules on contractual terms see *Clarion v National Provident* [2000] 1 W.L.R. 1888 Rimer J.; *Gorham v British Telecommunications Plc* [2000] 1 W.L.R. 2129; *Loosemore v Financial Concepts* [2001] Lloyd's Rep. P.N. 235.

[8] *Bowstead and Reynolds on Agency* (19th edn, 2010) at para.6–060 also doubts whether s.147 affects fiduciary obligations, although the authors suggest compliance might be evidence of statutory reasonableness or be a guide to the extent of the fiduciary obligation or trade usage.

[9] See Ch.6.

ally used to refer to the information barrier which protects a former client from the risk of misuse of confidential information, there is nothing in the COBS rules which so limits it. So the issue arises as to whether there may be a breach of the double employment rule. If so, how can SYSC, r.10.2.2 protect the firm against such a claim? Exactly the same issue was canvassed in the first edition of this book in respect of SIB r.36.[10] It seems surprising that the opportunity was not taken in FSMA to resolve the position.

The scheme established by the FSA Rules recognises that conflicts will occur in the regular course of business and provides that so long as appropriate steps are taken to manage them, the firm will be protected from (at least) regulatory criticism and action and will not be treated as having knowledge obtained on one side of an information barrier to those on the other side of the wall. The steps which may be taken are disclosure to the customer, declining to act, establishing internal arrangements (information barriers) and relying on a policy of independence. A policy of independence is intended to protect the interests of customers by requiring employees to disregard any material conflict when advising a customer or dealing for a customer in the exercise of discretion.

C. Financial services conflicts

The nature of the organisational structure of a financial conglomerate principally give rise to conflicts of interest and duty because of the range of products and services, the composition of the customer base, and the different capacities in which it conducts business. One may distinguish conflicts which arise from the structural organisation of a professional activity from difficulties that result from the fact that the professionals choose to carry on business in a way that may not comply with their fiduciary obligations.[11] It is in the financial services industry that conflicts arising from the organisational structure are most apparent. Thus stockbroking firms may have to be knowledgeable about insurance policies, unit trusts, managed funds and international and foreign securities as well as those listed on the Stock Exchange. If firms develop expertise in these, they will eventually put clients into their own business rather than intermediaries. There are compelling reasons for these various activities to be carried on within the same firm.

19–006

---

[10] 1st edn, para.11–03.
[11] Thus, to take examples given by the Law Commission Consultation Paper No.124, "Fiduciary Duties and Regulatory Rules" (1992), when an estate agent is paid a commission for arranging an endowment policy for a customer and does not disclose it or a valuer is retained by the estate agent department of the lender and who is under pressure because the lender for commercial reasons wants to make the loan, these are situations where professionals carry on business in a manner which could cause conflict with standard fiduciary norms. They have nothing to do with the structure of the industry.

"Big Bang" in 1986 abolished rules relating to outside ownership of members of the Stock Exchange and abolished the single capacity rule whereby a person had to act as stockbroker (agent acting for members of the public) or jobber (principal who made market in securities for his own account). In consequence, many Stock Exchange members were taken over by banks to form part of a financial conglomerate. The diversification of products and services has led to the fact that one of the principal services now provided by a firm is the exercise of discretionary control of customers' portfolios. This provides ample potential for a firm to prefer its own interests to those of its customers. A financial conglomerate may, therefore, at the same time be market maker, broker or dealer, provide asset management and customer advisory services, corporate finance services, underwriting of new issues or rights issues and services managing unit trusts. A firm will often itself deal either as agent or its own right. The problem here is the broker or dealer acting as principal and selling or buying stock to or from a customer off or for its own book in the course of a fiduciary relationship. Advance disclosure of the fact the firm may act as principal is probably sufficient, as is often done in discretionary management customer agreements. The difficulty is that advance disclosure does not enable the principal to know in what capacity his agent is acting on any particular transaction. One problem which arises in all these cases is that it may be impracticable to disclose the required information in advance of what may be regarded as breach of duty. The broker may not know at the time of a particular transaction whether it is executed off his own book. In these cases, strict compliance with the equitable rules as to fiduciaries is not merely inconvenient; it is simply not feasible.

The Law Commission set out a helpful summary of some of the most common conflicts which arise in firms providing financial services[12]:

> (a) Dealing off one's book or buying on own account this refers to the firm selling its own property to an advisory or discretionary customer or buying the property of such a customer. There will be a conflict between the firm's own interests and those of the customer, the vendor wanting the highest price, the purchaser the lowest and may breach the "no profit" fiduciary obligation.
> (b) Matching orders and riskless principal transactions where the firm executes an agency cross or a riskless principal transaction the firm acts for both parties to the transaction.
> (c) Dealing in property in which the customer has an interest if a firm has an interest in property in which the customer also has an interest their respective interests may conflict, as where both customer and firm

---

[12] See at the Law Commission Consultation Paper No.124, "Fiduciary Duties and Regulatory Rules" (1992), p.33.

have large shareholdings in a company, any disposal by the firm from either the customer's or his own holding may well affect the value of their respective holdings.

(d) Preferential or discriminatory treatment a firm must treat customers to whom it owes similar duties equally and cannot prefer one of them to others. So if the firm becomes aware of an investment opportunity, and only advises some of its customers, it will be in breach of duty. Thus if the corporate finance department is underwriting a share issue recommended by the broker/dealer department, the corporate finance department may treat some customers more generously than others, or, conversely if the issue is not a success, may persuade the broker/dealer department to purchase shares for discretionary managed accounts. Where a broker/dealer aggregates orders, this may lead to a less good price than if executed at once. Where a firm manages a general European unit trust and one restricted to a particular country, there will be difficulties in determining how investment opportunities in the particular country are allocated between the funds.

(e) Failure to utilise all information available when acting for a customer, a firm must utilise all the information available to it. The broker/dealer department may be advising the purchase of shares in a company advised by the corporate finance department which the latter knows to be on the verge of insolvency. The broker/dealer department will also obtain commission from any purchase order executed for a customer. Or the broker/dealer department may be instructed to purchase a substantial holding in a listed company at the end of the trading day and before the purchase an advisory customer seeks advice as to whether he should sell his shares in the relevant company.

(f) Breach of confidentiality. If a firm uses confidential information for another customer, it will breach its duty to that customer. Yet that information may be very important to another company to whom the firm owes fiduciary obligations.

(g) Self-dealing on the basis of confidential information. Problems will occur if the firm is dealing on its own account in a product about which some part of the firm has relevant price-sensitive confidential information.

(h) Takeovers: the commercial bank within a group may be advising the target of a hostile bid while the corporate finance department is advising the bidder. The corporate finance department may be advising a customer with respect to a rumoured bid from an anonymous bidder who turns out to be a former customer of the firm. The department managing discretionary accounts is selling the shares of a company which is making a hostile share exchange takeover and is being advised by the firm's corporate advisory department. The sale of the shares could depress the offeror's share price with obvious consequences as to the bid.

D. The use of information barriers in the City

19–007 Information barriers are very widely used in organisations offering financial services. The problem is that many of the conflicts which arise in financial services firms fall within Lord Millett's categorisation as an existing client conflict. Thus the concern is that where there is an existing client conflict the bar is based on conflict not confidentiality[13] and there is a potential breach of the "double employment" rule where the fiduciary owes conflicting obligations to two customers. Consideration has already been given to the potential defences which may arise to a claim of this nature for breach of fiduciary duty. For organisational information barriers the starting point is the protection which can be obtained from terms of business[14] so that the customer may be said to consent to the firm carrying on business using an information barrier as part of its organisational structure. Where the customer is in the same market, trade custom may provide an answer. Because the law treats separate companies in the same group as separate legal entities, where it is necessary for a group to ensure separation between different functions, it may be wise to set up separate corporate entities. But in many circumstances this simply will not be organisationally practical.

Information barriers are common as between corporate finance departments and other activities, between research and sales or trading, investment management and sales and dealing. Other circumstances in which they may be appropriate are between sales and trading, between loan officers and the firm's own account position in stocks, new issues and secondary market activities and between overseas branches and offices of the same organisation. It is likely to be difficult to maintain an effective information barrier in small organisations, where barriers are particularly difficult to construct.

The guidelines set out by Lord Millett as to when and in what circumstances information barriers may be regarded as effective are relevant here.[15] The firm will look at matters such as physical separation of departments, separate files whereby employees have no access to files or information networks on the other side of the information barrier, restrictions on the circumstances in which employees may cross the wall, and detailed codes of conduct enforced by a compliance officer, often accompanied by training courses. Some of the problems which regularly occur are as follows:

(a) Crossing the wall

19–008 A common problem is the need for penetration of the information barrier. This is not dealt with in SYSC 10.2.2. An industry or

---

[13] See Lord Millett in *Bolkiah* [1999] 2 A.C. 222.
[14] See 4–024 above.
[15] See para.7–015.

sector analyst may need to cross the wall to advise the corporate finance department with respect to a particular transaction.[16] This will inevitably cause problems. What happens to his customers when he is over the wall? This is a particular problem for a small firm: if the analyst ceases to deal with his customers the firm may not be able to provide a service. It is particularly difficult for a small firm to set up an effective information barrier. What happens when he comes back over the wall? He can in theory be put into quarantine[17] until the confidential information which has been imparted to him is stale and it is thus safe for him to return to his previous tasks. This may be a huge burden for a small firm. Plainly, the decision to bring an analyst over the wall should only be made after careful deliberation and at an appropriate level of managerial seniority. The initial request should usually be made through the compliance officer to ensure that information of a confidential nature is not unwittingly revealed by the department making the request to a senior officer of the analyst's department. The analyst should be provided with the minimum amount of information that he needs to know to perform his task. The compliance department should monitor the process including the analyst's conduct and dealings after he has returned over the wall.

(b) Personnel above the wall

Senior executives may be members of the main board or otherwise as a result of their management role may need to be "above" the wall. In order to discharge main board duties they will need to obtain information which is otherwise retained behind a information barrier. Sometimes a senior manager may learn information which is on the other side of the wall because of his overall management role. Ideally, personnel "above" the wall should not also have client or advisory functions which take them below the wall but this is not always feasible.

(c) Stop and watch lists

One practice which is employed is the use of "stop" or "watch" lists. These are practices where trading in a designated share is either prohibited (a stop list) or trading in a share is monitored (a watch list), the latter practice often being part of a firm's compliance programme with respect to employee trading. Where there are problems of straddling walls, the firm could simply decline to deal in the relevant security until the conflict had ceased to exist, or

---

[16] The FSA have given detailed consideration to the problems facing analysts in relation to conflicts of interest. See "Investment Research: Conflicts and Other Issues" D.P. 15, July 31, 2002; Consultation Paper No.205 Conflicts of Interest: Investment research and issues of securities, October 2003.

[17] That is, prohibited from resuming his normal duties.

for the firm to cease to recommend a share where this would create a conflict between the firm's interests and those of its customers but nevertheless executing unsolicited orders with respect to the share.

(d) Policing the effectiveness of the wall
The effectiveness of the wall will require monitoring. Ideally, the monitoring should be done by personnel who are not on one side or the other of the wall, such as compliance officers, to avoid compromising the effectiveness of the wall.

(e) Takeovers
The Takeover Panel has accepted that, in general, it is the intention of multi-service financial organisations to run their market-making operations independently and without regard to the interests of clients of the corporate finance arm of their organisation. The Panel thus accepts in this respect the principle of information barriers between parts of the business.

(f) The canteen factor
One reason for requiring training courses is to instil in employees the importance and culture of the information barrier. Employees must be aware of the importance of the wall and the sanctions available for breach. There is always the potential problem of social discussion between employees on different sides of the wall undermining its integrity.

2. Takeovers

A. The regulatory regime

19–009   The regulation of takeovers of UK public companies have in the past been governed by the City Code on Takeovers and Mergers.[18] The EU Takeover Directive required that the regime be put on a statutory footing. EU law required implementation of the Directive by May 20, 2006. As the Companies Act 2006 had not completed Parliamentary passage by that date, implementation was achieved by the Takeovers Directive (Interim Implementation) Regulations 2006.[19] This was unsatisfactory as other than a short term remedy because the power to effect primary legislation by regulations only extended to giving effect to the UK's treaty obligations to give effect to a directive. That meant that the Regulations could only deal with those aspects of takeover legislation derived from the directive, and not other matters. Now the position has been regularised by Pt 28

---

[18] 8th edn, May 20, 2006.
[19] SI 2006/1183.

of the Companies Act 2006,[20] which puts what was the Takeover Code on a statutory footing, and at the same time gives effect to the directive. The Takeover Panel has an obligation under s.943 to make rules for or in connection with the regulation of takeover bids, merger transactions and other transactions which have or may have, directly or indirectly, an effect on the ownership or control of companies.[21] It is also empowered to give directions to restrain actions in breach of the rules and to compel compliance with the rules.[22]

B. Issues for the director

Primary responsibility in the case of the bidder for the conduct of the bid and response in the case of the target rests with the board in each case. Appendix 3 to the Code sets out in detail the responsibilities of the board for the conduct of the bid. General Principle 3 of the Code emphasises that the directors must act in the interests of the company as a whole and must not deny the holders of securities the opportunity to decide on the merits of the bid. General Principle 2 states the board of the offeree company must give its views on the effects of implementation of the bid on employment, conditions of employment and the locations of the company's places of business.[23] Directors are under a statutory duty under s.172 (1) of the Companies Act 2006 to promote the success of the company, which requires having regard to a variety of factors in considering the interests of the company, including the interests of employees.[24]

19–010

There is no general rule that directors may not enter into a commitment to act in a particular way, including an agreement to make a recommendation to shareholders to accept a bid, but in many cases it will be difficult to square such an arrangement with the director's fiduciary obligations. In some cases it will be possible to justify the commitment as being of itself in the best interests of the company, for example where the very entry into the commitment facilitates a commitment or action by a third party which it is in the interests of the company to procure.[25] Another possibility is that the commitment is to be read as subject to an implied obligation

---

[20] See s.942 of the Act.
[21] s.945
[22] s.946
[23] There is no common law duty on the directors to give advice to the shareholders on whether to recommend a bid for their shares.
[24] The directors are not otherwise obliged to consider the interests of shareholders unless the company is insolvent. There is authority under the general law however that directors are obliged to deal fairly as between different shareholders: *Mutual Life Insurance v Rank Organisation* [1985] B.C.L.C. 11; *Re BSB Holdings (No.2)* [1996] 1 B.C.L.C. 155.
[25] *Fulham F.C. v Cabra Estates* [1994] 1 B.C.L.C. 363, CA; *Thorby v Goldberg* (1964) 112 C.L.R. 605-6, Australian High Court.

that it will continue subject to a continuing belief in the substance of the recommendation.[26]

Often the bidder will have nominee directors on the board of the target, where the bidder already holds a substantial shareholding in the target. Confidential information is one problem; the director will not be able without consent to pass on information confidential to one company to the other. Sometimes the information will be price-sensitive and will qualify as inside information for the purposes of criminal statutes. The conflict becomes particularly acute when the director has to consider his stance at board meetings. If he continues to receive papers on the issue but stays silent he risks getting the worst of all worlds—ignoring his fiduciary obligations as director to act, perhaps giving rise to allegations of bad faith. If he absents himself from board meetings during the relevant period, he risks being accused of failure to perform his fiduciary obligations.[27]

19–011   Before the bid is announced the director's position is at its most difficult. He will know from his position as a director of the potential bidder that the bid is about to be made but cannot take or refrain from taking any action sitting on the target board which will alert the target to the bid. If he participates in any board meeting or discussion, he risks getting himself into a serious mess given that he is unable to contribute on relevant issues without conflict. The conflict is at its most acute simply because the director cannot disclose the existence of the conflict. Once the bid is announced, the problem is identified and thus easier to deal with.

Nor does it seem that resignation solves the problems. First, resignation does not resolve problems of breach of duty which arose prior to the resignation. Secondly, resignation immediately prior to the bid may have the effect of tipping off the target. Thirdly, the Takeover Panel has generally preferred directors in this situation to remain on the board and explain their position clearly to shareholders. It has not approved of directors resigning principally to avoid participating in a recommendation or taking responsibility for documents because of a conflict.[28]

C. Buyouts

19–012   Where the company's business is to be sold under a buy-out transaction, the director faces conflict issues, particularly if he is to be part of the

---

[26] *Dawson Int v Coats Patons* [1989] B.C.L.C. 233, reported on the substantive issue in an obscure set of law reports (1991) Compliance Case Law 13; *Rackham v Peek Foods* [1990] B.C.L.C. 895; *John Crowther Group v Carpets Int* [1990] B.C.L.C. 460; *Heron Int v Lord Grade* [1983] B.C.L.C. 244.

[27] It may be a requirement of the articles of association that he attend a specified number of board meetings in a given period; if he fails to attend board meetings he may be in breach of his employment contract or if a non-executive director his terms of appointment.

[28] The Panel is prepared to accept that directors in position of conflict need not join in recommendation to shareholders in respect of the bid: see r.25.1, fn.3.

buy-out team. First, disclosure must be made of the interest of the director under s.177 of the Companies Act 2006. If the articles disqualify interested directors from voting or constituting a quorum, and all the directors are interested in the buy-out, the board may find itself constitutionally unable to do anything. Normally s.190, which requires shareholder consent where a company proposes to sell a non-cash asset to a director or a person connected with a director, will in any event make the transaction voidable unless specific shareholder approval is obtained.

A director who wishes to pursue buy-out proposals should seek prior consent to enable him to do so. Otherwise he may commit a breach of fiduciary duties as director and his obligation of fidelity as an employee. Although in one sense if the director forms the view that the buy-out is in the best interests of the company it may be said that pursuit of the proposal will not breach his fiduciary duties, that would be a path fraught with danger. First, it is never easy to persuade a court that a decision which happened to coincide with the personal interests of the particular director is one that he can properly say he decided was in the best interests of the company. Secondly, the tightrope the director walks by adopting such a stance is likely to become even more precarious when the remainder of the board disagree with his apparently altruistic view that the proposal is in the best interests of the company. Where there are competing buy-out proposals, even if the director has obtained clearance to pursue a buy-out proposal, he will have another problem where the board has to decide between different bids. He should normally absent himself from relevant board meetings and considerations of proposals.[29] He has problems of conflicts and of dealing with confidential information.

D. Takeover problems for conglomerates

The Takeover Panel considered at the time of "Big Bang" whether any part of a multi-service financial organisation might deal as principal, market-maker or otherwise in the securities of companies involved in a takeover when some other part of the same organisation is acting as a financial or other adviser to one of those companies. It also considered the effect of dealing by fund managers on behalf of discretionary clients in securities of companies concerned in an offer when the fund managers are part of the same organisation as the financial or other advisers to the offeror or offeree company. The Panel ruled[30]:

> "... when a multi-service organisation is (a banker, stockbroker or otherwise) advising an offeror, then all principal dealings in relevant

19–013

---

[29] For reasons set out above, he should seek clearance in advance for this stance.
[30] October 6, 1986.

securities by any part of that organisation will be presumed to be in concert with the offeror, with one important exception in respect of dealings in a market-making capacity, provided the market-maker concerned is an exempt market-maker . . ."

To obtain exempt status an application must be made to the Takeover Panel. In each case the Panel will need to be satisfied that the organisation has in place arrangements which ensure the market-making or fund management operations are operated independently of the other relevant parts of the business. The Panel has accepted that, in general, it is the intention of multi-service financial organisations to run their market-making operations independently and without regard to the interests of clients of the corporate finance arm of their organisation. The Panel thus accepts in this respect the principle of information barriers between parts of the business.

E. The adviser: acting for more than one party

19–014   The problem likely to confront the professional is likely to arise where there are a number of bidders and more than one wishes to retain the professional. This is probably particularly acute for the accountant, as there are a relatively small number of firms with the necessary expertise. Seeking consent will probably be wholly inappropriate, in circumstances where the bidders may not want others to be aware of their existence in advance and consent would probably not be given anyway. Thus the only effective way in which the professional can reserve himself a right to act is if he has covered the position in terms and conditions of engagement. A professional who is likely to be asked to act in such circumstances may want to consider whether terms and conditions should deal with this possibility.

There is a real distinction between merely doing a data exercise on the basis of information available to all bidders, which should be a largely mechanical exercise, and providing corporate finance advice. In the former case, there seems no reason why contractual terms of engagement should not make clear that the professional may accept similar instructions from other bidders, thereby in effect providing the required informed consent. In respect of corporate finance advice, where the matter is essentially adversarial, it seems unlikely to be feasible to act for more than one party.

F. Poison pills

19–015   The English courts have looked at "poison pills" provisions, which provide disincentives for takeovers or other changes to the current management structure of the company, in *Criterion Properties v Stratford UK*

Properties.³¹ Criterion through its managing director Mr Glaser invited Stratford UK, which was party to a property joint venture with Criterion, to amend the joint venture agreement to provide that if there was a takeover or change of management at Criterion, Stratford UK would be entitled to buy out the joint venture agreement on highly advantageous terms. The amendment could properly be regarded as a poison pill because of the disincentive it provided either to the making of changes in the management of Criterion or to a potential purchaser acquiring the shares of the company. When Mr Glaser was dismissed by Criterion, Stratford UK sought to enforce the amendment and Criterion asserted the amendment was unenforceable. The matter came before the court on a summary judgment hearing, and thus the court could not make findings as to the intentions of the participants. Mr Glaser alleged that he had acted in good faith in the best interests of Criterion to prevent a hostile takeover from asset strippers, and Stratford UK alleged it had acted in good faith having taken (incorrect) legal advice that such an agreement was unimpeachable before entering into it.

The Court of Appeal dealt with the "poison pill" issue in detail.³² They recognised that there may be some cases in which the directors of a company may use their powers to raise capital with a view to resisting a takeover which they think would be damaging to the company, but the purpose must be to protect or look after the interests of the company as a whole, as opposed to the interests of some or all of the existing shareholders.³³ Thus in the Australian case *Savory Corpn v Development Underwriting Ltd*³⁴ Jacobs J. said:

> "It would seem to me unreal in the light of the structure of modern companies and of modern business life to take the view that directors should in no way concern themselves with the infiltration of the company by persons or groups which they bona fide consider not to be seeking the best interests of the company".

The Court of Appeal recognised that there might be circumstances in which a "poison pill" of this nature could be a legitimate device decided upon by the directors in the interests of the company, for the purpose of preventing substantial damage to the company in the event of a takeover.

---

[31] [2004] 1 W.L.R. 1846, HL.
[32] [2003] 1 W.L.R. 2108.
[33] The leading authority is *Howard Smith Ltd v Ampol Petroleum Ltd* [1974] A.C. 821 at 834-6; see also *Re Smith & Fawcett Ltd* [1942] Ch. 304; *Hogg v Cramphorn Ltd* [1967] Ch. 254; *Cayne v Global Resources Plc*, Unreported, August 12, 1982, Megarry V.C.; *Teck Corp v Millar* (1972) 33 D.L.R. (3d) 288. See also in relation to poison pills; *Stena Finance BV v Sea Containers Ltd* (1989) 39 W.I.R. 83, Supreme Ct of Bermuda, and 347883 *Alberta Ltd v Producers Pipelines Inc* (1991) 80 D.L.R. (4th) 359, Saskatchewan Court of Appeal, especially at 392-3 where the "typical poison pill" is described and its use in the US and Canada.
[34] [1963] N.S.W.R 138 at 147.

What would not be permissible would be an improper desire to deprive an existing majority of shareholders of their position as such, because that would be having regard to the interests of part of the shareholders, or of the directors, rather than the company as a unit. However, the Court of Appeal took the view that the variation went rather further than might have been regarded necessary—it was said that the consequences of it being triggered were so dramatic that in effect it provided for a transfer of assets of the company to Stratford UK. Moreover, it applied not merely in cases of potential hostile takeover—it applied if Mr Glaser was dismissed or left. The Court of Appeal thus held that (whatever his motive) this was not something that Mr Glaser could have properly agreed to. When the case reached the House of Lords,[35] nothing was said on this point. The issue in the case was whether the amendment was enforceable.[36] Lord Scott made it clear that it was not appropriate to decide the issue on contested facts on a summary judgment issue, and recognised that the terms of the poison pill raised difficult issues as to actual and ostensible authority[37] which should be decided after the facts had been found.

G. Applications to restrain advisers acting

19–016   The decision of Lightman J. in *Mannesmann v Goldman Sachs Int*[38] repays detailed consideration because it is a spectacular object lesson in how not to restrain an adviser from acting on a takeover. Mannesmann had been advised by Goldman Sachs on its takeover by Orange. Goldman Sachs then appeared as advisers for Vodafone Airtouch in its plan to take over Mannesmann. Mannesmann applied for an injunction without notice and obtained an injunction restraining Goldman Sachs from acting. Mannesmann alleged that Goldman Sachs had assured them that they would not act against them in a hostile takeover. They also said that Goldman Sachs had acquired confidential information whilst acting for them which would not be protected if Goldman Sachs continued to act.

---

[35] [2004] 1 W.L.R. 1846.
[36] Hart J. had held, [2002] 2 B.C.L.C. 151, that Mr Glaser could not have had authority from Criterion to put forward an amendment in these terms, and as Stratford UK knew the material facts, they must be taken to have known that he did not have authority to put forward the amendment. The Court of Appeal agreed that Mr Glaser did not have authority from Criterion for the amendment but held that it was not unconscionable for Stratford UK to enforce the amendment because (for the purpose of the summary judgment application) they must be taken to have acted in good faith. The House of Lords said that the issue was not unconscionability at all but the actual or apparent authority of Mr Glaser. Difficult questions arose as to whether a director could ever have actual or apparent authority to sign an amendment of this nature, but it was necessary to look at the facts surrounding Mr Glaser putting forward the amendment before deciding such issues.
[37] para.29.
[38] November 18, 1999.

The matter came back with full evidence three days later. In the light of evidence from Goldman Sachs, Mannesmann withdrew the allegation that Goldman Sachs had assured them they would not act on a hostile takeover. Mannesmann were not permitted to amend their case as to what confidential information was learnt previously by Goldman Sachs because the matter was extremely urgent and Goldman Sachs had not had a chance to answer the changed allegations. The judge held that even if the confidential information originally relied on was genuinely confidential, Mannesmann had referred to the information at a public hearing so it could not be regarded as remaining confidential. The judge discharged the injunction amidst devastating criticism, describing it as a hopeless application based on false and misleading evidence which should never have been made.

There is a concern that in highly contested matters it may be seen as tactically advantageous to challenge the advisers of the other side. A decision that the advisers should cease to act will involve wasted costs, loss of time and, it is perceived, loss of morale. This is perceived as particularly attractive in takeover situations, where morale and public perception are vital. There are, of course, cases where a genuine complaint can and should be made. But attempts to get rid of the other side's advisers for tactical advantage is a deeply unattractive strategy. Courts should in such circumstances be alive to the motivation that may lie behind such applications and react accordingly. Lightman J. concluded his judgment by stating in open court:

> "All these considerations raise serious questions as to the good faith of the claim in the first place and whether it was indeed ... merely a sporting exercise designed to rule out of play Vodafone's first choice of advisers in the hostilities to come and pre-empt a bid by Vodafone ... It is to be hoped that there will be no repetition of this unseemly exercise in other cases ..."

In this case, the consequences of the application went far beyond immediate and humiliating failure. In the context of a hostile takeover of Mannesmann, it is hard to imagine a more spectacular own goal. The management of Mannesmann were made to look disreputable and incompetent, with potential consequences on the takeover. Particularly in highly-charged situations such as takeovers, those advising the application must always have an eye to the possible consequences of failure.

In the *Mannesmann* case, a successful application was initially made without notice[39] for an injunction. On urgent applications it is always tempting to apply without notice as a matter of urgency. But it will rarely be sensible in this area. If the court is willing to remove the adviser after hearing both

---

[39] In fact notice was given the same day as the application was made but this was tantamount to an application being made without notice as Goldman Sachs had no opportunity to deal with the allegations at that stage.

sides, then the object will have been achieved. However, if the case was a borderline one, (or if the application is unsuccessful) after the court has heard both parties, the party making the application is in a much worse position if he has obtained an injunction without notice. In *Mannesmann* the fact that the judge had granted relief previously on an application without notice led him to place critical focus during the inter partes application on the delay between Mannesmann learning the relevant facts about Goldman Sachs' involvement and making the urgent injunction application without notice. The judge would have had in mind that by obtaining an injunction in this way Mannesmann had had the benefit of stopping Goldman Sachs from acting for a short period already, with consequent disruption to the conduct of the bid. In disallowing new evidence from Mannesmann at the inter partes hearing, he would have had in mind that Mannesmann had had the benefit of an injunction which they were now seeking to justify on different grounds from those on which they obtained its benefit. And, most important, when the evidence of Goldman Sachs showed that the position was very different from what Mannesmann had originally asserted it to be, the option of withdrawing gracefully without a damning open court judgment against them was not open to them because they had already obtained an injunction. There was also potential liability on the cross-undertaking in damages.[40] The only circumstance in which it makes sense to apply without notice is when the risk of immediate transmission of confidential information is so great as to make essential an immediate application, which will probably not be in many cases.

19–017 Another bear trap which Mannesmann fell into was to seek to identify the relevant confidential information in non-confidential affidavits. Lightman J. said that even if the information identified in the affidavits could be regarded as confidential, by identifying it at a public hearing and in submissions of counsel, the information had been brought into the public arena. The information thus became common knowledge. He said there are well-known and established methods of preventing confidentiality being lost in this way: including the information in confidential exhibits, asking the court to sit in private. But this was not done.[41]

Marks and Spencer were rather more successful in their recent attempts to prevent Freshfields from acting for Mr Philip Green on his bid. The case is considered at para.00 above.[42] Here Freshfields' principal difficulty was that they had advised M&S on (among other things) a material contract. Both Lawrence Collins J. and the Court of Appeal held that the double

---

[40] Admittedly, it is hard to see what quantifiable damage could be claimed as a result of Goldman Sachs working on their affidavits rather than the takeover for three days.
[41] Indeed, it appears that Mannesmann opposed Goldman Sachs' application for the inter partes hearing to take place in private, which seems to have been another own goal.
[42] *Marks and Spencer Group Plc v Freshfields Bruckhaus Deringer*, Unreported, June 2, 2004, Lawrence Collins J.; Unreported, June 3, 2004, CA hearing the application for leave at the same time as the appeal and giving full reasons for refusing leave to appeal, see 00 above.

employment rule is not limited to "same matter" conflicts, but recognised obiter that there had to be "some reasonable relationship" between the two matters. There are open questions as to what is meant by "some reasonable relationship" in this context but there is a problem here specific to takeovers. The due diligence exercise will involve a review of all the assets and liabilities of the target. So, in one sense, it could be said that in this context everything is related. Does that mean that a firm which continues to advise a target on anything is debarred for acting for the acquirer? This would be an unattractive consequence, particularly where the firm may have offices in various parts of the world and the conflict may arise from something done through a foreign office. In large takeovers this might provide a significant restriction on the advisers available to the acquirer. If this is a problem for the lawyers, it may be a worse problem for the accountants. The way of resolving this problem, it is suggested, is to apply a test of materiality: if A had advised the target on a £1m contract, that might have a "reasonable relationship" to the retainer for the acquirer in a £10m takeover bid, because the £1m contract would be a material asset of the target and thus a conflict could be said to arise. But if the bid was £1bn, the £1m contract would be wholly immaterial and thus irrelevant to the retainer so that the position would surely be no different from the case where the two retainers are unrelated.

CHAPTER 20

Estate Agents and Insurance Brokers

1. Estate agents

A. The nature of the obligation of an estate agent

20–001 It has long been a legal conundrum whether the estate agent instructed to find a purchaser for a property enters into a bilateral contract with his client at the time of the instruction or whether the analysis is of a unilateral contract to the effect that if the agent finds a purchaser, the vendor will pay him agreed commission. The view expressed by the House of Lords in *Luxor (Eastbourne) v Cooper*[1] that the contract was unilateral in nature looks artificial and dated today and is undermined by legislation and authorities which assume the contrary is the case.[2] In particular, it would seem to follow from the unilateral contract view that the estate agent can be under no liability for failure to act until the commission-generating act has occurred and the contract crystallised, but the courts have generally rejected that view.[3] There may be circumstances in which the point does not arise at all. The estate agent may be a sole agent or given sole selling rights and there is some authority that the agent owes duties to use best endeavours to find a purchaser in such

---

[1] [1941] A.C. 108.
[2] The Estate Agents Act 1979, s.18 requires the agent to provide the client with specified information as to his services at the outset. *Kelly v Cooper* [1993] A.C. 205 is difficult to square with a unilateral contract because their Lordships assumed that the agent would subject to the knowledge of the client as to the practices of estate agents under a duty to pass on information prior to the contract becoming bilateral; see also *Keppel v Wheeler* [1927] 1 K.B. 577.
[3] Despite dicta in *Luxor*, per Viscount Simon L.C. at 117, Lord Russell of Killowen at 124 and Lord Romer at 153, the contrary view has been taken or assumed in *Kelly v Cooper*, above, and *Prebble & Co v West* [1969] 211 E.G. 831, CA (argued unsuccessfully that no breach of duty in failing to pass on offers).

circumstances.[4] And of course estate agents fulfil a range of functions which go beyond finding properties for potential vendors.

However, whatever the position in respect of duties owed in contract by estate agents, it does seem that the estate agent owes fiduciary obligations to the client before the commission-generating event occurs.[5] Thus the estate agent, it appears, has the same potential problems of conflicts that do other professionals,[6] subject to being able to act for vendors of competing properties within the terms established by *Kelly v Cooper*.[7] Thus conflicts problems have led to estate agents being fastened with liability where they failed to inform clients about intended resale of the property by a potential purchaser,[8] for concealing the existence of potential purchasers prepared to pay more than an applicant introduced by the agent but whose introduction would not entitle the agent to commission,[9] and who unduly favoured one potential purchaser on the ground that this purchaser would employ them in future transactions.[10] All these circumstances were cases where, expressly or by implication, the court found the agents liable for breach of fiduciary duty before the commission-generating act accrued.

B. Statutory disclosure of interests

The estate agent may carry out investment or property-related financial or other services as well as finding properties for purchasers. The problems here are no different in principle from those that apply in the City,[11] save that the regulatory regime is that of the Estate Agents Act 1979 rather than the FSMA.[12] Otherwise, the issues and problems of information barriers between departments are similar. The regulations on estate agents following an enquiry by the Office of Fair Trading[13] increase requirements of disclosure about remuneration and prohibit discrimination against purchasers who are

20–002

---

[4] *E Christopher & Co v Essig* [1948] W.N. 461; *Mendoza & Co v Bell* [1952] 159 E.G. 372; but see contra *Glentree Estates v Gee* [1981] E.G.L.R. 28, Ewbank J.
[5] Even though it seems anomalous if it is right that the contract is unilateral.
[6] See *Eric V Stansfield v South East Nursing Home Services* [1986] 1 E.G.L.R. 29 (estate agent retained by more than one client to look for similar property should disclose the potential conflict, at least once more than one client had shown real intent to buy); *Robinson Scammell & Co v Ansell* [1985] 2 E.G.L.R. 41 (attempt by agent on fearing arranged sale about to collapse to sell purchaser another house held by CA to be breach of duty to first client); see also *Kelly v Cooper* [1993] A.C. 205.
[7] [1993] A.C. 205, see para.4–016 above.
[8] *Keppel v Wheeler* [1927] 1 K.B. 577; *Dunton Properties v Coles Knapp & Kennedy* [1959] 174 E.G. 723; *Price v Metropolitan House Investment and Agency Co* (1907) 23 T.L.R. 630.
[9] *Heath v Parkinson* [1926] T.L.R. 693.
[10] *Henry Smith & Son v Muskett* [1981] E.G.L.R. 23.
[11] For example, the potential of conflict where the agent also markets insurance services and mortgage services and obtains commissions on these activities.
[12] Where an estate agent provides financial services, FSMA will apply.
[13] The Estate Agents (Provision of Information) Regulations 1991 (SI 1991/859); The Estate Agents (Undesirable Practices) Order 1991 (SI 1991/861). The regulation of estate agents

not accepting services from the agent or certain of his associates. These regulations reinforce rather than conflict with fiduciary duties and thus there is no significant practical scope for conflict or mismatch. By the Estate Agents (Undesirable Practices) (No.2) Order 1991, where the agent has or is seeking to acquire a beneficial interest in the land or in the proceeds of sale of any interest in the land, or where the agent knows that any "connected person" has or is seeking to acquire such an interest, the agent must inform the client promptly and in writing of the interest in question. Section 21 of the Estate Agents Act 1979 imposes duties of disclosure upon agents who are deemed to have an interest in the land which is being marketed. There is no civil or criminal remedy although breach may trigger enforcement powers of the Director General of Fair Trading.

2. Insurance brokers

A. The regulatory regime

20–003
The Financial Services and Markets Act 2000 fundamentally altered the regulation of insurance broking. FSMA sets up the FSA as a one-stop regulator whose remit includes insurance broking.[14] The general prohibition under s.19 prohibits the carrying on of a "regulated activity" without authorisation. The Regulated Activities Order (together with its amendments) treat "dealing with investments" as a regulated activity, which covers the buying, selling, subscribing for or underwriting of investments or other offer or agreement to do so as principal or agent. If the investment is a contract of insurance, which are specifically covered, it includes carrying out the contract. Participation in Lloyd's syndicates is included. Claims handling by a broker on behalf of an insurer is not. The FSA also regulates the sale and administration of general insurance and pure protection contracts. The conflicts of interest and information barrier sections contained in the insurance broking section of the handbook are the same as the rules which apply in FSA regulation more broadly.[15]

B. Conflicts in acting for insurer and assured

20–004
The principal area which has given rise to conflicts of interest is that the broker will act in different capacities as agent for both the assured and the

---

has been amended by the Enterprise Act 2002 and the Consumers, Estate Agents and Redress Act 2007.
[14] From January 5, 2008, the sourcebook is Insurance: New Conduct of Business Sourcebook ("ICOBS").
[15] See 19–001.

insurer. In a slightly different context, the problems which may arise for a lawyer in acting for an insured client where the lawyer's bill is paid by insurers and the relationship which gives rise to the instructions is in practice between lawyer and insurer are apparent from the notorious facts of *TSB Bank v Robert Irving and Burns*,[16] where counsel and solicitors instructed by insurers to act on behalf of a defendant insured valuer sought to trap the valuer into making admissions which would enable insurers to avoid cover.[17]

Despite the fact the Lloyd's broker is the agent of the customer for the purpose of effecting the insurance, in the past Lloyd's practice traditionally required him to act for the underwriters in certain respects in the settling of claims. In *Anglo-African Merchants v Bayley*,[18] Megaw J. held that even if the practice was known to persons seeking insurance and could be regarded as within the trade custom principle, it would not be upheld by the court as reasonable because it involved the broker serving two masters with conflicting interests at the same time. The decision was followed with a slightly different analysis in *North and South Co v Berkeley*[19] by Donaldson J., who started on the basis that informed consent before acting for two conflicting principals was the general principle then considered whether there was reasonable justification for a custom allowing deviation from the general principle. He was equally unimpressed by the custom in the market. In *Re Great Western Assurance SA*[20] Hobhouse L.J. said of insurance brokers:

> "An insurance broker is an agent for the insured or would be insured. He is not, when acting as an insurance broker, acting as the agent of the insurer in the relevant transaction. If he chooses to act for the insurer, he is ceasing, in at least that respect, to act as a broker and may be in breach of his duties to the insured, or would be insured. It is always important that a broker pay regard to his role in the relevant transaction and the duties which result from his accepting that role".

The principal conflicts of interest for insurance brokers arise from this curious position of acting in different respects for insurers and insured. In *HIH Casualty & General Insurance Ltd v JLT Risk Solutions*[21] the Court of Appeal held that in the particular circumstances of the case the broker owed

20–005

---

[16] [1999] Lloyd's Rep. I.R. 528, CA.
[17] The case is discussed at 15–018.
[18] [1970] 1 Q.B. 311. A claim was made under a theft policy and the underwriters argued non-disclosure by the assured. During the investigation of the claim the assured's brokers had made their files available to the underwriters and their solicitors but when asked by the assured's solicitors for the same facility, this was refused.
[19] [1971] 1 W.L.R. 470.
[20] [1999] Lloyd's Rep. I.R. 377 at 386.
[21] [2007] EWCA 710.

a duty after placing reinsurance to alert the reinsured to matters of potential concern on coverage. Auld L.J. said:[22]

> "The role of an insurance broker is notoriously anomalous for its inherent scope for engendering conflicts of interest in the otherwise relatively tidy legal world of agency. In its simplest form, the negotiation of insurance, the broker acts as the agent for the insured, but normally receives his remuneration from the insurer in the form of commission; he may in certain circumstances act for both. Where there is reinsurance of an insured risk, the same broker may act on behalf of the insured in placing the reinsurance".

Auld L.J. said, following *North & South Trust v Berkeley*[23] that the fact that a broker might in certain circumstances find himself in a situation of conflict could not be relied upon as negativing the existence of a duty of care.

Conflict problems for an insurance broker are particularly acute in two circumstances:

(a) *Binding authority to accept business* Where a broker has a binding authority from an insurer to accept business on the insurer's behalf, he must be certain that he is acting in the client's best interests. If he arranges the insurance in this way he must disclose this to the client and, where the client so requests, must inform him of the financial advantage he has gained.

(b) *Authority to settle claims* Where the broker has authority to settle claims, he may find it difficult to reconcile the client's best interests with those of insurers and should refer back to them for instructions where appropriate.

The binding authority problem raises a number of issues. The broker will often have an agency agreement with one or more insurers. Does the dual status of the broker enable the insured to sue the insurer on the basis that the insurer is bound by the acts or knowledge of the broker as its agent? What if in such circumstances disclosure is made to the broker, but he fails to pass it on? Is that treated as disclosure to the insurer? Where the broker is independent and acts solely for the insured, the insurer will not be fixed with the knowledge of the broker which he has failed to pass on.[24] The issue will depend on whether the broker has the authority of the insurer to

---

[22] At [60].
[23] See 20–004 above; see also *Youell v Blsnd Welch (No 2)* [1990] 2 Lloyds Rep. 431 at 447, per Phillips J.
[24] *Roberts v Plaisted* [1989] 2 Lloyd's Rep. 341, CA.

receive information on his behalf, which may not be a simple question.[25] What if the broker fills in the proposal form for the assured and does so incorrectly? Similar issues arise here.[26] Another variant considered in the authorities is where the broker makes negligent misrepresentations to the assured about the cover. Whose agent is the broker?[27] What duties in these circumstances are owed by the broker to the insurer? This will depend on careful analysis as to whether in carrying out a particular task the broker assumed responsibility to the insured.[28]

---

[25] Cf. *Julian Praet v HG Poland* [1961] 1 Lloyd's Rep. 187, CA; *Simner v New India Assurance* [1995] L.R.L.R. 240, Judge Diamond Q.C.; *Zeus Marine Tradition v Bell* [1999] 1 Lloyd's Rep. 703, Colman J.
[26] The Lloyd's Code prohibited a Lloyd's broker from filling in a proposal form. See on this point *Stone v Reliance Mutual* [1972] 1 Lloyd's Rep. 469, CA; *Bawden v London Edinburgh & Glasgow Life Insurance* [1892] 2 Q.B. 534, CA; *Newsholme v Road Transport & General Insurance* [1929] 2 K.B. 356, CA.
[27] *Stockton v Mason* [1978] 2 Lloyd's Rep. 430, CA.
[28] In *Re Great Western Assurance SA* [1999] Lloyd's Rep. I.R. 377; *IGI Insurance Ltd v Kirkland Timms Ltd*, December 5, 1985, Hirst J.; *St Margaret's Trust v Navigators & General Insurance* [1949] 82 Lloyd's Rep. 752, Morris J.

Index

Account of profits
  remedies, 8–008, 8–011
Accountants
  see also **Auditors**
  codes of conduct, 17–003
  conflict of interest, 17–002
  existing client conflict, 17–006, 17–007
  fiduciary relationship, 2–017
  former client conflict, 17–011—17–012
  insolvency practitioners, 17–013—17–023
  investment advice, 17–005
  powers rights and duties, 17–001
Actual conflict rule
  breach of fiduciary duty, 2–008
Ad hoc Chinese walls
  effectiveness of, 7–016
  meaning, 1–003, 7–015
Administration of justice
  persons involved in conflict of interest, 8–015
Adversaries
  duty to
    confidential information, 9–004—9–008
    examples of, 9–002
    generally, 9–001, 9–003
Advocate to the court
  perception of impropriety, 5–017
Arbitrators
  arbitrators' powers and duties
    disqualification, 14–005, 14–006, 14–008, 14–014
  contamination, 14–003
  enforcement, 14–009
  generally, 14–001, 14–007
  impartiality, 14–002

  International Bar Association guidelines, 14–004
  jurisdiction, 14–005, 14–006, 14–014
  relationships, 14–010—14–013, 14–014, 14–015
Auditors
  see also **Accountants**
  codes of conduct, 17–004
  fiduciary relationship, 2–017, 17–008—17–010
  role of, 17–001
Australia
  confidential information meaning, 1–010
  conflict rules, 1–010
  criminal proceedings, 5–012
  family proceedings, 5–011
  joint instructions, 4–007
  supervisory jurisdiction over solicitors, 1–010, 5–001, 5–006
Balance of convenience
  injunctions, 3–009, 8–002
Barristers
  cab rank rule, 16–001, 16–007
  codes of conduct, 16–002
  conflict between client and professional client, 16–005
  conflict of interest, 16–006
  duty to the court, 16–003
  fiduciary duty, 16–003, 16–004
  personal relationships, 16–009
  professional embarrassment, 16–002
  retainers, 16–007
  sharing chambers and facilities, 16–008
  solicitors, contrast with, 16–001
Beauty parades
  fiduciary relationship, 2–032

Bolkiah case
   injunctions, 8–004—8–005
   principles established, 1–008
   protection of confidential
      information, 1–006—1–008
Breach of fiduciary duty
   actual conflict rule, 2–008
   double employment rule, 2–007, 3–001
   Mothew case, 2–007
   no inhibition principle, 2–008
Burden of proof
   injunctions, 8–003
Buy-outs
   see **Management buy-outs**
Cab rank rule
   barristers, 16–001, 16–007
Canada
   conflict rules, 1–011
   double employment rule, 3–014, 3–015
Chinese walls
   see **Information barriers**
   see also **Confidential information**
City conflicts
   see **Financial services**
Clients
   existing client conflict
      accountants, 17–006, 17–007
      meaning, 1–002
   former client conflict
      accountants, 17–011—17–012
      changes of firm, 7–007
      meaning, 1–003
   identification of clients, 2–030, 2–031
Codes of conduct
   accountants, 17–003
   auditors, 17–004
   barristers, 16–002
   solicitors, 15–002—15–003, 15–012
Companies
   knowledge
      attribution, 6–026
Confidential information
   see also **Confidentiality; Information barriers**
   access to evidence of, 8–016

adversaries
   duty to, 9–004—9–008
   attributes of, 7–008
   Bolkiah case
      injunctions, 8–004—8–005
      principles established, 1–008
      protection of confidential
         information, 1–006—1–008
   'getting to know you' factors, 7–012—7–013
   identification of, 7–010—7–011
   relevant confidential information, 7–009
Confidentiality
   see also **Confidential information**
   fiduciary relationship, 2–003, 2–012
Conflict of interest
   commercial conflict, 1–004
   development of law, 1–001
   meaning, 1–002
   non-waivable conflict, 1–005
Consent
   contested litigation or takeovers, 4–012
   disclosure requirements, 4–013, 4–014
   implied consent, 4–016, 4–017—4–019, 4–020—4–021
   informed consent, 4–002, 4–008, 4–009, 4–010, 4–011
   risk management, 4–014
   undue influence, 4–015
Contempt of court
   recusal
      judges, 13–014
Contracts
   see **Retainers**
Contributory negligence
   damages, 8–012
Coroners
   bias, 12–012
Councillors
   decision-making, 12–011
Court of Appeal
   permission to appeal, 13–009
Criminal proceedings
   perception of impropriety, 5–012
Custom and usage
   implied terms, 4–022

Damages
  assessment of, 8–009
  contributory negligence, 8–012
  remedy, as, 8–008, 8–009
Directors
  conflict of interest
    duty to avoid, 18–004
  directors' powers and duties, 18–001
  disclosure of misconduct, 18–003
  engaging in competing business, 18–005
  fiduciary duty, 18–001
  groups of companies, 18–008
  joint ventures, 18–009
  management buy-outs, 19–012
  nominee directors, 18–007
  promoting success of the company, 18–002—18–003
  takeovers, 19–010—19–011
  transactions with directors, 18–006
Disciplinary tribunals
  apparent bias test, 12–007
  staff retiring with the tribunal, 12–008
  tribunal members' employment, 12–009
Disclosure
  advise, obligation to , 6–019
  attribution of knowledge
    Chinese walls, 6–024
    companies, 6–026
    knowledge split within the firm, 6–022—6–023
    partnerships, 6–025
  Barker Booth and Eastwood case, 6–010—6–014
  Chinese walls, and, 6–017, 6–018
  confidentiality, 6–010—6–013
  discreditable facts about clients, 6–012—6–013
  duty to disclose all information, 6–006—6–008, 6–020
  estate agents, 20–002
  exclusion clauses, 4–028
  failure to disclose
    judicial conflict, 13–005
  fiduciary duty, and, 6–003
  fraud, 6–021
  information learned from one client, to another, 6–001, 6–002
  informed consent precluding disclosure, 6–015—6–016
  loans, 6–004, 6–005, 6–006, 6–007, 6–008, 6–009
  money laundering, 10–001—10–002, 10–003, 10–004
  professional embarrassment, 6–018
Double employment rule
  acting for and against the client, 3–012—3–013, 3–014, 3–015
  acting without consent, 3–002
  actual conflict, 3–003, 3–005, 3–007
  balance of convenience, 3–009
  breach of fiduciary duty, 2–007, 3–001
  conflict with business interests of other client, 3–011
  generally, 3–016
  level of risk, 3–008
  no inhibition principle, 3–021
  non-waivable conflict, 3–005, 3–017, 3–018, 3–019
  personal conflict of interest, 3–022—3–026
  potential conflict, 3–003, 3–006, 3–007
  professional embarrassment, 3–018, 3–019, 3–020
  viewing the matter prospectively, 3–004
  'wait and see' approach, 3–009, 3–010
Duty to the court
  barristers, 16–003
Employees
  fiduciary duty, 2–014
Employment tribunals
  relationships and affiliations, 13–024
Estate agents
  breach of fiduciary duty, 20–001
  disclosure, 20–002
  powers rights and duties, 20–001
  regulation, 20–002
Exclusion clauses
  disclosure clauses, 4–028
  duty-defining clauses, 4–027
  legitimacy of, 4–024, 4–025

restrictions on, 4–025, 4–026
types, 4–023
Existing client conflict
accountants, 17–006, 17–007
meaning, 1–002
Expert witnesses
perception of impropriety, 5–013, 5–015
single joint experts, 5–014
Failure to disclose
judicial conflict, 13–005
Family proceedings
perception of impropriety, 5–011
Fiduciaries
see also **Fiduciary duty; Fiduciary relationship**
meaning, 2–002
Fiduciary duty
see also **Breach of fiduciary duty; Fiduciary relationship**
barristers, 16–003, 16–004
concept of, 2–005, 2–006
contractual duties, and, 2–001, 2–016, 2–019
directors, 18–001
disclosure, 6–003
ending of, 2–018
influence, 2–007
Mothew case, 2–007
non-fiduciary duties, and, 2–009
proscriptive / prescriptive nature, 2–010, 2–011
related parties, 2–023, 2–024, 2–030, 2–031
retainers
termination, 2–020, 2–021, 2–022, 2–025, 2–027
revealing discreditable matters about the client, 2–028, 2–029
Fiduciary relationship
see also **Fiduciary duty**
accountants, 2–017
auditors, 2–017, 17–008—17–010
beauty parades, 2–032
confidentiality, 2–003, 2–012
creation of, 2–003, 2–004
employees, 2–014
identification of clients, 2–030, 2–031

influence, 2–003
joint ventures, 2–013
meaning, 2–002
mutual trust and confidence, 2–003
shadow directors, 2–015
Final injunctions
see **Injunctions**
Financial services
attribution of knowledge, 19–002
Chinese walls, 19–001, 19–002, 19–003—19–005, 19–007
conflict of interest, 19–006
diversification of products and services, 19–006
financial regulation, 19–001
legislation, 19–001
organisational structure, 19–006
problems with information barriers, 19–008
Former client conflict
see also **Chinese walls**
accountants, 17–011—17–012
changes of firm, 7–007
meaning, 1–003
Fraud
disclosure, 6–021
Groups of companies
directors, 18–008
Human rights
right to fair and public hearing, 11–005
Husband and wife
see **Spouses**
Impartiality
arbitrators, 14–002
tribunals, 11–010
Implied terms
see also **Consent**
custom and usage, 4–022
Information barriers
see also **Chinese Walls**
ad hoc Chinese walls
effectiveness of, 7–016
meaning, 1–003, 7–015
adequacy of, 7–017, 7–018, 7–019
adverse interest, 7–005
effect of, 7–002
features of, 7–018, 7–019

INDEX

financial services, 19–001, 19–002,
  19–003—19–005, 19–007
former client conflict, 7–003—7–004
generally, 7–001
mergers, 7–006, 7–007
no real risk test, 7–014
restrictiveness of rules, 7–020, 7–021
structural Chinese walls
  effectiveness of, 7–016
  meaning, 1–003, 7–015
use of, 1–001

Injunctions
balance of convenience, 3–009,
  8–002
Bolkiah test, 8–004—8–005
burden of proof, 8–003
extent of, 8–006
final injunctions, 8–002
interim injunctions, 8–002
remedy, as, 8–002
'wait and see' approach, 3–009,
  3–010
without notice injunctions, 8–002

Insolvency practitioners
accountants, 17–013—17–023
perception of impropriety, 5–016
preventing solicitors acting for
  liquidators, 9–009

Inspection
solicitors' files, 8–014

Instructions
joint instructions, 4–006—4–007

Insurance brokers
conflict of interest, 20–004—20–005
regulation, 20–003

Interim injunctions
see **Injunctions**

International Bar Association
guidelines
  arbitration, 14–004

Investment advice
accountants, 17–005

Joint ventures
directors, 18–009
fiduciary relationship, 2–013

Judges
see **Judicial conflict**

Judicial conflict
see also **Arbitrators; Juries**

actual bias, 11–002
apparent bias
  contamination, 11–017
  dealing with allegations, 11–012
  discretion, 11–016
  fair-minded and informed
    observer, 11–014—11–015
  identification of the relevant
    circumstances, 11–013
  importance of, 11–010
  regulatory authorisation,
    11–021
  test of, 11–011
  waiver, 11–018—11–020
coroners, 12–011
councillors, 12–010
Court of Appeal
  permission to appeal, 13–009
disciplinary tribunals
  apparent bias test, 12–007
  staff retiring with the tribunal,
    12–009
  tribunal members' employment,
    12–010
duty to try a case, 13–001
facts
  importance of, 13–002
  failure to disclose, 13–005
generally, 12–012
Gough test, 11–011
independent tribunal, 11–006
judicial oath
  significance of, 13–004
Magill case, 11–011
meaning, 1–005
objections
  bias, 13–003, 13–006
prior legislative involvement, 11–007
prior views, 13–007—13–018
proprietary interests, 11–003,
  11–004
recusal
  judges, 11–001
relationships and affiliations
  choice of tribunals, 13–023
  court, party and advocate,
    13–019—13–020
  disclosure of, 13–001
  employment tribunals, 13–024

373

friends and relatives of the judge, 13–021
knowledge of parties and witnesses, 13–022
membership of organisations, 13–026
race and religion, 13–028
solicitor judge, 13–027
third parties, 13–025
right to fair and public hearing, 11–005
security of tenure, 11–008
separation of powers, 11–009

Juries
complaints against, 12–001, 12–002, 12–006
jurors with strong views, 12–005
jury deliberations, 12–001
police officers, 12–003, 12–004
prosecutors, 12–003, 12–004

Knowledge
attribution of knowledge
Chinese walls, 6–024
companies, 6–026
financial services, 19–002
knowledge split within the firm, 6–022—6–023
partnerships, 6–025

Legal professional privilege
money laundering, 10–006, 10–007

Litigation
defensive tactics, 8–019
offensive tactics, 8–018

Loans
disclosure, 6–004, 6–005, 6–006, 6–007, 6–008, 6–009
fraud, 6–021

Management buy-outs
directors, 19–012

Mergers
conflict of interest, 7–006—7–007

Money laundering
disclosure, 10–001—10–002, 10–003, 10–004
legal professional privilege, 10–006
offences, 10–002, 10–005
regulations, 10–002
tax evasion, 10–006
tipping off, 10–007

Mortgages
disclosure, 6–004, 6–005, 6–006, 6–007, 6–008, 6–009
fraud, 6–021

Mutual trust and confidence
fiduciary relationship, 2–003

New Zealand
conflict rules, 1–012
joint instructions, 4–007

No inhibition principle
breach of fiduciary duty, 2–007, 2–008
double employment rule, 3–021

Nominee directors
conflict of interest, 18–007

Oaths
judicial oath
significance of, 13–004

Objections
bias, 13–003

Other side
see **Adversaries**

Partnerships
knowledge attribution, 6–025

Perception of impropriety
advocate to the court, 5–017
criminal proceedings, 5–012
expert witnesses, 5–013—5–015
family proceedings, 5–011
Geveran principle, 5–009—5–010
inherent jurisdiction, 5–018—5–021
insolvency practitioners, 5–016
proper administration of justice, 5–008
Spincode case, 5–004—5–005
supervisory jurisdiction over solicitors, 5–001, 5–003, 5–006—5–007

Personal conflict of interest
double employment rule, 3–022—3–026
meaning, 1–004

Police officers
juries, 12–003, 12–004

Proceeds of crime
see **Money laundering**

Professional embarrassment
actual conflict, 3–019

barristers, 16–002
disclosure, 6–018
features of, 3–020
meaning, 1–005
non-waivable conflict, 3–018
Prosecutors
juries, 12–003, 12–004
Quia timet actions
double employment rule, 3–008
Recusal
see also **Judicial conflict**
judges, 11–001
Regulation
estate agents, 20–002
financial services, 19–001
insurance brokers, 20–003
takeovers, 19–009
Related parties
fiduciary duty, 2–023, 2–024, 2–030, 2–031
Relationship of trust and confidence
see **Mutual trust and confidence**
Remedies
see also **Damages; Injunctions**
account of profits, 8–008, 8–011
equitable remedies, 8–008, 8–010
loss of right to remuneration, 8–013
rescission, 8–007
Remuneration
loss of right to, 8–013
Rescission
remedies, 8–007
Retainers
see also **Consent**
barristers, 16–007
custom and usage, 4–022
exclusion clauses
disclosure clauses, 4–028
duty-defining clauses, 4–027
legitimacy of, 4–024, 4–025
restrictions on, 4–025, 4–026
types, 4–023
identification of clients, 4–004
informed consent, 4–002, 4–008, 4–009, 4–010, 4–011
interpretation, 4–005
joint instructions, 4–006—4–007
scope of, 4–002, 4–003
second retainers, 2–022

termination
close-out letters, 2–026
fiduciary duty, 2–020, 2–021, 2–022, 2–025, 2–027
revealing discreditable matters about the client, 2–028, 2–029
right to, 15–017
Right to fair and public hearing
see also **Judicial conflict**
human rights, 11–005
Risk management
consent, 4–014
Same matter conflict
meaning, 1–005
Shadow directors
fiduciary relationship, 2–015
Single joint experts
expert witnesses, 5–014
Solicitors
Chinese walls, 15–010—15–011
codes of conduct, 15–002—15–003, 15–012
common interest exception, 15–005
competing for the same objective, 15–006
confidentiality, 15–009
conflict of interest, 15–004
disclosure, 15–009
generally, 15–001
informed consent, 15–004, 15–008
inspection of files, 8–014
insurance cases, 15–018—15–019
liquidators
preventing solicitors acting for, 9–009
overseas practice, 15–013
reasonableness, 15–007
retainers
termination , 15–017
special position of, 15–014—15–016
supervisory jurisdiction over solicitors, 1–010, 5–001, 5–003, 5–006—5–007
Spouses
undue influence, 4–015
Structural Chinese walls
effectiveness of, 7–016
meaning, 1–003, 7–015

375

Takeovers
  Chinese walls, 19–008
  conflict of interest, 19–013
  contested takeovers
    consent, 4–012
    directors' powers and duties,
      19–010—19–011
  financial advisers
    conflict of interest, 19–014
    injunctions, 19–016—19–017
  'poison pills', 19–015
  regulation, 19–009
Tax evasion
  money laundering, 10–006
Tipping off
  money laundering, 10–007
Trade usage
  see **Custom and usage**
Tribunals
  see also **Judicial conflict**
  disciplinary tribunals
    apparent bias test, 12–007
    staff retiring with the tribunal,
      12–009
    tribunal members' employment,
      12–010

  employment tribunals
    relationships and affiliations,
      13–024
Undue influence
  consent, 4–015
  spouses, 4–015
  types of, 4–015
Unfair contract terms
  contracts, 4–026
United States
  conflict rules, 1–013
  information barriers, 1–013
Waiver
  see also **Consent**
  bias, 11–018—11–020
  forms of, 8–017
Wasted costs orders
  recusal
    judges, 13–013
Whistleblowers
  money laundering, 10–001—10–002,
    10–003, 10–004
Without notice injunctions
  generally, 8–002